NINTH EDITION

Communicating

A Social and Career Focus

Roy M. Berko
Communic-aid
Notre Dame College of Ohio

Andrew D. Wolvin
University of Maryland
College Park and University College

Darlyn R. Wolvin
Prince George's Community College

Houghton Mifflin Company   Boston   New York

Publisher: Patricia A. Coryell
Senior Sponsoring Editor: Mary Finch
Development Editor: Kristen Desmond LeFevre
Editorial Associate: Brigitte Maser
Project Editor: Amy Johnson
Senior Production/Design Coordinator: Jodi O'Rourke
Senior Manufacturing Coordinator: Marie Barnes

Cover illustration © Noma/Images.com, Inc.

Printed in the U.S.A.

Library of Congress Control Number: 2002109364

ISBN: 0-618-26015-3

23456789-QWV-07 06 05 04 03

BRIEF CONTENTS

PART ONE **Foundations of Communication** 1

1 THE HUMAN COMMUNICATION PROCESS 2
2 FOUNDATIONS OF VERBAL LANGUAGE 33
3 NONVERBAL COMMUNICATION 55
4 PERSONAL COMMUNICATION 82
5 LISTENING 104

PART TWO **Interpersonal Communication** 133

6 THE THEORY OF INTERPERSONAL COMMUNICATION 134
7 INTERPERSONAL SKILLS 171
8 THE INTERVIEW 206
9 THE THEORY OF GROUPS 236
10 PARTICIPATING IN GROUPS 264

PART THREE **Communicating in Public** 289

11 PUBLIC SPEAKING: PLANNING AND PRESENTING
THE MESSAGE 290
12 PUBLIC SPEAKING: DEVELOPING THE SPEECH 322
13 PUBLIC SPEAKING: STRUCTURING THE MESSAGE 346
14 INFORMATIVE PUBLIC SPEAKING 369
15 PERSUASIVE PUBLIC SPEAKING 388

CONTENTS

Preface   xiii

PART ONE Foundations of Communication   1

1   THE HUMAN COMMUNICATION PROCESS   2

Communication Defined   5
The Components of Human Communication   6
  Communicator Perceptions   8
  The Source and the Message   9
  The Channel   9
  The Receiver and the Message   9
  Feedback   9
  Noise   10
  Dealing with Noise   12
  The Context   13
Communication as a System   14
Models of Human Communication   15
  Linear Model of Communication   15
  Interactional Model of Communication   17
  Transactional Model of Communication   18
  The Models Compared   19
The Media as Communicator   20
Communication and Culture   22
  Intercultural and Intracultural Communication   22
  Multiculturalism   23
  Ethnocentrism   24
First Amendment Speech   27
Ethics and Communication   29

2   FOUNDATIONS OF VERBAL LANGUAGE   33

Origins of Human Language   34
  Selecting Symbols   35

Processing Symbols   35
Learning Symbols   37
The Concept of Meaning   39
The Functions of Language   42
Language Distortion   43
The Languages We Use   44
Standard American English   45
Slang   46
Nonstandard English Dialects   47
Using Verbal Language   50

3 NONVERBAL COMMUNICATION   55

Sources of Nonverbal Signs   57
Neurological Programs   57
Cultural and Intercultural Behavior   58
Emotional Influences on Nonverbal Communication   60
Verbal and Nonverbal Relationships   61
Substituting Relationship   61
Complementing Relationship   62
Conflicting Relationship   62
Accenting Relationship   63
Categories of Nonverbal Communication   63
Kinesics: Body Communication   64
Physical Characteristics   72
Proxemics: Spatial Communication   73
Paravocalics: Vocal Communication   75
Chronemics: Time as Communication   76
Olfactics: Smell as Communication   77
Aesthetics: Mood and Beauty as Communication   78
Gustorics: Taste as Communication   79
Using Nonverbal Communication   80

4 PERSONAL COMMUNICATION   82

Self-Talk   83
Cognitive Processing   86
Self-Concept   88
Understanding Yourself   90
Need Drives Affecting Communication   95
Survival   95
Pleasure Seeking   95
Security   96
Territoriality   96
Anxiety: Communication Apprehension   97
Communication Anxiety Defined   97
Causes of Communication Apprehension   98
Help for Communication Apprehension   99

5   LISTENING   104

The Importance of Listening   105
The Listening Process   106
   Reception   106
   Attention   108
   Perception   110
   Assignment of Meaning   110
   Response   114
   Listening Influencers   116
Purposes of Listening   118
   Discriminative Listening   118
   Comprehension Listening   119
   Therapeutic Listening   120
   Critical Listening   120
   Appreciative Listening   122
Listening Apprehension   122
Improving Your Listening   123

PART TWO   Interpersonal Communication   133

6   THE THEORY OF INTERPERSONAL COMMUNICATION   134

Basic Concepts of Interpersonal Communication   135
Self-Disclosure   137
The Self and Others   139
Seeking Approval   141
Gaining Compliance   142
Emotions   143
Power   144
Male/Masculine—Female/Feminine Communication   146
   Sex and Gender   147
   How Men and Women Communicate Differently   148
Sexual Harassment   151
   Responding to Sexual Harassment   152
Relationships and Their Development   153
   Development of a Relationship   154
   Continuing a Relationship   155
   Positive Relationships   156
   Communication in Relationships   157
   Ending Relationships   158
Computer-Mediated Interpersonal Communication   158
   Interpersonal Uses of the Internet   159
   Positive Aspects of Internet Use   160
   Negative Aspects of Internet Use   161
   Developing Personal Relationships Online   164
   Strategies for Effective Online Communication   165

7

INTERPERSONAL SKILLS   171

Participating in Conversations   172
Conversational Presentation Skills   172
Conversational Listening Skills   174
Conversational Nonverbal Skills   175
Giving Directions   175
Giving Details   176
Organizing Ideas   176
Using Understandable Terms   177
Requesting   177
Requesting Information   177
Asking Questions   177
Dealing with Interpersonal Conflict   179
Conflict Defined   179
Causes of Conflict   181
Levels of Conflict   182
Role of Personal Anger in Conflict   184
Dealing with Another Person's Anger in Conflict   186
Fair Fighting   186
Individual Approaches to Dealing with Conflict   187
Apologizing   190
Communication Approaches to Managing Conflict   192
Assertive Communication   193
Negotiation   197
Arbitration   198
Litigation   198
Mediation   198
Handling Criticism   200

8

THE INTERVIEW   206

Interviewing Roles   207
Role of the Interviewer   207
Role of the Interviewee   207
Interview Format   208
Opening of the Interview   208
Body of the Interview   209
Sequence of Interview Questions   209
Answering Interview Questions   211
Closing the Interview   211
Types of Interviews   211
Employment Interview   212
Information-Gathering Interview   220
Problem-Solving Interview   222
Oral History Interview   223
Counseling Interview   225
Persuasive Interview   225
Appraisal Interview   227
Reprimanding Interview   229

Interrogation Interview 230
Media Interview 231

9 THE THEORY OF GROUPS 236

Groups Defined 237
Group Versus Individual Actions 237
   Advantages of Groups 238
   Disadvantages of Groups 238
Types of Groups 240
   Work Teams 240
   Study Groups 241
   Support Groups 241
   Committees 242
   Focus Groups 243
   The Family as a Group 243
   Public Meetings 244
   Town Meetings 244
Group Operations 245
   Group Norming 245
   Group Storming 245
   Group Conforming 247
   Group Performing 248
   Group Adjourning 248
Making Group Decisions 248
   Formulating an Agenda 249
   Voting 250
   Decision-Making Techniques 251
Group Setting 255
   Seating Choice 255
   Table Configuration 256
   Effect of the Physical Environment 257
Mediated Meetings 258
   Types of Mediated Meetings 258
   Positive and Negative Aspects of Mediated Meetings 258
   How to Make Mediated Meetings Work 261

10 PARTICIPATING IN GROUPS 264

Cultural Differences in Groups 265
   Cultures and Groups 265
   Contrasts in Cultural Group Decision Making 266
   Cultural Contrast of the Role of Information for Groups 267
   Male and Female Roles in Groups 268
The Group Participant 269
   Responsibilities of Group Members 269
   Communicating as a Group Member 271
   Roles of Group Members 274
   Communication Networks 275
   Dealing with Difficult Group Members 276

The Group Leader and Group Leadership   279
 Types of Leaders   280
 Patterns of Leader/Leadership Emergence   281
 Why People Desire to Be Leaders   281
 Leader/Leadership: Communicative Perspective   282
 Effective Leader Questioning   283
 Responsibilities of Leaders   283

PART THREE **Communicating in Public   289**

11   PUBLIC SPEAKING: PLANNING AND PRESENTING THE MESSAGE   290

Preparing a Speech: An Overview   291
Parameters of Public Speaking   292
The Ethics of Public Speaking   292
 Plagiarism   293
 Fabrication   293
Prior to the Speech Analysis   294
 Demographics   294
 Psychographics   295
 Rhetorographics   296
 Applying the Prior Analysis   297
Process of the Speech Analysis   300
Postspeech Analysis   301
Presenting the Message   301
Modes of Presentation   301
 Impromptu or Ad Lib Mode   302
 Extemporaneous Mode   303
 Manuscript Mode   307
 Memorized Mode   310
Oral and Physical Presentation   310
 Vocal Delivery   310
 Vocal Variety   311
 Pronunciation   311
 Physical Elements   311
 Using PowerPoint   312
Public Speaking Anxiety   315
 Conquering Public Speaking Anxiety   315
Rehearsing the Speech   317
Dealing with Difficulties During a Speech   318

12   PUBLIC SPEAKING: DEVELOPING THE SPEECH   322

Sources of Information   323
 Books   324
 Magazines   324
 Newspapers   325
 Journals   325

Indexes   325
Government Publications   325
Special-Interest Group Publications   325
Nonprint Media   326
Interviews   326
Computer Searches   326
Computer-Based Retrieval Systems   326
Conducting a Computer Search   326
Use of the Internet   327
Selecting Sources   328
Analyzing Sources   329
Recording Your Research   330
Supporting Material   333
Illustrations   333
Specific Instances   333
Exposition   334
Statistics   334
Analogies   336
Testimony   336
Vehicles for Presenting Supporting Material   337
Internal Summaries   337
Forecasting   337
Signposting   337
Supplementary Aids   337
Preparing Presentational Programs   341
Developing PowerPoint Presentations   341

13

PUBLIC SPEAKING: STRUCTURING THE MESSAGE   346

Basic Elements of a Speech   347
The Introduction   347
Attention Material   347
Orienting Material   350
Historical Background   350
Definition of Terms   351
Personal History and/or Tie to the Topic   351
Importance to the Listeners   351
The Central Idea   351
The Body   352
Role of Culture on Speech Structure   352
Methods of Issue Arrangement   354
The Conclusion   359
Summary   359
Clincher   359
Methods for Formatting a Speech   360
Partitioning Method   360
Unfolding Method   363
Case Method   365

14 INFORMATIVE PUBLIC SPEAKING   369

Role of Informative Speaking   370
Concept of Informative Speaking   371
Characteristics of Informative Speaking   372
Classifications of Informative Speaking   372
    Speeches About Objects   373
    Speeches About Processes   373
    Speeches About Events   374
    Speeches About Concepts   375
    Informative Briefings   375
    Team Briefings   376
    One-on-One Briefings   376
    Technical Reports   376
    Professional Papers   377
    Lectures   378
    Question-and-Answer Sessions   379
    Speeches of Introduction   381
Developing the Informative Speech   382
Informative Process in Action   384

15 PERSUASIVE PUBLIC SPEAKING   388

Persuasive Speaking   389
Process of Persuasion   389
Persuasive Strategies   391
Role of Influence in Persuasion   392
Components of Persuasive Message   393
    Speaker Credibility   393
    Logical Arguments   395
    Organizing the Persuasive Speech   399
    Psychological Appeals   402
    Appeals to Motivate Listeners   405
Structure of the Persuasive Message   407
Persuasive Process in Action   408

Appendix 1: The Résumé   412

Appendix 2: Basic Rules for APA Style   417

Notes   419

Glossary   432

Index   444

PREFACE

This is the ninth edition of *Communicating: A Social and Career Focus.* As we look back, we are pleased with and amazed by the history of this text. It was first published in 1977. Since then many other competing books have come and gone. Few college texts reach their thirty-seventh anniversary. This one has, and it has prospered. Each edition has resulted in a growth in users. The eighth edition broke all records for sales. We are proud of the fact that we have continued to produce a book that is well researched, interesting to read, and pragmatic. We thank you, our readers, for your feedback and support. We look forward to many more editions.

A Message to Students

The average United States resident spends a great deal of his or her life in the act of communicating. The average student, for example, listens to the equivalent of a book a day and speaks the equivalent of a book a week.[1] Communication skills are the most important abilities a person can possess for career success.[2] The major competencies required of people in the workforce are working on teams, teaching others, serving customers, leading, negotiating, and working well with people of culturally diverse backgrounds. Communication competency has been identified as an important variable. For example, communication is at the core of success in college. It affects not only academic success but also social connectedness.[3]

Only a limited number of people are competent communicators. Twenty-five percent of the nation's people cannot adequately communicate orally.[4] Almost 63 percent of people cannot give clear oral directions.[5] About 20 percent of the children in any given school exhibit high levels of communication anxiety in most speaking situations.[6] The apprehension level of those who fear speaking in public is estimated to be 50 to 70 percent.[7]

Because of this need for communication skills, the National Communication Association, the nation's largest organization of speech and communication professors, teachers, and professionals, published *Speaking, Listening, and Media Literacy Standards for K through 12 Education.*[8] That document highlights the role of communication: "Communication shapes our sense of self and the way we interact in our environment, from gathering and presenting information to managing conflict."[9] It goes on to state, "Speaking, listening, and media literacy are fundamental to the process, purpose, and influence of interpersonal relations in the family, the workplace, and one-to-one social interactions."[10]

"Students must study and practice communication in order to achieve such competence; it does not come naturally."[11] Research shows that students report that "there was significant behavioral change due to the [communication] training."[12]

The purpose of this text is to give you the opportunities to achieve communication competency and not only to gain an understanding of the communication process but also to improve the skills that will accompany you for the rest of your life. Understandings and skills in communicating are necessary to your success as a human being in relational, family, social, and career settings.

A Message to Instructors

Communication is an ever-expanding field. As new editions of basic course texts are published, the trend has been for books to get longer and longer, making it difficult for instructors to cover all the material in the time allotted for a course. With this in mind, we have concentrated on stemming this tide. You will find this edition, as was the last, *concise, comprehensive, and creative*.

> *Conciseness:* The volume, though it continues to include the newest research and approaches to contemporary and emerging communication issues, carries on the trend of conciseness established in the previous edition.
>
> *Comprehensiveness:* We have updated many of the resources and added materials. Specifically, we have

- *made an additional investigation of mediated communication*
- *expanded the investigation of the role of culture on communication*
- *added an investigation of ethnocentrism*
- *reexamined First Amendment speech/freedom of speech/speech codes*
- *reinvestigated the origins of human language*
- *added a discussion of the Social Construct of Reality Theory*
- *reinvestigated the accuracy of polygraphs*
- *probed the concept of touch avoidance*
- *initiated an investigation of the acquiring and developing of language as a factor of inner speech*
- *examined of the implications of Dale's Cone of Learning*
- *reexamined the practice of therapeutic listening*
- *investigated the role of power in relationships*
- *added a section on the causes of conflict*
- *probed apologizing*
- *included information about how to answer the most common employment interview questions*
- *added sections on the telephone job interview and the oral history interview*
- *updated the material on groupthink*
- *clarified the process of operation of each of the communication networks*
- *added an explanation of how to deal with difficult people*
- *reexamined plagiarism in public speaking*

◆ *expanded the materials on preparing and structuring an outline*

◆ *added a new section on using PowerPoint slides in a speech*

◆ *reexamined public speaking anxiety*

◆ *adjusted the section on computer searches used in preparing a speech*

◆ *rewritten the section on preparing and developing computerized graphics for public speaking*

◆ *explained how to organize topical arrangement subdivisions*

◆ *added examinations of team briefings, one-on-one briefings, and presenting professional papers*

◆ *reexamined persuasive strategies, including studying propositions of fact, propositions of value, and propositions of policy*

◆ *added an appendix explaining the APA style of footnoting or endnoting*

◆ *updated the glossary*

◆ *evaluated and substituted sidebars*

◆ *retained the structure that allows instructors either to use chapters in order or to use only some of the chapters since they do not overlap or refer to features in other chapters*

Creativity: Historically, students and faculty alike have praised the writing style of this book. As has been the case with previous editions, we have given special attention to making this book readable, student centered, and practical. We have presented sidebars of enlightened and entertaining value. In addition, we have included custom-drawn cartoons. The cartoonist, a former communication student, not only is creative but also knows the field of communication.

Ancillary Materials

Support materials available to the adopters of *Communicating* include:

For the Instructor:

◆ **Instructor's Resource Manual and Test Bank**, fully revised and updated.

◆ **HM ClassPrep CD-ROM**, containing digital versions of the Instructor's Resource Manual and Test Bank items, as well as the HM ClassTesting test generator.

◆ **Instructor's companion website**, including updated web links, PowerPoint slides, and other ancillary materials.

◆ **On-Line Speech Studio,** a tutorial and classroom management tool.

For the Student:

◆ **Real Deal CD-ROM**, containing chapter objectives, chapter outlines, an interactive glossary, a guide to writing résumés, and self-test quizzes.

◆ **Student's companion website**, including ACE Quizzes/Self-Tests, a Speech Outliner Tool, interactive self-assessment tests, and additional content, exercises, and activities.

◆ **VideoLab student CD-ROM**, with interactive student speech video presentations, exercises, and applications.

◆ **On-Line SpeechStudio**, including self-assessments, speech design tutorials, and checklists for better-prepared speeches.

Acknowledgments

Without the assistance of Joan Aitken, University of Missouri–Kansas City, producing this edition would have been a much more difficult task. We appreciate her help with the sections on mediated communication, mediated meetings, and PowerPoint presentations as well as her editorial advice.

We thank Eunice Berko for editorial assistance and Adam Forrand, Kristen LeFevre, Brigitte Maser, Barbara LeBuhn, and Amy Johnson of Houghton Mifflin for their encouragement and dedication to this project. We also extend our appreciation to Laura Janusik, University of Maryland, for her research support and assistance with the Instructor's Resource Manual. Thanks also go to Tony Zupancic of Notre Dame College of Ohio and his students for their content suggestions and to Rebecca Ray for her assistance on the sexual harassment unit.

We are indebted to those professors who have been loyal users of this book through its first eight editions and hope that they will continue to use the text and to provide us with insightful and helpful comments for future editions.

Appreciation also goes to our professional colleagues who read and critiqued the manuscript throughout its development:

John Aber, College of Mount St. Joseph

James Cheseboro, Indiana State University

Betty Dennison, Marshall Community and Technical College

Tai C. Du, George Mason University

Jeffrey S. Hillard, College of Mount St. Joseph

Linda Hoyer, Madonna University

Kara Laskowski, Juniata College

Marianne Neuwirth, University of Utah

Andrea Pearman, Tidewater Community College and
    ECPI College of Technology

Bill Wallace, Northeastern State University

In Conclusion

COMMUNICATE COMPETENTLY!

R. M. B.
A. D. W.
D. R. W.

PART

Foundations of Communication

ONE

1

The Human Communication Process

After reading this chapter, you should be able to

- List and explain the components of human communication

- Explain the effects of perceptions on the human communication process

- Identify, define, and give examples of the noise factors that affect the human communication process

- Illustrate, define, and give examples of the linear, interactional, and transactional models of communication

- Understand the concept of communication as a system

- Relate to the role of the media as a communicator

- Understand the relationship between communication and culture

- Define and explain ethnocentrism

- Understand the role of First Amendment speech as a rhetorical tool

- Explain the role of the ethical value system in communication

When confronted with the requirement of taking a communication course, students sometimes ask, "Why do I need that? I know how to talk." Communication, though, is more than talking. When you answer a question in class, receive a compliment, challenge another person's ideas, interact with a family member, touch someone, participate in a job interview, take part in a group meeting, listen to a classroom lecture, do a victorious high-five, select clothing to wear, or go through the process of buying a car, you are involved in the act of communicating! Significant friendships, successful family relationships, and academic and occupational success depend on communication abilities.

Studying communication and learning how to be an effective communicator are not just academic exercises. One of the most important skills you will learn is how to use communication. For example, your academic success may well be linked to your ability to communicate. "Students must have speaking, listening, classroom management, and interpersonal communication skills for successful completion of a college degree."[1] In classes, students must be able to ask and answer questions, summarize opinions, distinguish facts from opinions, and interact with their peers and instructors.[2] Students also need good listening skills to comprehend the information presented in classes and good presentation skills to give briefings, reports, and team projects that are part of college course requirements.

Communication competency is indispensable for successful participation in the world of work. Interested in getting a job? A recent study indicated that the number one necessary ability is "communication skills."[3] The ability to communicate effectively often determines a person's perceived overall competency and level of success.[4] Today's workers need interpersonal skills even more than technical expertise.[5] Surveyed senior executives said they "want employees to be good listeners, to interact well with others, and to solve problems effectively."[6] Ironically these

Communication competency is indispensable for successful participation in the world of work.

executives indicated that the abilities most lacking in the workforce were those three skills.

Communication competency is not limited to the workplace and the classroom. We also need speaking and listening skills to function at the personal level. Relationships with friends and family depend on our listening and responding to each other. The business of life is a communication interaction—with the supermarket checker, the doctor, the college registrar, the meter reader, the repairperson, and the 911 operator.

Most people are not effective communicators. Twenty percent of the nation's young people cannot accomplish any of the simplest of communication tasks,[7] almost 63 percent cannot give clear oral directions,[8] about 95 percent of the population reports some anxiety about communicating with a person or in groups,[9] the apprehension level of those who fear speaking in public is estimated at 50 to 70 percent,[10] and adults listen at a 25 percent level of efficiency.[11]

To add to our woes is something that many think is a positive aspect of communication: the information explosion, resulting in information overload. We are bombarded daily with messages not only directly from other people but also from a number of technological sources. Cell phones, e-mail, pagers, televisions, and fax machines enable us to receive information quickly and incessantly. These are communication devices that carry communication messages.

The challenge is how to manage the information so that it doesn't become overwhelming. Given that information doubles approximately every three years, you can understand how difficult it can be to meet that challenge.[12] People are becoming more selective, turning off or tuning out messages that aren't relevant to them. Guided by daybooks and electronic reminders, some individuals have devised intricate organizational systems to file and retrieve information.

Okay, so there is a need to be able to communicate, but the question still is, "Why do I have to take a course in communication?" Although you are able to talk, you may not be able to communicate effectively. "Students must study and practice communication in order to achieve such competence, it does not come naturally."[13]

Skills in Demand

Skill	Percentage of Executives Who Ranked Skills as Very Important	Skill	Percentage of Executives Who Ranked Skills as Most Lacking in Employees
Listening	80%	Listening	28%
Interpersonal	78	Problem solving	27
Problem solving	76	Interpersonal	27
Technical within an industry	71	Technical	25
Basic computer knowledge	70	Creativity	24
Creativity	46	Administrative organizational	19
Administrative organizational	36	Basic computer knowledge	17

Source: Select Appointments North America, from Valerie Marchant, "Listen Up!" *Time,* June 28, 1999, p. 72. © 1999 Time, Inc. Reprinted by permission.

Communication Defined

Communication is a conscious or unconscious, intentional or unintentional process in which feelings and ideas are expressed as verbal and/or nonverbal messages that are sent, received, and comprehended. This process can be *accidental* (having no intent), *expressive* (resulting from the emotional state of the person), or *rhetorical* (resulting from specific goals of the communicator).

Being able to communicate effectively improves your facility to maneuver ideas. Vague impressions gain reality; ideas are examined, set in categories, and eventually added to other ideas.

Human communication occurs on the intrapersonal, interpersonal, and public levels. **Intrapersonal communication** is communicating with yourself. It encompasses such activities as thought processing, personal decision making, listening, and determining self-concept. **Interpersonal communication** refers to communication that takes place between two or more persons who establish a communicative relationship. Forms of interpersonal communication include face-to-face or mediated conversations, interviews, and small-group discussions. **Public communication** is characterized by a speaker's sending a message to an audience. It may be direct, such as a face-to-face message delivered by a speaker to an audience, or indirect, such as a message relayed over radio or television.

All communication is dynamic, continuous, irreversible, interactive, and contextual.[14]

Communication is *dynamic* because the process is constantly in a state of change. As the attitudes, expectations, feelings, and emotions of persons who are communicating change, the nature of their communication changes as well.

Communication is *continuous* because it never stops. Whether asleep or awake, we are always processing ideas and information through our dreams, thoughts, and expressions. Our brains remain active; we are communicating.

Communication is *irreversible*. Once we send a message, we cannot undo it. Once we make a slip of the tongue, give a meaningful glance, or generate an emotional outburst, we cannot erase it. Our apologies or denials cannot eradicate what has taken place.

Communication is *interactive*. We are constantly in contact with other people and with ourselves. Others react to our speech and actions, and we react to our own speech and actions, and then react to those reactions. Thus, a cycle of action and reaction becomes the basis for our communication.

The highly complex process of communication is *contextual* because it is a part of our entire human experience. The complexity of communication dictates that we develop the awareness and the skills to function effectively as communicators and to adapt to the setting, the people who are present, and the purpose of the communication. A word processing advertisement summarized this well: "You don't talk to your mother the same way you talk to your buddies. (Better not, for your sake.) That nice polite talk is perfect for Sunday dinners. Or when you're asking for money. That's why you've got Street talk. Small talk. Back talk. Coffee talk. Baby talk. And—even when you're not saying a word—Body Talk, which has absolutely no regard for syntax and grammar. Custom languages made to order."[15]

To be an effective communicator, you need to understand how the communication process operates as a system, how you send and process information, how you reason your way to conclusions and evaluate the ideas that others send, and the relationship between communication and culture. In addition, good communicators know what ethical standards they use in making their decisions.

Did you know?

The average person spends 30 percent of his or her waking hours in conversation.

The Components of Human Communication

As human beings, we are capable of **selective communication.** That is, from the wide repertory available to us, we can choose the symbol we believe best represents the idea or concept we wish to express. We can think in abstractions, plan events in the future, and store and recall information. Selective communication allows us to combine sounds into complicated structures and therefore describe events and objects.

When we communicate, we **encode** (take ideas and put them into message form), send the ideas through a channel composed of our **primary signal system** (the senses: seeing, hearing, tasting, smelling, and touching) to someone who receives them using his or her primary signal system, and **decode** (translate) the message (see Figure 1.1). We express our reactions to what we have sensed verbally and nonverbally. You may say, "I heard the bell" or "It feels soft." These are examples of verbal communication that are responses to what your senses have received. You also can respond on a nonverbal level. You touch a hot stove, pull your finger away quickly, and your eyes well with tears. The pulling away and eyes welling are nonverbal communication.

In any communication process, the degree to which the communication is effective depends on the communicators' mutual understanding of the signals being used. Suppose you are about to take an examination and suddenly realize you forgot to bring a pencil to class. You ask one of your friends, "May I please borrow a pencil?" She says, "Yes" and gives you a pencil. You have just participated in an effective communication transaction. You (*communicator* A) *encoded* a message ("May I please borrow a pencil?") and sent it out over a *channel* (vocal tones carried on sound waves) to your friend (*communicator* B). Your friend *received* the message (by using sensory agents, ears) and *decoded* it (understood that you wanted a pencil). Your friend's *feedback* (the word *yes* and handing the pencil to you) indicated that the message was successfully *received* and *decoded.*

Now suppose that the person sitting next to you is from France and speaks no English. The symbol that he uses for pencil is *crayon.* Unless both of you communi-

Your academic success may well be linked to your ability to communicate.

Figure 1.1   **Encoding and Decoding**

cate in French, he will be unable to decode your message. Or suppose that just as you start to ask your question, the public address system goes on, and a screech pervades the room. The receiver may not be able to hear the question, so no successful communication takes place.

Remember that *the act of speech is not itself communication*. Speech is only a biological act: the utterance of sounds, possibly of vocal symbols of language. Communication is broader: it involves the development of a relationship among people in which there is shared meaning among the participants. That is, the intent of the message received is basically the same as the intent of the message sent.

Figure 1.2 illustrates how the components of the communication process work. The circles representing the **source** (the originator of the message) and the **receiver** (the recipient of the message) overlap as each person sends **messages** (communication) and **feedback** (response to a message) to the other through a **frame of reference** (a perceptual screen). The overlapping circles suggest that communication is possible only when each communicator understands the other's message. The variables that affect the frame of reference make up the perceptual screen through which verbal and nonverbal messages are communicated.

Figure 1.2	**The Components of Communication**

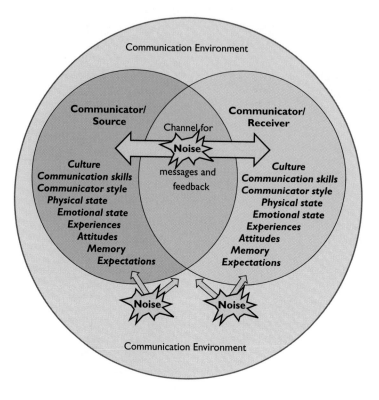

<table>
<tr><th colspan="2">Source</th></tr>
</table>

Source
1. Senses aroused by idea or need to communicate
2. Chooses to communicate the message using language symbols (the code)
3. Uses memory and past experiences to find language symbols to communicate the message (encoding)

Receiver
1. Senses aroused by stimuli or need to communicate
2. Receives symbols (the code) in distorted form
3. Uses memory and past experiences to attach meaning to symbols (decoding)
4. Stores information
5. Sends feedback

Communicator Perceptions

Your **perceptions**—the way you view the world—affect your interpretation of a communication stimulus. Many factors make up your perceptual filter. These factors, listed in Figure 1.2, include your *culture* (the background worldview you hold), *communication skills* (developed from experience and training), *physical and emotional states* (how you feel at this particular time), *experiences* (your cultural background), *attitudes* (negative and positive predispositions to respond to any particular stimulus), *memory* (ability to store and recall information), and *expectations* (what you anticipate will occur). Because of perceptual differences, two people reporting on an incident they have both seen may report their observations differently.

You encode and decode messages through your perceptual filters. These perceptual filters establish expectations for the outcome of the communication, and expectations guide your interpretation of the communicator's message. A person who expects to hear bad news from the boss, for instance, probably will interpret what the boss says in a performance review as negative even if the focus of the review highlights many of the positive aspects of the individual's work. In the early stages of the 2000 presidential race, Democratic candidate Albert Gore had to deal with the public's negative perceptions—fed by media comments—that he was a wooden, stiff, boring speaker. The press told people that Mr. Gore was not an effective speaker, and these messages shaped the perceptual communication "reality." Essentially, communicator perception creates our reality as we interpret messages: we see and hear what we want to see and hear or expect to see or hear.

The Source and the Message

The communication process begins when the source is consciously or unconsciously stimulated by some event, object, or idea. This need to send a message is then followed by a memory search to find the appropriate language (verbal or nonverbal or both) in which to encode the message.

The Channel

During a communicative act, the encoded message is carried through a **channel** or channels. If the communication occurs face to face, these channels may be some or all of the five senses. Typically, we rely on sight and sound as channels in speaking and listening. Instead of communicating face to face, however, we may choose to use an electronic channel that uses sound (e.g., the telephone) or seeing and hearing (e.g., television). In some instances, we may choose to send a message to someone by means of physical contact, such as by tapping the person on the shoulder. In this case, we use the touch channel.

The Receiver and the Message

At the end of the channel, the receiver must decode the message before communication can be accomplished. On gaining verbal and nonverbal signals, the receiver processes them through a memory search so that the signals are translated into the receiver's language system. This decoded message is not identical to the one encoded by the source because each person's symbol system is shaped by a unique set of perceptions. A chef and an amateur cook, for instance, may have different concepts of what "season to taste" means in a recipe.

Feedback

Once the receiver assigns meaning to the received message, he is in a position to respond. This response, called *feedback,* can be a verbal or a nonverbal reaction to the message, or both. Feedback indicates whether the receiver understands (e.g., by nodding), misunderstands

CULTURALLY SPEAKING

One thing I have found in general is that Europeans prefer directness, rather than subtlety, in negotiations and discussions. What we Americans perceive as diplomatic, they may see as not being direct, not getting to the point, and not saying what you need to say.

—**Nana Osei-Kofi,** owner of Scottsdale, Arizona–based GlobalReady, an international event management firm

Cultural noise results from preconceived, unyielding attitudes derived from a group or society about how members of that culture should act or in what they should or shouldn't believe.

(e.g., by shrugging the shoulders and saying, "I don't understand"), encourages the source to continue (e.g., by leaning forward and saying, "Yes"), or disagrees (e.g., by pulling back and saying, "No way!"). The act of responding, by which the receiver sends feedback to the source, actually shifts the role of the receiver to that of source.

Noise

Messages are influenced not only by the interpretations of each communicator but also by **noise,** which is any internal or external interference in the communication process.[16] Noise can be caused by environmental obstacles, physiological impairment, semantic problems, syntactic problems, organizational confusion, cultural influences, or psychological problems.

Environmental Noise   **Environmental noise** is outside interference that prevents the receiver from gaining the message. This can happen when you are in the kitchen running water and the sound muffles your friend's voice when he asks you a question from the adjoining room.

Physiological-Impairment Noise   A physical problem can block the effective sending or receiving of a message, thus creating **physiological-impairment noise.** For example, deaf persons do not have the sensory capabilities to receive a message in the same way as do hearing people.

Semantic Noise   Problems may arise regarding the meaning of words—*semantics*—creating **semantic noise.** For example, semantic noise may result when people use language that is common only to one specific group, a particular part of a country, another nation, or a particular field, profession, or organization.

　　Travelers frequently encounter semantic problems. The U.S. Midwesterner who goes into a store in many parts of the country's East Coast and asks for a *soda* will probably get a soft drink (*pop* in the Midwest) rather than a mixture of ice cream, fruit flavoring, and soda water (a *soda* in the Midwest).

Experts—professors, doctors, mechanics—sometimes forget that those who do not have as much knowledge of their field may not be familiar with its vocabulary. For example, clients often complain that lawyers fail to communicate clearly because they use legal jargon, which is confusing to non-lawyers.

Similarly, people sometimes use the initials of organizations, equipment, or activities rather than their full names. Computer specialists use such initials as LCD, GDSS, and CMC, forgetting that most people do not recognize these abbreviations. To avoid semantic problems, communicators must be aware that although they know the meanings of the words they use, those at the receiving end must assign similar meanings for communication to be effective.

Syntactical Noise   Each language has a *syntax,* a customary way of putting words together in a grammatical form. Various types of **syntactical noise,** that is, inappropriate grammatical usage, can interfere with clear communication. For example, receivers may become confused if someone changes tenses in the middle of a story ("She *went* down the street and *says* to him . . .").

The usual sequence of a grammatically correct English sentence is noun-verb-object (*I give him the book*). But other languages—Spanish, for example—do not follow this pattern. In Spanish, the same sentence reads *Le doy el libro* (*To him I give the book*). Thus, someone who is learning a new language must master not only its vocabulary but also an entirely different system of grammar. Until this new system becomes natural, the language may be quite difficult both to encode and decode.

We sometimes find ourselves in situations where stress causes us to send messages ineffectively.

Organizational Noise   When the source fails to realize that certain ideas are best grasped when presented in a structured order, **organizational noise** may result. A geography instructor presents ideas in a random fashion: first he talks about India, then China, then Greece, then India, and then China. After a while, his students become so confused they have absolutely no idea which country he is discussing.

Many methods of organization can provide a clear structure. In giving directions, a person may set a pattern by starting at the departure point and proceeding in geographical order (e.g., *Go to the first street, turn right, proceed three blocks, and turn left*). If material is presented in a specific pattern, the receiver is likely to grasp the meaning. If the material is not organized, the receiver must not only try to figure out what is said but also sort out the information.

Cultural Noise   **Cultural noise** results from preconceived, unyielding attitudes derived from a group or society about how members of that culture should act or in what they should or shouldn't believe. Individuals in a culture who believe in a set pattern of rules and regulations might say, "Nice people don't do things like that" and "We do it this way."

An instance of cultural noise is the attitude that any action by a representative of one's own group is always right whereas the actions by a member of another group are wrong. Thus, a person who has always voted for candidates of one political party may find it difficult to be open-minded when listening to information about the opposing political party's candidates.

Psychological Noise   We sometimes find ourselves in situations where **psychological noise**—stress, frustration, or irritation—causes us to send or receive messages ineffectively. Think of what happens when you are so angry that you "can't think straight." This is a normal example of psychological noise getting in the way of effective communication.

Some people have severe psychological problems that cause them to communicate in unusual ways. People with schizophrenia (a disintegration of personality) or catatonia (immobility and speechlessness) may have great difficulty communicating. They may talk in riddles and rhymes, make up words, switch personalities, or not speak at all.

These noise factors can interfere with effective communication in varying stages of the linear, interactional, or transactional models. For example, semantic noise may stop the sender from encoding a message if she does not have the vocabulary to create the message. The message may not get into the channel if there is physiological-impairment noise because the sender has laryngitis. The message may not get clearly out of the channel if there is environmental noise that creates static on the telephone line carrying the signal. The receiver may not be able to receive the message if she is deaf and can't hear the intended message. The receiver may be experiencing psychological noise: though he receives the message, he may be so disoriented that he doesn't really grasp the intent of the information. Or, due to semantic and syntactic noise, he may not be able to decode the message because he doesn't speak the same language as the sender (see Figure 1.3).

Dealing with Noise

Although noise interferes with communication, we must learn to adapt to and compensate for it because it is commonly present. For example, a source should offer opportunities for feedback to make sure that a message has been received and understood. Rather than assuming that someone in another room has heard your message, word the statement so that it requires an answer: "The phone is for you; are you going to answer it?" Another way to compensate for noise is to define terms that might be misunderstood or may not be part of the receiver's vocabulary. Rather than repeating exactly the same words in a message that has been misunderstood, you can change the terms or the sentence structure to aid the receiver in decoding the message. In the same way, a receiver should ask questions or repeat the message's general ideas to be sure that distractions have not interfered with comprehension.

The way a person does or does not respond may give you some clues as to how to compensate for a noise problem. For instance, consider what happens if you request a sheet of paper and the other person does not do anything. Environmental noise may have stopped the message from being received, or the person may not

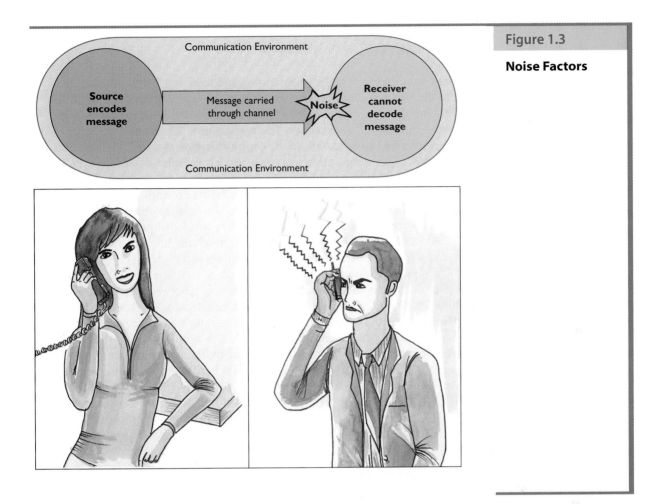

Figure 1.3

Noise Factors

have been paying attention because of psychological or cultural noise. Or the person may say, "I have difficulty hearing. Could you repeat what you said, and speak up a little?" In this case, you must increase the volume level when you repeat the message. A response of "No comprende!" to the question "Where is the Grande Hotel?" may indicate that the person of whom you asked the question does not speak English. You may then want to switch to Spanish, if you know the language, or show the person a brochure of the hotel. As a sender, you must keep your eyes and ears open to anticipate a problem and, if one exists, to adjust your communication.

The Context

Communication does not occur in a vacuum. It always relates to the **context:** who is present, where the communication is taking place, and the general attitude of those assembled. Where we are and who is with us affect our communication. Such factors as the size of the room, the color of the walls, and the type and placement of the furniture can all affect how we feel, the way in which we communicate, and the type of communicating we engage in. For example, placing a large number of people in a small work area, as is often the case with direct-phone salespeople, may bring about emotional stress that can be reflected by erratic communication.

Communication as a System

Think of your daily messages, your sending and receiving. There is a *system,* a pattern, to the way you communicate with others. The pattern centers on who speaks, what the speaker says or is allowed to say, the way in which the message is sent, and where the speaker and receiver are. The participants, the setting, the purpose, and how they interact form the basis of the **communication system.**

The flow of communication in a consistent pattern allows communication to be regular and predictable, not random, and gives everyone who participates a sense of assurance and security. Identify a communication system with which you are familiar (e.g., your family or work unit). You can probably anticipate what is going to happen and how your actions will affect others before you actually act. Your awareness of how well your ideas will be accepted or of how much encouragement or discouragement you will receive may well dictate what you do and do not say.

The type of communication system used affects who speaks. In a strongly parent-dominated home, for example, a parent may place restrictions on the type of language children may use and the topics they can discuss. Any attempt by the children to challenge the system may be met with strongly negative reactions and may result in verbal or even physical punishment.

A communication system can be shaped by the communicators' age, status, gender, attraction for each other, and cultural heritage. For example, in a family system, the rules for the male members may be different from those for female members, regulations may alter as the children get older, and favored children may be allowed more freedom than the others. Certain families may be influenced by a historical ethnic pattern that dictates how much public display of emotion is allowable and whether family members may express opinions. In many households, when children reach adolescence, their attempts to change the rules and not to be treated as children are at the core of many family conflicts.

A particular setting may encourage or discourage communication. In some settings, people may feel free to disagree whereas in others they may feel restricted. Some instructors, for example, encourage differences of opinion in their classroom; others demand adherence to their philosophy and discourage interpretations. Students quickly learn the rules in classrooms and conform accordingly; if they do not, they may be faced with lowered grades or verbal reprimands.

The purpose of the communicative act also may result in limits to the system. Trying to tell someone what you believe is a different task and experience from attempting to persuade that person to take some action you desire. Parents may be more than willing to hear children talk about what curfews their friends have, but when they try to persuade their own parents to extend their own curfew, they are rarely successful.

An artistic mobile is a good analogy to a system. It swings around until, by addition, subtraction, and other alterations, it attains balance. It remains that way until

The type of communication system used affects who speaks.

something disturbs the balance. In human communication, once a system is set up and operating, any attempt to alter that system and its pattern of rules can impair the system or cause it to stop functioning. This does not mean that all systems that are working are good ones. It merely suggests that when a system is functioning, regardless of whether the participants are happy with the pattern, at least there is a basis for understanding how the communication of the people within that system will take place. For instance, if you are aware that your supervisor is not going to accept anyone else's ideas, you learn to live with the system or find another job.

Interestingly, positive results can emerge from a system that is not working well because awareness of a problem may halt a negative system. For example, if a family unit has been operating under a reign of physical and verbal abuse, something that happens to stop the abuse could result in a much-needed change or could bring the system to an end.

Once rules become nonexistent or fuzzy, chaos may result. The basis of good communication patterns between any two or more people is the ability to alter the system with little chaos in the process. The inability to adjust within a reasonable period of time is often the basis for arguments and conflict.

In the complex process of human communication, it is not enough simply to be able to identify the component parts and realize that communication is systematized. We must also understand how these components fit together. A useful way of doing this is to look at models of the process of communication that illustrate how the various elements relate to each other.

Models of Human Communication

Any model is a simplification; communication does not, for example, have the clear-cut beginning and end that a model suggests (see Figure 1.4). Despite this limitation, models can help us to see the components of communication from a perspective that will be useful in analyzing and understanding the process.

Although there are many ways to describe the act of communication, three are used here to illustrate the process: the linear, the interactional, and the transactional.

Linear Model of Communication

Early theoretical work concerning verbal communication evolved from ancient Greek and Roman rhetoricians who were concerned with the proper training of orators. For this reason, early theories of communication stressed the role of the orator, the public speaker. The theories reflected what might be called a one-directional view of communication, according to which a person performs specific actions in a specific sequence during a speech and elicits specific desired responses from listeners. This view is called the linear model of communication (see Figure 1.5).

In the **linear model of communication,** a source encodes a message and sends it to a receiver through one or more sensory channels. The receiver then receives and decodes the message. For example, after you buy a computer, you listen to the tape-recorded message from the manufacturer. The tape explains how to insert the operating system disk and turn the computer on. When you follow the directions and the computer comes on, the communication has been successful.

Figure 1.4

A Simple Model of Communication

Although one-directional communication may be necessary, its effectiveness is limited. To illustrate this, let us consider an example. José (the speaker) says, "Please put the book on the table when you are done with it." He then turns and walks from the room. Brooke (the listener) has a stack of books in front of her; she is not certain which one to place on the table. In this example, José is assuming that this sending of a message is all there is to communicating. But this assumption ignores the important role of the receiver in responding to (and consequently affecting) the sender or the message, or both, by providing feedback. This feedback can enable the sender to check to see if an order is understood, a policy accepted, or a message clear.

Sometimes it is impossible to open communication for direct feedback; media newscasters, for example, must give careful consideration to figuring out the most appropriate language, clarifying examples, and structure to assist in avoiding listener or viewer communication noise because they normally have no avenue for direct feedback.

Employment managers, as well as teachers and parents, need to be aware of the limits of the linear approach to communication; issuing orders and directives does not necessarily mean that effective communication has taken place.

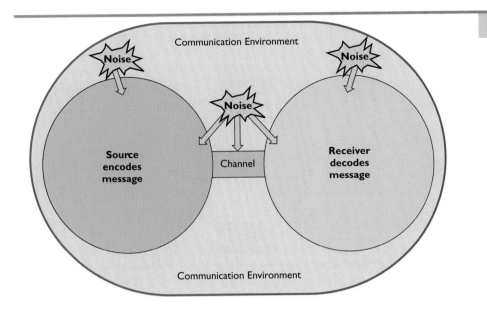

Figure 1.5

The Linear Model of Communication (One-Directional Communication)

Interactional Model of Communication

The linear model of communication does not take into account all of the variables in the communication process. Rather, it is a simple source-receiver model. For this reason, some early behavioral scientists, influenced by research in psychology, expanded the notion of the process to encompass greater interaction and to demonstrate the dynamic, ongoing nature of communication. The interactional model of communication is displayed in Figure 1.6.

In the **interactional model of communication,** a source encodes and sends a message to a receiver (through one or more of the sensory channels). The receiver receives and decodes the message, as in linear communication, but then encodes feedback and sends it back to the source, thus making the process two-directional. The source then decodes the feedback message. Based on the original message sent and the feedback received, the source encodes a new message that adjusts to the feedback (adaptation). For example, José says to Brooke, "Please hand me the book." Brooke looks at the pile of books in front of her and says, "Which one?" (feedback). José responds, "The red one on the top of the pile" (adaptation).

This view of communication accounts for the influence of the receiver's responses. It suggests a process that is somewhat circular: sending and receiving, receiving and sending, and so on.

Whenever possible, communicators should attempt to interact so that they can find out how effective their communication actually is. For example, José's analysis of the number of books available might have led him to the conclusion that he needed to be more specific, and he therefore could have said, "Please hand me the red book on the top of the pile." Or he might have wanted to ask, "Do you know which book I want?" Or he might have waited until Brooke put the book on the table to see whether she understood him. If she did not, he could have corrected his error by being more specific in his directions.

Managers in organizations, parents, and teachers should make use of this communication model in order to ensure that their employees and customers, children, and students have received and can react to their messages.

Figure 1.6

The Interactional Model of Communication (Two-Directional Communication)

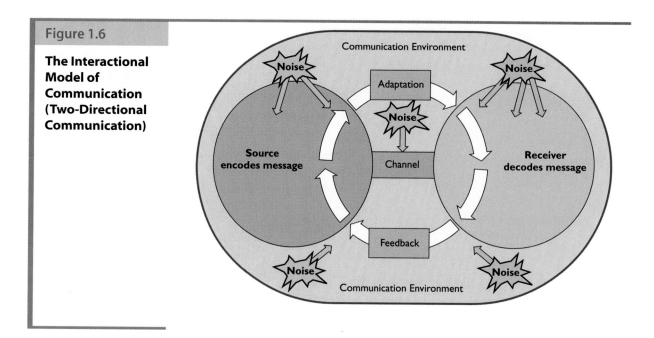

Transactional Model of Communication

Theorists have suggested that communication may not be as simple a process of stimulus and response as the linear and interactional models suggest. This view supports the idea that communication is a transaction in which source and receiver play interchangeable roles throughout the act of communication. Thus, a clear-cut model of the process is not easy to construct. Figure 1.7 illustrates the **transactional model of communication.** In this model, the communicators simultaneously process messages. Communicator A encodes a message and sends it. Communicator B then encodes feedback and sends it to A, who decodes it. But these steps are not mutually exclusive; encoding and decoding may occur simultaneously. Speakers may send a verbal message and at the same time receive and decode a nonverbal feedback message from listeners. Because messages can be sent and received at the same time, this model is multidirectional and the message overlaps.

Notice that one person is not labeled the source and the other the receiver. Instead, both communicators assume the roles of encoder and decoder in the transaction, thus simultaneously communicating—for example:

Miguele (source) says, "I love you," *while*

Miguele (receiver) sees Latica walk away as he is speaking, *while*

Latica (source) walks away from Miguele, *while*

Latica (receiver) says, "I love you," *while*

Miguele (source) stops, turns, frowns, and says, "I'm not sure you mean that," *while*

Latica (receiver) sees Miguele nod his head and walk toward her as she speaks, *while*

Miguele (receiver) hears her words, *while*

Miguele (source) nods his head and walks toward Latica as she speaks.

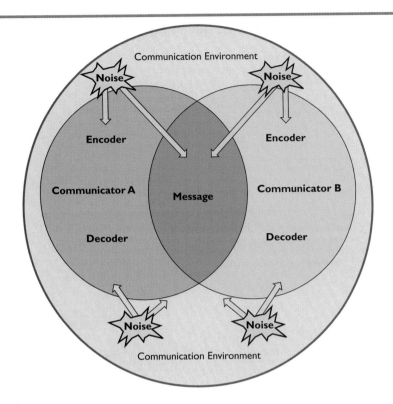

Figure 1.7

The Transactional Model of Communication (Multidirectional Communication)

Throughout the encounter, both Miguele and Latica are simultaneously sending and receiving (encoding and decoding) verbal and nonverbal messages. This is descriptive of how human communication often occurs.

The Models Compared

Comparing the three models in an example will give you an understanding of how each one differs from the others.

The director of public relations of a major corporation presents a speech over closed-circuit television from the headquarters' media studio to the marketing personnel at district offices located throughout the country. This is an example of the *linear model of communication* (see Figure 1.8a).

Next, the director gives the same presentation in the corporation's boardroom. She sticks to the manuscript she prepared, making no effort to seek feedback. Following the speech, she asks if there are any questions. A member of the board asks a question, which she answers. The question-and-answer session demonstrates the *interactional model of communication:* the sender encoded and sent a message, it was received and decoded, feedback was given (the question), and adaptation was made (the answer) (see Figure 1.8b).

Then the sales staff enters the room. The public relations director starts to speak. As she does, a salesperson asks a question. While the question is being asked, the speaker nods her head. She then verbally agrees with the salesperson. While this is happening, the salesperson also nods his head, indicating that he understood what was just explained, and says, "I get it." This is an example of the *transactional*

Figure 1.8	Comparing the Linear, Interactional, and Transactional Models of Communication

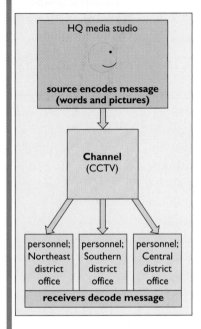
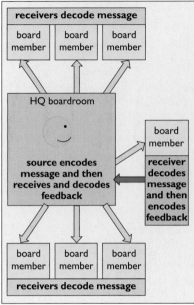
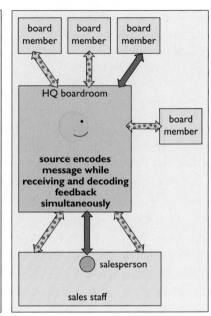

model of communication (see Figure 1.8c). Note that in Figure 1.8c, the red arrows indicate verbal and nonverbal feed back, while the dotted arrows indicate nonverbal feedback.

Besides understanding what the communication process is, it also is important to understand how we are affected not only by communication that is face-to-face but also by communication that is media derived.

The Media as Communicator

We are influenced by the **media**—radio, television, Internet, magazines, newspapers, film. Radio and television play a role in the communication lives of almost every person. When you consider that the typical person spends four hours and fifteen minutes a day in front of a television set, you can appreciate the potential influence the media can have.[17] Add to this the popularity of the Internet as a communication tool, and your awareness of the influence should increase even more. The Internet has allowed us instant access to information and to other people. In fact, many people are now using the Internet as a substitute for telephone and face-to-face interactions. Magazines, newspapers, and films abound. Some people are regularly tuned in to the media, listening to a personal radio while exercising, for example, or watching television while cooking dinner.

Many lives are shaped by the media. People develop role models based on seeing sports and entertainment celebrities on television, listening to them being interviewed on radio, or reading what is being said about them on the Internet. The images that the media project tell us how to dress, how to spend our time, and how to be a consumer. As political, business, and social attitudes are relayed, we form our beliefs on war, abortion, what stocks to buy or sell, or whom to vote for in the upcoming election. MTV and compact disks not only influence our music tastes but also send political, religious, and social messages.

The result of this media exposure can be positive. Children learn the alphabet and numbers through *Sesame Street.* They learn values from *Barney.* National Geographic specials and print sources provide information about people, animals, and places. We attend symphonies and dance performances without leaving our homes. Oprah introduces us to perspectives and to books.

A person's culture is passed to him or her through proverbs, family stories, fairy tales, songs, poetry, and literature.

But there is a downside to this exposure. As people spend time in front of television sets, listening to the radio, attending movies, and going online, they have less time to engage in direct conversations with others and in reading books and studying. Critics point to television, for example, as a key to the declining reading and academic scores of students and in the rising incidence of violence in the United States. The perception of the influence of media violence on the perpetrators of the 1999 shootings at Columbine High School in Littleton, Colorado, led then President Clinton to order the Federal Trade Commission to undertake a study. The goal was to determine if television and film companies use violent language and imagery to lure young, impressionable consumers and whether the amount of violence on television and in the movies has desensitized people to death and destruction. There is also the question of whether exposing people to information about violence can result in further violence. The number of copycat crimes after the Columbine shootings, for example, was perceived to have resulted from the exposure to the coverage of the murders on television. In addition, questions have been posed as to whether the media publicity about where on the Internet information on making and using bombs could be found and how weapons can be illegally obtained was instrumental in destructive acts.

Like television, the Internet has become a major mediated communication channel. It is estimated that more than 400 million people in the United States use the Internet.[18] As more and more people spend time at their computers getting information, e-mailing friends and family, and participating in online educational opportunities, the impact of this medium becomes profound. The rapid advances of the system now enable us to watch films, listen to the radio, place phone calls, do banking, watch each other, and shop, all online.[19] Some critics fear that this will turn us into social isolates who interact less with each other and more with our computer screens. Others point out, however, that the Internet brings friends and families together in meaningful ways as people maintain ongoing e-conversations and connections as well as allowing them to conduct personal and professional business without leaving their homes or businesses.

A media critic maintains that we are going to have to be trained to "read" television and other media in order to use them positively. He argues, "Only when we recover a critical distance from the technology which seduces us with its amusing appeal, can we recover the appropriate balance of mediums that will make us an intelligent culture."[20] An intelligent culture is one in which the inhabitants are competent communicators. Understanding how culture affects communication is another important concept to investigate in order to understand the world of communication.

Communication and Culture

What phrase or terms immediately come to mind when you are asked, "What is your culture?"

Intercultural and Intracultural Communication

"Each of us is a cultural creature. Each of us is furthermore a multicultural being."[21] You may not have thought about it, but you are the sum total of your environmental influences—the influences of your family, your community, your religious upbringing or lack of upbringing, your education, and the media with which you have come in contact. Because you have so many cultural influences, you are a multicultural being.

"It is culture that gives us our social and political ideals. It is culture that gives us our language, our music, our way of relating to others, and our expressive forms. It is culture that makes us human."[22] The words you utter and think, the actions you take, and your ability to interact with others have all been laid out for you by your cultural influences. You are a human because you have the ability to selectively use language to think about what has happened, use those experiences to perceive in the present tense, and project into the future. You can convey ideas, perceptions, and beliefs because of the language you have been taught.

"Culture penetrates into every aspect of our life and influences the way we think, the way we talk, the way we behave."[23] "Culture pervades the arts, beliefs, behaviors, ceremonies, concept of self, customs, ideas and thought patterns, ideals, knowledge, laws, language, manners, morals, myths and legends, religion, rituals, social institutions and values."[24] You are your culture, and your culture is you.

Usually "when one speaks of culture, nationality comes to mind."[25] **Nationality** refers to the nation in which one was born, now resides, or has lived or studied for enough time to become familiar with the customs of the area. Some nationality identifiers are Irish and Korean. Nationality is only one factor of culture, however. Other cultural group identifiers are the region of a country (e.g., the southern part of the United States), religious orientation (e.g., Jewish), political orientation (e.g., Democrat), socioeconomic status (e.g., upper middle class), gender (e.g., female), sexual orientation (e.g., gay male), age or generation (e.g., senior citizen), vocation (e.g., executive), avocation (e.g., stamp collector), family background (e.g., Italian Catholic from a large family), marital status (e.g., married), and parental status (e.g., single father). We are each culture filled, a combination of many cultures.

A great deal of your daily communication centers on your cultural identifications. As a student, for example, how many times do you refer to student-oriented topics, including the institution you attend and how your education will help you in the future? You probably compare and contrast your "studentness" with qualities of other students and nonstudents.

Communication and culture have a direct link. A **culture** consists of all those individuals who have a shared system of interpretation.[26] Culture is a communication phenomenon because it is passed among its adherents by communication: written and oral, verbal and nonverbal. "Culture is the software that allows the hardware (the person) to operate."[27] Your parents, the schools you have attended, and the media were all influential in aiding you to develop your belief system through communication. You were spoken to and listened to, and you saw and read about the rules, customs, and habits of those with whom you lived in your home, region of the country, and nation. This is an ongoing process; it was and is done through communication. Your culture has been passed on to you through proverbs, family stories, fairy tales, songs, poetry, and literature.

Culture is a communication phenomenon because it is passed from generation to generation through interactions.

When you interact with those with whom you have a cultural bond, you are participating in **intracultural communication.** For example, a baseball fan speaking to another baseball fan has a cultural bond. When you speak to those with whom you have little or no cultural bond, you are engaging in **intercultural communication.** A Japanese citizen with little knowledge of New Zealand and a New Zealander with little knowledge of Japan or its customs who are speaking with each other are involved on an intercultural level.

When people from various cultures live in the same place, unique multicultural situations can emerge.

Multiculturalism

The term **multiculture** refers to a society consisting of varied cultural groups.[28] The United States is a multicultural country as it relates to ethnic derivation; it is made up of African Americans, Hispanic Americans, Irish Americans, and many others. It is also multicultural as it relates to the broader definition of culture because it contains such differences as women and men, homosexuals and heterosexuals, and religious believers and atheists.

Much attention has been given to **multiculturalism,** a political and attitudinal movement to ensure cultural freedom. The movement came about because "a lot of people are ignorant about people of color, gay and lesbians, or whatever [Hispanics, Spanish Americans, Asians, and people from other cultures]. These groups feel like they are marginalized."[29]

Current estimates are that one in four residents of the United States is black, Hispanic, or Asian."[30] "By 2035, more than half of all United States residents younger than eighteen will belong to minority groups,"[31] and it is predicted that by 2056, non-Hispanic whites will comprise less than 50 percent of the population (see Figure 1.9). Many of these individuals have verbal and nonverbal patterns quite different from those of European Americans because of their cultural background—in this case, their ethnic or racial group.

People from ethnic and racial minority groups face a different and sometimes hostile and alien culture, value system, and communication system when entering such areas as school systems and corporate, social service, and governmental environments.[32] For example, many minority students perform poorly in school classes because they lack competence in the majority culture's rules for communication.

The ethnic majority often doesn't understand or has biases against those who are culturally different, and the culturally different don't understand the motives and patterns of the mainstream.

Accepting that you are a cultural being, understanding the process you use to discuss cultural affiliations as well as other aspects of yourself, is an important part of learning to be a competent communicator. Communication is the key to creating and maintaining a civil society in which people of differing cultures can live in harmony and peace.

Ethnocentrism

You are introduced to Aaron and think it is ridiculous that he wears a skullcap, a *yarmulke,* all the time. You are invited to Chan's home and are repulsed when you are told that the meat being served at dinner is snake meat. Were you amazed when you heard that in many Arabic countries women had to cover their entire bodies when they were in public? Your reactions centered on the concept of ethnocentrism. "**Ethnocentrism** is the belief that one's culture is primary to all explanations of reality."[33] When you encountered Aaron, Chan, or the notion of an Arabic woman enclosed in a *burka,* you put into effect your concept system of what you are used to, what your culture's rules are, what you believe to be the "right" way.

Generally, we view things in terms of our own group being the center of everything, and all others being scaled and rated with reference to it.[34] The founder of sociology in the United States explained the concept of ethnocentrism as the result of people's perception that they belonged to an **ingroup**, defined as a collectivity

Communicating Cross-Culturally

If you work with people whose native language is not your own, follow these tips to communicate instructions clearly:

◆ Avoid complicated and lengthy explanations. Keep instructions short.

◆ Make it clear that you welcome questions when something is unclear.

◆ Ask them to repeat your instructions in their own words. *Reason:* If they repeat the instructions in your words, they may have memorized the words but not the message.

Source: Sondra Thiederman, Ph.D., president of Cross-Cultural Communications, cited in *Leadership for the Front Lines,* 24 Rope Ferry Road, Waterford, CT 60386.

Figure 1.9

Shifting Population in the United States

Source: From "By 2056, White May Be A Minority Group," *Time,* April 9, 1990. Copyright © 1990 Time, Inc. Reprinted by permission.

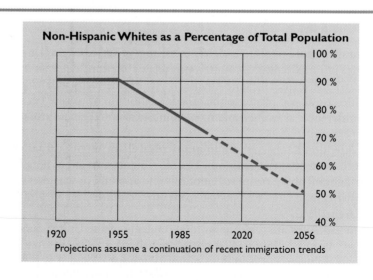

with which an individual identifies. An **outgroup** is a collectivity with which an individual does not identify. The ingroup's beliefs are perceived to be right, the outgroup's wrong.[35] Think of the clothing worn on campus by the majority of students. That's the "in" clothing. On most campuses in the early 2000s, that consists of jeans, T-shirts, and jogging shoes for males. A student showing up for class in an African *dashiki* or an Indian *sari* may be met with strange looks. That's ethnocentrism in action. The ingroup's style is considered the right one.

Ethnocentrism pervades every aspect of a culture's existence. "Examples range from the insignificant to the significant."[36] For example, "many students in the United States, if asked to identify the great books of the world, would likely produce a list of books by Western, white, male authors." You have been taught in your literature classes that these are the classics. Books written by women or by non-Westerners may be noteworthy, but they don't reach the high levels of being "classics." On the significant side, national conflicts often center on the perception that what is in our national interest is right. What is in the national interest of another country is not acceptable.

In reality, no one can claim that only certain groups have a cultural perspective or identity that is superior to another's perspective or identity.[37] Though we might like to think so, the "American way" is not superior to the "Chinese way." They are both valid in their own settings. The Chinese eat dogs and sparrows; Americans eat hamburgers and French fries. Which diet is better? Neither. What a person eats is based on cultural patterns, availability, and necessity.

Because our tradition centers on the separation of church and state, the study of religion in our public schools is not acceptable. However, studying the Koran in Iranian schools or the Old Testament in Israeli classrooms is acceptable. Which view is right? Both, if one accepts that cultures vary and that each culture has the right to act based on its historical and philosophical customs.[38]

Ethnocentrism "is a source of culture and personal identity."[39]

Ethnocentrism is not a new concept.[40] It was expressed, and reinforced, by the European colonizers in many ways. White-skinned colonists considered themselves more advanced than the natives, who were people of color. They subjugated the native peoples of Latin American, Africa, and Asia whom they considered inferior.[41] Strong attempts were made to convert the natives to the religion and views of the invaders. Often, if they would not convert to these cultural values, the natives were killed. Entire cultures were wiped out or nearly destroyed by ethnocentricism. Present-day missionaries act in much the same way when they attempt to get others to "see the light," which, of course, is the missionaries' view of the light.

Today our awareness of ethnocentrism has been highlighted by necessity. In the United States, for example, citizens are confronted daily with people from other cultures. Whether they like it or not, Americans need to accept that cultural diversity is in their collective face. "[B]y 2056[,] the 'average' U.S. resident will trace his or her descent to Africa, Asia, the Hispanic world, the Pacific Islands, Arabia—almost anywhere but white Europe. Minorities will soon constitute the majority."[42] See Figure 1.9 for a graphic illustration of this concept.

It is imperative for each of us to realize that ethnocentrism takes on a negative condition and becomes "destructive when it is used to shut others out, provide the basis for derogatory evaluations, and rebuff change."[43] Realistically, we must also recognize that the "propensity to see things from our own cultural viewpoint is very natural and, unless carried to an extreme, can have positive effects."[44] However, we must additionally realize that ethnocentrism has many negative impacts.

"First, ethnocentric beliefs about one's own culture shape a social sense of identity which is narrow and defensive. Second, ethnocentrism normally involves the perception of members of other cultures in terms of stereotypes. Third, the dynamic of ethnocentrism is such that comparative judgements are made between one's own culture and other cultures under the assumption that one's own is normal and natural. As a consequence, ethnocentric judgements usually involve invidious comparisons that ennoble one's culture while degrading those of others."[45]

Ethnocentrism can affect not only our view of nationality differences but also such factors as religion, political orientation, gender, sex, affectional orientation, rural/urban/suburban living environment, vocation, avocation, family, and family status. Thus, ethnocentrism can cause the alienation of cocultures from the dominant culture, or one group from another. Cultural beliefs in the superiority of males over females, for example, caused women in this country to be denied the right to vote or to enter certain professions, to receive lower wages, and to be denied access to opportunities to participate in sports for many years.

The blocking of interaction because one is locked in his or her own parochial view of the world prevents a person from seeing anything other than himself or herself and his/her own culture. In its highest forms, extreme ethnocentrism leads to a rejection of the richness and knowledge of other cultures. It impedes communication and blocks the exchange of ideas and skills among peoples. Because it excludes other points of view, an ethnocentric orientation is restrictive and limiting.[46] It can lead and has led to racism, sexism, and even war.

Understanding the negative effects of ethnocentrism may result in a fallout related to cultural insensitivity. However, the concept of the need to limit or eliminate ethnocentrism is easier to understand than to activate. "Putting aside our use of our own historical and cultural reference points to listen to the message of another is no easy task."[47]

In reality, can ethnocentrism be decreased or eliminated? Some theorists believe that two major actions can help change the behavior: "direct, personal (one-on-one) contact with an unalike other" and "intercultural communication training that is experiential." They propose that changes can be made by increasing contact between unalike individuals. In this way, through travel and interactions, people can become aware of others' patterns and learn to accept them as being as valid as their own patterns. And through training, individuals can understand the nature of their ethnocentric beliefs and increase their empathy by experiencing the unalike culture. An example is a two-week training course in India that was designed to decrease the sexism of male government employees. This Women's Awareness Training puts the male trainees in the daily role of an Indian woman. The trainees carry water from a distant well, wash their clothes and dishes, cook, and clean their living quarters. The male trainees are not allowed to go outside of their residences without permission of a female trainer. Nor are the trainees permitted to drive a vehicle. Thus, the Indian men are taught to empathize with the subservient role of Indian women. Individuals who have completed this training say that it has had a powerful effect on their sexist attitudes and has decreased their ethnocentrism.

An additional concept indicates that in order to decrease their ethnocentrism, individuals must realize that all cultures are not alike nor should be alike, that it is acceptable for people to be different, that one cannot expect all people to do things in the same way or to believe the same things, that there are cultural differences, that ethnocentricism causes problems, and that they should integrate cultural differences into their own worldview.[48]

Some communication experts feel that ethnocentrism must be replaced by cultural relativism through a concentrated effort to educate students about the dangers of being self-absorbed. **Cultural relativism** professes that individuals should judge another culture by its context and not by comparing one culture with another, with neither being right or wrong.[49]

They further contend that to counter ethnocentrism, students must be taught and given the opportunity to recognize individual differences and the uniqueness of each person/culture. The Semester at Sea program of the University of Pittsburgh is an academic attempt to help students gain such experience. Students travel to ten to fifteen countries during a single academic semester. Before visiting each country, students are instructed about the unique features of each nation, including their language, treatment of sexes, nonverbal patterns, and religions. A student who took an Intercultural Communication class expressed the point in a letter to one of your authors who was his instructor, "When people ask me about the voyage and what it taught me, I often respond with the statement, 'It's not good. It's not bad. It's just different.' Those words of yours brought home a new found awareness that I can use everyday as I continue to encounter people and cultures different from my own. I truly learned the meaning of differences."

In the United States one of our cultural cornerstones is freedom of speech. As a competent communicator, you should know your privileges and responsibilities concerning your constitutional rights. Your communication liberties are soundly influenced by the First Amendment to the U.S. Constitution.

First Amendment Speech

The First Amendment to the Constitution bans Congress from passing laws "abridging the freedom of speech." Therefore, when we are confronted with the question of the meaning of **freedom of speech,** the answer tends to be that it is the protected right to speak without restrictions—to be free to say what we want. In reality, however, since it is impossible to know the specific original intent of any of the items in the Constitution or its Bill of Rights, First Amendment rights have been broadly interpreted over the years to include many forms of expression.[50] The simple language of the First Amendment leaves much to interpretation. Because of this, the Supreme Court has been called on to establish standards and guidelines to resolve free-speech disputes. As a result of the many struggles over protecting First Amendment rights, it is perceived that free expression receives more protection in the United States than in other countries.

This lack of a clear definition of what is really meant by "abridging the freedom of speech" and the resulting differences of opinion in what is allowable have led to controversy and lawsuits. An examination of cases shows the complexity of the issue of freedom of speech:

- ◆ A student was expelled from Brown University for shouting racist, anti-Semitic, and homophobic epithets outside a campus dormitory while in a drunken state. The decision was challenged on the grounds that his First Amendment rights were violated by the university code, which restricts actions showing flagrant disrespect for the well-being of others.[51]

- ◆ The Iowa Board of Regents imposed a policy that requires professors to tell state university students when they are about to see explicit representations of human sexual acts. The policy stemmed from complaints over a film that was billed as an erotic comedy and a landmark in gay filmmaking. Some critics accused the regents of restricting academic freedom and taking away First Amendment rights.[52]

◆ For years, colleges and universities have had regulations regarding what speech acts and activities are acceptable and permissible on their campuses. "In June, 1993, a Supreme Court ruling dismantling a hate speech ordinance in Minnesota forced colleges and universities nationwide to rethink their hate speech policies."[53] The Court made it clear that hateful speech could not be banned because of its content.

Is there justification for limitations placed on freedom of speech, or are such restrictions unacceptable?

One of the justifications offered for limitations on freedom of speech is that *words are deeds.* It contends that some symbolic behavior may be so harmful that we are justified in restraining it. A presidential assassin might plead that he or she acted for the purpose of sending a political message to the public. To regard such a claim as legitimate may blur the line that must be maintained between speech and action.[54]

An argument against limitations on freedom of speech centers on the idea that *speech codes leave the judgment of whether the speech is good or bad to the speech code enforcer.* The reason for the First Amendment, it is contended, is that "the government is neither capable nor deserving of determining what is true, benevolent or moral speech."[55]

A further contention against limitations on the freedom of speech proposes that "more often than not, *the free-speech issue becomes a weapon to fight some other cause* . . . flag burning, blocking access to abortion clinics, pornography."[56] This assertion suggests that it is not freedom of speech or the First Amendment that is being dealt with in these cases but rather the causes themselves.

Also questioned is the issue of where to draw the line. "*If one speaker is banned, every speaker must be banned,* not only those who are not politically correct"[57] or with

Ethical behavior is guided by such values as integrity, fairness, responsibility, equality, confidentiality, honesty, respect, and freedom.

whom authorities disagree. The point can be carried to its extreme. Since almost all of us have someone who will disagree with us, no one would be allowed to speak.

The arguments about what freedom of speech really is and what the writers of the Constitution meant by First Amendment rights rage on. In her U.S. Supreme Court nomination hearings, Ruth Bader Ginsburg stated, "We are a society that has given, beyond any other, maximum protection for the speech that we hate, and on the other hand, are concerned for the quality and dignity of individuals. Those two principles collide in this area [hate speech]."[58]

Questions arise. Should schools and libraries be allowed to remove books which they, for whatever reason, believe are "anti-American, anti-Christian, vulgar, immoral, and just plain filthy," as was done by the Island Trees School Board in New York?[59] Can these schools and libraries restrict written speech? The Supreme Court said, "No."[60] Can schools prohibit students from wearing emblems of protest such as antiwar emblems, another form of speech? The Supreme Court indicated that "students may express their opinions orally and in writing, as long as they do so in a way that does not materially and substantially disrupt school activities."[61]

Colleges have attempted to set up speech codes that prohibit selective "verbal behavior" or "verbal conduct." Bowdoin College outlawed jokes and ways of telling stories "experienced by others as harassing."[62] A student at Sarah Lawrence College was convicted of laughing at something that someone else said. She was ordered as a condition of remaining in the college to read a book entitled *Homophobia on Campus* and to write a paper about homophobia.[63] Rutgers University included as forbidden communication "any manner likely to cause annoyance or alarm."[64] The University of Maryland–College Park outlaws not only "idle chatter of a sexual nature and comments or questions about the sensuality of a person"[65] but also "gestures that are expressive of an idea, opinion, or emotion including sexual looks such as leering and ogling with suggestive overtones."[66]

Following the September 11, 2001, terrorism attacks on New York and Washington, D.C., much controversy arose concerning how many and what kind of restrictions could or should be placed on individuals' rights. "Free speech versus public safety is familiar territory for the court, which has tended to side with those favoring less restriction on expression."[67]

How might this conflict affect you on a personal level? Should your speech instructor be allowed to limit what topics you may speak about in a speech class? Should Internet providers be allowed to censor what you send or receive? Should your collegiate organization be allowed to bring a speaker to campus who attacks others' religious or ethnic heritage? Should an instructor be allowed to lower your grade because you speak out in class in opposition to her view?

Not only is what you are allowed to and not allowed to communicate an issue, but also important is knowing what your ethical standards are as you act as a speaker and as a listener.

Ethics and Communication

Ethics is the systematic study of what should be the grounds and principles for acceptable and unacceptable behavior.[68] Ethics are not just something that individuals practice; they are values shared by society as a whole. Customs and characteristics pervade society—individuals, families, media, government, and organizations—and frame its ethical system. The significance of conducting our human affairs in an ethical, responsible way has been highlighted by the recent corporate financial scandals. The sleazy deal making and accounting lapses by big business have prompted a renewed emphasis on ethics.

Your ethics are the values that have been instilled in you, that you have knowingly or unknowingly accepted, and that determine how you act. Ethical behavior is guided by such values as integrity, fairness, responsibility, equality, confidentiality, honesty, respect, and freedom.[69]

Your **ethical value system** is the basis for your decision making and your understanding of why you will or will not take a particular stand or action. It is the basis for your communication ethics.

Over the decades, speech communication instructors and theorists have stressed that competent speakers should, by definition, be ethical speakers. "Potential ethical issues are inherent in any instance of communication between humans to the degree that the communication can be judged on a right-wrong dimension, involves possible significant influence on other humans, and to the degree that the communicator consciously chooses specific ends sought and communicative means to achieve those ends."[70] Therefore, it is contended that speakers should give the audience assistance in making wise decisions and that

Feel Your Way to Be Ethical

Thinking FEEL when you face an ethical dilemma can keep you on the right path, says James Melton, a consultant in Palm Springs, Calif.:

◆ **Feeling** Do you feel comfortable about the situation, or does something about it worry your conscience?

◆ **Equity** Will what you've decided to do be fair to everyone involved?

◆ **Emotion** Have you let emotion overrule reason in your decision-making process?

◆ **Legality** Will what you plan to do violate any laws?

Source: Management Review, March 1998, American Management Association, 1601 Broadway, New York, NY 10019. © Communications Briefings, www.briefings.com, 1101 King St., Alexandria, VA 22314. Used with permission.

speakers' decisions about what to say should be based on moral principles. Thus, Adolf Hitler and other hatemongers were certainly persuasive and compelling speakers; their ultimate downfall was their lack of ethical values.

Ethical communicators are usually considered to be those who conform to the moral standards a society establishes for its communicators. Although this definition seems plausible, it contains a major flaw: the words ring hollow because it is impossible to list or gain acceptance for universal moral standards. Although some people claim they have the true answer, in reality there is no universal agreement on what exactly it means to be moral.

Because most readers of this book live in a society that stresses Western philosophy, the discussion of what it means to be an ethical communicator centers on this viewpoint. Nevertheless, this perspective may not be appropriate or acceptable to you, based on your ethnic, racial, and other cultural influences.

Accepting the limitations of culture and perspective, research in the communication field has isolated some specific traits of an ethical speaker in the United States. The premise of ethical speaking can be stated as "You must understand that you are a moral agent, and when you communicate with others and make decisions that affect yourself and others, you have a moral responsibility because your actions have human consequences."[71] Specifically, ethical speakers

- Do not knowingly expose an audience to falsehoods or half-truths that cause significant harm.
- Do not premeditatedly alter the truth.
- Present the truth as they understand it.
- Raise the listeners' level of expertise by supplying the necessary facts, definitions, descriptions, and substantiating information.
- Present a message that is free from coercion.
- Do not invent or fabricate statistics or other information intended to serve as a basis for proof of a contention or belief.
- Give credit to the source of information; do not pretend that information is original when it is not.

Listeners too need to operate within an ethical framework. From the standpoint of the receiver, "in most public and private communication, a fundamental implied and unspoken assumption is that words can be trusted and people will be truthful."[72] This does not mean you should accept everything that is said; that would be naive. To be an ethical receiver, you should listen carefully to the information presented and determine whether the conclusions reached are reasonable and expected. In other words, can you, from the information presented, comfortably come to the conclusion that the sender presented, and does what the speaker said make sense?[73]

In Conclusion

Communication is a conscious or unconscious, intentional or unintentional process in which feelings and ideas are expressed as verbal and/or nonverbal messages sent, received, and comprehended. It can take the form of intrapersonal, interpersonal, or public messages. Three factors are present in any communicative event: the communicators, the purpose, and the setting. We communicate through our senses. The process of communication can be understood by investigating the linear, the interactional, and the transactional communication models and the components that make up the process. As a system, communication is directly influenced by culture. In the United States, multiculturalism is an important aspect of communication, as is freedom of speech and an understanding of what is meant by ethical communication.

Learn by Doing

1. Design a model of communication that differs from any of the three presented in this chapter, and explain it to the class.

2. Identify an experience in which your attempt to communicate was a failure. Use the classification of sources of noise given in the text to label the type of interference you encountered. Why did this happen? What, if anything, could you have done to correct the interference problem?

3. Describe a context in which you find it difficult to communicate. Describe a context in which you find it easy to communicate. Why did you select each one? What implications for communication are involved in your choices?

4. Describe the system of communication by which your family operates (or operated) by investigating the patterns of communication and the rules of operation. What were the advantages and disadvantages of that system?

5. Write one phrase or expression that is unique to your family or group of friends. It should be an expression that has meaning only for that group, not one commonly used in society as a whole. It may be an ethnic expression, an ingroup reference, or some other special phrase. The other students will read the expression and try to figure out what it means. Draw inferences about semantic noise from this activity.

6. Individually each student decides what he or she would do in each of the following situations. You will then be divided into small groups to discuss your answers and report back to the class as a whole on the choices made by each group.
   a. You are taking a public speaking course. The instructor requires three quoted references in the speech that you are to present in about five minutes. You had a week to get ready but did not have time to do the necessary research. Would you make up three references, not give the speech and get a failing grade, give the speech without the references and hope for the best, or take some other action? If you would take another action, what would it be?
   b. You have just finished eating in a restaurant. You check the bill and realize that the waiter has made a $10 error in your favor. The waiter sees your reaction and asks if anything is wrong. How do you respond?
   c. You look up during a test and see that your best friend, who needs a passing grade in this class to get off academic probation, is using cheat notes. You think the instructor also saw the action. As you hand in your paper, the instructor says to you, "Remember, this class operates on the honor system. Is there anything you want to say to me?" How do you respond?

7. Your class will discuss or debate the following resolution: A higher educational institution must be a platform for the debate of social issues. Therefore, it is resolved that [name of your college/university] allow, encourage, and invite *all* speakers to present their views in public forums on this campus.

8. Your class will discuss: Is it realistically possible to be an ethical communicator?

9. Write a list of words or phrases that answer the question "What factors or identities constitute my culture?" Your answers will be used by your instructor as the basis for a discussion of "What is culture?"

Key Terms

communication
intrapersonal communication
interpersonal communication
public communication
selective communication
encode
primary signal system
decode
source
receiver
messages
feedback
frame of reference
perceptions
channel
noise
environmental noise
physiological-impairment noise
semantic noise
syntactical noise
organizational noise
cultural noise

psychological noise
context
communication system
linear model of communication
interactional model of communication
transactional model of communication
media
nationality
culture
intracultural communication
intercultural communication
multiculture
multiculturalism
ethnocentrism
ingroup
outgroup
cultural relativism
freedom of speech
ethics
ethical value system
ethical communicators

Foundations of
Verbal Language

2

After reading this chapter, you should be able to

■ **Name and describe several theories of the origins of human language**

■ **Explain and illustrate how people select, process, use, and learn symbols**

■ **Identify the features common to all languages**

■ **Define and illustrate the emotive, phatic, cognitive, rhetorical, and identifying functions of language**

■ **Explain the roles of ambiguity, vagueness, inferences, and message adjustment in relation to language distortion**

■ **Define and contrast standard versus nonstandard dialects, and relate the effects of speaking a nonstandard dialect**

■ **Analyze slang as it relates to standard dialects**

■ **Compare and contrast Standard American English, Ebonics/Black English, Spanglish, Asian American Dialect, and Native American Languages**

■ **Relate the effects of speaking a dialect or nonstandard language**

■ **Be aware of the effects of using verbal language**

Each speech community conveys a value system to its children. These assumptions are reflected and reinforced in language, and language thus creates or recreates a social reality. Language is a giant, hidden structure that permeates life.[1] Those who study language and its effects have long contended that there is a connection between language and self-perception and self-esteem, as well as between language and behavior.[2] Language reflects our attitudes. Words can create categories and expectations so deep-seated that only such devices as affirmative action plans and anti-hate laws can force individuals to act differently than their language seems to allow.

What is **language?** It is "a system of human communication based on speech sounds used as arbitrary symbols."[3] It provides one of the means for encoding messages. The *study of language* involves the study of meaning,[4] meaning based on words, the way the words are placed together, and the backgrounds and experiences of the communicators.

The channels by which the words are conveyed help create their meaning. When they appear on a printed page, words are one-dimensional; the meaning is based on what the reader thinks the words mean, with no other clues for interpretation. But the words pick up additional dimensions when they are spoken because the rate, pitch, pause, and volume of the spoken words help us to figure out the meaning of the words and the intent of the sender. Even more dimensions are available when the receiver can see the speaker and note facial expressions, gesture patterns, and body positions.

Origins of Human Language

The origin of language remains one of human evolution's enduring puzzles. However, a recent study proposes that Gestural Theory explains how humans began to speak. **Gestural Theory** suggests that "long before early humans spoke they jabbered away with their hands."[5] The theory also contends that "speech was an ingenious innovation but not quite the freakish marvel that linguists have often made it out to be."[6] The theorist asserts that quite recently (he puts the date at around 50,000 years ago) our ancestors "could make voluntary movements of the hands and face that could at least serve as a platform upon which to build a language."[7] This view is not universally accepted since there is no fossil record to prove Gestural Theory.

Some anthropologists believe that two critical mutations in our human ancestors 200,000 years ago provided for a finer degree of control over mouth and throat muscles. They maintain that this control gave our ancestors new sounds that served as the foundation of language.[8]

Another researcher has proposed the Gestural Theory of Language Evolution. This psychologist argues that language has its roots in gestures, not vocalics. He suggests that speech evolved from grunts and vocal cries that were voluntary, emotional responses to human movements of the hands and face, gestures that people used to communicate with each other.[9]

Others maintain that language evolved from primate grooming behavior.[10] Still others link speech to the movements of the mouth made while chewing. A computer neuroscientist believes that speech is based on mental reflexes.[11]

However it started, "once speech caught on, it gave Homo sapiens a decisive advantage over less verbal rivals[,] including Homo erectus and the Neanderthals, whose lines eventually died out."[12] As one researcher puts it, "We talked them out of existence."[13]

Once the verbal language was developed to supplement gesture language, an additional way to convey messages was needed, which resulted in the creation of a written code.

Language does not remain static; it is constantly changing as it reflects changes in technology, lifestyles, and social attitudes. For example, a much-used dictionary has sixteen thousand new entries in its recent edition.[14] Among them are *boot up,* meaning to turn on (based on the computer usage); *Internet,* meaning to connect together (based on electronic-highway advances); and *womyn,* the plural for *woman* (a variant that avoids the sexism perceived in wo*men*).

Selecting Symbols

How are we able to select the symbols we want to use at the split second when the need arises to use them? The process can be clarified with an example. If I hold up a cylindrical piece of graphite about one-eighth of an inch in diameter, covered with wood, painted a yellowish gold, with an eraser on one end and a sharpened point on the other and ask you what the object is, you will probably respond, "A pencil."

Look at your surroundings, focus on an object, and identify it. Did you respond quickly with a word for the object? Now think back to the experience. Did you (as we did with *pencil*) think of all the parts that describe the object you just named? Probably not. Instead, you looked at the object, recognized it, assigned the symbol to it if you could, and then spoke or thought the relevant word.

Try another experiment. Picture these objects: a pen, an apple, a glass of milk. You probably had little trouble "seeing" these objects. This means that you have been exposed to the objects and can identify their symbols. Try the experiment again and picture these objects: a finger, a book, a jerboa. The first two words in the series were probably familiar, but what about the third? *Jerboa?* A jerboa is a mouse-like rodent found in North Africa and Asia that has long hind legs for jumping and looks a little like a miniature kangaroo with the head of a mouse. You had no trouble with the words *finger* and *book* because you have already come in contact with these objects and have been told what to call them. But few Americans—with the exception of those who have traveled or lived in Asia or Africa or who have stumbled on a book or a television show that included information about this type of rodent—have had any exposure to the word *jerboa.*

Consider our symbol selection in this way. As we acquire language, we do so by hooking ideas together. When you pictured the "pencil," you saw the form of what you have been taught was identified with the word *pencil.* You saw the image and searched for the word identification you have been taught, *the symbol.* It is easy to do this with those items in our vocabulary that we can visualize. It is more difficult with abstract words. For example, what is your image of *nice* or *good* or *bad?* Those conceptual words cause us problems since they have no exact definition, no image. In these cases we probably imagine a definition and hook the word that describes it to the concept. That explains why we can often get a universal agreement in English on what a pencil is but not on what a *good* person is.

Processing Symbols

A second question now emerges: How do we remember what we have been exposed to in our environment? In the human brain, the area that allows us to communicate

---

Language Mirrors Life

Within each speech community, the language spoken mirrors human life—the personalities of the speakers, their attitudes and beliefs, their styles of thought and expression, their interactions with one another. Language so interpenetrates the experience of being human that neither language nor behavior can be understood without knowledge of both.

Source: Peter Farb, *Word Play: What Happens When People Talk* (New York: Knopf, 1974), pp. 366–367.

selectively is the *cortex.* It is the center for memory and other activities necessary for communicating. The primary language areas of most human brains are thought to be located in the left hemisphere of the cortex because only rarely does damage to the right hemisphere (e.g., when one has a stroke) cause language disorders.[15]

Our senses bombard us with signals that beg to be interpreted and stored in our information bank. In response, the cortex stores, computes, and eventually processes some of these incoming signals and puts forth the necessary information. This operation, the **cybernetic process,** functions much like a computer. It is schematized in Figure 2.1.

By investigating the process you used to identify the pencil, you can gain understanding of the operation of the cybernetic process. You have been taught the word *pencil* (*input*), and it has been placed (*stored*) in your cortex along with the image of a pencil. Thus, when you see an object made of graphite, wood, and an eraser, the sight of the object (*stimulus*) activates your storage system to sort through its stored visual signals (*search*), find the symbol that represents the image (*recall*), and allow you to identify the combination of the stored term and the object and you say, "pencil" (*output*). You have just experienced the cybernetic process in action.

A mathematician/logician who played an important role in the development of high-speed computers coined the term *cybernetics.*[16] It comes from the Greek word for "steersman." The term is significant in that the means for internal control and communication in an animal—its nervous system—are similar to those of self-regulating machines, such as furnaces with thermostats. In each one, a measuring device feeds back information about performance. In human beings, the input comes in the form of a sense image (*taste, smell, sight, sound, touch*) that is tested against stored material (*symbols, images*); the output (*feedback*) represents the symbol or image. "The major difference between human and machine communication is that human communication is imperfect. You can program a computer to send and receive the messages exactly the way you intended, but this is not the case with human beings."[17] This error factor accounts for some of our language problems, such as why you sometimes can't remember the information when you take a test, even though you studied. Sometimes the stored information is incorrect. Sometimes not enough information has been stored. Sometimes an overload occurs. Just as machines trip circuit breakers because the demand placed on their circuitry is too great, so too can you trip psychological breakers from too much pressure. It is possible to get so upset that you block messages from coming forth. But when the emotional pressure is removed, the normal flow returns. That is why experts advise people taking a test or under other stress to "turn off" every so often—look out the window, put their head down, walk around, sing a song to themselves to break the tension—and then return to their work.

Cybernetic processing starts to develop in humans at about the third month after birth. It does not become fully operative, however, until a child is capable of processing the image-symbol relationship, selecting symbols, and articulating the symbols.

Figure 2.1

The Cybernetic Process

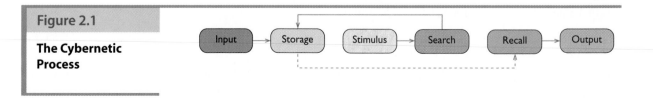

Some languages are pictographical.

Learning Symbols

Three views of how we acquire our unique language along with our beliefs, values, and attitudes are the Language-Explosion Theory, the Significant-Other Theory, the Language Instinct Theory, and the Social Construction of Reality Theory.

Language-Explosion Theory   The **Language-Explosion Theory** proposes that we build communication skills from the core of language we develop early in life. If you were asked to name the one person who had the most influence on your ability to communicate, you probably would name an immediate family member. The most common response is "my mother." In some instances the mother-infant **dyad** (pair) is replaced by a father-infant, sibling-infant, or grandparent-infant dyad. And in still other situations, the day care center or other caregiver may replace the family member. It all depends on who spoke to the child the most.

Language Development

Generally, oral language begins to emerge in infancy when undifferentiated crying patterns give way to cooing and babbling. By age 6 months, these sounds begin to take on meaning until single words appear between 9 and 12 months of age. Between the ages of 1 and 2 years, children begin to use telegraphic language, combining two words in meaningful ways, such as "me up" expressing a child's desire to be picked up. Between ages 2 and 3, a child's language evolves into more conventional sentence structure and gets more descriptive. The next year is an important one; most children begin to generalize their knowledge about language. This is when they make up their own grammar rules: "I goed to the store." Between 4 and 5 years of age, children use sentences that are more grammatically correct. This general developmental sequence means that most children are pretty adept at using oral language by the time they get to kindergarten.

Source: Joyce VanTassel-Basska, Dana Johnson, and Linda Neal Boyce, *Developing Verbal Talent* (Boston: Allyn and Bacon, 1996), p. 99.

Adults with a weak language base often were not themselves spoken or read to on a regular basis as youngsters.

Whatever the child's primary influence, his or her circles of influence quickly expand to include the communication patterns of many other people. The child's neighborhood, area of the country in which he lives, and schools attended all influence overall ability to communicate, as does exposure to the media.

Significant-Other Theory   When we are young, all of the sources around us influence us. But at a certain stage in our lives, we start selecting specific people or groups whose language, ideals, and beliefs we allow to influence us. These people become the significant others in our lives, and their effect is great. Indeed, social psychologists contend that we have no identity whatsoever except in relationship to others. This view is called the Significant-Other Theory.[18]

The **Significant-Other Theory** centers on the principle that our understanding of self is built by those who react to and comment on our language, actions, ideas, beliefs, and mannerisms. Thus, if we respect someone, we are likely to adjust our behavior and our messages to derive the most encouraging evaluation from that person. We may be influenced by such people's messages because of the position they hold, as is the case with politicians, sports heroes, or movie stars, or the control they have over us, as is true of a supervisor, teacher, or parent.

We constantly come into contact with people who have the potential to be significant others in our lives. If you think about who you are today and compare your current language, beliefs, values, and attitudes with those you held five years ago, you probably will find some noticeable differences. These very likely were brought about by your acceptance of someone else's influence. No one can change you except you, but the significant others in your life can alert you to new concepts and help lay the foundation for the changes that come if you accept them.

Language Instinct Theory   A neuroscientist has proposed a **Language Instinct Theory** that furthers our understanding of linguistic development.[19] His theory argues that language is a human instinct, wired into our brains by evolution much like spiders spin webs. Thus, language is a biological adaptation to communicate information. Infants are born with linguistic skills, skills that have developed as the brain forms in the fetus in the womb. Bombarded by sounds, the unborn child listens.[20] This neuroscientist disputes the notion that others have proposed that a child is born with a "blank slate." Thus, more of the language system may be in place at birth than linguists previously had realized.

Social Construction of Reality Theory   The power of language in human communication is profound. The **Social Construction of Reality Theory**[21] captures this significance. This theory suggests that our world and how we deal with it are shaped by how we talk about its various components. Our meanings and our understandings result from our communication with ourselves and with others. This communication frames our society. Recent history, for example, has transformed *bums in the street* to *beggars* and then to *homeless people.* These language changes reflect changes in the society's social attitudes toward the *less fortunate* and in the social construction of reality about how to deal with and view these individuals. As the language changed, the society's perceptions of the people being referred to changed as well.

Significant-Other Theory—Circles of Friends

A baby's first friends are usually the child's parents. Interaction with them prepares the child for future relationships in larger social circles. As a child grows, he/she comes in contact with others and is also exposed to media. These influencers are called the *significant others.*

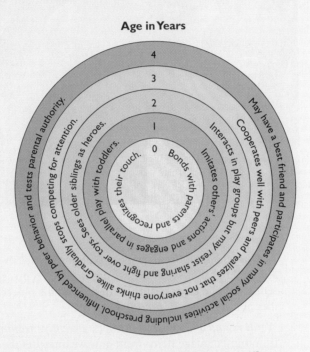

Source: "Your Child," *Newsweek* (Special Edition), Spring/Summer 1997. Copyright © 1997 Newsweek, Inc. All rights reserved. Reprinted by permission.

The Concept of Meaning

Understanding what language is, and how we acquire and access it, gives us an important basis for understanding how meaning results. The study of the sounds, structure, and rules of human language is **linguistics.** It tells us that certain features are common to all languages. Among these are the following:

Languages are based on a set of symbols, both verbal and nonverbal. We use the letters s-c-i-s-s-o-r-s, for example, to represent the instrument that is used for cutting. Or in the Euro-American culture, forming a circle with the thumb and index finger and extending the other three fingers signifies that everything is "okay."

Languages that are alphabetically based recognize the differences between vowels and consonants. In English, the vowel sounds are represented by the letters *a, e, i, o,* and *u,* singly or in combination. The consonants are such letters as *b, c, r,* and *m.* Not all languages use an alphabet. Some languages—for example, Chinese—are pictographical. A symbol represents a single word and is not made up of letters, as is the case with such languages as Turkish, English, and Hebrew.

We may be influenced by the messages of celebrities because of the position they hold, such as their being sports heroes or movie stars.

Languages have ordered structural categories, such as verbs, noun phrases, and objects. English is symbolic; we use words to represent objects and ideas. The sentence "The car is beautiful" designates the object (*car*) and expresses the idea about the car (*is beautiful*).

Words in and of themselves are not inherently meaningful. The meaning derived from our language stems from how we interpret the symbols used in that language. Because words carry no meaning as such, we derive our meaning for the symbols through our own backgrounds, experiences, and perceptions. This is well illustrated in the classic comic strip "Calvin and Hobbes." The boy, Calvin, says to his father, "The meaning of words isn't a fixed thing! Any word can mean anything! By giving words new meanings, ordinary English can become an exclusionary code! Two generations can be divided by the same language." Father to Calvin: "Marvy, Fab, Far out."[22]

Because we interpret symbols, we assign meaning to them according to our frame of reference: our backgrounds, experiences, and perceptions. Since each of us has **frames of reference** that are so different from those of others, our interpretation may be very far from the intent of the sender. To make matters even more confusing, all meanings for symbols are not easily definable. Symbols can carry both denotative and connotative meanings.

We asssign words **denotative meanings**—direct, explicit meanings—when we want to categorize them. For instance, the **denotative word** *dog* carries the denotative meaning of a "four-legged, furry animal; a canine." This denotation enables anyone to classify the animal and understand the literal characteristics of the term. In contrast, **connotative words** have an implied or suggested meaning. Words such as *good, pretty,* and *nice* have connotative meanings. It is difficult for people to agree on exactly what these words mean.

Our language is filled with connotative meanings that derive from denotative words. **Connotative meanings** are those that we associate with certain words or to which we attach particular implications. Thus, the denotative word *dog* may carry

Colors of a Rainbow

*W*hen you look at a rainbow, how many colors do you see? Each language encourages its speakers to tell certain things and to ignore others. All human eyes see the same colors because colors have their own reality in the physical world. But when speakers in most European [and U.S.] communities look at a rainbow, they imagine they see six sharp bands of colors. People elsewhere in the world, who speak languages unrelated to European ones, have their own ways of partitioning the color spectrum.

Source: From *Word Play* by Peter Farb. Copyright © 1973 by Peter Farb. Used by permission of Alfred A. Knopf, a division of Random House, Inc.

ENGLISH	red	orange	yellow	green	blue	purple

SHONA	cipsuka	cicena	citema	cipsuka

BASSA	ziza	hui

pleasant connotations, such as *lovable, friendly,* and *warm,* if we have had pleasant associations with these animals. Postal carriers, however, may find that the word has negative connotations; to them *dog* may carry the connotative meaning of *a mean, snarling, biting animal.*

Besides connotative problems, scholars who study **semantics**—the relationship of language and meaning—warn us to avoid a rigid orientation that sees everything as falling into one of two categories of value: good or bad, right or wrong. Instead of approaching the world with this either-or, **two-valued orientation,** we can remember that life is multidimensional and that meanings vary as the backgrounds and experiences of the communicators differ. (To test your two-valued orientation, complete Activity 6 in the Learn by Doing section at the end of this chapter.)

Teachers who say, "Alex is a good student" or "Manuel is not intelligent" reflect a two-valued orientation because such statements assign labels that do not allow for multiple dimensions of a student's performance. Perhaps Alex is strong in some subjects but weak in others. Or maybe Manuel has not been motivated to work in school but does have considerable academic ability.

A sender should attempt to use language as precisely as possible to reduce misunderstanding and thus avoid semantic noise. The use of definitions, examples, synonyms, and explanations can serve to clarify terminology. Consider an example: A dentist says to an assistant, "Hand me the instrument." The assistant looks at a tray of fifteen different instruments and responds, "Which one?" Obviously, the word *instrument* was so imprecise in this situation that the assistant was unable to determine the intended meaning.

Remember that not just the source has a responsibility in the transaction; the receiver is also an active participant. Giving feedback, such as asking questions and repeating the message, can aid in clarifying the meaning in a communication transaction. Further feedback can be beneficial; for example, asking the person to structure ideas in a different way can eliminate organizational noise, and stating that the words of the message need defining can eliminate semantic noise.

The Functions of Language

The way in which a person uses language is affected not only by the vocabulary available but also by the functions of language.[23] These functions are generally classified into five categories: emotive, phatic, cognitive, rhetorical, and identifying.

Emotive language employs emotional connotative words to express the feelings, attitudes, and emotions of the speaker. In discussing a movie, for example, a person who says that it is *riveting* and *gripping* is using emotive language.

Phatic language is used to reinforce the relationship between the participants in a communicative exchange. Language functions such as greetings, farewells, and small-talk exchanges are phatic aspects of language. The traditional "Hello. How are you?" and "Have a nice day" are examples of phatic language.

The function of **cognitive language** is to convey information. Cognitive language tends to be denotative. This section on the functions of language is an example of cognitive language.

The purpose of **rhetorical language** is to influence thoughts and behaviors. The speaker employs connotative terms to be persuasive by using emotionally vivid pictures and drawing implications while developing logical appeals. Advertisements to sell products or a speech supporting organ donations that uses examples of people who died because organs weren't available are examples of the rhetorical function of language.

The role of **identifying language** centers on naming things, thus being able to clarify exactly what we are speaking about—for example, "Ming went to Midway Mall." Using the name *Ming,* rather than *she* or *someone,* is identifying language.

But identification also carries implications beyond just hanging a name on something. In Sanskrit, the word for *name* is derived from *gna,* meaning "to know."[24] Naming defines people and influences communication responses. In the Bible, Genesis reports that Adam's dominion over animals was demonstrated by his being given the *power* to name them. And the North American Indian "regards his [her] name as a distinct part of his [her] personality, just as much as his [her] eyes or teeth."[25]

To be unnamed is to be unknown, to have no identity, such as the Unknown Soldier. Names can be positive, elevating the ingroup with positive terms, or negative, stigmatizing the outgroup. The outgroup is generally dehumanized, and this justifies oppression or even extermination. Hitler used this technique before and during World War II to attack Jews by labeling them *enemies of the country* and taking away their name identities and branding them with numbers, making them no more than cattle. Native Americans were debased when they were given the names *savages* and *primitives,* thus implying they were less than civilized, less than human. For years, male terms for females included demeaning names such as *chick* (dumb fowl) and *doll* (a toy to be played with). To avoid the results of negative labels, some groups have changed their names. For example, in the 1960s, civil rights leaders rejected the terms *Negro* and *colored* as historical terms that identified a weak and controlled people, and labeled themselves *black* as a clear identifier of their individuality, their skin color. Later came the belief that a name should connect the people to their country of origin, so the name was changed to *African American.*[26]

Much of what is called hate speech falls within the realm of identification. People use those images to construct their social reality, and the group being oppressed then starts to be a group at risk. The labels become the identification that demoralizes the recipient, and a tool to be used as the reason for psychological or physical destruction. From this perspective, it is acceptable to bash a *faggot,* burn down the store of a *rice-eater,* or sexually abuse a *bitch.*

Computer users have developed *technobabble,* which is computer language that has been adapted for use in other meanings.

Language Distortion

Words stand for different meanings, people intentionally or unintentionally distort information as they process it, and people intentionally or unintentionally use language that is unclear. These factors lead to **language distortion,** which is caused by ambiguity, vagueness, inferences, or message adjustment.[27]

Ambiguity can be present when a word has more than one interpretation. For example, does the word *hog* mean a *fat pig, someone who eats too much, a person who controls others' attention, a large car,* or a *motorcycle?* All of these definitions are appropriate depending on the context. Fortunately, ambiguity can often be overcome if the listener refers to the word's context to determine whether it describes an overindulging dinner guest or the purchase of a Harley motorcycle, or if the sender defines the term when used.

Vagueness results when words or sentences lack clarity. Use of words such as *they, he,* and *things like that* are vague unless we specifically know to whom or to what the speaker is referring. Many connotative words, because they have no specific definition, are vague.

A special form of vagueness that is deceptive, evasive, or confusing is **doublespeak.**[28] Examples of doublespeak abound. There are no *potholes* in the streets of some cities, just "pavement deficiencies." There are no longer any *street people,* just "non-goal-oriented members of society." Americans are not paying any *taxes;* they are subjected to "revenue enhancements" and "user fees." Patients do not die due to *malpractice;* "a diagnostic misadventure of a high magnitude" occurs. And some colleges are no longer administering *tests;* instead, students participate in "educational assessment opportunities."[29]

Doublespeak is a conscious use of language as a weapon or tool by those in power to achieve their ends at the expense of others. Some doublespeak is funny, but much of it is frightening. It can be a weapon of power, exploitation, manipulation, and oppression.[30]

Inferences result when we interpret beyond available information or jump to conclusions without using all of the information available. Because communicating is a creative process, inferences are an inevitable part of processing information. If we do not have enough material, we complete an idea with what seems logical to us, what we have experienced in the past, or what we hope or fear will be the potential outcome. Read the following sentence quickly:

The cow jump over
over thee noon.

Did you see *jump,* or did you read the word as *jumped?* What about the first and the second *over,* or *thee* and *noon?* Many people see the first couple of words and, based on their experience, instinctively infer the nursery rhyme statement "The cow jumped over the moon."

The Languages We Use

Language does not remain static; it is constantly changing. These alterations reflect changes in technology, lifestyles, and social attitudes.

Language, like chemical compounds, has a structure. There is a limited set of elements—vowels and consonants—and these are combined to produce words, which compound into sentences.[31] It is the responsibility of a **linguist**—a social scientist who studies the structures of various languages—to provide concepts that describe languages.

"Systematic and rule-governed differences exist between languages,"[32] reported one linguist. "Each language is a collection of similar dialects [a social or regional variation of a language]. Dialects, like languages, differ from each other in terms of pronunciation, vocabulary, grammar, and prosody [accent or tone]."[33] A **dialect** is a social or regional variation of a language. Over long periods of time, dialects may develop into separate languages. For instance, French, Italian, and Spanish were originally dialects of Latin.[34]

There are significant variations in language within the United States based on region, social class, religious and ethnic group, gender, and age. The same item may carry different word identifiers according to the region of the country. Philadelphia's *hoagie* is a *bomber* in upstate New York, *wedge* in New York City, *grinder* in Boston, *Cuban sandwich* in Miami, and an *Italian* in Kansas City.[35]

The dialects of the English language have more similarities than differences. For this reason, speakers of different English dialects can communicate with relative ease, though sometimes, an **accent**—the pronunciation and intonation used by a person—may cause some difficulty in understanding. Southerners, for example, may be difficult for some northerners to understand, and the "New York–New Jersey" sound is clearly identifiable yet often not always easily understood by those outside that area.

Each speaker of a language speaks some dialect of it or a combination of dialects. A common mistake is to view one dialect as best. No single dialect of a language is *the* language. But in every language, there is a continuum of prestige dialects from the lowest to the highest. High-prestige dialects are called **standard dialects,** and low-prestige dialects are **nonstandard dialects.** The dialects of those who are in power, have influence, and are educated become the standard dialects of a language; and the literature, science, and official records are written using the vocabulary and grammar that approximate the standard dialects.[36] "Powerful groups have held nonstandard speech against its speakers because it was a way of bonding their own social identity and manifesting their social status."[37]

Not only do dialects and accents create some difficulties, but the choice of which to use also can create controversy.

Standard American English

Some linguists contend that as long as no single pattern of language has been officially declared, there can be no such thing as a standard by which American English can be judged. In spite of this contention, there are generally accepted patterns of pronunciation, semantics, and syntax.

Standard American English is the language generally recognized by linguists as representative of the general population of the United States.[38] It is the oral form usually spoken by national news personalities and generally characterized by the oral sounds of the residents of the Midwest and West. The pronunciation is identified by articulating the final r (*father* versus *fa'da*) and the r before consonants in words (as in *park* versus *pok*). In these and other respects, Standard American English differs from the dialects spoken in the other principal regional-pronunciation areas: the Midland, New England, and the South (see Figure 2.2). In New England and the Midland, the *a* in such words as *fast* is generally pronounced like the *a* in *father,* and the r is not pronounced when it is a final consonant or precedes a final consonant. In the South, the r is not pronounced after vowels (*for* becomes *fo*), and simple stressed vowels are diphthonged (*him* becomes *he-im*). Out-of-the-mainstream pronunciation often is used as a source of humor. Entertainers Rosie O'Donnell and Fran Drescher, for example, have made their accents one of the focal points of their careers.

Although there may not be one "best" way of pronunciation, if some pronunciations are used, they become problematic. The words *pitcher* and *picture* do not have the same meaning and are not pronounced the same way. Such words as "hunderd" (*hundred*), "liberry" (*library*), "secatary" (*secretary*), and "alls" (*all*) linguistically do not exist. Words ending with *-ing,* such as *going* and *coming* when as "goin" and "comin" can result in negative listener reaction regarding the speaker's sophistication. Saying "jeet yit?" is not a substitute for *Did you eat yet? Many* isn't "minnie," and *didn't* is not "dint."

The Standard American English words and grammatical forms are those of nationally published magazines (such as *Time* and *Newsweek*) and newspapers (*USA Today* and the *New York Times*). These words tend to represent the vocabulary of the West, the Midwest, the Midland, and the southern section of New England. Notice, for example, that although New Yorkers tend to have their own pronunciation patterns, these do not carry over into their grammatical usage or word selection.

Standard American English is in a constant state of flux. A recently published dictionary has added 3,500 new words and phrases.[39] New entries include *bling bling* (a hip-hop term for flashy accessories), *six-pack* (a sculpted abdominal), *instant messaging* (a computer term referring to immediate conversation online), *road rage* (violent behavior exhibited by drivers), *beltway* (a roadway that

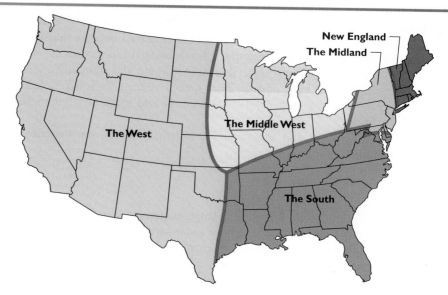

Figure 2.2

Principal Regional Pronunciation Areas

Source: From Wilbur Zelinsky, *The Cultural Geography of the United States,* A Revised Edition, © 1992, p. 118. Adapted by permission of Prentice Hall, Englewood Cliffs, New Jersey.

surrounds a city), *D'oh* (television character Homer Simpson's favorite exclamation), and *yada yada* (expression popularized on comedian Jerry Seinfeld's television show). "To be added to the dictionary, a word must be found in five different sources over five years."[40]

In addition to dialects and accents, slang plays a role in language.

Slang

The English language contains somewhere between 600,000 and 1 million words (see Figure 2.3). But the average American's vocabulary consists of only about 20,000 words, 2,000 of which may be slang.[41]

Slang denotes words that are related to a specific activity or incident and are immediately understood by members of a particular group. "Groups create their own language within a language. Peers recognize each other through its use. It's a way of belonging."[42] According to slang theory, "any group that wishes to bond together develops slang."[43] "Slang knows no color, class, or boundary."[44]

Types of Slang   Slang may come from anywhere. All it needs is a group of people who use and understand it. Computer users have developed *technobabble,* which is computer language used for personal communications. Technobabblers *interface with each other* and *debug their relationships.*[45] Because of the prevalence of computers in our society, technobabble is becoming a permanent part of Standard American English, so it is losing its status as slang. Once slang becomes mainstream language, it is no longer slang and is included in dictionaries, the chronicles of the language.

Regional slang is prevalent. In New England, a *flatlander* is anybody who does not live in Vermont, New Hampshire, or Massachusetts. People in the Midwest refer to a brown paper bag as a *sack,* whereas in some parts of the South, the same item is referred

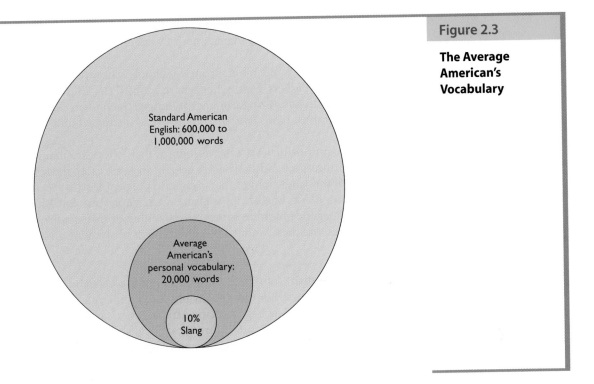

Figure 2.3

The Average American's Vocabulary

to as a *poke*. Among some southern Florida college students, *maxin'* means relaxing; *tossin' chow*, eating quickly; *shootin' the gift*, having a conversation; *jam*, partying; *phat flavor*, good music; *pop duke*, father; and *blaze*, leave. So in that environment it would make perfectly good sense to say, "We were maxin', tossin' chow, shootin' the gift, and listening to phat flavor at the jam, when the pop duke told us to blaze."[46]

Inarticulates   **Inarticulates** are uttered sounds, words, or phrases that have no meaning or do not help the listener gain a clear understanding of the message, such as the phrase *stuff like that*. They constitute what is considered to be "powerless language," language usage that diminishes rather than enhances the communication effect you wish to achieve. Studies of the negative perceptions of powerless language extend to tag questions ("Put away your toys, *okay?*"), hedges ("It's *like* difficult to concentrate"), hesitations ("*um*," "*you know*"), and intensifiers ("It's *so awesome* of you to come"). Such inarticulates become unassertive conversational mannerisms that can distract from the substance of the message and from the speaker's credibility.[47]

Nonstandard English Dialects

Many people in the United States speak languages or dialects that differ from Standard American English. Some of these speakers use a recognizable alternative language form, such as Spanish, French, Chinese, or one of the Native American tongues. In some cases, speakers present their ideas in identifiable dialects of Standard American English, such as Spanglish. Still others speak a separate but definite rule-based communication system called Ebonics, which fulfills the definition of language because it has a distinct grammatical and symbolic system; but because it has so many similarities to Standard American English, it is considered by some to be a dialect.

One of the major problems confronting schools is how to handle nonstandard American English speakers. Most schools have adopted the attitude that "we accept the language the students bring from home, but we teach them that Standard English is a tool they must have. They may not use it all the time, but when you need it, you need it."[48]

Any discussion of dialects must recognize that "there are many dialects and some get a lot of respect and some don't get any. In some cases, the respect given to the dialect is in the same amount that is given to the people who speak it."[49] A brief examination of Black English, Spanglish, Asian American English, and Native American languages can lead to some understanding of their nature, their history, the speakers who use them, and the perceived effects of speaking an alternative language or dialect.

Ebonics/Black English   On December 19, 1996, "the Oakland, California school board voted to recognize **Ebonics** (ebony phonics), sometimes referred to as **Black English,** as the primary language of many African American students and use it as a starting point to teaching Standard American English."[50] At that time the school board stated that Black English was recognized by many linguists as a legitimate language form with a unique and logical syntax, semantic system, and grammar.[51] Although, under pressure, the Oakland school board seemed to have backed off on its program, "the core of the initiative, known now as the Standard English Proficiency program, is growing."[52] It is still felt that "when teachers dismiss or demean the deep-seated speaking habits of some African American students, it has a corrosive effect on their self-esteem and interest in school."[53]

A "Vernacular Black English [Ebonics] is the most common dialect used by African Americans. This is not street talk; it is not broken English; and it is not slang."[54] It is "a private vocabulary of Black people which serves the users as a powerful medium."[55] Moreover, Black English is not a regional dialect. It reflects the common national culture of the African American community. The grammar that many African American adults in Los Angeles use in their home setting is virtually the same as that used by adolescent groups in New York. As a famous African American novelist stated, 'Black English is a vivid and crucial key to black identity.' "[56]

There is controversy as to the historical development of Ebonics. One theory holds that "Black English is rooted in a historical past that spans Africa, the Caribbean, the Creole heritage, the South, and now the northern U.S. cities."[57] Another proposes that "Africans came to the United States with no knowledge of English and developed the dialect [language]."[58] Still another version is that "it is a creole language formed out of mainstream American English and native African languages evolving from largely West African pidgin forms."[59]

Whatever its roots, linguists cite fifty characteristics of Black English that differentiate it from Standard American English, many of which have parallels with the linguistic structure of West African languages.[60] Among the most common speech markers is the use of the "invariant be" to denote an ongoing action ("He be going to work"). This usage is not present in Standard American English grammar but is parallel to the indefinite or habitual tense of languages such as French and Spanish.

"The distinctiveness of African American speech style has been problematic for group members [with mainstream speakers and in commerce]. On the one hand, speech that marks the individual as a member of the group can be important for in-

Vocal Behavior of African Americans and European Americans

African American children speak to each other less than do European American children. European Americans tend to talk to males for longer periods, while African Americans spend more time talking to females. Both African Americans and European Americans pause longer in response to racially oriented questions.

Source: From Michael Hecht, Ronald Jackson, and Sidney Ribeau, *African American Communication,* 2nd edition. Lawrence Erlbaum Associates, Publishers, 2003. Reprinted with permission of the author.

group acceptance."[61] One problem is that "children don't learn standard dialect so that they will be able to assimilate and demonstrate marketable skills in mainstream society."[62] Based on the latter viewpoint, some community leaders have encouraged African Americans to learn Standard American English and become **code switchers** who "selectively use Black English and mainstream American English depending on the situation."[63]

Spanglish   A significant group of Americans speaks a dialect referred to as **Spanglish**.[64] It is common linguistic currency wherever concentrations of Spanish Americans or Hispanics are found. Spanglish takes a variety of forms, from *hasta la bye-bye* to *lonche* (a quick lunch rather than a leisurely one), the description of a group of *los teenagers,* and the almost universally used *no problema*. Spanglish sentences are mostly Spanish, with a quick detour for a few English words and some fractured syntax.[65]

A professor of linguistics who speaks Spanglish with relatives and neighbors has characterized its use: "Among Latinos, Spanglish conversations often flow easily from Spanish into several sentences of English and back again. It's unconscious. I couldn't even tell you minutes later if I said something in Spanglish, Spanish, or English."[66]

Asian American Dialect   The last several decades have seen a large immigration of Asian Pacific language speakers into the United States. People have come from such countries as Vietnam, China, Korea, Taiwan, Japan, and Cambodia. They bring with them languages that differ from English and often from each other.

As with Spanish speakers, when Asian Pacific speakers develop an **Asian American dialect** by adapting their language to English, both vocabulary and pronunciation can be major stumbling blocks.

Aside from the vocabulary and pronunciation, Asian Pacifics confronted by English often have difficulty in developing arguments. "English is a language whose relative preciseness encourages not just argumentation and debate, but detailed analysis, Western logic, and thorough explanations."[67] This is not true of such languages as Chinese and Japanese, which are pictographic. In these languages, "precision is cumbersome and inelegant. Ordinary speech is necessarily vague and depends heavily on the cooperative imagination and sympathy of the listener."[68] Fewer words are required in Asian-language arguments because the concepts are shared in the experiences of the communicators.

Native American Languages   Controversy surrounds any attempt to discuss Native American or American Indian language. This centers on what constitutes "Indianness" and therefore their language(s). Indian identity is not the same as tribal identity because all tribes have differing languages and customs.[69]

Research in Native American language and customs has resulted in the identification of seven prominent modes of communication behavior: "(a) reticence with regard to interaction with strangers, (b) the acceptance of obligations, (c) razzing, (d) attaining harmony in face-to-face interactions, (e) modesty and doing one's part, (f) taking on familial relations, (g) permissible and required silence, and (h) a unique style of public speaking."[70] Since permissible and required silence is encouraged, many Native Americans are misperceived as communicative apprehensive.

The idea of harmony pervades the Navajo belief system of what things are and what they ought to be. "Rhetoric in such a universe has as its primary function not in discovery but in use, and its uses are carefully prescribed, sanctioned by ancestral tradition, and functional in maintaining the world as it ought to be."[71] The basic concepts are that talking it over is a way to straighten things out; talking is the most important means of persuasion; speaking and thinking are ways to energize and secure knowledge. Decisions must be discussed with all who happen to be around, which accounts for the importance of family councils.[72]

The use of razzing is a communication format unique to Native Americans. "**Razzing** is a collective form of storytelling in which participants take some episode, humorous or not, from a present or past experience and relate it humorously to the others in attendance. The story, which is often lengthy, is then characteristically embellished and altered by others who are present."[73] Razzing serves as a method to "determine cultural competency, identify ingroup and outgroup members, and as a form of instruction."[74]

A difficulty some Native Americans encounter in conversing with Standard American English speakers centers on the use of narration. Traditionally, Native Americans have relied on razzing and telling historical or experiential stories to clarify their points. Often the tales only allude to the general point being made rather than directly relating to the specific issue. It is called the **spiral structure of argument.** This is similar to the narrative communication patterns of many Hispanics and Arabs and strikes many Standard American English speakers as abstract and imprecise since it does not set up a clear purpose and use evidence to clarify and prove.

Effects of Speaking a Dialect or Nonstandard English   Recent studies have reinforced the concept that speaking a nonstandard dialect rather than Standard American English can be detrimental to a person's educational and economic health. The message seems clear: "You need to speak right to go to college, to get a good job."[75]

Children entering schools with weak Standard American English skills are at a definite disadvantage.[76] Since they don't know the alphabet or have the vocabulary, learning to read and understanding class discussions become extremely difficult. They often quickly turn off and eventually drop out.

In economic terms, nonstandard speakers are given shorter interviews and fewer job offers than Standard American English speakers. When job offers are presented, nonstandard speakers are offered positions paying as much as 35 percent less than those offered Standard American English speakers.[77]

In social terms, speakers of nonstandard dialects often are confronted with mistaken, negative assumptions concerning their intelligence, dependability, and creativity. Standard American English even contains prejudicial terms to describe those who speak nonstandard English (e.g., *hillbillies* and *crackers*).

Many different languages and accents make the United States a rich tapestry; however, people speaking dialects should be aware that in some instances, education and speech therapy can make alterations in their vocabulary and speaking patterns if they desire change. That desire is usually based on a person's awareness that his career and social goals include particular language requirements that the person does not possess.[78]

Using Verbal Language

Language "carries most of the rich and complicated symbolic freight that humans exchange."[79] To be effective, communicators must consider how most appropriately to use language.

Indian identity is not the same as tribal identity, as many tribes have differing languages and customs.

Because language is symbolic, it is necessary to be as clear and precise as possible when using words. You need to consider the other person's frame of reference and whether he or she will share your interpretation of the language used. If not, it is important to adjust your vocabulary level and word choice to fit the listener(s). For example, you must be careful not to use technical terms that are beyond your listener's experience. While exploring her run for the New York Senate seat she later won, Hillary Rodham Clinton, in a conversation with Lockheed/Martin plant employees, asked what they mean by the phrase *mag-lev railroad technology*. The employees forgot that she was not a railroader and would have no knowledge of the system they were talking about unless they clarified the term. You can increase your clarity by defining your terms, offering synonyms, or providing examples of the term you are using. Remember that slang expressions, words unique to a culture or a region, and euphemisms work against clarity and precision.

In addition to striving to be clear, it also is necessary to consider ways to make your language memorable. To be attention getting, words and phrases should be colorful, rhythmical, and compelling. After listening to a speech, a listener often will remember only one phrase. In fact, some speeches are identified by a single phrase. Martin Luther King Jr.'s stirring civil rights speech is identified as his "I Have a Dream Speech," based on a phrase he used over and over to make his point. As a wise communicator and an effective speaker, he was careful to include that phrase.

Words have an impact. "There are words whose effects are subtle and unperceived; there are words that comfort and words that pain, that support and that undermine; words that inform and that mislead, that foster rationality and that impede it; words that unite and words that divide."[80]

Martin Luther King Jr.'s stirring civil rights speech is identified as his "I Have a Dream Speech" based on the phrase he used over and over to make his point.

Research shows that the old adage "sticks and stones will break my bones, but words will never hurt me" is not true. Words can, according to the findings, "cause physical harm."[81] Investigations of emotionally abused women discovered that they suffered from illnesses strikingly similar "to those affecting physically abused women."[82] As a result of these findings, health care providers are being encouraged to regularly screen women for psychological abuse as well as for physical and sexual violence.[83]

A high school student who had slandered another student was asked to write an essay about the effect of his words. His essay, "The Impact Of Our Words,"[84] follows.

> It can build cities and destroy empires. It could move people to the brink of tears or inspire hate. It can be beautiful or disgusting. It can create love or destroy it. It can help people find common ground or destroy reputations. Using it carelessly has started wars. Such is the power of speesch and the words that accompany. According to many, speech is the most dangerous and oft used weapon in man's arsenal.
>
> Speech is the definition of a man, whether he is refined or crude, vulgar or complicated, appropriate or not. There is a good saying for this, "Better to remain silent and be thought a fool, than to open one's mouth and remove all doubt."

Words can hurt, too. Just think of insults and how they sting, especially from people whose opinion matters to you. Also, arguments can increase tensions between people until they snap, causing a fight. Psychological scars also take longer to heal than physical scars.

Speech can destroy reputations through slander: the vilest form of speech by far. Millions of people each year fall victim to this most heinous form of killing, for it not only destroys their reputations, it makes them wish they were dead, or at the very least someplace else.

Words and speech can be good, too. Many important cities and projects would not exist if the builders had not have had the force of will to continue, motivated by words. Words can also give encouragement, comfort, help, and sooth tempers, but used wrongly they can and will destroy anything.

Unfortunately, in the modern world, many people prefer slander, insults, and diminishing one's fellow man to make themselves feel big and important.

Also speech and words can entertain. Think of the happiness and release caused by a good joke. Comedy is the universal communicator. Where language can fail, humor can cross the gaps between cultures.

To conclude—speech and words can be used for good or evil. It all depends on the user. Unfortunately most people seem to prefer the more destructive uses of words and speech.

In Conclusion

In this chapter, the foundations of verbal language were discussed. Although there is no one accepted theory of the origins of human language, the operation of the human brain regarding its acquiring, retaining, and allowing for language usage can be explained by the cybernetic process. We acquire our language, beliefs, values, and attitudes from people and influences surrounding us. Languages are based on a set of symbols, both verbal and nonverbal. Successful communication takes place when the sender adapts the message to the background and knowledge of the particular person or audience being addressed. A dialect is used by people from the same geographical region, occupational group, or social or educational class.

Standard American English is the language usually recognized by linguists as being representative of the general society of the United States. Aspects of language are slang, inarticulates, and dialects.

Learn by Doing

1. A major controversy was ignited when the Oakland, California, school district recognized Ebonics as a language. Research the topic, and have a class discussion or debate that agrees or disagrees with this statement: Accepting Black English as a language is a sell-out to street slang and abandons good sense and kids' futures.

2. Find an example of doublespeak in a speech, a letter to the editor, or a newspaper or magazine article. Bring the material to class. Discuss what you think the speaker was trying to hide or manipulate by using doublespeak.

3. Write down one phrase or expression that has meaning only for a select group. It may be an ethnic expression or an ingroup reference. You will read the expression to other students, who will try to figure out what it means.

4. Make a list of five people who have had a significant effect on your own language use. Identify which of these people was the most influential and why.

5. List five words that have different meanings depending on the people who use them or the place in which they are used. See how many different definitions you can develop for each word.

6. This activity is geared at ascertaining your value orientation. Read each statement and indicate if it is *T* (true, proved accurate by information provided in the story); *F* (false, proved inaccurate by the information provided in the story); or *I* (inconclusive or cannot be proved accurate or inaccurate because the story does not indicate whether the information is true or false). [Your instructor will find the correct answers in the instructor's manual that accompanies this book.]

   Dale went to a travel agency to arrange some plane reservations. When Dale arrived in St. Louis, it was only two days before the wedding. After the wedding, the bride and groom took a trip to Hawaii.
   a. Dale arrived in St. Louis two days before the wedding.
   b. Dale got married in St. Louis.
   c. Dale went to a travel agency.

d. The plane reservation to get to the wedding in St. Louis was made by a travel agent.

e. Dale went to Hawaii on her honeymoon.

7. Identify someone who speaks a nonstandard dialect. Write down some examples of her or his pronunciation and/or language selections. Share the information with the class. (You are trying to learn about nonstandard dialects, not to belittle the user.)

Key Terms

language
Gestural Theory
cybernetic process
Language-Explosion Theory
dyad
Significant-Other Theory
Language Instinct Theory
Social Construct of Reality Theory
linguistics
frame of reference
denotative meanings
denotative word
connotative words
connotative meanings
semantics
two-valued orientation
emotive language
phatic language
cognitive language
rhetorical language

identifying language
language distortion
ambiguity
vagueness
doublespeak
inferences
linguist
dialect
accent
standard dialects
nonstandard dialects
slang
inarticulates
Ebonics
Black English
code switchers
Spanglish
Asian American dialect
razzing
spiral structure of argument

3

Nonverbal Communication

After reading this chapter, you should be able to

- Explain the importance of nonverbal communication as a message-sending system

- Categorize and discuss the origins of nonverbal messages

- State and explain the relationship between verbal and nonverbal communication

- List and illustrate the categories of nonverbal communication

- Analyze the role of culture in the development and use of nonverbal communication

D o you believe that when you communicate with another person, your *words* carry the majority of the meaning of the message? If you answered yes, you are mistaken. There has long been an awareness that it is possible to communicate a great deal even without using verbal language. We also are aware that nonverbal acts are symbolic acts closely connected to any talk in progress. They don't merely reveal information; they represent meaning.[1] "Nonverbal communication is a major force in our lives."[2] Nonverbal behaviors such as smiling, crying, pointing, caressing, and staring appear to be used and understood the world over.[3]

Nonverbal communication is composed of "all those messages that people exchange beyond the words themselves."[4] We have interpreted body talk, perhaps without knowing we were doing so, but only in recent years have attempts been made to analyze and explain nonverbal communication in a scientific manner.

Research has established that nonverbal language is an important means of expression. Experts in the field have identified patterns of body language usage through the study of films and videotapes and through direct observation. Nonverbal acts seem to have three key characteristics: they are sensitive to the relationship between the sender and receiver; they have meaning based on their context (the communicators, the setting, and the purpose of the communication); and they are part of, not a separate entity from, verbal communication.[5]

Because the study of nonverbal communication is more recent than the study of verbal communication, we do not yet have a dictionary of its terms or a thorough understanding of the process involved. But attempts are underway to apply the information that has been collected. One such attempt, known as **neurolinguistic programming,** has been developed to codify and synthesize research on nonverbal communication with that of other fields of communication, including cybernetics (the study of how the human brain processes information) and language study.

Traditionally, experts tend to agree that nonverbal communication itself carries the impact of a message. "The figure most cited to support this claim is the estimate that 93 percent of all meaning in a social situation comes from nonverbal information, while only 7 percent comes from verbal information."[6] The figure is deceiving, however.[7] It is based on two 1976 studies that compared vocal cues with facial cues.[8] While other studies have not supported the 93 percent, it is agreed that both children and adults rely more on nonverbal cues than on verbal cues in interpreting the messages of others.[9]

In the effort to read nonverbal communication, we must remember that no one signal carries much meaning. Instead, such factors as gestures, posture, eye contact, clothing styles, and movement must all be regarded together. This grouping of factors is called a **cluster.**

We also must remember that, just as in verbal communication, nonverbal signs can have many different meanings. For example, crossing the arms over the chest may suggest that a person is cold. But crossed arms accompanied by erect posture, tightened body muscles, setting of the jaw, and narrowing of the eyes would likely indicate anger.

Few of us realize how much we depend on nonverbal communication to encourage and discourage conversations and transactions.

A person's background and past pattern of behavior also must be considered when we analyze nonverbal communication. The relationship between current and past patterns of behavior, as well as the harmony between verbal and nonverbal communication, is termed **congruency.** When you say to a friend, "You don't look well today," you are basing your statement on an evaluation of the person's appearance today compared with her appearance in the past. In other words, something has changed, and you have become aware of a difference. If you did not have experience to draw on, you would not have noticed the change.

Few of us realize how much we depend on nonverbal communication to encourage and discourage conversations and transactions. For instance, we consciously wave at waiters and raise our hands to get a teacher's attention. Much of our opening and closing of channels, however, occurs without our consciously realizing it.

As you observe people conversing, you notice that they may indicate they are listening by moving their heads. If they agree with what is said, they may nod affirmatively. They may also smile to show pleasure or agreement. If, however, they glance several times at their watch, look away from the speaker, cross and uncross their legs, and stand up, they are probably signaling that they have closed the channel and wish to end the transaction.

Sources of Nonverbal Signs

We learn to read words through a step-by-step process in which we are taught to use our written oral and reading forms of communication. But how do we acquire nonverbal signs? There are two basic sources: innate neurological programs and behaviors common to a culture or a family.

Neurological Programs

Innate neurological programs are those automatic nonverbal reactions to stimuli with which we are born. These nonverbal "automatic reactions" are **reflexive** because of neurological drives. These reflexive drives seem to be tied to our need drives. For example, we blink our eyes automatically when we hear a loud noise (survival drive) or when a pebble hits the windshield of the car we are driving (survival and territorial drive). Our stomach muscles tighten and our hands sweat when we feel insecure (security drive).

That we are born with some of our nonverbal tendencies is illustrated by the fact that "people born blind move their hands when they talk, although they've never seen anyone do it."[10]

A study of eye-accessing cues indicates "whether a person is thinking in images, sounds, self-talk, or through their feelings their eyes move in patterns."[11] Most people, according to neurolinguistic psychological (NLP) research, will look up for visual accessing, down for linguistic accessing, to the left for past experiences, to the right for future perceptions, and straight ahead for the present-tense thinking.[12] "Some NLP experts consider eye movements to be an aid to accessing inner speech since the eye movements stimulate different parts of the brain."[13] If this is true, then following the advice that one should maintain good eye contact when speaking to someone would render "a person unable to make the accessing movements"[14] and could "interfere with and slow down the [person's] normal thinking style."[15] In academia, teachers often make the mistake of misinterpreting students' actions. For example, a teacher asks a question, and you struggle to visualize the answer, your eyes moving up or down and to the left or right [depending on whether you are looking for past learned ideas or inventing new material]. The teacher states, "Well, you won't find the answer on the ceiling." The teacher is wrong. The answer may be found by glancing up and to the left if your normal eye-glance pattern for past tense and picturing concepts is up.[16] (See Figure 3.1.)

A student who knows his or her eye-shift pattern may be able to access past-tense learning by moving his or her eyes in the direction of his or her past-tense triggering and looking up or down, depending on whether he or she is trying to access images or words.

Cultural and Intercultural Behavior

Some nonverbal behavior is learned in the same way as spoken language. When we display these culturally taught nonverbal behaviors, they are said to be **reflective**—reflective of the culture from which they were learned.

Figure 3.1	
Eye-Accessing Cues	The proponents of NLP (Neurolingistic Programming) believe that eye movements are linked to the sensory processing that goes on in a person's mind when he or she is thinking. The eye movement may be a flicker or it may be held for several seconds. This movement happens when a person is organizing incoming sensations, recalling past experiences, or imagining never previously experienced phenomena.

Eyes up and to the left: Recalling something seen before—a visual memory.

Eyes up and to the right: Visualizing something that has not been seen before.

Eyes centered, looking up: present tense visual memory; eyes centered, looking down: present tense verbal memory; eyes centered, staring (no matter whether eyes are up or down): daydreaming or not engaged in decoding any information being sent.

Source: "People Who Read People," *Psychology Today,* July 1979. Reprinted with permission from *Psychology Today* magazine, copyright © 1979 Sussex Publishers, Inc. For further information see *The Pegsasus Mind-Body Newsletter,* Issue 9, January 4, 2002, and research on neurolinguistic programming.

As children, we observe and imitate people around us; thus, we learn not only to speak but also to behave as they do. Every culture has its own body language, and the young learn its patterns along with those of spoken language. As a research anthropologist indicated, "The important thing to remember is that culture is very persistent. In this country, we've noted the existence of culture patterns that determine [physical] distance between people in the third and fourth generations of some families, despite their prolonged contact with people of very different cultural heritages."[17] These cultural patterns are readily identifiable. Italians, for example, are noted for using their hands when they speak. In contrast, the British are noted for controlling their use of gestures.

A person who uses more than one verbal language gestures according to the language he or she is speaking. Fiorello La Guardia, New York City's mayor in the 1930s and early 1940s, carried on his political campaigns in English, Italian, and Yiddish—the languages of the major voting blocs in the city. He used one set of gestures for speaking English, another for Italian, and still another for Yiddish.

Nonverbal gestures and behaviors convey different messages throughout the world. An Arabic male, for example, commonly strokes his chin to show appreciation for a woman whereas a Portuguese man does it by pulling his ear. But in Italy a similar kind of ear tugging is a deliberate insult.

In communicating nonverbally, people also operate on different action chains. "An **action chain** is a behavioral sequence with two or more participating organisms, in which there are standard steps for reaching a goal. If an individual leaves out a step, the chain gets broken, and you have to start all over again."[18] Different cultures operate under different action chains. For example, to an American, being on time normally means making contact within five minutes or so of a designated hour. To a Mexican, however, being on time often means within a reasonable time. A European American businessperson, having been kept waiting for twenty minutes in a Mexico City client's office, may decide to leave the office, feeling that she is being ignored and that the client's lateness is a sign of lack of interest in the business deal. But the Mexican client may not consider himself at all tardy and may be totally confused by the European American's quick exit.

Nonverbal Message Styles

My Son's Silent Language

An aboriginal mother wrote to her son's new teachers asking them to examine their own biases and expectations:

"He doesn't speak standard English, but he is in no way *linguistically handicapped*. If you take the time and courtesy to listen and observe carefully, you will see that he and the other Aboriginal children communicate very well, both among themselves and with other Aboriginees. They speak *functional* English, very effectively augmented by their fluency in the silent language, the subtle unspoken communication of facial expressions, gestures, body movement, and the use of personal space."

"You will be well advised to remember that our children are skillful interpreters of the silent language. They will know your feelings and attitudes with unerring precision, no matter how carefully you arrange your smile or modulate your voice. They will learn in your classroom, because children learn involuntarily. What they learn will depend on you."

Source: Jock Smith, "Inclusiveness in Learning Media, 27 January 1997," unpublished document. Originally from the Northian Newsletter, submitted by Jock Smith, Surrey School trustee and educational counselor for the Department of Indian Affairs to Focus on Equality, March 17, 1991.

European Americans engaged in business dealings with Arabs, for example, should understand and adhere to their customs of hospitality so as to be successful. The initial meeting with an Arab businessperson is typically devoted to fact finding. No commitments are implied or made, but the initial session is usually lengthy and thorough. Based on their pattern of working quickly so as not to waste time, European Americans often feel that the process is tedious. The next meeting is taken up with additional rituals. It is not unusual for a business deal to take as long as thirty days to complete.

Gesture patterns, which have verbal meanings, also vary. For instance, the thumb-and-forefinger-in-a-circle gesture means "okay" in the United States. In France or Belgium, however, it means the recipient is worth zero. The same gesture in Greece and Turkey is a sexual invitation. Similarly, an index finger tapping to the temple with the other fingers curled against the palm usually means "You're smart" in the United States whereas it communicates "You're stupid" in most of Europe.[19]

The use of space also varies widely around the world. Arabs, South Americans, and Eastern Europeans generally favor close conversational encounters, which may make European Americans feel somewhat uncomfortable and Germans and Scandinavians totally uncomfortable.

We tend to read nonverbal signs on the basis of our own personal background and experiences, and we assume that others share the same interpretations—an assumption that can be misleading, even dangerous. We must remember that in all forms of communication, an understanding of the receiver is necessary. And, as if matters were not complicated enough, we also must be aware that although cultural patterns are reported to be persistent, not all the people within a given culture share identical patterns.

Emotional Influences on Nonverbal Communication

Emotions have a direct effect on the size of people's personal territory and their resulting nonverbal responses. When people are insecure, they tend to avoid closeness. People who are emotionally upset may even become violent if someone invades their territory. Again, these are representative of the basic human needs and what happens when needs are not being satisfied.

When people are upset, their bodies may become rigid. For example, many people who are nervous about public speaking report that their throats tighten and their stomach muscles contract when they must present a speech. Under great tension, the pitch of the voice also rises because vocal cords tighten.

Those who attempt to mask their emotional upsets may become physically ill. The body must release its pent-up feelings. Suppressed emotions must get out somehow, and the result may be a headache or an upset stomach.

People under stress also find that others loom larger and closer than they actually are. To a frightened child, an adult can seem like a giant. Because of this, adults who are dealing with crying or hysterical children should kneel to talk with them. By the same token, police interrogators and trial lawyers know that moving in close to an interviewee may cause him to get upset and say something that would be controlled under normal conditions. This invasion of territory may result in the breaking down of defenses.

Sometimes nonverbal patterns change because of outside influences. For instance, a vast difference exists between normal nonverbal communication and deviant communication, such as that caused by drugs, alcohol, or shock. Patterns change as people lose control of their ability to make decisions and value judgments. A person under the influence of alcohol or drugs does not walk, talk, or have the same bodily controls as he or she would when sober. This has resulted in the development of drunk-driver-walking-a-straight-line and touching-the-nose tests, with the assumption being that a sober person can perform these acts while a drunk person can't.

Verbal and Nonverbal Relationships

Obviously, a link exists between verbal and nonverbal communication. Because they are so tightly interwoven, it is necessary to identify, analyze, and understand their various relationships. The main relationships of nonverbal to verbal communication can be described as substituting, complementing, conflicting, and accenting (see Figure 3.2).[20]

Substituting Relationship

Suppose someone asks you a question. Instead of answering verbally, you nod your head up and down. In doing so, you have used the **substituting relationship,** replacing the action meaning "yes" for the word *yes.*

		Figure 3.2
Substituting relationship Nonverbal message replaces the verbal message **Verbal message:** (none) **Nonverbal message:** Nod head vertically to indicate *yes*	**Complementing relationship** Nonverbal message accompanies the verbal message **Verbal message:** "Yes" **Nonverbal message:** Nod head vertically to indicate *yes*	**Verbal and Nonverbal Relationships**
Conflicting relationship Verbal and nonverbal message are in contrast to one another **Verbal message:** "Yes" **Nonverbal message:** Body language indicates *no*	**Accenting relationship** Nonverbal message stresses the verbal message **Verbal message:** "Yes" **Nonverbal message:** Body language indicates *yes*	

Complementing Relationship

Body language can complement a verbal message. For example, shaking your head horizontally from side to side while saying *no* reinforces the negative verbalization. The simultaneous saying and doing creates a nonverbal **complementing relationship,** in which a nonverbal message accompanies a verbal message and adds dimension to communication.

Conflicting Relationship

A person's physical movements sometimes can conflict with his or her verbal message. For example, suppose a professor is confronted by a student after a class session. The student asks, "May I speak with you?" The professor says, "Sure, I have lots of time." While making this reply, however, the professor is packing books, glancing at the clock, and taking several steps away. A conflict exists between the verbal and nonverbal messages.

When actions conflict with verbal messages, thus forming a **conflicting relationship** between the verbal and nonverbal, the receiver should rely more on the nonverbal aspect of communication. Nonverbal clues often are more difficult to fake than verbal ones. When you were young, you might have been surprised to find that your parents knew when you were not telling the truth. There you stood, looking at the floor, twisting your hands, with a flushed face, as you insisted, "I didn't do it." The father of the modern psychology movement said, "He that has eyes to see and ears to hear may convince himself that no mortal can keep a secret. If his lips are silent he chatters with his fingertips; betrayal oozes out of him at every pore."[21]

Lie detectors read the body's nonverbal reactions by measuring changes in blood pressure, respiration, and skin response—in other words, by attempting to detect a conflicting relationship between the verbal and the nonverbal. This is accomplished by hooking up a meter to the fingers, measuring perspiration, or checking heart rate on an electrocardiograph machine. Some researchers claim that the accuracy rate of poly-

Body shifts can encourage or discourage conversation.

On Nonverbal Communication

Here is a quiz, based on research, that will test your knowledge of nonverbal communication. Just answer "true" or "false."

1. Women are more sensitive to nonverbal cues—especially facial cues—and they transmit more accurate nonverbal cues to others.
2. When contradictory messages are sent through both verbal and nonverbal channels, most adults see the nonverbal message as more accurate.
3. People with low self-esteem use more eye contact when receiving negative messages than when receiving positive ones while those with high self-esteem do just the opposite in each case.

4. When people are conjuring up a lie, their pupils tend to become smaller. However, when they tell the lie, their pupils tend to dilate.
5. The three nonverbal cues an interviewer remembers most about a job applicant are gestures, posture, and handshake.

Answers: 1. true, 2. true, 3. true, 4. true, 5. false— interviewers remember eye contact, appearance, and facial expressions.

Source: NVC: *Nonverbal Communication Studies and Applications,* by Mark L. Hickson III and Don W. Stacks, Wm. C. Brown Communications Inc., 2460 Kerper Blvd., Dubuque, IA 52001.

graphs is "barely better than 50 percent."[22] Others "have pegged the accuracy rate at nearly 90 percent."[23] Another study indicates an 80 percent accuracy. Because of these differences in opinion, in light of the terrorist attacks on September 11, 2001, questions arose as to whether federal agencies should rely on lie detectors to screen workers and job applicants. The conclusion reached by the National Research Council was that "the machines are simply too inaccurate."[24] The report also contends that "almost a century of research in scientific psychology and physiology provides little basis for the expectation that a polygraph test could have extremely high accuracy."[25] However, this belief is not universal. A criminal justice expert counters by responding, "If what they're saying is that polygraph testing is not a useful tool in screening because it makes errors, I wouldn't necessarily agree with them."

Can nonverbal techniques be used to detect lying? A new technique, fMRI, functional magnetic resonance imaging, "scans the brain and could well morph into a forensic tool far more potent than the flawed polygraph test."[26] "Forensic experts are hopeful because fMRIs measure complex mental processes, while polygraph tests pick up skin and blood pressure changes that can be misleading."[27]

Accenting Relationship

Nonverbal behavior may accent parts of a verbal message, much as underlining or italicizing emphasizes written language. In the **accenting relationship,** the nonverbal message stresses the verbal one. Jabbing someone's shoulder with a finger as you turn the person to look at you while commanding, "When I speak to you, look at me!" emphatically accents the verbal message with nonverbal signs.

Categories of Nonverbal Communication

Nonverbal channels can be divided into many categories. Our discussion of these categories centers on kinesics, proxemics, paravocalics, chronemics, olfactics, aesthetics, and gustorics.[28] (See Figure 3.3.)

Kinesics: Body Communication

Kinesics is the study of communication through the body and its body movements. We communicate through the gestures we use, the way we walk and stand, the expressions on our faces and in our eyes, the manner in which we combine these variables to open or close channels, and what we look like. Specific areas studied in the area of kinesics are facsics; ocalics; gestics; haptics; posture, walk, and stance; artifactics; and physical characteristics.

Facsics   **Facsics** is the study of how the face communicates. "The 80 muscles of the face can create more than 7,000 expressions."[29] These expressions range from

Figure 3.3	**Categories of Nonverbal Communication**

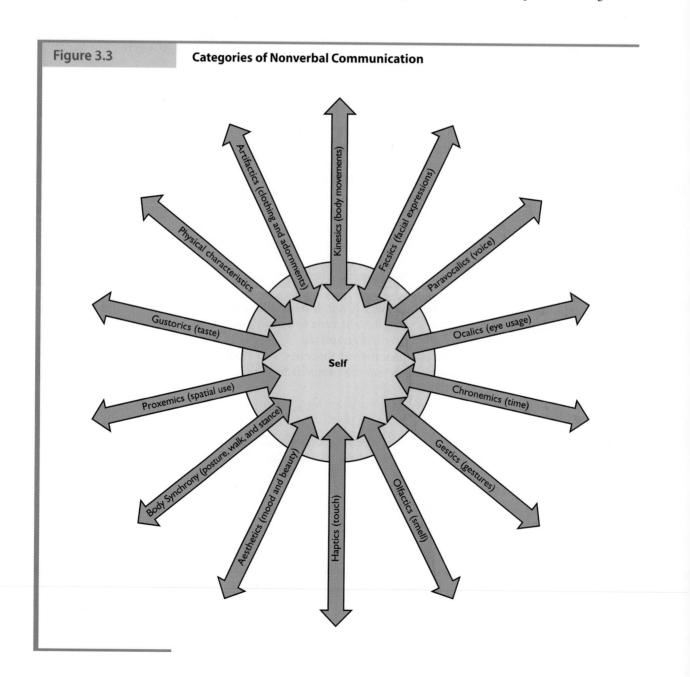

communicating our internal states such as anger or fear, to carrying messages to others of whether we want to interrupt what they are saying or are interested and want them to continue to speak. The face sends information about our personality, interests, responsiveness, and emotional states. How we perceive another person is often based on that person's facial expressions as we observe or interact with her.

Research on the face and its messages has been conducted through FACS (Facial Action Coding System). Through this process, we have more data about the face than about any other area of nonverbal communication.[30] What has been determined is that facial expressions are highly complex. Facial expressions are movements of such brief duration that if we don't watch carefully, we miss the message. They are also so subtle that they can just pass by us as an observer. An upturn of the corners of the mouth, nasal cavity expansions, an eyebrow arching, a dropping jaw, or open mouth are so subtle that they are often overlooked and the message is not conveyed.

Reading Body Language to Fight Terror

Learning to read body language is one skill FBI agents use to combat terror. Anxious people give off signals that trained personnel may be able to spot.

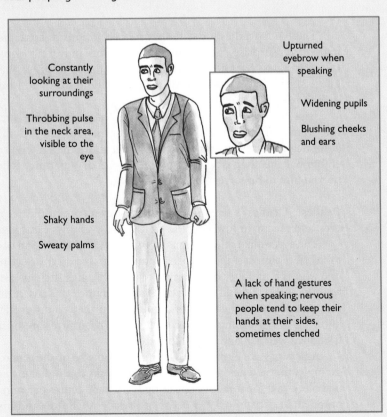

Constantly looking at their surroundings

Throbbing pulse in the neck area, visible to the eye

Shaky hands

Sweaty palms

Upturned eyebrow when speaking

Widening pupils

Blushing cheeks and ears

A lack of hand gestures when speaking; nervous people tend to keep their hands at their sides, sometimes clenched

Source: Christopher Newton, "New FBI Agents Get Terrorism Training," *Cleveland Plain Dealer,* August 28, 2002, p. A14. Orginal source: Center for Nonverbal Communication.

Research has established that nonverbal language is an important means of expression.

The FACS studies indicate that such emotions as anger, fear, disgust, sadness, happiness, surprise, and contempt may be universal signals. However, other research states that there is not enough evidence to prove this. Because each language system has its own words for these emotions, there would still be questions over the universal theory.[31]

Based on his early study of facsics, the leading FACS researcher summarized the importance of the face in communication when he said, "It's the one social fact that accurately reflects our subjective experiences. It's the only reflection of man's inner emotional life that is visible to the world." If anything, follow-up research has proved him to be correct.[32]

Ocalics   Ocalics is the study of how the eyes communicate. Winking, closing the eyes, and raising or lowering the eyelids and eyebrows can convey meaning.

The eye, unlike other organs of the body, is an extension of the brain.[33] Because of this, it is almost impossible for an individual to disguise eye meaning from someone who is a member of the same culture. Sayings such as "Look at the sparkle in her eye" and "He couldn't look me straight in the eye" have meaning. Of all our features, our eyes are the most revealing. Often they communicate without our even knowing it. For example, when the pupils of our eyes are dilated, we may appear friendlier, warmer, and more attractive.

A person's eye blinks have an effect on how he or she is perceived by others. For example, the slowness or rapidity of eye blinks can indicate nervousness. The normal blink rate for someone speaking is 31 to 50 blinks per minute. During the first presidential debate in 1996 between President Clinton and his Republican opponent, Bob Dole, polls indicated that Mr. Dole was considered to be very nervous. A review of the videotapes of the debate indicated that he had averaged 147 eye blinks per minute, almost three times the normal rate.[34]

A theory known as **pupilometrics** indicates that pupils dilate when the eyes are focused on a pleasurable object and contract when focused on an unpleasurable one.[35] Enlarged pupils signify interest, and contracted pupils reflect boredom. Thus, knowledgeable teachers often watch the pupils of their students' eyes to ascertain their interest in a particular lesson. The idea of wide-eyed wonder and interest is not new. In the late eighteenth century, European women placed a drug called belladonna in their eyes to keep their pupils large in order to make them look both interested and interesting.

Members of different social classes, generations, ethnic groups, and cultures use their eyes differently to express messages. European Americans often complain that they feel some foreigners stare at them too intensely or hold a glance too long. This is because a gaze of longer than ten seconds is likely to induce discomfort in a European American. But lengthy eye contact may be comfortable as long as the communicating people have sufficient distance between them. As you walk down a corridor, notice that you can look at someone for a long period of time until you suddenly feel uncomfortable and glance away. This usually happens at a distance of about ten feet.

When individuals in the European American culture are intent on hiding an inner feeling, they may try to avoid eye contact. Thus, the child who has eaten forbidden candy will not look at a questioning parent during the interrogation. (Euro-American children are often told, "Look me in the eye and say that.")

People in many cultures are very aware of the part played by eyes in communicating. This awareness has led some to try to mask their eyes. "Since people can't control the responses of their eyes," reported one source, "many Arabs wear dark glasses, even indoors."[36] This is especially true if they are negotiating.

Thus, in addition to watching a person's actions, an astute observer may ascertain what that person is doing by watching his eyes. For example, when 90 percent of people look up and to the left, they are recalling a visual memory they have experienced. Eyes up and to the right picture a future thought.[37]

Gestics   **Gestics** is the study of the movements of the body, such as gestures, which can give clues about a person's status, mood, cultural affiliations, and self-perception. Why do people gesture when they talk? A study indicates that speech and gesturing function together and may help us think and form words.[38] In addition, gesturing helps people retrieve words from memory. "When asked to keep their hands still by holding onto a bar, people had a more difficult time recalling words than those whose hands were free."[39] Nods of the head and body shifts can encourage or discourage conversation. Other movements may show internal feelings. For example, those who are bored may tap their fingers on a table or bounce a crossed leg.

As people attempt to communicate, they use gestures. These gestures may be classified as speech independent or speech related. **Speech-independent gestures** are not tied to speech. These gestures are referred to as emblems.[40] **Speech-related gestures** are directly tied to, or accompany, speech.[41] These gestures are illustrators, affect displays, regulators, and adaptors.

Emblems are nonverbal acts that have a direct verbal translation or dictionary definition consisting of one or two words.[42] The sign language of the deaf, gestures used by behind-the-scenes television personnel, and signals between two underwater swimmers are all examples of the use of emblems. It is important to realize that not all emblems are universal. In fact, they tend to be *culture specific,* meaning that an emblem's meaning in one culture may not be the same as that same emblem's meaning in another. For example, in Hong Kong, a diner signals a waiter for the check by making a writing motion with both hands. Extending the index finger and motioning toward yourself, as is done for calling a waiter in many parts of the United States, is used only for calling animals in Hong Kong.[43]

Illustrators are "kinesic acts accompanying speech that are used to aid in the description of what is being said or trace the direction of speech."[44] They are used to sketch a path, point to an object, or show spatial relationships. Saying, "*Josh, please stand up* (point at Josh and bring your hand upward), *go out the door* (point at the door), *turn to the left* (point to the left), and *walk straight ahead* (point straight ahead)" is an example of a cluster of illustrators.

Affect displays are facial gestures that show emotions and feelings, such as sadness or happiness. Pouting, winking, and raising or lowering the eyelids and eyebrows are examples of affect displays. Different people and cultures tend to use facial expressions in different ways. For example, many European American males mask and internalize their facial expressions because they have been taught that to show emotion is not manly; Italian males, however, express their emotions outwardly.[45]

Regulators are nonverbal acts that maintain and control the back-and-forth nature of speaking and listening between two or more people. Nods of the head, eye movements, and body shifts are all regulators used to encourage or discourage conversation. Imagine, for example, a conversation between a department manager and an employee who has asked for a raise. The manager glances at her watch, her fingers fidget with the telephone, and she glances through some materials on the desk. The manager's regulator signs indicate that she views the transaction as completed.

Adaptors are movements that accompany boredom, show internal feelings, or regulate a situation. People who are waiting for someone who is late, for example, often stand with their arms crossed, fingers tapping on upper arms, foot tapping the pavement, and checking the time every few seconds.

Haptics **Haptics** is the study of the use of touch as communication. Touch is defined as the physical placing of a part of one person's body on another's body, such as putting your hand on another person's shoulder. This may be done with or without permission. Your skin is a receiver of communication: pats, pinches, strokes, slaps, punches, shakes, and kisses all convey meaning. A doctor touches your body to ascertain sensitivity and possible illness. You shake hands to satisfy social and business welcoming needs. You intimately touch through kisses and use sexually arousing touch in the act of lovemaking. The messages that touch communicates depend on how, where, and by whom you are touched.

The importance of touch is well documented. Many people find that when they are upset, they rub their hands together or stroke a part of their body, such as the arm. We reassure others by touching them on the shoulder or patting them on the hand. "Touched and massaged babies gain weight much faster than unmassaged babies. They are more active, alert, responsive, better able to tolerate noise, and emotionally are more in control."[46]

Most people (except those who have been abused, raped, or brought up in a low- or no-touch family or society) associate appropriate touching with positive messages.[47] Those whose bodies have been invaded without permission, however, as in the case of sexual abuse, often pull back or feel uncomfortable when touched. In fact, touch avoidance is one of the signs counselors sometimes use to aid in the identification of clients who have been physically or sexually abused.[48]

If you have ever wondered why you felt comfortable, or uncomfortable, when you were touched, it could well have to do with your upbringing. Different cultures regard touch in different ways. Some avoid touch while others encourage it. The same is true within families. For example, in the United States, a moderate-touch society, "it is not unusual for an adult to pat the head of a small child who has been introduced by his or her parents. In Malaysia, and other Asian Pacific countries, touching anyone's head—especially a child's—is improper and considered an indignity because the head is regarded as the home of the soul."[49] In the United States, a handshake is appropriate as a business greeting, a bow fulfills the same purpose in Japan, and kissing on both cheeks is the French custom.

Touch is not only culture specific but also gender specific. Women in the European American culture tend to engage in more intimate same-sex touch than do men. Female pairs are more likely than male pairs to exchange hugs, kisses, and touches on the arm or back, and to do so for longer duration.[50] Men touch one another using only narrowly circumscribed behaviors, such as handshaking or, in instances of extreme emotion (e.g., athletic accomplishments), hugging, butt slapping, or kissing. The acceptability of showing physical affection by women may be one of the reasons lesbians may be less discriminated against than gay men.[51] Americans in the United States tend to react less to physical displays between women than between men. This is not true in other countries, such as Turkey, where it is acceptable for men to hold hands or kiss. In the United States, when men touch, kiss, or hug each other, attention is drawn to the activity, and since it is not generally part of the cultural norm, it is perceived by some in negative ways.

Permission to touch tends to follow an action chain sequence. If you have ever wondered why someone with whom you'd like to be intimate pulls away or gets rigid when you or the other person is touched, it may well be that you have jumped forward in the sequence too quickly. For a person brought up in a moderate- to low-touch society, there is an appropriate time not to touch, then to touch, then to kiss, and then to fondle. If one person feels he or she is at the no-touch stage, and the partner acts at the fondle stage, strong negative verbal and physical reactions may follow.

"Individuals differ dramatically in the degree to which they like or dislike touch."[52] The degree to which an individual dislikes being touched is identified as **touch avoidance.** If you would like to measure your touch/touch avoidance, fill out the questionnaire in Figure 3.4. Remember in evaluating your scores that your cultural background, including your nationality, sexual orientation, and gender, has a great deal to do with your score, your desire to touch, and whom you feel comfortable touching you. People in the American culture, no matter what gender, who are touch avoiders tend to have less overall intimacy, to be less open and less expressive, and to have somewhat lower self-esteem.[53] In addition, touch avoiders judge people who touch them less favorably than do touch approachers.[54] Further, people who like to touch and be touched by others are not only more communicative but generally also tend to be more self-confident.[55]

Body Synchrony: Posture, Walk, and Stance
Research in **body synchrony,** the study of posture as well as the way a person walks and stands, indicates that these nonverbal indicators do say something about a person.[56] A

Nonverbal communication is composed of all those messages that people exchange beyond the words themselves.

Figure 3.4	**The Touch Avoidance Scale**

The Touch Avoidance Scale

Directions: This instrument is composed of 18 statements concerning feelings about touching other people and being touched. Please indicate the degree to which each statement applies to you by circling whether you (1) Strongly Disagree, (2) Disagree, (3) Are Undecided, (4) Agree, or (5) Strongly Agree with each statement. While some of these statements may seem repetitious, take your time and try to be as honest as possible.

1. A hug from a same-sex friend is a true sign of friendship   1 2 3 4 5
2. Opposite-sex friends enjoy it when I touch them.   1 2 3 4 5
3. I often put my arm around friends of the same sex.   1 2 3 4 5
4. When I see two people of the same sex hugging, it revolts me.   1 2 3 4 5
5. I like it when members of the opposite sex touch me.   1 2 3 4 5
6. People shouldn't be so uptight about touching persons of the same sex.   1 2 3 4 5
7. I think it is vulgar when members of the opposite sex touch me.   1 2 3 4 5
8. When a member of the opposite sex touches me, I find it unpleasant.   1 2 3 4 5
9. I wish I were free to show emotions by touching members of the same sex.   1 2 3 4 5
10. I'd enjoy giving a massage to an opposite-sex friend.   1 2 3 4 5
11. I enjoy kissing persons of the same sex.   1 2 3 4 5
12. I like to touch friends that are the same sex as I am.   1 2 3 4 5
13. Touching a friend of the same sex does not make me uncomfortable.   1 2 3 4 5
14. I find it enjoyable when a close opposite-sex friend and I embrace.   1 2 3 4 5
15. I enjoy getting a back rub from a member of the opposite sex.   1 2 3 4 5
16. I dislike kissing relatives of the same sex.   1 2 3 4 5
17. Intimate touching with members of the opposite sex is pleasurable.   1 2 3 4 5
18. I find it difficult to be touched by a member of my own sex.   1 2 3 4 5

Directions for scoring:
A. Add up the circled numbers for items 1, 2, 3, 5, 6, 9, 10, 11, 12, 13, 14, 15, and 17: _____
B. Score items 4, 7, 8, 16, and 18 in reverse, so a circled 1 is scored as 5, 2 as 4, 3 as 3, 4 as 2, and 5 as 1, and add them up: _____
C. Add up items (A) and (B) above to get your score: _____

A score of 70 or higher indicates a very strong motivation to touch. Less than 14% (about one-seventh) of the population scores this high. If your score is right around 60, your motivation is about average, but still generally positive, since the midpoint between positive and negative on the scale is 54. A score of 50 or lower would place you approximately in the lower 14% in terms of motivation for touch.

Note: Item 15 from the original scale (Andersen & Leibowitz, 1978) has been altered from "when my date and I embrace" to "when a close opposite-sex friend and I embrace." Also, the scoring has been reversed from the original, so that a higher score indicates a more positive attitude toward touch.

Source: From *Environmental Psychology and Nonverbal Behavior, 3,* Human Sciences Press, Inc. Reprinted by permission of Plenum Publishing Corporation.

person's walk can give us clues about status, mood, ethnic and cultural affiliation, and self-perception.

Walking follows cultural patterns: Europeans, European Americans, and Asians have different walks. Some Europeans coming to the United States often ask why people are in such a hurry, an impression that comes from the quick pace at which European Americans typically walk.

In general, the way you walk and stand tells more about you than you probably realize. When someone enters a room, you instantly form conclusions about that person. Some people walk with confidence and stand with head high, shoulders back, and jaw set. Others walk slowly with a stance of sloping shoulders, eyes down, withdrawing within their bodies. This posture may indicate lack of confidence. Detectives and airline security personnel are trained to pick out suspicious people by the way they walk.

Artifactics   A person's clothing, makeup, eyeglasses, and jewelry carry distinct messages. **Artifactics** centers on the study of those things that adorn the body and send messages to others about us as well as saying something about ourselves and our selection of these items. It is known that the clothing you wear to a job interview may be the deciding factor on whether you are hired.

Clothing is probably the most obvious of the artifact communicators. It is almost like a substitute skin, telling an observer something about who you are. Because you have made a choice about what to wear, it follows that this is the image you want to portray, the attitude you want to present about the type of person you are, and the way you want others to perceive you. Wearing something out of the mainstream can influence reactions to you. Black trenchcoats were banned in many high schools in 1999 after two students who went on a shooting rampage at Columbine High School in Littleton, Colorado, were known to have worn such coats.

For those interested in climbing the business ladder, the corporate uniform is still considered essential for interviews. "A job interview is like any other ceremony that requires a costume."[57] "For women a dark blue suit, cream-colored shirt, hems on skirts should be at the knees, and no pants."[58] "For men, [wearing a] dark blue suit, white shirt and red tie is the way to go."[59]

In spite of the emphasis on corporate clothing for interviews, there have been some major changes in daily business wear. Originally started in California's Silicon Valley at such companies as Apple Computers, this trend has resulted in a major change in dressing at work. Seventy-four percent of U.S. companies allow casual dress, and what has become known as *casual Fridays*—employees are permitted to wear casual clothing on Friday—is a popular policy.[60] Even IBM, which had a notoriously stiff dress code, has eliminated it. "Here's stuffy IBM losing millions, and Microsoft, where the employees wear jeans and T-shirts, making millions. The irony is not lost on anyone."[61]

Although most Fortune 500 companies don't allow blue jeans, sneakers, and sweats, they will allow loafers, sweaters, and chinos. The guideline? Dress "the way men and women would dress to go to a singles bar Friday nights."[62] Many clothing manufacturers have developed whole lines of casual work clothing.[63]

Another new trend is workplace uniforms—not only at fast-food restaurants but also on bank officers, travel agents, runners at the stock exchange, and employees at funeral homes. The style, which started with the Century 21 gold-blazered real estate brokers, has expanded.[64]

Be aware, however, that casualness is not universal. Companies dealing in foreign markets know that the business suit, which rose in nineteenth-century Europe as a costume to make managerial workers stand out from production workers, is still very much the business garb. In countries like Japan, England, and Germany, casual is definitely not accepted.

Legal professionals also are aware of the effect of clothing for themselves and their clients. Lawyers advise clients to dress conservatively and reinforce their credibility with a professional appearance.

Physical Characteristics

A person's **physical characteristics**—for instance, height, weight, and skin color—communicate about him or her to others. We find some people appealing and others unappealing by how they appear physically.

Attractiveness is in the eye of the beholder.

Attractiveness   We can be drawn to or repulsed by a person's physical appearance. The prejudice against unattractive people is deeply ingrained in European American society. This attitude may, in part, be the result of the emphasis projected by the advertising industry on attractiveness in magazine, newspaper, and television ads, and the depiction of what makes a person attractive.

Attractiveness is in the eye of the beholder. What it means to be attractive differs from culture to culture. For example, judges at international beauty contests have difficulty determining the winner because of the vast physical differences among the contestants and the lack of a universal definition for beauty. Thinness for women might be important in the European American culture, but not necessarily to African Americans. In a study of teenage girls, white females thought an ideal attractive woman is five feet, seven inches, "between 100 and 110 pounds, with blue eyes and long flowing hair."[65] The African American girls in the study named full hips and large thighs as the signs of attractiveness.[66]

A jury's decision can be affected by both the plaintiff's and the defendant's physical appearances. In one study, participants in an automobile-negligence trial heard tape-recorded testimony. The first set of jurors was shown photographs of an attractive male plaintiff and an unattractive male defendant; the second set of jurors saw the reverse. A third panel saw no pictures but heard the testimony. The results: the attractive plaintiff received a 49 percent positive vote from the first jury, the unattractive plaintiff got only a

17 percent positive vote from the second jury, and 41 percent of the third group, which did not see any pictures, ruled for the plaintiff.[67]

Even salary can be affected by attractiveness. A study indicates that male attorneys who are attractive earn more money than their counterparts who are plain looking.[68]

Height   It should not be surprising that height can be a communicator. Men often are judged purely by their physical presence. "Size can affect a man's life. Short men are discriminated against."[69] Men under five feet, six inches are considered short, and people regard them as having less power. Short men are referred to as *submissive* and *weak;* tall men garner such titles as *mature* and *respected.* Even elementary students are aware of the height prejudice.[70]

A comparison of the starting pay of business school graduates indicates that tall males received six hundred dollars per inch more in yearly salary.[71] What are the implications? Short men need to be better prepared, be aware that they must exceed in grades and talent, and sell themselves during job interviews. Success is not impossible for short men; for example, former Clinton cabinet member Robert Reich is less than five feet tall; President James Madison was five feet, four inches; Attila the Hun, five feet; and, of course, there was small-structured Napoleon.

Although European American society seems to show a preference for taller men, "tall women often are labeled 'ungainly'; short businesswomen, in fact, may have an advantage in not acquiring whatever threatening overtones may attend to increasing height."[72] Mother Teresa was just five feet tall.[73]

Proxemics: Spatial Communication

A basic difference among people can be seen in how they operate within the space around them—how they use their territory. The study of how people use and perceive their social and personal space is called **proxemics.**

Every person is surrounded by a psychological bubble of space. This bubble contracts and expands depending on the person's cultural background, emotional state, and the activity in which he or she is participating. Northern Europeans—English, Scandinavians, and Germans—tend to have a need for a larger zone of personal space and often avoid touching and close contact. They require more room around them and structure their lifestyles to meet the need for this space. Thus, the English are stereotyped as being distant and impersonal, not showing great emotion through hugging, kissing, and touching. This stereotype derives from the respect they exhibit for each other's territory. In contrast, Italians, Russians, Spaniards, Latin Americans, Middle Easterners, and the French prefer close personal contact.

Personal space is important to us because we feel that if someone touches our body, he or she is attacking us because, in essence, we are our body.[74] Many of us do not like to be touched but do not really know why. This dislike may stem from cultural training rather than from something unique to us. When someone who does not like to be fondled meets a toucher, the situation can be quite uncomfortable. If the toucher places a hand on the arm of the nontoucher, who jerks away, the toucher may well get the idea that a rejection has taken place when in fact it is the touch, not the person, that has probably been spurned.

Culture has an effect on how people perceive themselves in space and how they use space.

Culture and Space   When people from different cultural backgrounds come into contact, they may assume they have the same concept of space. This, of course, is not true. In fact, "cultures can be distinguished by the distances at which members interact and how frequently members touch."[75] It has been proposed that there are **contact cultures**—those characterized by tactile modes of communication (e.g., Latin Americans, Mediterraneans, French, Arabs)—and **noncontact cultures** (Germans, Japanese, English, North Americans).[76] Although heterosexual men in the United States and England rarely touch other men, except in times of great emotion (such as athletic game victories) or for shaking hands when welcoming or meeting someone, arm linking between two men is common in Turkey, Morocco, and many Latin American countries.[77]

Even within our own culture, the space bubble varies according to our emotional state and the activity. Although European Americans usually keep well beyond the three-foot personal circle of space, this can change very quickly. If you are on a crowded bus and someone presses against you, you may tolerate it. If, however, you are standing at a bus stop and someone presses against you, you will probably object. This situation brings into play your idea of public distance.

Your emotional state also can change your idea of space. For instance, when some people are angry, they may grab someone by the front of the shirt, step in close, get "nose to nose," and shout.

Space Distances   An examination of space distances allows for an understanding of space as it relates to culture. Everyone has spatial needs. Studies of the space distances as they relate to white middle-class Americans indicate that there are four classifications that explain their spatial needs: intimate, personal, social, and public (see Figure 3.5).[78]

Intimate distance covers a space varying from direct physical contact with another person to a distance of eighteen inches. It is used for our most private activities: caressing, making love, and sharing intimate ideas and emotions. We can often get clues about a relationship by noticing whether the other person allows us to use his intimate space. For example, if you have been on a hand-holding/physically touching basis with someone, and suddenly he or she will not let you near or pulls away when you get very close, a change in the congruency patterns of the relationship may have occurred. If the other person suddenly encourages close body proximity, this also may indicate a change in attitude.

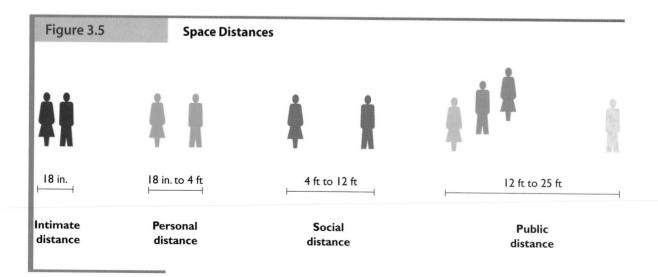

| Figure 3.5 | **Space Distances** |

| 18 in. | 18 in. to 4 ft | 4 ft to 12 ft | 12 ft to 25 ft |

| **Intimate distance** | **Personal distance** | **Social distance** | **Public distance** |

Personal distance, eighteen inches to four feet, is sometimes called the *comfort bubble.* Most European Americans feel most comfortable keeping at this distance when talking with others, and invasion of this personal territory will cause us to back away. If we are backed into a corner, sitting in a chair, or somehow trapped, we will lean away, pull in, and tense up. To avoid invasion of our territory, we might place a leg on the rung of a chair or on a stair. Some of us even arrange furniture so that no one can invade our territory. For example, businesspeople may place their desks so that employees must sit on one side and the boss on the other. In contrast, interviewers have reported a completely different atmosphere when talking to job applicants if the two chairs are placed facing each other about three to four feet apart instead of on opposite sides of the desk.

Social distance covers a four- to twelve-foot zone that is used during business transactions and casual social exchanges. Also part of social distance is the **standing-seated interaction,** in which the person in control stands and the other person sits. Standing-seated positions occur, among others, in teacher-pupil and police officer–arrestee transactions.

Public distance may dictate a separation of as little as twelve feet, but it is usually more than twenty-five. It is used by professors in lecture rooms and speakers at public gatherings as well as by public figures who wish to place a barrier between themselves and their audiences.

An important aspect of proxemics is the arrangement of seating and how people are spaced at meetings and in homes.

Small-Group Ecology   The physical placement of members of small groups in relation to one another has an effect on their behavior. This **small-group ecology,** which includes the placement of chairs, the placement of the person conducting a meeting, and the setting for a small-group encounter, clearly influences the group's operation. If, for example, people are seated in a tight circle, they will probably feel more comfortable and interact more than they would if they were sitting in straight rows. They will be able to see each other's nonverbal reactions, and because there is no inhibiting physical distance, they will lose their self-consciousness as they become members of the group.

Business organizations make considerable use of such nonverbal strategies in small-scale conferences. One technique is to seat key members of the group in prominent positions to stimulate discussion or even direct it.

Paravocalics: Vocal Communication

The vocal effects that accompany words, such as tone of voice—but not the words themselves—are called **paravocalics.**[79] Vocal quality communicates nonverbally to the listening ear. The rate (speed), volume (power), pitch (such as soprano or bass), pause (stopping), and stress (intensity) of sounds all have particular meanings. These paravocal tools are often referred to as vocal cues.

Vocal cues offer clues to determine the sex, age, and status of a speaker. We also can make some pretty accurate judgments about the emotions and feelings of the people with whom we communicate by their paralinguistic presentation. If you are very angry, the pitch of your voice may go up. And when you are very, very angry, you sometimes say words slowly and distinctly, pausing after each word for special effect.

Research indicates that the voice also may be important in some aspects of persuasion.[80] A faster rate of speech, more intonation, greater volume, and a less halting manner seem to be related to successful attempts at persuasion. If a

Formal time is the way in which a culture defines its time and the role it plays in regulating our lives.

person sounds assured, the receiver credits him or her with a higher degree of credibility. Network television anchors, for example, work to cultivate an assured broadcast voice.

Vocal cues can provide much information about a speaker, and our overall reaction to another person is colored at least somewhat by our reactions to these cues. Perceptions of vocal cues, combined with other verbal and nonverbal stimuli, mold the conceptions we use as bases for communicating.[81]

Chronemics: Time as Communication

You communicate to yourself and others by the way you use time. The way people handle and structure their time is known as **chronemics.** "Each of us is born into and raised in a particular time world—an environment with its own rhythm to which we entrain ourselves."[82] Time, as a communication tool, is sometimes greatly misunderstood. Only within certain societies, for example, is precise time of great significance. Some cultures relate to time as a *circular phenomenon* in which there is no pressure or anxiety about the future. Existence follows the cycle of the seasons of planting and harvesting, the daily rising and setting of the sun, birth and death. In **circular time,** there is no pressing need to achieve or create newness, or to produce more than is needed to survive. Nor is there fear of death. Such societies have successfully integrated the past and future into a peaceful sense of the present.[83] Many Native Americans have been raised with this cultural attitude toward time.

Other societies operate on **linear time,** centered primarily on the future. These societies focus on the factual and technical information needed to fulfill impending demands. In most of Western Europe, North America, and Japan, punctuality is considered good manners.

Another way of viewing time is to understand its technical, formal, and informal uses. **Technical time** is precise time, as in the way some scientists look at how things happen in milliseconds. Few of us come in direct contact with this usage.

Formal time is the way in which a culture defines its time, and it plays a daily role in most of our lives. It refers to centuries, years, months, weeks, days, hours, and minutes. As a student, you may think in the formal time terms of semesters or terms.

Informal time refers to a rather flexible use of time, such as "soon" or "right away." These terms often cause communicative difficulty because they are arbitrary and mean different things to different people. For example, how long is "pretty soon"?

Time has become a critical factor in the U.S. workplace. Throughout a person's career, punctuality is often used as a measure of effectiveness. A person who arrives late for a job interview probably will have difficulty overcoming such a negative first impression, and employees who arrive late or leave early may be reprimanded and even dismissed.

Time is culture based. European Americans, Euro-Canadians, and Western Europeans, in general, are clock bound; African, Latin American, and some Asian Pacific cultures are not clock bound. Time is based on personal systems.[84] European Americans traveling abroad often are irritated by the seeming lack of concern for time commitments among residents of some countries. In Mexico and Central America, tours may be late; guides may fail to indicate the correct arrival and departure times. Yet in other places, such as Switzerland, travelers can set their watch by the promptness of the trains. Businesspeople may get confused over what "on time" means as they meet those from other cultures. "In Britain and North America one may be 5 minutes late for a business appointment, but not 15 minutes and certainly not 30 minutes late, which is perfectly normal in Arab countries."[85] In Latin America one is expected to arrive late to an appointment. This same tardiness for Germans or European Americans would be perceived as rudeness.[86]

The differences in the use of time have been noted in regard to college students and when they arrive for classes and turn in assignments. For instance, one Euro-American professor notes, "Brazilian students showed few signs of concern for lateness, arriving as much as an hour late for a two-hour class, but also feeling comfortable about asking questions long after the class had officially ended."[87] Some cultures, such as gays and Hispanics, often are amused by their use of time and even have names that refer to habitual lateness such as *gay-late* and *mañana time.*

In cultures that value promptness, one of the questions raised about time centers on the person who is constantly late. What does habitual tardiness reveal about the person? Chronic lateness, in a formal time culture, may be deeply rooted in a person's psyche. Compulsive tardiness is rewarding on some level. A key emotional conflict for the chronically late person involves his or her need to feel special. Such a person may not gain enough recognition in other ways; people must be special in some way, so the person is special by being late. Other reasons include needs for punishment, power, or as an expression of hostility.[88] Tardiness can be a sign that a person wants to avoid something or that the activity or person to be met is not important enough to warrant the effort to be on time. Procrastinators are often not valued in a linear time-focused culture.

Olfactics: Smell as Communication

Olfactics is the study of smell. We communicate through our smells. Our sense of smell is extraordinarily precise. Growing evidence also suggests that we remember what we smell longer than what we see and hear.[89] Our sense of smell is very selective and helps us reach conclusions. We are attracted by the scents of certain colognes and repulsed by others. Some people find certain body odors offensive. This is especially true in a country such as the United States, where we have been taught by advertisers and medical people to wash off natural odors and replace them with neutral, fragrance-free, or substitute smells. This is not the case in other cultures.

We often make decisions without realizing that these choices are based on odors. Several phenomena provide insight into how smell serves as a nonverbal communication tool: smell blindness, smell adaptation, smell memory, smell overload, and smell discrimination.[90]

Each person has a unique ability to identify and distinguish smells. **Smell blindness** occurs when a person is unable to detect smells. It parallels color blindness or deafness because it is a physiological blockage. It accounts for the fact that some people do not smell their own or others' body odors or detect the differences in the odors of various foods. Because smell and taste are so closely aligned, this can explain why people who are smell-blind may also have taste-identification difficulties.

Smell adaptation occurs when we gradually lose the distinctiveness of a particular smell through repeated contact with it. When you walk into a bakery, you may be aware of the wonderful odors. The clerks who work there, however, may have become so used to the odors that they are not aware of them. The speed at which the odor message is adapted to depends on the strength of the odor and the length of time we are in contact with it.

If as a child your grandmother baked your favorite dessert, walking into someone's home years later and smelling that same odor may cause you to flash back to memories of your grandmother. This ability to recall previous situations when encountering a particular smell associated with them is **smell memory.** Smelling a crayon may trigger flashbacks to experiences you had in kindergarten, the odors of a dentist's office may cause your teeth to ache, or passing a perfume counter with samples of a cologne a former lover wore may trigger intrapersonal smell memories.

Have you ever entered an elevator and been bombarded by the heavy dose of perfume of another passenger? Onions in a salad are fine, but slicing several at the sink may cause you to cry. These are both examples of smell overload. **Smell overload** takes place when an exceptionally large number of odors or one extremely strong odor overpowers you. Walking down a detergent aisle in a supermarket or standing in a small room with several people who are smoking can trigger smell overload for some people.

The ability to identify people, places, and things on the basis of their smell is **smell discrimination.** The average person can detect more than ten thousand different odors.[91] You may have been able to distinguish someone who comes up behind you by the smell of her or his hair. The identification takes place through smell discrimination, which allows us to tell the difference between cinnamon and garlic, bananas and oranges, and one person and another.

Aesthetics: Mood and Beauty as Communication

The study of communication of a message or mood through color or music is **aesthetics.** When you are driving a car, the type of music on the radio affects your driving, alertness, and concentration. And the music in an elevator is almost never loud and pulsating because such strong sounds would be too emotionally stressful for people in a small, contained area.

As you stroll through the supermarket, you may not even be aware of how music affects you. During a nine-week test, the music in one supermarket was randomly played at a slow 60 beats a minute on some days and at 108 beats a minute on others. Not surprisingly, on slow-tempo days the store's gross receipts were 38.2 percent higher as people walked at a leisurely pace and purchased more.[92]

A study on the impact of rock music tested more than twenty thousand records for their effect on muscle strength. (This sort of activity is part of a science entitled **behavioral kinesiology,**[93] which holds that particular kinds of food, clothes, thoughts, and music strengthen or weaken the muscles of the body.) According to a behavioral kinesiologist, "listening to rock music frequently causes all the muscles in the body to go weak."[94] This relationship may well account for the drugged and dreamlike feelings of some people who attend rock concerts. It is theorized that some rock music has a stopped quality that is not present in other types of music—that is, the beat is stopped at the end of each bar or measure. Because the music stops and then must start again, the listener subconsciously comes to a halt at the end of each measure; this may tire the listener.

Other studies indicate that the effect of music also is based on tempo, rhythm, and instrumentation. Music can heighten a person's attention or induce boredom, thereby creating a nonverbal language that can change or stimulate various activities.[95] These effects, combined with the behavioral kinesiology studies, suggest that music can serve like a drug in regulating behavior. Music, for example, has been credited with easing pain, and a type of music therapy is being used in hospices in working with dying patients.

Colors also affect people, and many institutions are putting into practice this awareness. For example, hospitals are experimenting with using various colors for their rooms in hopes that the colors may motivate sick people to get well or ease pain. Hospitals also are painting large pieces of equipment, such as x-ray machines, the same color as the background walls so they do not appear as frightening to patients. Prisons are using pale pink shades because it is the most calming of colors. Similarly, bright colors are being added to classrooms to make students feel alert, but not in such amounts that the colors become overpowering.

Gustorics: Taste as Communication

Every time we place a substance in our mouths, our sense of taste communicates. Like our other senses, the sense of taste acts as a medium that carries messages of pleasure, displeasure, and warning to our brains.[96] **Gustorics** is the study of how taste communicates. It encompasses the communication aspects of such factors as the classifications of taste, the role of culture on taste, the role of food deprivation, food preferences, taste expectations, and color and textures as an encourager or discourager of eating and drinking.

Taste qualities have been classified: bitter, salty, sweet, and sour are taste identifiers with which you are probably familiar. We receive these signals much the same as we do smells. We come in physical contact with the object that brings about the sense reaction within us. These sense reactions are located not on our tongue but in various regions of our mouth and throat. The taste buds of the mouth are the most common tasters.

It is interesting to note that just as some people have smell blindness, and others can't smell all or some odors, some people have **taste blindness**—the inability to taste. This can either be a defect in their senses at birth or the destruction of the tasters through an accident or illness. This can be long or short term. It is estimated, for example, that 30 to 50 percent of all expectant mothers temporarily suffer taste loss during the first three months of pregnancy.[97] Other people have extremely sensitive tasting abilities. They react very strongly to the slightest taste, they may find slightly spicy foods to be very offensive, and the taste of certain foods may stimulate allergic reactions.

Another phenomenon associated with gustorics is taste adaptation. **Taste adaptation** takes place when a person becomes used to a taste to the degree that he or she can eat a substance and not taste it. People who eat a lot of very spicy foods may eventually develop an insensitivity to the tang.

Nonverbals' Role in Persuasion

Perhaps you believe visuals won't help you persuade. If so, consider a Columbia University study that shows the percentages each sense usually plays in interpreting messages.

Touch	65%
Taste	1.5%
Smell	6%
Hearing	11%
Sight	80%

Source: Creative Negotiating: Proven Techniques for Getting What You Want From Any Negotiation, by Stephen Kozicki, Adams Media Corp., 260 Center St., Holbrook, Mass. 02343.

Using Nonverbal Communication

A question arises as to why, if nonverbal communication is such an important aspect of communication, most people aren't aware of it or don't pay much overt attention to its powers. One reason is that most people have not been taught that actions communicate as clearly as words communicate, so they don't look for the nonverbal components. Schools don't generally teach courses in the subject, and what we do learn tends to be through subtle cultural communication. You may have been told that if you didn't look someone in the eye as you speak, that person might not believe you, or that you should stand up straight and walk with pride, or that you are judged by what you wear. These messages actually say, "Pay attention to the nonverbals," but most of us don't tie that to the fact that nonverbal communication is carrying messages.

Being aware that nonverbal communication exists, being aware that you need to listen to others with your eyes as well as your ears, and monitoring what you do as a nonverbal communicator will help you to become a more competent communicator.

In Conclusion

Nonverbal communication is composed of all those messages that people exchange beyond the words themselves. Nonverbal communication is a major force in our lives. There are two basic sources of nonverbals: innate neurological programs and behavior common to a culture. Research shows a relationship between nonverbal and verbal communication. In attempting to read nonverbal communication, we must remember that no one signal carries much meaning. Nonverbal communication centers on discussing the categories of the medium: kinesics, physical characteristics, proxemics, paravocalics, chronemics, olfactics, aesthetics, and gustorics. Through all of these channels, humans are always sending messages, even when no words are used.

Learn by Doing

1. Research one of these topics or people and be prepared to give a two-minute speech on what you have learned regarding the topic and nonverbal communication: neurolinguistic programming, Ray Birdwhistell, Albert Mehrabian, Edward Hall, pupilometrics, biorhythms, Muzak, behavioral kinesiology.

2. Give examples of your own recent use of substituting, complementing, conflicting, and accenting.

3. Carefully observe members of your family or think of the nonverbal patterns they display. Can you find any similarities between their patterns and your own?

4. Identify a cultural-specific nonverbal trait and describe it to the class.

5. Make a list of five emblems observed by you, by members of your family, or within your culture. Be prepared to demonstrate them. Compare your explanations of what they mean with those of your classmates.

6. Carry on a conversation with a person outside your classroom. As you speak, slowly move closer to him or her. Continue to move in on the person gradually. Observe his or her reaction. Did the person back up? Cross his or her arms? Report to the class on the results of this experiment.

Key Terms

nonverbal communication
neurolinguistic programming
cluster
congruency
innate neurological programs
reflexive actions
reflective actions
action chain
substituting relationship
complementing relationship
conflicting relationship
accenting relationship
kinesics
facsics
ocalics
pupilometrics
gestics
speech-independent gestures
speech-related gestures
emblems
illustrators
affect displays
regulators
adaptors
haptics
touch avoidance
body synchrony
artifactics

physical characteristics
proxemics
contact cultures
noncontact cultures
intimate distance
personal distance
social distance
standing-seated interaction
public distance
small-group ecology
paravocalics
chronemics
circular time
linear time
technical time
formal time
informal time
olfactics
smell blindness
smell adaptation
smell memory
smell overload
smell discrimination
aesthetics
behavioral kinesiology
gustorics
taste blindness
taste adaptation

4

Personal Communication

After reading this chapter, you should be able to

- **Define and explain the concept of intrapersonal communication**

- **State and discuss the theory of basic drive forces as they affect inner communication**

- **Explain self-concept and its role as a guiding factor in a person's actions**

- **Define self-talk and explain its relation to our communication accomplishments**

- **List some options and sources for improving self-concept, self-confidence, and self-esteem (or all of them)**

- **Define and explain the causes, results, and aids for communication apprehension**

A s you lie in bed at night before you fall asleep, you may review the events of the day. As you take a test, you may carry on a conversation with yourself to arrive at the answers. In both cases, you are participating in the act of **intrapersonal communication,** internally communicating with yourself.

The basis for communication with others is the ability to communicate with oneself. Those people who tend to know who they are, what they believe in, and what their attitudes are and have a clear understanding of their beliefs, values, and expectations are much more likely to be able to communicate these ideas to others. People who can internally process ideas and decide how to present them can communicate that information to others.

There is disagreement about where to draw the line as to what constitutes intrapersonal communication. For our purposes, assume that at times we talk to ourselves, such as when we debate during a test which of the multiple-choice answers is correct. Our bodies can "speak" to us nonverbally, as when muscles in the back of the neck tighten when we get emotionally upset. This nonverbal aspect of intrapersonal communication is an important part of the Gestalt theory of psychology, which centers on getting in touch with our feelings to gain awareness of our intrapersonal messages. Also, intrapersonal communication may occur below our level of awareness, such as when we daydream or dream.

One way of understanding your intrapersonal communication and, if necessary, improving your communication skills is by understanding your self-talk.

Self-Talk

There is a saying that it is okay to talk with yourself, but when you start answering back, it is time to worry! That tongue-in-cheek observation is basically incorrect. Indelible links exist between what we say to ourselves and what we accomplish. In addition, our self-talk has a powerful impact on our emotional well-being.

We all engage in **self-talk**—a nearly constant subconscious monologue or inner speech with ourselves. Sometimes we are conscious of our vocalizing aloud within our heads, but self-talk is often silent thinking, an internal whisper of which we are scarcely aware, or our automatic nonverbal reactions. Even though it may be quiet, its impact can be enormous. "Your behavior, your feelings, your self-esteem, and even your level of stress are influenced by your inner speech."[1] Everything that you do begins as self-talk. "Self-talk shapes our inner attitudes, our attitudes shape our behavior, and of course our behavior—what we do—shapes the results we get."[2]

Think of the inner struggles you have concerning whether you will believe something, will take a particular action, or will make a certain decision. Awake or asleep, you are constantly in touch with yourself. You mumble, daydream, dream, fantasize, and feel tension. These are all forms of inner speech.

The subconscious will work for or against you. It's up to you. Tell yourself you're clumsy or you aren't comfortable in social situations, and that is what you probably will be. "We have a choice each time we think, to think positively or negatively. Many of us don't believe it, but that absolutely is our choice. Once we understand that our private thoughts are ours alone to determine, we can select to program our brains with empowering, confidence-building thoughts."[3] One method to overcome negative self-talk is to (1) be aware of your negative messages; (2) collect

Mend Fences with Self-Talk

The kind of self-talk you employ can end or mend a relationship after a coworker criticizes you in front of your boss.

◆ **Negative self-talk:** "I'll show him. I'll arm myself with information I can use to undermine him."

◆ **Positive self-talk:** "I let this upset me too much. Maybe something's bothering him. I'll try to find out what it could be."

Source: Managing Workplace Stress, by Susan Cartwright and Cary L. Cooper, Sage Publications, Inc., 2455 Teller Road, Thousand Oaks, CA 91320.

Self-talk shapes our inner attitudes, our attitudes shape our behavior, and of course our behavior—what we do—shapes the results we get.

your recycled negatives, write them down, and regularly read them to yourself; and (3) replace the negative thoughts with positive ones by flooding your brain with such statements as "I'm an effective speaker," "I'm a people person." Once you start focusing on the positives, the negatives tend to go away. Negative self-talk can't survive if you don't feed it.[4]

This method has been used extensively with athletes to overcome negatives. In one study, basketball players were divided into three groups for foul-shot practice. The first group used imagery (internally picturing that they were shooting and making their shots) and negative-message elimination but did not practice shooting. The second group practiced shooting, and the third group did both corrective imaging and practicing. Although all three groups improved, the first and third

Listen to Your Inner Voice

Consider these ideas to help you think faster when you need to decide something in a hurry:

◆ **Treat so-called** gut feelings or hunches as information, not imagination. *Reason:* Your brain routinely fuses feelings, sensations, taste, sight, and smell and presents them as a quick impression.

◆ **Don't ignore** a hunch that, for example, tells you that you should make that phone call now. You'll find that respecting hunches can improve your sense of timing.

◆ **Switch to a** completely different activity when you're having trouble solving a problem logically. Doing so often sparks activity in the intuitive side of your brain.

◆ **Call on** the side of your brain that receives and blends data at high speed. To do so, relax, close your eyes and breathe deeply, and then let the intuitive side of your brain take over.

◆ **Build confidence** in using your intuition by acknowledging when a hunch or gut feeling gives you the help you need.

Source: Communication Briefings, as adapted from Laurie Nadel, writing in *The Take-Charge Assistant,* 135 W. 50th St., New York, NY 10020.

groups improved by the same amount while the second group improved less. "Positive self-talk really can turn your life around and make any life more successful."[5]

There is controversy about whether inner speech and symbolic thought are the same thing. A major theorist in thinking and speaking postulated that "inner speech is solely thinking silently to oneself while symbolic thought is used to make associations between or among words or concepts, thus creating word meanings."[6] For our purposes, "the term *inner speech* refers to subvocalized or silent intrapersonal spoken language used to generate symbolic and conceptual thought while in the process of creating word meanings."[7] This inner speech allows us to silently produce words that remind us of things we need to do, things that have happened, or things we want to do.[8] We tend to think, to self-talk, continually. The voice rarely stops.[9]

In order to understand how inner speech works, it is important to be aware of how people acquire and develop language. Children go through a series of stages that enable them to develop linguistic skills. These skills enhance the ability to develop concepts and are the basis for inner speech. Given a stable environment, normally functioning senses, and a functioning cortex, all children, no matter what their nationality, learn language in a series of sequential steps (see Figure 4.1).[10] There is no significant difference in the speech development of boys versus girls.[11] If a child is denied normal interaction with other humans, the child will probably not naturally develop proficient language abilities.

When a child is born, he or she is neurologically wired to learn language and develop the ability to think in abstractions.[12] "The human brain has been tuned for social learning. We have a general purpose device for acquiring culture, technology and language."[13] The first point of linguistic development is the involuntary cries of a child, expressing his or her being frightened, lonesome, hungry, wet, or in pain. At this stage the child is not selecting the sound, though cries of babies can be differentiated. A baby who is hungry, for example, will cry with a sucking sound.[14] The child, at this point, has no inner speech. Starting around the sixth to the ninth

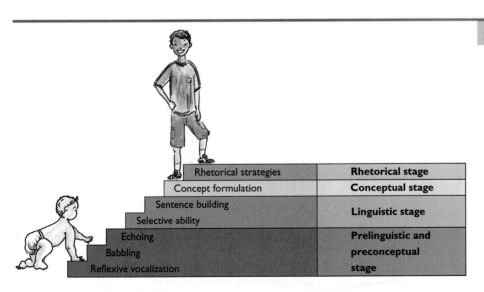

Figure 4.1

Sequential Steps of Linguistic Development

Rhetorical strategies	**Rhetorical stage**
Concept formulation	**Conceptual stage**
Sentence building	
Selective ability	**Linguistic stage**
Echoing	**Prelinguistic and**
Babbling	**preconceptual**
Reflexive vocalization	**stage**

Source: Roy Berko, Andrew Wolvin, and Darlyn Wolvin, *Communicating: A Social and Career Focus,* 3rd ed. (Boston: Houghton Mifflin, 1985), p. 56.

month, a child begins to make sounds beyond those of crying. By the ninth to twelfth month, there is an echoing of the words which surround the infant. Sometime between the twelfth and fifteenth month, the child starts to select words such as *coat* or *milk* to represent ideas. The word selected—for example, *milk*—generally represents whole ideas such as "I want some milk."

Children continue to develop language. A two-year-old child may have a vocabulary of three hundred to four hundred words but still externalizes instead of intrapersonally processing information. A child of four has learned the grammar of her language but still does not have internal speech. That is why if you watch four-year-olds playing, you will notice that they often "talk out" the activities they are performing to think things through. Younger children tell themselves to go, run, or hurry. The same thing happens when a child goes to bed and talks herself to sleep. A child's external speech parallels an adult's self-talk except that the child says the ideas aloud. Children often need to talk out loud to solve problems or make decisions. Teachers who insist on a silent classroom in the first and second grades may be closing off any means their students have for adding numbers, planning activities, or understanding what they are reading. Teachers and parents who tell children to "keep quiet" teach them to internalize, often before they are ready to do so. This forced silence can lead to emotional trauma and may restrict their ability to learn. You may have experienced this when your early grade teacher didn't let you count aloud during arithmetic class or let you talk as you tried to write a story.

Children normally don't develop internalized speech until sometime around age nine, when they can conceptualize, or think in abstraction. Interestingly, some adults find themselves needing external processing, including reading aloud and talking to themselves while writing or taking tests, in order to comprehend. This is especially true with creative, globally oriented people.

Once individuals have a usable vocabulary and the ability to think in abstractions, they start to learn the strategies to manipulate ideas and enter the rhetorical stage. In this stage, they can adjust their speech according to the person(s) to whom they are speaking, to the purpose of the communication, and to the place where the communication is taking place. This usually occurs at age twelve or thirteen. It is at this stage that the person also has fully functioning inner speech.

In addition to self-talk, one of the important aspects of intrapersonal communication is how we process information as we receive it.

Cognitive Processing

Your culture, background, family, education, and experiences all serve as the framework for shaping how you deal with incoming information and affect the way you decide on what actions to take or avoid. The act of **cognitive processing** is the comprehending, organizing, and storing of ideas. An aspect of intrapersonal communication, it is how we process information in relationship to our values, attitudes, and beliefs.

Each of us carries with us **values** (what we perceive to be of positive or negative worth), **attitudes** (our predispositions), and **beliefs** (our convictions). Most

Are You Sabotaging Yourself?

Check off the statements that apply to you.

_____ 1. My life often seems to be out of my control.

_____ 2. Much of my life is spent on other people's goals or problems.

_____ 3. I often get into trouble by assuming I know something when I don't.

_____ 4. I have a tendency to expect the worst.

_____ 5. I often find myself saying, "I don't feel up to it."

_____ 6. The fear of appearing stupid often prevents me from asking questions or offering my opinion.

_____ 7. I have trouble taking criticism, even from my friends.

_____ 8. If I'm not perfect, I often feel worthless.

_____ 9. I have trouble focusing on what's really important to me.

_____10. I often wish I were someone else.

_____11. I often feel irritable and moody.

_____12. I find that when I really want something, I'll act impulsively to get it.

_____ 13. I waste a lot of time.

_____ 14. I often do not live up to my potential because I put things off to the last minute.

_____ 15. I spend time with people who belittle me or put down my thoughts or ideas.

Total number of statements checked: _____

0–2: You are not likely to be sabotaging your life.

3–5: Like most people, you're doing some things that may be holding you back. A little effort at self-improvement will do wonders for you.

6–11: You may be undermining your life in a major way. Begin now to identify and remove your barriers.

12–15: Warning! Sabotage may be everywhere. Sustained effort may be needed to break down the walls of self-sabotage.

Source: From "The Sabotage Factor" course by Daniel G. Amen, M.D., author of *Don't Shoot Yourself in the Foot* (Warner, 1992). Reprinted by permission of the author.

people try to keep their actions parallel to their values, beliefs, and attitudes. If things are in balance, we feel fairly good about ourselves and the world around us. If they are not, we may intrapersonally become confused and frustrated, which may cause us to act negatively toward ourselves or others, maybe even blaming them for what's wrong. This imbalance happens, for example, when you know that a certain action you are about to take is wrong based on your value system. Your "internal voice" cries out, "Be careful! Don't do that!" Before the event, you may have a sleepless night as you toss and turn with the internal voice speaking messages, or you dream about the negative things that are going to happen as a result of your taking the action.

The *imbalance* between your values, attitudes, and beliefs is called **cognitive dissonance**.[15] Cognitive dissonance often leads to a **guilty conscience:** the real or perceived fear that we are going to get caught, get punished, or otherwise be "found out." For example, an individual who believes cheating is wrong yet cheats on a test may feel cognitive dissonance following the act, no matter what grade she receives.

If you become aware of cognitive dissonance before you act and decide not to do the deed, you could chalk it up to your conscience warning you and saving you from a perceived disaster. If you brood about the action afterward, then you may need to accept that you took the action, there is nothing you can do about it now, and go on from there, with the internal pledge of not doing it again. Our internal voice, through its self-talk technique, often continues to shout at us until we can put the imbalance to rest. Sometimes apologizing to someone else is in order if the action hurt someone else.

Another dimension of intrapersonal communication is self-concept.

internal voice reduces cognitive dissonance

Self-Concept

Your understanding of yourself is known as your **self-concept.** "Self-concept is the guiding factor in a person's actions. How a human being views himself or herself will determine most of his or her actions and choices in life. Essentially a person is going to choose what he or she feels he or she is worth."[16] Thus, the more positively you perceive yourself, the more likely it is that you will have **self-confidence,** that is, a sense of competence and effectiveness.

Each of us possesses a real self, an ideal self, and a public self (see Figure 4.2). The **real self** is what you think of yourself when you are being most honest about your interests, thoughts, emotions, and needs. For many people, the real self is dynamic and changing. This accounts for why you may feel as if you are in constant turmoil, searching for who and what you are, questioning your motives for doing and not doing certain things.

The **ideal self** is who you would like to be or think you should be. This is the "perfect you," perceived as being "perfect" by yourself or others (or both of you). It's often the you the significant others in your life (relatives, employers, the media, advertising) have told you that you should be, or who they want you to be.

The **public self** is the one you let others know. It is the you that you have decided to let others see. It is based on the concept that "if others believe the right things about me, I can get them to like me; I can persuade them and generally get my way." It acknowledges that "if others believe the wrong things about me, I can be rejected and blocked from my goals. Not only actors and politicians shape their public selves, we all do."[17]

Recognition of the importance of self-esteem and self-concept has a long tradition in the Euro-American culture. Psychologists and educators have been interested in the study of the self for many years and have developed different theories

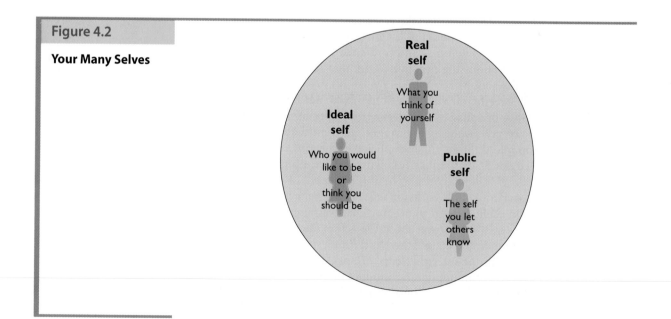

Figure 4.2

Your Many Selves

Real self

What you think of yourself

Ideal self

Who you would like to be or think you should be

Public self

The self you let others know

The more positively you perceive yourself, the more likely it is that you will have self-confidence, that is, a sense of competence and effectiveness.

about it. Communication theorists have examined the self and self-esteem based on observing and studying what we intrapersonally communicate to ourselves about ourselves and what we communicate to others.

The classic theory about the self is that it is composed of four aspects: the *spiritual,* what we are thinking and feeling; the *material,* represented by our possessions and physical surroundings; the *social,* represented by our interactions with others; and the *physical,* our physical being.[18] Much of our self-talk centers on how we perceive the four aspects.

Another theory stresses that the self evolves from the interactions we have with other people and how we intrapersonally integrate these interactions into our self-thought. This evolution takes place in stages. For example, a child aims for a sense of self as a separate person while developing gender identity; the adolescent tries to establish a stable sense of identity; the middle-aged person emphasizes independence while adjusting to changes in body competence; and the elderly person seeks to come to terms with aging.[19] As we go through these changes, our self-communication reflects the alterations that are taking place, and for this reason we experience over our lifetime multiple concepts, rather than a single one, of who we are. Thus, at any one time in our lives, we may perceive ourselves to be a different person than we were at another time. You are probably not the same person today that you were five years ago, and you are not the same person today that you perceive yourself to be five years from now.

Self-concept also seems to be situational. Who you are with one person or in one place may not be the same as who you are with someone else or in a different place. In one relationship, you may take on the role of student, and in another the role of friend. At work you may be the leader, and at home the follower. Many of these role plays are based on our intrapersonal perception of who we should or who we need to be with these people in this environment.

It is important that you understand yourself and your perceptions of yourself. This is the basis of self-awareness, which is the basis for much of your self-talk.

Understanding Yourself

Most people have only a general idea of who they are and what they really believe in. This explains why many of us don't understand why we think the thoughts we do and are intrapersonally motivated to act in particular ways.

It is often of great personal value to attempt to discover the you who is within you—the you who carries on your self-talk, cognitively processes, and acts on your self-concept.

Here is an activity to get you started in investigating your motives, beliefs, and self-concept. Complete these statements:

I am

I would like to be

I like to

I believe that

I have been

I wouldn't want to

The quality I possess that I am most proud of is

My biggest flaw is

Something that I would prefer others not know about me is

Once you are finished responding to these items, go back over your list of answers and write a two-sentence description of yourself based just on the answers to the statements.

A good part of our lives is devoted to communicating our pleasure or lack of pleasure as we exploit our conquests, stress our influences, and reinforce our accomplishments.

It has been said that you are what you are based on your verb *to be*.[20] What you have done in the activity you just completed is to describe yourself based on your perceived verb *to be*. You have used your intrapersonally stored data to examine your past experiences (*I have been/done*), current attitudes and actions (*I am*), and future expectations or hopes (*I would like to be/do*). If you were honest and revealed what you really think and feel, you have just gained a glimpse at your perceived self.

Another way of looking at yourself is through the model known as the **Johari window,**[21] which allows you to ascertain your willingness to disclose who you are and allows others to disclose to you (see Figure 4.3). From an intrapersonal perspective, the Johari window helps you understand a great deal about yourself and some cultural underpinnings of your self-thinking.

In the Johari window, area I, the *free area*, includes everything you know and understand about yourself and that all other people know and understand about you: your values, personality characteristics, and perceptions. For example, you may enjoy wearing nice clothes, and so you spend time selecting a wardrobe. This is communicated to others through the clothes you wear. Others, in turn, are aware of your enjoyment of wearing nice clothing because they observe what you wear and the care you take in selecting it.

The *blind area*, area II, represents all those things about you that others recognize but that you do not see in yourself. You may, for example, make a poor first impression

How to Accept a Compliment

Do you have a problem accepting compliments? Do you often answer with "Oh, it was nothing"?

Be aware that deflecting a compliment often draws unwanted attention and belittles both you and the person offering the compliment.

Instead, just say, "Thank you."

You'll be pleased at how well it works.

Source: Communication Briefings, as adapted from *The Wellness Book,* by Dr. Herert Benson and Eileen M. Stuart, Birch Lane Press, 600 Madison Ave., New York, NY 10022.

Deflecting a compliment draws unwanted attention and belittles both you and the person offering the compliment.

Figure 4.3

The Johari Window

	Known to Self	Not Known to Self
Known to Others	I. Free Area	II. Blind Area
Not Known to Others	III. Hidden Area	IV. Unknown Area

Source: From *Group Processes: An Introduction to Group Dynamics,* by Joseph Luft, 3rd ed., Mayfield Publishing Company, 1984. Reprinted by permission of the author.

on certain people because you are boisterous. Unless this behavior is pointed out to you, it will remain in the blind area. Information in the blind area is revealed only when you have the opportunity to investigate other people's perceptions of you.

In the *hidden area,* area III, you recognize something about yourself but choose not to share it with others. If you are a man, for example, you may have learned not to show certain types of emotions, such as crying, yet you sometimes face situations in which tears would express your true feelings. No one knows about your emotional feelings since you hide them from view.

The *unknown area,* area IV, represents all those things that neither you nor others know about you. Often these aspects are so well concealed that they never even surface. Since you don't reveal them, these traits remain unknown not only to you but also to everyone else. For example, in therapy a person may suddenly become aware of the forgotten experiences that he was sexually abused as a child, which may explain his strong aversion to being touched.

The following activity will help you chart your Johari window.[22]

Before each item in Part I, place a number from 1 to 6 to indicate how much you are *willing to reveal.* A 1 indicates that you are willing to self-disclose nothing or almost nothing, and a 6 indicates that you are willing to reveal everything or almost everything. Use the values 2, 3, 4, and 5 to represent the points between these extremes.

Before each item in Part II, place a number from 1 to 6 to indicate how *willing you are to receive feedback* about what you self-disclose. A 1 indicates that you refuse or resist feedback, and a 6 indicates that you consistently encourage feedback. Use the values 2, 3, 4, and 5 to represent the points between these extremes.

PART I: Extent to which I am willing to self-disclose my

_____ 1. goals
_____ 2. strengths
_____ 3. weaknesses
_____ 4. positive feelings
_____ 5. negative feelings
_____ 6. values
_____ 7. ideas
_____ 8. beliefs
_____ 9. fears and insecurities

_____ 10. mistakes
_____   Total

PART II: Extent to which I am willing to receive feedback about my

_____ 1. goals
_____ 2. strengths
_____ 3. weaknesses
_____ 4. positive feelings
_____ 5. negative feelings
_____ 6. values
_____ 7. ideas
_____ 8. beliefs
_____ 9. fears and insecurities
_____ 10. mistakes
_____   Total

Use Figure 4.4 to plot your scores. Circle the number on the top line of the square, designated "receive feedback," that corresponds to your score on Part II of the activity. Circle the same number on the bottom line of the square. Connect the two circles with a straight line. Then circle the number on the left side line of the square, designated "self-disclosure," that corresponds to your score on Part I of the activity. Circle the same number on the right side line of the square. Connect the two circles with a straight line.

You now have the four "panes" of your Johari window. Color in the four-sided figure in the upper left-hand side of the square as illustrated in Figure 4.5. Compare your pattern to those in the figure to ascertain your self-disclosure/receive-feedback style.

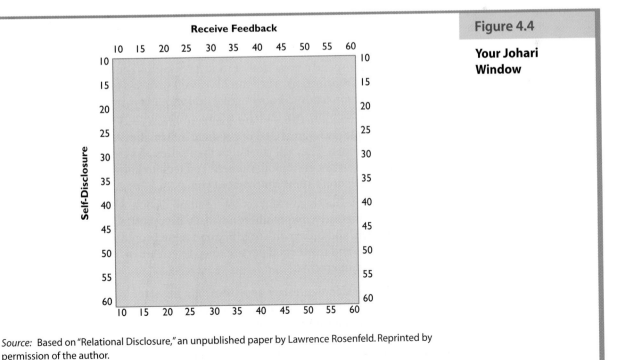

Figure 4.4

Your Johari Window

Source: Based on "Relational Disclosure," an unpublished paper by Lawrence Rosenfeld. Reprinted by permission of the author.

Figure 4.5

Sample Johari Window

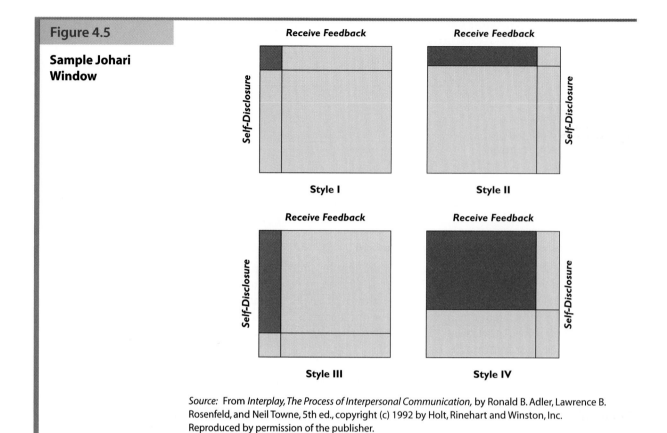

Source: From *Interplay, The Process of Interpersonal Communication,* by Ronald B. Adler, Lawrence B. Rosenfeld, and Neil Towne, 5th ed., copyright (c) 1992 by Holt, Rinehart and Winston, Inc. Reproduced by permission of the publisher.

- *Style I* people spend little time disclosing or giving feedback. They tend to be perceived as good listeners and fairly shy or quiet; sometimes they are labeled as introverts.

- *Style II* people spend a great deal of time listening and not much time sending out personal information. After you have been with this type of person for a while, the person tends to know a great deal about you, but you don't know much about the other person. This is also a style of introverts.

- *Style III* people give a great deal of personal information but don't like to receive very much. They tell you about themselves and are often perceived as great talkers but not very good listeners. You tend to know a great deal about them, but they don't know much about you.

- *Style IV* people like to give and get information. People who are very open and easily share themselves with others normally have a large, free area and smaller blind, hidden, and unknown areas. Because these people share, they are known to themselves and to others. They are often referred to as extroverts; they are outgoing and interactive.

If your four-sided figures are approximately the same size, you do not have a predominant self-disclosure/receive-feedback style.

What you should gain from the Johari window exercise is an understanding of not only your perception of yourself and how it affects your intrapersonal communication, but also how others may perceive you based on your willingness or unwillingness to disclose and receive information.

As you come to know yourself, you will gain an understanding of the need drives that uniquely shape you as a communicator.

Need Drives Affecting Communication

[handwritten: · survival · pleasure-seeking · security · territoriality]

We are each born with certain biological tools that allow us to communicate: a brain, sound-producing organs (mouth, tongue, larynx), and a receiving apparatus (ears, eyes). We also, according to **ethnographers**—researchers who study cultures—are born with need drives that must be satisfied. Some communication theorists think that these intrapersonal drives are the bases for our communication: what we think, what we express, what inspires us to act the way we do, and how we react to the way others express and use their drives. This concept explains why we communicate in ways that go beyond our usual understanding of communication.[23]

The basic forces that determine human behavior are survival of the species, pleasure seeking, security, and territoriality.[24] These drives are not manifested equally in every person. One person may have a pleasure need that is stronger than any of the other forces whereas another may have strong needs for security and territoriality. This view offers a contrast to the earlier proposed hierarchy of needs theory, which suggests that each need must be satisfied before a person can move on to the next one.

Survival

A person who is threatened screams out for help; when a pebble flies against the windshield of your moving car, you duck. These are examples of attempts to ensure *survival.* These are reflexive—inborn reactions that we instinctively use to communicate our fear of a possible ending of our existence.

Our ability to communicate selectively gives us a distinct survival advantage. For example, we can call for help, plead, explain our needs, or try to convince attackers that their action is unwise. In addition, we are aware of our own evolution, an awareness that is probably not found in other animals. Because of this, we can communicate about how we reproduce, what causes us to die, and how we can attempt to alter conditions to prolong our lives and those of our descendants. We have been able to communicate these ideas from person to person and thus build on the experience of the past in developing intrapersonal understanding.

Pleasure Seeking

We are basically *pleasure-seeking* beings. A good part of our lives is devoted to communicating our pleasure or lack of pleasure as we exploit our conquests, stress our influences, and reinforce our accomplishments. We talk about our awards, citations, and good grades to communicate to others that we have succeeded, thus satisfying our pleasure need.

People find different events pleasurable, and each of us may find both pleasure and pain in a single event. Moreover, we may find pleasure in satisfying not only our own needs but also the needs of others, or in fulfilling our long-term goals as well as our immediate desires. What pleases one person may well torture another. One person happily gives a speech before a large audience; another is petrified by any speaking situation.

We show our claim to territory by marking it with objects, fences, signs, and numbers.

If given the opportunity, we choose to communicate in those situations in which we perceive we will get pleasure. You raise your hand to answer a question in class if you think you know the right answer. Unless forced to do so, individuals who fear public speaking avoid putting themselves in a position of giving a speech. But a speaker who has received positive reactions from an audience is much more likely to try the experience again. We are constantly sending ourselves intrapersonal messages relating to whether some experience was or was not pleasurable, or whether a perceived activity will render pleasure.

Security

You enter a classroom for the first meeting of a class. You see a place that is unfamiliar, people you do not know, a professor who is an unknown entity. You feel insecure. Your desire to participate and your comfort in this situation can be affected directly by the messages you send yourself.

The need for *security* causes us to seek equilibrium, a balance. When security is absent, when we feel a lack of control, most of us are uneasy, overly cautious, and uncertain.

Our concept of ourselves in situations of security or insecurity motivates our verbal and nonverbal communication. Fear causes the vocal pitch to rise, the body to shake, and the stomach to churn. We find ourselves afraid to speak, or speaking incessantly, or stammering. But as we become more comfortable in a situation and learn the rules of the game, we find ourselves acting quite differently because we send ourselves positive messages. The first day of class, for instance, you may not say a word. But as you acclimate yourself to the situation, you may feel secure enough to participate.

Hearing intrapersonal messages of fear of the unknown explains why some people will not wander down the unmapped paths of life. The messages they send themselves center on the warning "beware of the unknown, the uncomfortable."

Territoriality

We intrapersonally define a particular *territory,* whether physical or perceptual, and then feel secure within that territory. We defend it from invasion and use it for protection. We mark off land by defining it precisely with a deed indicating length, width, and location. We mark our territory with fences, signs, and numbers that specifically say, "This belongs to me." We tend to feel most secure when we are in our own territory, and we often identify ourselves by our home town, our school, and our social groups, all of which are territorial markers.

We act differently in different territories. When friends come to visit you, conditions are not the same as when you go to visit them. The friend you invite over for dinner does not act the same way at your house as when you go to his house for dinner. In the same way, there is a definite difference between playing an athletic game at home and playing it on the road. The home team is estimated to have an advantage of about one touchdown in football and ten points in basketball.

In addition to physical territory, we have ideas and areas of expertise that we identify as ours. Inventors obtain patents to protect their inventions; writers copyright their books. Both are attempts to establish a territory and to communicate the boundaries to others.

The more insecure a person is within a territory, the greater is that person's intrapersonal fear of losing the territory. Once people have defined something as theirs, they will tend to defend it. Thus, an invasion of someone else's territory is likely to invite a counterattack.

Clearly, one's basic drives have a significant influence on intrapersonal communication.

The field of communication relies on research in psychology, sociology, and anthropology as well as communication to develop many of its concepts. One area related to intrapersonal communication is exclusively the property of the communication field: communication apprehension.

Anxiety: Communication Apprehension

Anxiety—excessive worry or concern—is an important variable that may affect our perceptions and performance. Anxiety is based on negative intrapersonal messages as they specifically relate to pleasure and security. Although many think of communication anxiety only in regard to public speaking, it is much broader.[25] Worries, concerns, and fears interfere with efficient listening, communicating in groups, talking in class and on the telephone, and verbalizing during interviews. Anxiety can make us so preoccupied that we do not get the message being communicated, or we become incapable of sending the message.

The communicatively anxious person is aware of the apprehension because intrapersonal messages convey the fear.

Communication Anxiety Defined

In the field of communication, the term used for speech anxiety is **communication apprehension.** It also is identified as shyness, social anxiety disorder, or social phobia.[26] The communicatively anxious person is aware of the anxiety because intrapersonal messages clearly warn of the fear. The messages warn of unfavorable outcomes, and the person experiences a sense of impending doom. These messages result in a wide variety of behaviors, including preperformance fears such as excessive worry, and can bring on sleeplessness, headache, and an upset stomach. Other signs include a racing heart, sweaty palms, dry mouth, vanishing words, cluttered thoughts, and an urge to escape from any communicative situation. It varies in its spectrum (see Figure 4.6).

"Shy people have inaccurate self-concepts."[27] They often believe that they are inadequate when they are not. "They tend to blame themselves for failure and credit others for success. They tend to erase themselves: They avoid eye contact, speak softly or less than others, and rarely take a strong

Figure 4.6	**A Spectrum of Shyness**			

NORMAL SHYNESS	EXTREME SHYNESS	SOCIAL ANXIETY	SEVERE SOCIAL ANXIETY
• You are jittery beginning a public speech, but afterward you are glad you did it. • Your mind goes blank on a first date, but eventually you relax and find things to talk about. • Your palms sweat in a job interview, but you ask and answer thoughtful questions.	• You clam up and your heart races when you know people are looking at you. • You tremble when speaking up at a meeting, even if it is only to say your name. • You avoid starting conversations for fear of saying something awkward.	• You will do anything, even skip work, to avoid being introduced to new people. • You have trouble swallowing in public, making it hard to dine out or go to parties. • You feel you never make a good impression and that you are a social failure.	• You are free of nervousness only when alone and you can barely leave the house. • You constantly worry about being embarrassed or humiliated by others.

Source: *U.S. News & World Report*, June 21, 1999, pp. 52–53.

position on a topic."[28] People who experience speech anxiety think poorly of themselves, feel fearful, and often perform in an inadequate fashion.[29]

Almost 95 percent of the population reports having apprehension about communicating with some person or group in their lives.[30] "A decade ago, 40 percent of people said they were shy, but in today's 'nation of strangers'—in which computers and ATMs make face-to-face relations less and less common—that number is nearing 50 percent."[31] It is reasoned that the increase may be due to people being able to avoid interacting directly with others by use of the electronic means. Thus, they avoid practicing the very skills that they need to hone. "Social phobia is the third most common mental disorder in the United States, behind depression and alcoholism."[32]

Research shows that "more women than men are thought to suffer anxiety, but because shyness and demureness are smiled upon in females and less acceptable in males, more men turn to professionals for help."[33]

Communication apprehension may be situation specific or general. For example, some people feel fear only when confronted with giving a speech. A survey indicates that 40.6 percent identified their major fear as speaking before groups, exceeding fear of heights, death, and loneliness![34] On the other hand, some people report perceived discomfort only in one-on-one conversations or in groups. Others indicate anxiety in any speaking situation. To find out if you perceive yourself to be situationally or generally apprehensive, do Activity 6 in the Learn by Doing section at the end of this chapter.

Causes of Communication Apprehension

Communication apprehension can result from heredity. Some people have a natural predisposition to be shy and uncomfortable with others. Ten to 15 percent of babies are reportedly born apprehensive, as demonstrated by their crying when being exposed to unfamiliar things. Tests on shy children progressing from two weeks of life to seven years indicated that at twenty-one months, they clung to their caretakers in new situations and hesitated before interacting with new persons; at four years, they remained quiet in the presence of an unknown adult, and at seven years they exhibited a greater reaction to imagined threats than other children did.[35] Biologically, shy children react more

Revised Cheek and Buss Shyness Scale

Instructions: For each statement, rate yourself on this scale: 1 = very uncharacteristic or untrue, 2 = uncharacteristic, 3 = neutral, 4 = characteristic, 5 = very characteristic or true.

_____ 1. I'm tense when I'm with people I don't know well.

_____ 2. It's difficult for me to ask other people for information.

_____ 3. I'm often uncomfortable at parties and other social functions.

_____ 4. When I'm in a group of people, I have trouble thinking of the right things to say.

_____ 5. It takes me a long time to overcome my shyness in new situations.

_____ 6. It's hard for me to act natural when I'm meeting new people.

_____ 7. I'm nervous when speaking to someone in authority.

_____ 8. I have doubts about my social competence.

_____ 9. I have trouble looking someone right in the eye.

_____ 10. I'm inhibited in social situations.

_____ 11. I do find it hard to talk to strangers.

_____ 12. I am more shy with members of the opposite sex.

_____   Total score

Ratings: Over 45 points, very shy; 31 to 45, somewhat shy; below 31, probably not shy, although you may feel shy in some situations.

Source: Jonathan M. Cheek and Bronwen Cheek, _Conquering Shyness._ Dell Trade Paperback Edition, 1990. © 1989 by J. M. Cheek and B. Cheek. Reprinted by permission of the authors.

---

intensely to the stimuli around them than other children do, as exhibited by racing hearts, widening pupils, and vocal cord tenseness.

Communication apprehension also can spring from social conditioning. Children may imitate or model such behaviors as they observe in others. Apprehensive parents often have apprehensive children. Another potential cause is having been brought up in an environment where perfection was stressed, often causing the person to fear being evaluated, which is a major fear of many communicatively anxious people.[36] In addition, a person may be reinforced in anxiety by the negative feedback received because of avoiding communicative activities.[37]

It should be noted that communication apprehension, as it is generally understood, focuses on _speaker_ apprehension. Receiver apprehension, however, is also significant as a communication barrier. Listener apprehension has been conceptualized as "the fear of misinterpreting, inadequately processing, and/or not being able to adjust psychologically to messages sent by others."[38] It is possible that a listener can be so anxious about the outcome of a communication (getting a test report from a physician, for example) that he approaches listening with a high level of apprehension. Receiver apprehension can stem from awareness of poor listening skills, fear of the speaker, or unfamiliarity with the speaker, the situation, or the subject itself.

Help for Communication Apprehension

Communication apprehension is not a mental disorder.[39] Since, except for those born with the anxiety, communication apprehension is a title given to a person by himself or herself, it can be removed. The simplest way, of course, is for the person to declare that he or she doesn't want or need the title. This is very difficult for many to do, so be reassured that aid is available to help rid those who want to rid themselves of the title. Skill training, systematic desensitization, cognitive modification, a willingness to communicate, and drug therapy are forms of aid.

COPING STRATEGIES

Skill Training   One of the factors that is perceived to be a problem among communicatively anxious people is their lack of oral communication skills. Not knowing how to structure or organize a speech, how to start and continue a conversation, or how to participate in a group can manifest itself into triggering the negative aspect of two of the basic human needs: security and pleasure.

Those who have learned the skills needed to be an effective communicator feel secure and anticipate pleasure. Many of the theories and concepts stressed in this book and taught in communication classes can teach the necessary skills.

Systematic Desensitization   Fear of humiliation and embarrassment when in the company of unfamiliar people and fear of being evaluated negatively by others are additional major apprehension inducers.[40] Through systematic desensitization, people are taught to recognize tension in their bodies and then how to relax.[41] As many as 80 or 90 percent of the people treated professionally by this system report the complete elimination of their apprehension.[42] Nevertheless, such a program works only if the person wants to change and has the skills to modify the negative behavior. If the individual lacks the necessary abilities, then skill training must precede systematic desensitization.

Cognitive Modification   The basic concept behind cognitive modification is that people have learned to think negatively and must be retaught to think positively. The first step in this process is for people to learn how to recognize when they are thinking negatively and to identify their own negative statements about their communication. Then they learn to replace negative statements with positive ones. Rather than saying, for example, "I really say stupid things," they may substitute "I can present clear ideas; it isn't that hard." The last stage of the training is to practice substituting positive statements for negative ones. This may sound very theoretical, but it works. The success of this technique is quite high.[43]

Willingness to Communicate   Your personal communication must stem from a willingness to communicate. People who are willing to communicate are willing to take risks, analyze their communication, and make adjustments as needed.

The willing communicator realizes that:

◆ There is no such thing as a perfect communicator. We all make mistakes.

◆ You need to interact with others, no matter what are perceived to be the negatives of that communication, such as being embarrassed.

◆ Most often, the perceived fear of what will go wrong never happens (speaking in public won't kill a person, for example).

◆ Accomplishing your communicative task is more important than your perceived fear of "what others might think."

◆ You must assume that if someone doesn't like what you say, or how you say it, it is that person's problem, not yours. This attitude allows you to be immune to the personal negative self-doubts that are often present in those who are communicatively apprehensive.

"Willingness to communicate is the one, overwhelming communication personality construct which permeates every facet of an individual's life and contributes significantly to the social, education, and organizational achievements of the individual."[44]

Drug Therapy   "Pasted on bus shelters nationwide, a poster asks passersby to imagine being allergic to people."[45] The purpose of billboards is to alert individuals who have social anxiety disorder that, in extreme cases, there may be some aid in dealing with the problem by using drug therapy as a support for psychological and speech communication assistance. Drugs such as Paxil have been found to aid in helping communicatively apprehensive people to manage their problems.[46]

In Conclusion

The basis for communication with others is the ability to communicate with oneself. The internal messages that we send to ourselves are called intrapersonal communication. Each person's culture, background, family, education, and experiences serve as the framework for shaping how he or she deals with incoming information and affects the way he or she decides on what actions to take or avoid. How a human being views himself or herself will determine most of his or her actions and choices in life; however, most people have only a general idea of who they are and what they really believe in. Some communication theorists believe that the intrapersonal drives we are born with are the bases for our communication: what we think, what we express, what inspires us to act the way we do, and how we react to the way others express and use their drives. Most people experience and subsequently deal with some form of communication apprehension.

Learn by Doing

1. Prepare a list of ten questions an interviewer should ask to get an accurate picture of who you really are. These questions should allow the interviewer to understand your personal history, beliefs, and future plans. Phrase the questions so that they require more than a one- or two-word reply. Your instructor will then match you with another member of the class. You will interview each other using the questions that each of you has prepared. Then introduce each other in a two- to three-minute presentation to the class. After the class presentation, answer the following questions:
   a. What did it feel like to reveal myself to a stranger?
   b. Did I conceal things about myself during the interview? If so, why?
   c. How did I feel and what did I do while my partner was introducing me to the class?

2. Bring to class a painting, poem, or piece of music you like. Share it with the class or a small group, and indicate why you have positive feelings about it. What does your choice indicate about you?

3. State whether you agree or disagree with these statements: "A person is change-able and can alter behavior patterns if she or he really wants to do so." "No one can change anyone else; only the individual can change himself or herself." Explain the reasons for your answers.

4. Fill out your Johari window (see pages 92–93). Get one of your friends to fill in the Known-to-Others part of the window about you. Compare that person's answers with yours. What did you learn about yourself from this activity?

5. Make a shieldlike coat of arms out of a piece of cardboard large enough for the class to see. Draw or cut out and paste at least four pictures, symbols, or words on the coat of arms that represent you: your beliefs, attitudes, bodily image, hobbies, future plans, past successes or failures. The class will be divided into groups. Each person is to explain his or her coat of arms and why he or she selected these things to represent himself/herself.

6. Personal Report of Communication Apprehension (PRCA-24)[47] directions: This instrument is composed of twenty-four statements concerning feelings about communicating with other people. Indicate the degree to which each statement applies to you by marking whether you (1) strongly agree, (2) agree, (3) are undecided, (4) disagree, or (5) strongly disagree. Record your first impression.

_____ 1. I dislike participating in group discussions.

_____ 2. Generally, I am comfortable while participating in a group discussion.

_____ 3. I am tense and nervous while participating in group discussions.

_____ 4. I like to get involved in group discussions.

_____ 5. Engaging in a group discussion with new people makes me tense and nervous.

_____ 6. I am calm and relaxed while participating in group discussions.

_____ 7. Generally, I am nervous when I have to participate in a meeting.

_____ 8. Usually I am calm and relaxed while participating in meetings.

_____ 9. I am very calm and relaxed when I am called upon to express an opinion at a meeting.

_____ 10. I am afraid to express myself at meetings.

_____ 11. Communicating at meetings usually makes me uncomfortable.

_____ 12. I am very relaxed when answering questions at a meeting.

_____ 13. While participating in a conversation with a new acquaintance, I feel very nervous.

_____ 14. I have no fear of speaking up in conversations.

_____ 15. Ordinarily I am very tense and nervous in conversations.

_____ 16. Ordinarily I am very calm and relaxed in conversations.

_____ 17. While conversing with a new acquaintance, I feel very relaxed.

_____ 18. I'm afraid to speak up in conversations.

_____ 19. I have no fear of giving a speech.

_____ 20. Certain parts of my body feel very tense and rigid while I am giving a speech.

_____ 21. I feel relaxed while giving a speech.

_____ 22. My thoughts become confused and jumbled when I am giving a speech.

_____ 23. I face the prospect of giving a speech with confidence.

_____ 24. While giving a speech, I get so nervous I forget facts I really know.

Scoring:

18+ scores for items 2, 4, 6; minus the scores for items 1, 3, 5 = Group discussion score

18+ scores for 8, 9, 12; minus the scores for 7, 10, 11 = Meetings score

18+ scores for 14, 16, 17; minus the scores for 13, 15, 18 = Interpersonal conversations score

18+ scores for 19, 21, 23; minus the scores for 20, 22, 24 = Public speaking score

Add your group, meetings, interpersonal, and public speaking scores = Total score

Your score should range between 24 and 120. If your score is below 24 or above 120, you have made a mistake in computing the score. (Your instructor will refer to the _Instructor's Manual_ for this textbook to tell you the meaning of your scores.)

Key Terms

intrapersonal communication
self-talk
cognitive processing
values
attitudes
beliefs
cognitive dissonance
guilty conscience
self-concept

self-confidence
real self
ideal self
public self
Johari window
ethnographers
anxiety
communication apprehension

5

Listening

After reading this chapter, you should be able to

- **Explain the importance of listening in daily communication**

- **Contrast hearing and listening**

- **Define and identify the roles of reception, perception, attention, the assignment of meaning, and response as they relate to the listening process**

- **List and explain some of the listening influencers**

- **Describe discriminative, comprehension, therapeutic, critical, and appreciative listening**

- **Understand how to listen to the media**

- **Identify and explain some of the techniques available for improving personal listening**

- **Discuss the causes of listening apprehension and approaches to dealing with it**

I f you are fairly typical, you have had little, if any, training as a listener. Most elementary schools operate on the assumption that you don't know how to read or write when you come to school, so they teach you how to perform those skills. They also assume that since you can talk and hear, you can communicate and listen. This assumption is incorrect. Talking and hearing are biological functions. Listening and communicating, like reading and writing, are learned skills.

How effective a listener do you think you are? How much of your time do you spend listening?

The average person in the United States spends 50 to 80 percent of the day listening but actively hears only half of what is said,[1] understands only a quarter of that, and remembers even less. Most people use only 25 percent of their capacity to listen.[2]

The Importance of Listening

Listening is an important skill that we use daily. Your academic success, employment achievement, and personal happiness may well depend on your ability to listen efficiently.

Listening is an important means for learning at all academic levels. In fact, listening is the most used scholastic skill. "Students listen to the equivalent of a book a day; talk the equivalent of a book a week; read the equivalent of a book a month; and write the equivalent of a book a year."[3] In fact, listening has been found to be more critical to academic success than reading or academic aptitude.[4] If you'd like to find out how you perceive yourself as a classroom listener, fill out the inventory presented in Activity 9 of the Learn by Doing section of this chapter.

listening- most used academic skill

"Listening seems, at first blush, passive, as it involves silence. But this image of passivity is an illusion. It requires a strong person to be a good listener, able to be patient and confident enough to suspend judgment, and yet not sacrifice one's capacity to analyze and reply. Not without reason people often indicate listening as a crucial skill for leadership, thereby linking listening with strength of character and judgment."[5]

The cost of poor listening can be catastrophic. A $10 listening mistake made by each of the 100 million U.S. workers would add up to a cost of a billion dollars. In a specific fact more telling than a theoretical number, federal investigators observe that poor listening is as much at fault as mechanical problems in airline crashes.[6]

Several years ago, the Sperry Computer Corporation launched a major advertising campaign to point out how important it is to listen effectively in both our personal lives and our careers. Like many other U.S. corporations, Sperry instituted training programs to prepare its executives, managers, and employees to be better listeners. Control Data, 3M, and General Motors are just a few other major companies that provide training in listening.

As an educated person, you have an obligation to strive to be an effective listener. And to be a responsible listener, you must know what the process is about, what it takes to

"Listen in Chinese"

The Chinese characters that make up the verb to listen explain the significance of this skill.

Ear

Eyes

Undivided Attention

Heart

be an effective listener, how to evaluate your own listening, and how to work toward improving your weaknesses while retaining your strengths.

The Listening Process

Many people assume that hearing and listening are the same, but they are not. **Hearing** is a biological activity that involves reception of a message through sensory channels. Hearing is only one part of **listening,** a process that involves reception, attention, perception, the assignment of meaning, and the listener's response to the message presented (see Figure 5.1).

Reception

The initial step in the listening process is the **reception** of a stimulus or message—both the auditory message and the visual message. The hearing process is based on a complex set of physical interactions between the ear and the brain. Proper care of the ear is important because auditory acuity enhances the ability to listen efficiently. It is estimated that approximately 28 million U.S. residents (more than one out of every twenty) are deaf or hard of hearing.[7] To keep these statistics from rising, people who work near loud machinery are now required to wear ear protectors. But the workplace is not the only source of potential danger. For example, individuals who expose themselves to loud music or listen to music through earphones should be aware that they can damage their hearing mechanism. Indeed, the use of earphones to listen to music is considered the source of much of the hearing damage.[8] An audi-

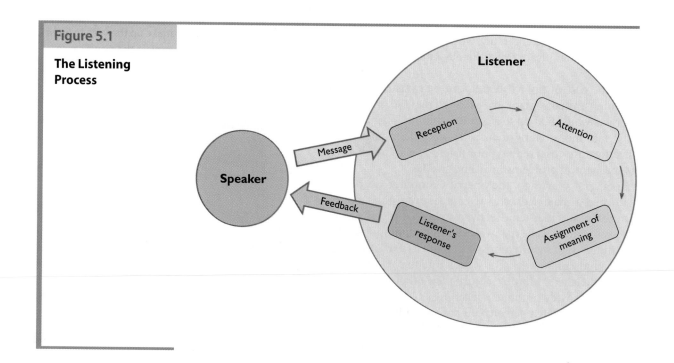

Figure 5.1

The Listening Process

ologist warns, "As you enjoy the blaring music in your car, home, or your headsets, or at a concert, be aware that you can be permanently damaging one of your most important biological tools . . . your hearing mechanism."[9]

In addition to using the hearing mechanism, people listen through their visual system. They observe a person's facial expression, posture, movement, and appearance, which provide important cues that may not be obvious merely by listening to the verbal part of the message. Research on how people learn indicates that the least effective method involves learning from information presented through verbal symbols, that is, listening to spoken words.[10] (See Figure 5.2, Dale's Cone of Learning.) As the figure illustrates, the most effective method, at the bottom of the cone, involves direct, purposeful learning experiences such as hands-on or field experiences. Both speakers and listeners must realize that listeners can only recall about 20 percent of what they hear. Thus, speakers must attempt to stimulate listeners by doing "the real thing," simulating a real experience, or doing something dramatic. Unfortunately, many speakers don't know this, so you, as a listener, must concentrate when hearing information. Try to get involved in the material and ask questions of the speaker so that you can be actively engaged.

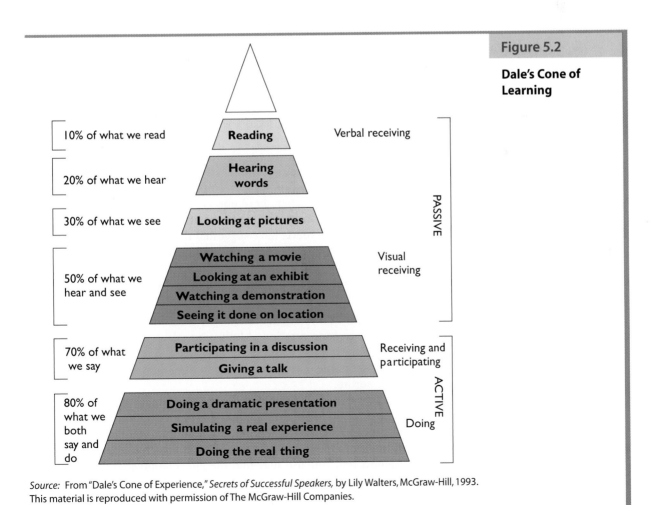

Figure 5.2

Dale's Cone of Learning

Source: From "Dale's Cone of Experience," *Secrets of Successful Speakers,* by Lily Walters, McGraw-Hill, 1993. This material is reproduced with permission of The McGraw-Hill Companies.

The research also demonstrates that the more concrete the experience, the more it actively involves the listener. Again, this means that speakers, such as briefers and instructors, should try and present material concretely. Many instructors don't know this. That means that you, the listener, in order to increase your attention, must ask questions that attempt to make academic materials as tangible as possible. This also means you should attempt to encourage discussions rather than acting like a note-taking robot in class.

Receiving the message through the visual and the auditory channels is but one component of the listening process. The listener also must attend to the message.

Attention

Once the stimulus—the word or visual symbol, or both—is received, it reaches the attention stage of the human processing system.

Role of Attention   In listening, **attention** represents the focus on a specific stimulus selected from all the stimuli received at any given moment. In this phase, the other stimuli recede so that we can concentrate on a specific word or visual symbol. Normally your attention is divided between what you are attempting to listen to, what is currently happening in the rest of the environment, and what else is going on in your mind. Consider, for example, what happens if you are attending a movie. Perhaps the person in front of you is constantly whispering to the person next to him, there is a buzz in the sound system, and you are worried because you left your car in a no-parking zone. Your attention is being pulled in several directions. "The more things [that are] in our mind, the harder it will be to use our attention, which really is a limited resource."[11] But if the film is interesting enough, you will focus on it, and the other factors will be relegated to the back of your consciousness.

Attention to a stimulus occurs in a person's short-term memory system. The capacity of the short-term memory—your **attention span**—rarely lasts more than forty-five seconds at any one time.[12] Thus, the listener's ability to focus attention is limited. In fact, teachers have observed that students cannot remain attentive much beyond a ten-minute time frame at best. The reasons are not yet fully understood, although experts have suggested that "it's entirely possible that our capacity for sustained attention and deliberate thought is being altered by television viewing."[13] Individuals who have been raised on television have come to expect a seven- to ten-minute viewing format followed by a commercial break.

Role of Concentration   Undoubtedly one of the most difficult tasks we have to perform as listeners is concentration. Motivation plays an important role in activating this skill. For example, if you really want to listen to a speaker, this desire will put you in a better frame of mind for concentrating than will anticipating that the speaker will be boring.

Two other factors that affect listening concentration are interest level and difficulty of the message. Some messages may be boring, but if you need to get the information, careful concentration is imperative. For example, you may not find the chemistry professor's ideas fascinating, but if you do not listen effectively, you probably will fail the next test. You also may find the information so difficult that you tune out. Again, if it is imperative for you to understand the ideas, then you have to force yourself to figure out what you do not understand and find a way of grasping the meaning.

We can think three to four times faster than the normal conversation rate of 125 to 150 words per minute.[14] And because we can receive messages much more quickly than the other person can talk, we tend to tune in and tune out throughout a message. The mind can absorb only so much material. Indeed, the brain operates much like a computer: it turns off, recycles itself, and turns back on to avoid information overload.[15] It is no wonder, then, that our attention fluctuates even when we are actively involved as listeners. Think back to any class you have attended. Do you recall a slight gap in your listening at times? This is a natural part of the listening process. When you tune out, the major danger is that you may daydream rather than quickly turn back to the message. But by taking notes or forcing yourself to paraphrase, you can avoid this difficulty.

Research with compressed speech illustrates the human capacity for efficient listening. In this technique, taped material is speeded up mechanically to more than 300 words per minute. Incredibly, there is no loss of comprehension at this faster rate. Tests even reveal increased comprehension, much as the tests given to people who have been taught to speed-read show an increase in their retention of information. Because of the rapid speeds, the test participants anticipated retention problems and thus forced themselves to listen more attentively and concentrate more fully than they would otherwise have done.[16]

Attention represents the focus on a specific stimulus selected from all the stimuli received at any given moment.

Concentration also requires the listener to control for distractions. As a listener, you probably have a whole list of things that you have to attend to in addition to the speaker's message. Rather than attempting to dismiss them, control your concentration by mentally setting these other issues aside for the moment to give the speaker your full attention. It takes mental and physical energy to do this, but concentration is the key to successful listening.

Role of Paraphrasing   **Paraphrasing**—making a summary of the ideas you have just received—will provide you with a concise restatement of what has been presented. It also will allow you to determine whether you understand the material. If you cannot repeat or write down a summary of what was said, then you probably did not get the whole message or did not understand it. Keep this in mind when you are listening to an instructor and taking notes. Try to paraphrase the material instead of writing down direct quotations. If you cannot do so, you should ask for clarification or make a note to look up that particular material later on.

Try verbally paraphrasing the next time you are engaged in a demanding conversation, such as when you are receiving directions. Repeat back to the speaker what you think she or he just said in order to check whether you both received and understood the same things. One of the benefits of paraphrasing is that it eliminates the common complaint that you weren't listening. Giving people back the ideas they have just presented makes it impossible for them to support the claim that you were not paying attention.

Perception

After the message is received and attended to, the listener's perceptions come into play. Perceiving is an active process. During the act of perception a person takes the material received and attempts to evaluate what has been input. The act of perceiving might be compared to a chef who is straining ingredients in order to filter what he wants from what he is not interested in using—for example, separating pasta from the water in which it was cooked by passing it through a strainer. The strainer can be compared to your **perceptual filter,** which strains the stimuli you receive and separates what makes sense from what doesn't. As you listen to information, your perceptual filter strains the information to which you are listening through your background, culture, experience, role, mental and physical state, beliefs, attitudes, and values.

Another approach to this stage of listening refers to the perceptual screen through which you receive and evaluate as your **sensorium.** This approach encourages you to listen emotionally, with all of your senses, including intuition, as well as logically. It is an approach akin to the Eastern philosophies.[17]

The process of narrowing your attention to specific bits or pieces of information is referred to as **selective perception.** An idea's distinctiveness or the satisfaction of your needs is often the basis for why you will pay attention to a particular stimulus. The louder, the more relevant, or the more novel the stimuli, the more likely they are to be perceived by the listener.

Assignment of Meaning

Once you have paid attention to the material presented, the next stage in the listening process is to categorize the message so as to assign meanings to its verbal and nonverbal stimuli.

It can be understood

A media interviewer uses paraphrasing, verbal feedback, internal summaries, and bridging.

Role of Assigning Meaning

The **assignment of meaning** —the process of putting the stimulus into some predetermined category—develops as we acquire our language system. We develop mental categories for interpreting the messages we receive. For instance, our categorizing system for the word *cheese* may include such factors as food, dairy products, taste, and nourishment, all of which help us to relate the word *cheese* to the context in which it is used.

The categorical assignment of meaning creates **schema**—scripts for processing information. The

COMMUNICATION BRIEFING

Listening: Send "Tell-Me-More" Signals

Good listeners use these techniques to get all the information they need before they act on what they've heard:

◆ **Examples.** "Please give me an example so I'll have a better idea of what you mean."

◆ **Illustrations.** "Could you illustrate that point to show me how it works?"

◆ **Statistics.** "What's the date on that information?" "Can you get more data on that?"

◆ **Authorities.** "Who said that?" "Do the experts you cite agree on this?" "Do these experts have other positions on this subject?"

◆ **Analogies.** "Can you compare that to the situation we faced last week?" "How does this model compare to the other one?"

◆ **Explanations.** "What are some of the specific problems you're having?" "Can you give me more details?" "Please explain how it works."

◆ **Restatements.** "Would you repeat that? I want to make sure I've got it right."

Source: The New Time Manager, by Angela V. Woodhull, Gower Publishing, Ltd., Gower House, Croft Road, Hampshire GU11 3HR, UK.

mental representations that we carry in our brains—**schemata**—are shaped by the language categories and the way our brains process information. An individual's culture, background, family, education, and experience all serve as the framework for creating the schema that enable us to deal with incoming information. The cognitive process draws on all of a person's schemata for the purpose of interpretation, and these schemata provide the mental links for understanding and creating meaning from the verbal and the nonverbal stimuli we receive.[18] Understanding a discussion of some of the customs and traditions on a college campus, for example, may be difficult for first-year students because they do not have the cognitive schema to relate to the information.

Role of Global/Linear Thinking/Listening

Each of us is unique in the way we listen and learn. Part of the differences among us is based on the way our brain works. The human brain is divided into two hemispheres, and research shows that some people are prone to use one side of the brain more than the other. This **brain dominance** accounts for learning and listening in patterned ways.[19]

The left hemisphere of the brain is most responsible for rational, logical, sequential, linear, and abstract thinking. People who tend to be left-brain dominant listen and learn best when materials are presented in structured ways. They tend to prefer specifics and logic-based arguments. Because they tend to take information at face value, abstractions and generalizations don't add much to their learning. Because they are so straight-line in their learning preferences, they are **linear learners/listeners.**

The right hemisphere of the brain is responsible for intuitive, spatial, visual, and concrete matters. It is from the right side of the brain that we are able to visualize. Those with this listening and learning dominance prefer examples rather than technical explanations. They prefer knowing that the information can be useful and applied. The right-brain-dominant person tends to be creative and rely on intuitive thinking, can follow visual and pictographic rather than written instructions, likes to explore information without necessarily coming to a conclusion, and enjoys interaction rather than lecturing. Because of their preference for a generalized rather than specific description, right-brain-dominant persons are often labeled as **global listeners/learners.** Many global learners find much of the traditional lecture method of teaching in U.S. schools and universities, a linear methodology, to be dull and frustrating.

Most people are a combination of global and linear learners and listeners. If you fall into this classification, you can be more flexible in how you listen and learn than those with extreme style preferences.

It is important for you to recognize your listening and learning style because this understanding can make a difference in the way you approach listening and learning environments. If you know that you need examples and the speaker is not giving them, you should ask for them. If the speaker is not drawing specific conclusions and not speaking in a structured format, and these are necessary for your understanding, then you must probe for information that will allow you to organize the ideas. Don't assume that the speaker knows how you need to receive information; the person doesn't. Most classroom instructors teach based on their own listening and learning style, forgetting that all students don't learn that way. If you are a global listener and learner, this may explain why you had trouble with some math or science classes. On the other hand, if you are a linear listener and learner, literature and poetry classes may have been difficult for you.

If you are interested in finding out your learner/listener style based on the hemispheres of your brain, complete Activity 7 in the Learn by Doing section at the end of this chapter.

A Comparison of Linear-Mode and Global-Mode Characteristics

Linear Mode

Verbal: Using words to name, describe, define.

Analytic: Figuring things out step by step and part by part.

Symbolic: Using a symbol to stand for something. For example, the drawn form 👁 stands for eye, the sign + stands for the process of addition.

Abstract: Taking out a small bit of information and using it to represent the whole thing.

Temporal: Keeping track of time, sequencing one thing after another: Doing first things first, second things second, etc.

Rational: Drawing conclusions based on reasons and facts.

Digital: Using numbers as in counting.

Logical: Drawing conclusions based on logic: one thing following another in logical order—for example, a mathematical theorem or a well-stated argument.

Linear: Thinking in terms of linked ideas, one thought directly following another, often leading to a convergent conclusion.

Global Mode

Nonverbal: Awareness of things, but minimal connection with words.

Synthetic: Putting things together to form wholes.

Concrete: Relating to things as they are, at the present moment.

Analogic: Seeing likenesses between things; understanding metaphoric relationships.

Nontemporal: Without a sense of time.

Nonrational: Not requiring a basis of reason or facts; willingness to suspend judgment.

Spatial: Seeing where things are in relation to other things, and how parts go together to form a whole.

Intuitive: Making leaps of insight, often based on incomplete patterns, hunches, feelings, or visual images.

Holistic: Seeing whole things all at once; perceiving the overall patterns and structures, often leading to divergent conclusions.

Source: From "A Comparison of Left-Mode and Right-Mode Characteristics," from *Drawing on the Right Side of the Brain* by Betty Edwards. Copyright © 1979, 1989, 1999 by Betty Edwards. Used by permission of Jeremy P. Tarcher, an imprint of Penguin Group (USA).

Role of Culture in Listening   Like brain dominance, a person's culture also influences listening and learning abilities. Some cultures, such as many in Asia, stress good listening by being a silent communicator in order to receive messages.[20] People in Japan, for example, are likely to spend less time talking on the job than do European Americans, stressing instead the listening aspect of communication. In addition, some cultures stress concentration, which results in longer attention spans. Buddhism, for instance, has a notion called "being mindful." This means giving whatever you are doing your complete and full attention. Training to have long attention spans starts in childhood. To those raised in a typical European American environment, these listening-enhancing concepts are not part of their background.[21]

Cultures have been identified as low context and high context.[22] In low-context cultures such as the United States and Canada, communicators expect to give and receive a great deal of information since these cultures perceive that most message information is contained in words. In high-context cultures such as Japan and Saudi Arabia, more of the information is situated in the communicators themselves and in the communication setting, so fewer words are necessary. "In high context cultures, it is the responsibility of the listener to understand; in low context, it is the speaker who is responsible for making sure the listener comprehends all."[23]

An investigation into the learning/listening style of the Navajos, a Native American tribe, demonstrates cultural effects. The Navajo listening/learning process, which is at the heart of the Navajo culture, has four components: observe, think, understand and feel, and act. This is in contrast to the "Anglo [European American] process of act, observe/think/clarify, understand."[24] Euro-Americans tend to learn from examining components in relationship to the whole. Native Americans spend much more time watching and listening and less time talking.[25] In an academic learning situation, this may result in "Anglo teachers seeing Native Americans as inattentive, laconic, and dull-witted, while students see their teachers as directive and bossy."[26]

Role of Evaluation   One of the greatest barriers to effective listening is the tendency to evaluate the stimuli we receive, regardless of whether the stimuli are relevant to the message. In fact, this tendency is thought to be the most persistent barrier to communication that we have to overcome.[27] Although assigning meaning to stimuli often requires a quick evaluation, listeners should attempt to avoid instant judgments based primarily on superficial factors. Sometimes if you feel you don't have enough information, or you need to study the information, it may be better for you not to come to a conclusion yet.

assignment of meaning uninfluenced by perceptions

A strategy useful to listeners in assigning meaning to messages is to differentiate *factual statements* (those based on observable phenomena or common acceptance) from *opinions* (inferences or judgments made by the speaker).

It also is helpful for the listener to sift through verbal obscurities and work for clarification of meanings. Unclear terms and phrases, euphemisms, and evasive language make interpretation difficult. The effective listener asks questions and seeks clarification from speakers and the contextual cues in their messages.

Listeners also benefit from recognizing what their emotional biases are and how those biases affect interpretations of messages. One way to discover such biases is to draw up a list of terms and phrases that serve as "red flags," triggering particular emotional responses. Recognition of such emotional barriers is a good first step toward compensating for the knee-jerk reactions that effectively tune out the speaker. Some people have strong reactions, for example, to such words and concepts as *skinheads, gay rights, taxes, abortion,* and, yes, *grades*.

Some cultures stress being mindful, giving complete and full attention, in order to be a good listener.

The assignment of meaning is a complex process involving categorizing, evaluating, filtering through verbal obscurity, and recognizing emotional biases.

Response

Once we have assigned meaning to a message, we continue the information processing with an internal and/or external response—an intellectual or emotional reaction—to the message. It is hypothesized that every stimulus we receive is stored internally somewhere in our brain. In addition, over time the information may be moved from our short-term memory to our long-term memory. Externally, we react to the stimulus by providing feedback to the speaker in order to further the communication.[28]

Role of Memory Techniques   Many people find remembering names a problem. In some cases, it may be that you don't remember because you don't listen when the name is spoken, or you don't immediately repeat the name to entrench it in your memory. "Thirty to 40 percent of people are unable to remember names because they don't hear the name in the first place. Most of us are so focused on ourselves in social situations that we fail to give any real attention to the other person."[29] But there are techniques that you can learn to improve your memory, including name recall. For example, when you are introduced to someone, you must first decide that you want to remember this person's name and then get ready to remember it. If you tend to remember things by pictures, picture the person in a particular setting—perhaps the location where you are meeting him. You can remember the person either by picturing him with a sign across his chest, emblazoned with his name, or you can tie the person's name to some other picture. (This is a good technique for right-brained people who tend to remember pictures, not words.) If you tend to remember words better than pictures, concentrate on the name and repeat it several times to yourself, or select a familiar word with which the name rhymes (a good technique for left-brained people since words, rather than pictures, are generally their way of remembering). Finally, repeat the name several times as you speak to the person. If you carry through on this process, the odds of your remembering the name increase greatly.

Role of Questions   One area of response that can assist listeners in storing information in long-term memory, and at the same time provide meaningful feedback to speakers, is asking questions. This enables listeners to ensure that the message they have received and interpreted is consistent with the speaker's original intent.

To be effective, questions must be relevant to the message that the speaker presented. When asking questions, try to figure out what you don't understand. Most commonly, difficulties in perceiving information center on a lack of understanding of vocabulary, a need for clarifying examples, or a need for the material to be presented in a different format or order. For example, let's say that you are taking notes in class and can't paraphrase the instructor's ideas so that you can write them down. One of the mistakes students often make is not to say anything. If it is important for you to gain the information, you must probe for meaning. If an opportunity is available, such as when a teacher indicates that questions are welcome, use that invitation to your advantage. When asking for information, don't say, "I don't understand." The instructor won't be able to clarify; you haven't provided the clues needed to be of help. It is common in certain academic subjects for the vocabulary to be new and unusual. If you don't understand the terms being used, ask, "Would you please define [fill in the term]?" Or, if you vaguely understand but need something more, you could ask, "Would you please give several examples to illustrate [insert the specific topic]?" (This is often what right-brained people need to grasp the idea because they require examples they can picture rather than words.) If you don't understand the concept, you could ask, "Could you restate the concept of [fill in the topic] in a step-by-step process?" (This is a technique for left-brained people, who need the structure to understand what may be confusing because it was not put in a patterned manner.) In each case, you are specifically centering on what needs to be done to help you gain the information. The same techniques work on the job and in other situations in which gaining information is important.

Role of Feedback   Good listeners are conscious of the role of feedback cues; they recognize the importance of giving the speaker an understanding of whether they received the message. Asking questions, nodding or shaking your head, smiling or frowning, and verbalization such as "uh-huh" or "um?" are all forms of listener feedback. Feedback responses can be verbal or nonverbal, and they should function to enhance or reinforce the communication.

Effective feedback should be readily perceptible to the speaker. Listeners must take a major responsibility for the outcome of the communication. Rather than enter into the listening process passively, assume an active, energetic role as a listening communicator. Assume responsibility for the outcome of the communication. Take seriously your part in sending feedback that will support the speaker's goals and further the communication, for this feedback plays a critical role in creating and maintaining the communication climate for listener and speaker alike.

Asking questions enables the listener to ensure that the message he or she has received and interpreted is consistent with the original intent of the speaker.

Listening Influencers

The process of listening, through which the listener receives, attends to, perceives, assigns meaning to, and responds to messages, is complex. To be effective, the listener must be actively involved throughout and work to overcome barriers that may arise. Certain key influencers can facilitate or hinder the process.[30]

Role of the Speaker   The speaker's credibility—that is, the listener's perception of the speaker's trustworthiness, competence, and dynamism—can lead the listener to accept or reject a message. Unfortunately, some listeners are so in awe of a particular speaker that they may lose all objectivity in analyzing the person's message. For example, if the speaker is a Hollywood celebrity, the listener may overlook that he is not an expert on the specific subject in question. If the listener accepts the speaker's message simply because he is a celebrity, the receiver may be overlooking the logical weaknesses of the presentation.

The speaker's physical presentation—animation, appearance, clothing—can have an instantaneous effect on listener attention. A speaker who is dynamic and humorous may be able to get past the critical listening abilities of certain listeners. To be a discerning listener, it is important to listen to the message, not just to the reputation or presentational style of the speaker.

Role of the Message   Another major influencer is the message itself. If the presentation is not clearly organized—if the arguments are not well ordered—the listener may have difficulty concentrating on and staying tuned in to the message.

The tone and the treatment of the message can also affect a person's listening abilities. Some religious speakers, for example, are known for their ability to put fear into the minds of their listeners when they prophesy eternal damnation. Listeners must ascertain whether the message is appropriate for them and whether they believe in the prophecies presented.

Role of the Channel   The communication channel can influence listening ability. Some people are more auditory, and some are more visual in orientation. The public speaker, for example, who couples the message with clear visual aids may assist listeners in comprehending the material. Electronic channels versus face-to-face presence also can have an effect. For instance, television has changed the nature of political campaigning. Historically, candidates had to appear in person before an audience, where listeners could have some physical contact with them. Now, sound bites, thirty-second spots, videotaped messages, and debates in which listeners can't actively participate in the experience have made for drastic differences. Likewise, candidates are making increased use of voice mail and the Internet to reach potential voters. For example, in 2002, Ohio's Tim Hagan, the Democratic candidate for governor, used the Internet almost exclusively in his campaign because he had limited campaign finances.

Students have reacted both positively and negatively to the concept of distance learning, in which television sets and computer screens replace a live instructor. Some like the fact that the instructor cannot call on the listener, that the message can be viewed whenever the receiver wants to listen or watch, and that they can replay the material for reinforcement. On the other hand, some students feel that the separation between listener and speaker causes a sterile environment and eliminates the feedback needed for effective communication.

Role of External and Internal Variables   Noise (any sort of interference) in the communication channel can diminish the effectiveness of the listener. Static on the telephone or distortions on the television screen can interrupt good listening. Noise from the environment also affects listeners. If the lighting is poor or the room temperature is too cold or too hot, the listener may have greater difficulty attending to the speaker's message. Control of or adjustment for the distraction may be necessary—for example, moving to a different spot so that you can see or hear the speaker more readily, adjusting the auditory or visual channel in some way, or negotiating with the speaker to move to a better environment.

Listeners are influenced not only by a vast array of external factors but also by internal ones. Receivers are affected by their physical state (general health, gender, age), experiences (background, life history, training), attitudes (predispositions), memory, and expectations.[31] The listener's culture also can be influential. People from different cultures have different ways of attending to each other, as indicated by the amount of eye contact, distance between each other, and amount of patience. For example, in some South American cultures, it is perceived as bad manners to look directly into the eyes of a speaker, especially if the presenter is an authority figure. Some Arabic and Asian cultures stress standing very close to people while conversing, which makes many European Americans uncomfortable, thus making concentration difficult.

The positive or negative attitude the listener carries into a listening situation (in conjunction with expectations of the experience) is important.

Listeners are influenced not only by a vast array of external factors but also by internal ones.

For example, a listener who goes to a training session convinced beforehand that it will be a waste of time will probably carry that negative attitude into the session and refuse to suspend judgment and listen comprehensively.

The listener's positive or negative attitude extends to himself or herself as a listener. Just as speakers have self-concepts, so too do listeners. Most people have had very little praise or external reward for good listening but have probably heard lots of negative messages: "Keep quiet and listen." "Why don't you ever listen to me?" These negative messages, which are often received from a very early age, can create a negative attitude in people about their listening abilities.

Role of Memory and Time   Throughout the entire process of listening, memory plays an important role. The listener must be willing to hold the message received in short-term memory long enough to perceive, attend to, and assign meaning to it. This activity requires sufficient auditory and visual memory to maintain focus long enough to process the message.

Coupled with the influence of memory is the influence of time. The listener has to have the time, and be willing to take the time, to listen with discrimination and comprehension. People lead busy lives and frequently have little time to engage in actively listening to another person. Well-intentioned listeners find it use-ful to recognize that they are busy. You must be willing, however, to mentally set aside or "bracket" the other internal factors competing for your attention ("Yes, I do have to finish that memo") and focus on the speaker and his or her message at the moment (". . . but first I need to listen to . . .").

Purposes of Listening

We listen on a number of levels, for a variety of purposes: to distinguish among sounds, gain ideas, discriminate among ideas, aid others, and appreciate sounds or symbols. Awareness of the purposes of listening sometimes aids a listener to select the listening techniques that best fit the desired outcome.[32]

Discriminative Listening

In **discriminative listening,** we attempt to distinguish among auditory and visual stimuli. Such distinctions are at the base of the listening we do. Through discrimination, we can come to understand differences in verbal sounds (dialects, pronunciation) and nonverbal behavior (gestures, facial reactions). By understanding such differences, we gain sensitivity to the sights and sounds of our world. We can then determine, for example, whether a person is being sarcastic, cautious, negative, or uncooperative because we realize that the same set of words can be taken in a variety of ways.

Discriminative listening also is important when we come in contact with some of the nonhuman features of our everyday lives. We may listen, for instance, to household appliances to determine whether they are functioning properly. People in professions such as music, medicine, and technology often find discrimination to be their most important listening skill.

It is interesting to check your own level of listening discrimination. Read the directions for the rest of this paragraph and then follow them. *Directions:* Stop reading. Close your eyes. Listen to the sounds around you. What sounds do you recognize? What sounds are unfamiliar to you? What effect do these environmental sounds have on you as you process them?

Is it important for you to be a discriminative listener? Of course, there are times when you must discriminate among the sounds around you. Daily you encounter sounds to the point that you just screen most of them out. However, if your car's engine is making an unusual whining noise, you should know that you need to get the car to a service technician right away. Or listen to your own voice as you are involved in a conflict. When the pitch and volume increase, these changes may indicate that you are getting stressed and could become physically abusive. Discriminative listening is an important but overlooked type of listening.

Comprehension Listening

In **comprehension listening,** the objective is to recognize and retain the information in a message. To comprehend a message, the listener must first discriminate the message to recognize its auditory and visual components. But listening for comprehension goes beyond the objective of discriminating a message. At this point in the process, heightened concentration is needed. In academia, comprehension is vital. "The classroom consists of the verbal and nonverbal transactions between teacher and students and among students. The ability to learn in a world of expanding information and cultural diversity demands competence in communication [listening]."[33]

(2nd level)

Some techniques have been found to aid listening comprehension. One strategy is to concentrate on getting the main points of a message rather than all the supporting details. That is, when you listen to an instructor, you should focus on the main points rather than on the elaboration and details. Even when taking notes, it is wise to sort the main points and the supporting details—for example, by drawing a vertical line down the middle of the paper, putting the main points in the left-hand column and noting the supporting ideas in the right-hand column. Abbreviation of commonly used words saves time in writing, which allows for more listening time. For instance, if this chapter were given as a lecture, the notes for it thus far might look like those in Figure 5.3.

The student whose notes are shown in Figure 5.3 obviously felt there were sufficient cues for understanding the material so that examples were not essential. Nevertheless, many note takers like to provide examples to help clarify material. Each note taker has to determine how much detail and how much reinforcement are necessary.

Some communication experts recommend a technique called *clarifying and confirming* to improve concentration. This strategy calls for the listener to ask for additional information or explanation. This system works well when added to a technique known as *acknowledging or bridging:* relating one part of the message to another. Good radio and television talk-show hosts use this system when interviewing guests. National Public Radio's award-winning interviewer Terri Gross is excellent at using paraphrasing (repeating ideas), verbal feedback ("uh-huh" and "that's an interesting idea"), internal summaries (summarizing one topic before going on to the next), and bridging (indicating what topic or idea she'd like to talk about next by referring to a quotation in a book or one just made by the speaker). The abilities of clarifying, confirming, acknowledging, and bridging are important tools for individuals going into listening professions such as counseling, social work, police work, newscasting, and reporting.

Remembering the main points at a later time also may require the development of a number of memory techniques. Some research indicates that a person can lose as much as half of any given information after the first day without taking notes and reviewing them. Because it is so easy to lose information in memory storage, good listeners work to gain the information presented. Some students have found, for example, that they retain ideas best if they review the information immediately after it is presented and then go over it daily rather than waiting until the night before an examination to cram.

Using comprehension and discriminative listening as the foundation, people listen for special purposes: to provide a therapeutic setting for a person to talk through a problem, critically evaluate a persuasive message, or appreciate aspects of a particular message.

Therapeutic Listening

Listening at the therapeutic level is important for those in such fields as mental health, social work, speech therapy, and counseling. **Therapeutic listening** requires a listener to learn when to ask questions, when to stimulate further discussion, and when, if ever, to give advice.

Therapeutic listening is not restricted to professional counselors. In daily life people often need a listener when dealing with a problem. The listener can help the speaker talk through the situation. To be effective in this role, therapeutic listeners must have empathy for the other person—the ability to understand that person's problem from her own perspective by momentarily putting themselves into her shoes and attempting to see the world as she sees it. This is difficult for many people to do as there is a tendency to want to solve the other person's problem and help rid her of the pain.

How can you learn to be an effective therapeutic listener? The empathic training given to hot-line volunteers includes teaching them to resist the temptation to jump in with statements such as "The same thing happened to me" or "If I were you, I would . . ." In addition, remember that there is nothing wrong with silence. Often we want the other person to keep talking. Listen patiently. The person in pain may need time to feel the pain and get in touch with her thoughts and feelings. The listener can help the speaker generate a list of possible alternatives from which that person may choose; then she will have some commitment to carrying out the self-generated action. Another negative technique is to diminish the fact that the person is feeling pain. Saying, "That's no big problem" doesn't help diminish the hurt.

Skill in therapeutic listening is important, not only for mental and medical health professionals but also for managers, parents, teachers, colleagues, and friends to provide for relational emotional support. Listening to each other's stories, experiences, and fears was a way many coped with the tragedy and terrors of September 11, with the Washington, D.C., area's 2002 sniper attacks, with the Columbine High School shootings, and with personal traumas.

Critical Listening

Critical listening centers on the listener's comprehending and evaluating the message that has been received. A critical listener assesses the arguments and the appeals in a message and then decides whether to accept or reject them.

Lstng	*Hearing – biological process*	**Figure 5.3**
Lstng Process	*Lstng – active processing of*	
	* info heard*	**Note-Taking**
	Reception – get message	**Format**
	Attention	
	* focus on ideas*	
	* anticipate next point*	
	* paraphrase – restate in*	
	* own words*	
	* get ready to lstn rapidly*	
	Perception – screen info	
	Assignment of meaning –	
	* categorize symbols*	
	Response – info storage	
	* choose to remember*	
	* visualize what is to*	
	* be remembered*	
	* associate info*	
	* practice material*	
Purposes of Lstng	*Lstng Influencers*	
	* speaker*	
	* message*	
	* channel*	
	* noise*	
	* internal variables*	
	* attitude*	
	* memory*	
	* time*	
	Discrimination	
	Comprehension	

An understanding of the tools of persuasion and the process of logic and rea-soning enables critical listeners to make judgments about the merits of the messages they receive. Judgments should take into account such factors as

when critically analyzing a speech

◆ *The personal appeal of the speaker.* The speaker's credibility stems from the position held (e.g., sports celebrity), expertise, trustworthiness, and dynamism. The critical listener needs to recognize how much this credibility is influencing how the message is being understood and analyzed.

◆ *The speaker's arguments and evidence.* Does the speaker present a logical argu-ment supported by substantive and relevant data?

◆ *The speaker's motivational appeals.* How is the speaker attempting to get the lis-tener involved in the message? What appeals to the listener's needs are used to get the listener to respond to a persuasive message?

◆ *Assumptions on the part of the speaker.* Does the speaker assume that some-thing is a fact before it has been established as such? Just because someone says, "It is readily apparent that . . ." doesn't make it so.

Therapeutic listening requires a listener to learn when to ask questions, when to stimulate further discussion, and when, if ever, to give advice.

◆ *What is not said.* In some cases, the speaker implies rather than states ideas, so the listener is forced to read between the lines to supply the message. "You know what I mean" is a remark to which the listener should be alert. What do you really know from what was said?

Critical listeners should be aware of these factors and assess the merits of a particular message. Sales pitches, advertising messages, campaign speeches, and persuasive briefings all require critical analysis.

As a communication student, you probably will be called on to critique the speeches of fellow students. In this mode of critical listening, your role is to provide information to help speakers improve their work. Offer comments on what the speaker does effectively as well as what the speaker needs to improve. Deal with content (topic choice, structure, supporting materials, clarity, and interest) and delivery (animation, vocal dynamics, and eye contact).

Appreciative Listening

Appreciative listening takes place when a person engages in enjoyment or sensory stimulation of a message, such as listening to humorous speakers, comedians, or music videos. Appreciation is a highly individual matter. Some people believe that the more knowledge they have about a particular subject or artistic form, the more they can appreciate it. Others feel that the more they know about something, the more they lose their ability to appreciate all but the best.

Listening Apprehension

Not only are some people apprehensive when they speak, but they may also be apprehensive when they must or are given the opportunity to listen. **Listener apprehension,** "the fear of misinterpreting, inadequately processing, and/or not being able to adjust psychologically to messages sent by others,"[34] is a major concern for many people. It may be a short-term fear, such as the anxiety associated with knowing you are going to receive a negative evaluation, or the fear of the person who is going to talk to you or what he might say. For example, in the context of physician-patient interaction, the difference in power roles between you as a patient and the doctor as the expert may interfere with your ability to listen to your physician calmly and accurately. You also might be afraid of what the doctor might say, so you dread listening.[35]

Listener apprehension also may be a long-term disability. There are individuals who have lived their entire lives being told they are poor listeners and have come to believe it. There are others who have a hearing or vision disability and fear that they will miss the core of the message in listening situations.

This type of anxiety makes it difficult to understand, process, and remember a message. It may make a person less able to interact effectively, less willing to communicate, and less confident about communication abilities. Further, if we are emotional about the content of the message, that may shake our confidence and increase our listener apprehension.[36]

Part of what you may be worried about is how you will respond in a listening situation, whether you will be able to adapt to what you hear, and if you can respond appropriately.[37]

In one study of employment interviews, the people with high listening apprehension did less to think about or prepare for the communication.[38]

If you experience listening apprehension, here are some suggestions that might help you:

- Realize that worrying isn't going to make you a better listener, so if you can't avoid the situation, then you must force yourself to participate and accept that you will do the best job you can.

- If appropriate, have a writing instrument and paper to take notes. Taking notes forces you to listen effectively and allows you to know if you understand. If not, ask questions to clarify what has been said.

- Repeat back the ideas of the speaker as you listen so that you can assure yourself that you are receiving the message and that you are letting the other person know that you are listening and understanding.

- Prepare ideas and arguments in advance if you know you are going to be evaluated or will need to defend yourself or your ideas.

- If there has been an agenda, memo, or outline of what will be discussed, such as for a meeting or a class, go over the material ahead of time and be ready to listen.

- Do your homework. Get ready for the session. If you are at work, have the ideas researched. In a classroom situation, read and prepare the assignment.

- Write notes to use during the discussion. That way you won't have to worry about not having anything of value to say.

✳ Improving Your Listening ✳

Effective listening is a complex, involved, and involving process requiring a great deal of commitment on the part of the listener. Despite its complexities, you can do a great deal to improve your skill as a listener.

Improvement of listening skills requires breaking old habits, putting new strategies in their place, and practicing these new skills until they feel comfortable and are part of your listening repertoire.

Here are some suggestions to help listeners develop greater skills:

1 *Recognize that both the sender and receiver share responsibility for effective communication.* If you are sending a message, you should define terms, structure your message clearly, and give your receiver the necessary background to respond effectively. As a receiver, you should ask questions and provide feedback if you cannot understand the speaker's point. If possible, repeat the major ideas so that the speaker can check to be sure you have grasped the meaning.

2 *Suspend judgment.* One of the greatest barriers to human communication is the tendency to form instant judgments about information we encounter. As listeners, we are prone to assess speakers prematurely, before we have even comprehended the entire message. Unstated thoughts such as "I don't like his voice" and "This is a boring lecture" set up barriers to effective listening. Good listening requires setting aside these judgments and listening for the message.

3 *Be a patient listener.* Avoid interrupting or tuning out until the entire message has been communicated. We often find ourselves beginning to act before we have totally understood what is being said. This is especially true of global listeners, who often act intuitively on perceived information.

Think about how difficult it is to assemble a new product until you thoroughly comprehend the instructions. Or remember the times you filled out a form, only to realize later that you put down your first name when the directions said your last name should come first. Patience in listening will help you avoid having to go back over messages you missed the first time or did not understand because you did not let the whole message come through.

4 *Avoid egospeak.* **Egospeak** is the "art of boosting our own ego by speaking only about what we want to talk about, and not giving a hoot in hell about what the [other] person is speaking about."[39] When you jump into a conversation and speak your piece without noticing what the other person is trying to communicate or listen only to the beginning of another's sentence before saying, "Yes, but . . . ," you are engaging in egospeak. As a result, you do not receive the whole message because you are so busy thinking of what you want to say or saying it. Although egospeak is a very natural temptation, it can easily become a real barrier to communication.

Several techniques can be used to control egospeaking. First, monitor your body. Individuals who are about to interrupt have a tendency to lean forward as if to jump into the conversation and poise an arm and hand so that they can thrust them

Be aware that your posture affects your listening.

forward to cut in. If you feel your body taking these actions, be aware that you are about to egospeak—and don't.

Another way to deter yourself from egospeaking is to repeat the ideas of the speaker before you give your point of view. Be aware that if you can't summarize, you may not have listened long enough to gain the message. In future conversations, see if you can repeat the message of the speaker to yourself before you jump in.

5 *Be careful with emotional responses to words.* Inciting words are those that trigger strong feelings, either

COMMUNICATION BRIEFING

Listening: Getting to What's Not Said

To find out what others are really trying to tell you but can't seem to say, use these approaches:

♦ **Summarize what you hear.** Preface your comments with phrases such as "Here's what I think you're saying …" "Let me check to see if I've got this right …" "I want to be certain I heard you right. You just said …"

♦ **Ask next-step questions.** Begin with phrases such as "Do you think that we …?" "If you plan to do that, would it lead to …?" "If you believe that, does it mean …?" *Caution:* Don't use this method to change the subject or to show off what you know.

♦ **Suggest feelings.** Gently hint at what speakers *might* be feeling with comments such as "I'd be angry if they had done that to me." "I imagine you must be feeling pleased about the way things turned out." *Caution:* Suggest only feelings that are clear from what speakers say, not those you think they should be feeling.

Source: Thank You for Being Such a Pain, by Mark I. Rosen, Harmony Books, 201 E. 50th St., New York, NY 10022.

positive or negative, within us. How do you react to the words *child abuser, rapist,* and *income tax?* Words like these often send us off on tangents. In an everyday situation, you may tighten up and block out the rest of the message when your friend mentions the name of a person with whom you have just had an argument. Or you might start daydreaming about the beach when your instructor uses the word *sunshine.* Speakers should be aware that listeners can be sent off on tangents by certain words, resulting in interference with the effort to communicate. As receivers, we should be aware that we can be led astray and lose our concentration through our emotional responses.

There is no quick way to prevent yourself from reacting to inciting words. By monitoring your body, however, you might catch yourself physically pulling in, feel yourself flushing as you become upset, or catch yourself daydreaming. These responses are typical of the emotional triggers that set us off while listening.

6 *Be aware that your posture affects your listening.* When you listen to an exciting lecture, how do you sit? Usually you lean slightly forward, with your feet on the floor, and look directly at the presenter. If you slump down and stare out the window, it's unlikely that you're actively participating in the communication act taking place.

POSTURE

Have you ever left a classroom and felt totally exhausted? You may have been concentrating so hard that you became physically tired. After all, good listening is hard work. An effective listener learns when it is necessary to listen in a totally active way and when it is possible to relax. An analogy can explain the concept. When you're driving a car with an automatic transmission, the car shifts gears when it needs more or less power. Unfortunately, people don't come equipped with automatic transmissions; we have to shift gears for ourselves. When you need to concentrate, shift into your active listening position: feet on the floor, posture erect, looking directly at the speaker to pick up any necessary nonverbal clues. Once you feel that you understand the point being made (a test is the ability to paraphrase what has been said), you may want to shift your posture to a more comfortable position. When a new subject arises or when you hear transitional words or phrases such as *therefore* or *in summary*, then you shift back into your active listening position.

7 *Control distractions.* All of us are surrounded by noise—the sound of machinery, people talking, music playing—which can interfere with efficient listening. If the message is important to you, try to adjust the interference or control it. If possible, turn off the machinery, or move away from it. Tell someone who is speaking to you while you are talking on the telephone that you cannot listen to both people at the same time. Turn off the radio, or raise your voice so that others can hear you over the sound. Remember that there is little point in continuing the attempted communication if you cannot hear the other person or that person cannot hear you.

8 *Tune in to the speaker's cues.* An effective speaker provides the listener with verbal and nonverbal cues. You should recognize transitions (words indicating a change of idea or topic: *therefore, finally*), forecasts of ideas (statements that show a series of ideas: "there are three ideas that . . . ," "the next point is . . ."), and internal summaries (restatements of ideas that have just been explained: "and so we have seen that . . ."). These are all vehicles for furthering your grasp of the major points the speaker is presenting.

The rate, volume, pitch, and pauses that the speaker uses can also help you to understand the points being developed. By stressing words, pausing before an idea, or increasing the volume of a phrase, the speaker is telling you that something is important or significant.

The speaker's physical movements can carry a meaning that may reinforce or contradict a verbal message. For example, a speaker who uses a forceful gesture or enumerates points with the fingers can assist listeners in following the main points. We often have to listen with our eyes as well as our ears to pick up all the cues to help us understand the real message.

9 *Paraphrase.* Paraphrasing can be one of the most effective ways to sharpen concentration because it requires careful focus and storage in short-term memory. By repeating the ideas in your answer, you let the speaker know what you have received. If your paraphrase is not correct, the speaker can clarify to help you understand what was really intended. The use of active feedback allows both of you to be sure that the message sent was the message received.

10 *Visualize.* To engage in successful communication, a good technique, especially for the global learner and listener, is to visualize the speaker's points or what he is doing when certain concepts are presented. Visual associations are a useful way to improve storage and retrieval in long-term memory. For example, a student relayed to a former instructor that even today when she hears certain topics discussed, she visualizes where the instructor stood in class and can remember what he said.

Not all the listening you do is one-on-one. People spend a great deal of time processing television, radio, and Internet messages. You need to understand "how words, images, and sounds influence the way meanings are created and shared in contemporary society in ways that are both subtle and profound."[40] One media specialist recommends these strategies for listeners to increase their media literacy:[41]

- ◆ Think about how realistic or how fantasized the images are.
- ◆ Compare media approaches to how a particular message is treated.

◆ Think about what is communicated in the presentation. Is it reasonable? Is it biased? Is it trying to manipulate you by appealing to your weaknesses?

◆ If you tend to believe the appeal, ask yourself why you are opening yourself to that belief.

◆ Be aware of when someone is trying to change your point of view. Apply this awareness by challenging the contentions before you go along with the idea.

◆ Recognize that much of what is on the media seeks to manipulate you to buy products or services. Recognize that commercials and factual news are not the same.

◆ Recognize that situation comedies, dramas, and other fictionalized stories are not reality. Real life doesn't always have happy endings, cures are not always found for diseases, and life doesn't go from beginning to end in thirty or sixty minutes.

In Conclusion

Listening is a central part of the communication process. Listening is a process of receiving, attending to, perceiving, assigning meaning to, and responding to messages. We listen to discriminate among auditory and visual stimuli, comprehend information, provide therapeutic support to other communicators, critically evaluate messages, and appreciate messages.

Various strategies can be undertaken to improve a person's listening skills, including shared responsibility for effective communication with the listener, suspending judgment and being a patient listener, avoiding egospeaking, being careful with emotional responses to words, being aware that your posture affects your listening, making a conscious effort to listen, controlling distractions, tuning in to the speaker's cues, learning how to use paraphrasing, and using visualization.

People spend a great deal of time processing television, radio, and Internet messages; therefore, they need to understand how words, images, and sounds influence the way meanings are created and shared.

Learn by Doing

1. Contrast hearing and listening. Develop a verbal analogy between listening and reading.

2. Analyze your own listening. Name one listening behavior you have that does not match the characteristics of a good listener as described in this chapter. Consider how you can change this listening behavior to be more effective.

3. Now that you are aware of some of the principles of effective listening, put them into practice. At the next speech or lecture you attend, sit up, concentrate on what the speaker is saying, and focus all your attention and energy on

comprehending the material. Make internal summaries and paraphrase to assist yourself. After the session is over, analyze your listening behavior and determine what you can still do to improve your comprehension.

4. Critically analyze an editorial on television. Listen for the arguments and appeals, and determine how those persuasive elements were arranged to get a positive response from you, the listener.

5. Make a list of your "red flags." Go back and review these terms. Why do you think they incite you? If class time is available, your instructor will divide the class into groups of four to six students. Discuss your "red flags" and what implications they have for your communication.

6. To learn how to paraphrase, do this three-step activity.
  a. Indicate whether you thoroughly agree (TA), agree (A), disagree (D), or thoroughly disagree (TD) with each of these statements:
  (1) Prayer should be allowed in the public schools.
  (2) Children who contract AIDS should not be allowed to attend public schools.
  (3) Homosexual marriages should be legally sanctioned.
  (4) College students should not have required courses outside of their major area of concentration.
  (5) Guns should be outlawed.
  b. Your class is divided into groups of four to six students. Your task is to get everyone in the group to accept one of the attitudes (TA, A, D, or TD) for each of the preceding statements. You must paraphrase during the entire discussion. You may not give your opinion until you have summarized the statement of the person who preceded you. One member of the group acts as referee and says, "Foul" if anyone speaks without summarizing. (If time does not allow for a discussion of all five questions, your instructor will select one for discussion.)
  c. Now make a list of the positive aspects of paraphrasing as a listening technique; then list the frustrations it causes.

7. Linear/global dominance.[42] Answer all of the questions quickly; do not stop to analyze them. When you have no clear preference, choose the one that most closely represents your normal attitudes or behaviors.
  1. When I buy a new product, I
     _____ a. usually read the directions and carefully follow them.
     _____ b. refer to the directions, but really try and figure out how the thing operates or is put together on my own.
  2. Which of these words best describes the way I perceive myself in dealing with others?
     _____ a. Structured/rigid
     _____ b. Flexible/open-minded
  3. Concerning hunches:
     _____ a. I generally would not rely on hunches to help me make decisions.
     _____ b. I have hunches and follow many of them.
  4. I make decisions mainly based on
     _____ a. what experts say will work.
     _____ b. a willingness to try things that I think might work.
  5. In traveling or going to a destination, I prefer
     _____ a. to read and follow a map.
     _____ b. get directions and map things out "my" way.

6. In school, I preferred
   _____ a. geometry.
   _____ b. algebra.
7. When I read a play or novel, I
   _____ a. see the play or novel in my head as if it were a movie or TV drama.
   _____ b. read the words to obtain information.
8. When I want to remember directions, a name, or a news item, I
   _____ a. visualize the information or write notes that help me create a picture and maybe even draw the directions.
   _____ b. write structured and detailed notes.
9. I prefer to be in the class of a teacher who
   _____ a. has the class do activities and encourages class participation and discussions.
   _____ b. primarily lectures.
10. In writing, speaking, and problem solving, I am
    _____ a. usually creative, preferring to try new things.
    _____ b. seldom creative, preferring traditional solutions.

Scoring and interpretation:

Give yourself one point for each question you answered *b* on items 1 to 5 and *a* on 6 to 10. This total is your score. To assess your degree of linear or global preference, locate your final score on this continuum:

Linear _____ Global
        1 2 3 4 5 6 7 8 9 10

The lower the score, the more linear tendency you have. People with a score of 1 or 2 are considered highly linear. Scores of 3 and possibly 4 show a linear tendency.

The higher the score, the more global tendency you have. People with scores of 9 or 10 are considered highly global. Scores of 7 and possibly 6 indicate a global tendency.

If you scored between 4 and 7, you have indicated you probably do not tend to favor either tendency and are probably flexible in your learning and listening style.

Bear in mind that neither tendency is superior to the other. If you are extremely linear or global, it is possible to develop some of the traits associated with the other hemisphere, or you may already have them.

8. The text mentions National Public Radio's Terri Gross as an excellent interviewer and listener. Listen to a radio interview or watch a television interview and critique the listening, feedback, and follow-up skills of the interviewer. Be prepared to discuss the interviewer and specifically what she or he did to enhance or distract from the quality of the interview.

9. To gain an understanding of how you perceive yourself as a listener, take this, the Janusik/Wolvin Student Listening Inventory (this activity was developed by Laura Janusik and Andrew Wolvin at the University of Maryland, 1999).

Janusik/Wolvin Student Listening Inventory

Directions: The process of listening includes the five steps of Reception, Attention, Perception, Assignment of Meaning, and Response. As a process, listening can break down at any of the five steps. This inventory will help you to identify your strengths and weaknesses in terms of the steps within the context of the classroom. After reading each of the following statements, code the item with the most appropriate response within the context of the college classroom. Remember, "speaker" can mean the instructor or fellow students, so you may have to average your responses. (1) almost never, (2) not often, (3) sometimes, (4) more often than not, and (5) almost always.

_____ **1.** I block out external and internal distractions, such as other conversations or what happened yesterday, when someone is speaking.

_____ **2.** I feel comfortable asking questions when I don't understand something the speaker said.

_____ **3.** When a speaker uses words that I'm not familiar with, I jot them down and look them up later.

_____ **4.** I identify the speaker's credibility while listening.

_____ **5.** I paraphrase the speaker's main ideas in my head as he or she speaks.

_____ **6.** I concentrate on the main ideas instead of the specific details.

_____ **7.** I am able to understand those who are direct as easily as I can understand those who are indirect.

_____ **8.** Before making a decision, I confirm my understanding of the other person's message with her or him.

_____ **9.** I concentrate on the speaker's message even when what she or he is saying is complex.

_____ **10.** I really want to understand what the other person has to say, so I focus solely on his or her message.

_____ **11.** When I listen to someone from another culture, I understand that the speaker may use time and space differently, and I factor that into my understanding.

_____ **12.** I make certain to watch a speaker's facial expressions and body language for further clues to what he or she means.

_____ **13.** I encourage the speaker through my facial expressions and verbal utterances.

_____ **14.** When others are speaking to me, I make sure to establish eye contact and quit doing other tasks.

_____ **15.** When I hear something with which I disagree, I tune out the speaker.

_____ **16.** When an emotional trigger is activated, I recognize it for what it is, set aside my feelings, and continue to concentrate on the speaker's message.

_____ **17.** I try to be sure that my nonverbal response matches my verbal response.

_____ **18.** When someone begins speaking, I focus my attention on her or his message.

_____ **19.** I understand that my past experiences play a role in how I interpret a message, so I try to be aware of their influence when listening.

_____ **20.** I attempt to eliminate outside interruptions and distractions.

_____ **21.** I look the speaker in the eye to focus on her/his message.

_____ **22.** I tune out messages that are too complicated to understand.

_____ **23.** I try to understand the other person's point of view and why she/he feels that way even when it is different from what I believe.

_____ **24.** I am nonjudgmental and noncritical when I listen.

_____ **25.** As appropriate, I self-disclose a similar amount of personal information as the other person shares with me.

Scoring

Directions: Write your responses in the appropriate positions. For example, if you gave yourself a "3" for the first statement, transfer the 3 to the first slot under Reception. When you have transferred all of your scores, add up all five scores for each step. The step with the highest score is your strength. The step with the lowest score is the step that can use the most improvement.

Reception	Attention	Perception	Assignment of Meaning	Response
1. _____	5. _____	3. _____	4. _____	2. _____
9. _____	10. _____	6. _____	7. _____	8. _____
12. _____	14. _____	15. _____	11. _____	13. _____
18. _____	20. _____	16. _____	19. _____	17. _____
21. _____	22. _____	23. _____	24. _____	25. _____

Total _____ _____ _____ _____ _____

Now add up your scores for all five steps, and use the following as a general guideline:

125–112   You perceive yourself to be an outstanding listener in the classroom.

111–87   You perceive yourself to be a good listener in the classroom, but there are some steps that could use improvement.

86–63   You perceive yourself to be an adequate listener in the classroom, but attention to some steps could really improve your listening effectiveness.

62–0   You perceive yourself to be a poor listener in the classroom, and attention to all of the steps could really improve your listening effectiveness.

Consider the following questions:

1. In which step or steps did you excel? What do you consciously do?

2. Which step or steps indicated the most need for improvement? What two specific actions could you take for each step to improve your listening effectiveness?

3. Did you find yourself averaging scores because you were considering both the instructor and peers? What does that say about your perception of both?

Key Terms

hearing
listening
reception
attention
attention span
paraphrasing
perceptual filter
sensorium
selective perception
assignment of meaning
schema

schemata
brain dominance
linear learners/listeners
global listeners/learners
discriminative listening
comprehension listening
therapeutic listening
critical listening
appreciative listening
egospeak

PART

INTERPERSONAL COMMUNICATION

TWO

6

The Theory of Interpersonal Communication

After reading this chapter, you should be able to

- Illustrate how self-disclosure plays a role in both self-understanding and understanding of another person

- Explain the roles of trust, approval seeking, emotions, and power as they relate to interpersonal communication

- Explain the similarities and differences in the communication of males and females and their effect on interpersonal communication

- Define what relationships are and demonstrate how they develop, continue, and end

- Explain the role of, positive and negative aspects of, and how to be a better online interpersonal communicator

The concept of interpersonal communication developed in the early 1950s.[1] As a result of research on the subject, the field of speech expanded from study focused on public speaking into the broader field of communication, encompassing such areas as self-disclosure, approval seeking, relational communication, family communication, conversational communication, and conflict resolution. Note that the field is called *communication,* not *communications* (with an "s"). The latter is reserved for topics such as electronic media, telephones, and computers.

The term *interpersonal communication* can be defined as "communication that is based on communicators' recognition of each other's uniqueness and the development of messages that reflect that recognition."[2] It also can be described as an interactional process in which two people send and receive messages. Two primary themes underlie this process: communication necessitates give and take, and communication involves relationships and information.

Because there can be no communication unless the communicators give and take information, the basis for interpersonal transactions is the sending and receiving of messages in such a way that they are successfully encoded and decoded. The more experiences the communicators have in common and the more openness they have between them, the more likely it is that their communication will be successful.

Our interpersonal relationships bring together the most important people, roles, contexts, and energies we experience. Interpersonal communication functions to combat loneliness, shape self-concepts, confirm experiences, renew personal and intrapersonal growth, and aid us in understanding who we are and how we relate to others.

Interpersonal skills have been identified by business executives as one of the three most important abilities that employees must have (good listening and effective problem solving are the others).[3] On the personal level, family and relational communication is dependent on your being a competent interpersonal communicator. A recent study, for example, revealed that interpersonal communication is at the core of success in college. Your interpersonal abilities affect your academic success, roommate rapport, and social connectedness.[4]

Basic Concepts of Interpersonal Communication

As you read about interpersonal communication, keep some basic concepts in mind:

1 *Communication takes place within a system.* As we enter into communicative relationships with others, we set a pattern by which we will interact. For example, in a family, there are flow patterns of message sending and receiving: who speaks to whom, who controls the interactions, who has the power to praise and punish, who can encourage or stop the message flow. If you examine any relationship you are in, you will recognize patterns by which the communication flows.

A change in the system results in a change of the communication. If someone in the system changes roles (e.g., a teenager leaves for college) or outside factors change the system (a grandparent gets ill and moves in), that changes the communicative system.

Our interpersonal relationships bring together the most important people, roles, contexts, and energies we experience.

There may be resistance to changing the system because this may also shift the power structure. If your supervisor, spouse, lover, or friend likes being in control, and you are proposing a change, problems may arise. At the other extreme, there also may be situations in which the system requires adjustment so that a person is forced to assume responsibility after having been dependent on someone else. Whatever happens, the communication system remains unchanged as long as the status quo is maintained.

2 *We teach others how to treat us.* The system in which communication takes place needs to be structured. Each person plays a role when a system is developing. If both people accept their roles, then those roles become part of the system. If a role is rejected, then it does not become a system rule. Often we wonder why people treat us as they do. In many instances it is because when they treat us in a particular way, we don't object; therefore, it becomes the pattern. For example, habitual physical abusers at one point hit people, who don't object or feel that they had the power to defend themselves. Consequently, the next time the abuser got angry, he or she repeated the action. The cycle is set unless the abused takes action to teach the aggressor a new way to act.

3 *We communicate what and who we are.* Every time we communicate, we tell a great deal about ourselves. Our selection of words, the tone of our voice, and the gestures we use combine to give a picture of our values, likes and dislikes, and self-perceptions. We give clues to our background by our pronunciation patterns and the attitudes we express. As receivers, we form conclusions about senders and react to these conclusions based on our own culture—our background, experiences, and beliefs.

4 *Much of our interpersonal communication centers on our wanting others to act or think or feel as we do; in other words, much of it is an attempt at persuasion.* In our interpersonal relations with parents, children, and friends, we often attempt to alter or reinforce behavior, gain compliance, give advice, or elicit some type of action.

5 *Meaning is in people, not in words.* A word has a meaning only by virtue of the meaning people give to that word. In communicating with others, we must be aware that what a particular symbol means to us is not necessarily what it means to the other person. A homeowner hearing the word *grass* may think of the *lawn*. A drug counselor probably thinks of *marijuana*. Unless some basis for understanding exists, ineffective communication may be the result. Thus, we must define terms and give examples, keeping our audience in mind and adjusting our messages accordingly.

6 *We cannot not communicate.* Communication does not necessarily stop simply because people stop talking or listening. Suppose you do not answer a question your instructor has asked. Or suppose you sit quietly at the dinner table instead of joining in the conversation. In these cases, you are still sending messages, although your lips are silent. Remember that much communicating is done below the verbal level. You may think that if you do not actively participate, you are not sending messages—but you are! In many instances, your body is communicating nonverbally, and the very fact that you are not saying something may be interpreted as if you were telling the other person that you are not interested, don't care, or disagree.

7 *People react to our actions.* We constantly are demonstrating the **action-reaction principle.** When we smile, others are likely to smile back; when we display anger, others tend to do the same. Try an experiment. The next time you walk down a hallway or a sidewalk, smile as others come toward you. You probably will find that the people you pass smile back, often saying *hello*—action-reaction. Think back to the last time you had an argument. If you raised your voice, what did the other person do? No doubt that person also raised his or her voice—action-reaction.

— reciprocity happens alot

8 We do what we do because in the end *we expect to achieve happiness.* When we choose to enter into communication, we do so hoping to gain from the experience, but certainly to be in no worse psychological shape than when we entered. Consequently, many people try to avoid any situation in which they feel they may get negative feedback or be unsuccessful in communicating their ideas.

9 *We cannot always have the same understandings and feelings as others.* As we communicate, we must recognize that because of differences in cultures, the only areas we share are those in which we have a common experiential background. To illustrate this, let us assume that all our knowledge and experience is contained within one circle and that all the knowledge and experience of the person with whom we are communicating is contained within another circle. The only commonality—the only place where our ideas, concepts, beliefs, and vocabulary will overlap—is where we have had similar exposure. Figure 6.1 illustrates this idea. Only in the area where the circles overlap are there any common unities.

If we add a third person to the conversation, the problem becomes even greater, as Figure 6.2 illustrates. Here, there are areas of overlap that exist between persons A and B, between persons A and C, and between persons B and C. But notice the small area of overlap among all three. The difficulty of communicating with large groups of people can easily be demonstrated when this process of drawing representative circles is continued.

Self-Disclosure

The starting point of any interpersonal communication is self-talk—intrapersonally communicating within one's self. The self-talk often triggers confidences and

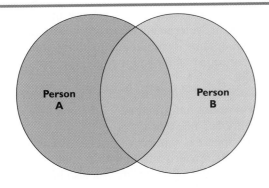

Figure 6.1

Commonality of Experience Between Two Persons

Person A

Person B

Figure 6.2

Commonality of Experience Among Three Persons

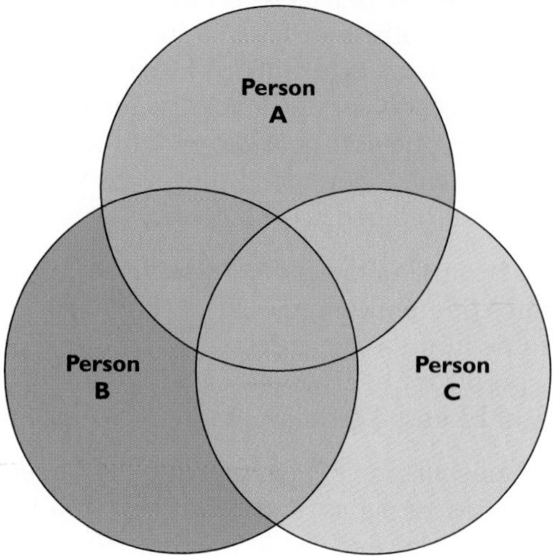

inquiries we have about ourselves, which then affect our interpersonal communication decisions. The view you have of yourself, your self-concept, determines what you will say and to whom you will say it. For example, if you perceive yourself to be a good communicator, then you are likely to feel confident in your communication. But if you label yourself as shy or apprehensive, then you may find it difficult to express yourself. At the heart of this dynamic process is the premise that if you do not accept yourself, probably no one else will either; your lack of confidence is easily picked up by those with whom you interact.

Some people worry about appearing too self-confident and being thought a braggart. But accepting yourself as a worthy person does not necessarily mean you are boasting. Sometimes you have to "blow your own horn" because no one else knows how to play the tune. You know yourself better than others and know more about yourself and your skills and talents than others do. Share your accomplishments, but don't oversell yourself, and let others share their accomplishments as well.

Self-love means accepting yourself as a worthy person because you choose to do so. Self-love has nothing to do with the sort of behavior characterized by telling everyone how wonderful you are. Self-love means to love yourself; it doesn't demand the love of others. Self-love is the basis for accepting who and what you are and realizing that if others can't accept you as you are, that is their problem and not yours. This is not to say that you can't listen to others and attempt to make changes in yourself, but the bottom line is your ability to accept yourself as a viable human being. This does not, of course, allow you to aggress against others physically, sexually, or psychologically.

Self-disclosure is "intentionally letting the other person know who you are by communicating self-revealing information."[5] This revealing can be accomplished through verbal or nonverbal messages.

Whether the atmosphere is supportive or defensive is a large factor in determining how much will be revealed and how vulnerable you will allow yourself to become. The amount and type of disclosure will also be based on the relationship between the people involved. The deepest level of self-disclosure occurs when two people open themselves in such a way that each can be hurt by the other's actions.

Self-disclosure allows others to understand you, and it allows you to understand yourself. As you talk about yourself, not only the other person is exposed to you; you may also learn something about yourself. One of the activities in psychotherapy, for example, is to get clients to talk about themselves in order to talk out what they think and feel, with the intent of having them learn who they really are.

The Self and Others

Your image of yourself makes up your "I."[6] The **self-perceived I** is the image you project, the way you perceive yourself. It is revealed through the words, ideas, actions, clothing, and lifestyle you choose. All of these communicate your "I" to others.

Those with whom you come into contact also build their own images of you for themselves, and they sometimes communicate this image to you. For example, friends comment about what they like and dislike about you; teachers and parents praise and criticize; significant others and supervisors evaluate. These collective judgments by significant others develop into a "Me." The **other-perceived Me** is the person that others perceive you to be. It may be the same as or different from your self-perceived I.

One of the best ways to understand how the I-Me dichotomy affects your communication is to examine the entire process as a mathematical formula. Under ideal conditions, we come as close to I = Me (I equals Me) as we can. Just as in algebra, when the equation balances, there is no basic error. If your perception of self (I) and the perception of you that significant others hold (Me) are basically the same—if these perceptions balance—then you maintain your equilibrium and continue to function as before. As a result, you continue to communicate in the same manner as previously (see Figure 6.3).

Self-disclosure can be accomplished through verbal or nonverbal messages.

Figure 6.3   I = Me

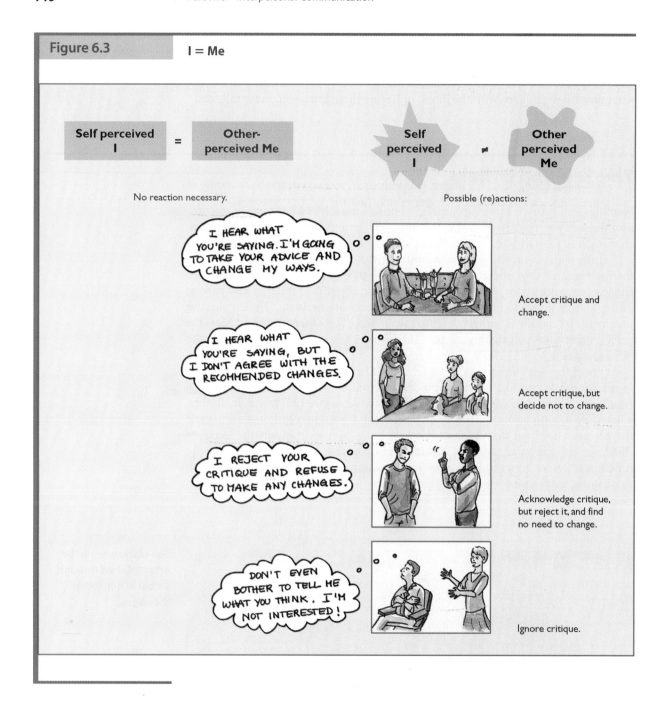

When the I and the Me are not in balance (I ≠ Me), you have four options for how to communicatively react:

1. *You can alter your communication actions.* You attempt to make the specific changes the significant other has indicated. In the play *Our Town,* George, one of the play's young lovers, must decide whether to alter his behavior as a result of a conversation with his girlfriend, Emily. She tells George that he is spending all his time playing baseball and that he has become stuck-up and con-

ceited. As the conversation continues, George offers to buy Emily an ice cream soda to celebrate not only their recent election as class officers but also his good fortune in having a friend who tells him what he should be told. The scene ends with George's promise to take Emily's advice and change his ways.

You can change on your own, or you can get help from mental health professionals, friends, or relatives. You have probably known someone whose personality changed suddenly, or even over a period of time, because of an alteration of attitudes and ideas as expressed through verbal and nonverbal communication.

2. *You can accept an evaluation by acknowledging that it exists, but you feel the recommended change is not desirable.* Consequently, you accept the evaluation but do not change. For example, a member may take the leadership role after a group makes no progress toward accomplishing its goal. Another member may accuse the newly emerged leader of exerting too much power. Because the group made no previous progress and is now well on its way to fulfilling its goal, the newly emerged leader may decide to accept the evaluation but not make any changes in her behavior pattern.

[handwritten: accept evaluation, but change not desirable]

3. *You completely reject the input.* You consider the information, decide it is not true, and do nothing about making any changes. This happens, for example, when a student in a speech class, rather than accepting comments about his presentation, refuses to consider any suggestions. It can take place in a work environment when an employee fails to make the adjustments presented by a manager.

[handwritten: completely reject evaluation after considering it]

4. *You can ignore any evaluation.* You don't seek out criticism, and if someone attempts to give it, you refuse even to listen to what is said. Ignorers use statements such as "Don't even bother to tell me what you think. I'm not interested." Sometimes you block out all criticism because you find it self-defeating. Think, for example, of people who adopt the attitude "I am what I am, and I'll be that way no matter what you say!"

[handwritten: ignore eval.]

Seeking Approval

A great deal of our interpersonal communication is spent on trying to get the approval of others. In some instances, people seek approval at the expense of diminishing their self-worth. Some people are so controlled by others and the fear that others (friends, relatives, employers) won't like them that they almost become immobile. Thus, not being able to make decisions for themselves, they turn over their destiny to others.

If you want to eliminate approval-seeking behavior as a major need in your life, keep these guidelines in mind:

[handwritten: (preventative Measures)]

◆ If you think someone else is trying to control you by withholding approval, say so.

◆ When you are faced with disapproval, ask yourself, "If they agreed with me, would I be better off?"

◆ Accept that some people will never understand you and that this situation is perfectly acceptable.

◆ You can refuse to argue or try convincing anyone of the rightness of your stance and still simply believe it.

- ◆ Trust yourself.
- ◆ Stop verifying your ideas by having them substantiated by others.
- ◆ Work at eliminating the apologies you make even when you are not wrong or sorry for what you have said or done.

The **self-fulfilled person**—the person who confidently chooses what to reveal and to whom—is not intimidated into a negative self-concept and realizes that there will always be problems, frustrations, and failures in life. These people have learned to be happy and are therefore confident of their ability in interpersonal communication.

Gaining Compliance

In our relationships with other people, we often need to get others to do something for us, agree with us, or otherwise engage with us. As a result, it is sometimes necessary to apply the skills of persuasion to our interpersonal communication to gain **compliance.** Physicians, for instance, must work to get patients to comply with their recommended treatment plan. Teachers must be persuasive in getting students to do the work required in a course. Parents rely on persuasive strategies to gain their children's compliance with their wishes.

Research on compliance-gaining strategies reinforces how much securing compliance is a transactional, give-and-take process. Some of the strategies that have been found to work effectively include:

Pregiving: In pregiving, you would give the person something he or she may want in order to help convince the person to act as you might want him or her to act. For example, you could give your significant other a gift and then request agreement with your plan to vacation in the mountains.

Liking: In order to assist in the persuasive interpersonal act, you may try and put the other person in a receptive mood by being friendly to him or her. For example, you could offer to help a coworker with a project she is doing so that she has positive feelings toward you and might, therefore, be open to a suggestion that she assist you on your next project.

Promise: In proposing assistance or conformity with your view, you might make a promise. For example, a candidate running for public office, in a face-to-face interaction with you, might promise that in exchange for your vote, he will attempt to get funding for the local YMCA, which is one of your favorite projects.

Threat: You could include in your proposal the intention to use influence or control over the other person if he or she doesn't conform to your request. A teacher does this, for example, when she discusses academic work with a student and warns that the student will fail if he doesn't study and pass the next test.

Self-feelings: You might include a statement of guilt in your proposal. A parent does this when, for instance, he tells his son that he will feel bad, and so should the child, if the child doesn't stop being a bully on the playground.

Esteem: One of our basic needs is pleasure, and people often strive to achieve personal recognition as part of that need. Indicating that there is a reward, recognition, or praise that could result from conforming with your request may sway the person to your side. For example, as a manager at a business, you might indicate to a worker that she could be a candidate for the Employee of the Month Award, which carries a $500 stipend. This knowledge might inspire her to work harder.

Debt: You may decide to indicate to a person who is indebted to you for a past favor that he "owes you one" in order to get him to comply with your request. For example, you could ask a friend to drive you to the airport and include the comment that he owes you a return favor since you gave him your sociology class notes when he had missed class.

Of course, these strategies can backfire if you aren't careful about when and how you use them. As always, you must consider the participants, the setting, and your purpose in evaluating which, if any, of these strategies you will use. It's necessary to assess the situation thoroughly so that you can anticipate how the other person will respond to your appeals. Consider how much is at stake. Realistically, people might consider your using any of these tactics as being manipulative, so be ready for a potential rejection. The bottom line is that you should determine what is the best strategy, make sure that you plan your proposal and compliance-gaining strategy as carefully as you can, and consider what the ramifications of your actions may be before you proceed.

Emotions

A theory that relates to how the brain works suggests that in the process of human development, two brains developed. These are parallel to the right and left lobes of the brain. The first brain to develop was the emotional brain (the right lobe), and therefore it triggers first. Then the second brain, the logical brain, is triggered.[8] The logical brain contains the information we are taught: reasoning patterns, the rules of civilized behavior, and cultural rules. This also parallels the concept that we instinctively act; then we logically reason to conclusions. It has been estimated that 90 percent of our actions are emotional, leaving only 10 percent intellectual.[9]

Any message we communicate is made up of both logic and emotion. Emotional states include fear, anger, disgust, grief, joy, surprise, and yearning. You probably have grown up believing that you can control your emotions—that anger, fear, and hate, as well as love, ecstasy, and joy, are things that happen to you but can be stuffed (held inside). This pattern of conduct is especially true if you are a typical European American male. If you were brought up to believe that it is good to control your emotions, whether love or hate, that nice people do not display their emotions, or that men do not cry, then this statement may startle you: *There is nothing wrong with expressing your feelings; it is normal and natural!*

One of the most feared interpersonal displays of emotion is anger, yet anger is a natural, normal emotion. To react with anger to a situation or set of events is not bad. Anger serves as an emotional defense mechanism to relieve the stress of an overly stressful situation. Suppressed anger leads to ill health, emotional disturbance, and a general feeling of unhappiness.[10] Expressions of anger, however, can be constructive or destructive. Letting out your anger by saying how you feel while not verbally or physically attacking another person can be a positive outlet. But physically or verbally abusing a person is not a positive way of showing emotions. If we use someone as a scapegoat, blaming him or her for our own shortcomings, we are not being fair to ourselves or the other person. Each of us must assume responsibility for our feelings and for our reactions to them.

Power

"**Power** is the ability to control what happens—to create things you want to happen and to block things you don't want to happen."[11] Power is the ability to choose for yourself or to control the choice of others.

Defining *power* as the ability to control what happens and to make choices clarifies several preconceptions. First, the power to choose is not bad, and it is something that is exercised in every human transaction. The view of power as bad may stem from its abuse (often in the form of winning at someone else's expense), from the perception that it contradicts the belief that all humans should be equal, or from its waste (as when there's really no opportunity to gain anything and large amounts of resources are being thrown away in the process, such as when a person spends time and money on a former romantic partner who does not intend to begin a new relationship with him). In fact, power, the ability to make choices, is desirable, not bad.

Every person may be more or less powerful or powerless, depending on the situation and its participants. Thus, you have power, and you are powerful—maybe not with everyone, at all times, and in every circumstance, but certainly with some people, at some times, and in particular settings. For example, a father may be powerful at home when dealing with his four-year-old son but powerless in a work situation in which his boss has made it clear that all decisions must be approved by her.

Power: ability to control what happens @ Make choices

One of the most feared interpersonal displays of emotion is anger.

People who feel powerless often lack the ability to make choices about their relationships, such as deciding which to maintain and which to terminate. They may feel that they don't have the ability to make choices, and therefore, they settle for unsatisfying relationships. Also, people who feel powerless in one situation may take out their hostilities and frustrations in other situations. For example, a parent having problems with her boss at work—and who feels powerless to do anything about it—may be unusually harsh with her children.

Many people in North American culture are raised to believe that they have great power over their own lives and even over the lives of others, that they are "masters of their own fate," and that they can "pull themselves up by their bootstraps." Not only do they want power and think that they deserve it; they also do not want other people to have power over them. They may leave home so that their parents will not have power over them. Women and minority groups ask for power so that they can have freedom from internal and external restraints. In short, North Americans are taught not to be powerless. This, of course, is not the case with all cultures. Most of the world's people, in fact, believe that an outside source or fate—be it "God," "the gods," "reincarnation," or "nature"—controls their lives. Muslims use the expression "It is Allah's will," and Hindus believe that their karma is being acted out. In both instances, these people do not feel powerless per se, but instead they believe in a philosophy of "what will be, will be." It is not their mission to seek power, nor in most instances do they rebel against the fact that they do not have power. In most situations, they hold the view that the legitimacy of power is irrelevant.[12] If you would like to investigate how you assess your own feelings of empowerment, complete Activity 10 in the Learn by Doing exercise at the end of this chapter.

Have you ever considered that there are different types of power and that you may possess all or none of these? The types include *expert power, referent power, reward power, coercive power,* and *legitimate power.*

Expert power is your capacity to influence another person because of the knowledge and skills you are presumed to have. Are you knowledgeable about how to operate a computer, throw a knuckle ball in baseball, or bake the world's best chocolate-chip cookies? To build expert power, you need to communicate or demonstrate your expertise to others. You can do this by mentioning your background and training, demonstrating that you are well informed on various topics, and accomplishing tasks competently.

People telling others about their power is not a universal trait. There are cultures, such as those in parts of Asia, in which people do not talk about themselves. First, too much self-focus is considered a form of bragging or boasting. Individuality is "systematically repressed."[13] Second, cultures that have a nonverbal rather than a verbal tradition believe that people possess intuitive *feelings* about each other and therefore do not have to state what is "known" by both parties. If an individual has power, others will just know it. In these cultures there is a belief that "it is the heart always that sees, before the head can see."

Referent power is probably the most important source of power because it's based on personal loyalty, friendship, affection, and admiration. The key to securing this power base is to demonstrate your friendliness and trustworthiness. For example, emphasize the similarities between yourself and the other person, such as your background, goals, attitudes, and values. It also helps to communicate your support for the other person, give her or him the benefit of the doubt, and create symbols that bind you together, such as in-jokes and a special language.

Reward power requires that you be perceived as the best or only source of desired rewards. To a child, for example, parents may be the ultimate possessors of reward power. Instructors and bosses also have reward power in the form of grades and pay increases.

based upon ability to dispense punishments →

Coercive power is based on possible negative outcomes that are used as weapons. To exercise coercive power, you need to (1) know what weapons the other person fears most, (2) acquire them, (3) communicate that you have them, and (4) persuade the other person that you're willing to use them. A boss who threatens to fire an employee unless she works overtime without pay is exercising coercive power, power that forces the person to decide between two options, neither of which is desirable. In this case, the employee can either work for free or get fired.

Legitimate power stems from one person's perception that another person has the right to make requests of him or her because of the position that the other person occupies or because of the nature of the relationship. For example, in an academic relationship, students perceive that the professor has the right to make requests of them such as asking them to do homework and take tests. In a committed relationship, companions often feel that their partners have the right to ask favors of them. To increase your legitimate power, you must either move into a new position or role that has more authority (for example, become the boss), change the nature of the relationship (from acquaintance to friend), or persuade another person that you have more authority by changing the expectations associated with your position.

When we are involved in interpersonal communication, we must recognize that we can lose a great deal by failing to realize the consequences of what we say and to whom. If a person has the power to control us, we must be willing to pay the price for any show of strength we may make. The price of challenging the power can include losing a job, failing a class, or getting a traffic ticket. If, however, we are in a position of power, we can, if we so desire, demand obedience based purely on our ability to manipulate, reward, and control.

Ideally, the use of power is controlled to the extent that it becomes a tool of cooperation rather than a weapon of punishment. A Hindu proverb says, "There is nothing noble in being superior to another man; true nobility is in being superior to your former self." Realistically, however, we must recognize that many people do not hold this attitude, and we should take this into consideration in our dealings with others.

Besides power as a communication factor, gender considerations are at the base of much of our interpersonal communication.

Male/Masculine—Female/Feminine Communication

"Some people become angry at the mere suggestion that women and men are different."[14] "Recent decades have witnessed two contradictory processes: the development of scientific research into the differences between sexes, and the denial that such differences exist."[15] This controversy as to whether men and women do, in fact, communicate differently has directly affected the field of communication.

In the early 1990s, research in gender communication seemed to indicate strongly that there were vast differences between the communication of males and females. Lately, however, there has been a reexamination of the early data. Communication scholars, for example, have investigated the research background of one of the first books to expose the differences between male and female communication and concluded that the text "makes quantitative claims based on thin sources, generalizes from small and unrepresentative study samples, and overlooks studies that support other explanations of differences in conversational styles."[16] They contend that "the best evidence on gender and communication suggests that men and women are far more alike than different."[17]

While one can accept that there are many similarities, there appears to be enough evidence beyond that of the initial writings in the field to indicate that differences do exist—enough so that the different tendencies deserve to be discussed.[18]

Sex and Gender

"Sex refers to one's biological or physical self while gender refers to one's psychological, social, and interactive characteristics."[19]

From the sexual perspective, biological research has "produced a body of findings which paints a remarkably consistent picture of sexual asymmetry. The sexes are different because the brain, the chief administrative and emotional organ of life, is differently constructed in men and in women. It processes information in a different way, which results in different perceptions, priorities and behavior."[20]

These biological underpinnings can have a profound effect on communicating. For example, scientists suggest that the differences in emotional response between men and women can be explained by the differences in the structure and organization of the brain. Because the two halves of a man's brain are connected by a smaller number of fibers than a woman's, the flow of information between one side of the brain and the other is more restricted. It is proposed, therefore, that a woman can express her emotions better in words because what she feels has been transmitted more effectively to the verbal side of her brain.[21]

Parallel to this view are findings about gender. This research shows that "gender is socially constructed. Because of the lessons we learn about ourselves and our world, people may develop differently. As children and later as adults, females and males often are treated differently, so it hardly is surprising that our ways of knowing and ways of being are distinct.[22] "From infancy on, males generally learn masculine traits—independence, self-absorption, competition, aggression."[23] "Men value power, competency, efficiency, and achievement. They are more interested in objects and things than people and feelings."[24] "Females learn feminine traits—dependence, other-absorption, nurturance, sensitivity."[25] However, recognize that there are some children who learn reverse gender roles.

Another factor to keep in mind is that the terms *men's traits* and *women's traits* really refer to "masculine traits" and "feminine traits." In fact, it has been suggested that discussion of male and female communication should refer to "mannish tendencies" and "womanish tendencies."[26]

The differences in the emotional responses of men and women can be explained by the differences in the structure and organization of the brain.

Remember that gender tendencies are not sexual descriptors. Someone whose gestures, walk, voice pitch, and language better fit the stereotype of what a member of the opposite sex uses does not make the user sexually that gender.

How Men and Women Communicate Differently

We have come to accept the general concept that communication between men and women is essentially cross-cultural communication and sometimes as confusion ridden as talk between people from two different countries. Because men and women often approach one another from distinct worlds, the simplest phrase can carry separate, and sometimes conflicting, meanings to members of the opposite sex. Men and women often use language to contrary purposes and effect. "Men use speech to report, to compete, to gain attention, and to maintain their positions in a social hierarchy. Women use speech to gain rapport, maintain relationships, and reflect a sense of community."[27] Women tend to use language to create intimacy and connection while men tend to use language to preserve their independence and negotiate their status.

> **Male and female communication can be cross-cultural. To a woman, "I'll call you" means *right now.* To a man, it generally means *sometime.***

How do these differences develop? Research shows that girls and boys grow up in different worlds of words. Boys and girls tend to have different ways of talking to their friends. Boys tend to play in large groups that are hierarchically structured; there is a leader and/or a competition for leadership; there are winners and losers in the games they play, as well as complex rules. The emphasis is on skill and who is best. Girls tend to play in small groups or pairs and usually have a best friend; intimacy is the key. Everyone gets a turn, there are usually no winners and losers, and girls are not expected to boast about their successes. Girls don't generally give orders; they express their preferences as suggestions. Boys say, "Gimme that!" and "Get out of here!" Girls say, "Can we do this?" and "How about doing that?" Gender differences in language can be observed in children as young as age three.[28]

Both male and female styles are valid in their own ways. Misunderstandings arise because the styles are different.

There are general patterns of communication that are identifiably male and female. For example, which of these do you think tend to be true?

- Women use more words to make their point.
- Men are more competitive in their speaking.
- Men tend to be more task oriented.
- Women are more supportive conversationalists.
- Men are more direct in their communication.

Perceptual Differences of Women and Men

	Women	Men
Love	A feeling	A ritual (evidenced by actions: send flowers, dinners, etc.)
Friendship	Verbally intimate: Express oneself	Buddy: No self-exposure
Commitment	A relationship to be nurtured, supported over time	Loss of freedom
Leadership	Facilitative	Directive
Communication	To understand and be understood	To win, outsmart; one-upmanship
Intimacy	Sharing and discussing innermost thoughts and feelings	Physically close

Source: From "Sex Stereotypes and Expectations: Classroom and Campus Strategies for Change," by Linda A. M. Perry, Phil Backlund, and Lisa Merrill, a short course at the Speech Communication Association Convention, October 29–November 1, 1992, Chicago, IL. Used by permission of the Speech Communication Association.

◆ Women disclose more personal information to others than men do.

◆ Women have larger vocabularies for describing emotions and aesthetics.

Yes, *women do use more words to make their point.* Much of this centers on their desire to fill in details and to explain more fully. They tend to be more sensitive to the needs of the listener. Men tend to say what they have to say, assume that the message is clear, and proceed from that point. Therefore, men may believe that women are wasting time, talking too much, or not getting to the point because of the additional effort women spend in clarifying and enlarging.[29]

Yes, *men are more competitive in their speaking.* They have been socialized to "take charge" and get things done. Typically men engage in **competitive turn taking,** grabbing the floor by interrupting another speaker. Women have been conditioned from childhood to believe that to interrupt is impolite. Indeed, research on male-female communication patterns found that 96 percent of the interruptions and 100 percent of the overlaps in mixed pairs in daily conversations were performed by men.[30]

Yes, *men do tend to be more task oriented; women tend to be more maintenance oriented.* Men tend to want results at any cost. Women are usually more concerned about the process used, about keeping things going smoothly, and about doing business in the least disruptive manner. Women characteristically use tentative phrases such as "I guess" and turn direct statements into indirect ones. For example, a woman may say, "Don't you think it would be better to send that report first?" A man will typically say, "Send the report."[31] Men will say, "What's next on the agenda?" and "What's the bottom line?" Women tend to ask, "You haven't spoken; what do you think?" or "How does everyone feel about this?"

Yes, *women are more supportive conversationalists.* They are much more likely to check the connection of conversations. Women tend to ask more questions and work harder than men do to keep the conversational ball rolling. In fact, women ask questions three times as often as men do. Women often feel that it is their role to make sure that the conversation goes well, and they assume that if it is not proceeding well, they have to remedy the situation.

Yes, *men tend to be more direct.* When men want something, they ask for it directly; women tend to be more indirect.[32] A man may ask a woman, "Will you please go to the

What we say and what we'd like to say are not necessarily the same.

store?" He wants something; he feels that he has the status to ask for it and get it. But a woman asking a man may say, "Gee, I really need a few things from the store, but I'm so tired." Often she speaks this way because she feels she is in a low-status position that does not include the right to make a request.[33] A man may well describe the manner in which a woman makes a request as "beating around the bush," and he may ask, "Why, if you want something, don't you just ask for it?" Women also tend to use more **tag questions**—questions added onto the end of statements, such as "That movie was terrific, don't you think?" The intent is to get the partner to enter the conversation. Men sometimes construe the tag question as continuing what has already been discussed.

Yes, findings indicate that *women disclose more personal information than men do.* In their vocabulary selections, females tend to be people oriented and concerned with internal psychological and emotional states whereas men are self-oriented and concerned with action.

Yes, *women have larger vocabularies for describing emotions and aesthetics.* Women have been taught to express their feelings, many men to hide or disregard theirs. Therefore, women tend to have a larger repertoire of words to describe what they are feeling. Women also have broader vocabularies that can finitely separate aesthetics such as colors. Men, for example, will describe the color as red; women describe specific shadings such as ruby, magenta, or rose. In addition, there may be some physiological reasons based on brain function that account for females being able to express their emotions and differentiate finite colors.

Other factors also seem to be present in male-female patterns:

◆ When a man resists a woman's suggestion, she feels as though he doesn't care and that her needs are not being respected. As a result, she may feel unsupported and stops trusting him.[34] But "when a woman resists a man's solutions, he feels his competence is being questioned. As a result he feels mistrusted, unappreciated, and stops caring. His willingness to listen understandably lessens."[35]

◆ The most frequently expressed complaint women have about men is that they don't listen. Underlying this is that she wants empathy, yet he thinks she wants a solution; she thinks she's nurturing him while he feels he's being controlled.[36]

◆ "Men are more interested in visual stimulation, physical details. Women are more interested in tactile sensations, emotional overtones, and intimacy."[37]

◆ Men offer solutions and invalidate feelings while women offer unsolicited advice and direction.

◆ Men tend to pull away and silently think about what's bothering them; women feel an instinctive need to talk about what's bothering them.

◆ Men are motivated when they feel needed; women are motivated when they feel cherished.

◆ Men primarily need a kind of love that is trusting, accepting, and appreciative; women primarily need a kind of love that is caring, understanding, and respectful.[38]

Whose communication patterns are right? Neither gender holds the key to being a competent communicator. For the past decade, some people have believed that men need to change since it is perceived that women are more effective communicators and more sensitive to human needs. In fact, a review of communication books leads to the conclusion that feminine patterns of being supportive, talking through issues, and not interrupting are positive; however, the task orientation, the directness, and the lack of tentativeness of males also gain points. Some communication theorists feel that one approach to a "best" communication pattern centers on a person who acts with **androgyny**—a person who communicates with both masculine and feminine patterns. That individual has the largest repertoire of communication behaviors to call upon. For example, this person may behave both emphatically and objectively, and both assertively and cooperatively, which increases the person's adaptability—one of the qualities of the competent communicator.

In recent years, based in part on the understandings of the communicative differences between men and women, and the expectations placed on each as they interact with each other, the area of sexual harassment has become an issue.

Sexual Harassment

Sexual harassment may be described as "generalized sexist remarks or behavior; inappropriate and offensive, but essentially sanction-free, sexual advances; solicitation of sexual activity or other sex-linked behavior by promise of rewards; coercion of sexual activity by threat of punishment; and assaults."[39] It also includes "unwanted and unwelcome sexual actions in work and educational contexts."[40]

Human communication performs a central yet complex role in sexual harassment. Communication is the primary medium through which sexual harassment is expressed. It is the means by which those who are harassed respond to harassment. It is also the primary means by which policies for eliminating sexual harassment can be implemented.[41]

The effect of sexual harassment, as a communicative event, was described by writer Toni Morrison in her 1993 acceptance speech for the Nobel Prize for literature: "Oppressive language does more than violence . . . it is violence."[42]

Sexual harassment is a serious and pervasive problem in modern organizational life. Both the targets and those accused (falsely or not) suffer personal anguish and dehumanization.[43] A survey of female employees found that 43 percent had experienced some form of sexual harassment.[44]

Sexual harassment takes place not only in the workplace but also on college campuses. Students at one university reported that as many as 89 percent of women experienced sexual harassment at least once and that many experienced it more than once.[45]

Although "sexual harassment is experienced primarily by women,"[46] this does not mean that men are not also victims. However, in our society, where men may perceive a come-on as positive, women perceive the same advances as negative. Instead of feeling like victims, men may perceive harassment as an ego booster, a cause for bragging.

Men's perceptions of what their behavior communicates are vastly different from women's. The harasser may see himself as intending to exercise his power over women, protect his professional turf, boost his macho self-image, and demonstrate his friendliness and helpfulness. The person who is harassed may want to stop the harassment; deter future incidents; preserve her reputation; avoid retaliation; maintain rapport; and preserve self-respect, physical safety, and psychological well-being.[47]

Sexual harassment has not changed over the years. "What has changed is that people now are more willing to label these behaviors as being sexual harassment, people are more willing to talk about it, and people are more angry about it."[48]

Responding to Sexual Harassment

One of the questions often asked regarding sexual harassment is "What should I do if I am a recipient of unwelcome behavior?" In general, if you question a person's actions as being inappropriate:[49]

◆ *Trust your instincts.* If you think it is harassment, it may well be harassment.

◆ *Don't blame yourself.* You are the victim, not the perpetrator. A common ploy by harassers is to intimate that the victim brought it on, encouraged the actions or advances by the type of clothing she or he wore, the way the person looked at him or her, or the type of language the person used. In almost all instances, this is a ploy to turn the innocent person into the guilty party. People with weak self-concepts often fall for this ploy.

◆ *Get emotional support.* Turn to a mental health professional, an expert in harassment, or a support telephone service or hot line that deals with harassment.

◆ *Say no clearly and early to the individual whose behavior and/or comments make you uncomfortable.* Don't allow the person to continue with the actions or ver-

---

A Sexual Harassment Quiz

How much do you know about sexual harassment? Here are some questions based on court rulings in sexual harassment cases. Answer "true" or "false."

1. A single incident or statement does not normally constitute sexual harassment.
2. If a person participates voluntarily in an unwelcome sexual relationship, sexual harassment is not an issue.
3. The courts recognize that fear of retaliation can prevent a victim from communicating that a harasser's conduct is unwelcome—even though the victim is expected to communicate this fact.
4. For vulgar language or sexual flirtation to be considered as creating a hostile environment, behavior has to adversely affect the working environment—in the judgment of a reasonable person.

5. If a sexual harassment problem is common knowledge at work, the employer is presumed to know about it.
6. Displaying "girlie" pictures can constitute a hostile work environment—even though some workers think they are harmless.

Answers: 1. True. Usually a sustained pattern is necessary—unless the incident was severe or physical. 2. False. The Supreme Court has ruled that voluntariness is not a defense. 3. True. 4. True. 5. True. 6. True.

Source: Adapted from *Working Together,* by Andrea P. Baridon and David R. Eyler, McGraw-Hill, Inc., 1221 Avenue of the Americas, New York, NY 10020

balizations. Call a halt to it immediately by saying emphatically, "I will not [allow you to speak to me like that, *or* put up with that type of talk, *or* allow you to touch me]."

♦ *Document every incident in detail.* Keep a record. Write down everything that happened, including exactly what was said and done, with dates and times, and any other supporting evidence. Share the information with another person to verify that the acts have taken place. If possible, get a witness to attest to the action(s).

♦ *Find a way to speak out.* Make a statement to someone in the personnel or human resources department of your organization or university, alert your supervisor or campus counselor, and confront the perpetrator.

♦ *Seek out supportive individuals.* More and more businesses and institutions are designating safe zones: a person or department responsible for providing resources for persons who perceive that they have been harassed.

♦ *Seek out institutional and company channels and use them.*

♦ *File a charge with a local, state, or federal antidiscrimination agency if necessary.* As with any other legal action, it will be your responsibility to prove the harassing actions or verbalizations. Be sure you can document the accusations.

If a friend tells you that he or she has been or is being harassed, you should:

♦ *Listen without judging.*

♦ *Validate that sexual harassment is wrong.*

♦ *Offer to help explore resources and support the recipient's efforts to seek help.*

♦ *Be prepared for displaced anger because the recipient may not be able to channel it appropriately.* In some instances, a person who is feeling stressed attacks the nearest source. So don't be surprised if the victim turns her or his wrath on you, even if you are trying to be helpful. The person is not really attacking you, but is just acting out of frustration.

♦ *Offer affirmation to the recipient that whatever feelings are being expressed are his or her right to have.* Victims sometimes are confused and don't trust their own judgment. They need affirmation as to their rights and responsibilities.

♦ *Reassure the recipient that you care and are there to be supportive.* Offer to be of assistance in whatever way you can, but be aware that you are not the person who was harassed.

♦ *Do not take matters into your own hands; rather, help the individual to find the appropriate channels either inside or outside the company or other institution.* Unless you are a lawyer or a mental health professional, be aware of your limitations.

Relationships and Their Development

Throughout our lives, we find ourselves in relationships with other people: parents, siblings, friends, and coworkers. After all, most of us do not suddenly grow up and no longer need caring and nurturing contact with others. This reality makes it extremely important that we understand how relationships develop, how they continue, what constitutes a positive relationship, how to communicate effectively within the structure of a relationship, and how to deal with relational endings.

Development of a Relationship

Relationships vary so greatly that it is almost impossible to formulate any rules about them. Nevertheless, some general principles explain how they develop.[50] Within the first moments of a relationship, internal (that is, intrapersonal) decisions are being formulated that can determine the functions and goals of the relationship. Whether the relationship will be primarily task oriented, friendship oriented, or intimate oriented more often than not is formulated with the initial interaction.[51]

When two persons meet for the first time, their levels of uncertainty about each other and themselves are fairly high. This uncertainty is generated because people can behave in a number of ways; thus, accurate prediction of behavior and beliefs is difficult. And initial encounters can cause uncertainty in the future as well because predicting behavior is always difficult, and little or no information has been exchanged between the two.

Powerful barriers to establishing intimate connections exist: *fear of exposure* (the decision not to tell certain things as they may be perceived as weaknesses or make you an undesirable partner); *fear of abandonment* (if the relationship begins, what happens if the other person decides to leave it?); *fear of reprisal or attack* (what if something goes wrong, and the other person physically or verbally assaults me?); *fear of loss of control* (especially a male issue, based on not being able to make decisions for and about oneself); *fear of loss of individuality* (the potential loss of *me* as *I* and *you* become a *we*); and *fear of creating a power imbalance* (the potential for relinquishing power to the partner, thus losing your own power).

Think back to your first meeting with a good friend, your spouse or lover, or a coworker. What went on during that first encounter? Why did you decide to pursue

First Impression

Try this simple tip to help you project a good first impression: Notice the color of a person's eyes as you shake hands. *Why it works:* You'll gain strong eye contact in a way that shows you care.

Source: Secrets of Power Persuasion, by Roger Dawson, Prentice Hall, Englewood Cliffs, NJ 07632. © Communication Briefings, www.briefings.com, 1101 King Street, Alexandria, VA 22314. Used with permission.

Intimacy depends on clear communication, maintaining a balance of independence and interdependence, and knowledge of the sequential patterns of relational development and maintenance.

the relationship? Did your attitudes change as you got to know the person better? How long did it take you to decide to pursue the relationship? We ask all these questions each time we encounter others and decide how far to allow the interaction to go.

It also is recognized that developing intimacy is difficult. Intimacy depends on acceptance of self, acceptance of others, clear communication, maintaining a balance of power, maintaining a balance of independence and interdependence, and knowledge of the sequential patterns of relational development and maintenance.

Relationships do have a sequential pattern: an *entry phase* (beginning), a *personal phase* (middle), and an *exit phase* (end) (see Figure 6.4). In the **entry relational development phase,** biographical information and general attitudes are exchanged. In the **personal relational phase,** information about central attitudes and values is exchanged. In the **exit relational stage,** questions concerning the future of the relationship are raised and resolved. This stage may include an agreement to continue the affiliation (continuing the personal phase) or terminate it. Each relationship does not necessarily move through the stages at the same rate. The personalities and needs of the participants determine the rapidity of the movement through the stage.

[handwritten margin note: 1) Entry 2) Personal 3) Exit]

Continuing a Relationship

People make judgments about interpersonal contacts by comparing relational rewards and costs—the **economic model of relationships.**[52] As long as rewards are equal to or exceed costs, the relationship will usually become more intimate; however, once costs exceed rewards, the relationship may begin to stagnate and eventually dissolves.

If one person believes that the investment (**relational costs**) of such factors as money, time, and emotion is met with such factors as security and affection (**relational rewards**), then that person will want to continue the relationship. If the person is doing all the giving and the partner is only taking, however, then the relationship will probably end.

[handwritten margin note: costs: money time emotion   rewards: security affection]

With this in mind, examine a relationship that you have. You probably have continued to associate with this person because you receive at least as much as you

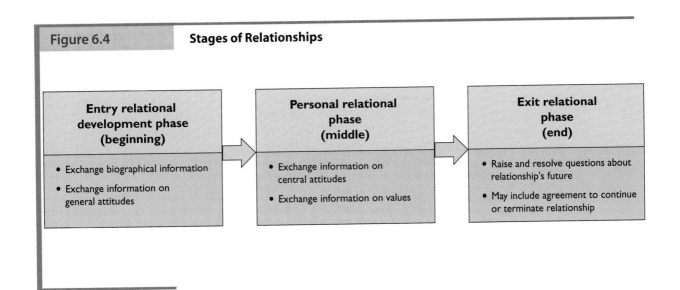

Figure 6.4	**Stages of Relationships**

Entry relational development phase (beginning)	**Personal relational phase (middle)**	**Exit relational phase (end)**
• Exchange biographical information • Exchange information on general attitudes	• Exchange information on central attitudes • Exchange information on values	• Raise and resolve questions about relationship's future • May include agreement to continue or terminate relationship

are giving from knowing and being with the person. In contrast, if you have taken the initiative to end an association with someone, you probably believed that you were giving too much and not receiving enough; the relationship was tilted against you, or it was one-sided.

Positive Relationships

A good relationship allows freedom of expression and reflects acceptance of the idea that the feelings of both people are important. We should remember, however, that any alliance experiences times of uncertainty and anxiety. The persons may change as individuals, what appeared to be fulfilling the economic model may no longer do so, and the reason for the relationship may cease to be.

We also must recognize that we cannot achieve happiness through someone else. If it is to be found, it must be found within ourselves. Unfortunately, this desire to find happiness in someone else causes us to try changing people we supposedly love when in fact we should allow them to be themselves and do what they feel is best for themselves. Love is the ability and willingness to allow those for whom you care to be what they choose for themselves without any insistence that they satisfy you. Unfortunately, this idea is easier to present as a concept than to live as a reality. Most of us spend a great deal of our time trying to alter and change the people we supposedly love.

Communication is the key to creating and maintaining positive relationships. Research shows that couples who are happily married argue no less vigorously for their own positions than do those who are not happily married. But happily married couples come to agreement fairly readily, through either one partner's conceding to the other without resentment or compromise. Unhappily married people tend to get caught in a situation that seems like cross-complaining. Neither partner is willing to come halfway to resolve a dispute; each must continue to have his or her own way.[53]

One approach to successful relational communication centers on five guidelines for making a relationship flourish:

1. *When you are speaking, get into the habit of using "I" messages instead of "you" messages.* Indicate what you are feeling or how you are reacting to the situation rather than accusing the other person. Say "I feel . . ." or "I think . . ." rather than "You did . . ." or "You make me. . . ." Report facts to back up your contentions. Rather than saying, "You are always late" try "I get angry when you tell me you will be here at 2:00 and you arrive at 2:45."
2. *Respond to what the other person has said.* When you go off on a tangent without first having replied to the original statement, you are catching the other person unaware.
3. *Give the other person freedom of speech.* If you want to have the opportunity to state your view, you must also be willing to hear out the other person.
4. *Set aside frequent talking time for just the two of you.* We often get so busy that we forget to talk to each other. Don't assume the other person knows what you are thinking.
5. *Do not put labels on either yourself or the other person.* Name calling doesn't solve issues; stating the issue and discussing it can possibly solve it or at least get it out into the open. Moreover, when people get angry, labeling can become the source of attack and conflict. Saying, "You're stupid," is an invitation to a battle.

Also, watch out for some specific communication patterns that cause conflict in intimate relationships. Included among these are blaming, putting someone down, or teasing. In the case of teasing, what can start out as fun usually has an underlying message behind it that is not humor.

Game playing can result in relational trouble. Such activities as trying to make a person measure up to preset expectations, making an individual prove how much he or she loves you, and forcing someone with whom you have a relationship to follow your wishes can result in conflicts that are unreconcilable.

Another problem is **relational fusion,** which takes place when one partner defines, or attempts to define, reality for the other. In other words, the controller dictates what is good, right, and acceptable for the partner. If the partner allows that to happen, the pattern for the future can be set. Then, when the defined partner wants to break the pattern, abuse may result.

People who are unhappy in their relationships tend to talk at each other, past each other, or through each other, but rarely with or to each other. Just because you're talking doesn't mean you are communicating. Although couples may spend time talking to each other, many lack the skills to get their messages across effectively, express their feelings, or resolve conflicts without hurting each other or provoking anger.

Communication in Relationships

All relationships have a structure, and each person has a role. As long as no one changes the system, and each member of the relationship maintains the assigned role, the structure is working. But if someone wants alterations, wants to do things that are not normally done, then the system becomes a **dysfunctional system.** A system that is operating to the general satisfaction of the participants is a **functional system.** Assume, for example, that you are dating someone. You and that person look forward to your times together. When conflicts do arise, you are capable of working out the problems without destroying the relationship or building up bad feelings. In contrast, a dysfunctional system is one in which its members are confused about the roles they are to play. For example, if a woman who has been a stay-at-home mother decides to go to college, there will have to be a redistribution of her former chores in the family, and the family's old system of operation will be thrown out of kilter. Some members in the system may not want to change roles. The husband may not want to do the cooking or child care, or the children may resent not having their mother around. Before the system can become normal again, a new balance has to be established. This does not mean that the system has to return to the past mode of operation, but a mode of operation in which a pattern of cooperation exists must be instituted.

This does not mean to suggest that dysfunctional systems are not operational. The individuals in the relationship may continue to function quite effectively as they make changes. The usual result of the dysfunction, however, is confusion because each person lacks clarity about what role to play and what rules to follow. For example, questions and protests may arise as to who is responsible for the tasks formerly done by the mother and wife who is now going to college. Common complaints may include "Why should I have to make the meals now?" or "I've never cooked before, and it's not fair for that job to be shoved on me."

The need to reestablish a system is not necessarily disastrous. In fact, most relationships go through adjustments on a regular basis. As a system is being recalibrated—that is, restructured—growth can take place. People learn to assume new roles, develop new respect for each other, or make a new team effort. On the other hand, chaos may result as people fight for new role identities, defend their emotional territories, or feel compelled to make changes not to their liking.

In a positive relationship, the participants attempt to adjust to alterations in the normal patterns so that the dysfunctional period is kept to a minimum. This usually

communication is a system

takes place because the partners in the *dyad* (a relationship of two people) have developed effective communication skills and a positive method for solving problems.

Ending Relationships

Whenever we enter any type of relationship, we pay a price for it. A relationship takes time, energy, and commitment. It means giving up freedom, and it means considering another person, adapting to another person, even changing our lives to accommodate another person. When we enter into a relationship, there are possibilities not only for mutual sharing but also for mutual or individual hurt.

Whether we are dealing with dating, friendship, or marriage, we also must realize that these relationships will not go on forever. Rather, we need to accept that the ending of relationships is part of the life cycle. We grow up, relocate, change jobs, have different needs, grow in different directions, and ultimately die. Just as change is inevitable, so are endings (unless you believe in life everlasting, life after death, or reincarnation).

The breakup of a relationship can be hurtful. And this hurt usually comes with the realization that there has been heavy emotional and sometimes physical investment. At such times, we feel loss, question who we are, feel alone, search for the reason for the break, and sometimes experience guilt. These emotional difficulties are compounded when one party wants to terminate the relationship and the other does not.

Relationship endings can take many forms. In some cases, the people decide on a mutual split, go their separate ways, and feel little regret. In some cases, as, for instance, when you were a child and your best friend moved, you tried to keep in touch for a while and then your interests and need for each other faltered, and eventually memories faded away.

Sometimes, it is possible to leave a relationship, if not on a positive note, at least with a feeling of not being rejected or with some gain from the experience. This sort of ending is most likely to occur in a face-to-face meeting in which the participants take time to discuss their own observations and inferences about the relationship and each other in a productive fashion. Although this is seldom done, it can be an insightful experience.

Some intimate relationships end with the individuals agreeing to "still be friends." This is very difficult. Being friends is not the same as being in an intimate relationship. Much time and effort often have gone into the relationship, and reverting to a shallow version of the former relationship is almost impossible. Unfortunately, the endings of most relationships tend to be charged with tension and hostility over feelings of loss, failure, and rejection.

The role of computer-mediated communication as means of interacting with others, including the development of relationships, is an important emerging interpersonal communication issue.[54]

Computer-Mediated Interpersonal Communication

"**Computer-mediated communication** [CMC] continues to grow in use and popularity among academic, business, and private users."[55] In fact, electronic mail, instant messages, and computer conferencing have become substitutes, in many instances, for the telephone, faxes, voice mail, letters, and even face-to-face interaction. **CMC** includes all forms of communication using computers.

The use of the computer as an interpersonal communication tool is growing at an astronomical rate. A few years ago, there were only a few hundred thousand people who used high-speed Internet access. Now, "every day about 55 million Americans go online, and more than a third of them spend at least an hour on the Internet. A hard-core 16 percent of the users admit to spending more than three hours online a day."[56] "The average e-mail respondent spends 19 hours per week on-line" while sending 2.2 billion e-mail messages a day, compared with the 293 million pieces of first-class mail that are sent.[57]

Although CMC is made possible through an electronic vehicle, in reality it is about intrapersonal and interpersonal communication,[58] not just about computers and technology. A person's success in communicating via the Internet depends on knowing how to be a competent communicator besides knowing how the technology operates. The technology doesn't communicate. You communicate as you use the technology.

Interpersonal Uses of the Internet

Research illustrates that "many people now maintain their major relational contacts on the CMC."[59] People are motivated to communicate with others face to face to fulfill interpersonal needs. Inclusion, affection, and control are three primary interpersonal communication needs. *Inclusion* means to be included or include others in a group; *affection* refers to the need to express love or be loved by others; *control* is the need to exert power over others or allow others to exert power over you. Other reasons for using the Internet for interpersonal purposes are to gain pleasure, to relax, and to escape from everyday concerns.[60]

[handwritten margin note: 3° interpersonal comm. needs.]

All of these needs can be met on the Internet. "You can flirt, you can have an affair, you can even consummate the relationship in some way. While on the

Chatrooms are group interactions that allow simultaneous communicating among people on the Internet who select to participate according to their interests.

Internet[,] the person has a sense of belonging, a sense of identity."[61] Someone is listening; you are getting attention. You can send and receive information; you can agree and disagree with others. You can take time off from your everyday stress, relax, and gain pleasure by writing a friend or getting into a chatroom concerning an interest or hobby.

Many individuals use the Internet to nourish existing relationships. They can maintain contact with friends and family, make long-distance relationships feel closer, meet people, create and sustain new relationships, and even indulge in fantasies. Some people use e-mail to compensate for their lack of interpersonal skills.[62] Those who are introverted may not be able to use the "natural" method of satisfying their need for social interaction and may instead choose a substitute, complementary method such as online communication.[63]

The Net can offer power without responsibility.[64] Although many people would not argue face-to-face with someone, on the Internet, especially when dealing with strangers, the meek can become bold. They feel they have nothing to lose.

If the person on the other end is a stranger, for example, that person can't punish, fire, or divorce the writer. Even when there are repercussions for certain actions, they may not be severe. If a moderator banishes an individual from an e-mail discussion group, for example, the person can simply join another group or use a new e-mail address and name to resubscribe to the group. The risks are often low compared with those of face-to-face communication.

"E-mail offers users chances to develop positive attitudes but can also offer some undesirable behaviors."[65] What are the positive and negative behaviors and consequences?

Positive Aspects of Internet Use

People list such benefits as receiving pleasure, relaxing, and escaping as positive reasons for using the Internet. Taking a break from school or job-centered work, interacting with someone you haven't seen for a while, catching up on what's happening, or being able to escape for a short time into a fantasy world can also have positive effects.

Many people use the Internet to improve themselves by taking courses or conducting school research online. Others use the Internet to look for employment and to conduct business (**e-commerce**). The rich variety and ease of access to the Internet makes information available to people as never before. The phenomenon of online stock market trading, for example, enables any consumer to access information previously only held by stockbrokers. New information, new ideas, new contacts, and new ways of developing and using creativity may result.

Through the Internet, people who would never come together under traditional, face-to-face circumstances have the opportunity to connect online. This interaction with strangers can offer unique opportunities for growth, confrontation of prejudices, and opening of the mind and heart. "The anonymity of the Net lets you judge and be judged on factors other than race, age, sex, disability and so on. That can be very intoxicating."[66]

The Internet also offers enormous flexibility. People can deal with e-communications when they have time to do so. There is no need to return a call at a particular time. There is no risk of interrupting an individual who is busy. The noninvasive nature of e-mail allows each individual to handle communications in his or her own time and own way. People can take a break from work while at their desks and talk to someone via e-mail. As the lines between work and play are blurred, individuals can use the Internet to make their work more pleasant.

The computer can serve as the "second self," engaging the individual in intrapersonal communication and self-exploration available in no other way. Writing via computer can be a form of self-expression, for example, a type of journalizing to an audience.[67]

E-mail is fast and inexpensive. Most people can type a message to an intended receiver faster than they can place a phone call. It also can be timesaving as e-mail messages tend to be brief and to the point with few or no side conversations, such as those that occur during phone calls.

Some people communicate better in writing than orally. They can write and rewrite, choose their words carefully, and not risk mistakes common to the spontaneity of oral communication.

Individuals can initiate, create, and sustain satisfying relationships online with people they meet and enhance relationships with those who are already in their lives. In addition, it has been found that collaborating by electronic mail leads to effective decision making.[68]

The collegiate environment offers many positive communication opportunities. Not only can the Net be used for research and for making contacts with other students in order to learn assignments and share class notes, but students can also contact instructors who otherwise might be unapproachable. "Seventy to 80 percent of U.S. university faculty report using electronic messages to communicate with students and colleagues."[69] Sometimes because of fear of negative face-to-face reactions, cultural patterns that restrict them from speaking directly to an authority figure, or shyness, students don't approach professors. For example, some Asian students have been brought up not to lose face by admitting that they don't know information or not to cause others to lose face, such as by asking questions of authority figures who may not know the answers. Such students feel more comfortable asking for the information online.

CMC can create a sense of community among people. Some schools have created virtual classrooms that bring together distance education students, allowing them to work online without ever stepping onto a conventional campus.

Some people have turned to chatrooms to supplement their psychological needs. Support groups can enable a person to interact with individuals who have similar problems or issues. People in remote areas can find others who can be of assistance. Isolated gay youth, women with breast cancer, and couples who have lost children can find willing interactive voices on the Net.[70]

Negative Aspects of Internet Use

In spite of all the positive aspects of CMC use, it also has its negative aspects and, therefore, has its detractors.

There is some evidence that an individual can become so involved in Internet usage that he or she can use it to the point of neglecting personal and work responsibilities and/or becoming socially isolated.[71] A study of college students, for example, found that 73 percent of students accessed the Internet at least once a week. Thirteen percent of these students indicated that their computer use interfered with personal functioning.[72]

Excessive computer users tend to be those who are described as having one or more of the feelings of loneliness, isolation, boredom, depression, anger, or frustration. One study indicated that "about 71 percent were diagnosed as suffering from bipolar disorder, commonly called manic depression."[73]

The psychological "causes" for excessive usage may be long- or short-term. For example, in the short term, a college freshman who feels isolated after leaving the security of home may turn to the Internet to deal with her social isolation until she makes school friends and feels secure in her new environment. Or a shy person may find that meeting people on the Internet can allow him to make initial personal contacts, thus allowing him to overcome the first fear of introductions and offer the possibility of meeting in person later after he has established some intimacy with an individual. On the other hand, the Internet is also a means for those who suffer sexual addiction and pedophilia to externalize their fantasies.

Excessive computer use may also be a symptom of other problems. Whether calling it *computer addiction, impulse control disorder, internet addictive disorder,* or the most commonly used term, **cyberaddiction,** Internet critics list addiction as the major negative aspect of Net usage.

Symptoms of cyberaddiction include lying about or hiding your level of Internet usage, being preoccupied with using the Internet, and neglecting almost everything else in your life. It's like a craving that a person continues to satisfy despite the problems it is causing.[74]

There is some evidence to indicate that those who are obsessive in their use of the Internet may experience such consequences as lost jobs, academic problems, marital problems, mounting debts, broken trust, and being caught in lies and cover-ups.[75]

Realistically, most people will use the Internet with discretion and experience few, if any, problems. In fact, research has shown that 90 percent of people go online to do what they need to do and then get off. It's the other 10 percent who are the problem users.[76]

The key question to ask yourself in regard to your Internet usage might be "Is my online time disrupting my face-to-face relationships, allowing me to hide from participating in face-to-face interactions, or forcing me to put on hold other elements of my life?"

If you think you are overdoing the media connectedness, ask yourself what you could do instead of spending all this time online. If your answers indicate that your time would be better spent in other pursuits, but you simply can't motivate yourself to cease your overuse, realize that there are ways to make changes. You might want to consider learning how to control the computer so that it doesn't control you and to set definite time limits for your computer use. If you can't do this on your own, getting involved in some face-to-face therapy or searching out a support group of cyberaddicts might be advisable.[77]

There may be other negatives in Internet usage. For example, "people who spend even a few hours a week online experience higher levels of depression and loneliness than if they used the computer network less frequently."[78] "Researchers were generally surprised by the findings, because they appear to be counter-intuitive to what we know about how socially the Internet is being used."[79] Analysis of the Internet probably brings to light why the study produced these results. "E-mail is totally devoid of social cues. It lacks any subliminal information—facial movement, body language, even dress or handwriting." "Without the normal face-to-face feedback, attachments form quickly. People move from casual chat to intimacy with startling speed. It requires a lot of care to avoid disappointment later." "What you saw in print and what you get in person are two different things." "People experiment with their identity on-line, both deliberately and unconsciously. It's not uncommon for someone with an introverted personality to be bolder on-line, or for people to be more playful than they normally would be face-to-face." The notion of a real self and a virtual self becomes outmoded in the wired world.[80] Because of this, people who are naive or trusting often get hurt and are disappointed.

People online can become the victims of flaming. **Flaming,** e-mail aggression or e-mail abuse, occurs when individuals exchange hostile or insulting remarks. Flaming can create problems in e-mail conversations. Because there is no direct personal contact, some people feel they can get away with verbally abusing others. There are few consequences for the abuser online. People who are controlled and nonassertive in face-to-face communication and don't have the skills to defend themselves may well become victims of flamers.[81] Or those same people may feel powerful in being able to flame and get away with what they wouldn't do in face-to-face conversations.

The opposite of flaming is **e-mail ignoring.** When someone takes the time and energy to write to write an e-mail or correspond, people expect a response within a day or two. That does not necessarily happen, and being ignored often prompts confusion about what the behavior means. The ignoring may be caused by a person's overwhelming

quantity of e-mail, wanting to avoid conflict, or wanting to end a time- or energy-consuming interaction.

Internet users may deal with ideas from a wide array of people, and sometimes doing that challenges their belief systems and threatens the values by which they live. Individuals may find it difficult to tolerate the intrapersonal conflict they experience when they are exposed to ideas that are not familiar, asked to evaluate long-held beliefs, or challenged to defend their ideas or values.

The amount of face-to-face interpersonal communication can be depleted as people spend more and more of their time on the Internet. Historically, businesspeople have screened their access so that they can use their time efficiently. E-mail allows anyone who can find a person's e-mail address to contact the individual quickly and directly. A barrage of work-related e-mail from unknown sources or continuous online business communication received during vacation or home time can negatively affect the use of a person's time. E-mail stifles conversation,[82] with a resulting decline in interaction with family members and a reduction in a person's circle of friends that directly corresponds to the amount of time he or she spends online.[83]

Another negative aspect of the Internet is that people may use it for devious means. Cases of rapes, teen runaways, invasion of privacy, harassment, and stalking that had their basis in e-mail and instant messages have been reported. Kids have sent bomb threats to schools and hate mail to teachers thinking that they could get away with these acts because they didn't use their real identity.[84] Be aware that there have been instances of cyberstalking on the Internet. **Cyberstalking** centers on following and harassing both males and females. In many cases, the cyberstalker and the victim had a prior relationship, and the cyberstalking began when the victim attempted to break off the relationship. However, there also have been many instances of cyberstalking by strangers. Relatively few states have laws against cyberstalking, but since 1995, the FBI has arrested almost three hundred individuals who stalked children online. Given the enormous amount of personal information available through the Internet, a cyberstalker can easily locate private information about a potential victim with a few mouse clicks or key strokes.[85] In order to protect yourself or your child from stalking, you might want to follow these suggestions:

1. Create a gender-neutral name, not one that reveals your interests or your gender.
2. Remove all gender and personal information from your user profile.
3. Make your e-mail signature dull, businesslike, and gender neutral.
4. Check your e-mail headers, which may be sending inappropriate information without your knowledge.
5. If you like controversial talk, use a remailer such as **http://www.well.com/ user/abacard/re-mail.html**.
6. If you find yourself being victimized online, the classic advice is to ignore the stalker. Even responding to the person's e-mail to say, "Leave me alone" just encourages him or her. Remember, those of us who are playing with a full deck don't send anonymous and menacing cyber threats. Your best bet is to hope that your cyberstalker will get bored by your lack of response.[86]

Developing Personal Relationships Online

The development of personal relationships is a pivotal issue in the larger debate about human relations in cyberspace. On one side are those who view online relationships as shallow, impersonal, and often hostile. The other side argues that computer-mediated communication liberates interpersonal relations from the confines of physical locality and thus creates opportunities for new, but nevertheless genuine, personal relationships and communities.[87]

When searching personal advertisements or entering chatrooms, you should remember that "CMC filters out demographic and socioeconomic information about the user, such as sex and social status, which also limits relational meaning."[88] People may lie because they feel that they cannot be discovered. They may switch their sexes, ages, locations, or personal appearance data. How are you to know? You can't see them! People are motivated to communicate by means other than face to face to fulfill interpersonal needs, and their needs may not include being honest with you.

Some people talk about their face-to-face relationships as their "real" friends as distinguished from their "online" friends. Although the relationships may differ, both are real, but they may serve different purposes. Associations maintained over long distances ultimately do not provide the kind of support and reciprocity that typically contribute to a sense of psychological security and happiness. Think about it. Why is your best friend your best friend? Probably because he or she has been there for you when you needed him or her. That person was there to pat you on the shoulder, bring you medicine when you needed it, and act as a support system. On the other hand, best friends can use e-interactions to enhance a relationship by providing contact between face-to-face meetings.

That person on the Internet who is many miles away isn't immediately with you. Before you break off any present-tense relationships, move, or fly thousands of miles to meet that "perfect" cybernet person, heed what was related by a couple who met and "dated" for almost two years on the Internet and who then actually decided to get married: "Despite the fact that we had been in steady communication—exploring each other's likes and dislikes and becoming intimate enough to marry—when we finally met face-to-face, we had a lot more exploring and adjusting to do."[89] This was the experience of a success-story couple. Most Internet relationships don't end up this happily.

Strategies for Effective Online Communication

Computer-mediated interpersonal communication is here to stay. You can now access the Internet through your cell phone. Imagine wearing a pair of glasses, in which one lens is actually a computer screen. Imagine wearing a computer on your body that recognizes individuals you have met previously and reminds you of the meeting even when your memory fails to recognize the person. Current ideas under development suggest that computers will continue to be integrated more closely into our personal communication.

How can you be a competent interpersonal cybercommunicator?

◆ Know that you may not get a response to your e-mail messages. Many people receive a large volume of e-mail, may delete days' worth of mail, may select "no mail," or may be selective about responding when they are busy. You may have to repeat your message or alter your channel of communication and use the telephone or fax machine to make sure that your message has arrived and will be answered.

◆ Remember that some e-mail users become irritated with comments that continue the sending of e-mails back and forth needlessly. Watch for cues that tell you that a correspondence has reached its climax. Such messages as "That about does it for this topic," "We seem to have concluded this," or "I'll get back to you when I have something more to say" are forecasters of conversational closings.

◆ Know that since the preference is for efficiency, there is no need for a standard letter salutation or closure.

◆ Be considerate. If you do not have time to answer an e-mail immediately, a short response telling the sender that you will deal with the matter within a set period of time is often appreciated. If you are going to be gone for a period of time, you might want to let people in your address book know so that they don't expect immediate responses.

◆ Be aware that there is no such thing as a private e-mail conversation. In many businesses, for example, the electronic window, a device that allows managers to monitor e-mail, exists. If you don't want others to know what sites you are visiting or the content of personal messages you are sending, don't use your business computer for such purposes.

◆ Recognize that software is available that can enable your employer, service provider, a disgruntled colleague, or the legal system to use your computer-mediated communication against you. Programs are available that supposedly can break the password of any account. Again, don't use your business computer if you don't want others to know what sites you are visiting or the content of your personal messages.

Netiquette

Here are some tips to keep in mind when minding your online manners:

1. **Always Respond**
Junk mail and forwards are one thing, but you should always respond to a real message, whether it's to invite you to a meeting or a hello from an old friend.

2. **What's the Story?**
Don't keep your readers in suspense. Use the subject line to alert the receiver to the subject matter of your message. You're likely to get a faster response.

3. **Addresses Ad nauseam**
When sending out an e-mail to a long list of recipients, consider using an address book function that doesn't list all recipients in the "to" header. Having to scroll past a long list of addresses to get to the message itself is annoying to many. Plus, many people may not like having their e-mail address displayed to others.

4. **Rapid Fire Responses**
If you only check your e-mail once a week, let people know. Otherwise, they may take offense at not receiving a timely (which when it comes to e-mail can mean immediate) response from you.

5. **Watch Your Language**
While our e-mail culture is full of its own shorthand, it's best to always reread your messages before sending to make sure there are no grammatical or spelling errors in your message.

6. Know Your Role

If you're sending out e-mail that is religious, political, or pornographic, be sure to know that your intended recipient wants to receive it. In many business settings, transferring pornographic materials via e-mail is grounds for dismissal.

7. Avoid Spam

When you surf or shop retail sites on the Internet, watch out for the "free newsletter" and "customer update" e-mail check boxes. If you sign up, you will be receiving regular e-mail that may not interest you.

8. Keep It Professional

At work, keep all personal information out of e-mail. This isn't the venue for dissing coworkers or spilling the beans about your weekend adventures with the copier man.

9. Selectively Select

"Send to All." Only the most relevant work-related messages should be sent to "all" recipients. Private messages or messages that apply only to a few recipients should never be sent this way.

Reprinted by permission from the Emily Post Institute, www.emilypost.com.

◆ An e-mail attachment can contain a virus designed to destroy your computer system. Be careful about what messages you open. Be aware of the latest computer bugs and their message titles. Don't open any message that you perceive might contain a virus.

◆ Remember, your computer provides "cookies" to most Internet sites so that companies, law enforcement, and stalkers can track back to you and your computer. The notions of Internet safety and anonymity are just illusions. Do not assume that you are anonymous and protected on the Internet.

◆ Be aware that your employer owns your e-mails and that e-mail messages that are encoded by the company's computers are being kept on its Internet provider. A rule of good sense is "Don't say anything on the Internet that you would be ashamed to have your family, boss, or best friend read."

◆ Remember that harassment charges can be lodged regarding e-mail. For example, if you send a private e-mail to a friend that contains gender-centered jokes or if you send racist humor to another person, you can be charged with harassment. Be careful about quickly sending out copies of those "funny jokes" you receive without considering the consequences. Be aware of what sexual, religious, racial, gender, and sexual-orientation harassment is and that you can be legally libel for both same- and other-sex harassment. "Two black employees brought a $60 million racial discrimination case against a U.S. investment bank after racist jokes were allegedly circulated on its e-mail system."[90]

◆ Be aware that you can't take e-mail back. Once it is sent, it is sent. Also remember that the receiver might forward the message to other people without your permission. Take your time when writing and sending e-mail. If you are angry or upset, don't pound your feelings out on the keyboard. Stop and think about whether that's really what you will want to say tomorrow.

◆ Be aware that most educational institutions and businesses prohibit chain letters, virus alerts, and similar e-mails because they overburden the server with useless e-mail.

◆ Be aware that voyeurs can use electronic devices to record your private moments, then rebroadcast your photos and videos on the Internet. Ask yourself, when sending photos and videos, whether you are willing for others to view them, and be aware that you are dealing with information that could be viewed by others.

◆ Before you flame, you might want to consider extinguishing the message. You are libel for any abusive, aggressive, or deliberately antisocial e-mail you send.

◆ Remember that "there is no intonation, affect, [or] facial expression . . . [as] e-mail offers only bare words."[91] To make your e-mail more expressive, pretend you are writing a novel. Include in the information necessary descriptive material so that your receiver can visualize what you are talking about and know the feelings you are expressing.

◆ If you use e-bbreviations, make sure that the person receiving your message will understand their meaning. If he or she wouldn't, don't use them. Though instant messages, individual chats, and e-mails tend to lend themselves to brevity, don't forsake meaning for that succinctness. Make sure that your message is complete.

◆ Be aware that there are those who manipulate. As with any type of good listening, ask whether what's being said is reasonable, whether it makes sense, if the sender is taking responsibility for what is being said, and if there are facts and examples that lead you to the conclusion or solution being proposed.

As a sender and receiver of CMC, be a wise and responsible consumer and communicator.

In Conclusion

This chapter dealt with interpersonal communication, especially self-disclosure and relationships. Interpersonal communication is an interactional process in which meaning is stimulated through the sending and receiving of messages between two people. Our interpersonal communication is made up of both logic and emotion. The role of power is important in any relationship. The sequential pattern of a relationship is the entry phase (beginning), the personal phase (middle), and the exit phase (end). People make judgments about interpersonal relationships based on comparisons of rewards and costs. In a functional system, members are clear about the roles they are to play. Males and females do not communicate in the same way. Computer-mediated communication (CMC) continues to grow in use and popularity among academic, business, and private users. As a sender and receiver of CMC, be a wise and responsible communicator.

Learn by Doing

1. Think of an interpersonal problem you have had. Then, on a three-by-five-inch card, describe your role and the role taken by the other person. The class will be divided into groups of three. Read your card to the other two people in your group, and find out how each of them would have handled the situation. After the discussion, tell them what you did and what the outcome was.

2. Relate to the class a recent personal experience that illustrates the action-reaction principle.

3. Think back to a relationship you had that has ended. Examine it from the standpoint of the costs and rewards theory discussed in the chapter.

4. What do you consider the most difficult part of developing a relationship? Give examples to back up your contention.

5. Relate an experience you had in which power was an important element in a relationship. Was the power used to aid or destroy the relationship? If the power structure had been eliminated, would the relationship have been the same? Why or why not?

6. Relate a personal experience in which your emotions totally dominated your logic and you said or did something for which you were sorry later.

7. Discuss the statement "Sometimes you have to blow your own horn because no one else knows how to play the tune."

8. Be prepared to take a stand on these topics:
   a. Men are being verbally bashed by women as women attempt to get what they call *equal rights*.

Family and relational communication is dependent upon one's being a competent interpersonal communicator.

b. Stereotyping males and females by their communication patterns is a disservice because it teaches people how others act and sets those patterns for others to follow.

c. The pop-psychology treatment of male and female communication has trivialized the valid research on the subject.

9. Select one of the following topics, and relate a personal experience or an incident a friend or relative has had: developing personal relationships online, cyberaddiction, people changing demographics online, flaming, e-lingo, e-bbreviations.

10. How Powerful Do You Feel?[92]

Think of one of your important relationships and keep it in mind as you respond to the following questionnaire. Each item has two alternatives. Your task is to divide 10 points between the two alternatives according to how well each describes you. You may give all 10 points to one alternative and none to the other; split the points evenly, 5 and 5; or assign any other combination of 10 points that seems appropriate.

1. When the other person says something with which I disagree, I
   _____ a. assume my position is correct.
   _____ b. assume what the other person says is correct.
2. When I get angry at the other person, I
   _____ a. ask the other person to stop the behavior that offends me.
   _____ b. say little, not knowing quite what to do.
3. When something goes wrong in the relationship, I
   _____ a. try to solve the problem.
   _____ b. try to find out who's at fault.
4. When I participate in the relationship, it is important that I
   _____ a. live up to my own expectations.
   _____ b. live up to the expectations of the other person.
5. In general, I try to surround myself with people
   _____ a. whom I respect.
   _____ b. who respect me.

Scoring:

Add all of your *a* responses. *a* = _____

Add all of your *b* responses. *b* = _____

Each of the two totals, *a* and *b*, indicate how powerful you feel in the relationship you chose. The total number of points is 50, so one score could be 50 and the other zero, although that is unlikely.

If your *b* score is greater than your *a* score by 10 or more points, you probably feel somewhat powerless in your relationship because you see the other person's choices as more important than your own.

If your two scores are within 10 points of each other, you are probably unsure of your own power and your potential to influence others.

If your *a* score is greater than your *b* score by 10 or more points, you most likely feel quite powerful and in control of the choices you make in the relationship.

11. Investigate the concept of *cyberstalking*. E-mail or cyberchat with a member of your class concerning your findings. Then summarize your results and e-mail them to your instructor. You might want to start your research by referring to the "1999 Report on Cyberstalking" at **http://www.usdoj.gov/criminal/cyber-crime/cyberstalking.htm** and **http://www.mgrossmanlaw.com/articles/1997/cyberstalking.htm**.

12. Use CMC to connect creatively with your friends and family. (a) Send an online greeting card for silly holidays (e.g., for a friend's non-birthday, passing a math test, or a twelfth-day anniversary). Yahoo.com, among others, offers a free greeting card service. (b) Use e-commerce to order a gift to be delivered to an acquaintance's pet. (c) Create and send an ASC art picture to a friend. (d) Set up an "add on to this" type of chain letter for a group of friends. Doing this will save the time of writing individual messages to each person on the list. Be prepared to report on what the reactions were to your efforts.

13. A rE-mailer can be an important tool to use in interpersonal communication. Do you know what a rE-mailer is? See **http://www.well.com/user/abacard/rE-mail.html**.

14. The following are some topics and questions that you might want to probe. Your instructor will tell you the format for processing your inquiry.

  a. Is it better to convey bad news via the computer rather than on the telephone or face to face?
  b. How can one convey nonverbals on the Internet?
  c. What are at least ten guidelines regarding writing style on the Internet?
  d. How does computer-mediated interpersonal communication differ from two-way direct communication in the workplace?
  e. What is the role of computer-mediated interpersonal communication for the college student?
  f. What is the effect of psychological distancing on interpersonal communication?
  g. What are some personal guidelines, beyond those discussed in the text, regarding cyberaddiction? Start your search by referring to the Internet Addiction Test at **//netaddiction.com/resources/iaindex.htm**, the Internet Addiction Survey at **www.stresscure.com/hrn/addiction.html**, and "Problems, and How to Cope with Addiction" at **www.stresscure.com/hrn/ iaddct.html**.
  h. What is an Internet relay chat?
  i. Define and explain the virtual community.
  j. What is the role of information overload on the Internet?
  k. Compare and contrast electronic and traditional mail.
  l. What is computer phobia?
  m. What are the advantages of teaching or learning via the Internet?

n. Make a list of twenty-five e-bbreviations.

o. What is meant by the term *online personalities*? Start your research by reading "A Guide to Cybercharacters," *U.S. News and World Report*, March 22, 1999, p. 61.

p. What are *techno prisoners*?

q. List five guidelines for the use of humor on the Internet.

r. Research David Greenfield's *Virtual Addiction: Help for Netheads, Cyberfreaks, and Those Who Love Them* (New Harbinger Publications) at **www.newharbinger.com**. Then summarize the advice of the author.

s. Research Patricia Wallace's *The Psychology of the Internet* (New York: Cambridge University Press) at **www.cup.org**. Then summarize the advice of the author.

t. Can anyone find a lasting relationship via an online international dating service? The U.S. government doesn't keep statistics on the topic, but investigate and see what you think about this exploding phenomenon. You may want to conduct this search via a lab computer so that you aren't tracked back to your home computer and end up receiving a lot of junk mail. Get online, start searching, and see what conclusions you reach.

u. Examine the report on the use of computers in the home from the National Science Foundation at **http://www.nsf.gov/sbe/srs/issuebrf/ sib00314.htm**. What are its implications for interpersonal communication?

Key Terms

action-reaction principle	entry relational development phase
self-love	personal relational phase
self-disclosure	exit relational stage
self-perceived I	economic model of relationships
other-perceived Me	relational costs
self-fulfilled person	relational rewards
compliance gaining	relational fusion
power	dysfunctional system
expert power	functional system
referent power	recalibrated system
reward power	computer-mediated communication
coercive power	CMC
legitimate power	e-commerce
competitive turn taking	cyberaddiction
tag questions	flaming
androgyny	e-mail ignoring
sexual harassment	cyberstalking

7

Interpersonal Skills

After reading this chapter, you should be able to

- Explain the presentational, listening, and nonverbal concepts of conversation

- State the rules for giving details, organizing ideas, and using appropriate terms in giving directions

- Discuss the process of ascertaining information, asking for change, and questioning

- Discuss the process of apologizing

- Define conflict and interpersonal conflict

- Define anger and explain it as a negative and positive emotion

- Explain negotiation, avoidance, accommodation/ smoothing over, compromise, competition, integration, and fighting fair as ways to deal with conflict

- Differentiate the win-lose, lose-lose, and win-win styles of negotiation

- Demonstrate the simple, empathic, follow-up assertions and DESC scripting

- Explain techniques for handling rejection and criticism

E very day you participate in the act of interpersonal communication. You converse with friends, negotiate with members of your family, become involved in conflicts, and send messages to and receive messages from your instructors. To participate successfully in all of these interactions, you need to master certain interpersonal skills, including how to participate in conversations, give directions, request, ask questions, resolve conflicts, accomplish goals, and handle rejection and criticism.

Participating in Conversations

A **conversation** is an interaction with at least one other person. Almost all of us possess basic conversational skills. Nevertheless, some people try to avoid conversations. Others have difficulty starting and maintaining social interactions even if they are not communicatively apprehensive. Still others need improvement in their conversational skills.

Conversational Presentation Skills

Conversations usually start with small talk and then move to more in-depth sharing. **Small talk** is an exchange of information with someone on a surface level. It takes place at informal gatherings, parties, bars, and meetings. The information exchange centers on biographics (name, occupation or college major, home town, college attended or attending) or slightly more personal information (hobbies, interests, future plans, acquaintances). Small talk usually lasts for about fifteen minutes, and then in-depth conversation starts. The ground level of communication has

finding common interest key to good conversation

Conversations usually start with small talk and then move to more in-depth sharing.

Handling Tough Conversations

If you want to avoid potential stress for you and those you're dealing with, consider these suggestions when you think you're going to be in a stressful conversation:

◆ **Begin** with agreement. If you know you're going to be disagreeing with someone, start off your discussion with some area on which you both agree. Even if it requires really digging to uncover that common ground, do it.

◆ **Say** "and"—not "but." "But" acts like an eraser inside people's heads. It erases the value of anything said before it in a sentence.

◆ **Use lots** of "I" statements. Limit "you" statements. "I" clarifies for the other person what you think and feel while "you" can make a person feel criticized. "I" also reduces defensiveness and fosters communication.

Source: Adapted from *Career Success: Personal Stress,* by Christine A. Leatz with Dr. Mark W. Stolar. McGraw-Hill, Inc., 11 W. 19th St., New York, NY 10011. © Communication Briefings, www.briefings.com, 1101 King Street, Alexandria, VA 22314. Used with permission.

been passed when people start talking about personal matters, such as attitudes, beliefs, goals, and specific ways of behaving, or express the desire for social or business interaction, such as a date, a business lunch, or a visit to each other's residence.

You will find that people usually like to talk about themselves and their experiences. For example, you can ask about where a person lives, what it is like to live there, what his or her job is. You can ask whether a person likes the job and how she or he chose it. The key to good conversation is to hit on a common interest between you and the other person.

Other approaches can help you to become a good conversationalist. Keep track of current events; watch nonverbal clues; show interest; if you disagree and want to state your opinion but do not want to offend, try to be tactful. You can say, for instance, "I see your point, but have you considered . . . ?" Another approach is to make a comment about an aspect of the situation you are both in or an observation about the person you are talking with. Say something positive about the person's appearance, ask for advice, or ask a question.

Questions are powerful devices for building conversations. In using questions, remember:

◆ *Questions encourage people to open up by drawing them out* (e.g., What university do you go to? What's your major? I've been considering switching my major to communication; do you think that's a good idea?).

◆ *Questions aid you in discovering the other's attitudes* (e.g., Why did you decide to be a communication major?).

◆ *Questions keep the conversation to the topic at hand.* Whenever a response is irrelevant, ask a follow-up question that probes for more information about the topic (e.g., What do you feel the future job market is for communication majors?).

◆ *Questions can be used to direct the conversation.* A question can change the topic, probe for more information, or keep the conversation going.

◆ *Questions help you gain information and clarify meanings.* If what the person says is not clear, ask for definitions or examples or for the source or basis of information.

To use questioning most effectively, start with easy questions; ask short questions; after each question, wait for an answer; and let your partner know you are listening by giving nonverbal feedback such as nodding or smiling while you are looking at the person.

One of the biggest problems for people who are nervous about conversations is staying calm and not giving themselves negative messages like "I'm really messing this up." Periods of silence are all right. If the other person does not want to talk to you, that is his or her loss, not yours. You are your own worst enemy if you convince yourself that you cannot carry on a conversation and that the other person is superior to you.

Specific suggestions for conversational improvement include the following:

- Turn the spotlight on the other person. Discover the person's interests. People are usually flattered by your interest in them.
- Listen closely for a nugget to explore that will interest you both. Follow these up with such comments as "What did you mean by that?" "Oh, that must have been exciting," "It sounds as if that was tough on you."
- Keep it light. Stay away from controversial subjects on your first meeting. If you need to voice your opinion, indicate it with a soft phrase such as "I can see we look at that differently," or "That's an interesting opinion."[1]

Remember that some people are difficult to get to know and that there are some people you may not want to get to know any better. The small talk at the start of a conversation often gives you and a new acquaintance an opportunity to determine whether a closer relationship merits exploring.

Be aware, too, that not all people converse in the same way. In the United States, people are constantly coming into contact with individuals who are from other cultures. In general, white European American males engage in focused conversations; they get right to the point. Behind this is the assumption that a speaker ought to know explicitly the idea or information he or she wishes to convey. European Americans speak in thought patterns emphasizing analysis, which dissects events and concepts into pieces that can be linked into chains and categorized. **Analytical thinking** is not typical for all cultures, however. **Holistic thinking,** which doesn't dissect events or concepts, is more typical in South American and some Asian cultures and for people descended from those cultures.[2] Storytelling, as a form of interacting, is common in holistic thinking. Although the stories may be interesting, they sometimes confuse European Americans since the stories don't answer questions and often don't come to conclusions.

In addition, European Americans generally are open to approaching strangers, often start conversations with strangers, and are responsive to strangers who approach them. Those from other cultures may not be as open to invasion of personal space. Asians are generally more standoffish toward strangers, are more reluctant to approach them, and respond less favorably to conversations initiated by people they do not know.[3]

Conversational Listening Skills

Listening is a very important part of conversations. People who can converse with strangers are invariably good listeners. To be a good conversationalist, repeat the person's name as you are introduced, continue to use the name during the conversation because the repetition will help you remember it and make the other person feel that you are centering on him or her, maintain eye contact, and listen to clues for what topics are of interest to the other conversant. Learn how to paraphrase the speaker's ideas, but be sure to allow the speaker to finish a point before you respond to it because interruptions can be very annoying, especially to European American women and those from mannerly cultures (e.g., Japan). Listening in conversations requires some strategies:

Listen to the concerns of others. Conversations should be two-sided, with both people having the opportunity to participate. Often people ask questions only so that they can give their own answers. You already know what you think. If you are interested in a conversation, not in giving a personal speech, find out what others think and address their ideas. An I-I conversation can be very unsatisfying.

Don't assume. Too often we assume one thing and later find we were mistaken. Because physical and oral first impressions are not always accurate, give the other person a chance to prove he or she is worthy of your conversation or repugnant enough to cast aside.

Before speaking, ask yourself what message is needed. Many people do not like to participate in small talk because it appears to offer no opportunity for in-depth discussion or because finding out little tidbits about people in whom they are not interested seems a waste of time. These contentions may be true, but you cannot get to know a person to the degree necessary to have in-depth conversations until you get to know him or her on a basic level and build rapport. People who start right off by stating strong viewpoints and getting too personal often are rebuffed.

Conversational Nonverbal Skills

Nonverbal communication plays an important role in conversation. If you do not think so, pay attention to the facial expressions and postures of the person with whom you are speaking. For example, quick glances away may indicate that the person is anxious to leave, and the same may be implied when that person glances repeatedly at a watch, looks around the room, or shifts from one foot to the other. If, however, the person leans forward, is intently looking at you, or is directly facing you, then the interaction is probably positive. Judge whether to continue or end the interaction based on these cues.

Giving Directions

We often find ourselves giving other people **directions**—for example, instructions for accomplishing a task, achieving an effect, or getting somewhere. In giving directions, include all the necessary details, organize the ideas in a specific order, and use clearly understood terms.

Giving Details

How many times have you asked someone for directions and been given only a very general description? Others assume that because they know what they are talking about, you do too. "Go down the street to the corner and make a right" may be very clear if you know what street and which corner the person means. Unfortunately, such is not always the case. On the other hand, too many details can be confusing.

Have you ever been frustrated by your attempt to assemble an electronic device that was accompanied by vague directions? Directions are commonly written by the experts who designed the item. They often assume that because they know what to do, you too can figure out how to do the assembly.

When providing directions, try to be as specific as possible. Include such information as names, references (north, south; left, right), descriptions (the size of the item, a sketch of what it looks like), and warnings about where confusion may set in. The procedure should be the same whether you are giving travel directions, assembly information, or a recipe.

Organizing Ideas

Directions are easiest to follow when they are given in a chronological or a spatial order. In a chronological order, you indicate the step-by-step procedure by telling what is to be done first, second, third, and so on. This is a good method to use when explaining how something should be assembled.

Spatial orders involve providing descriptions according to geographic directions. A travel plan from the auto club indicating the exact place where you start and the place-by-place order of the cities you will go through is an example of directions that are in spatial order.

Knowing if someone is a linear or global thinker (see Chapter 5 for details and a test to determine your style) can aid you in deciding how to package the directions. Linear thinkers prefer maps and written-out directions. Global thinkers pre-

We often find ourselves giving other people directions.

fer pictures and oral directions with specific landmarks (the identification of indicators such as restaurants and gas stations by name).

Using Understandable Terms

If a person cannot understand the directions, then the explanation is of no value. For this reason, make sure that any terms you use are clear; if you think they might not be, define them. The prospect of operating a computer is often more terrifying than it should be because in many instances the operational procedures are written in computer jargon rather than Standard American English. No wonder so many people have computer phobia! Unfortunately, the writers of many computer manuals appear not to have taken the potential users into consideration, although increased pressure has caused some manufacturers to make manuals more "user friendly" by defining terms, writing from the consumer's standpoint, and including visual aids.

Requesting

Requesting is the process of expressing a desire for something. The request, in some situations, takes on the form of a demand. Requests usually fall into one of two categories: requesting information or asking.

Be SPECIFIC in requests

Requesting Information

When you request information, specify the exact nature of the information you want and make the request in language that includes a suggestion as to how the request is to be carried out. If you ask the research librarian, for example, to tell you about Lucerne, Switzerland, she or he can give you volumes of information. But what specifically do you want to know? Maybe you are interested in finding out the most recent population statistics. Whatever your interest, try to be as specific as possible.

requesting change: be specific about problem + recommended soln.

If you are not presenting the request in person, indicate how you wish to receive the reply: by telephone, e-mail, fax, letter, or in person. If the information must be received by a deadline, be sure to specify this as well. This rounds off the entire process so that you and the other person both understand exactly what is wanted and how the request is to be processed.

Asking Questions

People often do not ask questions because they are afraid to do so, do not know how to ask them, or do not know what to ask. The reluctance to ask questions has become a major communication gap in academic, personal, and professional environments.[4] Students often sit in class not understanding the concepts being presented. However, when the instructor asks if there are any questions, they fail to take advantage of the opportunity for clarity. Employees, when given instructions for accomplishing a task, may not ask for clarification, even though they don't understand them. Personal relationships may be endangered because participants don't understand what another person is saying but won't state their lack of knowledge. Gaining the skills involved in **asking**—seeking out information by inquiring—will help you to eliminate misunderstandings, aid you in ensuring receipt of your

When you request information, specify the exact nature of the information you want.

intended message, reassure you that you gained the proper information, and convince the sender that you really do understand.

Asking questions is important to effective communication. If, for example, a person receives directions to institute a new procedure at work, he or she may need to ask questions of the supervisor or trainer who is providing the instructions. A worker who is reluctant to ask for clarification for fear of appearing uninformed is probably just creating more problems for himself. Later, when called on to perform the new procedure, he may be unable to do so. Remember that if something is important to know, it is important to ask questions.

When you ask questions that probe for information, word the queries in a way so that the listener will know exactly what you need. To do this, determine what it is that you do not understand. Ask a specific question that will clarify your dilemma. If you cannot identify what you do not understand, recognize that confusion usually centers on the need for restatement, definition, or clarification.

Don't understand, then ask for :
1) restatement
2) definition
3) clarification

Asking for Restatement   Sometimes in explaining, people state their ideas in such a way that the concepts are unclear. This confusion may be caused by the order in which the ideas were presented. For example, an explanation of an accounting procedure that does not tell the first step, the second step, and so on, will probably lead to confusion. In this case, ask for the ideas to be presented in a step-by-step sequence. This is especially true if you are a linear listener and learner. Linear listeners generally need a clear step-by-step structure to organize the ideas, thus leading to clarity.

Asking for Definitions   Unclear vocabulary is a major problem in understanding information. Asking someone to define terms often clears up the misunderstanding. This is usually the problem, for example, with physicians who use medical terms to explain a patient's illness. Many professionals forget that the average person does not have much expertise in the subject and therefore does not have access to technical terminology. An explanation appropriate to the layperson's vocabulary is necessary.

Each time you are introduced to a new subject area, you must learn its vocabulary. Chemistry, psychology, and communication, for example, all have a special vocabulary. Students who fail these subjects often do so because they are weak in the subject's vocabulary. In asking for definition, be specific. Ask, "What does [fill in the word] mean?"

Asking for Clarification   Sometimes the basic information in a communication message is simply not enough. In this case, clarification can be achieved through the use of examples, illustrations, and analogies for the clarification. For example, while listening to a lecture, you will find that the first few sentences dealing with each new concept tell the idea, and the rest of the statements clarify. Sometimes, however, senders forget to give examples, illustrations, or analogies. If the illustrations used are not clear, ask for new or additional ones. This is especially true if you are a global listener and learner. Global listeners generally need examples to clarify and make abstract ideas concrete.

As you sit in class, participate in a medical examination, or are being trained to operate a piece of equipment, try to paraphrase what the speaker is saying. If you cannot do so, you probably do not understand the message. In that case, ask questions—specific questions!

Dealing with Interpersonal Conflict

When you hear the word *conflict*, what do you think? If you are fairly typical, your list includes such terms as a *fight, dissension, friction, strife*, and *confrontation*. These terms tend to be negative, and many of us have been taught to think of conflict as a totally negative experience—something to be avoided at all costs. In truth, conflict in and of itself is a natural process that can be negative or positive, depending on how it is used. The Chinese word for *conflict* or *crisis* is made up of two components (Figure 7.1). The top figure stands for "danger" and the bottom section stands for "opportunity." Most people recognize the danger part in a crisis or conflict, but few recognize the opportunity. Conflict can promote relational changes, bring people together, precipitate personal growth, or aid in gaining personal and relational insights.

Conflict Defined

"A **conflict** is any situation in which you perceive that another person, with whom you're interdependent, is frustrating or might frustrate the satisfaction of some concern, need, want, or desire of yours."[5] "The source of conflict or crisis could be your perception of a limited resource (such as money) or an individual difference between you and the other person (such as differences in gender or differences in how you and the other person define your relationship)."[6] Conflict is part of everyone's life.

Figure 7.1

In Chinese the words *danger* (top) and *opportunity* (bottom) are components of the word *crisis*.

The process of conflict begins when one person perceives that another person has caused him or her to experience some type of frustration, thus they experience interference from each other in accomplishing their goals.[7] This frustration, if put into words, would sound like this: "I *want* [your personal concern, need, want], *but* [the person perceived as frustrating you] *wants* [his or her concern, need, want]." From these feelings or statements comes a conflict or crisis situation in which incompatible activities are present. These activities prevent, block, or interfere with each other or in some way irritate the participants. "Any situation in which one person perceives that another person, with whom he or she is interdependent, is interfering with his or her goal achievement may be defined as a conflict situation. . . . If it is not expressed in some way, but kept bottled up inside, it is an intrapersonal conflict."[8]

Some people try to avoid conflict at any cost. Indeed, one study indicated that "students try to avoid about 56 percent of their conflicts. They become skilled at turning away from conflict."[9] This sort of behavior is generally not desirable. Conflict can be healthy because it allows for the communication of differing points of view, which can lead to important awareness and changes.

Just as conflict can serve a useful function, so too can it be detrimental. Conflict is detrimental when it stops you from doing your work; threatens the integrity of a relationship; endangers the continuation of a relationship or your ability to function within it; causes physical, mental, or sexual abuse; or leads a person to give up and become inactive in a relationship or life in general.

Not all cultures deal with conflict in the same way. In most of the Middle Eastern and Mediterranean cultures, which are considered **conflict-active societies,** conflict is accepted as an important part of life, and men especially take great delight and pleasure in haggling and arguing. Haggling is expected when purchasing goods in many Central and South American and Arabic countries. People from **conflict-avoidance societies** believe that face-to-face confrontations are to be avoided.[10] Asians find haggling distasteful.[11] For example, a Chinese proverb states, "The first person to raise his voice loses the argument."

The conflict-avoidance aversion in Japan includes not resolving disputes with lawyers. It is estimated that the Japanese have only one lawyer for every ten thousand people; in the United States, a conflict-active society, there is one lawyer for every fifty people.[12] Since most of the readers of this book will be dealing with conflict in the predominantly Euro-American society, an investigation of that society's conflict patterns will be undertaken; however, even if you are European American, remember that because the United States and Canada are nations of immigrants, a great number of the people with whom you come in contact have strong other-cultural ties and may follow the patterns of their native culture.

Causes of Conflict

Think back to instances when you were involved in a conflict. What preceded the conflict? What were the causes of the conflict that ensued? Four major issues have been identified as the root causes of conflicts.[13] These issues center on goals, allocation of resources, decision making, and behaviors.

Goals to be pursued. Communication often centers on someone's desiring that you do what they want you to do while you are interested in doing what you want to do. A friend asks you to do her a favor that you don't want to do. A parent tells a high school senior what college to attend or what major to pursue. A boss insists that the only right way to perform the employee's job is the boss's way. All these are examples of goals one person is trying to set for someone else.

Allocation of resources. We only have so much time. We only have so much money. When someone asks us to expend our resources, we may get stressed. This stress can lead to conflict between parties. You have a term paper due in two days. A friend asks you to go to a party with her. You indicate that you are on a short calendar. She insists that you have lots of time and that the party will be fun. Or remember the time when you asked your parents for a new jacket, or a car, or a computer? They tried to explain that money was short, but that meant little as your needs were the most important issue. A battle followed. Often the acting out of these conflicts involves statements such as

[handwritten margin note: 4 major root causes of conflict]

Conflict is detrimental when it stops you from doing your work or accomplishing a goal.

"You're stingy," "Everyone else's parents get them what they need," and "You are a selfish brat."

Decisions to be made. Decisions that are appropriate for one person may not be appropriate for another. This situation becomes a source of conflict when someone attempts to force another person to go along with her decision. Another conflict can center on how decisions are made. People generally don't go along with or like decisions made about themselves that don't include their input. Employers who impose working hours on employees without obtaining their input may find themselves at the center of a storm. Teenagers often rebel over what they consider to be imposed solutions to their problems. Conflicts concerning whom a woman can date, what time she has to return from that date, and even what she can wear can cause wars.

Behaviors that are considered inappropriate. Each of us has certain parameters by which we live our lives, and we often expect others to follow our lead. If a person deviates from that course, we consider the person's behavior inappropriate. A person's displaying a lack of manners in a restaurant, wearing "inappropriate" clothing, or drawing unnecessary attention to himself or herself may be the cause of conflict. "You embarrass me when you act like that" may be the statement that stimulates conflict.

Levels of Conflict

As with all other heightening of emotions, conflict develops sequentially and can be understood by examining the levels it travels through. These steps seem present in every type of conflict, ranging from neighborly spats to family disagreements, marital problems, labor negotiations, and international incidents (see Figure 7.2).[14] The levels are:

Level 1: No conflict. The individuals face no key differences in goals.

Level 2: Latent conflict. One person senses a problem and believes that goal differences exist. Yet the other gives no sign of noticing such differences or tries to deny that differences exist.

Level 3: Problems to solve. The people express concerns that focus on interests. They choose to confront the problem and take the courage to face the risks associated with that confrontation. The goals do not include personal attacks that move the conflict toward a destructive orientation.

Figure 7.2

Levels of Conflict

Level 1
No conflict

Level 2
Latent conflict
- One person senses conflict
- Other person does not agree

Level 3
Problems to solve
- People express concerns
- People confront problems
- Avoid personal attacks

Level 4
Dispute
- Problem to solve carries needs-centered conflict
- Individuals fight about issue, but personal attacks move conflict toward destructive orientation

Level 5
Help
- People may get help when dispute becomes unmanageable
- Help can come from friends, mental health professionals, conciliators, mediators, arbitrators, or adjudicators
- Third party should be neutral and invited
- Help can be directive or non-directive
- Third party should manage procedure, not solve dispute (unless required to do so by law)
- Persons forced into solutions almost always resent them

Level 6
Fight or flight
- If help fails or help is not sought:
  - people move against one another
  - people try to defeat one another
  - people try to destroy one another
  - people try to escape the situation
- Fight: physical or verbal aggression, battering, or even murder take place
- Flight: Getting divorced or quitting job may be action chosen

Level 7
Intractability
- When people remain at Level 6 for a long time, sustaining conflict becomes more important than resolving it
- Conflict may continue until people destroy one another or give up

Level 4: Dispute. There is a problem to solve that carries with it a needs-centered conflict. The individuals fight about an issue but insert frequent personal attacks that move the conflict toward a destructive orientation.

Level 5: Help. When people can no longer manage their dispute because it has gotten out of control, they often seek help. The help can be from friends, relatives, or a professional such as a mental health worker, conciliator, mediator, arbitrator, or adjudicator. It is best if the third party is neutral and invited to participate rather than intrudes. The assistance can be directive or nondirective, but unless required to do so by law, the third party should manage the procedure, not solve the conflict. Individuals forced into a solution, such as in court-decreed divorces and child custody cases and arbitrated labor-management conflicts, almost always hold resentments.

Level 6: Fight or flight. If the help fails or the parties become so angry that they don't think of asking for help, they either move against and try to defeat or destroy one another (such as in declaring war), or they try to escape from the situation, such as when a teenager runs away from home. It is at the fight stage that physical and verbal aggression, battering, or even murder may take place. At the flight level, getting divorced or quitting a job may be the chosen action.

Level 7: Intractability. When people remain at the fight-or-flight level for a long period of time, sustaining the conflict becomes more important than resolving it. That is, the conflict gains a life of its own. People abandon hope for a constructive solution. The conflict may continue until the parties destroy one another or lose the will to continue to fight.

Role of Personal Anger in Conflict

Explaining their reactions to conflict, a person may say something like "He made me mad" or "I was so angry I couldn't control myself." These are statements expressing the emotion of anger.

Anger is the feeling of being upset with yourself or others (or both). "Anger is a signal, and one worth listening to. Our anger may be a message that we are being hurt, that our rights are being violated, that our needs or wants are not being adequately met, or simply that something is not right."[15] With the possible exception of anger caused by organic problems, such as illness, most angry episodes are social events. The participants are you and yourself, or you and someone or some group of others. You can be angry at yourself because you allowed yourself to be taken advantage of, for not standing up for your rights, or for doing something that you now know was not the right way to act. Or your anger may be aimed at another or others for what you perceive he, she, or they did to you or said to you or about you, or didn't say or do.

Anger is not a disease with a single cause; it is a process, a transaction, a way of communicating. You communicate to yourself first that something is wrong, and then, in some cases you communicate that knowledge to others. Sometimes your anger is below your level of awareness; you know something is wrong, but you don't know what it is. Anger assumes meaning only when you are aware of it or express it to yourself or others. Anger is emotional, not logical. You get angry emotionally, and you often express that emotion by attacking yourself or someone else. Anger isn't a problem, but the way you express that anger can make it into a problem.

Anger can be *implosive.* You can beat yourself up in various ways: negative self-talk; overuse of drugs, alcohol, or food; self-mutilation; or suicide. Or anger can be *explosive:* you attack others through physical or verbal abuse, cutting off verbal or social contact, removing love, restricting financial support, or disowning them.

Once you are aware of the feeling of anger, you identify what it is and its cause by putting the feelings into words. Think back to the last time you were feeling angry. Using that information, fill in the blanks in this statement: *I want/wanted* _____, *but* [name the person/s] _____ *wants/wanted or didn't want/didn't want to* _____. For example, "I wanted to leave to go to dinner, but James kept wasting time." Being able to verbalize what is bothering you often makes it possible for you to understand what is happening and decide what to do about it.

Normally we perceive anger to be a negative feeling. You get mad at yourself for not acting or because you did the wrong thing, and you deal with it negatively by getting depressed, reacting with defensive behavior, allowing it to affect you physically, or starting to doubt yourself. We know that internalized anger can result in headaches, tension, and depression. It can also result in legal and psychological effects if you attack someone verbally or physically. On the other hand, it can be positive if you use the anger to alert yourself to what's wrong, figure out how to deal with it constructively, and act in a responsible way.

Choices for Anger

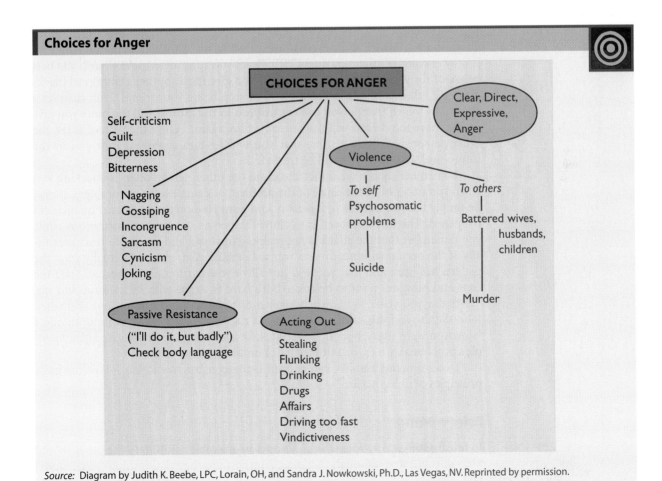

Source: Diagram by Judith K. Beebe, LPC, Lorain, OH, and Sandra J. Nowkowski, Ph.D., Las Vegas, NV. Reprinted by permission.

(handwritten margin note: Constructive ways to deal w/ anger)

(handwritten margin note: — Recognize diminished capacity for clear thinking)

There are some techniques that can affect your interpersonal expression of the anger so that it can be a constructive rather than a destructive action. Consider, for example:[16]

◆ *Do not react immediately when you are angered.* The count-to-ten technique is often effective. It stops you from acting on only your emotions and allows you to think through the ramifications of your actions.

◆ *If possible, don't make important decisions in the heat of an angry moment.* A moment of emotional stress is not the time to fire anybody or tell your spouse or lover that your relationship is over.

◆ *Use the extra energy generated by anger to act constructively.* When you experience anger (or its first cousin, fear), your body activates its **fight-or-flight** (stay and battle it out or run away) **mechanism.** This results in an increased flow of adrenaline that makes you temporarily stronger than usual. But instead of beating up someone, go for a fast-paced walk.

◆ *Apologize if necessary.* If you really behave badly during a fit of anger, an apology to those who have been affected is in order. A simple "I'm sorry; I was angry" will probably do. Sometimes you need to go further and make an "I" statement of what motivated your outburst.

Dealing with Another Person's Anger in Conflict

To deal with someone else's anger, one expert advises, "Don't let them dump on you; it only encourages their craziness."[17] Instead, you must determine what is the best behavior for you and then carry it out. If you give in to another's emotional blackmail (e.g., threats that he will leave you or stop being your friend), you have set a pattern by which that person can control you in the future. And the more you give in, the more the person will use the same ploy again.[18] Once the pattern is set, the other person will likely assume that you will let him aggress against you in the future, and that's how you will be treated.

Remember that in a conflict situation, the other person often is attacking you when you may not be the cause of the problem or cannot solve the problem. It may be simply that you are the first person who wandered on the scene after an incident happened. The best approach is to allow the person to vent her frustrations while you remember that the attack is not really against you and try not to react personally. If the person continually uses you as her scapegoat, recount factually what the pattern has been and that you will not allow yourself to be a scapegoat. State the facts and how you want to be treated. It's hard to argue with facts! You could say, "Yesterday you yelled at me when Mary didn't get her report in on time and when John didn't reach his sales quota. I wasn't responsible for either of those things. I know you were angry, but I'd appreciate it in the future if you discussed other people's problems with them, not take it out on me."

Disagreements actually can end up being constructive if you follow the basic principles of fighting fair.[19]

Fair Fighting

(handwritten margin note: participants keep both issue & relationship)

In **fair fighting,** participants work toward an amicable solution to the problem and keep in mind that although the issue is important, the relationship is also important, such as with marital or other relational partners, children and parents, and friends. Some fair-fighting strategies include the following:

Fair fighting strategies:

◆ *Get as much information as you can, and attempt to adjust to the problem based on this information.* Fact, rather than hearsay, may show that the supposed cause of the conflict is not the actual cause.

◆ *Keep arguments in the present tense.* Do not argue about what happened in the past; that can't be changed.

◆ *Do not try to make the other person change things that cannot be altered.* We cannot trade in our relatives, extensively alter our physical appearance, or become a totally different person.

◆ *Do not start a fight when it cannot be finished.* It is not appropriate to start a stressful discussion when a person is walking out the door on the way to work or on a tight schedule or when one or both parties are extremely tired.

◆ *The setting can affect a conflict.* Disagreeing in public *public v. private* or in front of individuals who are not part of the conflict is not a good strategy. It can bring about embarrassment not only to the participants but also to the observers.

◆ *A fight can take place only if both parties participate.* If the conflict is getting out of hand or has gone on too long, then one party should simply stop participating. The length of a constructive argument is normally about twenty minutes; people get tired, and their reasonable intentions break down after that. When the participants start repeating the same arguments, they have run out of concepts regarding the issue, and it is not uncommon, at that point, for one of the participants to start attacking the other person rather than dealing with the issue.[20]

◆ *Listen to your body.* If you are aware of your voice getting louder, your body tightening up, or you are making fighting fists, you should either physically leave or limit your role to that of a passive listener for a while.

◆ *Identify realistically what you need to get out of the transaction.* Often we enter into a conflict situation without having identified our goals, which means we have no clarity of purpose and don't even know if the conflict is over.[21]

If possible, don't make important decisions in the heat of an angry moment.

- walk thru argument before hand

Individual Approaches to Dealing with Conflict

People react differently in dealing with conflict. Some people pull back, some attack, and others take responsibility for themselves and their needs. Most of us use a primary style for confronting conflict. (To determine your usual conflict management style, do Activity 1 in the Learn by Doing section at the end of this chapter.) Knowing your style and its ramifications can be helpful in determining whether you are pleased with your interpersonal communication conflict management style. If you are not, you may need to acquire the skills to make a change in your habitual pattern. The styles of conflict management are avoidance, accommodation/smoothing

Negotiation— bargaining to reach agreement -requires explicit statement 1) Accommodation 2) compromise 3) competition

In most of the Middle Eastern and Mediterranean cultures, conflict is accepted as an important part of life, and men especially take great delight in haggling and arguing.

over, compromise, competition/aggression, and integration (see Figure 7.3).

Avoidance   Some people choose to confront conflict by engaging in **conflict avoidance**—not confronting the conflict. They sidestep, postpone, or ignore the issue.[22] They simply put up with the status quo, no matter how unpleasant. While seemingly unproductive, avoidance may actually be a good style if the situation is a short-term one or of minor importance. If, however, the problem is really bothering you or is persistent, then it should be dealt with. Avoiding the issue often uses up a great deal of energy without resolving the aggravating situation. Very seldom do avoiders feel that they have been in a win-win situation. Avoiders usually lose a chunk of their self-respect since they so clearly downplay their own concerns in favor of the other person's. Avoiders frequently were brought up in environments in which they were told to be nice and not to argue, and eventually bad things would go away. Or they were brought up in homes where verbal or physical abuse were present, and to avoid these types of reactions, they hide from conflict.

↗ Giving in

Accommodation/Smoothing Over   People who attempt to manage conflict through **conflict accommodation** put the needs of others ahead of their own, thereby giving in. Accommodators meet the needs of others and don't assert their own.[23] In this situation, the accommodator often feels like the "good person" for having given the other person his or her own way. This is perfectly acceptable if the other person's needs really are more important. But unfortunately, accommodators tend to follow the pattern no matter what the situation. Thus, they often are taken advantage of, and they seldom get their needs met. Accommodators commonly come from backgrounds where they were exposed to a martyr who gave and gave and got little but put on a happy face. They also tend to be people who have little self-respect and try to earn praise by being nice to everyone.

A form of accommodation known as **conflict smoothing over** seeks above all else to preserve the image that everything is okay. Through smoothing over, people sometimes get what they want, but just as often they do not. Usually they feel they have more to say and have not totally satisfied themselves.

As with avoidance and accommodation, smoothing over occasionally can be useful. If, for example, the relationship between two people is more important than the subject they happen to be disagreeing about, then smoothing over may be the best approach. Keep in mind, however, that smoothing over does not solve the conflict; it just pushes it aside. It may very well recur in the future.

Those who use this technique as their normal means of confronting conflict often come from backgrounds in which the idea was stressed that being nice was the best way to be liked and popular. And being liked and popular was more important than satisfying their needs.

Compromise   Conflict **compromise** brings concerns out into the open in an attempt to satisfy the needs of both parties. It usually means "trading some of what

-Both give in
Both parties don't
lose/win

Figure 7.3

Personal Styles of Conflict Resolution

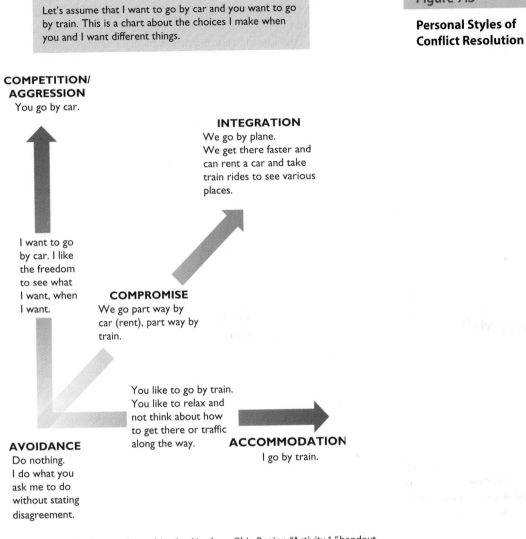

Let's assume that I want to go by car and you want to go by train. This is a chart about the choices I make when you and I want different things.

COMPETITION/ AGGRESSION
You go by car.

INTEGRATION
We go by plane.
We get there faster and can rent a car and take train rides to see various places.

I want to go by car. I like the freedom to see what I want, when I want.

COMPROMISE
We go part way by car (rent), part way by train.

AVOIDANCE
Do nothing.
I do what you ask me to do without stating disagreement.

You like to go by train. You like to relax and not think about how to get there or traffic along the way.

ACCOMMODATION
I go by train.

Source: National Conference for Community and Justice, Northern Ohio Region, "Activity 1," handout developed by Mary Adams Trujillo and Laurie Miller and distributed at the workshop "Responding to Conflict Around Issues of Difference," February 19, 1999, Cleveland, Ohio.

you want for some of what I want. It's meeting each other half way."[24] The definition of the word *compromise*, however, indicates the potential weakness of this approach, for it means that both individuals give in at least to some degree to reach a solution. As a result, neither usually completely achieves what she or he wants. This is not to say that compromise is an inherently poor method of conflict management. It is not, but it can lead to frustration unless both participants are willing to continue to work until both of their needs are being met. Those who are effective compromisers normally have had experience with negotiations and know that you have to give to get, but you don't have to give until it hurts. Those who tend to be weak in working toward a fair and equitable compromise believe that getting something is better than getting nothing at all. Therefore, they are willing to settle for anything, no matter how little.

Competition/Aggression   The main element in **conflict competition** is power. Its purpose is to "get another person to comply with or accept your point of view, or to do something that person may not want to do."[25] Someone has to win, and someone has to lose. This forcing mode, unfortunately, has been the European American way of operation in many situations—in athletic events, business deals, and interpersonal relations. Indeed, many people do not seem to be happy unless they are clear winners. Realize that if someone wins, someone else must lose. The overaggressive driver must force the other car off the road.

I wins ; I loses

The value of winning at all costs is debatable. Sometimes, even though we win, we lose in the long run. The hatred of a child for a parent caused by continuous losing, or the negative work environment resulting from a supervisor who must always be on top, may be much worse than the occasional loss of a battle. In dealing with persons from other cultures, European Americans sometimes are perceived as being pushy and aggressive. Many sales, friendships, and relationships have been lost based on the win-at-all-costs philosophy. Many of the aggressive behaviors in the personal lives of professional athletes are directly credited to their not being able to leave their win-at-all-costs attitude on the athletic field.

Integration   Communicators who handle their conflicts through **conflict integration** are concerned about their own needs as well as those of the other person. But unlike compromisers, they will not settle for only a partially satisfying solution. Integrators keep in mind that both parties can participate in a win-win resolution and are willing to collaborate. Thus, the most important aspect of integration is the realization that the relationship, the value of self-worth, and the issue are important. For this reason, integrative solutions often take a good deal of time and energy.

Win-win

People who are competitive, who are communication apprehensive, or who are nonassertive find it nearly impossible to use an integrative style of negotiation. They feel that they must win, or that they cannot stand up for their rights, or that they have no right to negotiate. In contrast, people who tend to have assertiveness skills and value the nature of relationships usually attempt to work toward integration.

Avoidance, accommodation, and smoothing over are all nonassertive acts; the person's needs are not met. Competition is an aggressive act in that the person gets his needs met at the expense of others. Integration is assertive since the objective is to get one's needs met without taking away the rights of someone else. Compromise, depending on how it is acted out, can be either nonassertive or assertive.

Apologizing

Have you ever angrily said something to another person? Have you offended someone by being sarcastic or joking around when your remark was perceived to be serious and not funny? Have you ever acted inappropriately toward someone whom you really like? If the answer to any of these is "yes," the question is, what did you do about it?

We all have said or done something we know has hurt or offended a personal friend, a significant other, or even a stranger. For many people brought up in the culture of the United States, one key to getting along with people is knowing when and how to **apologize,** to say you are sorry. How we react to having offended someone has a great deal to do with our background. If you've been brought up to fight for being right, not to give in, or to hold a grudge, you are not likely to consider apologizing. If you've been brought up to believe that the feelings of others supersede your own feelings, then making an apology is probably an automatic reaction.

Questions arise as to when it is appropriate to apologize and how to do it. For many people it is both hard to know when to apologize and difficult to apologize. You may be ashamed of your negative actions or have too much pride to admit to another that you did something wrong. Sometimes, even though you may want to apologize, you just may not know how. But remember that apologizing often solves the small problems and keeps them from getting bigger.

Traditionally, an apology basically has three stages. First, the person who has done the wrong should state exactly what he or she did. For example, the person could say, "I yelled at you after you told me that the idea I had presented at the meeting was wrong." Second, the perpetrator explains why he or she took the action. For example, the person could say, "I spent a lot of time on that solution, and I felt I had to defend myself." Third, a statement of remorse is made. For instance, the person could say, "I was upset, but I shouldn't have yelled. It didn't do anything to help deal with the task on which we were working." The reason the second step is optional is that you may not know why you took the action, or an explanation may incite further anxiety. If either of these situations is the case, it may be wise to skip that part of the process.

Does the process sound too formulaic or unnatural? It may well be, especially if you aren't in the habit of apologizing, but it lays out a pattern for verbalization that can and does work. Once you adopt the style, you may make adjustments to fit your own personality and situations, but at least you now have a format for the apology process.

The person who has been wronged may reject your apology. That is not your problem. If you offer an apology, and the apology is sincerely worded and felt, then whether the other person accepts or rejects the action is not the issue. You have fulfilled your obligation. You have recognized that what you did or said was wrong and have taken an action to let the other person know that you are remorseful. You can only be responsible for one person's actions, your own. You cannot make the other person act as you would like him or her to act. Therefore, acceptance of the apology is out of your hands. Don't go into the process of apologizing to receive forgiveness. Go in accepting that you are doing the right thing and that's your purpose.

Here are some additional tips that may make it easier to say you're sorry:[26]

Take responsibility. The starting point of any change of behavior is self-admission. Admit to yourself that you have offended someone. You may know this right away, the other person's reaction may let you know you have done something hurtful, someone else might alert you to the situation, or you may realize it yourself at a later time. However you find out, you must admit that you have done wrong and accept responsibility for your actions or you won't be prone to take action.

Explain. Recognize that your actions caused a problem for the other person. If you can do so, and it is appropriate, explain why you acted as you did. For example, if you were angry and blurted out something, you might say, "I was really having a bad day, and what I said wasn't really aimed at you. I was mad at myself, and I took my anger out on you. I'm sorry."

Show your regret. The other person needs to see that you are aware that what you did was wrong. That is, if you think you were wrong, say that you are sorry or ashamed with a statement such as "I felt bad the minute I told your secret. You trusted me, and I betrayed your trust. I shouldn't have done that." This, of course, is only appropriate if you are regretful. If not, the apology will sound phony and may cause a bigger conflict.

Repair the damage. To be complete, an apology should attempt to correct the injury. If you damaged someone's property, offer to fix it. If the damage is emotional, you might ask, "I'm really sorry. What can I do to make it up to you?" There may be nothing concrete you can do, but the offer is usually enough and shows your sincerity. You might follow up by saying something appropriate, such as "I'll try to keep my mouth shut in the future. In the meantime, let me buy you a cup of coffee."

Use good timing. If possible, apologize right away for little things. For example, if you bump into someone, say you're sorry right away. However, if you have done something more serious, like insult a friend out of anger, you may need some time to figure out exactly what to say. A quick apology might not give you time to realize what you've done, why you did it, and what the ramifications might be.

Choose an appropriate conduit. What's the best conduit for an apology? Letters, e-mail, voice mail, the phone, and speaking face to face are all message channels that are available. The first three are definitely impersonal. Using them may be easier and might save you from facing the person directly, but they are usually not as effective as other channels. Resort to using them only if there is no way to meet face to face. If a person lives far away, then there may be no choice. If that's the case, using the phone is probably a better alternative than a written presentation. At least hearing the tone of your voice can be a clue to the honesty of your message. If you do apologize by voice mail, "it is best to plan exactly what you want to say, and keep it to 30 seconds, never more than a minute."[27] Long, rambling messages quickly lose their impact.

A face-to-face apology is often best because you can display your honesty. It can be a humbling experience as you must see the other person's expressions, show yours, and probably hear a verbal reply. As one expert states, it is worth the anxiety since "you will be respected by the person [whom] you are addressing as well as by yourself more if you are able and willing to make your apology in this manner [face to face]. Smiles, laughter, hugs, handshakes, and other displays of appreciation and affection are added benefits for both parties that are all possible when apologizing this way!"[28]

It's not about who "won" or who "lost." Remember, life is not a war unless you or the other person makes it a war. Stubborn pride often leads to a loss of friends and can result in physical confrontations. "An apology is a tool to affirm the primacy of our connection with others."[29]

Communication Approaches to Managing Conflict

The communicative approaches to managing conflict are assertive communication, negotiation, arbitration, litigation, and mediation.

Assertive Communication

Have you ever found yourself saying, "I didn't want to come here, but she made me," or "I ordered this steak well done, and it's rare. Oh well, I guess I'll eat it anyway"? If so, the communication skill you probably were missing in either of these cases was the ability to be assertive.

Assertive Behavior Defined   **Assertive communication** takes place when a person stands up for and tries to achieve personal right without damaging others. It begins by acknowledging that you have a right to choose and control your life. A person who is assertive takes action instead of just thinking about it. Rather than saying, "Why didn't I tell her?" or "If the waiter was here now, I'd say . . . ," the assertive person takes action at the appropriate time.

The root of many communication problems is the lack of assertion. You know you are being taken advantage of and are upset because others are getting their needs met and you aren't. You may know how you feel but are afraid to state your needs because you're afraid somebody won't like you, you'll get in trouble, or you don't know exactly how to go about making your needs clear.

Assertion, Nonassertion, and Aggression   As illustrated in Table 7.1, the goal of assertive behavior is to communicate your needs through honest and direct communication.[30] **Assertiveness** does not mean taking advantage of others; it means taking charge of yourself and your world.

In contrast, the goal of **nonassertive behavior** is to avoid conflict. Nonassertive statements include "Think of others first," "Be modest," and "Let's keep the peace." The consequence of nonassertive behavior is that you do not get what you want. Because of this, anger may build, and you may be alienated from yourself and others.

The goal of **aggressive behavior** is to dominate, to get your own way. If you are aggressive, you are likely to make such statements as "Win at all costs," "Give them what they gave you," and "They only understand if they're yelled at." Aggressive behavior may well get you what you want, but it can also lead to alienation, thereby putting emotional distance between you and others that can lead to loneliness and frustration. **Direct aggression** is the outward expression of dominating or humiliating communication—for example: "That's the way it's going to be, and if you don't like it, that's tough. I'm bigger, and I'm stronger. You lose!" **Passive aggression** attacks or embarrasses in a manipulative way. This can be done by pretending that there is nothing wrong but, at the same time, derailing any attempt to solve a problem that isn't to your liking in a way that doesn't appear to be aggressive. Devices for passive aggression include using sarcasm that sounds like teasing, withholding something from the other person (some service, compliance with a request, or courtesy), or being sweet and polite but in fact controlling what is being done. Passive aggression is a common cultural pattern in places where direct aggression is considered bad manners, such as England, China, and Japan. In the United States, the direct aggressive sign would read, "No Dogs Allowed. This Means You and Your Mutt, Butt-Head!" In Britain it would say, "We Regret That in the Interest of Hygiene, Dogs Are Not Allowed on These Premises."

Principles of Assertiveness   To learn to use assertive communication, you might keep these basic principles in mind:

◆ *People are not mind readers.* You must ask for what you want. You must share your feelings if you are hurt, have been taken advantage of, or need assistance.

◆ *Habit is no reason for doing anything.* "That's the way it always has been," and "Our family tradition is . . ." are patterned statements. But the presence of a past pattern does not mean that change cannot occur.

◆ *You cannot make others happy.* Others make themselves happy, just as you make yourself happy. Much of our guilt has come from parents and friends who make us believe that if we do not act as they want us to, then we are causing them unhappiness.

◆ *Remind yourself that parents, spouses, friends, bosses, children, and others will often disapprove of your behavior and that their disapproval has nothing to do with who or what you are.* In almost any relationship, you will incur some disapproval.

◆ *Whenever you find yourself avoiding taking some action, ask yourself, "What's the worst thing that could happen to me?"* Before you let fear act on you, determine

Table 7.1	A Comparison of Nonassertive, Assertive, and Aggressive Behavior		
	Nonassertive	**Assertive**	**Aggressive**
Characteristics of the behavior	Does not express wants, ideas, and feelings, or expresses them in self-deprecating way Intent: to please	Expresses wants, ideas, and feelings in direct and appropriate ways Intent: to communicate	Expresses wants, ideas, and feelings at the expense of others Intent: to dominate or humiliate
Your feelings when you act this way	Anxious: Disappointed with yourself. Often angry and resentful later	Confident: You feel good about yourself at the time and later.	Self-righteous: Superior. Sometimes embarrassed later
Other people's feelings about themselves when you act this way	Guilty or superior	Respected, valued	Humiliated, hurt
Other people's feelings about you when you act this way	Irritation, pity, disgust	Usually respect	Anger, vengefulness
Outcome	Don't get what you want; anger builds up.	Often get what you want	Often get what you want at the expense of others. Others feel justified in "getting even."
Payoff	Avoids unpleasant situation, conflict, tension, and confrontation	Feels good; respected by others. Improved self-confidence. Relationships are improved.	Vents anger; feels superior.

Source: Created by Phyllis DeMark. Used with permission.

what the consequences of the action, the communication, are. If you would prefer to avoid these consequences, then by all means avoid the situation. But in most instances you will probably realize that the potential consequences aren't that bad.

◆ *Do not be victimized.* A *victimizer* is a person or establishment that interferes with another person's right to decide how to live his or her own life, and a *victim* is a person who is denied that right. Recent cases of sexual harassment illustrate that women and men have been made victims because they would not stand up to a victimizer. Victimization may be enacted by others, but it also can take the form of *self-victimization,* in which a person prevents himself or herself from deciding how to live. Self-victimizers often go through life thinking of themselves as failures or losers with no capability to achieve anything worthy.

   When people are functioning as assertive human beings, they use available resources to get out of victimizing situations and victimizing relationships. They report a sexual abuser or leave situations in which they are being victimized. These are communicative actions that say, "I am too valuable a person to be taken advantage of."

◆ *Worrying about something will not change it; only action will.* Worrying will not alter the past, the present, or the future. Instead, you must take some action to relieve yourself of anxiety.

◆ *Adopt the attitude that you will do the best you can, and if someone else does not like it, that is her or his problem, not yours.* You are responsible to only one person: you. If others cannot and will not accept that idea, that is their problem, not yours. This does not mean that you should not seek out information and advice from those whose opinions you respect; instead, it means that you do not need to seek reassurance for everything you do, think, and feel.

◆ *When you decide to be assertive, be aware of the consequences.* Actions have consequences. If you threaten to quit your job if you do not get a raise, you should be ready to start looking for another employer. Don't make a threat unless you are willing to accept the responsibility and take the action.

Assertiveness Skills   If you are not already assertive, you may have decided that you would like to be. Or if you are basically assertive but have not been extremely successful at it, it may be that you lack sufficient techniques to handle a variety of situations. In either case, some strategies can be of assistance to you.

   One assertiveness strategy is composed of the simple, empathic, and follow-up assertions. The use of this technique follows several stages. (See Table 7.2.) When you feel the need to be assertive, start with a **simple assertion** in which you state the facts relating to the existence of a problem. This may be enough to solve the problem because people are often unaware that something is bothering you or that they have done something you consider wrong. A simple assertion alerts them to the problem. If they act to eliminate the problem, the solution is at hand.

   Sometimes, however, you need to recognize the other person's position but state your own needs. This is an **empathic assertion.** It may follow a simple assertion or be the first step in the assertive process. By recognizing the other person's problems or rights, you may find that she understands that you are not on the attack and may then become quite cooperative.

   A **follow-up assertion** is used when the simple or empathic assertion is not successful in getting the desired action. It takes the form of a restatement of the simple

Table 7.2	1. *Simple assertion:* State the facts. If someone shoves ahead of you in the supermarket, you say, "I was here first."*
Three Types of Assertive Responses	2. *Empathic response:* You recognize the other's position but state your own needs. "I know you're probably in a hurry, but I was here first."*
	3. *Follow-up response:* Repeat a description of the person's behavior, then state your own position. "I was here first. I'd like you to go to the end of the line."*

*Remember that assertions should be made in a non-accusatory maner.
Source: Based on a concept of Judith Spencer. Used with permission.

or empathic assertion and then a statement of your own position, which may include a direct statement of the action you need or want.

Do not assume that by being assertive, you will always get your way. You may not, but you definitely have a better chance than if you are nonassertive. And you probably won't get the negative reactions that you might receive if you were aggressive.

DESC Scripting   **DESC scripting** is a way of dealing with interpersonal conflicts that centers on the process of **D**escribing, **E**xpressing, **S**pecifying, and stating **C**onsequences. This process allows you to "analyze conflicts, determine your needs and rights, propose a resolution to the conflict, and, if necessary, negotiate a contract for change."[31]

This process also allows you to plan ahead, if desirable, to avoid being unable to think of what to say. Most people, especially those who are communicatively anxious, tend to feel more secure if they know exactly what they are going to say. This system enables them to rehearse and eliminate bad scripts or self-defeating statements. There are four steps of DESC scripting:

1. **D**escribe. Describe as specifically and objectively as possible the behavior that is bothersome to you—for example, "I was told these repairs would cost $35, and I've been given a bill for $100."
2. **E**xpress. Say what you think and feel about this behavior—for example, "This makes me frustrated because I feel I was not told the truth."
3. **S**pecify. Ask for a different, specific behavior—for example, "I would like my bill adjusted to the original estimate."

The Five Ps of Negotiation

You'll boost your chances of getting what you want in a negotiation if you're

◆ **Prepared.** Before you seat yourself at the table, make sure you know as much as possible about the needs of both parties and any external factors that may affect your negotiations.

◆ **Poised.** Negotiators who become emotional lose points in the negotiation. Those who remain calm win points.

◆ **Persuasive.** This boils down to two things: You must be able to explain your position and provide support for it.

◆ **Persistent.** This doesn't mean you should fight for a point until you're "the last one standing." But it does mean that you should not give in at the first sign of resistance to an issue that's important to you.

◆ **Patient.** Pressing too quickly to conclude the negotiations may cause you to compromise more than you should and leave you with a hollow victory.

Source: Adapted from Right Associates, Philadelphia, cited in *Industry Week,* 1100 Superior Ave., Cleveland, OH 44114.

4. Consequences. Spell out concretely and simply what the punishment will be for not changing the behavior. The consequence should be something that you are willing to do and are capable of doing. Threats that go beyond reasonableness will be ignored. For example, you may say, "In the state of Ohio, I know you can only charge me $50 over the amount of the estimate. If the change isn't made, I'll contact the state's consumer protection office and lodge an official complaint." (Since this is the law, you can carry through.)

DESC scripting can be used for requesting an adjustment, asking for information or help, clarifying instructions, reconciling with someone, saying *no* to unreasonable demands, protesting annoying habits, and dealing with unjust criticism.

Negotiation

In contrast to assertion, which is the act of one person attempting to meet her or his needs, **negotiation** is the act of bargaining to reach an agreement with at least two people working on a mutual problem.[32] When negotiating, both parties must be explicit about what they want and why. If you are unable to work out an amicable solution, you must accept that invoking consequences may be necessary. If this is the case, both parties must make clear what the consequences will be; they must also make sure that the consequences are relevant to the other person or organization and can be carried out.

A number of considerations must be kept in mind during negotiating:

Look closely at the other party's point of view to understand where you differ. Conflict is often cleared up as soon as one party realizes that he did not understand the other person's viewpoint—or his own.

Identify your needs. What do you really want? What does the other person want? Are your needs similar or different?

Decide on a negotiating style. One pattern does not work in all situations. Because of this, one of your basic considerations should be whether you are interested in a win-lose, lose-lose, or win-win resolution (see Figure 7.4). **Win-lose negotiation** centers on one person getting what is wanted while the other comes up short. In a **lose-lose negotiation,** neither person is satisfied with the outcome. In a **win-win negotiation,** the goal is to find a solution that is satisfying to everyone. Although win-win seems to be the ideal for which most people strive, some may aim for a different option. There are times when people feel they must win at all costs, and if they cannot win, the other person is not going to win either.

Figure 7.4	Negotiation Resolutions	
Win-lose negotiation	**Lose-lose negotiation**	**Win-win negotiation**
• One person gets what s/he wants • Other comes up short	• Neither person is satisfied with the outcome	• All parties try to find a solution that is satisfying to everyone

Set up a conducive climate for negotiating. If the atmosphere is positive, the negotiation will probably go forward. If the atmosphere is negative, however, there may be no way of avoiding a win-lose or lose-lose situation, both of which are fostered by competition. Are you really interested in amicably settling the issue? If so, make an effort to be cooperative. Try to set up a "we" rather than a "you versus me" atmosphere.

Consider the impact of the setting on the process. Trying to negotiate in front of others often places a strain on the participants that can result in a less-than-desirable solution. If the participants feel rushed, tired, or under pressure to meet a deadline, this can influence both their thinking and their emotional attitude.

Keep the discussion focused. Avoid attacking the other person; rather, deal with the issue.

No one has to lose in a negotiation. If both people are satisfied with what is decided, then their needs are met, and a win-win situation results.

Arbitration

authority figure decides.

In **arbitration** a third party is brought in to settle a dispute. The third party hears evidence and makes a decision on how the conflict will be resolved. Both parties have previously agreed that they will abide by the decision. This is a common technique that is used when negotiation has failed. The major communication factors that the disputants should practice include honestly answering questions and being an active listener so that the questions asked are the questions answered.

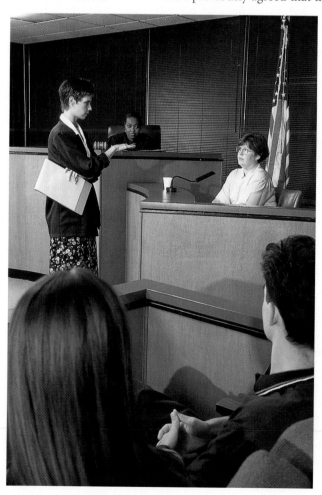

Litigation is conducted by lawyers who call witnesses and question them to reveal information.

Litigation

Litigation is adversarial communication in which a dispute is settled by presenting evidence to a judge or a jury, who decides who is right. Litigation is usually conducted by lawyers who call witnesses and question them to reveal information while following a prescribed set of rules that have been established by law and interpreted by the person in charge, usually a judge.

Mediation

Mediation is a process in which a neutral person, who has no vested interest in the outcome, facilitates communication between parties and, without imposing a solution on the parties, enables them to understand and resolve their dispute.[33] Mediators are specially trained in specific communication techniques and are often licensed to perform the act of mediation. Mediation is becoming a communication technique that many courts are mandating instead of litigation in such matters as child custody, divorce, and neighbor disputes.

Tips for Getting Along with a College Roommate

- Be respectful.
- Appreciate differences.
- Communicate.
- Be patient and flexible.
- Compromise, while still asserting your rights.
- Ask your resident assistant for help in mediating a discussion when a problem arises that you cannot solve yourselves.

When problems arise, consider these suggestions:

- Start by setting up a good time to talk in private.
- Remember that everyone has an equal right to be heard.
- Set aside your desire to "win" and focus on succeeding together.
- Create a comfortable environment where all room-mates feel able to talk honestly about their feelings, without being interrupted.
- Avoid blaming each other and focus on a solution.

- Stick to the topic.
- Avoid generalizations or blanket statements.

Steps to resolving conflict:

- Express your feelings to your roommate. Try to see the situation from all viewpoints. Communication is the key to any relationship.
- Come to an agreement about the conflict. Create a compromise and work together to develop a solution.
- Talk to your resident assistant.
- Make a plan of action and set a time frame for these changes to take place. Be committed to implementing personal changes.
- Set a date to evaluate the situation and discuss the next step.

Source: "Building Community Begins With Two: Your Guide to Roommate Success," John Carroll University, as appeared in *Plain Dealer*, August 26, 2002. Reprinted with permission of John Carroll University, Cleveland Heights, OH.

The basic principle in mediation is to get those in conflict to communicate with each other so that they can reach a win-win decision, thus ensuring that the dispute remains settled.[34] It is imperative in mediation that the participants stay in the present tense and discuss how to solve the issue. Therefore, mediation rules usually indicate that in the first session, disputants may be allowed to blame, and then they are not to revert to blaming again during the rest of the mediation sessions.

There are times when people feel they must win at all costs, and if they cannot win, the other person is not going to win either.

The mediation participants use a joint problem-solving approach, which focuses on their interests. Since most people are not trained to deal with each other in a nonbiased manner of problem resolution, the mediator acts as both guide and teacher in getting the disputants through the process.

The mediator structures the process, encourages information gathering, assists in defining the issues and generating possible conclusions, guides an exploration of the consequences of various solutions, keeps participants focused, and draws out the parties. The mediator does not advise either disputant or advocate a particular solution.

Although most mediators are professionals, specifically trained to carry out the

procedure, anyone can use the techniques that mediators use. The stages of mediation are:

1. Establish the rules.
2. Explain the process and the role of the mediator.
3. Begin assessment of the problem.
4. Begin information gathering.
5. Discuss possible solutions.
6. Evaluate the solutions.
7. Work toward selection of a mutually agreed-on solution.
8. Obtain signatures on an agreement that validates the solution.

The most difficult role of a mediator is to remain neutral and not step in with advice for either party, even when one of the participants appears to be getting the worst of the agreement or you, as the negotiator, think you know the "best" solution.

An issue that often leads to conflict is criticism. An understanding of what criticism is and how to handle it can help diffuse its being a cause of conflict.

Handling Criticism

Criticism—the act of judging—is typically considered to be a negative act by the receiver. Few of us handle criticism well. In many instances we attempt to deny or dismiss it. Criticism often triggers within us memories of being corrected by our parents, teachers, coaches, or clergy. It may make us feel inadequate and unacceptable.[35]

But like it or not, sometime in your life, you are going to be the recipient of criticism. To handle criticism as constructively as possible, without feeling the need to justify yourself, get angry, withdraw, or counterattack, you can try these strategies:

When criticized, seek more information.

When criticized, seek more information. If someone accuses you of having done something, ask for specifics. For example, if a friend says that you are selfish and do not respect anyone's feelings, ask for some specific examples or the specific instance that led to the comment.

Paraphrase the ideas of the person making the criticism to clarify them for both of you. Repeat the accusation, and ask if that is what he or she really meant. That way, you will be dealing with exactly what has been said.

Ask yourself what consequences will result from your not altering the behavior being criticized. Will you personally gain from making the changes, or is the criticism based on satisfying the needs of the criticizer?

Listen to the person; if the criticism is just, accept the opinion. Use such techniques as agreeing with the truth, agreeing with the odds (if it is a projection into the future, agree with the odds for its occurrence), agreeing in principle (if the criticism comes in the form of an abstract ideal against which you are being unfavorably compared, you can agree with it in principle without agreeing with the comparison), or agreeing with the critic's perception (agreeing with the right of the critic to perceive things the way he or she does). For example, if you are accused of spending too much time studying and not enough socializing, and you feel this is true, why not simply agree rather than arguing that you have a right to spend your time as you wish?[36]

In dealing with criticism, recognize that much of it is well intentioned. Often family members, friends, and your supervisor are telling you how to change for what they perceive is "your own good." This does not mean that they are right or wrong or that you have to take their suggestions. Remember that none of us has a crystal ball allowing us to see into the future. Your desires, needs, and goals are ultimately your responsibility, and you can do as you wish as long as you are also willing to accept the consequences.

> ### COMMUNICATION BRIEFING
>
> ### Feedback: Try This Response to Criticism
>
> Benefit from both positive and negative feedback with STAFF:
>
> ◆ **Say thanks.** Even if the feedback is negative, avoid the urge to defend yourself. If you agree, say so and thank the person. If you don't agree, say nothing except "Thank you."
> ◆ **Think about what the person said.** Walk away and take time to honestly answer this question: "Was the feedback accurate?" Don't waste time trying to think of ways to defend yourself or to criticize your criticizer.
> ◆ **Ask for more information if you feel you need it.** Even if you disagree with the feedback, it can help to know the reasons for it. Also, you both need to agree on the problem and how serious it is before moving to the next step.
> ◆ **Find out what you need to change.** Ask for specifics. If the other person has none, and if you feel you deserved the criticism, try to think of how you might do better. But also consider this: The lack of specifics could also mean the criticism was unfounded.
> ◆ **Follow through on any changes you've agreed to try on your own.**
>
> *Source:* Dawn Hudson, writing in *Office Hours*, The Economics Press, Inc., 12 Daniel Road, Fairfield, NJ 07004. © Communication Briefings, www.briefings.com, 1101 King Street, Alexandria, VA 22314. Used with permission.

In Conclusion

Every day we participate in interpersonal communication. The basic principle of good conversation is to find a common interest between yourself and the other person. Directions include instructions for how to accomplish a task, achieve an effect, or get somewhere. Requesting is the process of seeking out information or change. Conflict is natural, the inevitable result of individual differences, limited resources, and differences in role definitions. Apologizing is saying you are sorry. The communicative approaches to resolve conflict include assertive communication, negotiation, arbitration, litigation, and mediation. Knowing how to handle criticism is an important communication skill.

Learn by Doing

1. We each have a general pattern by which we deal with conflict. To learn your approach to dealing with conflict, circle T (true) or F (false) to indicate how you would respond in each of the situations. Although you may not agree with either choice, you must select either T or F. Read quickly, and react quickly.

Directions: Circle T (true) or F (false) to indicate which of the following statements best describes how you would respond in each of these situations. Although you may not agree with either choice, you must select either true (T) or false (F). Your first response will be your best.

	1	2	3	4	5
1. When there is a difference of opinion, wants, or needs, I would rather explore our differences than try to convince the other person that I am right and he or she is wrong.	F				T
2. When there is a difference of opinion, wants, or needs, I would rather disagree openly and explore our differences than agree with the other point of view simply to have someone agree with my point of view.				F	T
3. When asked to perform an unpleasant task, I would rather postpone the task indefinitely than follow orders without discussion.		F	T		
4. When there is a difference of opinion, wants, or needs, I would rather try to win the other person over than withdraw from the conversation.	T		F		
5. Sometimes it's easier to agree and appear to go along with something without discussion than to avoid making any comment on a controversial subject.		T	F		
6. During a disagreement, I would rather admit that I may be half wrong than try to convince the other person that I am 100 percent right.	F		T		
7. When there is a difference of opinion, wants, or needs, I would rather give in totally than try to change the other person's mind or opinion.	F		T		
8. I would rather postpone a potential disagreement than explore our different points of view.			T		F
9. During a disagreement, I would rather meet the person halfway than give in totally.		F		T	
10. Sometimes it's easier to agree without discussion than to try to convince the other person I'm right.	F	T			
11. During a disagreement, I would rather admit that I am half wrong than not say anything and withdraw from the conversation.			F	T	
12. When asked to perform a task I don't want to do, I would rather postpone it indefinitely than make someone else do the task.	F		T		
13. During a disagreement, I would rather try to win the other person over than to split our differences.	T			F	
14. When there is a difference of opinion, wants, or needs, I would rather explore our differences and reach a mutually satisfactory solution than withdraw from the conversation or conflict.	F		T		
15. When asked to perform a task I don't want to do, I would rather postpone the task indefinitely than discuss my feelings and attempt to find a solution we can both agree on.			T		F
16. During a difference of opinion, wants, or needs, I would rather try to convince the other person that I am right than explore our differences.	T				F
17. During a disagreement, I would rather admit that I am half wrong than explore our differences.				T	F
18. Sometimes it is easier just to agree without discussion than to give up half of what I believe to reach an agreement.		T		F	
19. When there is a difference of opinion, wants, or needs, I would rather explore our differences than give in without a discussion.		F			T
20. During a difference of opinion, wants, or needs, I would rather try to win the discussion than sacrifice my point of view by not discussing it.	T	F			

	1	2	3	4	5
21. During a disagreement, I would rather try to find a solution that satisfies both of us than to let the other person find a solution without my input.		F			T
22. During a disagreement, I would rather try to win the other person over than give in totally	T	F			
23. When asked to perform a task I don't want to do, I would rather agree to perform just half the task than to find a solution that is mutually satisfactory.				T	F

Scoring Instructions

1. Count the number of items circled in each of the five columns. Record your totals in the boxes below. Multiply each score by 10.

	1	2	3	4	5
× 10 =					

2. Chart your score on the graph below. Place an X next to your score for each of the five strategies. Draw a straight line connecting the Xs from one column to the next. This will give you your conflict management strategy pattern.

	1 Competition/ Aggression	2 Accommodation/ Smoothing Over	3 Avoidance	4 Compromise	5 Integration
120					
110					
100					
90					
80					
70					
60					
50					
40					
30					
20					
10					
0					

2. Select a place on your campus, and write directions from your classroom to that place. Your instructor will divide the class into pairs. One partner gives the directions orally to the other partner without revealing the chosen destination. See if by following your directions, your partner can figure out the place you selected. Then reverse roles.

3. Select an object and write a description of it without revealing its identity. Then read your description to your classmates. At the end of the entire description, they will attempt to name the object. When everyone has read his or her description, discuss why the class members could or could not identify certain objects.

4. Do this activity over a period of several days, completing the tasks in the order given. When you are finished, share your experiences with the class, and discuss what you learned about the process of assertiveness. In the discussion, figure out why activities a and b were assertive acts.
   a. Do something you have wanted to do for yourself but for some reason have not (e.g., call a friend you have wanted to talk to for a while). This is an assertive, selfish act. Record what you did and how you felt.
   b. Do something you have wanted to do for someone else but for some reason have not (e.g., visit an ill relative). This is an assertive, selfless act. Record what you did and how you felt.
   c. Think of something that someone is doing that bothers you. Using the DESC or the simple/empathic/follow-up assertion format, tell that person how you feel, remembering to be assertive, not aggressive (e.g., tell your roommate you would appreciate her not borrowing your clothes without asking). This is an assertive act. Record what you did and how you felt.

5. Think of a specific situation in which you should have been assertive but were not. Why did you not assert yourself? How could you have asserted yourself? What do you think might have happened if you had asserted yourself? Use your answers as the basis for a discussion on assertiveness.

Key Terms

conversation
small talk
analytical thinking
holistic thinking
directions
requesting
asking
conflict
conflict-active societies
conflict-avoidance societies
anger
fight-or-flight mechanism
fair fighting
conflict avoidance
conflict accommodation
conflict smoothing over
conflict compromise
conflict competition
conflict integration

apologizing
assertive communication
assertiveness
nonassertive behavior
aggressive behavior
direct aggression
passive aggression
simple assertion
empathic assertion
follow-up assertion
DESC scripting
negotiation
win-lose negotiation
lose-lose negotiation
win-win negotiation
arbitration
litigation
mediation
criticism

8

The Interview

After reading this chapter, you should be able to

- **Define what an interview is and identify the types of interviews**

- **List and explain the different purposes for interviews and how those purposes affect what happens in the interview**

- **Demonstrate the organizational structure of an interview**

- **State the principles of preparing for and functioning as an interviewee and an interviewer**

- **Identify and illustrate the types of questions used in an interview**

An **interview** is a purposeful conversation between two or more persons that follows a basic question-and-answer format. Interviewing is more formal than most other conversations because the participants usually share a preset purpose and use a focused structure.

Although there are many types of interviews, the employment interview is one of the most prevalent. In fact, some people mistakenly believe that it is the only variety of interview. Some other formats are the information-gathering interview (e.g., medical personnel gathering patient data), counseling interview (participating in a psychotherapy session), interrogatory interview (a detective examining someone suspected of a crime), and radio-television interview (talk shows).

Interviewing Roles

The most effective interviews are conducted at a highly conversational yet structured level. In the process, the communicators assume fundamental communication roles. In some transactions, the people involved can reverse roles as the interview proceeds. Mainly, however, the roles remain somewhat fixed: one person maintains the position of interviewer; the other, the role of interviewee.

Role of the Interviewer

The **interviewer** is responsible for the interview's arrangements and takes the lead in conducting the activity. This person usually establishes the time, location, and purpose of the meeting. Careful preparation is a key to success as an interviewer. Therefore, the interviewer often prepares an **interview format,** which outlines the procedures that will be used to achieve the interaction's purpose.

One of the most common mistakes interviewers have been found to make is that they tend to talk too much.[1] "The general rule is that the interviewee should do about 80 percent of the talking."[2]

A good interviewer works at establishing a rapport with the interviewee by providing a climate of trust and support. The successful interviewer must be a sensitive communicator who is aware of the nonverbal cues of the interviewee and can adapt to these responses. The interviewer should also be a good listener so that she or he can adapt to the needs and concerns expressed by the interviewee and acquire the information that is the basis for the interview.

Role of the Interviewee

The **interviewee,** the person who is being interviewed, should prepare for the session by knowing the purpose of the meeting, what her role and responsibilities are, and the information she needs to provide. As an interviewee, anticipate what you will be asked and think about how you can best respond. But don't assume that your only role is to answer questions. Just as a candidate for a position in an employment interview, for instance, responds to the questions asked by the interviewer, so too can the candidate shift roles and ask questions about the position, company, and benefits.

Want That Job?

10 "Must Do's" for Your Next Job Interview
1. Be on time.
2. Introduce yourself in a courteous manner.
3. Read company materials while you wait.
4. Have a firm handshake.
5. Listen.
6. Use body language to show interest.
7. Smile, nod, and give nonverbal feedback to the interviewer.
8. Ask about the next step in the process.
9. Thank the interviewer.
10. Write a thank-you letter to anyone you have spoken to.

Source: jobweb.com

A good interviewer works at establishing a rapport with the interviewee by providing a climate of trust and support.

Interview Format

In interviewing, the participants usually have a preset purpose.

Once the objectives of the interview are established, the interviewer should prepare the interview format. The basic format, regardless of the interview's purpose, is divided into the opening, the body, and the closing.

Opening of the Interview

The opening of the interview focuses on establishing rapport between the two communicators. The interviewer should try to make the interviewee feel comfortable. One of the best ways to do this is for the interviewer to do most of the talking at the outset. This technique serves two functions: it establishes the goal of the interview for both communicators, and it gives the interviewee time to become comfortable with the situation and the interviewer.

For example, a journalist conducting an information-gathering interview with Whoopi Goldberg about black-white relationships in the United States as we enter the twenty-first century started with a conversation about the movie

Ghosts of Mississippi. The discussion of how Goldberg portrayed the wife of the slain civil rights leader Medgar Evers offered her the opportunity to feel comfortable communicating with the journalist before going into the substance of the interview.

Body of the Interview

The body of the interview is the heart of the process. At this stage, the interviewer asks questions in an attempt to accomplish the purpose of the session.

Types of Interview Questions   An interviewer has a variety of questions to use:

Direct questions are explicit and require specific replies—for example, "Where did you last work?"

Open questions are less direct and specify only the topic—for example, "What is your educational background?"

Closed questions provide alternatives, narrowing the possibilities for response, and probe for opinions on opposite ends of a continuum—for example, "Do you think knowledge of a product or possessing communication skills is the most important asset of a salesperson?"

Bipolar questions, a form of closed question, require a yes or no response— for example, "Would you like to work for this company?"

Leading questions encourage a specific answer—for example, "You wouldn't say you favor gun control legislation, would you?" This is a leading question because it implies how the interviewee should answer the question.

Loaded questions, a type of leading question, are designed to elicit an emotional response. Asking a job applicant who was an officer of the union at a previous job to defend this company's policy of nonunion affiliation would, for example, be a loaded question.

Yes-response questions, another form of leading question, are stated in such a way that the respondent is encouraged to agree with the interviewer—for example, "You would agree with me, wouldn't you, that this company's policies are fair?"

Leading, loaded, and yes-response questions are used by interviewers who feel that the only way to get responses that reveal the true personality and beliefs of the interviewee is to put him or her on the spot. Consequently, interviewees should be aware that questions can carry implications going far beyond what is actually being asked.

The mirror question and the probe are used to follow up on initial questions:

Mirror questions are intended to get a person to reflect on what he or she has said and expand on it. For example, the interviewee may say, "I've worked for this corporation for years, and I'm getting nowhere." The mirror question might be "Do you feel you're not moving ahead in the corporation?" Such a response may encourage the interviewee to disclose more about her or his feelings.

Probes are used to elicit a more detailed response—for example, "Why do you feel that way?" This question encourages the interviewee to discuss his or her point with more direction and depth.

Sequence of Interview Questions

To accomplish the purpose of an interview, the interviewer should set up a checklist of questions, a schedule, in the categories he or she wants to cover. To do this, the interviewer must first determine the categories needed. For example, in the following job interview outline, the interviewer selected four categories: educational background, experience, job-related outside activities, and communication skills. These categories and the questions within them are set up ranging from those that are easiest to answer to those that are more difficult. The interviewer also sets up the questions so that they move from finding facts to seeking attitudes. The schedule of questions may take the form of a funnel schedule in which the questions are sequenced to take the interview from more general to more specific information.

The interviewer should provide the interviewee with transitions at the end of each category of questions so that he or she knows what direction the interview is taking, can think along with the interviewer, and consequently can provide appropriate responses. Specifically, the interviewer could say, "Now that we've covered your educational background, let's turn to your on-the-job experience."

Interviewer: Personnel director seeking to hire a civilian computer programmer to work on a military base

Interviewee: Computer programmer applying for a programming position

I.   Open interview
     A. Specify details of position
        1. Duties
        2. Workdays, hours, benefits, and pay
     (Transition to next topic)

II. Education
     A. Why did you choose computer science as your educational major?
     B. Which courses do you feel best prepared you for this position?
     C. Why?
     (Transition to next topic)

III. Experience
     A. Describe one problem for which you devised a solution on your last job.
     B. If you were rushing to meet a deadline, how would you complete the assignment while keeping quality high? Give an example from your last job.
     (Transition to next topic)

IV. Job-related activities
     A. In which computer language or languages are you fluent?
     B. Which language do you like the most? Why?
     C. What specific computer-security measures do you feel should be carried out to protect military information?

V.   Communication skills
     A. We cannot read the VTOC on any of a string of disk drives. The CE is stumped and strongly suggests that it is a software problem. You are 100 percent sure that it is a hardware, not a software, problem. If I am the CE, convince me that I am wrong and you are right.
     B. If I were to offer you the following two jobs, which would you choose and why?
        1. One with a $65,000 salary and a job description and responsibility level with which you are not very happy.
        2. One with a $50,000 salary and a job description that fits the type of position you really want.

VI. Conclude interview
   A. Summarize briefly.
   B. Ask for any questions.
   C. Tell interviewee when to expect to hear from you regarding the final hiring decision.

Answering Interview Questions

Although the interviewer carries the burden of determining the sequence of questions, the interviewee should answer with accuracy, clarity, and specificity. The answers should be backed up with supporting material for clarification and evidence. Following are some suggestions for answering questions.

If you don't understand the question, ask for clarification. For example, "Would you please restate the question?"

Restate the question in the answer. For example, if asked, "What are your responsibilities in your present job?" the answer might start, "In my current job, I . . ." In this way, the questioner knows you are listening, and you are clarifying exactly what you are answering.

Answer one question at a time. Often interviewers group questions together. In general, it is best to answer one question at a time to make sure that the questioner knows specifically which piece of information you are giving. For example, assume that the interviewer asks, "Would you describe your working conditions and what you like best about your job?" Divide your answer into two parts, such as "My working conditions are . . ." and "I like the fact that at my job I can . . ."

Try to turn negative questions into positive answers. A commonly asked job interview question is "What do you think your greatest weakness is?" This negative can be turned into a positive by stating, for example, "I am aware that I am rather compulsive about my work, so I spend a great deal of time making sure that what I do is done correctly."

Closing the Interview

An interview's conclusion should summarize what has been accomplished. If appropriate, discussion of the next step to be taken after the interview has ended should finish the session. When the interview is nearing its end, the interviewer should give the other person an opportunity to make statements or ask questions. A real estate broker, for example, ended a sales interview with a potential buyer in this way: "I'll write up the contract at the $350,000 price you'd like to offer plus the provision that all the electrical fixtures remain. Do you have any further questions before I leave?"

Types of Interviews

There are numerous types of interviews. The commonly used formats are employment, information gathering, problem solving, counseling, persuasive, appraisal, interrogatory, and media. Although not all the varieties may be relevant to you at this point in your academic or employment career, you may well be called on to participate in them at some time. Therefore, it is useful to investigate some considerations of each type.

Employment Interview

The most crucial interview for many people in their careers is the **employment interview.** It is both a way of entering the job market *and* a means for changing positions, getting promotions, and achieving salary increases. The job interview format sometimes may be part of the admission processes for colleges and universities, internships or assistantships, and graduate and professional programs.

Since the interview usually follows the prospective employer's examination of prior work experience, grade point average, and personal recommendations, the interview is often the last hurdle to be jumped before work employment, academic admission, internship appointment, or promotion.

A study of company recruiters revealed that six communication factors are especially important to the success of a candidate's interview:[3]

1. Resourcefulness (leadership, initiative, goals)
2. Written credentials (résumé, application letter, follow-up letter)
3. Support for arguments (clarifying issues, relating familiar to unfamiliar, organization of thoughts)
4. Social attributes (attitude, motivation, personality)
5. Comportment (image, appearance, delivery)
6. Style (euphemisms, assertiveness, use of transitions)

It has been recommended that interviewers go beyond the standard interview questions and ask some queries that will allow the interviewer to gain a realistic and in-depth view of the potential employee. These questions might include:[4]

The most crucial interview for many people in their careers is the employment interview.

◆ What would your former employer say about you?

◆ What would your former subordinates say about you?

◆ How do you recognize incompetence?

◆ What would you do about incompetence in someone whom you are assigned to supervise?

◆ What is something about yourself that you would like to improve?

◆ What makes you extremely irritated?

Employment Interviewer   In an employment interview, the interviewer's purpose is to find out about the job applicant. At the same time, the interviewer attempts to sell the organization or the position. Research suggests that interviewers vary widely in their selection decisions and are highly idiosyncratic in their approach to employment interviews. Consequently, selection interviewers are advised to develop selection criteria, determine how the criteria will be assessed, and establish a criteria-based interview guide.[5] Legal ramifications may result from the failure to have clear criteria and procedures because of federal, state, and municipal employment laws.

Employment Interviewee   The interviewee also has the responsibility to provide information about her background and experiences and, at the same time, convince the recruiter that she is the best applicant for the position. As the job seeker, don't overlook the importance of preparing for an employment interview.

Preparing for the Employment Interview   If you are applying for a job at a new place of employment, you should provide a résumé and a letter of interest so that the recruiter has background information.[6] A résumé is a vital part of your communication image and can often make the difference in whether you are even called for an interview. A résumé and cover letter ought to be tailored to the specific company and particular position for which you are applying. (Information on preparing a résumé and a sample résumé are presented in Appendix I at the end of this book.)

Another important aspect of preparation is to be ready to answer the questions posed. Here is a list of the most-asked interview questions for entry-level positions and some ideas about how you might answer them:[7]

1. *What are your future plans?*
   Connect your response to the goals of the organization with which you're interviewing. For example, since your preinterview investigation revealed that the company is growth oriented, you might state, "Since I have strong training and experience in computer graphics, I really want to be part of an organization that is exploring new and innovative ways of entering into the graphics field."

2. *In what school activities have you participated?*
   Highlight any activities that demonstrate your leadership abilities and how you are good at time management, assuming responsibility, and multitasking. An appropriate answer would be "I was involved in the Blue Key Honor Society. I served as president of the Student Government Association and was on the Student Government Council for two years. These activities allowed me to assume leadership responsibilities, balance school work and other responsibilities, and develop skills in working well with others."

3. *How do you spend your spare time?*

   Be selective in what you disclose. Focus on those activities that reflect your physical, intellectual, and community service activities. Consider including your religious or ethical activities only if you perceive that the organization and interviewer are aligned with your views. Usually, it is wise to avoid making political comments or talking about social activities, especially those that would put you in a bad light. A solid answer might be "I enjoy working out at the gym, going to professional sports games, working with Habitat for Humanity, and volunteering as a Big Brother." If your list is not strong, you might add wishes for the future by stating, "I have been busy getting my degree, but as soon as I have a job, I'm planning on becoming involved in Habitat for Humanity and volunteering as a Big Brother."

4. *In what type of position are you most interested?*

   Try to tailor your response to this company and this position. If you are interviewing for an entry-level position, it would be appropriate to state, "As a recent college graduate, I am interested in your opening because it will give me the necessary basis for understanding the field of accounting." If the interviewer asks, "Is that your career goal?" you could respond by saying, "Realistically, I need to know more information about the field, which I can acquire in this position, before I can make decisions about the future." This response doesn't close doors on your ambition and indicates that the job is at your appropriate level.

5. *Why do you think you may like to work for our company?*

   In answering this question, refer to your preinterview research about the company and reflect on those features of the firm that are attractive to you and which the organization also stresses. For example, you could say, "I'm very excited that your company has on-the-grounds recreation facilities, encourages its employees to participate in community service projects, and recently was recognized as one of the area's most family-friendly places to work."

6. *What jobs have you held?*

   Include those positions that are relevant to the job for which you are interviewing. Even if you have only had part-time jobs, you can successfully weave those into your answer. If you are interviewing for a customer-service position at a bank, try stating something like "Working at McDonald's taught me how to deal calmly with people who become irritated about waiting for their orders. While at Home Depot's customer-service department, I also learned to understand why people become frustrated with organizations and their rules. I think this background will be helpful in this job."

7. *What courses did you like best? What courses did you like least?*

   Be sure in answering these questions that your response doesn't contradict what your transcript reveals. If you got a D in Introduction to Physics, you'll have to substantiate your answer if you mention that as your favorite course. If you are interviewing for your first teaching position, you could say, "I've always wanted to be a history teacher, so I was really pleased with the fact that my university had a top-notch history department and a strong education program. As for what courses I liked the least, science isn't my favorite subject. Given a choice, I would always take a history class over a science course."

8. *Why did you choose your particular field of work?*

   Demonstrate that you have passion for the field, not that you just fell into it for lack of anything else to study or do. An acceptable answer might be "When I was in junior high, I came home and asked my father what career someone goes into if everyone is always asking her for advice and if when she gives it, they take it. My dad said, 'Sounds like a psychologist to me.' So I set my goals right then to become a psychologist, and here I am today interviewing for a position on your psych staff." Or you might respond, "When I started college, I wasn't sure what field I wanted to go into. When I took my first speech and hearing class, I realized that I could combine my interest in working with children and older adults with my interest in biology."

9. *What are your strengths? Your weaknesses?*
   Interviewers know that in communication and job preparation courses students are usually prepped to answer these questions. The general rule is that when answering these questions, try not to sound conceited but let the interviewer know of your strengths as they relate to the potential job. And try to turn your weaknesses into strengths. Consider saying something like "I've been told over and over that my strength as a person is my ability to analyze what's going on around me and to assume a role in dealing with the circumstances. I work creatively and efficiently. My creativity sometimes gets me into trouble because I think of solutions that others haven't considered. If they are fairly traditional, they might think my ideas are off the wall. In the long run, however, my solutions do give people some options to think about."

Dressing for the Employment Interview   Appearance is an important factor for success in employment interviews. An extreme, but probably wise, opinion is that "a lot of people out there have the credentials, the degrees, and the experience. Success comes down to image."[8] A leading consultant who advises businesspersons on what to wear states, "Walk though a door into an office, and instantly people draw a dozen conclusions about you, from how much money you make (or should make) to how trustworthy you are."[9] And although you may not want to believe it or wish it weren't so, "even the best credentials aren't enough to overcome a poor physical image."[10] Appearance can even have an effect on salary. "An initial salary of 8 to 20 percent higher is a result of upgrading a mediocre business appearance to one that is crisp and effective."[11]

Although some organizations have turned to a more relaxed look, this doesn't normally apply to clothing choices for employment interviews. If you want to succeed, you must package yourself to turn off the least number of people and turn on the greatest number of opportunities. This generally translates into the conservative, trustworthy look.

For men that "means dark blue and gray suits in solids or muted patterns. Sport coats are not recommended. Accessories, from ties to shoes to watches, should all be the type that project solidity and never draw attention to themselves."[12] In other words, leave the Nike running shoes, earring, and Mickey Mouse tie at home. A double-breasted suit transmits more authority than a single-breasted suit.[13]

Women should "stick to the classic look—skirt suit or dresses with jackets—in dark colors."[14] Choose natural fabrics over synthetics and avoid polyester. Wear neutral-colored stockings. Avoid gaudy jewelry, leaning toward conservative earrings such as pearls or small gold loops.

Researchers have identified the five biggest mistakes that men and women make in dressing for interviews:[15]

Men

1. Dirty, wrinkled, ill-fitting clothes
2. Shirt that is too tight at collar or waist
3. Dirty hands, nails, or hair

Dressing Up at Work

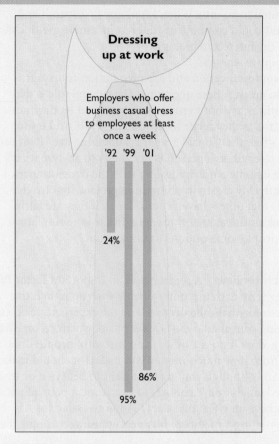

Dressing up at work

Employers who offer business casual dress to employees at least once a week

'92 '99 '01

24%

86%

95%

4. Dirty or improperly colored shoes
5. Improper style clothing for body composition

Women

1. Too much or inappropriate jewelry
2. Too much or too little makeup
3. Inappropriate or scuffed shoes
4. Inappropriate clothing
5. Ill-fitting clothes

Actions During the Employment Interview   What should you do during the interview? In general, it is wise to keep in mind this advice:[16]

◆ Be pleasant and friendly but remain businesslike.
◆ Tell the employer your job preferences as specifically as possible. Avoid a comment like "I'll do anything" because it shows a lack of clarity about your desires and skills and sounds desperate.

- Stress your qualifications without exaggeration.
- When you discuss your previous jobs, avoid criticizing former employers and fellow workers.
- Be prepared to state what salary you want, but do not do so until the employer has introduced the subject.
- Few people can fake a role or lie well. Even if you can, employers will hire you for what they see and hear, and if you are not the person you have pretended to be or cannot perform at that level, you'll be terminated.
- Ask questions when appropriate. For example, ask about what your initial duties will be and what kind of training you will receive.
- Be enthusiastic; listen for ideas; maintain eye contact.
- Take notes during the interview that you can use to remind yourself of questions you want to ask or refer to later.
- If the employer does not definitely offer you the job or indicate when you will hear about it, ask when you may call to learn of the decision.
- Thank the interviewer for granting you the interview. It is also appropriate to send a letter of appreciation within a day or two after the session.

Answering the Employment Interviewer's Questions   One of the common questions interviewees ask is "How should I answer the questions?" A specialist who trains interviewees offered these recommendations:

- Listen to the questions asked.
- Avoid making assumptions if you do not understand the question.
- Answer ambiguous questions to your best advantage.
- Make use of pauses and silences to formulate your thoughts.
- Establish a rapport with the interviewer.
- Treat every question as an important one.[17]

Legal Restrictions on the Employment Interview   An important consideration for both the interviewer and the interviewee is the legal issues that relate to the selection process.[18] Both the interviewer and the interviewee should know the federal guidelines as to what questions can and cannot be asked in employment interviews. Unfortunately, the laws are constantly being changed, so a review of the current standards must be made. At the time this book was published, these were some of the regulations:

An interviewer *may* ask:

How many years' experience do you have?

What are your career goals?

Who were your prior employers?

Why did you leave your previous jobs?

Are you a veteran? Did the military provide you with job-related experience?

If you have no telephone, where can we reach you?

What languages do you speak?

Do you have any objection if we check with your former employer for a reference?

Interviewers *can't* ask:

What is your age?

What is your date of birth?

What is your race?

What church do you attend?

Are you married, divorced, separated, widowed, or single?

Have you ever been arrested?

What organizations or clubs do you belong to?

What does your spouse do?

Have your wages ever been attached or garnished?

What was your maiden name?

Unfortunately, in spite of these guidelines, job applicants still report that they are subjected to inappropriate questions. If you have experienced this situation and feel that you may have lost a position because of it, you have the right to make a formal complaint against the interviewer and the company, and possibly take legal action.

In addition, if you feel that you have been discriminated against because of gender, age, or any of the other classifications approved by your state or legislative district, you have the right to take action. A midwestern utility company, for example, was judged by the courts to have placed too great a reliance on the subjective judgment of its interviewers. As a result, the firm was required to establish a structured means of conducting interviews and a clear rating system for evaluating job applications to make sure that all people were treated fairly. If you plan to take action, be certain that you can document the questions that were asked or the procedure that was followed.

What should you do if an illegal question is asked? You might say, "I'm not trying to be difficult, but I was told in one of the classes I took that asking that question is illegal. I'm afraid if I answer it we could both get into trouble, so, if it's all right with you, I'll not respond." Another approach is to compliment the questioner but refuse to answer the question—for example, "That's an interesting question. Normally I'd love to answer it, but in my business class, the professor told us that we aren't legally allowed to answer that." On the other hand, if you think the answer will not be negatively perceived, you might decide to answer the question and hope for the best.

Second Employment Interview   Many organizations use the initial employment interview as a recruitment tool to gain the pool of applicants for a particular position. The candidates whom the company wishes to consider seriously are invited to a second interview.

Second employment interviews provide more detailed information about the position and, at the same time, further determine the candidate's fit to the organization and the job. In turn, the candidate may be able to raise questions about salary, benefits, retirement plans, and projected plans or profits of the company.[19]

Behavioral Interview   As part of the second employment interview, a prospective employee may be asked to participate in a **behavioral interview,** which is designed to allow employers to know what skills you, the applicant, may have and how these skills would translate into performance on the job. The interviewer may stress questions that ask you to talk in detail about your skills or demonstrate those skills. For instance, you might be asked about a time that you assumed leadership: How did you do this, and how did you perform? You also might be asked to perform a function. A favorite is to give the candidate an "in-box" and ask the individual to prioritize the work in the in-box and set out a plan for accomplishing the work.

If you know you are going to participate in a behavioral interview, you might want to review the types of skills needed for the position and what potential skills might be tested, and then prepare for the potential test by rehearsing your abilities.

Case Interview   The **case interview,** popular with investment firms and consulting companies, asks you to work through a particular case study or set of case studies. It is helpful to learn as much as possible about the company so that you will have a solid foundation for dealing with the problem that is presented in the case study. Go to the company's literature, check out its website, and talk with people in the organization if you can. If you find yourself having to participate in a case interview, you might want to investigate the website of the consulting firm McKinsey & Company (www.mckinsey.com). It provides a sample case interview dealing with a client that needs to improve its credit card business.

Stress Interview   The **stress interview** is designed to determine how you might function under pressure. Because many employment positions operate in a crisis management mode, an employee's ability to handle stress can be a necessary criterion for employment. You may face two or more interviewers who are firing questions at you, or the interviewers may act in ways that induce stress, such as standing very close to you while interviewing or asking you personal questions that are intended to embarrass you. They may ask rapid-fire questions, interrupt before you are finished with an idea, or belittle your answers. These are all meant to see how you react.

The key to handling this type of interview is to stay as calm as you can, realizing that this is a type of game with the purpose of rattling you. Assume the attitude that you personally are not under attack. You win the game when you don't allow the harassment to bother you.

The stress interview may be of value to you as a potential employee. It may be an indication that this is not the right job for you. If you can't handle the stress, you may not be happy with this position.[20]

Telephone Job Interview   At some organizations the **telephone job interview** has replaced the first personal interview that an applicant used to have with a company.[21] This is being done in an attempt to save time and money. Weeding out undesirable candidates; cutting down on airplane, hotel, and meal costs; and eliminating the interruption of the normal organizational routine are regarded as offsetting the lack of face-to-face interaction. Some feel that this is a positive step because it eliminates the interviewer's possible prejudice toward certain people regarding their race, physical appearance, or disabilities. On the other hand, if the interviewer doesn't see the person face to face, the best candidate could slip through the cracks.

As a result of this trend, the principles of employment interviewing must be adapted to how best to use the telephone as the conduit for the message. In general, you must recognize, if confronted with this interview option, that your vocal delivery is crucial. You need to communicate energy and enthusiasm as you respond to the questions. Conciseness and clarity of ideas are also imperative. In face-to-face encounters, you have the luxury of greater conversational informality because more nonverbal channels are present. In the telephone interaction, however, the limits can be significant.

Here are some suggestions for being a participant in a telephone interview:

◆ Practice responding orally to potential questions so that you're comfortable with the way you want to respond and sound. You might want to record yourself so that you can listen to the tape.

◆ Confirm the time of the interview and be sure your telephone is going to be available.

◆ Select a quiet setting, one in which you will not be interrupted. If other people use the phone, tell them not to place a call between *x* time and *y* time. Make your setting secure by informing others not to enter your space and, if possible, put up a sign asking for privacy and quiet.

◆ Prepare your desk or working space with items you may need. These might include a writing instrument, a pad for taking notes, your résumé, and any materials to which you might want to refer, such as the organization's financial report or research notes you've made about the company.

◆ Use a corded phone so that you don't run the risk that the signal will fade or a battery will expire during the interview.

◆ Do a relaxation exercise before answering the phone. Try to maintain a positive attitude and high energy throughout the interview. Smile as you answer the phone. Sit erect in the chair, feet on the floor, to ensure an active listening posture. Don't play with anything on the desk. Concentrate on the phone and the caller. Don't get distracted by objects in the room.

◆ Hold the phone in one hand and leave the other free to gesture. Animated speakers are vocally more expressive. Be sure that the hand you write with is free for taking notes.

◆ Listen carefully. Write down the name(s) of the interviewer(s) during the introductions. Refer to the interviewer(s) by name when addressing them. Directing questions and answers to specific people is imperative if there is a team of interviewers.

◆ Ask questions. You may prepare these questions in advance, or you can generate them during the interview. Because the interviewer can't see you, you can write down the questions as they occur to you so that you don't have to interrupt the interviewer's flow of questions. If the interviewer clarifies something you have been curious about, remove that question from your list.

◆ Stay alert!

Information-Gathering Interview

In an **information-gathering interview,** the interviewer sets out to obtain information from a respondent. This type of interview is important to journalists, law enforcement authorities, health care workers, students, businesspeople, and mental health professionals. As a student, for example, you may want to conduct an information-gathering interview to collect data to use in a speech or a term paper. Reporters and newspeople depend on information-gathering interviews to obtain information.

Conducting an Information-Gathering Interview   Information-gathering interviews may be transacted in person, by telephone, or through e-mail. Here are some guidelines for information-gathering interviews:

1. Make an appointment to interview the potential interviewee if you are appearing in person or conducting a telephone interview.
2. Preplan the questions you want to ask.
3. If possible, send your list of queries to the interviewee in advance of the session. However, avoid sending the questions if you wish to catch the interviewee off guard and get a spontaneous response.
4. Consider using the *five-Ws-and-an-H approach* developed by journalists for getting facts: who, what, when, where, why, and how? *Who* has to do with the person or persons involved in an event. *What* asks for a description or explanation of the event. *Where* indicates the place the incident happened. *When* provides such information as the date and time of the occurrence. *Why* is an explanation of the reason the event took place. And *how* centers on the exact details of what occurred.
5. Actively listen during the interview. Ask follow-up questions. Make sure that you understand and get all the information you need; you may not be able to do a follow-up session.
6. Take careful notes. If you are going to use quoted material, repeat back what the person has said to be certain you have the information correctly recorded. Or to ensure that you have the exact information, use a tape recorder. Be sure to ask permission when you make your original appointment as to whether recording equipment can be used.
7. Remember that you are taking up valuable time. Ask your questions and leave.
8. Be aware that "certain people can be highly evasive, hard to pin down. You just have to persevere and keep after them. 'I understand what you're saying, but you haven't answered my question.' You've got to try to control the interview without alienating the interviewee so he'll cut off the interview."[22] Sometimes, of course, alienating the interviewee is inevitable. If this person has something to hide or if the information could be used in a legal action, then it well may be impossible to find out exactly what you want.

Being the Subject of an Information-Gathering Interview   You may find yourself in the role of the interviewee, giving information. If so, be sure that you understand the questions being asked and that you don't feel pressured into answering against your will.

If you are a witness, say, to a traffic accident, you may be asked to provide information as to what happened. If you are unable to give facts, make sure the interviewer is aware that you are transmitting an opinion. There is a vast difference between saying, "The driver turned left on the red light," and "I couldn't see the light clearly, but I think it was red when the driver turned left."

It is advisable, if you know you could possibly be called as a witness, to write down or tape-record everything you can remember as soon as you can following the incident. Time often alters memory.

A research surveyor or journalistic interviewer may ask for information that you do not want to reveal. You need to make a decision about what and how much you are willing to share. Do not allow yourself to be pressured into an answer you may regret later. Remember that even in a court of law, you always have the right not to reveal information.

In an information-gathering interview, the interviewer sets out to obtain information from a respondent.

A concern is whether what you share is being used faithfully. You may want to stipulate that the information may not be used until you are given a copy of the article or speech in which the ideas are to be used.

Problem-Solving Interview

In a **problem-solving interview,** the interviewer and interviewee meet to solve a problem. Problem-solving interviews are very common in business and industry. If a company has a slump in new sales, for instance, it would be strategic for the marketing division to conduct interviews with sales personnel to determine why sales are down and what can be done to recover the lost business.

In this type of interview, structure the questions in the body of the interview so that the dimensions of the problem—its causes and effects—are discussed before specific solutions are addressed. If the full implications of the problems are not covered first, then a solution may never be derived. Indeed, the greatest drawback to the effective use of the problem-solving format is people's tendency to deliberate about solutions before having a clear understanding of the problem.

An effective problem-solving format relies on extensive give-and-take in which the interviewer and interviewee shift roles and discuss the matter thoroughly.

Managers in organizations frequently use problem-solving interviews to deal with problems with specific employees. In this context, both parties are encouraged to identify their stake in the problem so as to develop a plan that will be acceptable to both. "The problem-solving style is characterized by questions and descriptive language. . . . Questions are used to seek information, probe feelings and discover other points of view. . . . The language is non-judgmental . . . and the amount of time spent talking and listening is equally balanced between the two people."[23]

Knowing a problem-solving technique, such as the one illustrated in Figure 8.1, can aid considerably in keeping the action on track.

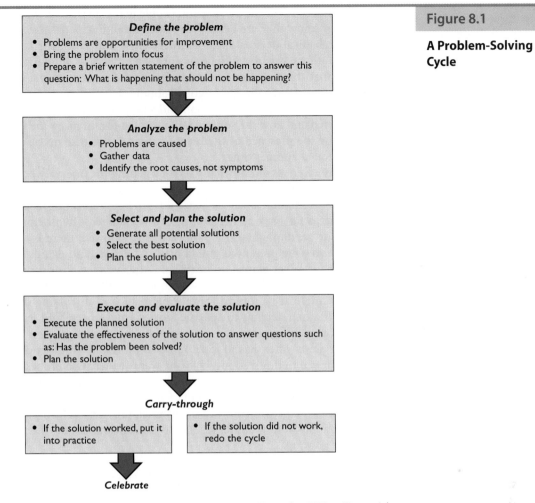

Source: "Tool Kit for Quality," by Joann Horai, *Association Management,* November 1993, p. 65, copyright 1993, American Society of Association Executives, Washington, D.C. Reprinted with permission.

Oral History Interview

A valuable application of informative interviewing is the **oral history interview.** It is a way for families to preserve their history by interviewing members of the family who have stories and customs they can share on audiotape or videotape. Organizations are also using the oral history interview to establish and maintain an archive of people and their stories. Knowledge of historical events is also stored this way, as in the series of interviews done with Jewish survivors of the Holocaust. The recordings can be kept in family archives or by organizations. The Smithsonian Institution, for example, conducts oral histories at the annual Summer Folklife Festival in Washington, D.C., in order to preserve the story of America and makes the histories available through its various museums.

A successful oral history is best conducted in an informal atmosphere so that the interviewee feels free to tell his or her story with minimal interruption. It's important to make a recording of the session in order to preserve the authenticity of the events in the words of the participant. People may experience a sense of discomfort when they know they are being videotaped or audiotaped. Most people forget about the mechanical devices once the interview is underway. For instance, when one of the authors began conducting such an interview with his mother, she objected to "that thing" being on. Interestingly, as soon as the first question was asked, and she started to talk, she forgot all about the tape recorder. Afterwards, she asked if she could hear the taped version and was quite pleased with how much she had remembered and how she sounded. If, in spite of assurances, the interviewee is still stressed by the presence of the recorder, turn it off, take notes, and try for a recorded session at another time.

The interviewer should normally start by getting the interviewee to talk auto-biographically, usually asking for the person's name, age, and any other relevant background information such as place of birth. Establishing a chronological order, starting as far back as the person can remember, often helps the speaker organize his or her thoughts. If a pattern is not followed, there is a danger that random ideas may be presented, much history left out, and details omitted. Use prompts such as "What happened next?" or "After you left Pittsburgh, where did you live?" If the person objects to this method or can't remember things chronologically, you might try a topical arrangement, such as discussing individuals in the person's life or referring to specific stories you've been told and asking for clarification or amplification.

The interviewer often has to learn to be comfortable with silence. Allow time for the interviewee to think about what she wants to tell. Use probes when necessary, but only if the person is having trouble coming up with the next topic. Don't interrupt unless you want further amplification. Even then, you might want to take notes and, when the person runs out of material, provide a return prompt such as "You told me about your grandfather Morris. I'm curious about when he was born and where he grew up."

The interviewer ought to be prepared to participate in the interview. You might want to model an answer by stating, "I remember a story about how you and your sisters finally got Grandma's Russian tea biscuit recipe written down. I'd love to hear that story again from your viewpoint. What happened?" You might be able to fill in any gaps of information by asking questions about things that you've discovered in family documents and genealogy records. If this is an interview about an organization, such information might be found in company publications.

Some interviewers find that a subject who is agitated often will reveal things that a calmer person would omit, and thus they intentionally will attempt to arouse the anxiety of an interviewee. A determination was made to try this tactic during some of the interviews with Holocaust survivors who had resisted being interviewed because of the trauma of their experiences. Since it had been deemed psychologically therapeutic for the individuals to "let loose," interviewers were sometimes encouraged to push the people. In general, doing this is not a good idea unless the consequences have been clearly considered, and the decision has been made that this would be the most appropriate approach.

As you proceed with the interview, be aware that an older person might tire easily. If that's the case, divide the session into segments with breaks. Each time you reenter the interview, remind the person what was discussed at the last session. Again, keep in mind that as people age, their memories may tend to falter.

The conclusion of the oral history interview should include a comment of appreciation and a discussion of what will be done with the information. If possible, present the interviewee with a final copy if one is produced.

Counseling Interview

We all have problems; some of them require that we have assistance in working through them. The **counseling interview** is designed to provide guidance and support to the interviewee. It is used by mental health professionals, friends, and family members, among others.

In some organizations, managers have been urged to develop basic skills in counseling to improve communication with their employees. In this way, "counseling can provide a service to both the organization and to individuals within it who have particular problems. Counseling can provide a release for the frustrations that are an inevitable part of human interaction in an organization."[24] Any person who is not a trained therapist, however, should keep in mind that harm as well as gain can result from trying to play amateur psychologist.

One approach to the counseling interview centers on the concept that it should not include any evaluation by the interviewer. Using this approach, you would not say to your friend who is not doing well in school, "Have you considered that your study habits may be the cause of your problem?" Instead, you could encourage the person to talk until she got to the heart of the difficulties. Such a strategy can be valuable in helping people see their own problems and giving them a firm foundation for a commitment to solve them. But such **nondirective techniques**—not taking an active role in a solution—can work only if the troubled person accepts that a problem exists, has the skills to identify what is wrong, and wants to deal with it.

Some mental health professionals believe that allowing unlimited talk by patients who are not capable of solving their own problems in the first place only wastes time and leads to even more problems. These professional counselors might elect to use **directive intervention:** the counselor takes a stand that there should be active probing; that specific activities should be carried on outside the counseling session (e.g., writing a letter to or directly confronting a person who has abused the client); that there should be role-playing and activities during counseling (e.g., releasing emotions by envisioning that the victimizer is sitting in a chair nearby so the client can tell the imagined person exactly how he or she feels); and that therapeutic hypnosis should be used in some cases to deal with certain types of problems.[25] An effective mental health professional fits the nature of the counseling approach to the client and the nature of his or her perceived problem. Many of these techniques, which are based on Gestalt psychological counseling principles, are used by Dr. Phillip McGraw on his syndicated television program, *Dr. Phil.*

Therapeutic interviews go through a series of stages: the expectations and objectives of the counseling are spelled out by both interviewer and interviewee; there is an emotional release during which the interviewee elaborates on his or her perceptions of the problem; the problem is explored and, ideally, all its ramifications are probed; the interviewee is reassured or consoled; a confrontation occurs in which the interviewee's contradictions, or "blind spots," are examined; further probing for more information takes place to gain a better perspective about the problem; the interviewee's options are discussed; and finally, there comes a time when the interviewee's feelings or behavior may be changed or when the interviewer may wish to refer the person for another type of counseling.[26]

Persuasive Interview

The purpose of a **persuasive interview** is to change a person's beliefs or behavior. The selection and organization of persuasive points depends on the initial position of the interviewer. If she or he agrees with the beliefs or purpose of the interviewee,

Helping Others Solve Problems

Want to encourage others to work on problems that are bothering them on the job? The key is to get them to open up and express themselves.

Here are two approaches:
◆ Ask open-ended questions—such as those that begin with "what," "which," "why," "how," etc. Also use open-ended comments—such as "Tell me more." Examples:
　—"How do you feel about ...?"
　—"What do you think of ...?"
　—"Give me a complete picture of how you see things."
◆ Mirror others' feelings by reflecting what they say or imply. Examples:
　—"I sense that you're ..."
　—"When you talk that way, it seems to me ..."

Source: Adapted from *Why Didn't I Say That?! What to Say and How to Say It in Tough Situations on the Job,* by Donald H. Weiss, AMACOM. American Management Association, 135 W. 50th St., New York, NY 10020.

then the interviewee's task is to reinforce the agreement. For instance, if a woman comes to a volunteer agency already convinced that she wants to volunteer, then the volunteer coordinator does not have to persuade her to give her time to the cause. Instead, the coordinator can concentrate on explaining the opportunities available.

If, however, the interviewee disagrees with the interviewer's beliefs or purpose, then the interviewer should find some points of agreement and try to build on these before leading the interviewee into areas of controversy. In this way, the interviewer can build an argument to secure the interviewee's acceptance of other points. For example, a management consultant may have to begin with praise and recognition for some aspect of a company's management program before attempting to persuade its executives that their organization needs to develop better internal communication.

The uncertain or neutral interviewee may require more background information before persuasive appeals can be introduced. If, for example, a voter does not know anything about your candidate for mayor, you will have to provide that person with some background information on the candidate before giving any reasons to vote for her or him.

Persuasion and influence researchers demonstrate how compliance-gaining strategies can be applied to influence people to do what you want them to do. Among the more familiar techniques are asking for a favor, calling in a debt, and appealing to guilt.[27]

A persuasive interview should maintain a conversational style so that the interviewee is free to raise questions and respond to the interviewer's message. In addition, the interviewee should apply the principles of critical listening and be alert to biased or leading questions.

Sales Interview   The sales process is a persuasive interview. As with all other communication, the sales interview process is cultural specific: that is, in different cultures the procedure will vary. In many Middle Eastern cultures, for example, an exchange of personal information and establishment of a friendship are imperative for a successful sale. Negotiation and haggling are part of the customs of some cultures, such as those of many parts of Mexico and South America.

On the other hand, in the United States and Canada the procedure is quite different. The **sales interview** usually begins with the salesperson's establishing rapport, arousing interest, and getting the customer involved; then the salesperson explores the customer's needs through probing, careful listening, and observing so that the product and the presentation can be linked to these needs. The next step is to present the product or service and illustrate how it will meet the customer's needs. This is followed by an acknowledgment of the potential buyer's objections, in which the salesperson probes and answers them. Finally, on closing the sale, the salesperson reiterates the reasons to decide favorably, asks for a commitment, and paves the way for future business.[28]

Just as the persuasive interviewer should be well organized and be prepared to adapt to the needs of the interviewee, it is crucial that the interviewee also actively participate in the process, critically analyzing the sales approach and appeals, particularly when a great deal of time and money are at stake.

An understanding of what the interviewer is attempting to do to get the potential purchaser to buy a product or idea can be strong ammunition for dealing with any sales approach. Asking questions, reading the available literature, and going to several different suppliers to compare opposing points of view should prepare you to handle hard-sell techniques.

If the sales pitch is legitimate, and the product or proposal is going to meet your needs, then your acceptance of it may well be in order. But remember that many salespersons are trained to close a sale in order to make a commission or reach a quota; thus, they have strong motivations to do whatever they can to disarm and manipulate you during the negotiation.

As a salesperson seeking to counter the often negative perception of salespersons, keep in mind that trust can be built by showing knowledge of the product and concern for the needs of the customer, using sales techniques that are not manipulative, being sincere without being condescending, and showing concern for the finances and welfare of the customer. Most important, however, the successful sales interviewer must listen. One sales expert has found this to be the case in her own entrepreneurial career: "The more mature I get, the more I recognize the importance of really listening to the customer. . . . I won't find out what he needs if I'm doing all the talking."[29]

The sales interview usually begins with the salesperson establishing a rapport, arousing interest, and getting the customer involved.

Appraisal Interview

In an **appraisal interview,** sometimes referred to as a *performance review*, the interviewer helps the interviewee to realize the strengths and weaknesses of his or her performance. An appraisal interview takes place when you meet with an instructor to review your English theme or in-class speech; however, this type of interview is usually more associated with employment settings.

Employees are consistently rated on their performance. It is estimated that "over 90 percent of companies and . . . nearly 80 percent of all governmental units have formal systems of personnel assessment."[30] Performance appraisal interviews are useful in improving individual performance by (1) clarifying job requirements and standards, (2) providing feedback on an employee's progress in meeting the requirements, and (3) guiding future performance on the job.[31] A survey of U.S., Canadian, and European companies determined that 66 percent of the employees believed that appraisals helped to motivate them to do good work.[32]

Unfortunately, appraisal interviews may be misunderstood and abused and too frequently are used only for negative criticism instead of positive reinforcement. But when handled well, an appraisal interview can present methods for change while reinforcing the positive aspects of a person's performance.

Twelve points characteristic of effective performance appraisal interviews have been identified. These include:

1. Identify the positive behavior your employees should strive for.
2. Identify the criteria by which you will evaluate their performance.
3. Maintain a balance between positive and negative in the performance assessment.
4. Do not overemphasize differences between ideal and actual job performance.
5. Bring up performance concerns as needed, not just at the scheduled periodic review time.
6. Distinguish between an employee who *will not* work from an employee who *cannot* work.
7. Separate the performance discussion and the salary discussion of the review for counseling purposes.
8. Avoid becoming defensive.

9. Encourage employees to participate in the development of a performance appraisal system.
10. Keep performance appraisals open, honest, and informal.
11. Develop effective communication channels within the organization so that performance appraisals will be part of an open system of communication.
12. Give employees full, factual, and complete information.[33]

Performance appraisals should be two-way communication. Both supervisor and subordinate should view the process as a careful analysis and, if necessary, problem-solving session. This, of course, is very difficult to carry out in practice because of the nature of the supervisor-worker, professor-student power relationship. Nevertheless, in organizations in which the supervisor or instructor has built trust by dealing honestly with the persons with whom she or he works, there is a better chance for true participatory evaluation. This usually takes place when the person in the position of power indicates what is and what is not negotiable, encourages openness regarding questions of authority and does so without repercussions, and does not feel she or he is the only one with the ability to think of solutions to problems. Unfortunately, this type of leader is quite rare.

Just as it requires skill to present constructive criticism in a performance appraisal, so too does it take ability to receive criticism. Unfortunately, criticism can engender a great deal of defensiveness; people are ego centered. Most people have a need to be right. Even when we recognize we are wrong, we want to defend our actions. Performance appraisals, from the viewpoint of the receiver, will be most productive when the interviewee:

1. Listens carefully to the criticism.
2. Paraphrases the criticism.
3. Asks for specifics.
4. Monitors nonverbal behavior and is aware of the physical signs that indicate possible upset: hand twisting, teeth grinding, face flushing, wiggling in the chair or shifting from foot to foot if standing, or feeling sudden tightness in the back of the neck or the temples.
5. Responds by agreeing to take the steps necessary to change the situation, or, if he or she feels the criticism is not legitimate or beneficial, refusing to take the recommended actions and indicating why.[34]

Remember that if you refuse to accept the recommendations or input, you may be punished for that action: fired, denied a promotion, put on warning for insubordination, fail a course. Therefore, if you choose to take such an action, be sure you are willing to accept the consequences.

Much of the research on performance appraisal methods deals with the manager in the workplace. It should be apparent, however, that the same principles apply to a teacher who is trying to improve a student's performance or a parent who wishes to change or improve a child's behavior.

The goal of performance appraisal in any field is to improve performance, but improvement can result only if a specific plan is established during the interview. For this reason, the performance appraisal interview should conclude with a concrete plan in which both parties jointly explore several possible actions; concentrate on one or two specific actions; specify to whom those actions will happen, what will happen, and when; provide for follow-up on the work; and set out in writing the plan to be followed.[35] The Motorola Company, for example, has designed a "Tell the

Truth" interview in which a substandard employee's problems are reviewed and then a performance improvement plan is discussed so that the employee knows specifically how to improve to keep the job.[36]

Reprimanding Interview

In a **reprimanding interview,** the interviewer helps the interviewee to analyze problems caused by the latter so that corrections can be made. Usually a reprimand happens only after an appraisal interview so that an employee has had an opportunity to correct the situation in the meantime. Unlike most of the other types of interviews that function through the funnel schedule, the **inverted funnel schedule** is most appropriate for the reprimand. In this format, the interview starts out with a clear, specific statement of the performance problem so that there is no question as to what the problem is. After this discussion, the interview should move to a more general discussion of the person's work, such as how he or she feels about it, and what barriers are interfering with a high level of performance.

Ideally, the interviewee should suggest a desirable solution to the problem. In fact, some employers like to build counseling techniques into the reprimand, beginning with identification of the problem and then leading to the employee's own explanation of why the problem persists and how to resolve it. Suppose, for example, a lab technician continually fails to return equipment after using it, a practice causing other technicians to complain to the employer. Through an interview, the employer tries to help the technician to understand the problem, suggests the necessity for correcting the behavior in the future, and encourages the employee to propose an acceptable procedure for correction.

The National Labor Relations Board and the U.S. Supreme Court have ruled that an employee has the right to have third-party representation at any disciplinary interview—a witness, attorney, or some other person.[37]

The reprimanding interview is difficult to conduct because the interviewer carries the burden of establishing grounds for the disciplinary action. Using a preset list

---

If You Must Criticize Someone

Here are some suggestions for giving criticism in a way that motivates others to do a better job:

◆ **See yourself** as a teacher or coach—as being helpful. Keep in mind that you're trying to help someone improve.

◆ **Show you** care. Express your sincere concern about sharing ways the other person can boost his or her success.

◆ **Pick the** right moment to offer criticism. Make sure the person hasn't just been shaken by some incident.

◆ **Avoid telling** people they *"should* do such and such" or *"should* have done such and such.""Shoulds" make you appear rigid and pedantic.

◆ **Avoid giving** the impression that you're more concerned with seeing your recommendations put into practice than in helping the other person improve.

◆ **Show how** the person will benefit from taking the actions you suggest.

◆ **Give specific** suggestions. Being vague might only make the situation worse by creating anxiety and doubt.

Tip: Be sure you can take criticism yourself. If not, you may not be perceived as a credible source.

Source: How to Love the Job You Hate, by Jane Boucher, Thomas Nelson Publishers, P.O. Box 141000, Nashville, TN 37214.

Law enforcement officers are commonly trained in interrogation interviewing.

of questions for which answers are provided may not make the process any less painful, but what is wrong and what is going to be done will be clear:

1. What did I do wrong?
2. Why was it wrong?
3. What is the penalty?
4. Is the penalty fair?
5. What will happen if I do it again?
6. What can I do to improve my performance or behavior?[38]

The reprimanding interview, whether used by managers with workers, parents with children, or teachers with students, ought to be considered the procedure of last resort. The risk in this interview is great because the procedures can create considerable defensiveness on the part of the interviewee unless the process is handled skillfully.

To be careful communicators in these situations, interviewers should avoid accusatory statements starting with "you are" and instead use phrases such as "I feel" and stick to factual statements. They should ask questions that permit the person to express feelings or explain behavior, stay away from verbalizing conclusions during the interview, and try to conclude the interview on a neutral note.[39] Because the interviewer can be held legally liable for any type of punishment that is given, she or he must use factual evidence as a basis for any final decision. The evidence should be available for any legal action that may follow.

Interrogation Interview

An **interrogation interview** is designed to secure information from an interviewee through extensive use of probing techniques. Lawyers, credit officers, tax specialists, and law enforcement officers use such interviews. Because of the circumstances, the interviewer is sometimes dealing with an interviewee who is reluctant to respond to questions. Consequently, through the phrasing of questions and the manner in which they are verbally and nonverbally presented, the interviewer often uses psychological pressure to elicit responses.

Law Enforcement Interrogation Law enforcement officers are commonly trained in interrogation interviewing, a format designed to scrutinize an interviewee and, in the case of an arrest, to secure a confession to a crime. As a result, the interviewer often works to create a climate of stress during the interview to pressure the interviewee into admitting wrongdoing.

Investigators who must use this interview format are advised to attempt to maintain emotional control throughout the interrogation. Whatever your personal feelings toward the person being questioned, keep those feelings to yourself. Try to remain even-tempered. In spite of this recommendation, there are situations in which strong emotion may be needed to extract the necessary information.

Because the interviewee in a police investigation is likely to be quite hostile, the questioning strategy is very important. A good interrogator works to break through the hostility and get the information needed to complete the case. The interrogator begins this process by informing the suspect of his or her rights. The U.S. Supreme Court's far-reaching *Miranda* decision requires that police officers inform suspects that they have the right to remain silent, that anything they say may be used as evidence against them, and that they have a right to have an attorney present at the interrogation.

An interrogator must establish credibility and take control of the situation. By using different types of questions, the officer constructs a picture of the incident depicted by the suspect. Lies are difficult to maintain. By noticing contradictions or improbable statements, an interrogator can undermine the suspect's story, which weakens resistance and self-confidence and makes compliance with the investigator's demands easier.[40]

Obviously, the less practiced a person is in resisting an interrogator's techniques, the less will be his or her ability to lie effectively, and the more likely that the interrogator will be successful.

Interrogation techniques displayed by television and movie detectives and police officers can be misleading. Remember that the scripted interaction is based on various theatrical techniques and restrictions: the length of the show, the need for dramatic tension, and the general philosophy that the "good guy wins and the bad guy loses." License is often taken with the legalities that is not allowed in real-life situations.

Through the phrasing of questions, the interviewer often uses psychological pressure to elicit responses.

Legal Interrogation   Interrogation in court is a firmly established practice. Some trial lawyers attempt to trap a witness by asking questions that elicit information outside his or her factual knowledge. For this reason, witnesses should be on guard so they do not place themselves in the position of answering questions on the basis of opinion rather than proof.

For example, one of the authors appeared as a character witness for a former student who was on trial for possession of illegal drugs. The prosecutor asked, "Do you think that the defendant has ever used drugs?" and "Would you say that there is a drug problem at the school the defendant attended?" In both questions the prosecutor was asking for information beyond the factual knowledge of the witness. The answers given were, respectively, "I have no way of knowing whether the defendant has used illegal drugs," and "I don't know what you mean by 'drug problem,' and if I did, I would have no way of knowing whether the school has such a problem." The witness was not trying to be evasive or hostile, but the questions were posed for the purpose of leading the witness to conclusions that the prosecutor could then use to influence the jury.

The courtroom interviewee always must be on guard to answer only those questions for which he or she has accurate, factual information.

Media Interview

The **media interview** takes place when an interviewer asks questions of a guest. The most popular format is the talk show, which can be on radio or television and can be

The media interview takes place when an interviewer asks questions of a guest. It may take place in a studio or on-site.

an entire program or a segment of it. Formats vary greatly: one guest, one host, one host and open lines for listeners to phone in, multiguests with a single or several hosts. Such shows may cover a wide range of topics.

The host's responsibility is to set the format and tone for the program. Some choose the attack-dog approach, others the nice-person role; some are looking for facts, others to incite reaction; some hold strong biases while others try to be more centrist. There is no one way to format such shows; therefore, the techniques vary greatly. Some hosts ask questions and politely wait for the guest to answer. Others interrupt, badger, and incite. Some hosts insist that all calls be screened; others let any call come through.

If you appear on such a show as a guest, be sure you know and approve of the format. Know if you will be asked to submit questions in advance and whether the host or the listening audience will ask the queries. Agree in advance on the topic, and set any guidelines of what subjects you are and are not willing to answer. Some guests have been amazed by both the type of the questions asked and the manners of those who ask them.

When you participate as an interviewee in a talk show, consider the implications of what you say. Try to avoid getting trapped with any line of questions, and steer the conversation to the message that you want to present as best as you can. Use transitional bridges such as "Yes, that's an interesting point, and in addition . . ." or "What's really important to consider . . ." to allow you to emphasize your message.

An interesting reversal of roles takes place when a listener calls a talk-show host and asks questions, such as on an open-line segment when a question on any topic can be asked. In that case, the person "in charge" becomes the interviewee. In other cases, callers wish to interrogate the guest expert. If you are a caller and truly want information, here are some suggestions for probing:

1. Ask a short question with only one point. Long, complicated questions confuse the listener and are seldom answered in whole. If you need to ask more than one thing and are permitted to do so, break the question down into parts and let the listener know that there are several sections to the inquiry.

You can introduce this with such a phrase as "I have a two-part question I'd like to ask ..."

Media Relations: Answering Questions on TV

Whether you're prepared for a TV interview or surprised by it, these tips can help you get good footage:

◆ Avoid these three signals that a tough question has fazed you: looking away, crossing your legs, or clasping your hands in front of you. Instead, keep your posture open and maintain friendly eye contact.

◆ Answer questions briefly. *Reasons:* Viewers have no patience for lengthy comments. And time limits usually will force editors to cut your comments to a sound bite, so anything extra you say won't make it to the screen anyway.

◆ Move on if you misspeak, even if the cameras are rolling. *Reason:* Both reporters—and audiences—may not notice what you said the first time. But they'll focus on it if you apologize or try to defend what you said.

◆ Prepare for a planned interview by having three points you want to make and rehearsing four or five ways to say the same three things.

◆ Deliver your main point first if the show is live. *Reason:* If you save it until last, you may never get to say it.

Source: Morey Stettner, writing in *Investor's Business Daily.*

2. Many shows are on what is called a seven-second delay. If you try to listen to the radio or television and ask your question on the telephone, you will hear yourself coming out of the speaker in what sounds like an echo. The sound also feeds back into the telephone and is distracting to the host. Turn off your receiver.

3. Ideally, the purpose of your call is to ask a question. Unfortunately, some people want to give speeches. Don't be surprised if you get cut off if you start on a tirade.

4. If you tell the screener what subject you would like to speak about, stick to that topic. The reason the hosts know your name before you come on is that the screener inputs a message to the host using a computer. The host knows all about you before you are on. If you deviate from the topic, you may be cut off.

5. Get right to the point. This is not a social engagement. Asking about the health of the host, or telling that you are a "first-time caller, long-time listener," is of little interest.

6. If you are calling to get advice, listen to the answer, ask clarifying questions, and hang up. Debating the value of the advice is generally not appropriate. You asked, the person gave what she or he thought was right, and that's about as far as this can go.

In Conclusion

The interview is a communication form used extensively to accomplish many goals. Effective participation requires that interviewers and interviewees recognize that an effective interview involves an opening that enables both parties to establish rapport and clarify their objectives, a body of questions and responses that accomplishes the communication objectives, and a close that ties up the conversation and identifies any further steps to be taken.

Interview communicators participate in many different types of interviews, including the employment, the information-gathering, the problem-solving, the oral history, the counseling, the persuasive, the appraisal, the reprimanding, the interrogation, and the media interview.

Learn by Doing

1. Make an appointment with a person who is or was employed in your current career or career choice. Interview the person to determine what academic courses she or he took to qualify for the job, what specific skills are required for success in the career, what the specific job responsibilities are, and what helpful hints he or she can give you about being successful in the field. Report to the class on both the results of the interview and what you learned about the interviewing process.

2. You are paired with another student according to your academic major. Each student independently researches job descriptions within the field; employment opportunities; communication skills, special talents, and abilities that are needed; types of organizations employing people trained in the field; working conditions; and salary. You are given several weeks to complete your research. You and your partner then conduct a seven- to ten-minute information-gathering interview concerning the selected career during one of your class periods. One of you acts as the interviewee and the other as the interviewer. Before the interview, develop an interview agenda and questions. If your professor prefers, the interviews can be done on audiotape or videotape and submitted for evaluation.

3. Two students are assigned to read the same book, short story, or magazine article. In class, one of the students interviews the other concerning what she or he has read. This can be done in small groups or in front of the entire class.

4. Write down five items you want an interviewer to know about you; then write a sentence about how you plan to convey each of these items. The class is then divided into groups of three, each group having an interviewee, an interviewer, and an observer. After a ten-minute interview, the observer states what he or she believes the applicant has communicated. The interviewee shares the list of five items, and then the entire group discusses how the interviewee might have communicated any items he or she failed to get across. Then change roles and repeat the process until all three members of the group have had a chance to be interviewed.

5. You are paired with another student. You are to select a subject of mutual interest and ask each other a series of questions about the topic. You should first ask each other a direct question, then an open question, then a closed question. Repeat the procedure three times to practice the types of questions. Continue the interview by asking a leading question, a loaded question, and a yes-response question. Follow up with a mirror question and a probe.

6. Prepare a résumé for yourself, following one of the formats given in Appendix I at the back of this book.

7. Select an ad from a newspaper for a job you would be interested in applying for. It should be one for which you are qualified now. Use the advice given in this chapter on how to prepare to be interviewed, and write a paper with specific examples describing what you would do to get ready for the interview.

8. Your class will be divided into groups. One person from each group is to call a radio talk show and engage the host in a discussion. Other members of the group listen and then critique the interviewing style of their classmate.

9. Your instructor will assign groups of two people in your class various segments of Richard Bolles's *What Color Is Your Parachute?*[41] to read. Each pair conducts an information-gathering interview about the segment read. These interviews may be done in front of the entire class, outside class, or in dyads while the class is in session. If either of the latter is done, each team is asked to share observations in a class discussion after the interviews have been completed.

10. Your instructor will appoint one person to be the interviewer and another to be the interviewee. The interview is to be tape-recorded. The interviewer is to ask the interviewee each of the most-asked interview questions for entry-level positions as presented in the chapter. The tape-recordings can then be used for a class discussion or can be evaluated by your instructor.

11. Search the Web for advice on preparing for and responding to interview questions. See, for example, **CareerPerfect.com**.

12. There are numerous family history software programs such as *Reunion, The Family Tree Software* by Leister Productions. Online sites are also of value. For example, search "Oral History Internet Resources" in Yahoo! or Google. The Indiana University Oral History Research Center offers a pamphlet on how to organize and conduct oral history interviews. Using these sources, prepare a list of statements that expand beyond the text's discussion on how to conduct a family history interview. Be prepared to share your list with your classmates.

Key Terms

interview

interviewer

interview format

interviewee

direct questions

open questions

closed questions

bipolar question

leading questions

loaded questions

yes-response question

mirror question

probe

employment interview

second employment interviews

behavioral interview

case interview

stress interview

telephone job interview

information-gathering interview

problem-solving interview

oral history interview

counseling interview

nondirective techniques

directive intervention

persuasive interview

sales interview

appraisal interview

reprimanding interview

inverted funnel schedule

interrogation interview

media interview

9

The Theory
of Groups

After reading this chapter, you should be able to

- Define what a group is and compare and contrast large and small groups

- Explain the advantages and disadvantages of group decision making

- List and define the kinds of groups

- Explain and illustrate the norming, storming, conforming, performing, and adjourning group phases

- Enumerate the Six-Step Standard for Decision Making and the 1-3-6 Decision-Making Technique

- Define voting and explain the four common voting methods: consensus, majority, plurality, and part of the whole

- Clarify the role of the setting in group actions

The hink back over the last several weeks. How often have you been involved in group activities or heard others speaking about attending a meeting of some type? If you are typical of most people, you probably came up with a considerable list. Businesspeople hold conferences at all levels in an organization, scientists work in teams, educators serve on committees, families meet and discuss mutual joys and problems, students attend classes and hold meetings, citizens serve on juries, and athletes play on a team. All of these are examples of groups in action. Each of us will spend on average more than nine thousand hours—roughly one year—in meetings over our lifetime.[1]

In the United States, people join groups for various reasons. You may join because you are required to do so, such as in a work environment or classroom when there is a group project. You may affiliate because you like the members of the group. This is a common reason that individuals join fraternities or sororities. You may join because you believe in the causes that the assemblage espouses, such as their political beliefs. Organizations such as Save the Whales and the Human Rights Campaign gain membership because of their stances. Some people join because of the meaning or identity a group gives their lives. For example, you might join a church, synagogue, or the Nation of Islam because of your philosophical or religious leanings. Some people affiliate because they think they can gain some contacts or socialization from the members. Joining the American Society for Training and Development, for example, is a way of making business contacts. Social groups allow you to meet new friends.

In the United States, why a person joins a group has a noticeable effect on the productivity and cohesiveness of the group.[2] People who do not willingly become members tend to shun responsibilities and do not actively participate in collective efforts. Think of activities you were required to join. Did you actively participate? Probably not, or, at best, you did so reluctantly.

Groups Defined

A group is not just any collection or aggregate of persons. Groupness emerges from the relationships among the people involved.[3] A **group** traditionally has been defined as "an assemblage of persons who communicate, in order to fulfill a common purpose and achieve a goal."[4]

Groups often are classified by their size. **Small groups** usually consist of three to twelve persons; **large groups** normally have more than a dozen. Research shows that participation rates are affected significantly by differences in group size. For example, six-person juries offer greater vocal participation than do twelve-person juries.[5]

Group Versus Individual Actions

Groups, by the very nature of their collective identity, offer participants both advantages and disadvantages over working alone.

Advantages of Groups

The group process provides an opportunity for input from many people with different points of view. Groups also offer the advantage of challenging ideas before they are put into action. Since a group is composed of people with varying backgrounds and interests, an idea probably will receive the scrutiny of many evaluations before it receives group acceptance. Because any one person's experiences are limited, the aggregate viewpoints should result in a better-thought-out decision.

In addition, taking part in group action can lead to greater commitment among participants to the decisions reached. Workers who discuss new procedures, for instance, may approach their tasks with more enthusiasm because they helped to develop those procedures.

Research has revealed the **risky shift phenomenon,** which holds that decisions reached after discussion by a group display more experimentation, are less conservative, and contain more risk than decisions reached by people working alone before any discussion is held.[6] A group of managers who come together to solve a problem of worker morale, for instance, are more likely to adopt a radical strategy than any single one of the managers acting alone. A manager by himself or herself is likely to be more careful and assume less risk because he or she is acting alone rather than together with others.

Disadvantages of Groups

A group is not just a collection or aggregate of persons.

Although the group process offers important advantages, it also has some disadvantages. For example, group decision making takes much longer than individual decision making because there are discussions among many people with diverse points of view. The group process also requires participants to give up some individuality for the purpose of compromising with other group members.

Yet another disadvantage of the group process may surface when people blindly commit themselves to group cohesion at the expense of careful analysis. This phenomenon, **groupthink,** is "the mode of thinking that persons engage in when concurrence-seeking becomes so dominant in a cohesive in-group that it tends to override realistic appraisal of alternative courses of action."[7] Although it happened almost half a century ago, the disastrous Bay of Pigs invasion in Cuba in 1961 is cited as a classic example of groupthink. President Kennedy's group of advisers blended so well as a group and felt that any negative comments would be perceived as being disloyal to the group that even those who disagreed didn't speak up.

On January 28, 1986, almost twenty-five years after the Bay of Pigs incident, the same problem presented itself. The space shuttle *Challenger* was launched from Kennedy Space Center. Seventy-three seconds after

I'M GLAD I'M HOME! YOU GUYS ARE THE BEST SUPPORT GROUP I'VE EVER HAD!!

'PPl clrtan of groupdecsion commit binduy to group cohesion

the launch, the *Challenger* exploded, killing all seven astronauts aboard. "The Presidential Commission that investigated that accident pointed to a flawed decision-making process as a primary contributory cause."[8] It determined, as illustrated in Figure 9.1, that the decision makers *failed to form a group that had different perspectives,* thus falling into the same pattern as the Bay of Pigs resolution proposers. The commission further found that the decision-making team had been operating under a *time pressure* that was unrealistic. Further, the *leadership* of the group *failed to heed the known consequences of groupthink* and did not carefully monitor the proceedings. In addition, the commission found that the group had *made the decision without considering alternatives, without seeking out expert opinions beyond those of the group, and rejecting negative information* that might have cast a negative light on their preferred procedure. The *outcome was disastrous.*

Some have suggested that the decision of the George W. Bush administration in 2003 to attack Iraq was another example of groupthink. The president had surrounded himself with a vice president and cabinet members who were hawkish, and prowar. In addition, after the September 11, 2001, terrorist attacks, Bush had established an atmosphere in which people who did not support his actions were labeled anti-American. This environment made the situation ripe for groupthink.

To prevent groupthink:[9]

♦ Recognize the problem of groupthink and that it stems from pressure to conform to group norms.

♦ Seek information that challenges an emerging concurrence.

♦ Develop a norm in the group that legitimizes disagreement.

♦ Be aware that although cohesion is normally a positive aspect of group maintenance, the more cohesive a group is, the greater is the danger of groupthink.

Because a group usually has made so much effort to reach its conclusion, the members often just assume that the solution will work. This can lead to the **Pollyanna-Nietzsche effect:** excessive optimism (*pollyannaism*) and an idealized belief (*nietzschism*) that the group is superhuman and can do no wrong. This results in assuming that all is well. To avoid this, groups must evaluate the implementation of any solution and constantly be vigilant to adjusting the recommendations if things do not go as assumed.[10]

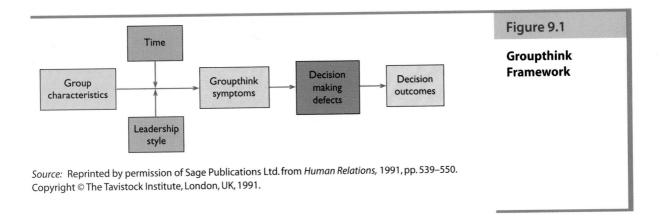

Figure 9.1

Groupthink Framework

Source: Reprinted by permission of Sage Publications Ltd. from *Human Relations,* 1991, pp. 539–550. Copyright © The Tavistock Institute, London, UK, 1991.

Groupness emerges from the relationships among the people involved.

Members of any group must be aware that although participation in the decision-making process can lead a person to greater commitment to his or her work or to the decision made, in some cases social loafing may take place. **Social loafing** occurs when group membership leads people to work less than they would individually. An individual who thinks that his or her own contribution to the group cannot be measured may tend to slack off.[11]

Types of Groups

We communicate in various types of groups, including work teams, study groups, support groups, committees, focus groups, family as a group, public meetings, and town meetings.

Work Teams

In the professional setting, people may be involved in a number of different kinds of groups. One of the most prevalent groups in U.S. industry is the **work team:** small groups of workers who function as teams to make and implement decisions about their own work. As organizations work to accomplish their goals, they have found, based on the success of the Japanese and the Swedes, that it is important to set up work teams. For a work team to achieve its goals, management must commit to "empowering" the team: training the members to work in a group and allowing the group the time to carry out its functions and the decisions it makes.[12] Organizations have found that the use of work teams leads to improved employee morale, greater responsiveness to and flexibility in meeting customer needs, and better quality of services and production of goods.[13]

Study Groups

Study groups are established to enable individuals to work together to study and learn with the assistance of others. Students planning to take the Graduate Record Examination, for example, often join together, with or without a tutor, to work toward learning the materials on the test.

To be productive, a study group should follow some basic principles:

1. Limit the group to participants who will help in the learning process.
2. Meet on a regular basis in a location that lends itself to studying, not to socializing or allowing interruptions, and insist that beepers and cell phones be turned off.
3. Insist that all members of the group attend all meetings and participate.
4. Require that each member be prepared for sessions.
5. Allow each member to take a turn in leading and providing explanations.[14]

Support Groups

A **support group** is a system that allows people to interact with others who share similar goals or problems. "The purpose of a support group is to increase people's knowledge of themselves and others, assist people to clarify the changes they most want to make in their life, and give people some of the tools necessary to make these changes."[15]

"People are coming together in record numbers both to cope with affliction and to deal with normal processes in life."[16] It is estimated that nearly 1 million special types of support groups exist. Growth groups have a vast number of purposes: to deal with preventive and remedial aims (e.g., Alcoholics Anonymous), treatment of eating disorders (Weight Watchers), learning coping skills (Adult Children of Alcoholics), managing relationships (Marriage Encounter), offering support for grieving (Mended Hearts), making family adjustments (Parents Without Partners), and being the parent or friend of a gay man or lesbian (P-Flag).

One of the most prevalent groups in U.S. industry is the work team.

In the counseling setting, some therapists believe that support groups may be more effective than individual counseling because they can provide the empathy and knowledge of other people who have had similar experiences and can share their thoughts and feelings.[17] Support groups are considered an effective means for working through trauma caused by rape, incest, physical abuse, battering, physical illness, and phobias. One study indicated that women with advanced breast cancer who had group therapy, in addition to medical treatment, lived twice as long as women who were given medical treatment alone.[18]

A newspaper advice columnist encouraged the use of support groups when she told a troubled correspondent: "I can't say enough about the groups that operate on the theory that people who share the same problem can get strength from one another. If you are having a problem with children, parents, family, friends, or with yourself, there is probably a self-help group for you."[19]

Committees

Most organizations rely heavily on committees. Because it is often difficult for a large group of people to accomplish much more than voting on policy matters, it may become necessary to send certain tasks to a **committee:** a small group responsible for study, research, and recommendations about the issue at hand. The committee's actions usually are brought back to a larger group for action. Unfortunately, some individuals use the "refer to committee" technique as a ploy to make sure the issue is never discussed again. They know that referring a subject to committee often means no one will actually deal with it or that it will be forgotten.

Committees work best when they have clear objectives.

To ensure that committees work effectively, a series of guidelines have been proposed:

- ◆ Have clear objectives,
- ◆ Include a diversity of members from throughout the organization,
- ◆ Be flexible in allowing members to move in and out of the committee,
- ◆ Be sure that everyone is allowed a voice in the deliberations,
- ◆ Balance the needs of the committee with the needs of the rest of the organization,
- ◆ Cooperate,
- ◆ Work as a team,
- ◆ Enjoy the experience,
- ◆ Share the results throughout the organization, and
- ◆ Assume the responsibility for study, review, guidance, direction, and evaluation but allow the implementation to be handled by management.[20]

Organizations often have to discover information to help lead them to make decisions. One of the ways, for example, that advertising agencies discern market trends, logo favorites, or attitudes of particular potential groups of consumers is to use focus groups.

Focus Groups

Motivational research has led many organizations to the use of **focus groups,** which are designed to test reactions to a particular product, process, or service offered by an organization. A randomly selected group of participants who are representative of the user or consumer group are brought together with a professional facilitator to discuss, for example, a new product. The reactions are carefully recorded and quantified in a report to the organization as input for decision making.

The Family as a Group

Although you may not have ever thought of it as such, the family is a group. In fact, it is one of the primary groups in which most of us participate. Families are groups operating as a system by the very nature of their purposes and functions: decision making, interpersonal relationships, and mutual dependency.

A **family** is an assemblage of people who have legally been declared a group or who have defined themselves as such. Typical kinds of families are natural families (a married couple with or without children), blended families (families created by divorce and remarriage or death and remarriage), single-parent families (one parent with a child or children), extended families (a cluster of relatives who may also include friends), and self-declared families (e.g., heterosexuals living together, homosexuals living together, communal groups, religious cults).

Families are groups operating as a system.

There is no one best way for a family to operate. Some families learn to operate under stress and chaos. Some have open channels of communication and operate in cooperative harmony.

Most family communication follows a structure that resembles a mobile. The parts (family members) are segments of the same unit, and any reverberation of a problem goes through the system and throws off the mobile's balance. How well the family functions depends on the members' abilities to communicate with one another and balance the various parts of the system.

Family discussions center on answers to some basic communication questions. What are members allowed to talk about (e.g., death, alcohol use, sex, money)? What words can be used to talk about certain subjects (e.g., death is "passed on"; alcoholism is "Daddy is sick")? Where can members talk (e.g., in the kitchen, at the table while eating, in the bedroom, in the car, "only in our own house—this is nobody else's business")? Who can talk about it (e.g., mother and father only; father talks, others listen)?

Most families typically enforce rules randomly and lack consistency in their methods of operation. In some families, however, rules of communication are established and upheld at all costs, resulting in praise, cooperation, abuse, punishment, and/or banning.

Public Meetings

In addition to the use of internal group interactions, some organizations find it necessary to conduct **public meetings,** in which members or interested individuals may attend the sessions. Corporations must hold stockholders' meetings. Government organizations, such as school boards and city councils, may need to conduct their meetings in public to ensure that the decisions they reach are in the best interests of the public they serve and to fulfill the legal requirements of many states to hold open meetings.

Public meetings can follow a number of formats. The members may discuss the issue among themselves and then let the audience ask questions. Or there may be a series of experts or witnesses in a **symposium** format, in which participants give prepared speeches with no interaction among themselves or with the audience. These presentations are often followed by a **forum:** an interaction during which questions are fielded by the participants from each other as well as from any audience present.

Town Meetings

In a **town meeting,** the presenter opens with a short, prepared statement that establishes the framework for the meeting. Individuals in the audience then engage in a forum with the speaker. In the ensuing dialogue, both speaker and audience members explain their positions and share viewpoints on issues. The town meeting has a long history in some areas of the United States, such as New England, where some communities still use it for town decision making. It came into contemporary prominence when President Clinton conducted town meetings in various parts of the country in his 1992 campaign. Clinton met with people in their hometown settings to talk about their needs and wants. It was one of the formats selected for a 1996 presidential debate between candidates Bill Clinton and Bob Dole.

Group Operations

Groups are continually evolving. Normally they evolve through five phases: norming, storming, conforming, performing, and adjourning (see Figure 9.2).[21]

Group Norming

Group norming is the orienting aspect of people coming together and starting a group or welcoming new people into an existing group. Depending on the nature of the assemblage, an exchange of names and other demographic information usually occurs. In new organizations, discussion is often cautious and doesn't deal immediately with the purpose or goals of the group. The norming process usually proceeds more rapidly when new people enter an existing group.

During this stage, **group norms**—the rules by which the group will operate—are developed. The obligations of the members, what they can and can't do, and the mode of operation are decided. These norms can be explicit (written and agreed on, as in a constitution) or implicit (understood but not formalized).[22]

The source of the group's norms may be influenced from outside the group. They may be rules preset by others, such as when a judge charges a jury; handed down, such as when a local chapter of an organization is given rules by the national organization; developed by group members based on their past experiences or through trial and error; or influenced by a member or leader who has either experience in the group process or strong enough persuasive skills to influence others. Whatever the means, setting boundaries is a critical group function.

Group procedures that should be determined include[23]

♦ *Planning an agenda.* Group meetings normally follow an **agenda:** the list of the topics to be discussed or the problems that must be dealt with in the order in which they will be acted on.

♦ *Handling routine housekeeping details.* Such details include taking attendance and agreeing on the rules for decision making.

♦ *Preparing for the next meeting.* An ongoing group must decide when it will reconvene. It is sometimes necessary to designate who will be responsible for certain details for the next session.

Group Storming

Although it might be ideal and make group decision making much easier, groups seldom norm and work toward their goal without some disagreements. Most groups, during either the process of setting rules or working toward their goal, enter into a period called **group storming,** when conflicts erupt. The disagreements may be caused by a power struggle among those interested in being the leader, conflict

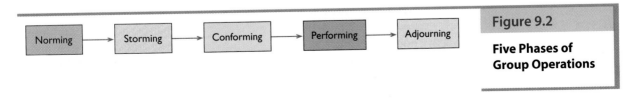

Figure 9.2

Five Phases of Group Operations

Norming → Storming → Conforming → Performing → Adjourning

over the rules of operation, or personality conflicts among group members. Storming can be a positive aspect of group operation since it often alerts the group to underlying problems. It brings the conflicts into the open, allows the members to deal with them, and permits the establishment of an open communication environment. Although storming is common, don't assume that something is wrong if a group you are in doesn't go through storming. Just be sure that the lack of storming is not caused by groupthink.

Types of Group Tension   Two types of social tensions are at the base of storming. **Primary group tension** refers to the normal jitters and feelings of uneasiness that group members experience when they first congregate. Think of an experience you've had when entering a group for the first time—for example, entering a class on the first day or going to work on a new job. Group interaction at this point is usually of very low intensity. Often there are long periods of silence, discussion of frivolous topics, tentative statements, and overpoliteness. Interruptions evoke profuse apologies. This phenomenon can be compared to boxers' feeling each other out.[24] There is a tendency, especially among European Americans, to want to get through this "meaningless stuff" quickly and get down to business. However, people in other cultures are interested in this relationship stage and are willing to put time into it. It is fairly common in Japan and in Arabic countries, for example, for social interactions to take initial precedence over getting down to work.

Your strategy as a competent communicator is not to avoid primary tension but to let it take its natural course. Primary tension tends to be short-lived and cause for little concern unless it escalates to an unmanageable level. With time, it normally disappears.

The other type of social tension is referred to as **secondary group tension;** it is the stress and strain that occur within a group later in its development. Frequent causes of this problem are having to make a decision, shortage of time to accomplish the task, differences of opinion, and difficult members.

Signs of secondary tension include abrupt departure from the group's routine, a sharp outburst by a member, a sarcastic barb, or hostile and antagonistic exchanges between members. Extreme secondary tension can be unpleasant. If it is left uncontrolled, the group's existence may be threatened. The goal is not to eliminate the tension, but to use it in a positive way. Tension can be energizing—a source of creative thinking—and if effectively dealt with, can bring a group together.

Role of Power   One of the major triggers of storming is the role of power. Competition appears to be unavoidable in human transactions, and one of the major centers of competition is who holds the power. **Power role** is the ability to influence another's attainment of goals. Power can center on controlling another person or persons, influencing the efforts of others, and/or accomplishing a goal.

All groups have a power structure. One person may exert power because he or she has information or expertise that will allow the group to reach its goal. For example, a group dealing with a financial crisis may turn for advice to the person most knowledgeable about economics or accounting. In some cases, power centers on legitimate authority. The person who is appointed chairperson of the committee by the company president holds the position legitimately and therefore can act as the leader no matter what the feelings of the group may be. Sometimes the power figure has the ability to give rewards or punishments. A parent, for instance, often has the ability to decide on allowances and curfew times, thus putting her or him in a control position over children.

Another type of power centers on personal qualities. That is, some people have the charisma or likability to become a power source. It is often believed that our most effective leaders, whether presidents or athletic coaches, are those who get others to follow them willingly, to do so because of their charisma.

Unresolved Storming   Do not assume that all groups make it through the storming stage. Some find that because of the personalities of the members, the inability to decide on norms, or the lack of clarity of purpose, they simply cannot work their way through storming. In this case, they may disband or continue to operate in a storming fashion, or members gradually fade away, and the group folds when members stop coming to meetings because nothing is being accomplished.

Storming Strategies   In order to deal with storming so that it does not remain an unresolved issue, consider the following:

◆ Provide a get-acquainted period before the first meeting so that group members meet each other informally.

◆ Schedule an informal chat period before each meeting so that there is unpressured interaction between participants.

◆ Remind the group both that disagreement can help to achieve a superior outcome and that the purpose of the assemblage is to achieve the group goal, not individual goals.

◆ Tolerate, even encourage, disagreement and deviance. The trick is to keep disagreement within tolerable limits. Be aware, however, that some people can't tolerate any disagreement. They may have a history of physical or verbal abuse and panic when bickering starts, fearing it will escalate into a full-fledged war. Others have been brought up to avoid fighting at all costs. Whatever the situation, even though allowing some disagreement can be a positive force in a group, be aware of the possible deep-seated sensitivity of some members.

◆ If appropriate, use humor, joking, and shared laughter to lighten the mood.

◆ Stick to attacking the issues, not the person who disagrees with your stand. Don't keep repeating the same argument over and over.

◆ Be an active listener. Even though you have a clearly defined viewpoint, be aware that the other person believes his or her viewpoint is as valid as yours. If you really listen, you might find that the other's view has some validity.

◆ Look for possible places to compromise. Be careful, however, in reaching a compromise that you don't water down the solution so much that it will not achieve its goal of relieving the problem.

Group Conforming

Groups that work their way through the storming stage are those that can go on to work together. This coming together is called **group conforming.** The group will know that it is in the conforming stage when such issues as norms, the group's purpose, and how to handle the role of power have been settled. At this point, members feel commitment to the group. The group is ready to work toward the agreed-on mission, recognizing that it may revert back to storming and will then have to work again toward conforming.

Group Performing

Group performing is the action stage of group process. During this phase, the members clearly start to work toward goals. They have developed a history and know each other, have worked out their mode of operation, and have agreed to move forward to accomplish their task and maintenance roles.

All decision making in a group is influenced by both task and maintenance dimensions. These are not independent entities that stand in opposition to each other; they are interrelated.

The **task dimension of groups** includes decision making, informing, appraising and examining, problem solving, and creating interest in staying on track. Some consider accomplishing the goal the entire purpose of the group and concentrate solely on making sure that the group stays "on task." However, most groups also need to attend to the **maintenance dimension of groups:** meeting the interpersonal needs of the members. The main purpose of maintenance is developing **group cohesion:** the interconnectedness of the members.

As social beings, most people like to be with others, interact with them, express opinions and feelings. Ignoring these aspects of group process by concentrating only on task functions can lead to an empty experience for some of the participants.

Group Adjourning

Groups also find it necessary to go through **adjourning:** going out of existence. In business settings, certain groups are constituted to accomplish a particular task. At the completion of the task, the group disperses. Study groups are formed to prepare the participants for a test. Once the test is over, the group's purpose is completed. Such adjourning requires no specific action other than awareness that the task is done.

On the other hand, some groups have no specific end goal but are ongoing. Even these groups may come to an end. Members may lose interest; people may leave the organization, therefore depleting the membership; or group members determine that the group no longer has a purpose. In these cases, the members vote the group out of existence or simply stop holding meetings. It is advisable that group members take formal action to bring the group to an end. Otherwise, they may feel that they have not reached a true ending and feel incomplete, similar to not completing the process of saying good-bye to someone who dies suddenly.

How to Run a Good Meeting

Here are some tips on how to run a meeting:

♦ Don't compete with group members. Give their ideas precedence over yours.

♦ Listen to everyone. Paraphrase, but don't judge.

♦ Don't put anyone on the defensive. Assume that everyone's ideas have value.

♦ Control the dominant people without alienating them.

♦ Realize that your interest and alertness are contagious.

♦ Keep all participants informed about where they are and what's expected of them. Keep notes on flip charts or a board that everyone can see.

♦ Check with the person who owns the problem to find out if an idea is worth pursuing or if a proposed solution is satisfactory.

♦ Give others a turn at running the meeting. Those who learn to lead learn how to participate.

Source: Financial Times.

Making Group Decisions

One of the most prominent functions of the group communication process is that of decision making. Traditionally in the European American culture, effective decision making tends to follow a step-by-step procedure that allows group members to explore the dimensions of a problem, seek out solutions, and select a solution the members think is most appropriate.

Developing a process leads a group to consider the rules of operation to be followed to reach decisions. Formal organizations, such as city councils and sororities and fraternities, develop a constitution and bylaws clearly spelling out procedures. A set of parliamentary guidelines, such as *Robert's Rules of Order,* usually is adopted as a framework for handling procedural agreements and disagreements.[25] Individuals who chair formal meetings should learn these rules of order. Less formal organizations may allow the leader of a group to determine the operational procedures. Whatever method is used, however, it should be agreed on before any formal work is undertaken by a group in order to clarify how action will occur.

Formulating an Agenda

For the members of a group to be aware of the order in which items will be handled, an *agenda*—the order of business for a meeting or discussion—is prepared. It allows the group to cover topics systematically and accomplish the task in the most efficient way possible. An agenda should be used like a road map. It should contain just enough detail to allow the group to travel the path to the task but should not be so rigid that it does not allow for any detours.

Most meetings have a similar agenda:

I.   Calling the meeting to order
II. Reading the minutes of the previous meeting
III. Presenting committee reports
IV. Discussing unfinished business
V.   Proposing of new business
VI. Adjourning the meeting

Sometimes the agenda specifies not how the meeting should be run but rather how to go about solving a specific problem. The participants start their work by wording a **discussion question**—the issue or problem that will be dealt with. For example, if the group's purpose is to decide what type of grading system should be used on campus, the question could be "What should be done to solve the problem of inconsistent grading policies on campus?"

Some guidelines are useful for wording a discussion question:

◆ *Propose the issue in a question form.* Since the major issue of a problem-solving discussion is what the group should do to solve a specific problem, the discussion should center on answering the question.

◆ *Keep the question short and simple.* Clarity is important.

◆ *Word the question so that it does not show bias.* You cannot honestly discuss a question that states the expected conclusion.

◆ *Word the question as an open question so that it cannot be answered with a yes or no.* You need to allow for other alternatives.

In some instances, the group is formed because the dilemma is clear and the group's task is to solve the preworded problem. On the other hand, some groups may be given a general idea of what is wrong and need to begin by formulating the discussion question. One way to plan a discussion question is for each member to prepare one in advance. Then the group can meet for a short time to share individual questions and blend them into a question on which the group can agree. No discussion of the issues should take place while the question is being put together.

Once the question is agreed on, a format for a discussion may be in order. This step of the process involves developing a discussion agenda. Assume that you are in a group that is going to discuss the question "What can be done to solve the problem of computer hardware and software incompatibility?" Your problem-solving agenda might look like this:

Set an Agenda with Questions

When writing an agenda for a meeting, ask these four questions for each topic on the list:

◆ What specific issues will we discuss?
◆ What outcome do we want from the discussion?
◆ What system will we use to move the discussion along?
◆ How much time will we devote to the issue?

Source: Adapted from Robert Levasseur, author of *Breakthrough Business Meetings,* cited in *Successful Meetings,* 355 Park Ave., S., New York, NY 10010.

Dewey's critical thinking sequence

I. What is the problem?
   A. What terms do we need to know to deal with the problem?
      1. What is computer hardware and software?
      2. What is meant by computer hardware and software incompatibility?
   B. How does this problem concern us
      1. As professionals?
      2. As consumers?

II. What are the causes of the problem?
   A. Is the desire for profits the cause of computer hardware and software incompatibility?
      1. Is competition among leading companies a cause of incompatibility?
      2. Is the purposeful creation of more profitable products a cause of incompatibility?
   B. Does the swiftly growing and changing nature of computer design cause incompatibility?
   C. Does a lack of standards contribute to incompatibility?

III. What are possible solutions?
   A. Would government guidelines bring about greater compatibility?
   B. Would public encouragement of hardware and software compatibility solve the problem?
   C. Would forming a group of manufacturers bring about greater compatibility?
   D. Could groups dedicated to enforcing standards solve the problem?

IV. What is (are) the best solution(s)?
   A. Which of the solutions proposed is workable?
   B. Which of the solutions proposed is desirable?
   C. Which of the solutions proposed is practical?

V. How can the best solution(s) be put into effect?

Following such an agenda allows for complete discussion and contributes to a well-thought-out solution.

Voting

In addition to developing a system for conducting business and arriving at results, a group has responsibilities for determining how decisions will be made by members. **Voting** takes place when members are given an opportunity to indicate agreement, disagreement, or no opinion on an idea or candidate. The purpose of voting is to ensure that members know of the outcome of the discussion and the decision made. It is imperative that the method of voting be agreed on before the group starts working toward the solution, for any alteration of the method can affect the outcome of the group's action.

There are four common voting methods:

Consensus. *Consensus* means "all."[26] Thus, in a consensus decision, every member of the group must agree on a proposal before it can be put into action. This is often the method used for decisions in which dire consequences can result from the outcome of the action. For example, most juries operate by consensus.

Majority vote. The winner must receive more than half of the votes, excluding those who do not vote or who abstain (i.e., do not want to vote).[27] For example, if there are ten people in a group and all vote, it will take six votes for a majority to rule. If, however, one of the people abstains, then it will take five votes for passage according to the majority method.

Plurality. *Plurality* means "most."[28] Often when more than two options are available, a group may turn to plurality voting. If, for example, three candidates are running for an office, in plurality voting the one getting the most votes is declared the winner. In the same way, if five ideas have been proposed as solutions to a problem, the solution selected will be the one receiving the greatest number of votes.

Part-of-the-whole voting. This method occurs when a specific number or percentage of those who are eligible to vote is required to bring about some action. For example, some of the rules of operation of an organization can be changed only if 75 percent of those eligible to vote agree to the change. A group has the right to set any number or percentage it wishes to allow action to take place. These numbers need to be set before starting the decision-making process.

The method selected for the voting can have a profound effect on the outcome of a proposed action. In a historic case, the proposed federal equal rights amendment was not enacted as a U.S. constitutional change, even though more than a majority of the states approved its inclusion. This happened because the part-of-the-whole method was used, and a two-thirds vote was needed but was not obtained. If a majority voting system had been used, the amendment would have passed. Juries, which use consensus, require all twelve jurors to agree on the vote. If the vote is eleven to one, which is a majority, there is no decision.

Decision-Making Techniques

In the European American culture, there are a number of approaches to structuring a decision-making discussion. All of these center on two concepts. First, "effective group decision-making requires an analysis and understanding of a problem before members search for solutions,"[29] and, second, "effective decision-making groups normally engage in creative exploration of unusual, even deviant, ideas

Making Decisions in Small Groups

Decision making in small groups is most effective when all members of the group believe in the decision. *Some suggestions:*
◆ Try for consensus first, but don't force it. Forced consensus often means some members hide their opinions because of pressure from others to reach agreement. True consensus allows for all opinions to be expressed.
◆ If you vote, incorporate the concerns of the people with fewer votes into the final decision so no one "loses." When every member "wins," every member will work to make the decision successful.

Source: Adapted from *From Pyramids to Circles; Taking Hierarchy Out of Small Groups,* by Paula Kramer, Woodrose Press, P.O. Box 93, Nelsonville, WI 54458.

Voting takes place when members are given an opportunity to indicate agreement, disagreement, or no opinion on an idea or candidate.

...ming consists of
...ng possible
...without
...n of them at the
time of their proposal.

during initial discussions."[30] These two steps ensure that the group works toward solving an agreed-on problem and that all the resources and creativity of the members are used. Two methods of decision making are the Six-Step Standard Agenda and 1-3-6.

Six-Step Standard Agenda   The **Six-Step Standard Agenda for Decision Making**[31] is a direct outgrowth of the traditional reflective-thinking process, which stresses that a problem be identified and analyzed, solutions sought, and a solution selected and implemented.[32] The procedure for this method is comprised of six steps:

Step 1   *Problem identification.* A question is worded that states the problem. The query may be a **question of fact** (whether something is true, and to what extent); a **question of value** (whether something is good or bad, right or wrong, and to what extent); or a **question of policy** (whether a specific course of action should be undertaken in order to solve a problem).

Step 2   *Problem analysis.* Collect the information needed to identify the problem. Gather the facts, determine how serious the problem is, determine what harm is associated with the problem, decide whether the harm is serious and widespread, and identify what causes the problem.

Step 3   *Solution criteria.* Before the solutions are addressed, determine what criteria will be used to evaluate the possible solutions. One of the most common sets of criteria centers on workability, practicality, and desirability. *Workability* is whether the solution will solve the problem. *Practicality* is whether the solution can be put into effect. *Desirability* is whether harm will be caused by implementing the solution.

Step 4   *Solution suggestions.* Brainstorm for possible solutions to the problem.

Brainstorming consists of generating possible solutions without evaluation of them at the time of their proposal. Guidelines for brainstorming include[33]

◆ Don't evaluate ideas while brainstorming.

◆ Don't clarify or seek clarification of an idea during the collection.

◆ Encourage zany ideas. Some of the best solutions are those that haven't been tried before or are out of the normal stream of action.

◆ Record all ideas without reference to who contributed the idea.

◆ Encourage participation by all group members.

Step 5   *Select a solution.* Explore the positives and negatives of all the ideas collected during brainstorming, and apply the agreed-on criteria. Another method of selecting the solution is to apply an evaluation technique known as RISK, which has these basic steps:[34]

    a. Think of any risks, fears, or problems associated with the solution.
    b. Brainstorm potential negative consequences either individually or as a group.
    c. Post all potential consequences on a chart or blackboard for all members to see.
    d. Give time for additions to the list.
    e. Discuss each negative point again.
    f. Weigh the risks and consequences against the perceived benefits.
    g. Make a decision to implement, delay for further study, modify, or kill the proposal and search for (a) better alternative(s).

Step 6   *Solution implementation.* Put the solution into effect and monitor it by follow-up testing and observation to make sure it is working. If it is not working, repeat Steps 4 through 6.

1-3-6 Decision-Making Technique   The **Nominal Group Technique of Decision Making** centers on the concept of brainstorming without direct group interaction in the initial stage. This technique encourages idea generation from all individuals but avoids criticism, destructive conflict, and long-winded speeches.[35]

The **1-3-6 Decision-Making Technique** is a format for using the nominal group technique.[36] It takes place after the specific decision to be made or problem to be solved is agreed on by the group, and members are ready to work toward solution. The technique gets its name from how the participants work: alone (1), then in a group of 3, and then in a group of 6. The steps, illustrated in Figure 9.3, are

Step A   Each individual in the group lists what he or she thinks should be done to solve the problem or the best possible decisions regarding the issue. This process is a brainstorming session.

Step B   Participants are divided into groups of three. Each group combines its members' lists. No items are deleted, but possibilities are combined and solutions or decisions reworded. There should be no discussion of the value of the ideas during this step.

Step C   Each subgroup meets with another one, and they combine their lists. Again, duplicate ideas are eliminated and solutions or decisions reworded. No evaluations are made.

Step D   The whole group reassembles. A spokesperson for each subgroup reads its list aloud. All items are written on a long sheet of paper or on a chalkboard.

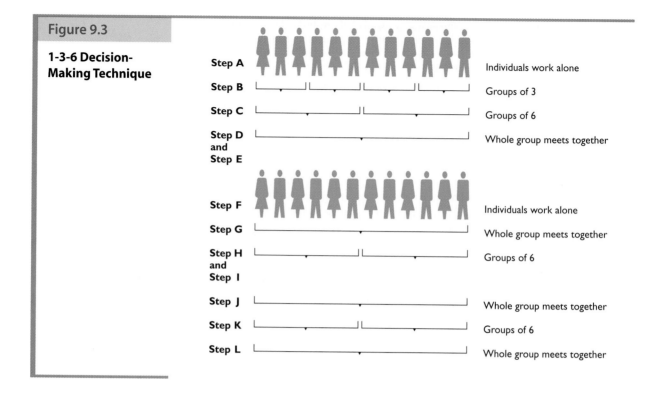

Figure 9.3

1-3-6 Decision-Making Technique

Step A — Individuals work alone

Step B — Groups of 3

Step C — Groups of 6

Step D and Step E — Whole group meets together

Step F — Individuals work alone

Step G — Whole group meets together

Step H and Step I — Groups of 6

Step J — Whole group meets together

Step K — Groups of 6

Step L — Whole group meets together

(It is important that everyone in the room be able to read the lists, so large writing is imperative.)

Step E   The items are numbered.

Step F   Each person prioritizes the entire list, ranking in order all items with no ties. The most important or best solution or decision should be numbered 1, the next 2, and so forth. Each person's rankings are recorded on a sheet of paper.

Step G   The rankings are collected and tallied. The top items are identified, the final number of which should be a proportion of the number of items generated in Step D. If thirty or more items were generated, the top ten would be a reasonable final list. For fewer items, about one-half to one-third of the total is appropriate. (Determine this in advance to avoid conflict over how many should be included in the final list.)

Step H   Individuals select their top choices and then are randomly divided into subgroups of no more than six persons. If possible, a representative of each of the subgroups in Step C should be in each of the newly formed units. (This is not imperative, but in cases where there is lack of clarity in a statement, the individual from the subgroup that generated the idea may be able to clarify its meaning.)

Step I   Each subgroup selects what it considers the best solution using the individual selections from Step H. At this step, evaluations are made. Statements may be reworded, but no new solutions may be introduced.

Step J   Spokespersons for each subgroup report on the decision of the subgroup. If all subgroups have selected the same solution, the process is completed. If not, solutions that received the support of at least one subgroup are retained and the others eliminated.

Step K   Subgroups reassemble and select what they consider the best solution from those remaining on the list.

Step L   A spokesperson for each subgroup reports on the selection of his or her subgroup.

Steps K and L are repeated until a single solution is chosen.

Some smaller groups adopt an alternative approach, using only Steps A through F, and then have all members meet together to reach a final solution. Smaller groups also can adapt the procedure to be a 1-2-4 process.

Recognize that communication factors (i.e., members are willing to listen to one another, members are comfortable expressing ideas, and members analyze information and ideas) have a major impact on the outcome of the decision making in a group. Research suggests that people believe that decisions are of high quality "when group members participate fully in the process and the group climate is characterized by the presence of respectful behaviors and the absence of negative socio-emotional behaviors."[37]

Group Setting

Although you might not have given it much consideration, where a group meets—the size, shape, color, temperature, and decor of the room—and where participants sit can affect the success of a group. Group meeting spaces represent a particularly important type of microenvironment that can influence the quality and quantity of communicative interaction, the participants' perceptions of each other, and the task performance of a given group.[38]

Two specific variables of importance in group settings that can affect group action are seating choices and the configuration of the tables.

Seating Choice

Where you sit at a meeting may determine whether you are selected as the leader, how much you will participate, and how others perceive you. This is an important concept for you to consider if you aspire to be the group's leader. For example, the person who sits at the head of a rectangular table significantly increases his or her chances of being perceived as the leader.[39]

Studies about seating have arrived at these findings:

◆ "It seems to be a norm, in the United States at least, that leaders are expected to be found at the head or end of the table."[40] At family dinners, for example, the head of the household is usually seated at the head of the table. Elected group leaders generally put themselves in the head positions at rectangular tables, and the members place themselves so they can see the leader.

◆ At a round conference table, whoever sits at the twelve o'clock position is the most powerful, with power diminishing as it moves around past positions at three o'clock, six o'clock, and nine o'clock. The least powerful person sits at the eleven o'clock position.[41]

The person who sits at the head of a rectangular table significantly increases his or her chances of being perceived as the leader.

◆ Individuals who choose to be seated along the sides of a table not only decrease their chances of being perceived as leaders but also are likely to be perceived as individuals with lower status and less self-confidence.[42]

◆ People seated in a circle will feel more comfortable and interact more than they would if they were in straight rows or seated around a rectangular table.

◆ In a group consisting of all women, the person at the head of the table is perceived as the leader. However, in a mixed-gender group, a woman at the head position is less likely to be perceived as the leader than a man who occupies the end position.[43]

◆ At round tables, if several people sit at one arc of the table and the others spread themselves around the rest, the two seated together tend to be perceived as the leaders. This is considered the visual center of the table because the others tend to turn to face the two seated together.[44]

Table Configuration

Table configuration or shape is an important variable in group interaction. Rectangular arrangements foster more and better communicative interaction than do T-shaped or L-shaped seating arrangements, and a round configuration is better in this regard than a rectangular table. The round configuration is the most neutral.[45] At rectangular tables, communication usually flows across the table rather than around it.[46]

People seem to be aware of the different perceptions related to different seating positions. Interestingly, when asked in one study to select seats to convey different impressions, respondents chose end positions to convey leadership and dominance, the closest seats to convey interpersonal attraction, and seats that afforded the greatest interpersonal distance to indicate they did not wish to participate.[47]

In classrooms arranged in rows, students who participate the most tend to form a triangle from the center of the room. For example, in a room with six rows of chairs, most class participation tends to come from those seated in the first four seats of the row closest to the front, the three seats behind them, the two seats

Meeting Seating

Have you ever paid attention to where people decide to sit in a business meeting? Seating arrangements are often left up to chance, but where meeting participants sit can actually influence overall meeting effectiveness and can have a profound impact on your perceived power in the group.

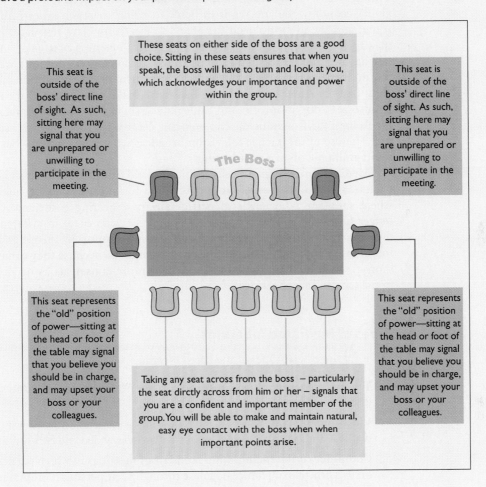

This seat is outside of the boss' direct line of sight. As such, sitting here may signal that you are unprepared or unwilling to participate in the meeting.

These seats on either side of the boss are a good choice. Sitting in these seats ensures that when you speak, the boss will have to turn and look at you, which acknowledges your importance and power within the group.

This seat is outside of the boss' direct line of sight. As such, sitting here may signal that you are unprepared or unwilling to participate in the meeting.

The Boss

This seat represents the "old" position of power—sitting at the head or foot of the table may signal that you believe you should be in charge, and may upset your boss or your colleagues.

Taking any seat across from the boss – particularly the seat dirctly across from him or her – signals that you are a confident and important member of the group. You will be able to make and maintain natural, easy eye contact with the boss when when important points arise.

This seat represents the "old" position of power—sitting at the head or foot of the table may signal that you believe you should be in charge, and may upset your boss or your colleagues.

behind them, and the one seat behind them. The least participation comes from the very back corners and those seated in the end rows.[48]

Effect of the Physical Environment

The physical environment should be comfortable. A meeting can unravel if the room is too large or small, if it is too warm or cold, and if the lighting or the acoustics are not conducive to seeing and hearing one another. Groups often function more effectively if snacks are provided. Attention to these kinds of details will pay off in member satisfaction with the group and contribute better to the group process and product.

On the other hand, the **meet-while-standing theory** requires a meeting place without any furniture. The concept is that people forced to stand will make decisions more rapidly because the participants get tired and want to finish their business and find someplace to sit.

Mediated Meetings

It is estimated that 20 million face-to-face meetings are held every day in the United States.[49] Increasing competition that creates a need for faster decisions, a global economy that makes it difficult to bring together expertise in a single room, and the growing need for access to electronic data resources in decision making has brought about the need to change "business as usual."[50] As technology has become increasingly sophisticated, organizations do not always have to rely on in-person meetings to conduct their business. Corporations such as Marriott, Bank of America, and Aetna Insurance make regular use of mediated conferences, as do nonprofit and collegiate associations. Many universities and hotels have their own media-conferencing centers for their own as well as public use. The use of interactive television broadcast to various settings has become a multi-million-dollar-a-year business.

Mediated meetings are electronically held audioconferences, videoconferences, or computer conferences that allow for meetings to be held anyplace where someone who needs to participate in a meeting is located. Groups no longer have to meet in a conference room; they can meet in cyberspace.[51] Not only are they cost-effective, but electronically supported meetings have been found to be "more satisfying to the group members, because they can participate more equitably. They result in as much or more consensus as occurs in traditional face-to-face meetings."[52]

Types of Mediated Meetings

There are three basic types of mediated meetings:

Teleconferencing, which consists of telephone conference calls and speakerphone meetings.[53]

Videoconferencing, which includes meetings conducted with one-way video and two-way audio as well as fully interactive two-way video and two-way audio.[54]

Computer conferencing, which consists of meetings in which participants log on to a central conference database through their personal computer. It is similar to their sending or receiving e-mail. Computer meetings can take place as a **real-time conference,** in which all participants are at their computers at the same time, or as an **asynchronous conference,** in which participants contribute to an online conference database at different times. These meetings may go on for weeks, depending on their purpose.[55]

Positive and Negative Aspects of Mediated Meetings

As with any other method of operation, there are advantages and disadvantages with each type of mediated meeting. Understanding these differences can help potential users or participants.

Teleconferencing   Most organizations have the equipment and procedures in place for multiway calls. Therefore, one of the major advantages of teleconferencing is the ease of use. On the other hand, participants typically are sitting alone in their offices, and they may feel isolated. If there are several people in a single room with a speaker-phone, regulating who will speak can be difficult. Participants cannot observe their coparticipants' nonverbal feedback, so it often is hard to read feedback cues. Other drawbacks are that member participation may be inconsistent, members can do other things while participating such as work at their desks and not pay strict attention, and it is difficult to share visual elements such as charts or diagrams unless they have been distributed in advance or can be faxed to others while the discussion is ongoing.[56]

COMMUNICATION BRIEFINGS

Teleconference ABCs

Here are three teleconference tips for you to follow:

◆ Make sure that ALL conversation is directed at the telephone. Even if a team member is responding to the person next to him, he and everyone else should make it a point always to talk "to" the phone, looking at it and speaking "to" it in loud, clear voices.

◆ Shared rituals help to bond people—but they're tougher to create when people only "meet" around a speakerphone. One virtual ritual that has been found effective is the initial "check-in." Attendees each get fifteen seconds to tell the group what they're clearing from their minds so they'll be mentally "present" for the meeting.

◆ If you're conducting regular teleconferences across time zones, be fair. Rotate call times so that no single group or country gets the persistent "hit" of a really early—or late—call time.

Source: Christopher Avery, www.partnerwerks.com.

Videoconferencing   Because many organizations have on-site video equipment, such as a voice-sensitive camera and sound system, a large-screen television set, and speakers, the equipment for videoconferencing is often readily available. Most hotels and conferencing centers have video facilities, so even holding video-conferences away from the home office is convenient.[57]

"Group videoconferencing's three most distinguishing features are its interactive capabilities, the ability to originate from any number of locations, and the capacity to reach multiple worldwide locations simultaneously."[58]

Videoconferencing is effective for introducing new products to a team of sales-people or potential users, having collaborative meetings among project members in distant places, holding corporate town meetings when employees are at various worldwide sites, conducting training sessions, and participating in trade shows without leaving the office.[59]

It should be recognized that videoconferencing technology is expensive and, thus, not accessible to every group. Also, as sometimes happens with electronic equipment, technical difficulties and poor usage can cause communication problems.

Computer Conferencing   Computer conferencing is fairly inexpensive. Most employees have personal computers, and the only other costs are covering the toll for local or long-distance calls and special computer programs, if they are desired. The conferences can take place wherever a computer and telephone can be activated. General training is minimal because most people are computer literate. Participants report that often dynamic interactions take place as people get involved in each other's messages.[60]

The fact that the conference can take place over an extended period of time can be an advantage. "Members of asynchronous conferences often report being able to mull over their comments before entering them, resulting in deeper and more thoughtful discussions."[61]

COMMUNICATION BRIEFINGS

Make Videoconferencing Work

Your videoconference will be as good as a face-to-face meeting if you

♦ **Prepare questions.** You'll need them to get the discussion going.

♦ **Wear only camera-friendly clothing.** Avoid plaids, prints, reds, and whites.

♦ **Speak naturally and clearly,** just as you would if all those taking part were in the same room.

♦ **Start with roll call, and add something personal**—the weather or business conditions in your location, for example—to help relax participants.

♦ **Stay aware of which camera you're on.**

♦ **Give participants a little extra time** to answer questions to allow for possible delays in image transfers.

♦ **Rotate the order** in which you call on participants to make sure they all take part.

♦ **Make any graphics you use large and simple.** And be sure to alert participants when you're about to use one.

♦ **Summarize the discussion and any decisions visually,** and follow up immediately with written minutes.

Source: Tools for Virtual Teams, by Jane E. Henry, Ph.D., and Meg Hartzler, ASQ Quality Press, 611 East Wisconsin Ave., Milwaukee, WI 53202. © Communication Briefings, www.briefings.com, 1101 King Street, Alexandria, VA 22314. Used with permission.

Computer conferencing has weaknesses as well as strengths: some view computer meetings as impersonal, it takes longer to type a thought than to speak it, and not everyone feels comfortable with computer technology.[62]

Additional weaknesses include that even with interactive messaging, there is a delay in message sending and retrieval and a tendency to use short and incomplete messages. Moreover, there is no nonverbal presence; the interactions are dependent on the keyboarding speed of the participants; overlapping messages can cause confusion; and with numerous participants, direct interactions become very difficult.[63]

Attempts to overcome the negative aspects of computer conferencing have led to the development of **groupware:** specially designed software that meeting participants use to perform tasks such as brainstorming and decision making.[64]

In a typical meeting in which groupware is used, each participant sits at a computer terminal. The leader begins the meeting by telling participants what problem must to be solved or what decision they need to make. Participants input ideas and cast votes on their individual screens, which are integrated by the groupware and shown on a public screen at the front of the room. The content of the meeting is saved for later reference.[65]

"Most research suggests that groupware does improve the quality of meetings." It is reported to save time, help build consensus, and guide the uninitiated through meeting procedures.[66] On the other hand, it doesn't automatically make meetings more productive. Slow typists complain that they can't participate or that decisions are made before they can respond. It limits the amount of discussion that can take place. Extroverts complain that they can't participate enough. And because of the ease of operation, so many ideas may be presented that the volume becomes unmanageable. Examples of groupware are *Optifinder* and *Lotus Notes.*

With *Optifinder* each participant is given a ten-digit keypad wired to a computer. The system can support more than one hundred keypads. At critical points in the meeting, the leader asks questions of the participants, who register their votes by pushing buttons on the keypad that correspond to their opinions or choices. When the voting is completed, the computer processes the responses and displays them on an overhead projector. Participants then explain or clarify their opinions, compare them with others, offer new ideas, discuss areas of disagreement, and ultimately reach a decision. *Optifinder* is mainly used for planning and designing and opinion-gathering meetings.[67]

Lotus Notes is a highly flexible software program that enables its users to organize, access, share, and track information through databases that they create, access,

and manipulate. One of its most powerful advantages is that its users can pose a question or ask for information without knowing who might have the answer or data. Anyone with the network can respond. It has been found that users can accomplish a task in a few days instead of weeks.[68]

How to Make Mediated Meetings Work

Business meetings and meeting teams are here to stay. They need tools to help get their jobs done. Mediated meetings seem to be at least part of the answer as to how meetings should be conducted.

These techniques are useful for planning and implementing electronic meetings:[69]

◆ Speakers should be close enough to the microphones so they can be easily heard.

◆ Participants should control the noise of papers, tapping on the table, and other distracting habits that the microphones will pick up.

◆ High-quality graphics must be prepared to fit the television format.

◆ Audio or materials that are too complex to be seen on video should be mailed or faxed to the participants in time to be used for reference during the session.

◆ Participants should identify themselves continuously during the process.

◆ Participants should announce when they leave or enter the discussion.

◆ Wait until the camera is on you if you are participating in a videoconference.

◆ Limit the agenda to no more than one hour. If it is longer, a break should be scheduled.

◆ Select the appropriate participants: people who are willing to work with the media and are not being forced to do so.

◆ Make sure the technology is operating properly and the participants know how to work the equipment.

VC Etiquette

Have you ever turned on the TV to a talk show and watched a guest's clothing take on a life of its own? Obviously, the guest did not have a fashion consultant around when he was getting dressed that morning. Well, video-conferencing is comparable to TV, and the following are some dos and don'ts, not only on what to wear but also how to present yourself.

✔ Introduce yourself.
✔ Speak slowly.
✘ Do not shout.
✘ Don't ask if they can hear you—they'll let you know if they can't.
✘ Don't interrupt others.
✔ Avoid unrelated conversation.
✔ Sit still, and when you do move, don't move quickly.
✘ Don't upstage the person speaking by getting up and walking around the room.
✔ Find out the color of the backdrop and avoid that color.
✘ Don't wear patterns; red, white, or black colors; or baggy clothing.
✔ Do wear blue, gray, or teal.
✔ Have someone videotape you while you're practicing your presentation—and critique it.

◆ Have an orientation with the participants before the actual presentation in order to answer questions about the procedure and the media.

◆ Prepare and distribute a written agenda in advance of the session.

In Conclusion

A meeting should be a purposeful interaction; therefore, no matter the setting or the technique, the basic questions always to be asked are why a meeting is being held, who should attend, when the meeting should take place, and what materials need to be prepared and present for accomplishing the purpose.

Groups are an assemblage of persons who communicate in order to fulfill a common purpose and achieve a goal. Group members influence one another, derive some satisfaction from maintaining membership in the group, interact for some purpose, assume specialized roles, and depend on one another. Groups often are classified by size, with small groups containing three to twelve persons and large groups more than a dozen. One of the most prominent functions of the group communication process is that of decision making. There are advantages and disadvantages to both participating in a group and having groups make decisions, versus working alone. Groups normally go through five phases: norming, storming, conforming, performing, and adjourning. Where a group meets and where participants sit can affect the success of a group. Besides face-to-face meetings, organizations are using mediated meetings, which include audioconferencing, videoconferencing, and computer conferencing.

Learn by Doing

1. Be prepared to defend or counter this statement: "The advantages of working in a group outweigh the disadvantages." Go beyond the arguments given in the chapter and use personal examples to develop your answer.

2. Consider a group in which you have worked that was *not* successful in reaching its goal or that had difficulty in reaching its goal. What specifically was the problem? How could the problem have been solved?

3. For your next examination in this class, students will be divided into study groups to prepare for the test. After the exam, a class discussion will be held on the value or lack of value of this approach.

4. Mentally revisit a group in which you have participated. Write a short paper (which may be given as an oral presentation) analyzing its norming, storming, conforming, and performing stages and adjourning.

5. Your class will be divided into groups. Each group is to contact at least two representatives of an organization that is conducting mediated meetings. Interview

them in person, by telephone, or online about the pros and cons of conducting mediated meetings. Write a short report on your findings. You will present a group report to your classmates on your findings.

Key Terms

group
small groups
large groups
risky shift phenomenon
groupthink
Pollyanna-Nietzsche effect
social loafing
work teams
study groups
support group
committee
focus groups
family
public meetings
symposium
forum
town meeting
group norming
group norms
agenda
group storming
primary group tension
secondary group tension
power role
group conforming
group performing
task dimension of groups

maintenance dimension of groups
group cohesion
adjourning
discussion question
voting
consensus
majority vote
plurality
part-of-the-whole voting
Six-Step Standard Agenda for Decision
    Making
question of fact
question of value
question of policy
brainstorming
Nominal Group Technique of Decision
    Making
1-3-6 Decision-Making Technique
meet-while-standing theory
mediated meetings
teleconferencing
videoconferencing
computer conferencing
real-time conference
asynchronous conference
groupware

10

Participating in Groups

After reading this chapter, you should be able to

- Explain that people from different cultures possess varying attitudes about being a group participant and about procedures for working in groups, about making decisions, about procedural structure, and about using information

- Discuss the role of gender as a factor in group activities

- Define and explain the role of the participants, the leaders, and the leadership in groups

- Compare and contrast the role of disagreement in the group process

- Acknowledge the role of the hidden agenda in the group process

- List the types and explain the communicative role of group networks

- Define the authoritarian, democratic, and laissez-faire leader types

- Explain why a person would want to be a group leader and demonstrate how the person would proceed to acquire the leader or leadership role

G roups are made up of people. Those who comprise a group play the roles of leaders, leadership, and participants. **Participants** are those members of a group who interact to bring about the actions of the group. **Leaders** are those who guide the group. **Leadership** refers to those who influence the group to accomplish its goal.

Members of groups, whether they are assuming the participant or leader role, come to that group with cultural influences. These influences affect the way in which group members function.

Cultural Differences in Groups

Each of us is a product of the culture in which we were brought up. We learn the customs and patterns of our culture, and these carry over into all phases of our lives. Research shows that people from different cultures possess varying attitudes about making independent decisions and being a group participant, procedures for working in groups, making decisions, procedural structure, and using information.

Cultures and Groups

"The United States has the highest individualism index. We [European Americans] are, without doubt, the most individualistic culture on earth."[1] This individualism—putting oneself before group loyalty—has a strong historical base; the United States was founded by adventurers and dissidents. In this culture, membership in groups (except those that are mandatory because of a person's work or academic environment) tends to be voluntary. While recognizing that there may be traditions, such as membership in a particular religion, European Americans tend to decide on their own whether they want to belong to a group. You, for example, choose whether to participate in a social group or a fraternal organization. Once a part of the group, if you don't like being a member, you can resign.

Because of this ability to join and leave a group, allegiance tends not to be a lifelong commitment. This, however, is not the case in other parts of the world. For example, in many East Asian countries, Confucianism is the basic philosophy of much of the population. The **Confucian principle of i** requires that a person be affiliated and identify with a small and tightly knit group of people over long periods of time. These long-term relationships work because group members aid and assist each other when there is a need; sooner or later those who assisted others will have to depend on those they aided. This mutually implied assistance pact makes for group interdependence.[2]

Native Americans use group discussion "as a means to maintain or restore harmony."[3] It is important for group members to work toward consensus. "In the absence of consensus, talk goes on interminably, with great respect for the conventions of oratory."[4] Discussion continues "until those in opposition feel it is useless or impolite to express further disagreement."[5]

Not only does the attitude toward being in groups vary by culture, but there also is a difference in the training needed in certain cultures for group participation. Because they participate in groups to a limited degree, many European Americans need to learn about group operational methods when they enter into organizations. The same is true of people from other countries having a high degree of individualism, such as Australia, Great Britain, Canada, New Zealand, and Denmark.[6] In contrast, people

Group actions are based on proposing actions, putting forth ideas, and proposing solutions to problems.

from societies in which group adherence is stressed have a clearer sensitivity about how groups operate since they are encased in groups all their lives. Those areas and countries that are the least individualistic are found in Asia (Japan, China, Vietnam) and South America.[7]

Cultural differences also are reflected in the way a person works in a group. In many East Asian countries, for example, the Confucian principle of i leads to a strong distaste for purely business transactions. This is carried over into meetings, where the tendency is to mix personal with public relationships. Business meetings, for example, may take place over a long period of time in order for people to establish personal relationships, include activities like sports and drinking, foster an understanding of the personalities of the participants, and develop a certain level of trust and a favorable attitude.[8]

A good example of where the business is mixed with the personal is in Japan, which is known as a nation stressing group culture, where individualism is submerged, and expression occurs in hidden ways. This, of course, is almost the opposite of how European Americans operate. In the United States, individuals work in groups to get *tasks* accomplished. In Japan, the individual's sense of identity *is* the group. This is based on a long history of ruling families who created a social structure that bound families, villagers, and strong leaders together. In the United States, the stress has been on rugged individualism, with the group coming second to the individual. In Japan, the word for describing a group is *we*. In the United States, groups often are divided between "us" and "them." For instance, administrators and faculty members are part of the same group—the university—but too often find themselves on opposite sides in decisions.

Contrasts in Cultural Group Decision Making

If the assumption is made that one of the important tasks of a group is decision making, another cultural variation comes into play. It is important to realize, when working in decision-making groups, that there are vast cultural differences in how people think, apply forms of reasoning, and make decisions.

In the Western view, it is generally believed that people can discover truth if they apply the scientific method of the decision-making process. The familiar problem-solving sequence has four segments: identify the problem, search for solutions, test those solutions, and put a solution into practice. The final decision is often based on a majority vote of the membership, with those who will have to implement or live with the decision often not part of the decision-making team. For example, few students are included in university discussions on curriculum requirements. In Japan, on the other hand, everyone affected by the decision is included in the process.[9]

COMMUNICATION BRIEFING

Cross-Cultural Considerations

These guidelines can help you speak the right business language when you deal with those from other cultures:

◆ **Find out** if the culture you'll do business in is high-contact—expects lots of details—or low-contact—prefers a broad overview.

◆ **Realize that** you may have to ask permission to take meeting notes. *Reason:* Some in other cultures object because they feel it may "pin them down."

◆ **Assume that** in most cultures it's safer to let your counterparts bring up business issues first. That allows them to set the pace and provides signals you can use to adjust your behavior.

◆ **Be more** formal. Use titles and last names—and be sure to pronounce them correctly.

◆ **Talk clearly,** avoid slang and sports terms, and learn and use a few key phrases in the others' language. *Examples:* "Good morning,""Yes,""No,""Please," and "Thank you."

◆ **Adjust your** tempo to your counterparts' concept of time. Some cultures have little concern for punctuality.

◆ **Learn to** read cultural differences in nonverbal signals. *Example:* A smile can signal embarrassment in some cultures.

Source: Speaking the Language of Business Overseas, Prudential Relocation Global Services, Flatiron Park West, 2555 55th Street, Boulder, CO 80301. © Communication Briefings, www.briefings .com, 1101 King St., Alexandria, VA 22314. Used with permission.

Other societies use different decision-making approaches. For example, for the Chinese, "decision-making is more authoritative than consensual; decisions are made by higher authorities without the inclusion of subordinates."[10]

"Middle-Easterners can be described as using an **intuitive-affective decision-making approach.** Broad issues that do not appear to be directly related to the issue at hand are brought up; issues are linked together on the basis of whether or not the speaker likes the issues."[11] Although subordinates are consulted informally, the leader always makes the final decision.[12]

Work groups in Mexico tend to use a **centralized decision-making process.** Mexicans often view authority as being inherent within the individual, not his or her position. Making trade-offs is common for Mexican negotiators, including adding issues that are not part of the original business at hand.[13]

Cultural Contrast of the Role of Information for Groups

Even the information or ideas that are used for making decisions may differ among cultures. European American negotiators tend to compartmentalize issues, focusing on one issue at a time instead of negotiating many issues together. "They tend to rely on rational thinking and concrete data in their negotiations."[14] In the United States, negotiating toward the final decision usually takes on a form of **proposal counterproposal negotiating,** in which a plan or solution is presented and then a counteroffer is made. For example, in a group meeting concerning salary negotiations, the employees propose a particular salary and explain why they think this is the appropriate amount. Management then typically makes an offer of a lesser amount

Emergent leaders exhibit a significantly higher rate of participation than do non-leaders.

and offers counterarguments. This process continues until an amount is agreed on. The negotiations may be accompanied by a threat of the workers' going out on strike, an action unheard of in some other cultures.

The French, on the other hand, seem to "have no problem with open disagreement. They debate more than they bargain and are less apt than Euro-Americans to be flexible for the sake of agreement. . . . They start with a long-range view of their purpose, as opposed to Euro-Americans, who work with more short-range objectives."[15]

"Japanese negotiators make decisions on the basis of detailed information rather than persuasive arguments."[16]

Because this book is directed primarily at individuals who will find themselves most often participating in groups in the U.S. culture, the material in this chapter deals mainly with participant and leader conventions and patterns typical in the United States. However, because of the multiculturalism of this country, you likely will be working with people and in social situations with individuals from a variety of cultural backgrounds. Also, with the internationalization of business, it is becoming more and more common for the businesspeople from the United States to be working in international settings, so knowledge of other cultures' group procedures can be helpful.

Male and Female Roles in Groups

Besides cultural differences based on nationality, the cultural roles of males and females play an important role in leader and participant operational modes.

Is gender a factor in group tasks or maintenance? Generally, studies on leader, leadership, and group process indicate that differences do occur in the way men and women operate in a group. For example, "women tend to be more process-oriented than men. Men are more goal-oriented. For women, the process is as important, or more important, than the product."[17] Other studies indicate that "individuals prefer managers who possess masculine characteristics."[18] This carries over into courtrooms, where men are more likely than women to be selected as foreperson of a jury.[19] Research in educational groups indicates that students believe classes led by women are more discussion oriented, and classes taught by men are more structured and emphasize content mastery.[20] In addition, male college professors are perceived to be less supportive and less innovative than are female instructors.[21]

"Being the only member of one's sex in a mixed-gender group affects the perceptions of other group members and often skews the opportunities to communicate and the feedback one receives."[22] In addition, men are perceived to be more dominant and women more submissive during group communication that includes both men and women, whether the communication is verbal or nonverbal.[23] And research on juries shows that male jurors typically offer 40 percent more comments during deliberation than do female jurors.[24] It also has been shown that "male students initiate more interactions with teachers than female students initiate" and that males tend to dominate classroom talk.[25]

Thus, it appears that there are differences, or at least perceived differences, between the genders as they participate in groups in the European American culture.

The Group Participant

Participants in groups have various responsibilities to themselves and to the group. They normally perform communicative maintenance and task roles, form networks by which they relay messages, and must deal with other members.

Responsibilities of Group Members

All participants should remember that an entire group is responsible and accountable for final decisions. Thus, being a member of the **silent majority** (those who say nothing during the decision-making process) does not release you from accountability for that decision. For example, if the group decides that each member should pay fifteen dollars more in dues, you must pay the extra fee, even though you may not have said anything during the discussion and may not have even voted on the issue. Despite your lack of participation, if you expect to remain a member of the group, you cannot announce after the decision is made, "I didn't say anything and I didn't vote, so I don't have to pay!"

All group members should be knowledgeable. In the Western logic system, although personal beliefs are important, expert opinions and facts reveal what authorities believe and what testing has proved, and this is the basis for sound

Japanese negotiators make decisions on the basis of detailed information rather than persuasive arguments.

When Participants Disagree

If you're in charge of a meeting or just a participant, you might want to use some of these suggestions to help deal with disagreements:

◆ **Find a** way to agree. *Example:* "I agree that this is an unfortunate situation, and I would remedy it differently from the way you suggested."

◆ **Use humor** to defuse tension. A spontaneous laugh can sometimes offer the fresh perspective the group needs.

◆ **Use peer** pressure to keep off-the-topic comments to a minimum. Ask the group early in the discussion to remind one another to stay on the topic. Agree on a signal that members can use to suggest the speaker get back to the point.

◆ **Avoid** "triangling," complaining about a person who is not part of the conversation. Speak directly to a person if you want a conflict resolved.

◆ **Restate** a person's critical comment and ask if you understand it correctly. It shows that you're taking the disagreement seriously.

◆ **Seat a person** who is hostile toward you to your side rather than across from you. Confrontations will be less likely to occur.

◆ **Describe** observations in nonthreatening, nonjudgmental language. Don't say: "You claim that …" This suggests that the person might be lying. A better response: "Is my understanding correct? Are you saying that …?"

Source: As adapted from *Busy Manager's Guide to Successful Meetings,* by Karen Anderson, Career Press, 180 5th Ave., Hawthorne, NJ 07507. © Communication Briefings, www.briefings.com, 1101 King St., Alexandria, VA 22314. Used with permission.

decision making. In other words, the use of supporting evidence can help ensure that your conclusions have substance and will probably be perceived as having credibility. Consider how you can apply evidence such as statistics, testimony, and illustrations to your discussions. Your participation is enhanced if you use this research to support your comments clearly and concisely.

Some groups are plagued by people who insist on dominating the discussion and the decision-making process. These people may, at worst, destroy the group and, at best, irritate members and make decision making difficult. Although it is sometimes very difficult when you have strong opinions and believe you are right and others wrong, each participant should try to respect as much as possible the rights of the others. This does not mean you should not participate if your views differ from others. It does mean that a point can be reached where continued bickering can be destructive to the group's mission. Suppose that after presenting your point of view, it appears that your ideas are not going to be accepted. Your task, then, is either to try to work toward reaching a compromise into which you can enfold your ideas or to accept the fact that you have done everything you could to get your viewpoint presented and accepted but have failed to achieve your goal.

It is important not to assume that rejection of your idea is a rejection of you personally. Unfortunately, many people have difficulty making this distinction. They assume that if one of their ideas is rejected, they have been deemed unworthy. Not understanding this concept causes people to "fight to the death" for acceptance of their beliefs. In reality, what they are fighting for is to establish or retain their own legitimacy. This may lead the rejected person to start attacking others rather than sticking to the issues. Personal attacks often do little to get your stand accepted; rather, they cause alienation within the group. Personal issues lead other people to take stands not on what solution is right or wrong but on who is right or wrong. This choosing up of sides often divides the group, causing internal rifts and destroying the chances for group cohesion and goal accomplishment.

Normally group members should assume an active role in communicating with each other so that the entire group can benefit. Of course, there are times when, for

Group participants should remember that the entire group is responsible in making a decision.

whatever reason, you may feel that you do not want to participate. You may think that you do not have the necessary information, or that you might not have strong enough feelings to interject, or that your beliefs have already been presented by someone else. Whatever the reason, if you knowingly and willingly don't participate, this is your privilege. However, choosing not to participate is an act of abdicating responsibility as a group member.

Participants in a group discussion, much like therapeutic listeners, also must try to set aside their own prejudices and beliefs so as to listen and respond to what others have to say. This ability to suspend judgment is difficult. Deal with conflicts by adopting an openness to compromise and conciliation—that is, if you feel this is in the best interests of the group process and you can live with the compromise. Remember that compromises can result in giving up beliefs and moving to watered-down solutions, unsatisfying to all concerned. Do not allow a verbal bully to force you into a compromise or to adopt a solution you feel is not in the best interests of the group. Note that the focus is on the best interest of the *group*, which may not necessarily be in *your* best interest!

Communicating as a Group Member

As a group member, you perform varied communication activities. Foremost of these are speaking and listening. In the process of participation, you probably evaluate information, propose concepts, and agree and disagree with the ideas of others. Group interactions seem most effective when participants are aware of their maintenance and task roles.

Performing Group Maintenance Tasks   In general, group participants should treat other members with respect. For most people this is not a great problem. No doubt you and others realize that you will not always agree. There should be an understanding that disagreement can be helpful because it opens the decision-making process to a variety of viewpoints and allows differences of opinion to be aired.

It is generally understood that having positive attitudes about what you are doing makes for a more committed and active group member. Think back to times when you have been proud of how your group acted and its achievements; perhaps you have been on a winning athletic team or planned an event and been pleased with the results. Accomplishments help build group pride.

The hope is that group members have pride in their group and show commitment to it. If this is not the case, maybe one of the tasks of the group should be to investigate why there are negative attitudes. Dealing with this issue may make working in the group more pleasant and increase the productivity of the membership.

Taking an active role in a group through volunteering ideas, showing willingness to work on subgroups and committees, and making supportive comments is important for helping a group to work cohesively.

Research shows that individuals who are communicatively supportive of maintenance functions reinforce others' ideas, participate in a constructive way, separate people from ideas, try to remain flexible, express their feelings, and describe their reactions.[26]

Performing Task Roles   Besides maintenance roles, participants need to perform task roles, which include initiating ideas, encouraging diverse ideas, using reasoned thought, staying open-minded, being aware of hidden agendas, being cognizant of time constraints, encouraging other participants, and attending to nonverbal messages; in other words, making sure the group accomplishes its goal.

Initiating ideas   Group actions are based on someone's first proposing actions, putting forth ideas, and proposing solutions to problems. Initially, people in most groups tend to be a little shy about presenting ideas. But as the group moves from norming to participating, this reluctance to put forth ideas is overcome. If the others in your group aren't proposing ideas, make a suggestion. This may encourage others to participate. If you know that suggestions will be sought, and you know the topic of the discussion or the nature of the problem, come to the meeting prepared to propose ideas.

Encouraging diverse ideas   Another important aspect of task roles is to encourage diverse ideas. Conservative thinkers hold to the tried and true. They tend to recreate past solutions to problems, sticking mainly to the status quo. Creative idea generators go beyond the norm and search for different solutions. Their ideas may seem crazy at first, but many daft ideas have satisfied major needs. Historically, space travel, the invention of the computer, and even the light bulb were all "far-out" ideas. Don't be stifled by the tried and true; think creatively, even if you risk being called a dreamer or an idealist. Join Alexander Graham Bell, Michelangelo, George Washington Carver, Madame Marie Curie, and other inventors, scientists, and explorers who have made a difference.

Using reasoned thought   One of the important roles of task communication is to operate on the basis of reasoned thought. Being able to support sound ideas, develop well-thought-out concepts, separate fact from opinion, criticize weak or unsubstantiated ideas, use critical thinking, offer evidence, and integrate ideas are important obligations of a constructive task communicator.

Staying open-minded   In general, most of us come to a conclusion, believe it is correct, and defend it no matter what. But ideally we are open to the possibility that

The effective group communicator attends to nonverbal messages.

someone else's ideas may be as valid as, if not more valid than, ours. There are often ideas we haven't thought of, approaches we haven't been exposed to, ideas that challenge our beliefs. Don't overlook the possibility of joining ideas together to make for a blended solution.

Being aware of hidden agendas   Be aware that not all members of a group will be as open, caring, and responsible as you are. Some individuals attempt to accomplish their goals at the expense of others. Some members of a group enter the task process with a **hidden agenda:** an objective or purpose that goes beyond the constructive interests of the group as a whole. When individuals work for their own unstated ends rather than for the group's objectives, the result is usually counterproductive. A hidden agenda is apparent, for example, when a department manager, discussing budget allocations, promises to support any plan that divides the resources equitably among departments but then opposes every plan presented. In this case, the manager has a hidden agenda: he may want most of the funds for his department and thinks a delay will tire the participants and lead to a decision that favors that department. Thus, the manager is trying to manipulate the group toward a personal goal.

In your role as an effective task communicator, listen carefully to the proposals and arguments of other members and be alert to the possibility of hidden agendas.

Being cognizant of time constraints   A group participant should be sensitive to time factors, both to ensure that time is used wisely and that the group is not manipulated by a clever user of time.

If you use a great deal of time and dominate a discussion with too many statements or lengthy comments, you run the risk that you will be tuned out or that your contributions will be so overpowering that the group process will be lost in your dominance. Use time effectively, and make sure that you allow others the time they need.

Be wary of the participant who knows the meeting is coming to a close and that time is short, yet suggests a new, untested, or undiscussed solution. This is a device commonly used by individuals who know that when time pressures become a dominant factor, group members may act impulsively. If someone suggests a solution late in the discussion, make sure it is not acted on immediately, before the group has time to think about the advisability of taking the proposed action.

Encouraging participants   Being encouraging rather than discouraging also can aid in task accomplishment. Negative messages during a group discussion can easily shut down communication. **Communication stoppers** are phrases that put down the ideas of others in a way so that they stop participating, possibly cutting off valuable input. Statements such as "That will never work," "We've tried that before," or "That's ridiculous" will shut down a group's communication.

Attending to nonverbal messages   The effective group communicator also attends to nonverbal messages. It is important to maintain eye contact with those speaking and to engage physically in the discussion. The person who faces the speaker usually is showing attentiveness. The person who looks away or turns away from the speaker could be communicating that he or she really does not care about the discussion or disagrees with the comments being made.

Research shows that a rapid speech rate, fluid gestures, relaxed posture, and verbal fluency (e.g., avoiding "uh," "things like that," or "you know") are positive nonverbal communicators.[27] "To keep a meeting moving along and under control," suggests one meeting management specialist, "let your own body language be one of your strongest allies."[28]

Roles of Group Members

Participants in small groups function in a variety of roles. It is helpful to recognize these roles and monitor not only your own behavior but also that of others. Monitoring often allows you to understand why you and others are doing what you all are doing. And this awareness opens the possibility of altering behavior or alerting others to the role they are playing if actions being taken are detrimental to the group's progress. It also allows for self-praise and for praising others if you discover that the roles being played are productive. Remember that titles and role descriptions are only classifications to explain the roles that group members may assume in their task and maintenance functions within groups. These designations are by no means all-encompassing, nor are they mutually exclusive. Like any other model, they are simply ways to identify certain patterns of role behavior in task and maintenance.[29]

As a participant in a group, you or others may assume roles that are considered positive for group action—for example:

Initiator-contributor—presenting new ideas or perspectives

Information seeker—asking for facts and clarification

Opinion seeker—asking for opinions to get at group values

Information giver—presenting facts and opinions

Opinion giver—presenting values and opinions

Elaborator—providing examples and solutions and building on the contributions of others

Coordinator—identifying relationships among the ideas presented

Orienter—clarifying ideas for the group through summaries and identification of the group's direction

Evaluator—analyzing the group's decisions

Energizer—stimulating the group to greater productivity

Procedural technician—handling mechanical tasks such as paper distribution and seating arrangements

Recorder—recording the transactions of the group

Encourager—supplying positive reinforcement to group members

Harmonizer—mediating various differences among group members

Compromiser—attempting to resolve conflicts within the group

Gatekeeper—keeping channels of communication open by encouraging the members

Standard setter—establishing group norms and patterns of behavior

Communication Networks

Groups operate by different formal and informal patterns that link members together. As participants speak, they develop patterns that result in their talking to, through, or at others. These patterns can be analyzed and help the group to understand why and if their communication patterns encourage or discourage communication. These patterns are called **group communication networks.**

Early research on communication networks indicated five basic network patterns. These are illustrated in Figure 10.1. Each of the dots represents an individual

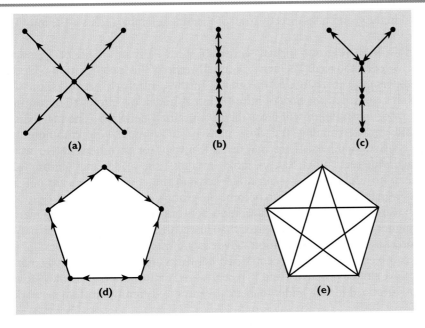

Figure 10.1

Communication Networks:
(a) wheel
(b) chain
(c) Y
(d) circle
(e) all-channel

Source: From Roy M. Berko, Andrew D. Wolvin, and Ray Curtis, *This Business of Communicating,* 5th ed., p. 273. Copyright © 1993 Wm. C. Brown Communications, Inc., Dubuque, Iowa. All rights reserved. Reprinted by permission.

communicator; the arrows, the way the information flows. The leader, or the person of influence, is at the center of each flow of information. For example, in the wheel, the chain, and the Y, there is a clear leader or power figure. All information flows toward and through that person. Therefore, these patterns are referred to as **centralized group communication networks.** In general, centralized networks are most effective for groups dealing with simple problems. They often depend on a strong leader to guide the proceedings. They can work more rapidly than other patterns because the leader normally has a great deal of influence and can direct participation toward accomplishing the task.

In the circle and the all-channel patterns, there is no central focal person; information does not flow from or through a single person. **Decentralized group communication networks** describe these patterns. In decentralized networks, ideas flow freely. They are more effective for solving complex problems. Decentralized networks can often result in greater member interaction and satisfaction because there is more interplay among participants and less influence by a power figure. The leader in a decentralized network plays less the role of director and more that of a participant.

no central focal person

Specifically, in the wheel flow of information (a), each person in the group speaks to the leader, the leader speaks to each of the participants, but the participants do not speak directly to each other. The leader is in total control of the discussion. The chain communication network (b) follows a format in which specific members of the group speak to each other, but they all do not communicate directly. The lynch pin is the leader who is in the center of the message chain. In the Y (c), two of the group members speak directly to the leader—but not to each other—while two of the other members speak to each other and send messages to the other members through the leader. In the circle (d), each person speaks to two other people but doesn't speak directly to the others. The flow of messages is not controlled by the leader. In the all-channel communication network (e), each person in the group talks directly to all of the other members. This is the most interactive format.

How do these group formats get established? Early in the life of a group, the patterns get established. The network usually reflects the leader pattern philosophy of the person(s) in charge of the group. In the centralized networks, the leader maintains control of the flow of information. A leader less interested in controlling the flow of information will favor the decentralized networks. The members also can aid in determining the flow pattern. In groups with communication-apprehensive members, there may be a tendency for members not to want to interact with each other. Or, in some instances, the leader may encourage the members to use a more decentralized network, but the members do not assert themselves, forcing the leader to become the group's guide.

Research concerning communication networks indicates that group members have higher morale in a decentralized than in a centralized communication network; that decentralized communication networks are more efficient when groups must solve complex problems, but centralized networks are more efficient when groups must solve simple problems; and that centralized networks are more likely to result in work overload for the leader than are decentralized communication networks.[30]

Dealing with Difficult Group Members

Many people in groups are a joy to work with. They are cooperative, participate, assume leader and leadership roles in noncontrolling ways, and are willing to be open-minded in dealing with others. Unfortunately, there are some who create dissent, are self-centered, attack others rather than deal with the issues, and won't stick to the agenda.

A theory about problems that groups encounter centers on the idea that 90 percent of the people who are members of groups are reasonable most of the time. There are conflicts and differences of opinion, but people contribute to the good of the group and work things out. Another 9 percent of the members are somewhat difficult to work with. These people have hidden agendas and disagreeable personalities, and seem to be marching to the tune of a different drummer much of the time. Then there is the remaining 1 percent. Their obstructive nature gets in the way of any attempt to deal cooperatively with them.

Using this theory as a basis, you can understand an aspect of conflict in a group and how to deal with different group members. To deal with the 90 percent, applying the concepts presented in this chapter on effective group communication should be sufficient to work things out and work toward task.

As for the 1 percent—the impossible people—there is very little you can do to work constructively with them. Reasoning with them or giving in to their demands accomplishes little. These individuals are out to make life miserable for themselves and everyone around them. They often are incapable of listening, processing, and working toward group cohesiveness. They tend to be so self-absorbed that there is no way to work things out short of giving in. But giving in seems only to encourage their behavior, which escalates their negative actions because they know that eventually the group will give in to their tantrums and negativism again.

One coping method is to expel the impossible ones from the group. Another is to ignore them. A third is recognizing that they must have their say, but it is no one's obligation to listen. Unfortunately, if one of these is the group leader—the supervisor, the professor, the parent—the problem is compounded. Even group experts and psychologists have no recommendations for what participants should do if this is the case. Quitting a job, withdrawing from the class, or leaving a group may be your only salvation if things get too bad.

That leaves the 9 percent who are considered difficult group members. Difficult people are those who cause problems regarding the task or maintenance functions of a group—actions such as frequent disruptions, long speeches, irrational requests, insulting behavior toward others, and interruption of participants.

These labels describe counterproductive group members:

Aggressor—attacks the group and its members

Blocker—provides negative feedback and opposition, with no constructive suggestions

Recognition seeker—attempts to focus attention on himself or herself and ignores group issues

Playboy/playgirl—thinks that the purpose of the group is for this person to have a place to play around, with little or no regard for the group or its task

Dominator—attempts to take over the group and, if he or she can't do that, does everything possible to stop group progress

Help seeker—turns group sessions into self-help sessions with her or his problems at the center of the process

Special-interest pleader/evangelist—disregards what is best for the group and presents only the case for some special group or cause

Before taking any action, be sure that the scenario is actually taking place and that the person is in fact difficult. Sometimes we perceive a person to be difficult because his or her ideas are different from ours. Is the person really difficult, or is the problem yours?

Experts seem to agree that to deal with difficult people, six general axioms should be followed:[31]

♦ *Don't placate the troublemaker.* Allowing the disrupter to manipulate the group in order to keep the peace rewards the troublemaker for objectionable behavior and only encourages similar future actions. For example, the person might interrupt a vote by saying, "I don't want us to vote at this point. It's not fair to cut off discussion until we have all had our say." You could respond by saying, "The motion to call for the vote was made and seconded. The result was almost unanimous—except for your vote. Therefore, we have followed parliamentary procedure, and we will go ahead with the vote." To give in to the person would encourage him or her to continue to be an obstructionist in the future.

♦ *Refuse to be goaded into a reciprocal pattern.* Resist the temptation to meet fire with fire. Someone might say to the chairperson, "You and your people are always making decisions that cause problems for this group. You need to be more honest in dealing with the rest of us." The person's intent is to get the chairperson upset and have her or him apologize or back down. The chair should not be pulled into such goading.

♦ *Try to convert disruption into a constructive contribution.* There is a difference between being disruptive and being constructive. Use the person's idea to ask for other ideas. Doing this takes the discussion away from the person and allows others to speak. If, for example, a member of a committee indicates that the decision-making process of the group was tainted by a lack of input, the chair might state, "That's an interesting point of view. Let's review the minutes of the meeting and relist the arguments for and against the selected decision." Doing this not only stops the disagreement but may also aid in alerting the group to whether or not groupthink has been precipitated.

♦ *Confront the difficult person directly.* If her or his tirades or other actions are disruptive, tell the person so. Continual disruptions and other negative actions that stop task and maintenance progress are not in the best interest of the group and need to be dealt with. Ideally, the confrontation should be assertive, factual, and focused on the issue—in other words, state exactly what the person has done. For example, instead of saying, "You are always making stupid and irrelevant remarks," state, "The last two times we have discussed the issue of selecting a new membership campaign, you changed the subject to why you believe the club should have more social events and why you believe you should be serving on the finance committee. Neither of these statements had anything to do with the topic being discussed, and they didn't help us to solve the issue at hand."

♦ *Separate yourself from the difficult person if all else fails.* Some individuals leave no other option but ostracism by the group. Quitting the job or leaving the group may be your only recourse. Before quitting, make an assertive statement that clearly indicates why you find the person's actions disruptive to the group and why you find yourself unable to continue working with the person. Make sure that your statements contain only facts that led you to your conclusion.

You can control only your own communication behaviors and your own responses to others' communication. Unless you are in a total power control position, you cannot change or control the actions of another person, so concentrate on dealing with yourself, and avoid getting frustrated.

The Group Leader and Group Leadership

The strength of a group is found not only in effective participation but also in meaningful guidance and decision making. The leader of a group is the person who is recognized as being responsible for guiding it through its tasks (see Figure 10.2). The leader may be *elected* (e.g., president of the speech honor society), may be *appointed* by an outside source (e.g., the board of trustees appoints the university president), may *volunteer* (e.g., a person volunteers to chair the social committee), or may *emerge* by taking control (e.g., a parent in a family). A group may also have more than one leader; for instance, a group may have several chairpersons. Furthermore, in some groups, the recognized leader may not be the only one guiding the group; other members may share this function by being appointed or assuming such responsibility.

The ability to influence others' opinions and actions is known as *leadership* (see Figure 10.2). It can be demonstrated by one or more people in a group, and the use of the power that derives from leadership can be viewed as enforcing obedience and/or the ability to influence others to perform.

Leadership power can be defined, first, as enforcing obedience through the ability to withhold benefits or inflict punishment. In this sense, power is coercive. **Coercion** centers on offering a selection of choices, all of them undesirable. For example, in a meeting of nurses to discuss whether shifts should be rotated, many of the participants may not want this action to be taken. But if the head nurse is in favor of rotating shifts, then the power of the position may come into play. He may

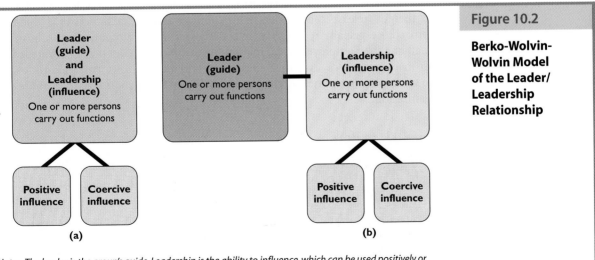

Figure 10.2

Berko-Wolvin-Wolvin Model of the Leader/Leadership Relationship

Note: The leader is the group's guide. Leadership is the ability to influence, which can be used positively or coercively. Both leader and leadership functions can be carried out by (a) the same person(s) or (b) separate persons.

say that it's his responsibility to determine staff assignments and that anyone who cannot accept his proposal can request a transfer to another department. Thus, the decision has been made through coercive power because neither of the options offered may be desirable to the nursing staff. Similarly, in a family, a mother can control the members by stating, "As long as you are living in my house, you will do as you are told or get out."

But leadership power also can be defined as the ability to influence others to perform or produce results. This kind of power does not use force or coercion. With this type of power, the influence of the person, rather than the authority of the position, is paramount. For example, in the meeting of nurses, the head nurse may suggest a solution whereby those nurses who want to work on a rotating shift may do so, and those who do not may select a permanent shift. The head nurse presents reasons for his two options and asks the others for suggestions. Eventually the group accepts the head nurse's suggestion, with or without changes, because it was explained well and because he was willing to accept alterations and perhaps has a record of being flexible in such situations. This influence through positive leadership is a productive way to use power for the benefit of the entire group.

The tendency of certain people in leadership positions to act coercively has given rise to an examination of alternative leadership styles. One of these styles is **transformational leadership** in which the person takes on the role of transforming agent. A transforming agent can change both the behavior and the outlook of his or her followers. This person keeps the interest of the group and its goals in mind rather than forcing her or his will on the group. Therefore, she or he gives up the command-and-control model of leadership.[32] This approach closely resembles the way most managers operate, getting others to perform or produce by offering rewards or punishments in the process: "Leaders approach followers with an eye to exchanging one thing for another: jobs for votes, or subsidies for campaign contributions. Such transactions comprise the bulk of the relationships among leaders and followers."[33] Transactional leadership may be well suited to short-term goals of a group, but the group, to be successful, may require a more visionary approach in the long run.

Another style is **superleadership,** in which people are led to lead themselves and thereby release the self-leadership energy within each person.[34] Such an approach is especially appropriate in today's scaled-down organizations, in which not all qualified employees have the opportunity to move up the corporate ladder into management or executive positions. This leadership format allows everyone to develop his or her leadership skills and to stay productive in changing an organization.

Types of Leaders

Regardless of leadership style, leaders use their power to influence the process of group effort. As such, leaders exhibit characteristics by which their style can be categorized. Three basic types of leaders have been identified:[35]

An **authoritarian leader** dominates and directs a group according to personal goals and objectives, regardless of how consistent or inconsistent these goals are with group members' goals.

A **democratic leader** facilitates a group according to the goals of its members and allows them to form their own conclusions.

A **laissez-faire leader** is nondirective and empowers group members to "do their own thing."

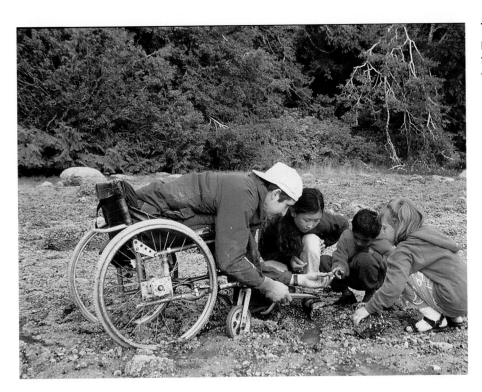

The leader of a group is the person who is responsible for guiding the group through its task.

Evidence suggests that neither the directive nor nondirective approach is consistently more effective. Each approach works under certain conditions. "The key to leader effectiveness is matching the appropriate style to the group environment."[36] Thus, if group members are very task oriented and are empowered to make decisions, they may be productive working with a laissez-faire leader. The laissez-faire style may be disastrous, however, if group members are unable to function productively on their own. A democratic leader works well with a group that requires minimal supervision. If group members cannot accomplish their tasks because they lack self-discipline, an authoritarian leader may be needed to direct activities and assign specific responsibilities. Research on leader style suggests that the power position of the leader, the task at hand, and the needs of the group should determine how and when a leader must adapt his or her style to any given group.[37]

Patterns of Leader/Leadership Emergence

If a leader is not appointed for a group, one of the questions that arises is how a person interested in becoming a leader should proceed. Research shows that emergent leaders exhibit a significantly higher rate of participation than do nonleaders.[38] In addition, "leaders become leaders when they exert influence over others on behalf of the group."[39] Leaders also tend to conform to the group's norms, values, and goals while displaying the motivation to lead. They know the rules of order, have charisma, are positive about themselves, encourage others to communicate, and are supportive listeners.

Why People Desire to Be Leaders

Recognizing that a great deal of responsibility is laid at the feet of leaders, that leaders often find themselves the target of attacks, and that they are blamed if things don't go right, why would anyone want to be a leader? People seem to want to be leaders for five basic reasons:

◆ *Information*   The leader is privy to special information. Many leaders like to be "in the know."

◆ *Rewards*   Leaders receive praise, attention, payment, power, and special privileges for being in their positions. Being a corporate executive who makes several million dollars a year can be highly satisfying in spite of the responsibilities and time constraints. Some people also like to be in the public eye. A number of corporate and business leaders do advertisements for their companies.

◆ *Expectations*   Certain people have enough faith in themselves to believe that they can accomplish a task or that they have better solutions than someone else. Listen to politicians campaigning for office. They have platforms that attempt to explain why they are more capable of making things better than are their opponents.

◆ *Acceptance*   Some people equate the title of president, chairperson, or boss with being accepted, liked, and admired.

◆ *Status*   Acquiring status in one group can bring status in other groups. That is, a record of having been a leader often is the basis for selecting someone for another leader position. Members of boards of directors of hospitals and banks are often the same people who hold the leader role in other organizations. The president of the United States almost always has been in public office as a senator, member of the House of Representatives, or state governor.

Leader/Leadership: Communicative Perspective

There is a fundamental link between human communication and leader/leadership. Influential leaders such as Winston Churchill, Golda Meir, Martin Luther King Jr., Sitting Bull, Gandhi, Mao Tse-tung, Barbara Jordan, and César Chavez were compelling communicators. A communicative perspective on leader/leadership emphasizes the group as a product of communication and the leader as a catalyst for the

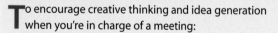

Advice for Meeting Leaders

To encourage creative thinking and idea generation when you're in charge of a meeting:

◆ **Ask open-ended** questions. *Reason:* Participants will have to answer with more than just a "yes" or "no."

◆ **Encourage people** to continue—even if they start to back off because they're repeating points made earlier.

◆ **Paraphrase ideas** when someone makes an unclear point.

◆ **Don't force** your views on others. Always remain neutral. *Reason:* A dominant tone will repress discussion.

◆ **Make sure** everyone contributes to the discussion. *How:* Direct questions to people who have not spoken. *And:* Ask for examples and elaboration.

◆ **Have opposing** sides state one another's opinions when conflict occurs.

◆ **Direct questions** to other people—or ask to hear another view—when one person tries to dominate the discussion.

◆ **Say to** the last person who spoke, "Tell me more."

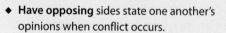
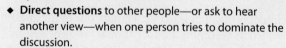

Source: Adapted from *How to Facilitate a Productive Group Session,* by Floyd Hurt, 1004 East Jefferson St., Charlottesville, VA 29902. © Communication Briefings, www.briefings.com, 1101 King St., Alexandria, VA 22314. Used with permission.

communication.[40] Leaders not only use words well but also "exhibit significantly more nonverbal cues than do nonleaders in task-oriented and informal small groups."[41]

Effective Leader Questioning

One of the most important responsibilities of a leader is to monitor the proceedings and interject appropriate questions to stimulate discussion, clarify ideas, and resolve conflict. Here are some ways to deal with common problems:[42]

Issue: Drawing out a silent member

Question to ask: "Does anyone who hasn't spoken care to comment?" Or, "Amad, what is your opinion of . . . ?"

Issue: Calling attention to points that have not been considered

Question to ask: "Does anyone have any information about this matter?" Or, "Lamont, would you care to explore this angle of the topic in more detail?"

Issue: Keeping the discussion focused on the subject

Question to ask: "That's interesting, but just how does this point fit in with the issue being considered?"

Issue: Using conflict constructively

Question to ask: "Since we do not seem to be able to resolve this difference now, could we move on to the next point?"

Issue: Suggesting the need for more information

Question to ask: "Is it agreeable to the group if we ask a subcommittee to investigate and bring back the needed information to our next session?"

Issue: Calling attention to the source of information

Question to ask: "Where did this information come from?"

Issue: Preventing a few from monopolizing the discussion

Question to ask: "May we hear from someone who hasn't expressed an opinion?"

Issue: Suggesting the need for closing the discussion

Question to ask: "We're scheduled to finish discussion in about five minutes. Is there a final comment?"

Responsibilities of Leaders

Regardless of style, a leader has the responsibility for guiding the group toward accomplishing its task and maintaining the group as a functioning unit. An effective leader needs to know when to sit back and let the group work on its own, when to step in and make suggestions, when to warn about such potential problems as groupthink, how to motivate the building of cohesion, and how to instruct on the need to evaluate ideas critically and express doubts. In other words, an effective group leader needs to know her or his responsibilities and how to carry them out.

A leader has responsibilities before, during, and following a meeting:[43]

Two Questions Leaders Ask

Changing one word when you question decisions can say a great deal about your leader ability. *Examples:*

◆ A good leader asks, "What's *right* with it?" *not* "What's *wrong* with it?"

◆ A thoughtful leader asks, "Who will it *benefit*?" not "Who will it *hurt*?"

Source: Reality Leadership, by Mark B. Jacobs, Performance Press, Inc., 10585 North Meridian St., Indianapolis, IN 46290. © Communication Briefings, www.briefings.com, 1101 King St., Alexandria, VA 22314. Used with permission.

Not only do attitudes toward being in groups vary by culture, but cultural differences are also reflected in the way a person works in a group.

Leader's responsibilities
· don't dominate
· open discussion
· establish topic
· set ground rules

In Preparation for a Meeting

◆ Define the purpose of the meeting.

◆ List specific outcomes that should or must be produced from this meeting.

◆ Establish the starting and ending times of the meeting.

◆ Notify members of the purpose and the agenda, their necessary preparations, and the time and place of the meeting.

◆ If specific resource persons are needed, advise them and prepare them for the meeting.

◆ Make necessary physical arrangements.

◆ Get necessary work items (e.g., pencils, paper, charts, data sheets, reports).

During the Meeting:

◆ Describe the importance and purpose of the meeting.

◆ Make an effort to establish a climate of trust and informality (if appropriate).

◆ Stimulate creative thinking (if appropriate).

◆ Stimulate critical thinking.

◆ Promote teamwork and cooperation.

◆ Equalize opportunities to participate and influence.

Follow-Up to the Meeting:

◆ Remind members who agreed to do after-meeting work.

◆ If minutes are kept, see that they are written and distributed.

◆ If the group decision should be forwarded to another person, see that this is done immediately.

◆ If work is necessary before a future meeting, be sure it is done.

In Conclusion

Groups are made up of people. People from different cultures possess varying attitudes about making decisions or being group participants. Participants are those members of a group who interact to bring about the actions of the group. Leaders are those who guide the group. Leadership refers to those who influence the group to accomplish its goal. Group members, their leaders, and their leadership perform task and maintenance roles.

Learn by Doing

1. Your class will be divided into groups. Each group is to take twenty minutes in which to agree on what a time traveler should take into the future, using this information for the decision:[44]

> A time machine travels to the year 5847. By then, the world has been destroyed in a nuclear holocaust, and all that remains are a few men and women living a primitive existence and having no record or memory of the past. The traveler in the time machine decides to rebuild the world but can make only one trip back and forth in time. On the trip, which can encompass any years between the dawn of humanity and this year, the traveler may collect such useful items as living things, printed materials, food, toilet paper, and so forth. The only limitation is one of weight: excluding the weight of the time traveler, no more than 200 pounds of material may be carried through time. What should the time traveler take into the future?

After the small-group discussion, the class meets to discuss these questions:
   a. What effect did differences in members' backgrounds have on the group's decision?
   b. What was the role of the leader in the group?
   c. What was the greatest problem the group encountered in reaching its decision? Could this have been resolved? How?
   d. What inferences about how groups operate can be drawn from this experience?

2. The purpose of this exercise is to illustrate how groups operate and the roles of members of a group.
   a. Before coming to class, indicate whether you thoroughly agree (TA), agree (A), disagree (D), or thoroughly disagree (TD) with each of the statements.

You must illustrate your attitude for all statements.

(1) Prayer should be allowed in public schools.

(2) Corporations have an obligation to their stockholders to make profits; this obligation supersedes all obligations.

(3) We have little control over what we communicate about ourselves to others.

(4) Every member of an organization should be permitted to present views at a meeting, regardless of how long this may take.

(5) The changing ethical structure of current society has led to confusion and a breakdown of traditional morality.

(6) Television is a major factor in desensitization of people to violence.

(7) Advertising is necessary for continuation of the free-enterprise system.

(8) War is an inevitable result of international conflict.

(9) Same-sex persons should be allowed to legally marry.

b. Your instructor will assign each member of the class to a group. Each group is to elect a leader who will be responsible for leading the discussion. Each group will be assigned one of the topics to discuss. If you finish your discussion of your topic, proceed to the next numeric topic. (e.g., if you are assigned 5, and complete your discussion, discuss 6, etc.) the group must reach consensus—total agreement—on one of the four responses (thoroughly agree through thoroughly disagree). Group members may rewrite a statement if it will help them come to consensus.

c. At the end of the discussion, each person will write answers to these questions:

(1) What one thing did the leader do that helped the group in reaching its goals?

(2) What one thing could the leader have done that would have helped the group in reaching its goals?

(3) One thing I did as a participant that pleased me was . . .

(4) One thing I did as a participant that I should not have done was . . .

(5) This group did/did not work well because . . .

d. After each student has completed Step c, each group will meet and discuss the member's answers. Be prepared to report back to the class of your group's overall strengths and weaknesses and the process of group decision making.

3. Using the discussions that were held for either Activity 1 or Activity 2, each person in your group is to analyze all of the group members, including himself or herself, by identifying the roles each played, using the identifiers in the "Roles of Group Members" section of this chapter (pages 274–275). Share your lists with the members of the group, and discuss the observations.

4. Identify a specific culture (e.g., ethnic, racial, or gender group), and prepare a short paper (which may be given as an oral presentation in class) indicating what the research shows about characteristic patterns of the specific culture as group members.

Key Terms

participants
leaders
leadership
Confucian principle of i
intuitive-affective decision-making
    approach
centralized decision-making process
proposal counterproposal negotiating
silent majority
hidden agenda
communication stoppers
group communication networks

centralized group communication
    networks
decentralized group communication
    networks
leadership power
coercion
transformational leadership
superleadership
authoritarian leader
democratic leader
laissez-faire leader

PART THREE

Communicating in Public

11

Public Speaking: Planning and Presenting the Message

After reading this chapter, you should be able to

- Define public communication/public speaking
- Explain the ethical responsibility of a public speaker, including the implications of plagiarism and fabrication
- Explain the role of the participants, setting, and purpose/topic in public communication
- Define and explain the roles of prior, process, and postspeech analyses
- Clarify the role of the statement of central idea of a public speech
- Discuss how to develop impromptu (or ad lib), extemporaneous, manuscript, and memorized presentations
- List pointers on preparing an oral-style manuscript
- Explain the advantages and disadvantages of the impromptu, extemporaneous, manuscript, and memorized modes of presentation
- Identify the oral and physical factors that lead to an effective presentation
- Clarify how to use visuals in a presentation
- Explain public speaking anxiety and some ways of dealing with it

For many, the thought of giving a speech is exciting. For others, standing before an audience conjures up feelings of terror. No matter what your attitude is, you can learn to be a competent public speaker! Really!

The act of **public communication** involves a transaction between a speaker and an audience. You may think that public speaking is something you do not need to be concerned about, but this is not the case. In fact, "a surprising number of persons . . . do speak to audiences of ten or more people fairly frequently."[1] No matter what your college major or current position, odds are that you will be doing some type of public speaking.

Preparing a Speech: An Overview

Research shows that preparation is an important key to effective public speaking. The quality of a speech performance normally correlates positively with the total preparation time, the amount of research done, the time and effort spent in preparation of speaking notes, the time spent preparing visual aids, the number of rehearsals, and the time spent rehearsing out loud.[2]

Although there is no universally agreed-on one best way to prepare a speech, there is a process that works well for many people:

Step 1   *Decide on a topic or accept the topic assigned to you.*

Step 2   *Formulate a statement of central idea.*

Step 3   *Collect research that develops the statement of central idea.*

The act of public communication involves a transaction between a speaker and an audience.

Step 4   Prepare an introduction that will grab the attention of the listeners and provide them with the necessary background so that they will be ready to hear the particulars of the topic.

Step 5   Formulate the body of the presentation so that the goal can be achieved.

Step 6   Prepare the necessary aids, such as visuals and computer-generated graphics.

Step 7   Develop the conclusion, which summarizes the points and wraps up the presentation.

Parameters of Public Speaking

Any act of communication is based on three parameters: the participants, the setting, and the purpose of the communication. In a speech, these three parameters may affect the topic selected, the language used, the types of examples and illustrations chosen, and the aids needed to support and/or clarify ideas.

The **speech participants** are the speaker and the members of the audience. The **speaking setting** encompasses where the speech is given, what the time limit is, when the presentation is made, and the attitude of the audience. The **purpose of the speech** centers on the speaker's expected outcomes for the presentation.

To give effective speeches, analyze the three parameters in three stages: prior analysis, process analysis, and postspeech analysis. The majority of the work takes place in the **prior to the speech analysis,** before the speech is given. But observing the audience for feedback (the **process of the speech analysis**) and paying attention to reactions following a speech (the **postspeech analysis**) are also very important.

The Ethics of Public Speaking

A major concern of any communicator is the matter of ethics. An ethical public speaker

- Speaks with sincerity.
- Does not knowingly expose an audience to falsehoods or half-truths that cause significant harm.
- Does not premeditatedly alter the truth.
- Presents the truth as he or she understands it.
- Raises the listeners' level of expertise by supplying the necessary facts, definitions, descriptions, and substantiating information.
- Employs a message that is free from mental as well as physical coercion by not compelling someone to take an action against his or her will.
- Does not invent or fabricate statistics or other information intended to serve as a basis for proof of a contention or belief.
- Gives credit to the source of information and does not pretend that the information is original when it is not.

Two specific areas of ethical concern in public speaking are plagiarism and fabrication.

Plagiarism

Plagiarism occurs when a speaker uses the ideas and words of others as his or her own without giving credit to the originator of the material.

Plagiarism can be as seemingly innocent as overhearing someone's idea on a solution to a problem, presenting that idea in your speech, and not giving credit to the originator of the idea. Or the speaker can copy an entire essay someone else prepared and present it as a speech with no reference to the source.

The extent of plagiarism may extend from using an idea to replicating an entire speech. There are unscrupulous people who encourage plagiarism by supplying opportunities to participate in the act. For example, theme and speech sales organizations sell prepackaged presentations. Be aware that using one of these in a classroom can result in your failing a course or even being expelled from school, plus the personal embarrassment of being identified as a cheat.

The number one fear of Americans is speaking in public.

Also be aware that there are federal laws regarding the illegal use of someone else's materials, especially if the ideas are copyrighted. Materials published in a book or magazine are almost always copyrighted.

One of your authors was at a national convention and attended a session at which a graduate student presented a teaching activity that she credited as being her own. She supplemented her speech with a drawing. During the question-and-answer session, the author asked if this was the speaker's own material. She assured him that it was original and developed specifically for this presentation. He knew better. Following this session he was to present a workshop on creative teaching and had a copy of an instructor's manual, published several years previously, that he had written and that contained the *exact* exercise, complete with the *exact* drawing, which he pointed out to the presenter. You can imagine how difficult and embarrassing it was for the plagiarist to make a public apology.

Every idea you present in a speech does not have to be original; however, if the concept comes from another source, you are obligated as an ethical speaker to give credit.

The consequences for plagiarism can be severe. "At some colleges, students who plagiarize are expelled."[3] In 2001, at one prestigious southern university, thirty-three students were expelled after a professor employed software that he had designed to detect plagiarism.[4]

All plagiarism, intentional or unintentional, is stealing! Someone else has done the work; you are taking credit for it. That is not ethical.

Fabrication

Fabrication is making up information or guessing at information and making it appear as being true. If research doesn't reveal the desired statistics you need for proving a point of a speech, you can just make them up. Right? Wrong!!!!

Don't assume that listeners are stupid. They read, and they watch television; they can be experts on the particular topic about which you are speaking. How would you feel if you had fabricated statistics and, during the question-and-answer session following your presentation, an audience member indicated that the information was not accurate and had proof to back up the inaccuracy? How would you feel if during a business briefing your employer was made aware by an audience member that the material you were using was made up, not accurate, and had no substantiation?

Telling half-truths because you haven't completed your work or you didn't have enough time for proper research is no excuse for making up information. Fabrication is lying, and lying is unethical.

As an ethical public speaker, you must understand that you are a moral agent. When you communicate with others and make decisions that affect yourself and others, you have a moral responsibility.

Prior to the Speech Analysis

In determining what you are going to say, you need to consider several factors. This information will aid in dealing with selecting or refining a topic, developing the speech, selecting appropriate language, and deciding what information to include in the presentation. This **audience analysis** consists of assessing the demographic, psychographic, and rhetorographic characteristics of your prospective listeners.

Demographics

Demographics—your listeners' characteristics based on their descriptions and backgrounds—include such factors as age, gender, religion, ethnicity, education, occupation, and race.[5]

Age   The general age level of your audience should be considered. Make sure that the examples and language you use are appropriate for the age level of the group you are addressing.

Gender   Knowing whether the audience will be made up primarily of males or females may help you in deciding how to approach the topic or what types of examples to use. It is important not to stereotype all men or women as being universally the same; however, using examples that are appropriate to the gender makeup of the group can draw in the listeners. Further, be aware that sexist statements can turn listeners against the speaker.

Religion   A speaker can establish or destroy a common bond with specific religious groups through language and examples. If the group is all of the same religious persuasion, using examples of people or principles of that group could lead to the acceptance of your views, just as an inappropriate reference might turn listeners against you.

Ethnic Background   The ethnic background of an audience often is as important as its religious affiliation. Appropriate ethnic references, if they fit the topic, can enhance a speaker's credibility. Select references that put the ethnic group in a positive light.

Educational Background   Understanding the educational background and training of your listeners is important so you can choose material appropriate to their level. For example, a highly expert audience at an informative briefing will expect a more detailed analysis of Internet capabilities than would a group of listeners who have just purchased home computers.

Occupation   Occupational interests and experiences often serve as the communication bond for speakers and listeners. Using examples that are specifically aimed at members of a particular work group can result in clarity, pride, and a feeling of togetherness.

Racial Background   Like ethnic background, the racial composition of your audience may be a critical consideration. Just as it is important not to make stereotyped statements when addressing all men or all women, so too it is important not to make assumptions about any particular racial group, especially if you, the speaker, are not of the same race as your listeners.

Psychographics

The audience's **psychographics**—its attitudes and beliefs—are an important consideration. This profile can be determined by analyzing the listeners.

Attitudes   Attitudes are the predispositions that your listeners bring to the communication event. They will have attitudes toward you as the speaker based on their perceptions of your trustworthiness, competence, and presentational style.

Your listeners also have attitudes toward the occasion. Usually they are part of a voluntary audience, participating in the speech event because they want to be there; but if they are a captive audience (e.g., a collegiate assembly, a required training seminar, a military briefing), it is important for you to know that. Audiences who are required to listen to a speech are less receptive, and you may need to add humor or drama to get and hold their attention. You also may want to recognize that you realize that they are not there voluntarily, empathize with them, and make sure that you do an effective job of using devices to make them want to listen.

Your listeners also have attitudes toward your subject. They may agree or disagree with your stand on the subject. If they agree with you—for example, they are pro-choice when you are speaking on that subject—then they will probably need less persuading. On the other hand, if the majority of the audience is pro-life, your task is going to be more difficult, and you are going to have to use devices to attempt to change their attitude. In this case, you may want to anticipate that the pro-life audience may verbally attack you in the question-and-answer session, so you might prepare for that eventuality in assembling your materials.

Conservative/Liberal   In dealing with issues such as abortion, the death penalty, genetic engineering, homosexuality, and school prayer, you are taking on topics about which the listeners may well have an emotional investment that comes out of

Psychographics—attitudes and beliefs of the audience members—are an important consideration.

their conservative or liberal disposition. It is helpful to know the predispositions of your listeners as you select arguments and appeals to get them to respond.

Political Affiliation   The listeners' political affiliations usually correspond to their conservative/liberal dispositions, and may have religious roots as well. You may want to know if your listeners were primarily independent voters or registered members of a particular political party before putting together your message in order to trigger the responses you desire by appealing to their loyalties.

Rhetorographics

Just as you analyze your audience, so must you analyze the **rhetorographics:** the place, time limit, time of day, and emotional climate for the speech.

Place   The place can affect the tone and topic of a speech. Such factors as the size of the room, temperature, lighting, arrangement of the furniture, and physical comfort or discomfort of the audience all affect your communication. Do the acoustics of the room enable the listeners to hear you clearly? Is there a microphone? When using slides or PowerPoint-generated graphics, can you dim the lights, or do you have to turn them off completely? How is the seating arranged?

Time   Both the time limit and the time of day affect a speaker's performance. Whatever the reason for the time limit, a speaker has an obligation to stay within the prescribed boundaries, so it is important to prepare carefully so that you don't ramble on.

Speakers also should be aware that time of day can affect an audience. Early morning and late night hours, for instance, often are difficult times to hold the attention of an audience. You might want to plan a shorter speech if you know you are speaking near the end of the day or the finish of a conference.

The settings for public communication may be affected by its emotional climate.

Emotional Climate   The setting for public communication may be affected by its emotional climate—the overriding psychological state of the participants. A community recently devastated by a tornado, for example, certainly would have a special emotional climate. Thus, a speaker called on to present a speech in such a setting would have to adapt his or her message to the tragedy and deal with the fears, bitterness, and trauma that the audience has been experiencing.

From the information obtained in the prior analysis, you should be able to reach a reasonable conclusion about a topic that will fit you and the audience concerning the language and the supporting materials needed to develop the speech.

Applying the Prior Analysis

Assuming you have completed your prior analysis, how do you use the information?

Topic Selection   Typically speakers are asked to make presentations because of their knowledge, experiences, or expertise. For example, a businessperson is told to present a new plan for reorganizing her department. Or a speaker decides that he has something to say and finds an audience who should and will listen to the message.

On the other hand, sometimes a speaker is given limited or total leeway in selecting a topic. In the academic setting, for example, to help students learn how to plan and prepare speeches, instructors may let the students figure out what topic to use for a class assignment.

If you are given latitude in selecting your topic, know that you are your own best resource. An examination of your life experiences and interests can be useful for selecting topics. For example, consider your hobbies and special interests, places you have lived or traveled, or the skills you have. Some people like to develop a speaking inventory to help them in the topic identification process. To develop such a list, do Activity 1 in the Learn by Doing section at the end of this chapter.

Using the information presented so far, let's examine the process leading up to the presentation of the speech:

Picking a General Topic: An Example

Chan is a twenty-year-old college sophomore. In filling out his speaker inventory, he discovered that his interests and knowledge all center around his having worked at McDonald's restaurants for the past four years. He is now in the management training program and is in college to fulfill requirements for becoming a district manager. He would like to talk about McDonald's! He now has a general topic. The next question is, What specifically will he speak about? The answer takes further analysis.

Using Demographic Information: An Example

Chan remembers that during the first day of his speech communication course, everyone was introduced. Almost all of the students are health care, premedicine, social work, preschool, education, and psychology majors. He is one of two business majors. A number of the older students have young children. The topics he considers include how a McDonald's restaurant is managed, what his job consists of, his possible future employment with the restaurant chain, and the Ronald McDonald House program. He would feel comfortable talking about all of these, but which would be best for this audience? Based on the major academic fields of the audience, he eliminates managing the restaurant and possible employment; these would be more appropriate for business majors. He eliminates speaking about what his job consists of because it is of interest to him but probably not to anyone else. He selects the Ronald McDonald House program because it deals with health care and social service issues and is aimed at working with children and parents, which fits the audience demographics.

Using Psychographic Information: An Example

Chan reconsiders his choice based on psychographics. It doesn't appear, from what he can tell of the class, that any political or conservative/liberal disposition would be negatively stirred by his topic selection, so he decides to stick with his choice.

Using Rhetorographic Information: An Example

Chan now needs to test his topic regarding place, time limit, time of day, and emotional climate. The classroom doesn't seem to have any negative effect on the topic selection, though he is aware that his idea of showing snapshots isn't going to work in the large room, with a class of thirty students, so he decides to use PowerPoint graphics instead. There doesn't seem to be any existing emotional climate he has to deal with. The time limit of the speech, however, is going to be a factor. He has a maximum of five minutes to speak. There is no way he can inform the class about all the activities of Ronald McDonald House in that time, so he is going to have to limit the breadth of the topic. He decides to tell the purpose of Ronald McDonald House and give two personal examples of children he has assisted as an active volunteer with the local project and university hospital.

Language Selection   Like the topic, the language selected for use during a speech must be adapted to the audience. The average thirteen-year-old's vocabulary is not the same as an adult's, for example. By the same token, certain terms that are common to a specific occupational or cultural group may be baffling to individuals who are not members of that group. And a person who is well versed on a specific subject can easily forget that the audience may not have the same knowledge or know the same terms.

It is important to adapt your vocabulary to the level of the audience. Be careful not to talk down to your listeners—and just as careful not to use language that is so technical or abstract that they do not understand.

Selecting Appropriate Language: An Example

Chan, in thinking about the subject, the audience, and language, realizes that he has to make sure not to use terms that are unfamiliar to those not working at McDonald's or unfamiliar with the facility. For example, he must avoid calling the site "Willard's Place," the volunteers' nickname for it. (The first person to portray Ronald McDonald was the now nationally known TV weatherman Willard Scott, who has been strongly identified with the agency.)

Statement of Central Idea   In developing a message, a speaker should know specifically what she or he wants to communicate. Thus, before even starting to put together the actual presentation, public speakers find it useful to compose a **statement of central idea,** which defines the subject and develops the criteria by which to evaluate the material to be included in the speech. A statement of central idea centers on what you want the audience to know, to be able to do, to believe. The statement of central idea typically consists of three parts: the goal of the speech, the statement of the topic, and the method or process used to develop the speech.

The **goal of the speech** is expressed in terms of its expected outcome. To *inform* (impart new information and secure understanding or reinforce information and understandings acquired in the past) or to *persuade* (attempt to get the listener to take some action, to accept a belief, or to change a point of view) are the speech goals.

The **topic of the speech**—the subject—should be stated as specifically as possible.

The **method of speech development** encompasses how you plan to approach the presentation. A topic that requires an in-depth study of one fact—for example, how cast members are chosen for a theatrical production—presents a detailed development of a single issue. If the topic requires a complete survey of ideas, a multiple number of topics may need to be covered—for example, how a play is cast, rehearsed, and performed. Just as in language selection, the method of development depends a great deal on your determination of how much your listeners know about or, indeed, need to know about the topic you have selected.

Key words can assist in developing a statement of central idea for an informative speech—for example, *by explaining, by summarizing, by contrasting, by describing, by demonstrating, by analyzing.*

In a persuasive speech, key phrases for the method of development section of the statement of central idea can include *to accept that, to attend, to support, to agree with, to contribute to, to serve, to share, to vote for.*

The statement of central idea thus consists of the goal of the speech, the statement of the topic, and the method or process to be used to develop the speech. Here are two examples of the statement of central idea prepared by an informative speaker:

To inform the audience why competency testing is being used as a determination for high school graduation by discussing the three major reasons for its use.

I want the audience to know of the important effect that Latino music has had on changing the self-image of Hispanic Americans. To do this, I will list and explain the effects on Hispanic Americans brought about through the cross-cultural popularity of Ricky Martin, Chayanne, Graciella Beltran, and Selena.

Here are two examples of persuasive statements of central idea:

> I want the audience to fill out and sign living wills. To do this, I will list five reasons for them to take the action.

> To persuade the audience to accept the concept that getting help from a mental health professional can be a positive act by examining the five most common reasons people seek mental health help and the statistics showing the success rate of treatment for those problems.

By keeping these factors in mind, you can avoid some of the major pitfalls of neophyte speakers: not finishing the speech in the time limit, not accomplishing the speech's purpose, and not allowing the audience to gain the information.

Writing the Statement of Central Idea: An Example

Chan is now ready to prepare his statement of central idea: "To inform the audience about the Ronald McDonald House project, by explaining the purpose of the project and presenting two examples of children who have been aided by Ronald McDonald House." He checks to make sure his statement contains a goal (to inform), a topic (the Ronald McDonald House project), and a method of development (explaining and presenting). Chan is now ready to develop his speech.

The speaker's preparation thus extends to doing a careful prior analysis of the audience and the setting and drawing up a statement of central idea that will be appropriate to his or her level of expertise and knowledge and to the intended listeners.

Process of the Speech Analysis

As the speech is being presented, actively analyze the feedback you are receiving. This process of the speech analysis is important to the accomplishment of your speaking goal. Speakers frequently need to adjust the materials as they present. For example, President Clinton adapted good process analysis to defuse a hostile situation during his first term when he was presenting a speech about his proposed health care plan. A man in the audience suddenly jumped up and started to verbally attack the president's efforts regarding AIDS research. Clinton paused, dissuaded the Secret Service from removing the heckler, and invited the man to present his point. The president then responded to the arguments, went back to his prepared remarks, and built references to this unplanned interaction into the remainder of the presentation.

Verbal interruptions are not typical. More typical are nonverbal cues of attentiveness and agreement, or of boredom or hostility, conveyed through posture and facial expression. Some speakers are sensitive to the *cough meter*. If you have lost your audience's attention, you may hear increasing numbers of people clear their throats, cough, and become physically restless.

Effective process analysis requires that you interpret cues accurately and then adapt to them. Be careful not to assume, for instance, that one person nodding off represents boredom on the part of all of your listeners. However, if most of the audience looks bored, you should be concerned.

You can adapt to the feedback you receive in various ways. For example, if you feel the audience does not understand a point, add an illustration, clarify your terms, or restate the idea. If you sense that the audience is not attentive, change the volume of your voice, use a pause, move forward, or insert an interesting or humorous story. Another technique used in the classroom or training session is to ask questions of the audience members to involve them in the presentation.

Most people don't feel totally comfortable in departing from their preplanned notes during a speech. The more confidence you have in your speaking abilities and the more comfortable you are with the topic, the more willing you will be to adjust to the feedback. Some people make mental notes about what is happening and then try and figure out afterward what went wrong so they can adjust their material or presentational style for the next speech. Besides noting what is going on during the speech, postspeech analysis can be of help in perfecting your speaking skills.

Postspeech Analysis

Postspeech analysis enables you to determine how a speech affected the audience, which gains you useful information for preparing and presenting future speeches. A direct way to conduct a postspeech analysis is to have a question-and-answer session. The questions your audience asks may reveal how clear your presentation was. The verbal and language tone of the questions may reflect the general mood of the listeners, telling you how positively or negatively they received you and your message. Informal conversations with members of the audience after the speech also can reveal a great deal.

Other postspeech techniques include opinion polls, tests, questionnaires, and follow-up interviews. These techniques are often used by professional speakers, such as politicians, to evaluate their presentations.

In addition to planning your speech, you need to attend to the presentation of your message.

Presenting the Message

To prepare for a speech, recognize that there are several basic means of presenting a message. These include the oral and physical elements of the presentation. You also should be aware that these elements are sometimes affected by the mode of presentation that is selected and used.

Modes of Presentation

Four basic **modes of speech presentation**—the preparation method and reference aids to be used during the speech—are the impromptu, extemporaneous, manuscript, and memorized.

Impromptu or Ad Lib Mode

Sometimes a speaker uses information acquired from experiences, speaks with little or no preparation, and organizes ideas while he or she is communicating. This approach is referred to as **impromptu speaking.** Some speech theorists distinguish this from **ad lib speaking,** in which a speaker has no time to organize ideas and responds immediately when answering a question, volunteering an opinion, or interacting during a question-and-answer session. The impromptu mode gives a speaker a short period of time to decide what to say; therefore, the speaker does not communicate quite as spontaneously as when ad libbing. For example, when a teacher asks a question in class and gives students a minute or so to think of the answer, students use the impromptu mode when responding. Getting called on and being required to give an immediate answer is an ad lib.

These forms of speaking offer the advantage of being natural and spontaneous and tend to represent a speaker's true feelings because so little time is available to develop defenses and strategies.

Both of these modes are weakened, however, by the lack of time a speaker has to develop organized and well-analyzed statements. Another drawback, which derives from the impossibility of doing research, is the speaker's lack of opportunity to use statistics, examples, or illustrations to explain ideas clearly unless he or she is an expert on the topic. Still another liability is the speaker's tendency to ramble or use unnecessary phrases such as "you know" and "stuff like that" to gain thinking time or gloss over nonspecific information. Finally, lack of preparation also can result in oral uncertainty—a speaker's inability to present a coherent speech.

Putting together an impromptu speech requires quick work and immediate decisions. The process is the same as preparing for any other type of speech, except that there is less time to get ready. As you try to organize your thoughts, keep these ideas in mind:

Step 1   Determine what topic you wish to present.

Step 2   Word a statement of central idea that represents the topic.

Facing a Last-Minute Speech

If you have to present with little notice, follow these tips:

◆ Write down a single phrase describing what you need to communicate to your audience. Then, write three actions, reasons, or qualities supporting that phrase. *Example:* If you want to communicate how to increase sales, three actions to do so could be: make more cold calls, ask for referrals, and survey customers. Mention the points during your speech. *Tip:* Write them on the back of a business card for easy reference.

◆ Answer the questions who, what, when, where, why, and how. *Example:* If you're talking about change that will occur in your organization, tell the audience who will be in charge of the change effort, what the change is, why it's necessary, when it will occur, where it will take place, and how it will be achieved.

◆ Refer to a current event or personal story and link either to your main point. Audiences will remember these more easily than facts or figures.

◆ Use an analogy to help get your message across. *Example:* If speaking about a new product, say, "Our new widget is like a stealth fighter because it gets the job done, and you don't even know it's there."

◆ Memorize four or five quotes about motivation, communication, or teamwork and include them in your talk.

Source: Adapted from *Smart Moves for People in Charge,* by Sam Deep and Lyle Sussman, Addison-Wesley Publishing Co., 1 Jacob Way, Reading, MA 01867. © Communication Briefings, www.briefings.com, 1101 King St., Alexandria, VA 22314. Used with permission.

Step 3   List the major headings that develop the statement of central idea. If paper is available, jot down the ideas. Write these in the vertical middle of the sheet of paper so you have time to add the introduction about them later, if time is available. Leave space between the major headings so that if you have time for developing subpoints, you will be able to write them in.

Step 4   Arrange the major headings according to one of the methods of organization—time or space order, problem-solution, or a topical approach. Use the list you developed in Step 3 and number the order of each heading.

Step 5   Decide on an introduction. Most ad lib speakers tend to use a question or a reference to the topic, but often you can think of a story that relates to the topic. Because you probably will not have time to write out the whole introduction, jot down several key words so you will remember what you want to say.

Step 6   Restate the major points you made as the conclusion.

Step 7   If you have time, go back to see if you can think of any illustrations, examples, or statistics that develop the major ideas you want to present. Write them in at the appropriate place in the outline. If there is no time, try to think of some as you speak. Make sure that you clarify or define any words that may be unfamiliar to your listeners.

Extemporaneous Mode

People who have more time to prepare for their presentations often use the **extemporaneous speaking mode,** developing a set of "talking points," such as notes or an outline to assist them in presenting their ideas. The speaker knows in advance that she or he will be giving a speech and can prepare by doing research and planning the speech.

The extemporaneous mode offers significant advantages: time to find the information needed to help accomplish the statement of central idea; the security of having notes or an outline to refer to throughout the speech; use of quotations, illustrations, and statistics in written form for backing up ideas; and a more spontaneous and natural oral presentation and physical presentation than are likely in the manuscript or memorized mode.

As with any other presentational mode, the extemporaneous mode of delivery has some disadvantages as well. For example, a speaker who does not allow sufficient time for preparation and rehearsal may get mentally lost during the presentation. Furthermore, if a speaker refers to the notes or outline too frequently during the speech or has too many notes, she or he may fail to interact with the audience. And because extemporaneous material is never written out word for word, there will be no permanent record of the speech.

Preparing the Extemporaneous Speech   Most speakers use either notes or an outline when they present an extemporaneous speech. Notes can consist of a list of words that guide the speaker through the presentation or a series of phrases or sentences to act as clues. Most commonly, extemporaneous speakers use an outline.

Many speakers start out with a **speech planning outline,** a brief framework used to think through the process of the speech. This outline contains the major ideas of the speech, without elaboration. It is a means of thinking through the things you wish to say and putting them in a structured order. Some speakers use this for practice and while speaking. Others prepare a **speech presentation outline** in which they flesh out the outline with examples and illustrations and write in internal summaries and forecasts.

Eye span is an effective method for establishing eye contact with an audience in an unobtrusive way, while following a manuscript.

Outlining   The basic concept in outlining is that the speaker has a clear step-by-step structure of what will be said and in what order. Some speakers simply list the headings and subordinate points in a sequential order. Others use a formal outlining method.

Numerous rules have been developed for how to structure an outline.[6] Some speech instructors are very specific as to what the outline is to look like, indicating that the discipline of developing the outline aids the speaker in making sure that all parts of the speech are well developed and ordered. Others believe that the outline is for the speaker's benefit. They advise preparing it so that you are comfortable with the material and can remember what you need to say.

The following are some considerations for preparing an outline:[7]

An outline has a balanced structure based on four major principles: parallelism, coordination, subordination, and division.

Parallelism   Whenever possible, when preparing an outline, you should express coordinate heads in parallel form. That is, nouns should be made parallel with nouns, verb forms with verb forms, adjectives with adjectives, and so on (*Example:* Nouns: *computers, programs, users;* Verbs: *to compute, to program, to use;* Adjectives: *home* computers, *new* programs, *experienced* users). Although parallel structure is desired, logical and clear language should not be sacrificed simply to maintain parallelism. (For example, there are times when nouns and gerunds at the same level of an outline are acceptable.) Reasonableness and flexibility of form are preferred to rigidity.

Coordination   In outlining, those items that are of equal significance should have comparable numeral or letter designations: an *A* is equal to a *B*, a *1* to a *2*, an *a* to a *b*, and so on. Coordinates should have the same value. Coordination is a principle that enables a writer to maintain a coherent and consistent document.

Here is a sample of good coordination:

A. Types of programs
    1. Word processing
    2. Desktop publishing

B. Evaluation of programs
    1. Word processing
        a. Word
        b. WordPerfect
    2. Desktop publishing
        a. PageMaker
        b. Quark XPress

Subordination   To indicate levels of significance, an outline uses major and minor headings. Thus, in ordering ideas, you should organize the outline from general to specific or from abstract to concrete—the more general or abstract the term, the higher its level or rank in the outline. This principle allows your material to be ordered in terms of logic and requires a clear articulation of the relationships among the component parts used in the outline. Subdivisions of each higher division should always have the same relationship to the whole.

Here is a sample of good subordination form of major headings:

A. Word
   1. Positive features
   2. Negative features

B. WordPerfect
   1. Positive features
   2. Negative features

Division   The purpose of the divisions is to flesh out the major ideas by adding clarifiers, examples, and illustrations. Some outlining purists contend that "for every *A* there should be a *B* and for every *1* there must be a *2*."[8] In general, this makes sense. If you are subdividing an idea—that is, breaking it into parts—then by definition, you must have at least two subideas. This does not mean, however, that if you are supporting an idea with an example, you must have two examples.

Here is a sample of good division form:

A. Computers
   1. Mainframe
   2. Micro
      a. Floppy disk
      b. Hard disk

B. Computer uses
   1. Institutional
   2. Personal

Form   The most important rule for outlining form is to be consistent! Most speech outlines use either a topic structure or a sentence structure.

A **topic outline** has words or phrases for all entries and usually has little or no punctuation after entries. One advantage of this format is that it presents a brief overview of the ideas. In addition, speakers often find that they will speak more and read less with the abbreviated material on the page.

A **sentence outline** has complete sentences for all entries and usually has correct punctuation. One advantage of this format is that there is a more detailed overview of the ideas to be presented. Therefore, it may give the speaker more security since whole ideas rather than word clues are presented.

An outline can use a combination of Roman numerals and letters or a decimal form. An outline composed of Roman numerals and letters follows this format:

I.
   A.
   B.
      1.
      2.
         a.
         b.
II.

An outline composed of decimals would follow this format:

1.0
    1.1
    1.2
        1.2.1
        1.2.2
            1.2.2.1
            1.2.2.2

Here are some additional speech guidelines:

◆ *Include internal summaries and forecasts.* Internal summaries restate each major point before proceeding to the next major point. Forecasts tell the listener what is coming next. To ensure that they remember to include these in the oral presentation, many speakers write the statements into the outline.

◆ *Write notes in the margins to remind yourself of necessary information.* If you need a reminder to slow down in certain sections or to use a visual aid to emphasize a point, write yourself a note in the margin of the outline. Use a color of ink that stands out. Although the marginal notes are not an official part of the outline, they are yet another device to help make the speech effective and to help you feel comfortable and gain confidence.

◆ *Avoid overoutlining.* To avoid having an excessive number of notes, limit the quantity to those you absolutely need to trigger your thoughts. In determining what is essential, you are wise to consider this analogy. The first time you drive to a particular site, you may need a detailed set of directions complete with route numbers, road markers, and indications of exact mileage. On your second trip, you need less information, and by the third trip, you need almost none. So it is with your use of notes and outlines. You should have enough information to feel comfortable and free to navigate through the presentation with no fear of getting lost. The only way to discover the extent of your readiness is to take several test drives through your speech to ascertain how much prepared information you really need to have with you in the form of written prompts.

Mind Mapping   An alternative to using an outline for the extemporaneous mode of presentation is mind mapping. **Mind mapping** is a method of arranging materials visually rather than in list form. This is a mode often favored by right-brained people, who are stimulated by pictures rather than words. Mind mappers can use the procedure to develop the speech or to develop and then use the visual images for the presentation stage of speaking.

To mind-map, the potential speaker makes a list of all the ideas to be included in the speech. Then major headings are selected, each major idea is placed in a circle, and the subpoints are grouped around the major heading circles and connected to the circles with spokes. The speaker indicates the major heading, then orally flows from one spoke to another. When one circle and its spokes are finished, the speaker proceeds to the next circle and discusses its topical spokes. Let's say you are planning on speaking about a visit to Washington, D.C., the nation's capital. You make a list of the things you did and the sights you saw (Table 11.1). You then set the major theme ideas in circles and group the subhead ideas around those major themes (Figure 11.1). This drawing forms the basis for the extemporaneous speech.

Mind Maps

"If I'm concerned about having too much to say or what to cover in a speech, I organize it by mind mapping the material. I put the topic or theme in the middle of the page. Then [I] brainstorm everything I can think of about that topic. I write just a word or so that represents each of those thoughts. I put little squiggles around each word, just for fun. I then look at the thoughts and number each one in the way I might use them. I don't draw pictures or get elaborate in terms of colors—my wife, Marge, does like to organize her talk that way."

Dr. Ken Blanchard

Yellow elephant.

As you read that phrase, did you think of letters Y-e-l-l-o-w-e-l-e-p-h-a-n-t. Or did you see an image? Of course, you saw the image. The mind thinks in images and pictures. Mind mapping was developed by Tony Buzan, author and brain researcher, as an alternative to outlining. He suggests you organize your material by drawing pictures. For example, you might draw a simple picture of a yellow elephant (assuming you were doing a talk that involved a yellow elephant), then a line with an arrow to the next thought you want to talk about.

When you try to force your mind to think in a traditional outline form—with words and sentences—you may wait around forever, staring at a blank paper, waiting for Roman numeral I to bounce into your head. But in mind mapping you draw each idea as it pops up, then connect the pictures later into a speech.

As you draw your mind map, you can more easily see when you've got too much stuff in one place and not enough in another. If you can't easily connect one line to another, then you can see it may not belong in the presentation at all.

Source: From *Secrets of Successful Speakers* by Lilly Walters, McGraw-Hill, 1993. This material is reproduced with permission of The McGraw-Hill Companies.

Manuscript Mode

In the **manuscript speech mode,** the material is written out and delivered word for word. This method offers the advantages of providing accurate language and solid organization. In addition, it gives the speaker a permanent written record of the speech.

But the manuscript mode also has some disadvantages. Because the manuscript provides a word-for-word record of the speech, the speaker cannot easily adapt it to suit the audience during the presentation. The speaker is stuck with the message as written. As a result, the speaker must depend on prior audience analysis to ensure that the message is tailored to the listeners.

The manuscript mode of delivery also requires the ability to read effectively from the written page. An effective speaker should use extensive eye contact, vocal inflections, and physical actions to maintain rapport with the listeners. Unfortunately, most people are not very good oral readers. They read monotonously, make reading errors, get lost in the script, and fail to establish good eye contact. Many novice speakers turn to the manuscript mode because they feel more secure with it. However, manuscripted speeches, in the hands of many people, are dull and boring presentations.

As a result, accomplished speakers use the extemporaneous mode rather than the manuscript mode because it allows them to interact more freely with the audience and to adapt better to feedback. At times, however, preparing an exact word-for-word presentation is necessary. For example, the manuscript mode must be used when speakers are going to be quoted, when they must meet specific time requirements, or when they need precise word selection.

Preparing the Manuscript   Unlike a reader, who has the opportunity to reread a passage, the listener has only one opportunity to receive, understand, and interpret

Table 11.1	A. Listing of topics	B. Mapping visual outline

Mind-Mapping Procedure	*Subject: Visiting Washington, D.C.*
	Smithsonian Museums
	Georgetown
	Kennedy Center for Performing
	  Arts
	Tyson's Corner Center
	Korean Memorial
	Metro
	*Outdoor things to do
	Vietnam Memorial
	Ford's Theater
	Jefferson Memorial
	Beltway
	Bureau of Engraving and Printing
	The White House
	Capitol Building
	Mazza Gallery
	*Indoor things to do
	Holocaust Museum
	Washington Monument
	Arlington Cemetery
	National Zoo
	FBI Building
	Parking lots
	*Transportation
	Roosevelt Memorial
	Corcoran Art Gallery
	Lincoln Monument
	The Mall
	*Shopping
	Tidal Basin
	Pentagon
	Old Town Alexandria
	Smithsonian Gift Shops
	Fashion Mall at Pentagon City
		Outdoor Things to Do
		Arlington Cemetery
		National Zoo
		Korean Memorial
		Vietnam Memorial
		Lincoln Monument
		Jefferson Memorial
		Roosevelt Memorial
		Washington Monument
		Tidal Basin
		The Mall
		Shopping
		Old Town Alexandria
		Mazza Gallery
		Smithsonian Gift Shops
		Fashion Mall
		Georgetown
		Tyson's Corner Center
		Indoor Things to Do
		Smithsonian Museums
		Kennedy Center for Performing
		  Arts
		Bureau of Engraving and
		  Printing
		The White House
		FBI Building
		Corcoran Art Gallery
		Pentagon
		Capitol Building
		Holocaust Museum
		Ford's Theatre
		Transportation
		Beltway
		Parking Lots
		Metro

*Main topics

the oral message (unless he or she uses an audiotape or videotape recorder and can replay passages).

When composing something that will be heard rather than read, you must write as though you are speaking, not reading. To do this, write as you would talk, say the material aloud as you are writing, and practice reading the material aloud. These pointers may help you prepare a manuscript:[9]

◆ Use the active, not passive, voice.

◆ Keep sentences short.

◆ Use short, simple words.

◆ Use repetition to reinforce major ideas.

◆ Express ideas that create emotional or sensory allusions for the listener.

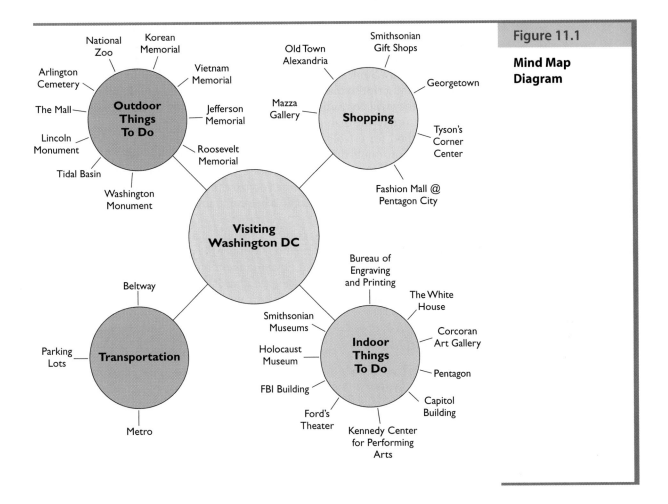

Figure 11.1

Mind Map Diagram

◆ Avoid using technical terms that the audience may not understand.

◆ Be careful in your use of pronouns so that listeners will not be confused about which "he" or "she" you are referring to.

◆ If a member of the audience is expected to apply the material to himself or herself, then the word *you* is appropriate. If the reference is to an experience that you, the speaker, had or something you are going to do, then use *I*.

◆ The word *we* is more involving than the word *you*.

◆ Unless it is absolutely necessary not to do so, round off any numbers you use.

◆ Use language with which you are comfortable. The purpose of language is to convey a message, not impress the audience.

◆ Remember the rule for wording a bumper sticker: Express specific ideas by employing clear ideas in a few well-chosen words.

Reading from the Manuscript   Using a manuscript can be difficult because you must look at the audience at the same time that you are trying to read your material with animation and naturalness. You will have to work out some system for following the script in an unobtrusive way so that you also can look at the audience without losing your place. Be careful not to move or flip manuscript pages unnecessarily; this draws attention away from you and toward the manuscript. Also, try to avoid a flat-sounding reading style. Instead, read according to the meaning by stressing important words and ideas, and vary your tone of voice so that you are speaking naturally. Some speakers run the index finger of their left hand down the side of the manuscript so that they are continuously pointing to the start of the next printed line they will be reading. Then when they look up, they can find their place when they return to the manuscript.

One method for establishing eye contact with an audience while following a manuscript in an unobtrusive way is *eye span.* You can train your eyes to glance down quickly, pick out a meaningful phrase, and deliver it to the audience. As you reach the end of the phrase, but before you have finished saying it, glance down and grasp the next phrase to be spoken. It is helpful to underline key words and to mark off phrases.

It also helps to arrange the script in a manner that keeps you from getting lost. Double- or triple-space the information, number the pages, do not divide sentences by starting them on one page and finishing them on another, do not write or type on the backs of the pages, and use a large font. If you are going to use note cards, write on only one side so you don't get lost, and number each card.

Memorized Mode

In the **memorized speech mode,** a speech is written out word for word and then committed to memory. Public speakers seldom use this mode of communication because it is potentially disastrous. Whereas speakers who use the extemporaneous or manuscript mode can refer to written information, those who use the memorized mode have nothing available for reference as they speak. Forgetting one idea can lead to forgetting everything. Also, the memorizer may be so concerned about getting the exact word in exactly the right place that the meaning of the words becomes secondary. The few advantages of the memorized mode include the ability to select exact wording and examples, the opportunity to look at the audience during the entire speaking process, and the ability to time the presentation precisely. The disadvantages of memorized speaking usually so overshadow its advantages that few people choose to use this mode.

Oral and Physical Presentation

People who capture their listeners' attention are likely to share certain qualities: confidence, ease, authority, conviction, credibility, sincerity, warmth, animation, enthusiasm, vitality, intensity, concern, and empathy. They also make effective use of eye contact, conversational tone, and a variety of pitch, pacing, projection, and phrasing.[10]

Vocal Delivery

A well-prepared speech can be enlivened by effective vocal and physical delivery. Audience members tend to listen with attention when a speaker is dynamic and enthusiastic.

Vocal Variety

Someone who speaks in a *monotone*—a flat, boring sound resulting from constant pitch, volume, and rate—eventually will cause the audience to tune out. Most people speak about 125 to 150 words per minute, the equivalent of one-half to two-thirds of a double-spaced keyboarded page, which is a comfortable pace. Speaking slower than that can lead to listener boredom. On the other hand, speaking so rapidly that the listener can't understand will result in confusion.

Pronunciation

"There are many different and acceptable ways of pronouncing American English, because our language is spoken differently in various parts of the United States."[11] Standard American English—the language generally recognized by linguists as representative of the general population of the United States—tends to be the most acceptable of the regional dialects. Speech becomes substandard if pronunciations cause misunderstandings and set a negative tone for the presentation.[12]

Because you will be evaluated on the basis not only of what you say but also on how you say it, you should be aware of some common pronunciation problems and their causes:[13]

◆ *Sloppy or incorrect articulation.* If you say "air" for *error* and "dint" for *didn't,* you are mispronouncing because of lazy use of the articulators (tongue, jaw, teeth). Be conscious of dropping the *g* sound at the end of words ending in *-ing,* such as *going, doing,* and *watching.* Also be aware of slurring words together. "Alls-ya-godado" is not an understandable substitute for *all you have to do.*

◆ *Ignorance of correct pronunciation.* Listening and reading vocabularies are far greater than speaking vocabularies. In preparing a speech, look up in a dictionary or a pronunciation guide any word whose pronunciation is unfamiliar.

◆ *Vowel distortion.* Some of us have grown up in environments in which words are mispronounced because of vowel substitutions. *Milk* may have been pronounced as "melk"; *secretary* may have been "sekatury"; and *many* may have been "minny." Being aware of the distortions allows some people to begin monitoring their own pronunciations and correcting themselves.

◆ *Pronunciation outside the normal pattern.* If we assume that Standard American English is the norm, certain pronunciations usually are not considered acceptable in the marketplace of business, education, and the professions. *Asked* is not "ax" and *picture* and *pitcher* are not the same word.

Physical Elements

The physical elements of public communication include gestures and eye contact. The way you use visual aids is another physical element.

Gestures   Gestures involve the use of hands, body movements, and facial expressions. Researchers have determined that speakers who use hand movements appear to be free, open, and more honest to an audience than less active speakers.[14]

Knowing the importance of movement, students in speech classes sometimes ask their instructors to teach them how to gesture. Unfortunately, it is impossible to do so because gesturing is the result of the speaker's degree of involvement, excitement, dynamism, and personality. Each person uses his or her own characteristic

---

Rest Your Hands When Speaking

Unsure of what to do with your hands while giving a speech? Rest them lightly on the corners of the lectern.

Don't drop them at your sides or touch your notes except when "absolutely necessary."

This will permit you to begin your speech without appearing unsure and use gestures naturally as you "get into" the substance of the speech.

Source: Adapted from Dr. Jim Vickrey, professor of speech communication, Troy State University, Troy, AL 36082. © Communication Briefings, www.briefings.com, 1101 King St., Alexandria, VA 22314. Used with permission.

gesture pattern while communicating. Some people use a great number of gestures whereas others use just a few.

Gestures should be natural. That is why you should not worry about what to do with your hands; forget them, and they will take care of themselves. Your hands will be active when your body calls for movement. Avoid gripping the lectern so tightly that you cannot let go or have your hands jammed inside your pockets and cannot get them out. If you are orally dynamic, so will be your body. If you are orally boring, so will be your body.

Eye Contact   Establishing **eye contact**—looking into the eyes of your audience as you speak—is another key to effective speaking. Members of an audience will tend to feel involved in the presentation if you look at them. Maintaining eye contact also helps you receive feedback so you can adjust your presentation accordingly. To use eye contact effectively, look directly at listeners, not over their heads. Shift your focus so that you are not maintaining contact with just one section of the audience, and be especially careful not to overlook those in the front or back rows.

People who use hand movements when they talk appear to be freer, more open, and more honest to an audience.

Use of Visual Aids   Keep these basic suggestions in mind when you use visual aids in a presentation:

◆ Do not stand between the visual aid and the audience; you will block their view.

◆ Speak toward the audience, not toward the visual aid.

◆ Know the visual aid well enough so that you do not have to study it while you talk.

◆ Point to the particular place on the aid that you are discussing.

◆ Use the aid at the point in your presentation at which it will have the greatest impact.

◆ If you do not need the aid for part of the speech, put it down, cover it up, or turn it over. If it is electrical, turn it off.

Using PowerPoint

If you are using PowerPoint or a similar presentation program, recognize that like any communication strategy, using a computer presentation program probably will not be comfortable for you at first.

Here are some suggestions on how to make your presentation work well:

1. *Practice thoroughly.* One of the questions often asked is "How

The Magic V

Let's say there are 500 people in your audience. It's very difficult to make actual eye contact with 500 people. However, there's a trick to help called the Magic V (see the figure). When you look at someone, all of the people in a V behind that person think you are looking at them.

Divide the room up into a tic-tac-toe board. Look at one of the "squares" and use the V and the mind touch to lift that section. Once you have them, move to another square.

When the crowd is large, use the Magic V. Draw a "tic-tac-toe" in your mind over the crowd. As you look at each square, you are actually looking at all the people in a "V" behind the person you are really looking at.

After you have made contact with that group emotionally, switch to another square. Make sure you work the squares at random.

Source: From *Secrets of Successful Speakers,* by Lilly Walters, McGraw-Hill, 1993. This material is reproduced with permission of The McGraw-Hill Companies.

much should I practice with my supplementary aids?" A valuable rule here is to spend at least as much time practicing your delivery as you spend on preparing the visuals. If it takes an hour to pull together the visuals, then plan to spend an hour with those slides in actually practicing your delivery. Because of differences in equipment, it is best to practice with the actual equipment that you will use during the presentation. Once you get your materials developed, work with the computer and/or the projector so that you can use the equipment smoothly.

2. *Learn how to use the mouse or remote control so that you can get to the right slide at the precise time in the sequence of your talk when it should appear.* While practicing, remember that listening to a speaker read word for word from a slide that is visible to all is both uncreative and boring.

3. *Be patient.* Accidentally advancing two slides instead of one takes control away from the speaker. If something goes wrong—and with use of electronic equipment, it well may—don't panic. Adjust to the place in the presentation where you need to be and go on. Some people apologize or make a joke about the problem. Theories differ about whether to try and cover

up the error or not. If it's a one-time occurrence, the best advice is just to correct the problem and go on. Doing this does not draw attention to the error. If the cause of your errors is your apparent lack of preparation or familiarity with the equipment, the audience will probably be less forgiving than if the cause is a mechanical glitch or a slip of the finger.

4. *Maintain control of the presentation.* The speaker, not the technology, must maintain control. Just as you should cover your poster-board visual aid until you want the audience to see it, an effective speaker controls the use of the projection equipment throughout the presentation.

5. *Be prepared for the worst.* Have a contingency plan available in case of equipment failure. Ask yourself what you will do if at the start or during the speech, the equipment malfunctions. Many speakers print copies of the necessary graphics for distribution as a hedge against negative possibilities while others present the material as if no visual had been intended. In general, avoid statements such as "If I had the slide to show, it would illustrate . . ." or "This point would be clearer if I had the visuals." Statements such as these add nothing to the message development and diminish your credibility as a speaker.

6. *When you get to the place where you will make your presentation, check out the facilities.*
   a. If you did not bring your own equipment, make sure any equipment that has been ordered is present and working. If you are using computer equipment, be sure the right software has been loaded.
   b. Pull down the projection screen.
   c. Check the lighting to determine the appropriate level for the audience's viewing.
   d. Check the power connections to be sure that they are operational.
   e. If you are using an overhead projector, check to ensure that the machine comes with a spare light bulb, just in case the bulb burns out.
   f. Check the focus and size. Walk around the room to make sure that the visuals are readable from all seats in the room.

Unfortunately, examples abound of speakers who failed to use presentation tools effectively. Consider, for example, Alex's biology instructor. She prepared a PowerPoint presentation for every class meeting in the course, an activity that probably took many hours of work on her part. Sounds like a good idea? Not the way she did it! The slides were a dark background with white lettering, and the projector was so weak that the room had to be totally dark the entire presentation time. The students found it hard to stay awake. Plus, the instructor's controls were located at the back of the room, so she stood behind the class. As a result, they couldn't see her, nor could she read feedback on the students' faces. Instead of using bullets, phrases, and outlines, the instructor wrote a paragraph on each slide, which she read aloud. The students felt that if she had intended to read to them, she should have just put the information on a handout, let them read the material themselves, and skipped the class session. The biology instructor's intentions were good, but her lecturing with the overused and poorly developed PowerPoint program was a boring, nonadaptive disaster. Don't be like Alex's biology teacher when you prepare and use an electronic program for your speeches.

In addition to your preparation for speaking, understanding and dealing with speaker anxiety can help you be a more effective speaker.

Public Speaking Anxiety

Very few speakers escape the "butterflies." "Speech anxiety is a serious problem for a large number of people and has been found to affect career development as well as academic performance."[15] "Millions of professionals make themselves sick at the thought of having to get up in front of people to give a speech."[16] "The fear of public speaking is the No. 1 rated fear in America."[17] (If you would like to ascertain your public speaking anxiety level, complete Activity 2 in the Learn by Doing section at the end of this chapter.)

Public speaking anxiety is known as **speechophobia.** It is a phobia because of its characteristics: (1) there is persistent fear of a specific situation out of proportion to the reality of the danger, (2) there is a compelling desire to avoid and escape the situation, (3) the fear is unreasonable and excessive, and (4) it is not due to any other disorder.[18] As with most phobias, it is curable. A lack of knowledge of how to prepare and present a speech leads to anxiety.[19] As you read this book and practice developing speeches, you will gain the knowledge to overcome this roadblock to public speaking.

Conquering Public Speaking Anxiety[20]

Here are some principles that might help you both understand public speaking anxiety and work toward conquering it:

◆ *Speaking in public is NOT inherently stressful.* "Most of us believe parts of life are inherently stressful. In fact, most of us have been taught to believe that life as a whole is very stressful! To deal with any type of stress effectively, you first must understand that life itself, including public speaking, is *not* inherently stressful. Thousands of human beings have learned to speak in front of groups with little or no stress at all."[21] "If they can conquer the fear of public speaking, so can you!"[22]

◆ *You don't have to be brilliant or perfect to succeed.* "You don't have to be brilliant, witty, or perfect to succeed. That is not what public speaking is all about. I know it may look that way, but it's not. You can be average. You can be below average. You can make mistakes, get tongue-tied, or forget whole segments of your talk. You can even tell no jokes at all and still be successful."[23] "The essence of public speaking is this: give your audience something of value."[24] If you have a clear statement of central idea and have developed it effectively, you will have succeeded.

◆ *When you speak in public, nothing that bad can happen!* "One thing that adds to the fear of public speaking is the dread people have that something awful, terrible, or publicly humiliating will happen to them."[25] The odds of this happening are remote. In all the years your authors have been teaching public speaking, no student or client has ever passed out from nervousness, and no one has died. A few speakers have forgotten what they intended to say, or didn't say exactly what they had intended, but no one has been humiliated because of it unless a speaker imposed the humiliation on himself or herself. No one is perfect. Unless you are totally unprepared, all you can do is the best you can do, and that is not a crime.

◆ *You don't have to control the behavior of your audience.* "To succeed as a public speaker, you don't have to control the behavior of your audience. There are certain things you do need to control—your own thoughts, your preparation, arrangements for audiovisual aids, how the room is laid out—but one thing

America's Number One Fear: Public Speaking

Americans fear more than just things that go bump in the night—a lot more, like public speaking, financial problems, heights, and deep water. In a nationwide survey American adults were asked about the things of which nightmares are made, American fears. Speaking before a group is the top terror, frightening 45 percent of American adults.

Fear	Total	Women	Men
Speaking before a group	45%	54%	34%
Financial problems	40	42	38
Heights	40	50	29
Deep water	33	45	19
Death	31	34	28
Sickness	28	34	21
Insects and bugs	24	34	13
Loneliness	23	27	18
Flying	22	30	15
Driving/riding in a car	10	13	7
Dogs	10	11	8
Darkness	9	14	4
Elevators	8	13	4
Escalators	8	13	4

Source: From Bruskin/Goldring Research Report, February 1993. Reprinted with permission of Roper ASW.

you don't have to control is your audience. They will do whatever they do."[26] This does not mean that you should ignore the audience. Audience analysis and adaptation are important, but thinking you need to change or control other people is a hidden cause of stress in many areas of life. This is just as true for relating to a group as it is for relating to your friends, spouse, children, or other acquaintances.

◆ *Your audience truly wants you to succeed.* "Your audience truly wants you to succeed. Most of them are scared to death of public speaking, just like you. They know the risk of embarrassment, humiliation, and failure you take every time you present yourself in public. They feel for you. They will admire your courage. And they will be on your side, no matter what happens."[27] "This means that most audiences are truly forgiving. While a slip of the tongue or a mistake of any kind might seem [like] a big deal to you, it's not very meaningful or important to your audience. Their judgments and appraisals will usually be much more lenient than yours. It's useful to remind yourself of this point, especially when you think you've performed poorly."[28]

These suggestions for dealing with speaking anxiety may also be helpful:

Do not avoid the experience of giving a presentation. The more you speak, the more comfortable you will get. Although your nervousness may not go away completely, it should let up as you get more practice.

Accept that you will experience some anxiety. All speakers encounter at least a moment of anxiousness as they begin because they are, essentially, facing the unknown. Indeed, a study reveals that public speaking is our greatest fear![29]

Do not take drugs or alcohol because you think they will relax you. Though there has been some recent research that shows that in extreme cases such prescription drugs as Paxil can help in containing physically caused anxieties, self-prescribed drugs and alcohol tend to dull your reflexes and increase your chances of forgetting and making a fool of yourself.

Use relaxation techniques. Before beginning a presentation, some speakers find it helpful to take several deep breaths and expel all the air from their lungs. Others like to shake their hands at the wrists to "get out the nervousness." Some people favor grabbing the seat of their chair with both hands, pushing down, holding the position for about five seconds, and repeating this movement about five times. This tightens and then loosens the muscles, which causes a decrease in physical tension.[30]

Recognize the anxiety. Another approach is to think of the experience of getting up before the audience and to feel the anxiety. Let it stay in your mind, imagining that you are going through the experience. Let yourself be as nervous as you can; psychologically push it as far as you can. Some people report that by imagining the upcoming experience in its worst way, the actual experience becomes much easier.[31]

Prepare. Highly anxious speakers are less likely to spend time preparing and rehearsing their speech.[32] Ironically, this avoidance of getting ready is exactly the opposite of what most research shows aids a person to overcome speechophobia. It is well documented that preparation and rehearsal are keys to effective speech performance.[33]

Practice visualization. We all tend to perform the way we expect to perform, so expectancy restructuring is based on the idea that if you expect to do well, then you will do well. To overcome the fear, prepare a well-structured and well-documented speech so that you have confidence in your material. Then go through the process of visualization—seeing yourself in the actual setting in which you are going to give the speech and making a successful presentation. Picture yourself getting out of your chair, walking to the front of the room, arranging your materials on the podium, looking at the audience, and giving the speech. As you see yourself presenting the material, look at various people. They are nodding their heads in agreement; they are interested and are listening attentively. Finally, imagine yourself ending the speech, the audience applauding, and returning to your chair, feeling good about yourself. The more you visualize this positive experience, the more your expectation level of success should increase. Soon you will be expecting success, not failure.

Individuals who, after following the suggestions just presented, are still traumatized by the prospect of giving a speech may need mental health support. Many hospitals and mental health centers have phobia clinics that should be of assistance.[34]

Rehearsing the Speech

If possible, start to prepare far enough in advance so that you have sufficient material, the speech is well structured and well organized, and you have a chance to practice it. Some speakers try to convince themselves that they will do better if they just get up and talk, with little or no thought about what they will say. This is a fool's contention. It is usually the excuse of a procrastinator or a person who is not properly aware of his or her responsibility to audience and self. Yes, some speakers can get up and "wing it," but the normal mortal usually cannot. Rehearsal is a key to effective speech performance.[35] So prepare and practice!

There is no one best way to rehearse. For some people, sitting at a desk and going over the material by mumbling through the outline or notes is the starting

---

Rehearsing the Speech

Common sense can also dictate the forms your rehearsal might take. The following are some of the possibilities:

1. Read the speech over several times, silently.
2. Read the speech several times aloud.
3. Practice your delivery, including the entire address, standing in front of a mirror. This gives you the opportunity to observe not only your general attitude but also your gestures, posture, and facial expression.
4. Read the speech into a tape recorder and listen to the results. Then listen to them again. At this stage you will make an astounding discovery. Things begin to become apparent to you at a second listening (or, for that matter, a tenth) that had escaped your attention earlier.

5. If you have access to videotaping equipment, make a record of your performance in that way.
6. If you have cooperative family members, deliver the speech to them and ask for their honest comments. Don't make the mistake of welcoming only compliments and tuning out messages that are analytical or critical. If your spouse says something like "I think it's quite good, but you were talking too fast," don't argue the point, whether or not your ego will permit you to agree at that moment. Just absorb the message and let it bounce around in your internal computer.

Source: From *How to Make a Speech,* McGraw-Hill, 1986. Material reproduced with permission of Steve Allen.

point. This will alert you to ideas that do not seem to make sense, words you cannot pronounce, places where you go blank because you need more notes, and areas that need more or fewer examples. Make the changes, and continue to review your notes orally until you are satisfied with the material. Another approach is to ask someone to listen to the speech. The person can then give you feedback on your presentation.

Once you are satisfied with the material, try to construct the setting in which you are going to speak. Duplicate as closely as possible what you are going to do. If you are going to use visual aids, use them. The more familiar you become with exactly what you are going to do, the more likely it is you will be comfortable doing it.

Stop practicing when you are comfortable with your material and have worked out the problems related to using notes and supplementary aids. You are striving to become as comfortable as you can in what is a stressful situation for almost all of us.

Dealing with Difficulties During a Speech

As you proceed through the speech, you can do several things to assist in making this a positive experience for both you and the audience:

◆ *Try to be relaxed as you speak.* Some interesting research has shown that how you stand affects your ability to avoid your body's tightening. The tightening often results in shallow breathing, dry mouth, and shaking hands and legs. Using the *triangle stance* can help you stop your body from stiffening. In the triangle stance (Figure 11.2), you place one foot—foot A in Figure 11.2—at a slight angle and foot B at about a forty-five-degree angle, as if it were coming out of the arch of foot A. Keep your feet about six inches apart. Shuffle your feet slightly until you feel comfortable and balanced. Place your weight on foot A. You will feel leg and foot B relax. You may also find that it helps if you slightly extend the hip on the foot-A side of your body. As you proceed through a speech, you can alter your stance by changing the positions of feet A and B, but always remember to put your body weight on the foot that is farther back.

Figure 11.2

Foot Placement to Aid in the Relief of Speaker Anxiety

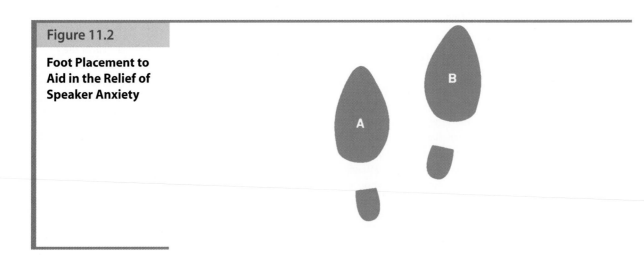

◆ *Look at the people in the audience who are alert during the presentation.* You can find these people by watching for those who nod in agreement or smile at you as you speak. Typically presenters feel good when they get positive reactions.

◆ *Remember that we all make mistakes.* Even professional speakers and media announcers fumble words. If you make a minor error, just ignore it and keep going. If it is a major error, fix it. Simply repeat the correct word or words and continue your speech, recognizing that you can't erase the mishap.

◆ *Take time to get yourself organized at the lectern.* Arrange your notes on the lectern so that page 1 is on the left and the rest are on the right. Halfway through page 2, slide (don't flip) the page over to cover page 1. Continue to do this so that you are not pausing at the end of each page to move it over. Sliding allows you to move pages without calling attention to the act; flipping pages can be distracting as it draws attention to the pages for no reason.

In Conclusion

The act of public communication involves a transaction between a speaker and an audience. As in any other act of communication, the participants, the setting, and the purpose of the communication affect a public speech. These three parameters may affect the topic selected, the language used, the types of examples and illustrations chosen, and the aids needed to support and clarify ideas. To investigate the parameters, an audience analysis is done through prior speech analysis, process of speech analysis, and postspeech analysis.

The public speaker can use one of four basic modes of presentation: impromptu or ad lib, extemporaneous, manuscript, and memorized. In presenting the speech, the vocal elements and the physical elements are important. Some people have a fear associated with giving a speech. Techniques are available for lessening the fear.

Learn by Doing

1. One of the keys to giving an effective oral presentation is to choose a subject you are interested in and about which you have some knowledge. To learn your interest and knowledge base, fill out this speaker inventory:
a. Hobbies and special interests _____
b. Places I have traveled _____
c. Things I know how to do (sports I can play, skills I have) _____
d. Jobs I have had _____
e. Experiences (accidents, special events) _____
f. Funny things that have happened to me _____
g. Books I have read and liked _____
h. Movies and plays I have seen and liked _____
i. Interesting people I have known _____

j. People I admire _____
k. Religious and nationality customs of my family _____
l. Talents I have (musical instruments played, athletic abilities) _____

2. This instrument is composed of six statements concerning feelings about speaking in public.[36] Indicate the degree to which each statement applies to you by marking whether you (1) strongly agree, (2) agree, (3) are undecided, (4) disagree, or (5) strongly disagree. Work quickly. Record your first impression.

_____ a. I have no fear of giving a speech.
_____ b. Certain parts of my body feel very tense and rigid while I am giving a speech.
_____ c. I feel relaxed while giving a speech.
_____ d. My thoughts become confused and jumbled when I am giving a speech.
_____ e. I face the prospect of giving a speech with confidence.
_____ f. While giving a speech, I get so nervous I forget facts that I really know.

Scoring: Add 18 to your scores from items a, c, and e, and then subtract your score from items b, d, and f. This is your final score.

Interpretation: Scores can range from a low of 6 to a high of 30. If your score is 18 or above, you are like the overwhelming majority of Euro-Americans in that you display public speaking apprehension.

3. What questions would you ask a person who has invited you to give a speech on the topic of your choice to a club or organization? Why did you pick these questions?

4. Use a topic related to your academic major to develop a statement of central idea for an informative speech to be presented to a group of classmates. Then prepare another informative statement of central idea for the same topic but for a nonclassroom audience. Based on the different statements of central idea, how will the speeches vary?

5. Prepare a statement of central idea informing a group of high school students about your college for a speech of fifteen minutes. Now write a statement of central idea for the same speech in which you will have only five minutes to speak. Why did your statement of central idea change according to the time frame?

6. The class sits in a circle. The instructor throws a ball to someone in the circle and passes an envelope to that person. The person selects a statement from the envelope, takes a minute to prepare, and gives a one- to two-minute presentation on the topic. Before speaking, the first person tosses the ball to someone else, who will be the second speaker. While the first person is speaking, the second person selects a topic and prepares a speech. Each speaker tosses the ball to another speaker until all members of the class have spoken.

7. On a three-by-five card, list three topics you think you could speak about for a minimum of two minutes. Your instructor selects one of these for you to give an impromptu speech about. You have two minutes to get ready. You may use any notes you can prepare within that time.

8. Some of the most commonly mispronounced words in Standard American speech are listed here. Look up each word in a dictionary or pronunciation guide. During a class session, you will be asked to pronounce these words and

use them in sentences: *across, acts, actually, all, ambulance, any, asked, because, catch, doing, familiar, fifth, genuine, get, going, horror, hundred, introduce, just, library, next, nuclear, particular, picture, prescription, probably, pumpkin, recognized, sandwich, secretary, Washington, with.*

Key Terms

public communication
speech participants
speaking setting
purpose of the speech
prior to the speech analysis
process of the speech analysis
postspeech analysis
plagiarism
fabrication
audience analysis
demographics
psychographics
rhetorographics
statement of central idea
goal of the speech

topic of the speech
method of speech development
modes of speech presentation
impromptu speaking
ad lib speaking
extemporaneous speaking mode
speech planning outline
speech presentation outline
topic outline
sentence outline
mind mapping
manuscript speech mode
memorized speech mode
eye contact
speechophobia

12

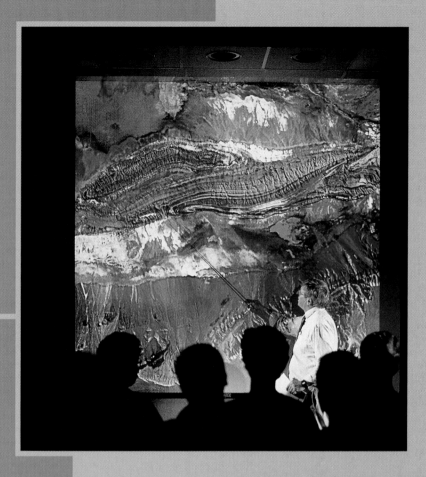

Public Speaking: Developing the Speech

After reading this chapter, you should be able to

- Identify the sources used to develop public speaking messages

- List basic reference sources used for the development of public speeches

- Illustrate the value of using and the method for finding books, magazines, newspapers, journals, indexes, government publications, special-interest group publications, and nonprint media

- Record research information

- Explain the role of support material in the development of a speech

- Identify and illustrate means of presenting and focusing supporting material

L istening to a speech can be an exciting, interesting, or uplifting experience. It also can be a frustrating, boring, or confusing one. The differences between positive and negative listening experiences are often based on whether the speaker has defined terms, offered clarifying examples, explained abstract concepts, presented proving statistics, restated ideas, and illustrated thoughts with supplementary aids.

Sources of Information

Most of the information we use to develop messages is based on personal experiences, personal observations, or learning acquired through school, the media, and reading. As we are exposed to information, we retain a certain amount of it, and this knowledge forms the core of our communication. We select words and examples from this storehouse that we use to organize messages. Sometimes, however, we need information that is not in this core to develop a message. In such cases, you need outside sources to aid you.

Since the advent of the World Wide Web, some speech researchers have relied entirely on doing a quick web search for materials and using only what is revealed in that search. Be aware that search engines find only so much. Also be aware of the limited number of sources that a web search can reveal.

As you search for sources of information to support your points, you should make every effort to locate **primary sources of information:** sources that represent the original reports of the observations or research. When the original work is not available to you, you may find it necessary to go to **secondary sources of information:** sources that report, but did not originally generate, the observations or research.

Research from major sources has been made easier with access to computerized databases. "The past decade has seen a remarkable expansion in digital networks in the U.S. research and educational community, from a state where networking was the purview of the privileged few to one where it is considered an essential tool by millions of researchers and educators."[1] Because of the wide use of computers, research data may be accessed from places outside libraries. Many libraries have made their holdings list available through the Internet or similar access systems. The National Science Foundation is heading an effort to develop ways to digitize all the world's library holdings. This system, known as the **information highway,** is an assemblage of networks hooking primary and secondary schools, public and private institutions, commercial enterprises, individuals in their homes, and foreign institutions together for collaboration. They include the traditional reference sources, plus national telephone directories, sound and voice recordings, images, video clips, scientific data, and private information services such as stock market reports and private newsletters.

In addition to locating information, a speaker must assess its validity. All sources of information reflect certain perceptions and biases. Consequently, it is wise to attempt to determine the bias of a source and interpret its information accordingly.[2] Thus, when doing research for a presentation, it is a good idea to find several agreeing authoritative sources so that your supporting details will be credible to your listeners.

THE 12th GRADE CLASS CAN'T MAKE IT TO YOUR SPEECH ON THE DANGERS OF DRUNK DRIVING. YOU'LL HAVE TO GIVE THE SPEECH TO THE KINDERGARTENERS.

Make sure the topic, examples, and language are appropriate for the age level of the group you are addressing.

Sources of information that speakers seek out include books, magazines, newspapers, special journals, indexes, government publications, and the publications of special-interest groups. Additional sources include nonprint materials such as tape recordings, records, films, videotapes, charts, and models, as well as interviews with knowledgeable people in a particular field and computer searches.

Books

Personal, academic, and public libraries can be the sources of much information; nevertheless, you must know how to find the materials you need. In academic and public libraries, books are shelved according to a numerical system and can be located by looking in the electronic card catalog under the title, the author's name, or the general subject.

Unfortunately, not all subjects are easy to locate. For example, an average library's electronic card catalog would reveal no information if you looked under the word *Arapesh.* Thus, to learn which books contain material about this subject, you would need some additional information. By looking in an encyclopedia, you would discover that the Arapesh are a primitive, mountain-dwelling people of New Guinea, whose society was investigated by anthropologist Margaret Mead and discussed in her book *Sex and Temperament in Three Primitive Societies.* Based on this information, you could look in the electronic card catalog under such subjects as *anthropology, Margaret Mead, New Guinea,* and *Sex and Temperament in Three Primitive Societies.*

Books are of great value in supplying information, but they can quickly become out-of-date. It generally takes at least a year for an average book to move from the author's draft through the printing process and onto the shelves of a library. Some subjects change little, and in these areas books are a good research source. But for quickly changing subjects, more up-to-date sources are needed for a thorough investigation.

Magazines

Most magazines are designed to provide recent information quickly. Many magazines are published weekly, so their information is current.

At one point the only way to access a magazine was to locate a copy of the publication. Now, however, magazines have piled up on the information highway.[3] The publications have bought into the electronic distribution and can be electronically accessed quite readily.

Researchers must be aware, however, that because these sources gather their data so quickly, some inaccuracies may occur. In addition, the editorial staffs of magazines—like the authors of books—sometimes have political and ideological biases that may temper what they write or influence what subjects they include.

To find information in magazines, you can search electronically or start with the *Readers' Guide to Periodical Literature,* a publication that indexes magazine articles by subject, title, and author, or the *International Index*. Key word or topic searches of the World Wide Web and other accessing devices will often reveal materials.

Newspapers

Newspapers, like magazines, contain current information that is published daily, weekly, or monthly. As is the case with magazines, because of the speed with which newspapers are written and printed, you must be aware of the possibility of error. Many libraries do not keep past issues of newspapers, but some store the information on both microfilm and microfiche, or make them available through electronic sources. Most newspapers can be directly accessed on the Web.

Journals

Professional organizations often publish journals reporting research and theories in their specific fields. The National Communication Association, for example, publishes *Communication Education, Quarterly Journal of Speech, Communication Monographs, Journal of Applied Communication Research, The Communication Teacher,* and *Critical Studies in Mass Communication.* Thus, students who are interested in finding out about some area of speech communication can refer to these journals. The organization also has a CD-ROM for doing word, topic, and article searches.

Indexes

Encyclopedias, atlases, and bibliographical guides are indexes that provide descriptive information in certain categories. An index gives a minimal amount of information. Thus, if you want in-depth material, indexes may not be the best sources.

When using encyclopedias, recognize that many of them are expensive to produce and therefore are not totally updated each year. This has been somewhat rectified by CD-ROMs, which update the indexes on a regular basis.

Government Publications

The U.S. government publishes materials, available at minimal cost, on a variety of subjects. These can be found at bookstores in federal buildings in many major cities of the country and also can be accessed through the U.S. Government Printing Office's homepage. In addition, many major universities are designated as government depositories; all government documents are housed in those campus library systems.

Special-Interest Group Publications

Special-interest groups such as the American Cancer Society and the American Society for Training and Development publish information regarding their research and programs. A telephone call or letter to such an organization often brings a prompt response, or materials can be accessed through an organization's homepage on the Web. To find the name of an organization, its e-mail address, and/or its website, look in *Gale's Encyclopedia of Associations.*

Nonprint Media

Much information is available from nonprint media. Libraries and audiovisual departments of colleges and universities have collections of tape recordings, records, films, filmstrips, and videotapes from commercially and locally prepared sources covering a variety of topics. These sources usually are cataloged in a manner similar to that used for books and periodicals. Some nonprint materials are available for general circulation, but others must be used on the premises. Local and national radio and television stations and networks often sell audio or visual copies of their programs. For example, ABC News has a catalog of programming videos available for sale.[4]

Interviews

Interviews can be used to find information that is not available from written or audiovisual sources. After all, what better way is there to find out, for example, how the budget of your college is developed than by talking to the treasurer or the budget director? Such interviews can be conducted in a variety of ways. If someone is not available for a face-to-face or telephone session, you can submit a series of questions to be answered through either writing or tape-recording. In addition, contacting a person on the Internet often brings an immediate response.

Computer Searches

Traditionally, a researcher would obtain information by going to a library and looking in the card catalog or the *Readers' Guide to Periodical Literature* or by asking the reference librarian what sources were available. Now you may be able to access many of the same library materials online from your home computer. When going to a library, you can ask for help in adapting to its system, and then you will be on your way to finding sources efficiently and effectively. Online research requires knowledge of what search engine to use as well as how to access information.

Computer-Based Retrieval Systems

A **computer-based retrieval system** allows the researcher to compile a bibliography or a set of facts relevant to a specific topic. Searches may be used for a variety of purposes, including gathering research or references, compiling a reading list, acquiring statistical information, or simply keeping abreast of developments in a field. Naturally, a major advantage to this method is the time saved, as a computer retrieves in minutes information that otherwise takes much longer to compile. The search is also quite comprehensive and can locate references that the most careful conventional searches may not. Another feature is the timeliness of the material since these databases are updated frequently.[5]

Conducting a Computer Search

Once you have the database you plan to search, you need a method to find what you need. There are several steps in conducting an effective computer search. The principles apply no matter what search engine or index you use.

1. *Select a database* that is relevant to the kind of information you seek.
2. *Narrow the hits.* Depending on the database and what you seek, you may want to select options to narrow the hits to a manageable number (e.g., 20–100).
3. *Examine the hits* you have for clues to what is working and what isn't working. If you have trouble finding the right sources, check to be sure you're using the right words by consulting the database's thesaurus. On the other hand, what do you do if your search is too successful? What do you do when you get 10,000 hits and need to narrow your search?

   a. Select a database with focused content.
   b. Use a search engine that is more focused.
   c. Select only English-language articles (or articles written in whatever languages you read).
   d. Narrow to recent dates.
   e. Select only abstracts or full-text articles.
   f. Search by author, title, or subject.
   g. Conduct a **Boolean search,** a search that combines multiple words connected by *and* or *or.*

4. *Mark the sources.* When you find sources you like, check the boxes or mark them.
5. *Save your sources* by printing, e-mailing them to yourself, or saving to a disk. If they are abstracts, then go to the library and look up the full articles. If they are full text, you have all the information you need.
6. *Cite your sources.* Be sure to cite the source of the information in your speech and have the full bibliographic reference available for anyone who wants that information.

From the screen you can cut and paste information for your presentation. The way you do so is by opening your word processor (e.g., Microsoft Word). Highlight the material you want, use the "Edit" function to "cut," and then move the material to your e-mail program (or wherever you are creating the speech) and "paste" it there.

Remember, cite the source of your ideas and information unless the ideas are ones that you already know (common knowledge) or that are truly your own. You want your speech to flow, so integrate the citation into your message. You might say something like:

"According to the November 2002 issue of *Time* magazine . . ." or "In looking at the womenandlanguage.org website, I discovered . . ."

Speakers are seldom criticized for citing too many sources. But do so in a way that makes sense in your speech, and be sure to have additional information available for your listeners who might request it during the question-and-answer session. You need to record all citation information so that if listeners want to look up your sources, they can find them.

Use of the Internet

Researchers should realize that the Internet is not always a perfect search source. As one Internet expert states, "The Internet makes readily available so much information that students think research is far easier than it really is. Students are producing superficial research papers [and speeches], full of data—some of it suspect—and with little thought."[6]

An investigation concerning the use of the Internet as a means of finding material reveals these potential problems for speech researchers:

It is difficult for the uninitiated to find their way around the Internet. Some instruction and practice can yield the expertise needed to unlock the code to finding all of the potential sources of information on the Internet. Unfortunately, most students simply tinker around until they think they have found the information. One of the major components that is missing is a reference librarian—someone to aid you in your search!

"The Internet is commonly thought of as a library, although a poorly cataloged one, given limitations of the search engines available."[7] "Search engines are imprecise."[8] The quality of databases available and the format design of the software can greatly limit the quality of the search for information.

"Because information is so accessible, students stop far too quickly."[9] Researchers often assume that everything about a particular topic will be revealed through an Internet exploration. Consequently, they often stop short in looking for other information. In addition, using only the Internet eliminates one of the best research sources—the interview. The best advice that can be followed is to use the Internet as a part of, not as the whole, process of researching a topic.

"Many sites neglect to stay up-to-date."[10] Don't assume that because something appears on the Internet, it is up-to-date and accurate. For example, one kind of computer software that was supplying information regarding a specialized program went out of business and left its homepage active. Individuals who took information from that site were using concepts that were totally out of date. In addition, information is sometimes entered and then forgotten about.

Some information is fabricated by the source. People with biases and prejudices who manipulate information for their own means enter material on the Web. Anyone can enter anything she or he wants. Just because information has been posted on the Internet doesn't mean that it is true, well researched, or up-to-date. Some websites are refereed journals, but for most there are no editors, evaluators, or research scholars who screen much of what appears.

Selecting Sources

An expert on research offered some excellent advice on using the Internet for research when he explained:

Academic research is a three-step process: finding the relevant information, assessing the quality of that information and then using that information either to try to conclude something, to uncover something, to provide something or to argue something. As its best the Internet, like a library, provides only data. The Internet mainly is only useful for that first part, and also a little bit for the second. It is not useful at all in the third.[11]

With these warnings in mind, follow these suggestions for locating the best possible Internet sources:

Find valid sources. Look for sources noted for generally doing accurate research such as universities, scholarly organizations, and the government. If you are looking for statistics for a speech about rape, for example, you may be able to find information from your local police department, the FBI, or a local rape crisis center. In addition, associations like the American Psychological Association and the American Counseling Association have homepages that can lead you to information that has been published after being reviewed by experts in the field. "Search engines, such as Google and Ask Jeeves, are not bad places to start, but the results aren't always reliable or relevant, because popularity or paid placement can determine which sites turn up first."[12] Some sites to consider are Library spot (www.libraryspot.com), Bigchalk (www.bigchalk.com), and the Library of Congress (www.loc.gov).[13]

Use the databases available through college libraries. Your university or college is probably part of a library consortium. Each consortium member pays a fee for a site license so that you and other students can have full access to the sources available in all of the libraries that are part of the consortium. These databases give citation information, abstracts, and often full-text articles, so you can find the articles you need. Sometimes they tell you whether or not the sources are available at your local library. Because these databases are academically based, you are likely to get more accurate material than you would from a generic database.

The main values of using electronic sources for speech research are:

1. The accuracy of information
2. The speed of access to information
3. Having unique sources

Remember, some Internet sources are completely inaccurate. You'll want to check carefully for accuracy. There's plenty of incorrect information in books, but on the Internet, anyone can have a site, and its content can be totally fallacious.

Set a stopping point. How much time will you spend on your research? Theoretically, you could research your topic for months or years. Realistically, you only have so much time to prepare a speech. Set a logical stopping point. This is usually when you think you have enough information to flesh out the speech and have the aids you need to assist in the speech's development. If necessary, as you prepare the speech itself, you can go back and find some additional support to plug some holes in your message. Of course, this theory is based on the supposition that you have left yourself enough time to research, prepare, practice, and adjust the speech. If you are a procrastinator, you may be rushed to find material and not find enough or the right kind.

Analyzing Sources

It is important, as you identify and collect information, to do a careful analysis of the validity of the information that you plan to use in your speech. Unfortunately, some people are so happy just to find information that they use it without any thought that they have an ethical responsibility to present accurate, truthful support to the claims that they make.

Realize that all sources of information have perceptions and biases that can distort the information presented.[14] Consequently, you should consider what stake the

Research has been facilitated by easy access to computerized databases.

source has in the information so that you can locate the most objective material possible. This has become a major issue in assessing Internet sources because any individual or group with little or no credibility can post almost anything on the Web.

While every institution has its own perspective, information from government agencies and educational institutions is generally perceived to be credible since they tend to have less of a vested interest in persuading people to a particular point of view. For instance, the Central Intelligence Agency's *World Factbook* offers an exhaustive collection on the population, geography, government, and economy of other countries: www.odci.gov/cia/publications/factbook. Subscription-based sites that provide reliable, advertising-free information also can be dependable alternatives. Publications with long-standing reputations such as the *New York Times* and the *Economist* are generally considered credible sources. Like panning for gold, the quality of information that you use is central to the quality of your communication: "Use credible information providers. Identify sources. Authenticate what they say. Then ask yourself: Is this gold or garbage?"[15]

Recording Your Research

When you do research, keep a record of where your information came from so you can refer to the source to find additional information, answer questions about a source, or give oral footnotes during a speech. When you write a term paper, you must footnote **quotations**—material written or spoken by a person in the exact

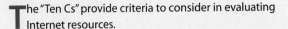

The Ten Cs for Evaluating Internet Sources

The "Ten Cs" provide criteria to consider in evaluating Internet resources.

1. **Content.** What is the intent of the content? Are the titles and author identified? What is the date of the document or article? Do you have the latest version?
2. **Credibility.** Is the author identifiable and reliable? Is the content credible?
3. **Critical Thinking.** Can you identify the author, publisher, edition, and so on, as you would with "traditionally" published resources?
4. **Copyright.** If the material falls under the copyright laws, is the credit given?
5. **Citation.** Is credit given to the author? Does the format of the citation follow a standard style?
6. **Continuity.** Will the Internet site be maintained and updated? Can you rely on this source over time to provide up-to-date information?
7. **Censorship.** Does your search engine or index look for all words, or are some words excluded?
8. **Connectivity.** Does access to the resource require a graphical user interface? Are you familiar with the tools and the applications required to access the material?
9. **Comparability.** Does the Internet resource have an identified comparable print or CD-ROM data set or source? Does the Internet site contain comparable and complete information (e.g., full text versus partial information)?
10. **Context.** How does the Internet information fit in the overall information context of your subject?

Source: Adapted from "The Ten C's for Evaluating Internet Sources," McIntyre Library, University of Wisconsin—Eau Claire; and "Evaluating Internet Research Sources" at <http://www.VirtualSalt.com/evalu8it.htm>.

words in which it was originally presented—and **paraphrases**—someone else's ideas put into your own words. You do the same in public speaking, except orally. For example, in a speech concerning male-female communication, this **oral footnote** would be appropriate:

> Deborah Tannen, in her book *I Only Say This Because I Love You: How the Way We Talk Can Make or Break Family Relationships Throughout Our Lives,* observed, "It's true that women, on average, tend to say 'I'm sorry' more frequently than men do. And because they do, others often conclude that they lack self-confidence or are putting themselves down."[16]

In some instances, you also may feel that it is necessary to establish a quoted author as an authority. You do this because you think the audience doesn't know the author's credentials or the person or because you want to reinforce the author's credibility. In this case, for your oral footnote, you might say:

> Deborah Tannen, the author of the best-selling book *You Just Don't Understand,* which introduced the concept of gender communication to the general public, has received grants from the National Endowment for the Humanities and the National Science Foundation to probe male-female communication. She is a professor of linguistics at Georgetown University. In her newest book, *I Only Say This Because I Love You,* she states, "It's true that women, on average, tend to say 'I'm sorry' more frequently than men do. And because they do, others often conclude that they lack self-confidence or are putting themselves down."

In recording your research, you may select from a variety of formats. The most commonly used patterns are those of the Modern Language Association (MLA) and the American Psychological Association (APA). (For the APA style, see Appendix 2 in this book.)[17]

When actually inscribing your bibliographical information and notes that result from your research, you need to be careful to keep track of where you got the material. Notes can be taken on three-by-five-inch or four-by-six-inch cards or on sheets of paper. They can also be keyboarded into a computer. Whichever method you use, be sure to note the source of the material, including the writer, where the material was obtained (newspaper, book, the Internet), the date of the publication, and the page number.

One method of recording the research is to use a running bibliography. The list is numbered so that it can be used while you are taking notes.

For those who are unfamiliar with formats for coding bibliographical entries, patterns for (1) a book, (2) a newspaper story, (3) a magazine or journal article, and (4) an online article are presented.

Bibliography

1. Deborah Tannen, *I Only Say This Because I Love You: How the Way We Talk Can Make or Break Family Relationships Throughout Our Lives* (New York: Random House, 2001).
2. Erica Goode, "Study Offers New Look at How Females Respond to Stress," *Cleveland Plain Dealer* (May 19, 2000), p. 13-A.
3. R. Traci Kann and Fred J. Hanna, "Disruptive Behavior Disorders in Children and Adolescents: How Do Girls Differ from Boys?" *Journal of Counseling and Development* (Summer 2000), pp. 267–274.
4. Audrey Nelson, "Men, Women & Work." Retrieved October 30, 2002, from <http://www.corvision.com/gencomm.htm#INVISRULESGENCOMM>.

As you do your research and record information, you can refer to the source by number, thus eliminating the necessity of continually keyboarding or writing out the same bibliographical material. You can refer to Tannen's apology quotation, for example, as 1-98 (source 1 in the bibliography, page 98). Because the material is directly quoted, put quotation marks around it. If it is paraphrased, the use of quotation marks is not necessary, but make sure you remember that the material is not original to your speech but from another source.

If cards are used, a footnote reference would look like this:

Topic: Gender Communication
Reference: 1-98

Information: "It's true that women, on average, tend to say 'I'm sorry' more frequently than men do. And because they do, others often conclude that they lack self-confidence or are putting themselves down."

If the notation is keyboarded, it might appear like this:

1-98   "It's true that women, on average, tend to say 'I'm sorry' more frequently than men do. And because they do, others often conclude that they lack self-confidence or are putting themselves down."

If a computer is used, keyboard a running bibliography and enter the reference material by keyboarding or scanning it. Double-space between entries.

After assembling all of your research, if you used a computer, print out the material. Then cut the reference material into strips, separate them by topic, and write or outline directly from these slips of paper. Some people arrange the slips on sheets of blank paper and attach the slips to the pages with transparent tape, and use these as their outline for the speech. An alternative is to connect the strips and then duplicate them on a copying machine, thus creating a final outline. The advantages of using or copying the actual slips of paper center not only on saving time but also on allowing you to have all your footnote sources available if you are asked about them during the question-and-answer session.

If you used notecards, arrange them in a sequential order and follow the procedure described in the previous paragraph to complete the speech.

Supporting Material

Supporting speech material should clarify a point you are making in the speech or offer proof of the validity of the argument presented. The forms of support you select depend on your purposes, but the most common are illustrations, specific instances, exposition, statistics, analogies, and testimony.

Illustrations

Examples that explain a subject through the use of stories are **illustrations.** They are intended to clarify a point, not to offer proof. They may be hypothetical or factual.

If the illustrations are hypothetical, the speaker should make this clear by saying, for example, "Suppose you were . . ." or "Let us all imagine that . . ." Hypothetical illustrations can be used, for instance, by a medical technician who is taking a listener on a theoretical trip through the circulatory system.

In contrast, a factual illustration is a real or actual story. It can be introduced by statements such as "When I came to school this morning . . ." A speaker developed a speech on safety codes with this illustration:

> Where Memorial School stands today, Jefferson School once stood. One day a devastating fire struck Jefferson School. Eighty students and four teachers lost their lives in that tragic fire, and hundreds of others were seriously injured. The new Memorial School can never eradicate the memories of those who died during the tragic fire.

Stories are the most interesting form of supporting material. "The delivery of the message is enhanced with stories because stories help us reach our deepest level of understanding."[18]

Think back to some of the more memorable speakers you have heard. Undoubtedly, they used a number of relevant, interesting stories to support their points.

Specific Instances

Condensed examples that are used to clarify or prove a point are **specific instances.** Because they are not developed in depth, you can say a great deal quickly by using them and provide listeners with evidence they can relate to your point.

If you want to develop the idea that speech communication is an interesting major for college students, for example, you can support your point with specific instances of careers that employ communication majors: speech writing, teaching, research and training in business and industrial communication, political campaigning, health communication, and public relations.

Exposition

An **exposition** gives the necessary background information to listeners so that they can understand the material being presented. Sometimes, for example, a speaker needs to define specific terms, give historical information, explain the relationship between herself or himself and the topic, or explain the process that will be used during the presentation. In using exposition, the speaker must also anticipate or alter a message to provide listeners with the background information they need for understanding the transaction.

The speaker, realizing an obligation to aid the audience in understanding the message, may feel a need to define terms and ideas that will be used in the presentation. For instance, a speaker who wants to explain the advertising campaign to be used in marketing a product may find it necessary to clarify such terms and phrases as *bandwagoning* and *plus-and-minus factor of surveying.*

An audience may need historical information as well. For listeners to understand the outcome of the Whitewater investigation, for instance, they may need to know the specific events that led to the decision, during the Clinton presidency, to launch the investigation.

Listeners may need a bridge between the speaker and the topic to understand why the speaker is discussing the subject or to establish the speaker's expertise. For example, a student nurse who is explaining the nursing program he recently completed should share his educational background with the audience.

In addition, indicating the process to be followed during a presentation or the results the speaker wants to achieve may be helpful to listeners. An outline of the major points to be made can be distributed or displayed, or the speaker can explain what she or he will do and will want the audience to do as the speech proceeds.

Statistics

Any collection of numerical information arranged as representations, trends, or theories makes up **statistics.** Communicators use statistics to provide a measurement (e.g., The upper limit of hearing by the human ear is 20,000 Hz per second), to compare (The normal intelligible outdoor range of the male human voice in still air is 200 yards; female screams register higher readings on decibel meters than male bellows),[19] and to demonstrate amounts (The census indicates that the population of Ecuador is 8,053,280 people).[20]

Nevertheless, before accepting statistics as proof, the wise speaker asks:

- ◆ Who says so?
- ◆ How does he or she know?
- ◆ What is missing?
- ◆ Did somebody change the subject?
- ◆ Does it make sense?[21]

Any collection of numerical information arranged as representations, trends, or theories makes up statistics.

When statistics have been accurately collected, are properly interpreted, and are not out-of-date, their use is a valid aid in reaching conclusions. Unfortunately, not all statistical studies are accurately conducted, properly interpreted, or current.

Statistical Surveying   Statisticians have developed methods for collecting data—statistical surveying—that can be used with some degree of assurance that the resulting information will be correct.[22] Ideally, to discover everyone's opinion on a particular issue, everyone should be asked, but of course this is usually impossible for large groups of people. Thus, to make educated guesses, statisticians have devised methods of random sampling that allow less than the entire population to be surveyed. These methods recognize the probability of error, and a speaker should indicate this fact when giving the statistical results of a survey.

Proper Interpretation of Data   If a particular group or person is trying to get a specific result, that tester may keep testing until she or he gets the desired conclusion or ignore results that do not agree with the goal. For this reason, be wary of statistics that are taken out of context, are incomplete, or do not specify the method used to collect the data.

Currency of Data   Studies and surveys conducted in the past may have been perfectly accurate at the time they were done. This does not mean that they are accurate now. It is important that you use or receive the latest data and not allow yourself to be influenced by information that is out-of-date.

Reporting the Data   Remember that a person can retain only a limited amount of information. Thus, extensive lists, complicated numerical combinations, and long numbers may well be lost if you do not help listeners by simplification or visualization. For example, a long list—such as the figures representing the cost of each material used to produce a piece of machinery—can be written on a chalkboard or poster or projected on a screen. In this way, listeners view as well as hear, and they can refer to the numbers as needed.

Simplify numbers. A statistic such as $1,243,724,863 is difficult to comprehend, but the phrase "approximately $1.25 billion" is within the grasp of an audience. If a statistic is important enough to include in a speech, you must be sure that the listener can grasp the information.

Analogies

A speaker may use an **analogy** to clarify a concept for listeners; that is, the speaker compares an unfamiliar concept to a familiar one. For example, in the section of this text dealing with the processing capacity of the human cortex, an analogy was drawn between a cybernetic process and a computer process. This comparison was not intended to indicate that the cortex and the computer are one and the same, but to demonstrate that if a reader understands the functioning of a computer, he or she may also understand the basic operation of the cortex.

Remember that an analogy is effective only if the listeners are familiar with the object, idea, or theory being used as its basis. Contrasting a patient on an operating table to stars in the sky may confuse listeners who are unfamiliar with either astronomy or surgical techniques.

A speaker also should be careful not to overextend the comparison or contrast. A college president once developed an inaugural speech by comparing the school to a football team. The analogy compared faculty members to team players, students to spectators, the president to the coach, and on and on and on! After a while, the listeners became confused and stopped paying attention; the intended effect was lost.

Testimony

Testimony may be a direct quotation (actual statement) or a paraphrase (reworded idea) from an authority. Speakers provide testimony to clarify ideas, back up contentions, and reinforce concepts. Thus, a speaker may turn to this type of supporting material when it is believed that an authority is more knowledgeable than the speaker about the topic being discussed or that the opinion of an authority will make listeners more receptive to a particular idea.

An **expert** is a person who, through knowledge or skill in a specific field, gains respect for his or her opinions or expertise. We trust experts' opinions because their knowledge has been acquired through personal experience, education, training, research, and/or observation. We also respect people who have academic degrees, who are licensed or accredited, or who are recognized by peers as leaders in their fields. Many useful quotations are available to speakers on "The Quotes Home Page" at <http://www.lexmark.com/data/quote.html>.

Selected quotations should be true to the intention of the source. Before you accept testimony as support, assess its validity by asking some basic questions:

◆ *Is the material quoted accurately?*

◆ *Is the source biased because of position, employment, or affiliation?* A quotation by the chairperson of the board of directors of a major tobacco company that cigarette smoking may not lead to cancer should be suspect because of the speaker's biased position.

◆ *Is the information relevant to the issue being discussed?*

◆ *Is the source competent in the field being discussed?* For example, what qualifies an actor to recommend changes in U.S. foreign policy?

◆ *Is the information current, if currency is important?*

Vehicles for Presenting Supporting Material

Three means of presenting and focusing supporting material are internal summaries, forecasting, and use of supplementary aids.

Internal Summaries

As a listener, have you ever been on the receiving end of a message and found yourself totally confused because of the amount of material involved? To avoid listener confusion, summarize each segment of a presentation by providing an **internal summary,** a short restatement of what just has been said in the section that you are about to leave, before proceeding to the next segment. For example, after spending several minutes proposing that the United States should adopt a more aggressive foreign policy, the speaker could bridge out of that unit with the internal summary "Our nation, then, needs to pursue a more vigorous, definitive approach to its international relations."

Forecasting

A **forecast** is a statement that alerts the audience to ideas that are coming. An example of a forecast is "Let's now examine the three examples of how bulimics purge food." This forecast alerts the audience to get ready to listen for the three points.

Signposting

An additional vehicle for presenting supporting material is signposting. In **signposting,** a speaker forecasts where the listeners have been, where they are presently, and where they are going. This aids the listener by recapping what has been learned and telling where the speech is going. An example of a signpost is "We've seen how being aware of the effects of cholesterol could result in clogged arteries. I've just reinforced this idea by presenting information from the American Medical Association proving the theory to be correct. Now, let's examine what you can do to lower your cholesterol and, therefore, lessen your chances of having a heart attack."

Supplementary Aids

Many speakers find **supplementary speech aids**—visual, audio, audiovisual, and computerized graphics—valuable in augmenting the oral segments of their presentations. Aids are intended to facilitate listener understanding, not to function as decorative touches; therefore, a speaker should ask two questions before using aids: Is the aid relevant to the presentation? And, will listeners better understand the material through the use of an aid?

Reasons for Using Visual Aids

Using visual aids when you present can make you more persuasive, credible, and interesting, according to these research results:

◆ Combining visual aids with what you say makes you 40 percent more persuasive than talking alone and boosts audience retention rates by 50 percent.

◆ Using visual aids in a meeting reduces meeting time by almost 30 percent.

◆ Including overheads in a meeting presentation spurs 80 percent of participants to agree more quickly to a proposal. Without overheads, the agreement rate drops to 60 percent.

◆ Restricting a group to no more than ten people yields the best results when you use posters, flip charts, and "white" boards. Also, an audience will endure viewing posters and flip charts slightly longer than slides or overheads.

Source: Simple Steps to a Powerful Presentation, Quill Corp., 100 Schelter Road, Lincolnshire, IL 60069.

Visual aids appeal to our sense of sight. As in using any other supplementary aid, speakers must be careful that the visual aids truly aid the presentation.

In a speech, statistical differences can be greatly enhanced by the use of charts. In a classroom, supplementary aids can be used to teach particular techniques. For example, student nurses sometimes inject needles into grapefruits so they can learn how to give shots, and a videotape of an interrogation can supplement a discussion on how to question suspects for law enforcement students. These aids are intended to supplement the speaker's voice.

Visual Aids   Visual aids appeal to our sense of sight.[23] And since so many listeners are visual in orientation, visual support of a speaker's message can be a key to enhancing comprehension. As in using any supplementary aid, speakers must be sure that the visual aid truly *aids* the presentation; that is, be sure that it doesn't just replace you and your message. Some speakers use the basic rule that if something can be said orally, without any assistance, then an aid should not be used. Others contend that right-brained listeners often depend on visual stimulation both in order to comprehend and to pay attention. Too many speakers bring in a huge number of pictures or PowerPoint slides and proceed to overwhelm listeners with no real supporting purpose.

A speaker can choose from a variety of visual aids:

1. *Real objects.* To demonstrate the process of swinging a hammer, why not use a real hammer? Or use an actual form to show how a traffic ticket is filled out. These are examples of using real objects as visual aids.

2. *Models.* At times, it is impossible to use real objects. In such cases, a scale model (in exact proportion to the dimensions of the real object) or a synthetic model (not in proportion but nevertheless representative) may be used. For example, although a Boeing 757 jet cannot be brought into an aviation classroom, a scale model certainly can be.

3. *Photographs, pictures, and diagrams.* A photograph of a death scene and the victim can be shown to a jury in a murder trial in order to reconstruct the scene or the violence.

4 *Charts.* A chart is a visual representation of statistical data that gives information in tabular or diagrammatic form. For example, a series of columns representing the number of doctors available to a hospital compared with the number needed presents a striking visual image of the problem.

5 *Cutaways.* It often is difficult to look inside certain objects. A cutaway allows us to see what we normally would have to imagine, thus enabling us to visualize and understand better. To show the layers of materials used to construct a house, a wall is cut in half so that we see the siding, the insulation, the studding, the wallboard, and the wallpaper.

6 *Mockups.* A mockup shows the building up or tearing down of an article. For example, a biology textbook may include an outline drawing of the human body on a page with a series of clear plastic sheets attached. Each of these plastic overlays shows a specific drawing that, as it is flipped onto the original sketch, adds an aspect of the human anatomy.

7 *Flip charts and chalk/white boards.* You may be presenting in a classroom or training room with little or no technological support. In such a setting, make use of the chalkboard or white board or bring a flip chart with newsprint paper so that you can list your major points or illustrate numbers as you speak. A good rule is to start at the far left and let your material "flow" across the board in the sequence in which you present it. Write legibly and large enough for your writing to be seen from the farthest point of the room. A traditional chalk mark or wide-tipped felt marker line can be seen clearly up to a distance of about twenty feet. If you know in advance that you will be using a flip chart, you can prepare the pages before your presentation and flip through them as you speak.

8 *Presentation graphics.* **Presentation graphics** are a series of visuals that are projected using an overhead projector while the speaker is discussing each point. The slides enable the speaker to illustrate visually with statistics, cartoons, short quotations, maps, and other materials.

In order to supplement the computer-generated materials in lengthy presentations, it often is helpful to provide listeners with a copy of the slides and space for taking notes.

Audio Aids   **Audio aids** appeal to our sense of hearing. Such devices as records, tape recordings, or duplications of sounds may be the only way to demonstrate particular sensations accurately for listeners. For example, playing a segment of Martin Luther King's "I Have a Dream" speech is an excellent way to demonstrate his dynamic oral style.

Audiovisual Aids   **Audiovisual aids** such as films, videotapes, and tape-slide presentations combine the dimensions of sight and sound. A video clip of a seeing-eye dog assisting his or her person can illustrate the support that such animals can provide. In the same way, a videotape of an executive's speech is an excellent way to illustrate his or her vocal and physical mannerisms.

Computerized Graphics

In many ways, presentation graphics have revolutionized the way people give speeches. Computerized programs such as PowerPoint provide speakers with the opportunity to outline a speech, create slides with animated bullets that follow that outline, and import visual graphics, photos, video or audio clips, and Internet connections. Many

---

When Preparing Audiovisuals

When preparing slides or overheads, you should limit punctuation. Specifically, avoid using

◆ Slashes. *Example:* "yes/no." *Why:* When seen from a distance, slashes can resemble letters. They'll confuse your audience, who may think you're using longer words that don't make sense.

◆ Em-dashes, short dashes that serve to separate expressions. *Example:* "…is of course—hypothetically speaking— …" *The problem:* When these expressions are knocked to the next line as a single word, you'll get awkward line breaks.

◆ Exclamation points. *The problem:* When projected, an "!" may resemble a "1."

Source: Adapted from Roger C. Parker, writing in *Technique,* 10 Post Office Square, Boston, MA 02109. © Communication Briefings, www.briefings.com, 1101 King St., Alexandria, VA 22314.

Presentation graphics are a series of visuals that are displayed via a projector while the speaker is discussing each point.

courtrooms, classrooms, and organizations are now equipped with projectors so that speakers can display computerized graphics. As a result, a speaker who uses the program effectively can provide listeners with multimedia messages, stimulating their visual and auditory senses.

Computer graphics allow people who are not artists to prepare attractive visuals. In addition, apprehensive speakers may be less fearful because they perceive that the audience members are looking at the visuals, not at them.

A computerized presentation allows for varying the visuals through a variety of media and media techniques. It has been observed that "a true multimedia experience keeps a person's attention longer and gives you the ability to leave a visual impression in [his or her] mind."[24]

Besides the advantages, recognize that there are also drawbacks to using computer programs:

◆ If the projection equipment is substandard, it may be necessary to turn out the lights so the audience can see the slides, a move that creates a sleep-inducing environment and makes it difficult for people to take notes.

◆ There is a risk of putting so much on the screen that the material becomes overwhelming.

◆ A speaker can get so carried away with the program's technological abilities to dissolve, fade, or fly transitions that the medium becomes more important than the message.

In addition, a controversy exists regarding whether public speaking students should use or learn how to use such programs as PowerPoint. "The debate centers around the utility of the software for making presentations, as the wizards often lead students down organizational paths that may not be best for their presentations, and around whether there is still a demand for use of presentational software in professional settings [when,] in fact, some managers have banned the use of presentational software for internal reports."[25] In addition, there is a question of whether class time in speech courses should be spent in teaching students how to prepare and use computerized presentational techniques.[26]

Preparing Presentational Programs

Since many speakers want to and may even be required to use electronic techniques and equipment, this text presents a discussion of their preparation and use. It is understood, however, that some instructors may request that their students not use computer-assisted presentational programs, just as some organizations are requesting that their employees avoid using this type of equipment. Be aware that this attitude is not universal; many organizations expect their employees to be proficient in the use of presentation graphics.

In planning the use of PowerPoint, remember that presentation graphics, like any visual aids, are designed to assist your oral presentation, not replace it. As a result, you will want to plan carefully how best to incorporate the graphics so that they reinforce or clarify your verbal points. Recognize that some speakers rely far too extensively on visuals, putting their entire presentation on the screen. Remember that audiences are expected to comprehend word slides at a glance, without breaking their concentration on the speaker. When bombarded with word slides, audiences can only pretend that they're taking in both the visuals and the voice. Also be aware that depending on your projector system, the audience may have to sit in the dark during the use of the equipment. Darkness can be depressing, lead to sleepiness, and make it difficult for people to take notes.

Keep in mind the purpose of supplementary aids. If you can say something without any visual assistance, do so. Do not use visuals as decoration or to show off your computer skills. Make sure that the materials aid your speech, not detract from it. After a while the novelty of graphics wears off, and audience members find themselves bored, or they pay attention to the process rather than to what you are saying.

Developing PowerPoint Presentations

The materials should be easy to read, visible to all, and simple to understand (see Figure 12.1). Each slide or visual should focus on a single idea and convey that information clearly. Punctuation and capitalization should be consistent throughout. Spelling and punctuation should be correct. Select a neutral color for your ending slide. This way you avoid having a glaring white screen after your last visual.

Make sure that when preparing the graphics, you parallel your speech materials with the visuals. Listeners shouldn't have to struggle to comprehend the connection between the visual and verbal message.

If you are going to prepare and use electronic presentational programs to their full advantage, you also need to understand not only how to input the information but also how to use the process during a presentation. Many colleges and organizations offer classes on how to prepare and use the programs, and some packages have video or computer tutorials. The PowerPoint package, for example, comes with PowerPoint Wizard, a program that directs you through each step of creating the visuals. For those who prefer to read instructions, books specifically written for the presentational packages are available. A guide for use in classes at Western Kentucky University is available at <http://www.wku.edu/~downijr/classes/161/PowerPointManual.htm>. Another course is <http://www.depts.washington.edu/catalyst/ quick/ppt.html>.

Figure 12.1	Design Elements and PowerPoint Slides

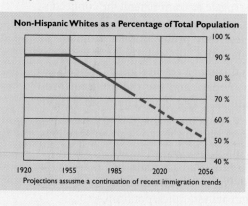

You'll want to give careful consideration to the design elements of your Power-Point presentation. For clarity, keep these suggestions in mind:

◆ Use a clean-looking font, such as **ARIAL**.

◆ Use the rule of 5×5, which indicates that no slide should use more than five words per line and no more than five lines per slide.

◆ Phrases are easier to grasp than full sentences, but full sentences may be useful to express complete thoughts.

◆ Bulleted and/or numbered lists and topic outlines are useful.

◆ Be aware that different computers may project colors differently, so standard colors may work best.

◆ Use the same font and format on all slides so that your words don't seem to jump all over the screen with each new slide.

◆ Keep the lights on during the speech (in most rooms).

◆ Use a very light background with black or dark lettering.

◆ Plan the presentation so that you deliver one page in thirty seconds (or more).

◆ Use one visual per minute.

◆ Present only one major idea per slide or viewgraph.

◆ Use no more than four subordinate ideas per minute.

◆ Each bulleted point should be horizontal on the slide.

◆ Use colors that can be seen (avoid putting black print on a dark-blue background).

◆ Pay attention to the print and background colors in the preformatted designs.

◆ Incorporate video and film clips, maps, graphs, and charts, if appropriate.

◆ Use the same graphics, colors, and fonts on all of your slides.

◆ Prepare a slide that lists the main points of your speech to use as an overview of the body of your speech and to show at the end as you present your summary.

◆ Preview your visuals before using them. Stand back and look at your visuals as your listeners will see them. This is the only way you can determine if the colors, layout, and format work.

In Conclusion

The sources of information available to a speaker include personal experiences, personal observations, and accumulated learning, plus information derived from research and interviews. Research information may be found in books, magazines, newspapers, journals, indexes, government publications, publications from special-interest groups, and the Internet. Additional information can be found in nonprint media and interviews. When doing research, keep a record of where the information came from. Supporting material is used in a speech to clarify the speaker's point or to demonstrate that the point has some probability of being true. Supporting material can include illustrations, specific instances, expositions, statistics, analogies, and testimony. Three means for presenting and focusing supporting material are internal summaries, forecasting, and the use of supplementary aids.

Learn by Doing

1. Select a controversial subject area (e.g., abortion, euthanasia, legalization of drugs, confiscation of handguns), and identify an authority on the subject. Interview that person (in person or via the phone or Internet), and give an oral presentation to the class about your interview. You should clearly state the interviewee's stand concerning the issue and the reasons for the stand. After all of the presentations have been made, participate in a class discussion on the value of the interview as a means for collecting data for a speech.

2. Use the information collected from the interview in Activity 1 to research the same topic. Look for the views of other authorities on the subject. Prepare a presentation in which you compare and/or contrast the results of your interview with the results of your research.

3. Make a presentation to the class in which a supplementary aid is absolutely necessary for the listeners' comprehension of the message (e.g., a description of Van Gogh's style of brush stroke, the music of the Grateful Dead in comparison with that of the group Chicago, the architectural styles of the Maya of the Yucatan).

4. Research each of these items and compile a set of notecards or notes and a running bibliography as explained in the chapter:
   a. The name of one book about the teachings of Aristotle
   b. A magazine article about nuclear-waste disposal
   c. The longitude and latitude of Omaha, Nebraska
   d. Three encyclopedia entries about the White House
   e. The name of a journal exclusively about nonverbal communication
   f. The definition of the word *cacophony*
   g. The 1950 population of the United States
   h. The name of the university that sponsors the Semester at Sea academic program
   i. The title of a government pamphlet dealing with AIDS
   j. The gross national product of the United States in 1996
   k. The name of the lyricist for the musical *Rent*

5. Use the format explained in the chapter to make three notecards or notes for a speech with the purpose statement "to inform the class of the effects of the Salk polio vaccine." Two are to be quotations; one, a paraphrase. Use a different source for each entry.

6. Find a factual or hypothetical illustration that could be used for the speech described in Activity 5.

7. What background information do you think would be needed by members of your class if you were to present the speech in Activity 5?

8. Locate and footnote three sources of testimony concerning the effects of secondary smoke on nonsmokers.

9. Find a humorous story that you could use as an introduction for a speech about the United States' educational system, gender similarities or differences, or sports.

10. Prepare a three- to five-minute speech that depends on the audience's viewing a PowerPoint presentation.

11. Select one feature of preparing a PowerPoint presentation that you can demonstrate to the class in a speech of three minutes or less. Since everyone in the class will be doing this assignment, try to select an aspect of the program that is unusual. Then present the speech to the class.

Key Terms

primary sources of information
secondary sources of information
information highway
computer-based retrieval system
Boolean search
quotations
paraphrases
oral footnote
supporting speech material
illustrations
specific instances
exposition

statistics
analogy
testimony
expert
internal summary
forecast
signposting
supplementary speech aids
visual aids
presentation graphics
audio aids
audiovisual aids

13

Public Speaking: Structuring the Message

After reading this chapter, you should be able to

- Explain why it is important to structure speeches carefully

- Structure a speech to meet the needs of the listeners

- Explain what makes an effective introduction, central idea, body, and conclusion for a speech

- List and give examples of introduction attention-getters for a speech

- Identify the purpose and various types of orienting materials

- Explain the purpose of and develop a central idea for a speech

- List and give examples of the methods of issue arrangement for the body of a speech

- List and give examples of the methods for concluding a speech

- Identify and illustrate the methods for the overall organization of a speech

H ave you ever sat through a class lecture and found yourself thoroughly confused because the instructor kept jumping from idea to idea and then back to a previous one while discussing still another thought? If so, you were experiencing organizational confusion.

If a speech is well ordered, the chance of its success increases. One of the most effective approaches to enhancing listener comprehension of a message is the development of well-supported points.[1] "Experienced speakers know (1) that if a presentation is to be effective, it must be understood and (2) that if a presentation is to be understood, it must be organized logically."[2]

Speakers who can plan and then build in repetition of their points foster listening comprehension. Television commercials, for example, repeat extensively to reinforce the message in viewers' minds. They present an idea, clarify it, and then represent it.

Listeners have limited attention spans, constantly tuning in to and out of speakers' messages. Consequently, it is important to present a carefully structured message that enables listeners to get back on track when they tune back in to the speech.

A careful plan for putting together a speech is a major part of the process of preparing and developing effective presentations.[3] The plan should aid in eliminating confusion, produce a well-supported presentation, foster listening comprehension, and maintain attention.

Basic Elements of a Speech

A public communication message should be arranged in four parts:

I.   Introduction—attention-gaining and orienting material.

II. Central idea—the purpose of the presentation and a specific statement of its main idea.

III. Body—the major points to be expressed in the presentation. The body of the speech may be organized into as many divisions as necessary to develop the intent of the message.

IV. Conclusion—a summarizing and possibly a motivating statement.

The Introduction

The purposes of the **introduction to a speech** are to gain the listeners' attention and orient them to the material that will be presented.

Attention Material

It is imperative to gain the listeners' attention at the start of the speech. If the speaker fails to convince the audience to listen immediately, getting them to tune in

COMMUNICATION BRIEFING

Test Yourself: Rate Your Presenting Skills

Labeling each of these statements as true or false will tell you if you know what it takes to be a powerful presenter:

1. Visuals will keep the audience's attention better if you use a variety of type fonts and sizes.
2. Memorizing a speech isn't a good idea.
3. Each visual should include no more than two key concepts.
4. Casually leaning back on one hip tells an audience that you're less formal and thus more believable.
5. To get an audience to think creatively, project information on the right side of a screen.

Answers: 1. *False.* Audiences react better to consistency, so use no more than one or two fonts. Also, it's best to use a sans serif because it's easier to read in the larger sizes you need for the screen. 2. *True,* but some experts recommend that you memorize the first minute or two to help you build confidence by starting strong. 3. *False.* Limit each visual to only one key concept or risk confusing an audience with too much to recall at once. 4. *False.* It signals—nonverbally—that you wish you didn't have to be there. 5. *True.* Research also shows that you should put the image or the words as high on the screen as you can get them.

Source: © Communication Briefings, www.briefings.com, 1101 King Street, Alexandria, VA 22314. Used with permission.

later is almost impossible. Attention-getting techniques include presenting personal references, humorous stories, illustrations, rhetorical questions, action questions, unusual or dramatic devices, quotations related to the theme, and a statement of the theme.

Personal References Introductions containing personal references give a speaker's reasons for undertaking a presentation on a specific topic. For example, to introduce a presentation that appeals for funds, a speaker may relate the personal experience of receiving aid from the Muscular Dystrophy Association.

Humorous Stories People like to laugh and enjoy themselves; therefore, humorous stories often are an effective way to start a presentation. The humor should fit the audience and the occasion, be relevant to the material being presented, and set the desired tone.

The humor should parallel the intent of the speech. A speaker, for example, could begin a presentation with a humorous anecdote: "A railroad agent in Africa had been bawled out for doing things without orders from headquarters. One day headquarters received a telegram from the agent which read, 'Tiger on platform eating conductor. Wire instructions.'"[4] From this story, listeners would expect a speech about worker empowerment or creative decision making.

It is important to consider, too, whether humor is appropriate to your own communication style. Some people are not very comfortable telling funny stories or jokes, and that discomfort will be revealed to the audience. Other speakers have a good ear (and memory) for relaying humorous anecdotes and find the form successful for them.

Illustrations Illustrations such as stories, pictures, and slides help to make ideas more vivid for listeners because they create a visualization or image of the topic to be discussed. For example, showing pictures of the results of a new skin-grafting process for burn victims clearly illustrates the topic. Similarly, a speaker who is going to talk about the need for well-equipped police cars can begin a speech by saying, "Picture yourself on a dark road some night with car trouble or maybe even an injury that prevents you from driving. Suddenly you see the headlights of a car. It could belong to almost anyone. But wouldn't you feel better if it turned out to be a police officer with all the equipment you needed?"

Rhetorical Questions Questions for which no outward response is expected are **rhetorical questions.** For example, a speaker may say to an audience, "Have you ever asked yourself what you would do if someone tried to rob you?" In this case, the speaker does not intend to count how many people in the audience have or have not asked themselves the question. Instead, the purpose is to have audience members ask themselves the question so as to build their curiosity or interest.

Although they are sometimes overused, rhetorical questions can be an effective method of getting the audience to ponder a topic.

COMMUNICATION BRIEFING

Try These Speech Starters

Successful presenters use these techniques to quickly establish a connection with their audiences:

- ◆ **Quiet** a talkable group with the silent treatment. Just stand there and look at them until all the eyes—and the ears—in the room focus on you. At the precise moment that occurs, hit them with a statement that gives them a good reason to keep listening.
- ◆ **Imply that** you need their help. "I have something on my mind, and I'd like to share it with you to see what you think."
- ◆ **Dramatize what** you're planning to tell them. *Example:* "I'm deeply troubled by something, and I'm wondering if the same thing is also troubling you."
- ◆ **Ask them** how they feel about the topic of your presentation. *Example:* "I'm fed up with the tax system. Are you?"
- ◆ **Say something** that will involve them. *Examples:* "I'm going to ask you to think about an important topic." "I'd like you to do something for me."

Source: Steve Adubato, Ph.D., Emmy Award–winning author and communication trainer, Bloomfield, NJ, writing in *Business News New Jersey,* Snowden Publications, Inc., 104 Church St., New Brunswick, NJ 08901. © Communication Briefings, www.briefings.com, 1101 King Street, Alexandria, VA 22314. Used with permission.

Action Questions **Action questions** are a means of getting the audience involved in a speech and making listeners think and respond. For example, a speaker started a presentation by asking, "How many of you have been involved in an auto accident?" After the hands went up, the speaker said, "For those of you with your hands up, do you remember that instant when you knew the accident was going to happen and you couldn't do anything about it? What flashed through your mind?" After getting some answers from the audience, the speaker said, "Yes, a common response is helplessness and fear." Thus, the speaker involved the audience and was able to move their attention to the next segment of the speech, which centered on how to overcome the feelings of helplessness caused by fear and despair.

Humorous stories often are an effective way to start a presentation.

Unusual or Dramatic Devices Unusual or dramatic devices get the audience's attention because of their curiosity or shock value. In one dramatic opening, a medical lab technician set up equipment and drew blood from a student volunteer to show how blood is analyzed.

Quotations Related to the Theme Speakers sometimes begin by quoting a famous person or expert, reading an account of a specific event, reciting a section of a poem or play, or reading a newspaper editorial. The quotations should be relevant to the topic and be read meaningfully. The greatest mistake many speakers make in presenting a quotation is to select an appropriate piece and then speed through the reading or fail to stress the meaning.

Stating the Theme   Theme statements indicate to the audience exactly what the speaker is going to talk about. Unfortunately, many untrained speakers start out their presentations by saying, "Today I am going to tell you about . . ." This is not a creative or attention-getting opener.

A more creative theme statement is likely to hold the audience's attention. For example, a mechanic started her presentation by saying, "There is a right and a wrong way to change a tire. Doing it the wrong way can result in death or permanent injury. I'm going to share with you a simple technique to ensure you do it the right way."

Orienting Material

Orienting material gives the audience the background necessary to understand the basic material of the speech. It is designed to tie the material to the central idea, provide necessary information, establish personal credibility for the speaker, and make the subject important to the listener. Orienting material can include such clarifiers as providing a historical background, defining terms that will be used in the presentation, tying the speaker's personal history to the subject, using statistics to identify how many people are affected, and illuminating the importance of the ideas to the listener.

Historical Background

Often a speaker has to explain what led up to the present so an audience can gain the necessary historical background. For example, a speech intended to persuade the audience to vote for a renewal of a school levy ought to include the facts that illustrate the history of the levy.

Unusual or dramatic devices get the attention because of their curiosity or shock value.

Definition of Terms

Although terms usually are defined at the place they are used in a speech, sometimes the very nature of a speech depends on the audience's having an understanding near the start of the presentation. For example, in a speech about agoraphobia, the definition of it as an emotional illness that manifests itself in the person's not wanting to appear in public should appear near the beginning of the presentation. Only terms that are universal to the speech should be included in the orientation.

Personal History and/or Tie to the Topic

A speaker often can gain credibility if she or he has some personal tie or experience related to the topic. A speaker intending to demonstrate the steps in mouth-to-mouth resuscitation could refer to his Red Cross training and his background as a lifeguard. This documentation establishes the speaker's authority to speak about the subject.

Speakers who don't have a clear purpose risk not getting their point across to the audience.

Importance to the Listeners

One of the most critical parts of the orienting material is relating the subject to the listeners in some way. Listeners pay attention to ideas and issues that are relevant to them, so it is helpful if the speaker makes that link at the outset. One good strategy is to show the importance of the topic based on the interests of the audience—for example, "The Internal Revenue Service reports that an average of 107 million income tax forms are filed yearly. Many of these are incorrect and result in millions of lost refunds. Hopefully, your tax form was not one of these."

The Central Idea

The **statement of the central idea of a speech** is intended to keep the speaker on course for developing a purposeful and well-organized speech. It also indicates the response the speaker wants from listeners. If, for example, the central idea of a speech is stated as "I will present to you two reasons why we should all vote for the school bond issue on November 2," both the speaker and the audience are clear about the topic, the method of developing that topic, and what is desired from the audience.

The importance of stating the central idea in a speech cannot be overemphasized. Speakers who skip this important part of the speech deprive the listeners of the clue they may need to be sure of what the exact point of the speech is. The central idea should be presented as a statement because a speaker who uses a question (e.g., "Should the federal government provide financial aid to private educational institutions?") is not indicating to listeners what the main point really is. But a speaker who presents the point as a statement ("There are three reasons that I believe the federal government should not provide financial aid to private educational institutions") is clarifying the stand that will be advocated.

The Body

The **body of a speech** develops through major points as well as any subpoints pertaining to a speaker's central idea. In this way, the listeners should have little trouble in understanding the message. However, this is not always the case. Culture plays an important role in the organization of ideas. It must be remembered, however, that not all audiences will be U.S.-American.

Role of Culture on Speech Structure

"Languages differ in the very assumption of how information should be organized, of what is to be or not to be described and expressed."[5] In other words, as we develop our language skills, we hear ideas presented in certain patterns. If concepts are presented in an alternative pattern, it can cause listener problems.

Historically, speakers of Western cultures, based on the concepts developed by the Greek rhetorician Aristotle, make use of a process that calls for stating a contention, supporting that contention, and drawing a conclusion for the listeners. This is accomplished in a step-by-step manner. In some other cultures, a **spiral**

COMMUNICATION BRIEFING

Words to Use in Speeches

Your speech will be more "listenable" for your audience if you follow these guidelines when you write a manuscripted speech:

- **Choose simple** sentences over those that contain dependent clauses. *Original:* The reorganization plan, *on which I have worked for two months,* is almost complete. *Revised:* "I've worked on the reorganization plan for two months. And it's almost complete.
- **Get rid** of *that* whenever you can. *Original:* "It's possible *that* we'll be in the black by April." *Revised:* "I predict we'll be in the black by April."
- **Don't bury** verbs in nouns. *Original:* "There's a *belief* among many managers ..." *Revised:* "Many managers *believe* ..."
- **Shrink long** connecting words. Use *still* or *but* for *nevertheless* and *also* or *and* for *furthermore.*
- **Stress your** ideas by repeating words. *Example:* "Why should we adopt this plan? *Because* it's fair. *Because* it's feasible. And *because* it will give us a competitive edge for at least the next four years."
- **Use contractions** such as *you're, you'll,* and *we're* as much as possible.
- **Insert** *I* when appropriate and *you* and *we* every chance you get.

Source: Presentations for Decision Makers, by Marya Holcombe and Judy Stein, Van Nostrand Reinhold, 115 5th Ave., New York, NY 10003. © Communication Briefings, www.briefings.com, 1101 King Street, Alexandria, VA 22314. Used with permission.

form of explanation is used. In this mode, a statement is made and then a story or analogy that deals with the statement is presented. It is left to the listener to apply the parallels and draw outcomes related to the original statement. This is a method often used in Arabic, Native American, and some Asian cultures.

Here are some examples of how culture affects the organization of ideas:

◆ Presentations by Koreans may be characterized by indirectness and nonlinear development. This format is used because memory research shows that "Koreans have more difficulty recalling information when that information is presented in a linear rhetorical style."[6]

◆ Arabic speakers value telling a story or a series of parables and letting the listeners figure out the moral of the narrative. This indirect presentational style, with little structure, often confuses those who are used to a direct format in which a statement is made and evidence is presented to clarify the proposition.

◆ "African-American rhetoric depends on a unique style of language, for its effectiveness."[7] Thus, European Americans who are listening to black speakers may be confused when the presenter fails to set a specific theme but strings together stories, anecdotes, and biblical quotations in a random order.

◆ Spanish writers and speakers use loose coordination of ideas, elaboration, and narrative in the form of stories.[8]

◆ Because discourse for Navajos is designed to secure order, harmony, and balance, they are interested in dialogue, not a speaker who is expounding a point of view to silent listeners. Public speaking, Navajo style, is interactive, with no prescribed structure.[9] European American and Navajo speakers and listeners often disagree not over what is said but how the material is organized and presented. Most Native Americans start presentations with an homage to their forefathers.[10]

African-American rhetoric depends on a unique style of language for its effectiveness.

◆ U.S. Americans have been schooled to emphasize a purpose early, advance their argument linearly by connecting ideas with clear and concise bridges, and omit any material that does not obviously contribute to their linear progression. By contrast, the German tradition promotes a logical progression but imposes fewer restrictions on the inclusion of material. Germans may appear to digress from the main point if they feel that the additions contribute to their purpose.[11]

◆ English writers and speakers tend to follow a strict deductive (the thesis is in the initial position) and inductive (the thesis is in the final position) organization pattern. Japanese, Chinese, Thai, and Koreans follow an organizational pattern that is quasi-inductive—that is, the thesis is often buried in the materials, with the topic implied rather than stated.[12]

◆ The Chinese tend to present ideas through a variety of indirectly related views. This may take the form of an eight-legged essay:[13] the opening, amplification, preliminary exposition, first argument, second argument, third argument, final argument, and conclusion. The most important part is the amplification, which consists of two or three sentences that express the topic. This is in contrast to the European American tradition of the body being the most important part of the presentation because it amplifies the reason for taking specific actions.

◆ Arabs use "a completely different persuasive style than that set in Western logic. The Arabic argumentative style depends greatly on parables from the Koran, which are based on the concept 'because Islam says so.'"[14] This organizational style often causes Western listeners to disregard the information because it is not based on logic proofs, such as statistics and research findings.

Because this book is written primarily for public speakers for whom the Western mode of reasoning and organization is the general format, the discussion of how to develop a speech will follow those guidelines. This is not to say that other formats or approaches should not be learned or used when appropriate. In fact, a European American whose analysis shows that the audience is composed primarily of individuals who are not European Americans should adapt the message and its presentation to that audience.

Methods of Issue Arrangement

The **method of issue arrangement for the body of a speech** normally takes one of six forms: spatial arrangement, time arrangement, topical arrangement, causal arrangement, comparison-contrast arrangement, or problem-solution arrangement. The method selected acts as a guide for sequencing information for listener clarity.

Spatial Arrangement   Many people organize information automatically even though they are not aware of it. Suppose some friends are visiting you at your college. They have never been on your campus before, so they ask you to tell them about the institution. You start by describing the buildings located on the south end of the campus and then proceed to talk about all the other buildings, noting their locations from south to north. You have organized your presentation according to the **spatial method of issue arrangement.** You have set a point of reference at a specific location and followed a geographic pattern. The pattern can be left to right, north to south, or from the center to the outside. This is a common method for giving directions or describing something by its location.

We can see how spatial arrangement can be used for the body of a speech whose central idea is "to inform the audience of the financial tax base of the state of Maryland by examining the state from west to east." Here is a possible outline of the body of the speech with the major headings spatially arranged according to geographical location:

III. Financial Tax Base of the State of Maryland
    A. Western Maryland
        1. Cumberland
        2. Hagerstown
    B. Central Maryland
        1. Baltimore
        2. Rockville
    C. Eastern Maryland
        1. Annapolis
        2. Ocean City

Time Arrangement The **time method of issue arrangement** orders information from a beginning point to an ending one, with all the steps developed in numerical or time sequence. Research shows that using a time method of issue arrangement increases a listener's retention of a speaker's information.[15]

For example, chronological arrangement can be used to develop the body of the speech whose central idea is "to inform the audience of the accomplishments of the last four Chinese dynasties." The body outline for the speech would read:

III. Last Four Chinese Dynasties
    A. A.D. 960–1280: Song (Sung)
        1. Paper money invented
        2. Primitive printing press developed
        3. Scholars active
           a. Books printed
           b. Painting reached zenith
    B. A.D. 1280–1368: Yuan
        1. Became part of an empire that stretched to Europe
        2. Silk Road reopened
        3. New religions introduced
    C. A.D. 1368–1644: Ming
        1. Agricultural methods of production developed
        2. Great sea expeditions undertaken
    D. A.D. 1644–1911: Qing (Ching)
        1. Tobacco and corn industries developed
        2. Lost Korea, Taiwan, and the Pescadores Islands

Topical Arrangement Ideas can be organized on the basis of their similarities. Thus, in using a **topical method of issue arrangement,** a speaker explains an idea in terms of its component parts. For example, in speaking about dogs, a speaker may discuss cocker spaniels, poodles, and then collies, developing ideas about each breed (the component part) completely before going on to the next one. The speaker also can organize the presentation of ideas by talking about the temperament of each breed, then about the size of each breed, and finally about the coloring of each breed. In this way, the speaker is organizing the ideas by classifying the animals according to specific identifiable characteristics (the component parts) and then developing each subsection into identifiable patterns of information.

Though there is no set sequence in which topics should be arranged in the topical arrangement, some speakers put the entries in *alphabetical order* (e.g., see the WordPerfect for the Macintosh example that follows this explanation). Another structural device would be arranging the topics according to their *order of relevance.* Or one could place the items according to their *order of importance or priority.*

Whatever mode you chose, with a topical arrangement, it is incumbent on you as the speaker to create and communicate a rationale for the order of the main points. One way to do this is to explain to the audience how you are organizing the topics. This will allow the audience to understand why some items are included and others are excluded and will alert them as to how the points are to be presented. You might say, "In speaking about word processing programs, it must be recognized that there are many to choose from. My research shows that the two most popular are WordPerfect and Word. I've chosen to speak about the program that has been judged by computer magazines and writers as the best program, Correl's WordPerfect. I will discuss three parts of the program: editing, page formatting, and merging operations."

To illustrate this process, here is an outline of the main headings of the body of a speech whose central idea statement is "to inform the audience about three operations of WordPerfect for the Macintosh: editing, page formatting, and merging operations":

III. Three Operations of WordPerfect for Macintosh
    A. Editing
        1. Inserting and deleting text
        2. Starting a new line
        3. Wraparound typing
        4. Inserting text in paragraphs
    B. Formatting
        1. Setting margins
        2. Changing point size
        3. Adding a heading
    C. Merging operations
        1. List processing
        2. Fill-in forms
        3. Automatic printing

Causal Arrangement   The **causal method of issue arrangement** shows how two or more events are connected in such a way that if one occurs, the other will necessarily follow. In other words, if one incident happened, it caused the second incident to happen. This is a good method to use when a specific observable result can be understood by determining what happened.

This outline was developed for the body of a speech whose central idea was "to list and discuss the theory that a series of identifiable events can result in the development of agoraphobia":

III. Series of Events Resulting in the Development of Agoraphobia
    A. Sequence of events
        1. First event
            a. Physical symptoms such as heart palpitations, trembling, sweating, breathlessness, dizziness
            b. No apparent cause for the physical symptoms

2. Second event
   a. Duplication of physical symptoms in a place similar to the site of the first event
   b. Increasing awareness of fear of going to certain places
3. Third event
   a. Symptoms occurring when there is a thought of going to a place similar to the site of the first event's occurrence
   b. Feeling of being out of control when thinking of leaving the safety site (usually the home)

B. Result—agoraphobia
   1. Personality changes
      a. Frequent anxiety
      b. Depression
      c. Loss of individual character
   2. Emotional changes
      a. Impassiveness
      b. High degree of dependence on others
      c. Constant alertness

Note that the events leading up to the final result are listed, with the final result discussed last. An alternative form would have been to give the final result first and then list the events leading up to it. The former method is called *cause(s) to effect;* the latter, *effect from cause(s).*

Comparison-Contrast Arrangement   Suppose you are asked to explain the similarities between a community college and a four-year institution. Your explanation could follow the **comparison method of issue organization,** in which you would tell how two or more examples are alike. In the case of the colleges, you could talk about the similarities in curriculum, staff, facilities, activity programs, and costs. If, however, you are asked to tell the differences between the two, you would use the **contrast method of issue arrangement,** developing the ideas by giving specific examples of differences between the two types of institutions. A speech based on the **comparison-contrast method of issue arrangement** tells about both similarities and differences.

The body of a speech with a central idea of "informing the audience of some similarities and differences between state-supported two- and four-year colleges in Ohio" would be:

III. Similarities and Differences Between Two- and Four-Year State-Supported Ohio Colleges
   A. Similarities
      1. Are governed by the Board of Regents
      2. Receive state funding
      3. Offer general studies courses
      4. Must receive permission to add new curricula
      5. Are governed by a Board of Trustees appointed in part by the governor
   B. Differences
      1. Two-year colleges: funded in part by their local communities; four-year colleges: not funded by local communities
      2. Two-year colleges: offer associate degrees; four-year colleges: bachelor's and advanced degrees

3. Two-year colleges: have certificate and two-year terminal programs; four-year schools: no certificates or terminal programs
4. Two-year colleges: less expensive; four-year colleges: more expensive

Problem-Solution Arrangement The **problem-solution method of issue arrangement** is used when a speaker attempts to identify what is wrong and to determine how to cure it or make a recommendation for its cure. This method can be used to think through a problem and then structure a speech. A person dealing with the problem of child abuse, for instance, may wish to begin by analyzing the problem: the influence of family history, lack of parental control or knowledge, and the different types of child abuse. Such an analysis then may lead to a consideration of various solutions, such as stricter legislation mandating penalties for child abuse, stronger enforcement of child abuse laws, improved reporting procedures, and greater availability of social services to parents and children alike.

An alternative form of the problem-solution method is the *see-blame-cure-cost method.* In this approach, the evil or problem that exists is examined (see); what has caused the problem is determined (blame); solutions are investigated, and the most practical solution is selected (cure); and what finances, time, or emotions will have to be expended (cost) are examined.

When you develop a problem-solution message, state the problem, its cause, the possible solutions, and the selected solution. This organization allows your listeners to share a complete picture of your reasoning process.

Here is an example of a speech outline using problem-solution for the body of a speech with the central idea "to inform the audience why I believe that one of the solutions for the acid rain problem is to require coal-burning companies and smelting plants to build taller smokestacks, use scrubbers, and wash their coal before using it":

> When developing a problem-solution message, a speaker should state the problem, its cause, the possible solutions, and the selected solution.

III. Solution to Acid Rain Problem
    A. Problem
        1. Acid rain is caused by substances such as sulfur oxides and nitrogen oxides.
        2. Acid rain falls anywhere that is downwind of urban or industrial pollution.
        3. Acid rain has significant negative effects.
            a. It decreases the fertility and productivity of soils.
            b. It causes freshwater lakes and streams to become barren of fish, amphibians, invertebrates, and plankton.
            c. It damages such materials as stone, marble, and copper.
            d. It affects human health through contamination of the water we drink and fish and wildlife we eat.
    B. Solution
        1. Coal-burning companies and smelting plants should be required to build taller smokestacks to disperse the pollution.
        2. Scrubbers—traps in smokestacks that can catch up to 90 percent or more of the sulfur oxides emitted—should be required for all industrial users of smokestacks.
        3. All coal burned by industrial users should be washed before it is used.

A more detailed presentation of the speech can include discussions of the testing of each element of the solution. This can be accomplished by including subdivisions under each of the statements of the solution to explore whether it is *workable* (developing why the suggestion will solve or help solve the problem), *desirable* (explaining why the suggestion will not cause greater problems), and *practical* (indicating if and how the suggestion can be put into practice).

Major and Internal Methods of Arrangement   For each speech, the speaker usually selects one major method of development, always keeping in mind that other methods may be used as necessary to present subdivisions of the complete idea. For instance, in developing a presentation on the causes of World War II, a speaker may decide to use a chronological arrangement as the major method of development and a spatial method for some of the subtopical segments of the presentation. Thus, the speaker may talk about the political and social changes in the 1920s in England, France, Germany, Russia, and Japan; then proceed to tell about events in the early 1930s in these countries; and then discuss happenings in these countries in the mid-1930s. In this way, the audience can develop a listening pattern that allows for clarity of comprehension through the year span and then place.

No matter which pattern you use to develop a message, maintain that pattern consistently throughout your presentation. Otherwise, your audience will be confused by sudden shifts or failure to follow a sequence to its logical conclusion.

The Conclusion

Depending on the purpose of a speech, the **conclusion of a speech** can be used to summarize, pull thoughts together, or motivate listeners to take a prescribed action.

Summary

Whatever the purpose, a presentation should end with a **summary of a speech** that restates the major points to recap what has been covered. The guide for developing the summary is to refer to the major headings in the body of the speech and indicate how they develop the statement of central idea.

Clincher

Many communication theorists believe that all speeches should end with a summary of the major points, followed by a **clincher to a speech,** which gives the speaker one more chance to reinforce the major ideas presented and then wraps up the presentation with a final message to clinch the selling of the central idea. The outline of the conclusion section of a speech that includes a clincher would be:

IV. Conclusion
    A. Summary
    B. Clincher

Summarize

Don't end your presentation with "Here's one final thought." *Reason:* You'll only confuse your audience by introducing a new idea in your conclusion.

Source: Communication Briefings, as adapted from *Communicate to Win,* by Heinz Goldman, cited in *The Competitive Advantage,* P.O. Box 10828, Portland, OR 97210.

Clincher techniques are similar to attention-getting introduction methods—for example:

Personal reference. A speaker who established expertise at the start of a speech can reestablish his or her authority in the conclusion.

Humorous story. A humorous story summarizes the speaker's ideas. For example, a presentation about public speaking anxiety could end, "The mind is an amazing thing; it starts working the moment you are born and never stops until you get up to give a speech."

Illustration. A drug counselor can end a speech on substance abuse with a story about a client's success in turning away from the drug scene.

Rhetorical question. A speaker who posed a rhetorical question at the beginning of a presentation can conclude by answering it.

Unusual or dramatic devices. A speaker concluded a speech about the necessity of proper dental hygiene by passing out a small cup of disclosing solution and small mirror to each member of the audience. She then asked each of them to rinse out their mouths with the solution, which turned plaque and other substances on or between the teeth bright red. This activity effectively illustrated the importance of proper brushing—and the value of unusual or dramatic devices.

Quotations. A quotation that restates the major theme of a presentation can be used in ending it. A speaker could summarize a speech against the death penalty, for example, by reading the vivid description of an execution presented in Truman Capote's classic book *In Cold Blood.*

Repetition. Closing a speech with repetition ties it back to the introduction. It makes for a circular presentation.

Methods for Formatting a Speech

In organizing a speech, you make decisions about the type of introduction, statement of central idea, methods of arranging the material in the body of your speech, and various techniques you can use to conclude. Some theorists believe that a speaker should go beyond this basic four-step structure to an overall organizational pattern that uses the partitioning, unfolding, or case methods.

Partitioning Method

The **partitioning organizational speech structure** depends on a great deal of repetition and is the easiest of the three overall methods for listeners to follow.

When using this type of organization, you start with the introduction and lead into the central idea. Then you state the central idea, restate it, and divide it by listing the main issues you will cover in the order in which you will cover them. This restatement and division constitute what is called the **partitioning step.** For example, a speaker whose central idea is that "there are several problems with the use of radiation therapy" could state: "To understand these radiological difficulties, we will look at the harmful effects of radiation therapy and the poor quality of radiation facilities in hospitals."

From the partitioning step, you move into the first issue of the body of the speech by using a transition that forecasts the first issue. For example, the speaker could say, "Turning, then, to our first point, let us consider the harmful effect that radiation therapy has had." Restatement is also important, for as new material is added, the speaker should hold the audience's attention and clarify by repeating the points in different words.

In moving from one issue to the next in the body of the speech, a speaker should use **transitions** that provide a connection between the points. A good transition consists of two parts: a restatement of the previous issue and a forecast of the next one. For example, a speaker presenting a talk on marine biology provided a transition between two issues by stating, "From the evidence presented, it appears that the problems of water pollution are massive. How, then, can we tackle these problems?"

Once the last issue in a partitioned speech has been discussed, the presentation concludes with a summary that restates the central idea and the main issues. This summary gives listeners a chance to review in their own minds the points that have been discussed.

Successful partitioning organization follows the format of "Tell the audience what you're going to tell them, then tell them, and then tell them what you've told them."

A general outline for the partitioning sequence looks like this:

I.   Introduction
    A. Attention material
    B. Orienting material

II. Central Idea
    A. Statement of central idea
    B. Restatement of central idea
    C. Division (listing of issues by some method of issue arrangement)
       1. First main issue
       2. Second main issue
       3. Third main issue (and so on)

III. Body (Transition: forecast of the first issue)
    A. First main issue
       1. Discussion of first main issue through examples, illustrations, and explanations
       2. Discussion of first main issue through examples, illustrations, and explanations (and so on)
          (Transition: restatement of first main issue and forecast of second issue)
    B. Second main issue
       1. Discussion of second main issue
       2. Discussion of second main issue (and so on)
          (Transition: restatement of second main issue and forecast of third issue)
    C. Third main issue
       1. Discussion of third main issue
       2. Discussion of third main issue (and so on)

IV. Conclusion
    A. Summary (restatement of issues and central idea)
    B. Clincher

This next outline develops a speech according to the partitioning method of organization. Its central idea is "to inform the audience of the alternatives an intake counselor has by listing and discussing the alternatives available":

I.   Introduction
    A. Attention material: Each of us probably makes hundreds of decisions every day. We decide what to eat, what to wear, what television program to watch, what time to go to bed.
    B. Orienting material: In my work as an intake counselor with the Department of Juvenile Services, I must make decisions that can seriously affect a child's life. An intake counselor gets the police report when a juvenile commits a crime, calls in the parents and the child to decide what actions should be taken, and counsels them. An investigation of such work can help you to understand some of the procedures that local governments use to combat the problems of juvenile delinquency.

II. Statement of Central Idea
    A. Let us consider the alternatives an intake counselor has.
    B. The counselor can select from three major decisions.
    C. These decisions are to
        1. Send the case to court.
        2. Close the case at intake.
        3. Place the child on informal supervision for forty-five days.

III. Body
    (One decision a counselor may make is to send the case to court.)
    A. The law states that you must send the case to court if
        1. The charge is denied.
        2. The juvenile has a prior record.
        3. You notice signs of trouble in the family.
        4. The case is like Felicia's. Felicia . . .
        (Thus a case may be sent to court. A counselor also may decide to close a case at intake.)
    B. There are several reasons for closing the case at intake.
        1. The child admits guilt.
        2. The incident was a first offense.
        3. The parents are supportive, and the home life is stable.
        4. An example of a case closed at intake was Henrietta's. Henrietta . . .
        (As a result, a case may be closed at intake. A counselor also may decide to put a juvenile under informal supervision.)
    C. Supervision for forty-five days is warranted if
        1. The child or the family is in need of short-term counseling.
        2. The procedure is not used often.
        3. The court has never ordered this in the past.
        4. The case is like Lamont's. Lamont . . .
        (Through informal supervision, some children can be helped.)

IV. Conclusion
    A. Summary: The basic decision is whether to arrange court appearances, stop the action at the beginning, or supervise the client.
    B. Clincher: The goal of the whole intake process is to provide whatever is best for the child so that he or she will have proper care, treatment, and supervision.

Although partitioning organization can be used for a speech of any purpose, it is especially well suited to informative speaking and informative briefing. Because the aim of such a speech is to increase the listener's comprehension of a particular body of information, a clear structure and repetition of the major points are warranted.

Unfolding Method

The **unfolding organizational speech structure** can be used for a speech of any purpose, but if the goal is to persuade listeners, this format is the most useful. Unfolding organization differs from partitioning organization in two important ways: it does not restate the central idea, and it does not include the division step.

The unfolding format may be appropriate for an audience that initially agrees with the central idea and issue the speaker plans to develop. Here is one possible sequence for an unfolding format:

I.   Introduction
    A. Attention material
    B. Orienting material

II. Statement of Central Idea

III. Body (organized by some method of issue arrangement)
    (Transition)
    A. First issue
        1. Discussion of first issue through examples, illustrations, and explanations
        2. Discussion of first issue through examples, illustrations, and explanations (and so on)
    (Transition)
    B. Second issue
        1. Discussion of second issue through examples, illustrations, and explanations

The unfolding format may be appropriate for an audience that initially agrees with the central idea and issue the speaker plans to develop.

      2. Discussion of second issue through examples, illustrations, and explana-
        tions (and so on)
   (Transition)

IV. Conclusion
    A. Restatement
    B. Clincher

If members of the audience oppose your stand, it does not make sense to alien-
ate them by stating your central idea early in the presentation. Instead, lead them
through the main points, moving from areas of shared agreement into areas of controversy. If you arrange the main issues subtly and word them carefully, you may be
able to establish acceptance of your purpose statement just before you reach the
conclusion. In proceeding, follow this variation of the unfolding format:

I.   Introduction
    A. Attention material
    B. Orienting material
    (Transition)

II.   Body (organized by some method of issue arrangement)
    A. Discussion of first issue
       1. Examples and illustrations
       2. Examples and illustrations (and so on)
    B. Statement of first issue
    (Transition)
    C. Discussion of second issue
       1. Examples and illustrations
       2. Examples and illustrations (and so on)
    (Transition)

III. Statement of Central Idea
    (Transition)

IV. Conclusion
    A. Restatement
    B. Clincher

For instance, if you are trying to persuade a group of people to vote for a candidate, and you know the audience is not committed to the person, you are wise to
develop your position by stating the issues, stands, and actions of the candidate.
Stressing the positive aspects of your candidate will help build strong support for
him or her. After establishing this argument, you then reveal the voting action you
want from the audience. Some members may be swayed.

The unfolding method is considerably more flexible than the partitioning
method because it lends itself to a variety of formats. For example, in the unfolding
method of organization, you can move the statement of the central idea anywhere
in the speech as long as it comes before the conclusion. And your transitions do not
have to restate and forecast issues; they simply have to establish clear connections.
Furthermore, in this method, you do not have to restate all the issues and the central
idea in the conclusion. Remember, however, that a good conclusion should summarize and conclude your presentation.

As a speaker, you want to maintain a clear framework so that the speech moves
forward sequentially. Remember that a speech is of no value if the audience does not
clearly understand your central idea at the conclusion.

This outline develops a speech according to the unfolding method of organization. The central idea is "to persuade each member of the audience, by listing and discussing the reasons, that he or she should donate his or her body to science":

I. Introduction
   A. Attention material: Picture a three-year-old girl attached to a kidney dialysis machine once a week for the rest of her life. Picture a little boy whose world is blackness, or a father who is confined to his bed because he has a weak heart.
   B. Orienting material: Such pictures are not very pleasant. But you can do something about them.

II. Statement of Central Idea: You should donate your body to science.

III. Body
   A. Organ banks need organs so that people who need them may function normally.
      1. List of organs that can be donated
      2. The need for speed in transplanting organs (thus specific organs can be used)
   B. Your body can be used as an instrument for medical education.
      1. Who can donate and how
      2. The need to eliminate shortages
         (As a result, your entire body can continue to serve a useful purpose.)

IV. Conclusion
   A. Summary
      1. Organs are needed so that others can function normally.
      2. Your body can be used for medical education.
   B. Clincher
      1. I am a benevolent person who believes that everyone is born with a benevolent nature. I know that you and I will help those less fortunate than we are. I am a potential organ and cadaver donor through my will. A donor's card can be obtained through any medical foundation. I cannot overemphasize the need for body and organ donations.
      2. Don't, as the proverb states, wait for George to do it. You do it! Take immediate action to become an organ and cadaver donor.

Case Method

In some respects, the **case method of organizational speech structure** is less complex than the partitioning and unfolding methods because the speaker discusses the central idea without breaking it into subpoints. As a result, this format is especially suitable for speeches designed to entertain, commemorate, or present a single issue. If, for example, your central idea is that "kids say the funniest things," then the body of a speech you organize using this method includes a series of examples of children's clever sayings connected by clear transitions.

When you use the case method, be careful not to develop subpoints in the body of the speech so that they become main points in themselves. The danger of subdividing is that you may not develop each subdivided point fully, and your listeners may become confused. If, for instance, in the "kids say the funniest things" example, you say in one of the transitions, "Kids say funny things at school and at camp," you have subdivided your central idea into two issues.

Here is the general format for a speech developed by case organization:

I.   Introduction
     A. Attention material
     B. Orienting material
     (Transition)

II. Central Idea
     (Transition)

III. Body (organized in a sequence)
     A. Example (a case)
     (Transition)
     B. Example (a case)
     (Transition)
     C. Example (a case, and so on)
     (Transition)

IV. Conclusion
     A. Summary
     B. Clincher

This outline develops a speech according to the case method of organization. The central idea is "to inform the audience of some ways in which left-handers are discriminated against by listing some examples":

I.   Introduction
     A. Attention material: Have you ever pondered the design of a butter knife or the structure of a gravy ladle?
     B. Orienting material: These structural problems are important to all of us who are afflicted with a key social problem: left-handedness.
         (Those of us who are left-handed believe that . . .)

II. Statement of Central Idea
     A. Left-handers are discriminated against.
     B. Let's look at some examples.

III. Body
     A. Example: Tell a story of the difficulties encountered when using scissors.
     (Transition: Another experience I've had . . .)
     B. Example: Tell a story of the problems with school desks designed for right-handed people.
     (Transition: This experience points out another one . . .)
     C. Example: Tell a story of the problems with words such as *gauche* and *south-paw.*
     (Transition: So you see . . .)

IV. Conclusion
     A. Summary: Left-handers are discriminated against all the way from the design of scissors to the names they are called.
     B. Clincher: If you are left-handed, however, no matter the discrimination, you are in good company: eleven presidents of the United States have been left-handed!

In Conclusion

A public communication message is usually divided into four parts: introduction, central idea, body, and conclusion.

Attention material can be personal references, humorous illustrations, references to the occasion or setting, rhetorical questions, action questions, unusual or dramatic devices, quotations related to the theme, or statements of the theme.

Orienting material, which includes historical background, definition of terms, personal history and/or the speaker's tie to the topic, and the topic's importance to the listeners, gives an audience the background necessary to understand the basic material of the speech.

The body of a speech in the Western world normally takes one of six forms: spatial arrangement, time arrangement, topical arrangement, causal arrangement, comparison-contrast arrangement, or problem-solution arrangement. It must be remembered, however, that not all audiences will be European American and that cultures and languages differ in the very assumption of how information should be organized, of what is to be or not to be described and expressed. A speaker is wise to take into consideration the general culture of the audience and adopt the speech materials accordingly.

A summary restates the major points of the speech. Clinchers can include personal references, humorous stories, illustrations, rhetorical questions, unusual or dramatic devices, or quotations.

The basic approaches to overall speech organization are the partitioning, unfolding, and case methods. The structure of a speech is crucial to listener comprehension.

Learn by Doing

1. Your instructor asks for a volunteer and gives him or her a card with a drawing on it. Each member of the class has a sheet of paper and a pencil. The volunteer explains to the class how to draw the diagram exactly as it appears on the card. No one is allowed to ask any questions. When the volunteer has finished giving directions, the members of the class compare their drawings with the original. After the activity, the class discusses these questions:

   a. If the volunteer did not do so, would it have helped if he or she had given a general overview of what to draw before beginning to give directions? Discuss this question in relation to your reading about the purpose of an introduction.

   b. Did the instructions have a conclusion? How could a conclusion restating the major points have helped you?

   c. Did any words used in the directions confuse you, causing you to make an error or not be able to follow the instruction? What were they? How did they cause problems?

   d. Was the structure of the directions clear?

   e. Do you think a question-and-answer session following the instructions would have been valuable? Why or why not?

2. Do Activity 1 again using a different diagram. This time, a different volunteer builds on the positive things the first volunteer did and makes improvements based on the class discussion. This time the activity is followed by a question-and-answer session. Note how many people altered their drawings during the question-and-answer session. Reach some conclusions about the value of question-and-answer sessions.

3. A speaker informs the class about an unusual topic—something that the audience probably has no knowledge about. Sample topics are the language of bees, the Christmas customs of Puerto Rico, rafting on the Colorado River, or organic architecture. Be sure the speech has a clear structure and lasts no more than five minutes.

4. Select a subject about which you are expert, and present a speech to your classmates in such a way that when you finish, they too have an understanding of the topic. Clearly structure the speech, and take no more than six minutes to deliver it.

5. Prepare a speech of no more than five minutes informing the class about a controversial theory. Sample topics: The Loch Ness monster exists; Rational emotive therapy can alter behavior; Alcoholism is an inherited disease. Explain the theory and the various arguments concerning the theory. Do not include your own views in the presentation. Be sure the speech is clearly structured.

6. You are assigned to give a speech about your education (elementary, high school, college). Prepare an introduction for the presentation representing each of these introductory devices:
   a. Personal reference
   b. Humorous story
   c. Rhetorical question
   d. Unusual or dramatic device

Key Terms

introduction to a speech
rhetorical questions
action questions
orienting material
statement of the speech's central idea
body of a speech
spiral form of explanation
method of issue arrangement for the body of a speech
spatial method of issue arrangement
time method of issue arrangement
topical method of issue arrangement
causal method of issue arrangement
comparison method of issue organization
contrast method of issue arrangement

comparison-contrast method of issue arrangement
problem-solution method of issue arrangement
conclusion of a speech
summary of a speech
clincher to a speech
partitioning organizational speech structure
partitioning step
transitions
unfolding organizational speech structure
case method of organizational speech structure

14

Informative
Public Speaking

After reading this chapter, you should be able to

- **Define informative speaking**

- **Discuss the need for informative speaking in the information age**

- **List and explain the classifications of informative speeches**

- **Explain how to develop an informative speech**

- **List and explain the steps a successful informative speaker takes in developing a speech**

W̲e live in an era that has been dubbed "the information age," with knowledge "doubling at the rate of 100 percent every twenty months."[1] Oral briefings and informative presentations have become major vehicles for disseminating, managing, and dealing with information.

One societal commentator suggests that the need for people who can retrieve and explain information is going to increase greatly in the future.[2] Many employees are called on to do oral presentations, train others, and participate in briefings in order to give and get the information necessary to do their work.

Role of Informative Speaking

With the ever-expanding development of information, we need to have reliable sources for obtaining the information. The traditional sources, such as television, radio, and the newspapers, have been supplemented by the Internet and CD-ROMs. In addition to the usual sources, institutions depend on information resource people, professors, and guest speakers to provide information that employees and students need.

Businesses recognize the need for information. According to one corporate communication expert, "A factor vital to the health of any corporation is the constant exchange of accurate information. Although written forms of business communication remain important, the oral exchange of information occupies an increasingly important role in the functioning of today's companies."[3]

As the amount of information that we have to process expands, organizations no longer have time for lengthy written documents. As a result, oral briefings and informative presentations have become major vehicles for disseminating, managing, and dealing with information in most organizations. Thus, many employees are called on to present and listen to oral presentations, to be trained and instruct others, and to present and listen to briefings.

Informative speaking is not limited to the workplace. As a student, you have been or will be called upon to do informative oral presentations in classes. Educators, knowing that students learn best from personal involvement, have increased the number of public communication assignments in classes. For example, you may be asked to give an informative speech on the life of an author, a psychological theory, or the operational method of a computer system.

Informative speaking is also a function in governmental, community, and cultural venues. Clarifying a zoning change that has been enacted, sharing the design specifics for the new high school, or giving information about the upcoming seasonal offerings at the local community theatre are all examples of informative speaking.

Concept of Informative Speaking

Traditionally, **informative speaking** has been defined as discourse that imparts new information, secures understanding, or reinforces accumulated information. At present, however, controversies persist among communication theorists about this definition. For instance, some scholars argue that all speaking is persuasive in nature and that the traditional distinction between informative speaking and persuasive speaking is simply a matter of theoretical degree.

This textbook assumes that all communication contains elements of persuasion. After all, the audience in the traditional informative speaking format must be persuaded to accept information that the speaker presents. Indeed, even the act of using materials to gain attention is persuasive because the speaker is asking listeners to pay attention to the speaker rather than to any other competing stimuli. If there are distinguishing elements between an informative and a persuasive speech, they center on the structure of the message and the appeals used in the persuasive format. The importance of understanding this argument, for you, the student, is to be alert that an informative and a persuasive speech are not exactly the same as you have different communication goals. Some informative presentations are designed to create awareness of the latest information about a topic while others are more explanatory, being designed to enhance understanding of information that the speaker already knows. As you study this and the next chapter, you will be

In most organizations, oral briefings and informative presentations have become a major vehicle for disseminating, managing, and dealing with information.

introduced to the differences between them and to your responsibilities as a preparer, presenter, and listener of speeches.

Characteristics of Informative Speaking

As in any other type of speaking, the development of an informative presentation depends on audience analysis. Consideration must be given to the listeners' knowledge about the subject, the concepts they know that can function as a foundation to their gaining the information, and the extent to which definitions, understandable analogies, examples, and clarifiers need to be used. A speaker also must determine the appropriate language level, attention devices, and structure of the message that will best fit the group. Research suggests that the speaker, as the information source, may think his or her listeners lack necessary information whereas the listeners themselves may not feel the same way.[4] An astute speaker determines the real needs of the audience members by thorough audience analysis and uses that information to develop the speech.

In an informative presentation, a speaker always must keep the purpose of the presentation in mind. Thus, a clear statement of central idea is essential. Consider these two examples:

> To inform the audience of what the Heimlich maneuver is, how it was developed, and how this technique can prevent people from choking to death.

> At the conclusion of this speech, I want the members of the audience to know what the Heimlich maneuver is and what steps are necessary to do the maneuver.

In the examples, the subject is the same, but the goal is different. The first statement explains the maneuver and its value. The second explains the maneuver and then teaches the steps for performing it. Both, however, are stated in a manner that narrows the subject and indicates specifically what will be included in the speech. Thus, the statement of central idea serves as a fence around the territory to be covered in a presentation and indicates how to "corral" the information. If you do not set up boundaries, you may find yourself discussing many things but not achieving your desired outcome.

Classifications of Informative Speaking

There is no universally accepted classification of informative speeches. One classification system examines presentations about objects, processes, events, and concepts. At the same time, this system recognizes other specific types of informative speeches that can be identified by the setting in which they are used or by their uniqueness—for example, informative briefings, technical reports, lectures, question-and-answer sessions, and speeches of introduction.

Speeches about objects
describe a particular thing
in detail.

Speeches About Objects

Speeches about objects describe a particular thing in detail. The object may be a person, place, animal, structure, machine, or anything else that can be touched or seen. First the object is identified, and then details concerning some specific attribute of the object are discussed.

Here are some examples of statements of central idea for informative speeches about an object and each presentation's method of arrangement: "To inform the audience about the three purposes of the Office of Global Communication" (topical arrangement), "To inform the audience of the experiments being conducted to identify the language capabilities of dolphins by discussing two of the experiments" (topical arrangement).

Speeches About Processes

Speeches about processes instruct the audience about how something works, is made, or is done so that they can apply the skills learned.

COMMUNICATION BRIEFING

The Right Spot When Speaking

Maintain audience interest in you—and in your visual aids—with these moves:

◆ Stay on the audience's left. *Reason:* People read left to right—in most languages. So capitalize on that by placing yourself where you can point to the left margin of your visuals without blocking them.

◆ Limit your movement to an imaginary triangular area on the right side of the screen—the audience's left. *Benefits:* Use the triangle's center as your rest position. From there, you can easily move to the screen or a point closest to the audience. And you'll never block the screen.

◆ Stand at a 45-degree angle to the back wall in your rest position. *Reason:* The audience will see this as a nonthreatening stance, and it will make it easier to point to the screen.

Source: Angela Kay Larson and Tom Mucciolo of MediaNet, Inc., a presentation skills firm based in New York City, writing in *Currents,* Council for the Advancement and Support of Education, 11 Dupont Circle, Washington, DC 20036. © Communication Briefings, www.briefings.com, 1101 King St., Alexandria, VA 22314. Used with permission.

Speeches about processes
instruct the audience about
how something works.

The purpose may be to gain understanding of the process or to be able to do something. This technique is used in training workers to operate a piece of equipment or in explaining a manufacturing process. Statements of central idea for informative speeches about processes include "To inform listeners of the step-by-step process of creating a PowerPoint slide" (time sequence arrangement) and "To demonstrate the process used to fill out the income tax short form" (sequential order).

Speeches about processes often lend themselves to development according to a chronological method of organization. In this method, the speaker describes the first step of the process, then the second, and so on.

Speeches About Events

Speeches about events inform the audience about something that has already happened, is happening, or is expected to happen. This type of presentation tends to work well in a chronological, comparison-contrast, or spatial arrangement. Here are statements of central idea for informative speeches about events: "To inform the audience of the spread of the AIDS virus in the United States through a statistical examination of the years 1980 to 1999" (time sequence arrangement) and "To inform the audience of the similarities and differences in the American and Russian Revolutions based on their economic causes" (comparison-contrast arrangement).

Speeches about events inform the audience about something that is happening or is expected to happen.

Speeches About Concepts

Speeches about concepts examine theories, beliefs, ideas, philosophies, or schools of thought. Much of the formal educational process deals with speeches about concepts.[5] Concept topics include explanations and investigations of business theories, philosophical movements, psychological concepts, and political theories.

Because many of the ideas relating to concepts are abstract, the speaker must be sure to use precise language, define terms, give historical background, avoid undefined slang and jargon, and use clarifying support materials such as audio, visual, and audiovisual aids. Examples of statements of central ideas for informative speeches about concepts are "To inform the audience about the theory that abused children grow up to be child abusers through an examination of three classic research studies" (cause-to-effect arrangement) and "To inform the audience that musical theater composers Alan Jay Lerner and Frederick Loewe used the theme of the search for a perfect time, perfect place, and perfect love story as the basis for their musicals" (topical arrangement).

Informative Briefings

Business, organizational, and technical communicators often gain up-to-date knowledge in their fields as a result of informative briefings. The fundamental objective of an **informative briefing** is to present information to a specialized audience, followed by the exchange of data, ideas, and questions among participants.[6] Organizations, for example, use this technique to explain new or existing organizational policies, procedures, and issues. For example, a sales manager of an automobile agency may inform her staff about the new models, or a dean of students may explain a college's academic policies to a group of entering freshmen.

As with any other speech, preparation for an informative briefing requires careful analysis of the audience to determine what background and definitions will be needed to ensure audience comprehension. If the audience has extensive knowledge, the speaker does not have to cover background material in as much depth as he or she would for uninformed listeners. For example, the automobile agency sales manager does not have to go into detail with her experienced staff about the auto manufacturer and the history of the agency. On the other hand, she would give this background for a meeting of new salespersons.

Team Briefings

In a college course or at work, you may find yourself acting as part of a team asked to complete a project. The group may be asked to present a **team briefing** on its findings or recommendations. Team briefings are, for example, used in technology organizations in which design projects or project proposals must be pitched to potential clients or funding agents. In a classroom, teams often are formed to do research or perform an experiment. The team is then asked to present a final report to the class.

Like individual briefings, team briefings must be well planned and rehearsed. The rehearsal stage could be complicated because the group has to work with each individual's time schedule. In order to use group time efficiently, each member should first prepare and rehearse her or his individual briefing. Then, when the team meets, the entire presentation should be blended together. This will entail deciding the speaking order for the presentations, the format for the program, and whether each speaker will have a question-and-answer session or whether there will be an inquiry session for the entire group.

Since a common communication format for team briefs is to have one individual serve as the facilitator, that person will have to be selected, appointed, or elected. The facilitator's role is to introduce the presentation and the speakers, make transitions between each of the speakers, process the question-and-answer session, and then provide a final summary.

One-on-One Briefings

You may find yourself giving a **one-on-one briefing** to a person or a small group of individuals. Intelligence and financial analysts, for example, often are called upon to brief key decision makers in an informal, across-the-table presentation. Though the presentational climate is informal, the briefing still must follow the basic rules of effective public speaking regarding audience adaptation, clear structuring, and dynamic presentation.

In some instances, the briefer may be told that he or she is to make an opening statement about the topic and then present a short statement of the findings, which will be followed by a question-and-answer session. In this setting follow the basic rules of the question-and-answer session as discussed later in this chapter to ensure that you stay "on message."

Technical Reports

The **technical report** is a concise, clear statement describing a process, explaining a technique, or discussing new elements to either people within a business or industry or people outside it. In spite of the fact that the technical report is a major communicative activity in corporate America, recent college and university graduates do not seem prepared to give such presentations.

In presenting a technical report, the speaker must know who will be in the audience. If the report is to be given to nontechnical people, all technical words must be defined, and analogies familiar to the audience should be included to clarify the ideas presented. This does not mean a speaker has to water down the material so that it is invalidated. Instead, the speaker should be sure to define words, give examples, and present ideas in a variety of ways to make sure that the audience understands the concepts being set forth.

If your presentation includes technical drawings or a number of statistics, use handouts so that everyone can examine the materials closely. If the group is small, consider allowing audience members to ask questions as you develop your ideas so that they have the opportunity for immediate clarification.

One of the major factors in the development of a technical report is determining the structure. When you structure a technical report that involves a recommendation, start with a statement of the proposal unless there is a compelling reason not to do so. (You may want to hold the recommendation until the end if you know the audience will be hostile to the proposal or if you want to lead up to the recommendation by giving total background before revealing your solution or recommendation.) After you have proposed the idea, explain how you arrived at the conclusions or recommendations. Make sure you know exactly how much time has been allotted for your presentation, and plan the speech so that you can stay within that time limit.[7]

> A speaker should know exactly how much time has been allotted for the presentation and plan to stay within that time limit.

Professional Papers

Another type of speaking that you may encounter is the professional paper. A **professional paper** is a speech in which the presenter briefs his or her audience on some findings that relate to the listeners' area of interest. For example, you may be selected to go to a national conference of your college honor society where you would present the results of a research project you did for a class to your peers. Many college campuses also stage undergraduate research conferences for students to present their work. Communication graduate students and college professors may often present their research findings at the National Communication Association's yearly convention.

Some presenters choose to read through their papers while the listeners follow along, but, as you can imagine, that is not a very engaging presentational style. The most effective presenters will speak extemporaneously and,

following the presentation, hand out copies for listeners to read at another time. This method avoids having the listeners glancing at your paper while you are speaking.

Another format for presenting research at these conferences is the poster session. In a **poster session** you prepare a poster or series of charts that visually highlights your research or idea. The posters are usually set up in a room with other charts, displays, and speakers. You will be asked to explain your work and answer questions posed by those who have come to look at your work. For example, if you have ever been to or participated in a school science fair or a product sales show, you've been part of a poster session. Most of the presentations will be made one-on-one or to a very small group. Since the audience will be circulating, you must be aware of the time factor and the setting. In general, you will want to prepare a one- or two-minute briefing and be prepared to answer questions when they are asked.

Here are some guidelines for preparing for a poster session:

◆ Divide the contents of the poster into appropriate sections: title, author, affiliation, project abstract, method of determining the idea or recommendation, data, results, and conclusions.

◆ Use a font larger than 16 point for headings or major information.

◆ Avoid fonts that are difficult to read (for example, avoid using letters with serifs (flags) such as *APPLE CHANCERY*, as they are difficult to read, or erratic fonts such as MISTRAL).

◆ You don't have much space, so be concise.

◆ If appropriate, use graphs, pictures, and tables to display your results or conclusions.

◆ Generally, use a neutral-colored poster board unless you are trying for a specific result (e.g., a student at a college science fair who was making a presentation on explosives intentionally selected a red poster board to visually highlight her work).

◆ If possible, have copies of your entire paper available for people to take with them.

Lectures

Probably the most familiar type of informative speaking is the **lecture,** the formal presentation of material to facilitate learning. Lectures are an integral part of academic life, serving as the main vehicle for presenting information in many subject fields. Lectures also are used in other settings, including invited speakers for lunch or dinnertime seminars in corporate headquarters and public lectures by distinguished authorities in museum, arts, religious, or public settings.

A good lecture should be carefully adapted to the intended audience so that the speaker does not make inaccurate assumptions about the listeners' level of knowledge and vocabulary. An effective lecture should be clearly organized, with transitions that allow listeners to stay on track and anticipate what is coming next. The speaker should use supporting details to elaborate each of the points made. Like all other informative speaking, lectures often tend to be top-heavy with explanations and consequently risk boring the listeners. A variety of supporting materials (stories, statistics, analogies) enhance explanatory details and draw in listeners more readily. Humor is also a way of getting and holding attention, as is the use of interaction that involves listeners by asking them questions, probing for information, and inviting inquiries during the presentation instead of waiting until the question-and-answer session. Supplemental aids (charts, handouts,

Lectures are an integral part of academic life, serving as the main vehicle for presenting information in many subject fields.

PowerPoint graphics) can facilitate listeners' understanding and keep them interested in the presentation.

The timing of a lecture is another key to success. Lecturers should be aware of the time frame available. The audience expects a lecturer to stay within the framework of the assigned time (such as a class period).

We have all sat through good and bad class lectures—lectures that held your attention and from which you learned and those that put you to sleep. If you are ever asked to present a lecture, ask yourself what the good lecturers did. Then duplicate that style.

Question-and-Answer Sessions

The **question-and-answer session** that follows many speeches is a type of informative speech in itself. It is an ad-libbed, on-the-spot set of unrehearsed answers that measures a speaker's knowledge, alerts a speaker to areas in a speech that were unclear or needed more development, and gives listeners a chance to probe for ideas.

In some instances, a question-and-answer session allows receivers to point out weaknesses in a speaker's arguments or present alternative views. These occur more frequently after persuasive speeches than after informative presentations. If confronted by a hostile questioner, the speaker has to determine

In a question-and-answer session, the speaker has to determine whether to deal with the issue or remind the prober of the purpose of the speech.

COMMUNICATION BRIEFING

Presenting: Use Nonverbals to Aid Q&A

Here are some nonverbal signals you can use to make sure your question-and-answer session adds power to your presentation:

◆ **Raise your** hand when you ask for questions. *Reasons:* This signals that you're in charge. And it tells people how they should seek your attention.

◆ **Break eye** contact with questioners when they finish asking a question and shift your gaze to another person. *Reason:* This signals the audience that your answer will interest—and is intended for—everyone.

◆ **Look at** questioners again as you answer, and tie your answer to your presentation. *Reason:* You can check the reaction to your answer and reinforce the main points of your presentation.

◆ **Fix your** eyes on questioners as you finish your answer only if you want to continue that discussion. If you don't want another question or have said all you want to on that subject, look at someone else as you close.

◆ **Raise your** hand for the next question. Your gesture signals that you consider the question answered and invites others to speak up.

Source: Kevin Daley, DEO, Communispond, 300 Park Ave., New York, NY 10020. © Communication Briefings, www.briefings.com, 1101 King St., Alexandria, VA 22314. Used with permission.

whether to deal with the issue or remind the prober that the purpose of this part of the speech is to ask questions, not give a counterspeech or engage in debate.

When you enter into a question-and-answer session, set the ground rules. Ask the program chairperson about the process to be used and the time limit. Tell him or her of any restrictions you wish to place on this segment of the speech and inform the audience of the rules. Some speakers like to call on participants; others prefer that the chairperson entertain the questions. Some presenters want all questions written out beforehand so they can select the questions they will answer.

The most difficult part of many question-and-answer sessions is to get the first question asked. Once this hurdle is overcome, questions usually flow readily. To overcome the first-question trauma, you may want to have someone in the audience prepared in advance to ask a question. Another technique is to ask a question yourself. This can be accomplished by stating, "I've often been asked my views concerning . . ." and then answering by indicating your views.

Here are some additional suggestions for conducting a question-and-answer session:

> *Before you answer a question, restate it so that everyone hears the inquiry.* If the question is complicated, simplify it in the restatement.

> *Speak to the entire audience rather than only to the questioner.*

> *Be patient.* If you have to repeat material you have already covered, do so briefly.

> *If a question goes on and on, prompt the questioner to summarize the question.*

> *Keep your answers short.* Restate the question, give your response, clarify any vocabulary necessary, give an example if appropriate, and then stop. Following the response, some speakers ask the questioner whether the answer was satisfactory.

> *Back up your responses with examples, statistics, and quotations.*

> *If a question is overly complicated or of interest only to the asker, suggest a discussion with the questioner after the speech or via correspondence.*

> *If a question is irrelevant, indicate that it is interesting or thought provoking but does not seem appropriate to the presentation.* Do not get sidetracked from the purpose of the speech or pulled into a private debate with a questioner.

> *If you do not know an answer, say so.* You can offer to find out the answer and report back later.

> *Limit the discussion to one question per person, and avoid getting caught in a dialogue with one person.* Others who have questions will become frustrated, and those who do not will get bored.

Pause Before You Answer

During Q&As, always pause before every answer. The extra two seconds give you a chance to refine your response. Also, if you get an unexpected zinger, the audience will already be used to your pattern of pausing; you won't telegraph the fact that you really *are* grappling with a difficult issue and actually need more time.

Be willing to be corrected or at least to recognize another's viewpoint. Thank a person for clarification or acknowledge that more than one point of view is possible (e.g., "That's an interesting idea," or "The idea can be viewed that way"). You may win a battle of words by putting down or insulting a questioner, but you will usually lose the respect of the listeners in the process. It is futile to get involved in a battle of words with a heckler or a person with a preconceived attitude or bias.

Know when to end a session. Do not wait until interest has waned or people begin leaving. You can lose the positive effect of a speech by having an overly long question-and-answer session.

Speeches of Introduction

The purpose of a **speech of introduction** is to identify the person who will be speaking to the audience and give any other information that may spark listeners' interest in the speaker or the topic. Too often, speeches of introduction are ineffective because the presenter has not carefully prepared remarks appropriate to listeners' needs. When you introduce a speaker, clearly identify who the speaker is by the name, title, and the identification he or she wants used. You can talk about where the speaker is from as well as his or her accomplishments and when they were achieved. Establish the credibility of a speaker by highlighting aspects of his or her credentials and background that indicate knowledge or expertise in the subject being discussed.

Remember that listeners have come to hear the speaker, not the person making the introduction, so a speech of introduction should be short and to the point. Here are some suggestions for a speech of introduction:

Get the information you need from a speaker as far in advance as possible so that you have time to work on the presentation.

Be sure you can pronounce a speaker's name as he or she wants it pronounced.

If possible, ask what background information a speaker wishes to have highlighted.

Do not overpraise a speaker. Indicating that he or she is the best speaker the audience will ever hear, for example, gives the presenter an almost impossible goal.

Avoid using statements such as "It is an honor and a privilege" or "This speaker needs no introduction." These are overused and often sound insincere.

Set the proper tone for the speech. If, for example, you know that the speech is going to be humorous, try to fit humor into the introduction.

Developing the Informative Speech

Every informative speaker has a challenge: to get the audience to understand and retain the information presented. And this is a significant challenge: the typical listener remembers only about 10 percent of an oral presentation three days after hearing it.[8]

Learning theory specialists stress that the basis for retention and understanding is the establishment of relationships (associations and connections) with physical or mental activities. We can learn through repetition—hearing ideas over and over again. We can learn too through experiencing—doing a task to see what it is.[9] We are more likely to remember things that have relevance to us. We remember information we are exposed to that will somehow make life easier or teach us something we did not know before or for which we will be rewarded. In other words, we remember when we see a reason to do so. We also remember when something makes sense to us—when the order in which the material is presented makes the idea(s) easy to understand or the examples and other developing materials make the idea clear.

When you plan an informative speech, consider using supplementary aids to help your listeners remember your message. Understanding how people learn can be of assistance in determining the approach to take. It is estimated that we learn 1 percent through taste, 1.5 percent through touch, 3.5 percent through smell, 11 percent through hearing, and an astonishing 83 percent through sight.[10] Thus, your best chance of getting people to remember is to have them hear and see the content of your presentation. Such devices as slides, charts, illustrations, pictures, and models help to reinforce and clarify what you say. Keep in mind these pointers when developing an informative speech:[11]

Order your ideas clearly. Select a method of organization that helps your audience follow the step-by-step development of the speech.

Use a time sequence method of delivery if a speech lends itself to a first-second-third progression or is date oriented (years or ages). Sample subject: Explaining an experiment that requires a specific progression.

Use a spatial method of organization if a speech has some geographical basis that lends itself to an east-west, top-bottom, or inside-out organization. Sample subject: Tracing the voyage of Christopher Columbus from Spain to the New World.

Use a topical method of delivery if a broad subject area can be divided into specific parts. Sample subject: Describing the life cycle, characteristics, and dangers of the killer bee.

Use comparison-contrast when a topic centers on illustrating similarities and differences. Sample subject: Comparing Nebraska's unicameral (one-house) legislature with the two-house legislative system of other states.

Use the familiar to explain the new. An excellent clarifying technique is to use an analogy that compares something unfamiliar to the familiar. For example, you can explain how an AM radio signal travels by comparing it to the way a bow and arrow works. The arrow goes as far as the bow projects it. If something gets in its way, the arrow stops moving. Similarly, an AM signal goes as far as its thrusting signal power allows it to move unless something gets in its way and stops it.

Use vivid illustrations. Descriptions, stories, comparisons, contrasts, and verbal pictures add to the possibility of gaining and holding the audience's attention. An audience member who can visualize something is likely to remember it.

Avoid being too technical. If you have ever tried to follow directions for using a computer program when you knew nothing about computer language, you know the difficulty of understanding materials geared for an expert, not a layperson. If your subject is technical, evaluate the vocabulary level of audience members and choose terms that are unlikely to confuse or clarify the technical terms you do use. The purpose of a speech is not to impress an audience with your vast vocabulary; it is to accomplish an informative objective. Select words that will help, rather than hinder, your task.

Personalize your message. Audiences are more attracted to real, human-element examples than fictional or hypothetical examples. If at all possible, use illustrations that allow your audience to identify with the plight of a victim, understand the joy of what happened to someone who mastered the process you are teaching, or learn how someone's life was altered by the historical event you are sharing.

Do not speak down to your audience, but do not overestimate audience knowledge. There is no clear guideline for evaluating an audience's knowledge level other than to learn as much as you can about what the audience knows, specifically and generally. It is senseless to draw an analogy to the familiar if it is not familiar. For example, professors who grew up in the 1960s, when John Kennedy was president, often forget that most college students today were not even born during JFK's presidency. Drawing comparisons between today and that time may be beyond the conceptual level of students in a freshman-level class.

Use as much clarification and detail as you think necessary to ensure listener understanding. If anything, err on the side of overexplanation. Most audience members appreciate a speaker who makes an effort to communicate clearly.

When Analyzing Data

- ◆ **Use the** data correctly. Don't try to adjust the information to produce the results you were hoping for. Don't give prominence to favorable evidence and lose negative data in the shuffle.
- ◆ **Make solid** and reliable deductions. Don't try to read big news into commonplace results.
- ◆ **Keep the** results as simple as possible. Don't let any analysis develop into a mass of statistics that few can understand. Remember that the goal is to produce summary information out of raw bulk details.
- ◆ **Be sure** the sample size is big enough to project comfortably. If you want to use the results based on a small sample, flag them with a warning that they are based on an insufficient sample.
- ◆ **Don't equate** opinions with facts. Point out the difference in the data presented. When looking for cause-and-effect relationships, be thorough. Misreading the relationships can severely damage the validity of an analysis.

Source: Adapted from *Marketing for Nonmarketers,* by Houston G. Elan and Norton Paley, AMACOM, 135 West 50th St., New York, NY 10020. © Communication Briefings, www.briefings.com, 1101 King St., Alexandria, VA 22314. Used with permission.

Informative Process in Action

It is helpful to study the process of speech preparation by investigating the steps in developing a speech. Table 14.1 outlines a speech that follows the principles you've learned for developing informative speeches.

Table 14.1	Information Process in Action

Statement of Central Idea: To inform the audience about the importance of maintaining a routine of regular physical exercise by examining what "exercise" really is, what a healthy amount of exercise is, and what the benefits of regular exercise are.

Attention material using reference to an authority with statistics	**I. Introduction** A. *Attention Material:* According to a recent study by the Centers for Disease Control and Prevention, more than 60 percent of American adults do not get the recommended amount of physical exercise.
Orienting material demonstrating how topic affects listeners	B. *Orienting Material:* Furthermore, studies show that approximately 25 percent of American adults do not engage in any physical activity, causing risk to their physical and mental well-being.
Topic of speech	**II. Central Idea** A. The key to achieving a healthy lifestyle for your body is sustaining an appropriate exercise program of moderate daily activity that recognizes the importance of physical activity and exercise.
Partitioning steps (preview of issues)	B. Let us explore the topic of exercise by looking at what "exercise" really is, what a healthy amount of exercise is, and what the effects of regular exercise are.
Statement of the first issue	**III. Body** A. Identify what exercise is and how it differs from physical activity.

Discussion of distinction between exercise and physical activity with information and examples	1. To many, it appears that physical activity and exercise are one and the same, but in actuality they are not.
	  a. Physical activity is any type of body movement in which muscles are contracted and metabolism is increased.
	  b. Exercise is a subcategory of physical activity geared toward achieving and maintaining fitness.
	2. Types and levels of physical activity and exercise
	  a. Physical activity includes everything from washing the dishes to running a marathon.
	  b. Exercise is a structured program of regular physical exercise in which fitness is attained.

Transition	(Understanding what exercise really is is crucial in promoting the development of one's own exercise routine.)
Statement of second issue	B. The amount and type of exercise that are sufficient to achieve and sustain physical fitness

Discussion of the amount and type of exercise that are needed	1. A well-rounded exercise program should include the enhancement of three key fitness areas.
	    a. Resistance (strength) training includes exercising the major muscle groups of legs, trunk, arms, chest, and shoulders.
	    b. Aerobic activity involves elevating the heart rate by brisk walking or its equivalent.

Discussion of specific exercise needs	2. Stretching and flexibility exercises require a basic stretching routine of all major muscle groups. To reap the benefits of exercise, the heart rate must be elevated and breathing increased.
Explanation and elaboration of needs	a. Today's emphasis is not on bursts of high-intensity exercise but is on longer, more frequent sessions of moderate activity. b. Moderate activity exudes between 50 and 60 percent of maximum capacity and includes accelerated heart rate, light sweating, and deep breathing. c. In addition, between 700 and 2,000 calories should be burned weekly.
Transition	(Now that we have defined *exercise* and discussed what is needed to obtain fitness, it is important to recognize the vast benefits of physical exercise.)

Identification of the benefits of exercise	C. Identify the effects of regular physical exercise on the body and mind.
	    1. Exercising lowers the chances of developing physical illnesses that could potentially be fatal.
	        a. Reduces risk of heart disease by increasing the oxygen supply to the heart
	        b. Lowers the risk of high blood pressure
	        c. Reduces risk of osteoporosis and increases bone density
	        d. Prevents disease such as arthritis, cancer, and diabetes
	        e. In addition, exercise controls weight and reduces the amount of body fat.
	    2. Exercising also has significant benefits to the mind.
	        a. Lowers risk of depression, anxiety, and tension
	        b. Increases energy levels and elevates mood
	        c. Improves the quality and duration of sleep and the ease of falling asleep
	        d. Improves self-image

IV. Conclusion

Reiteration of main points	A. Summary
	    1. It is helpful to recognize what exercise is and how it differs from physical activity.
	    2. It is important to recognize the amount and type of exercise that are sufficient to achieve and sustain physical fitness.
	    3. There are numerous benefits of regular physical exercise to the body and mind.

Restatement of theme to emphasize importance of exercising	B. Developing a consistent schedule of challenging physical exercise is important for the body and mind.

In Conclusion

Informative speaking imparts new information, secures understanding, or reinforces accumulated information. Types of informative speaking include presentations about objects, processes, events, and concepts. Informative speeches, when classified by setting or uniqueness, include informative briefings, team briefings, one-on-one briefings, technical reports, lectures, professional papers, poster sessions, question-and-answer sessions, and speeches of introduction. The challenge for an informative speaker is to get the audience to understand and retain the information presented. To develop an informative speech, order ideas clearly, use the familiar to explain the new, use vivid illustrations, avoid being too technical, personalize the message, and do not speak down to the audience.

Learn by Doing

1. In class, your instructor will match you with a partner. With the assistance of your partner, select a topic for a speech based on audience analysis (your class), setting (your classroom), and purpose (an informative speech of three to five minutes). After both of you have selected your topics, meet with another duo. Each person will present a short informative speech indicating what topic you have selected and why this subject suits you, the audience, the setting, and the purpose. The speech should have an introduction, statement of central idea, body, and conclusion.

2. Bring to class an object or piece of machinery (e.g., a camera, food processor, or microscope) that you feel members of your class cannot operate or that you have a different approach to operating. Be prepared to teach someone else how to use the equipment. In class, you are placed in a group with four of your classmates. Decide the order in which you will present the material. After this is done, the first speaker gives a two- to four-minute presentation on how the object works. Then the second speaker demonstrates how the object operates. Your success as a speaker is based on whether the person following you can operate the object.

3. Before a series of speeches is to be given by class members, your instructor assigns you the name of a person in your class whom you will later be introducing. Interview that person, and collect all the information you will need to prepare a speech of introduction (topic of the speech, some background information on the speaker, why the subject was chosen, the qualifications of the speaker to present a speech on this topic, and so on). On the day of your partner's speech, introduce her or him.

4. You are going to give a "what-if" speech. On each of three 3-by-5-inch notecards, indicate something that could go wrong immediately before, during, or after a speech (e.g., you drop your speech outline in a puddle of water just outside your classroom building, an audience member challenges your statistics during the question-and-answer period). The instructor collects the cards, shuffles them, and hands them out one by one. When you get your card, immediately give a presentation that includes a restatement of the occurrence and a

contingency plan for dealing with the situation. (This assignment may take place when a short amount of time remains at the end of any class period.)

5. All students present one-minute speeches in which they state something that bothers them in everyday life. They should tell what the peeve is, why it is a peeve, and what they would like to see done about it, if anything.

6. Use your vocational preference, or an occupation you may be interested in, to investigate some phase of the career and present an informative speech about it. The presentation must include the use of a supplementary aid. *Sample speech topics:* a future audiologist explains the differences among several brands of hearing aids; an accounting major illustrates how a balance sheet is prepared; an aspiring musician demonstrates how music is scored.

Key Terms

informative speaking
speeches about objects
speeches about processes
speeches about events
speeches about concepts
informative briefing
team briefings

one-on-one briefings
technical report
lecture
professional papers
poster session
question-and-answer session
speech of introduction

15

Persuasive
Public Speaking

After reading this chapter, you should be able to

- Explain how people are influenced by persuasive messages

- Explain how people are influenced by coercive messages

- Illustrate how speaker credibility, logical arguments, and psychological appeals can affect listeners

- List and explain how speaker credibility, logical arguments, and psychological appeals can be used in the preparation of a persuasive speech

- Analyze a persuasive speech to ascertain its potential effectiveness based on logical arguments and psychological appeals

- Prepare a persuasive speech using credibility, logical arguments, and psychological appeals

Every day you, as a listener, are bombarded with messages intended to convince you to take some action, accept some belief, or change some point of view. And almost every day you, knowingly or unknowingly, attempt to bring about these changes as a speaker. You have been participating in the act of persuasion.

Persuasion is the process of influencing attitudes and behaviors. The bottom line in being a successful persuader is to find the means to answer the question "What's in it for you?" The bottom line for the person who is the recipient of a persuasive message is "Is what the speaker proposing in my best interests?" Most people will take actions or adopt beliefs if they can figure out how they can benefit from them—monetarily, socially, physically, philosophically, spiritually.

Persuasive Speaking

A **persuasive speech** is intended to influence the opinion or behavior of an audience. Its materials are derived from problems about which people hold differing beliefs and opinions, such as controversial matters that call for decisions or action. The persuasive speaker tells listeners what they ought to believe or do.

A persuasive speech or presentation may have as its end goal either conviction or actuation.

In a **speech of conviction,** the speaker is attempting to convince the listener to believe as the speaker does. Topics that fall into this category could include "There is no real danger of nuclear fallout from atomic plants" or "XYZ Corporation has developed a clear set of equal opportunity guidelines."

A **speech of actuation** should move the members of the audience to take the desired action that the speaker has proposed—for example, buy the product, sign the petition, go on strike, or adopt the plan presented.

Process of Persuasion

Much is known about what motivates people to act. Unfortunately, in spite of our knowledge, there are flaws in the system, or no candidate for office would ever lose, no charity would fail to reach its goal, and no product would ever go unsold. This chapter presents the theories that explain the process of persuasion and how—if you are developing a persuasive speech to individuals from the European American culture—you might use those theories to accomplish your goal.

The basic process of persuasion centers on making a claim, then backing up the claim with reasons and emotional appeals that will lead listeners to accept the claim. To do this, you must analyze the audience and develop arguments that will appeal to that particular group.

Several concepts, including the theories of field-related, group, and individual standards, help explain what to do.

The **theory of field-related standards** establishes that not all people reach conclusions in the same way and thus may react differently to the same evidence or

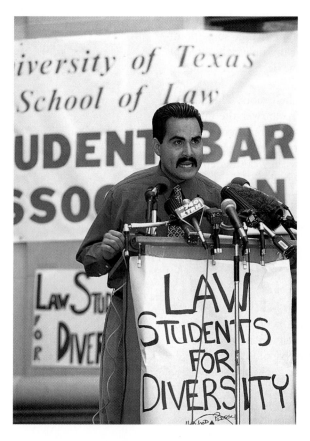

In a speech of conviction, the speaker is attempting to persuade the listener to believe as the speaker does.

psychological material. Therefore, in establishing your arguments, you may want to include as many appeals as you can to cover the various thought processes of members of your audience. For example, in establishing arguments for why your listeners should vote for a particular candidate, you can list several of the candidate's positions rather than just one.

Group norm standards—the thinking of a particular group—may be used as a guide for developing your arguments. For example, if you are speaking to a group of union members, you can assume that on labor-related issues, they will have views that favor the union rather than management. Thus, if you are going to propose a change in the plant operation, show how it will be good for the union and its members.

Individual norm standards—the thinking of those people within a group who have influence over the group's members—also might be included in the criteria for persuasion. If these influential members can be persuaded to go along with a proposal, then the entire group will probably go along. But who are the leaders? If your presentation deals with your need to use this appeal, find out. For example, if the elected president of the city council agrees, the rest of the group who elected her may follow her lead.

To be persuasive, you also should develop your materials so that listeners believe that the solution, plan of action, or cure that you are presenting is reasonable. Two methods you might consider using are critical thinking and comparative-advantage reasoning.

To apply **critical thinking,** you establish criteria and then match the solutions with the criteria. For example, if you are proposing a plan of action for solving a club's financial problems, you can set criteria that include not having to raise members' dues and planning an activity that can raise money quickly, without extensive planning. You may then propose that the club stage a lottery and sell raffle tickets, establishing how the lottery fulfills the established criteria.

In contrast, when you use **comparative-advantage reasoning,** you begin by stating possible solutions. Then you demonstrate how the proposal is the most *workable* (can solve the problem), *desirable* (does not cause any greater problems), and *practical* (that it can be put into operation). Establish why your particular proposal has fewer disadvantages than any other. To achieve the goal of raising funds, for example, use the comparative-advantage reasoning process. Propose that a lottery be set up, explain why this is a workable plan by referring to other organizations that have used the process, and present statistics on the amount of money these groups have raised. Then indicate that a lottery is desirable because it will not cost members a great deal of money and the risk that the organization will lose money is not great. Next, show that the proposal is practical because the tickets can be ready by the next week and the finance committee has worked out a plan for distributing the tickets and handling the money. Finally, you explain why this system is better than raising dues.

The persuasive process can be presented in the form of a **motivated sequence.**[1] This plan uses a psychological process by which a listener is taken through a five-step persuasive message:

1. Attention—cutting through competing stimuli to get the listener to attend to your message.
2. Need—identifying a problem and showing how it relates to the listener.
3. Satisfaction—proposing a plan of action that will meet the need that has been identified.
4. Visualization—describing the beneficial results if the plan is implemented (or the detriments if it is not undertaken).
5. Action—challenging the listener to do as requested.

Accomplishing your persuasive goal is a complex challenge. One of the reasons that politicians fail to persuade the voters to elect them, advertisers fail to get their products sold, and organizations don't convince the public that they are good community citizens interested in the welfare of communities rather than just in profits is that they fail to understand and use persuasive techniques effectively.

Persuasive Strategies

Persuasive strategies are currently under scrutiny. The aftermath of the September 11, 2001, terrorist attacks has led to increasingly worse news. Americans have been bombarded with news of nonspecified security warnings, reports on the dangers of drugs and food products, financial upheaval, West Nile virus, drought, SARS, bioterrorism, sniper attacks, and obesity warnings. Because we receive so much bad news, it's become too easy to obsess about it, ignore it, or deny it. Consequently, persuaders are hard-pressed to know how best to get our attention and how to target appeals that will lead to a desired response.

Researchers, therefore, have renewed their efforts to ascertain how people are influenced.[2] Their research centers on such factors as personal involvement, saving face, the Elaboration Likelihood Model, values clarification, and the sense of social support.

It is understood that a person who has something at stake will be most likely to be persuaded by a message that solves a personal problem, gives advice on how to fulfill a personal desire or need, or allows him or her to "save face," fulfill an ego need, or feel better about himself or herself. If the message has little or no relevance to the listener, he or she is not going to focus much energy on processing it.

The **Elaboration Likelihood Model** has been used to explain how listeners process persuasive messages.[3] The model maintains that if the issue being discussed is one that the listener has encountered before, is interested and involved in, and enjoys thinking about, he or she is more likely to engage in processing the persuader's arguments. This attention does not necessarily mean that the listener will be persuaded, but at least it gives the speaker the attention of the receiver and, if the arguments are emotionally and logically sound, there is a chance for persuasive results.

The listener also may be persuaded because the message resonates with his or her values. Such factors as personal responsibility, good health, ability to communicate your feelings, faith in God, job fulfillment, and financial security have been ranked highly as very important U.S. American values.[4] Messages that tap into these values probably have the greatest effect in eliciting change because listeners can connect with the appeals.

To be persuaded, listeners may also rely on a strong sense of social support. The long-term staying power of messages depends not only on how the appeal resonates with the individual but also on the degree to which the individual perceives that he or she has the support of others, thus enabling the person to feel that "we are all in it together."

Six principles that persuaders should consider when attempting to get people to respond have been identified:[5]

◆ *The principle of liking.* People like those who like them, so find a common bond and offer genuine praise and support.

◆ *The principle of reciprocity.* People will repay in kind, so a good strategy is to give what it is you want to receive.

◆ *The principle of social proof.* People will follow the lead of those similar to them, so use the examples of peers to reinforce your effort.

◆ *The principle of consistency.* People will make their commitments if they're based on active, voluntary choices.

◆ *The principle of authority.* People defer to experts, so don't assume that your expertise is self-evident. Let people know your background and experience.

◆ *The principle of scarcity.* People want more of what they can only have less of, so limiting opportunities to act will have a mobilizing effect.

Persuasiveness is a complex matter that requires careful understanding of your listeners and adaptation of your message to them.

Role of Influence in Persuasion

The purpose of the persuasive process is to influence. The persuasive process, for instance, occurs when salespersons from different data processing corporations present speeches in an attempt to sell their systems to the purchasing agents of clients. Based on the presentations, the purchasing agents may be influenced to buy products from salesperson A, say, because of her arguments stressing her product's lower cost and ease of operation.

Normally, the intended audience has a choice of what actions to take. However, a particular form of influencing takes place when listeners are not given a voluntary choice. For example, a speaker at a union meeting says, "Either we accept the proposal as presented, or we go on strike." You might not want to choose either of those options, yet if the vote is set up with only those two, you must choose. This attempt to change behavior relies on force and is known as coercion.

Another form of influence includes various psychological appeals aimed at emotionally stirring audience members to action. Such factors as fear, hatred, social pressure, and shock can be used to dull listeners' senses to the point where they perform acts they may not consider if they were to step outside the emotion of the situation and objectively evaluate potential consequences. German dictator Adolf Hitler before and during World War II used emotional appeals focused on building a "master race" that included killing all those he deemed inferior: Jews, gypsies, homosexuals, and his political enemies. Many people responded to these appeals and participated in the destruction of other human beings as a result. Most of them later came to regret their actions.

Persuasion is accomplished by repeated exposure to messages. Seldom does one persuasive message result in any major change of belief on the part of the receiver. As a result, massive amounts of time and money are spent waging persuasive campaigns by systematically and repeatedly exposing listeners to a message with the objective of enhancing retention of its basic persuasive thesis. This is the reason that the electorate is inundated with speeches and other publicity about candidates during political campaigns.

Do not assume that all persuasion is negative or immoral. Persuasive communication strategies are essentially amoral—neither good nor bad. It is only the ways in which the strategies are used, and to what ends, that give communication a dimension of morality. By knowing this, and being equipped to recognize manipulative and coercive methods, you may be able to protect yourself from being taken advantage of.

Psychological appeals are aimed at emotionally stirring audience members.

Components of Persuasive Message

The classical Greek philosopher-rhetorician Aristotle first described Western culture's system of persuasion as based on the use of three components: speaker credibility (**ethos**), logical arguments (**logos**), and psychological appeals (**pathos**).[6] Although Aristotle wrote more than two thousand years ago, his theory still characterizes what are considered to be the components of the development of an effective persuasive message.

Speaker Credibility

The reputation, prestige, and authority of a speaker as perceived by the listeners all contribute to **speaker credibility.** In most persuasive speaking situations, listeners' acceptance of the speaker as a credible person will make it easier for the speaker to gain acceptance of the message. If you, as a listener, dislike, mistrust, or question the honesty of a person, she or he will have difficulty persuading you to accept her or his beliefs.

Credibility, or lack of it, may exist even before you speak. A person's prior reputation with an audience can help or hinder his or her persuasive ability. For example, if

Dr. David Ho, the AIDS researcher who is a former *Time Magazine* Man of the Year, addressed an audience about the need for increased funding for research on communicable diseases, he would have initial credibility, and his views would have an excellent chance of being accepted. But an unknown or negatively perceived speaker would have a much more difficult persuasive task.

A speaker who has a reputation for being knowledgeable about the topic, is a celebrity, or has a positive personal reputation with the audience comes with credibility. One of your authors has been invited for many years to speak on a communication topic to a group of cosmetologists at their annual conference. Each time, audience members say how much they are looking forward to the presentation. He has no problem persuading them to take the actions he proposes during the speech.

Credibility is sometimes characterized as being composed of the three Cs: competence, charisma, and character.

Ethos
(speaker credibility)

Competence *Competence* refers to the wisdom, authority, and knowledge a speaker demonstrates. For an audience to feel that you are competent in the subject area being discussed, you must demonstrate that you know what you are talking about. This ordinarily means including up-to-date information and showing your familiarity with the material. A salesperson who has just made a presentation to a group of executives can ruin a potential sale, for example, if he displays a lack of knowledge about the product during the question-and-answer session.

Another way to establish credibility is to build on someone else's knowledge. For example, if you aren't an expert on a topic, you can strengthen your position by quoting recognized experts in the field. In this way, listeners draw the conclusion that if experts agree with your stand, then your contention must have merit.

If possible, associate yourself with the topic. Suppose you are proposing a plan of action concerning safety regulations. If you have had experience on a construction crew and refer to this experience, your listeners will more readily accept your point that the construction industry needs more stringent safety regulations than if you did not have the personal experience. To establish the tie, use statements such as "It has been my experience that . . ." and "I have observed that . . ."

Charisma   Another characteristic of credibility is **charisma.** Words synonymous with charisma are *appealing, concerned, enthusiastic,* and *sincere.* People with charisma are compelling and have the ability to entice others. A charismatic speaker grabs and holds attention. John F. Kennedy and Martin Luther King Jr. were masters of getting masses of people to follow them because of their ability to mesmerize audiences. Oprah Winfrey has that effect on television viewers. Some religious speakers are capable of getting their followers to give vast amounts of money because of the power of the listeners' unwavering belief in the messenger.

Character   Your reputation, honesty, and sensitivity all aid in developing your *character.* People who are assumed to be of high character based on the experiences they have had, the positions they hold, or the comments others have made about them engender trust.

Positively perceived speakers often find audiences receptive to their messages. Speakers who are negatively perceived need to try to alter their listeners' beliefs by emphasizing qualities about themselves that the audience may respond to positively. For example, a former convict, speaking to an audience about the need for altering prison procedures, started his presentation with these comments:

> I am a paroled convict. Knowing this, some of you may immediately say to yourself, "Why should I listen to anything that an ex-jailbird has to say?" It is because I was in prison, and because I know what prison can do to a person, and because I know what negative influences jail can have on a person, that I want to speak to you tonight.[7]

People with charisma are compelling and have the ability to entice others.

Sometimes speakers can change the attitudes of audience members who disagree with their views by directly taking on the issues of disagreement and asking listeners to give them a fair chance to be heard. For example, a Democratic candidate speaking before a predominantly Republican audience stated:

> I realize that I am a Democrat and you are Republicans. I also realize that we are both after the same thing: a city in which we can live without fear for our lives, a city in which the services such as trash and snow removal are efficient, and a city in which taxes are held in check. You, the Republicans, and I, the Democrat, do have common goals. I'd appreciate your considering how I propose to help all of us achieve our joint objectives.

Not only are competence, charisma, and character important, but developing a logically constructed speech is critical to persuading listeners.

Logical Arguments

If it doesn't make sense, the audience is less likely to be swayed. To a European American audience, "making sense" generally means that statements and the

What is perceived to be the most persuasive form of supporting material—evidence—includes testimony from experts, statistics, and specific instances.

supporting evidence add up to a reasonable match. Listeners, especially when they are dealing with information about which they know little or are skeptical, look for logical connections in the messages they are receiving.

Be aware that the use of logic, though important in the Western world, is not universal. If you are speaking to an audience primarily composed of Arabic or Hispanic members, for example, know that their basic method of conveying information is through the use of stories that illustrate the point being made but do not necessarily state the conclusion to be reached. Therefore, in planning a presentation, be sure to recognize that cultural adjustments may be necessary. If you are to speak outside of your norm culture, you may need to consult an expert in the persuasive cultural patterns of the listeners.

Structure of Logical Arguments   There is no one best way to get everyone to agree with you. However, these qualities of a presentation will provide a good foundation:

◆ A clear statement of the purpose of the speech so that the audience knows what you are proposing

◆ Reasons that you believe or want the audience to believe in the proposal

◆ Reference to credible sources if you are not a recognized expert on the topic

◆ Arguments that follow some structure for ease of understanding and that develop the main point(s)

◆ A statement of the desired outcome, stand, or action

◆ Absence of false facts, partial information, and biased stands

To lead your listeners to your conclusion, it often is wise to choose an argumentative structure that fits your analysis of what approach is most likely to sway the listeners. The most familiar Western logical structures are the inductive or deductive formats.

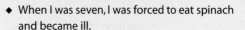

Logical Reasoning

by Jeanine Walters Miranda

Deductive Process

Spinach makes me sick.
Spinach souffle is tonight's main dish.
Conclusion: By deductive process, I will get sick if I eat tonight's main dish.

Inductive Process

If we are to draw our conclusion about spinach, the evidence might be …

◆ When I was five, I ate spinach and became sick.

◆ When I was seven, I was forced to eat spinach and became ill.

◆ When I was nine, creamed spinach made me ill.

◆ When I was thirteen, spinach salad also made me ill.

◆ At twenty, I tried spinach again and became ill.

Conclusion by inductive process: Spinach makes me ill.

Source: From *Secrets of Successful Speakers,* by Lily Walters, McGraw-Hill, 1993. This material is reproduced by permission of The McGraw-Hill Companies.

An **inductive argument** is based on probability: what conclusion is expected or believed from the evidence. The more specific instances you can draw on in an inductive argument, the more probable your conclusion will be. Inductive argument can take one of two forms: the generalization conclusion or the hypothesis conclusion.

In a **generalization conclusion,** a number of specific instances are examined. From these, you attempt to predict some future occurrence or explain a whole category of instances. Underlying this is the assumption that what holds true for specific instances will hold true for all instances in a given category.

Speaking at the National Conference on Corporate Community Involvement, a representative of the American Association of Retired Persons described the "graying" of America by developing this inductive argument:

> Because of better medical care, nutrition, and activity, more people are gliding into their 60s and beyond in good physical shape. . . . Mental ability does not diminish merely because of age, according to researchers. In fact, it may improve. . . . The economic health of today's older generation has improved to the point where advertisers are already targeting the "maturity" market.

Using evidence to support each of the claims, he drew an inductive conclusion:

> The upshot of all this change in better physical, psychological, and economic well-being is that we are looking at a new breed of older person vastly different from former negative stereotypes.[8]

In the **hypothesis conclusion,** a hypothesis is used to explain all of the evidence. For the argument to have substance, however, the hypothesis must provide the best explanation for that evidence. Reviewing a number of cases in which terrorists had been tried and convicted throughout the world, a U.S. Department of State ambassador-at-large for counterterrorism argued that "the rule of law is working against terrorists, and fewer terrorists are being released without trial" in an effort to convince his audience that "we, the people of the world's democracies, will ultimately prevail over those who would through terror take from us the fruits of two centuries of political progress."[9]

The other logical structure is the **deductive argument,** which is based on logical necessity. If you accept the premise of the deductive argument—the proposition that is the basis of the argument—then you must also accept its conclusion.

Major premise → conclusion

One type of deductive argument is the **categorical syllogism,** an argument that contains premises and a conclusion. For instance, in a speech with the central idea of persuading the listeners of what the symptoms are that lead doctors to diagnose chronic fatigue syndrome, a speaker might state:

(Premise) A proven sign of chronic fatigue syndrome is an off-balance immune system.

(Premise) A proven sign of chronic fatigue syndrome is a positive diagnosis for human herpes virus 6.

(Premise) A proven sign of chronic fatigue syndrome is a positive diagnosis for human B-cell lymphotropic virus.

(Conclusion) Therefore, a person diagnosed with an off-balance immune system, human herpes virus 6, and human B-cell lymphotropic virus can be diagnosed as having chronic fatigue syndrome.

A syllogism also may take the form of an **enthymeme,** in which a premise usually is not directly stated. The omitted premise is shared by the communicators and therefore does not need to be verbalized. For example, while speaking to those attending a conference on writing assessment, a speaker concluded, "If we can teach our children, from all backgrounds, to write with joy, originality, clarity and control, then I don't think we have much else to worry about," a conclusion based on the premise shared by his listeners that children should be taught effective writing skills.[10]

Another type of deductive argument is the **disjunctive argument**—an either-or argument in which true alternatives must be established. Talking about the United States and the collapse of the Soviet empire, a speaker pointed out that the United States faced an either-or choice: "To follow our fears and turn inward, ignoring the opportunities presented by the collapse of the Soviet Empire, or to answer the summons of history and lead toward a better future for all."[11]

Still another form of deductive argument is the **conditional argument,** which sets up an if-then proposition. In this form, there are two conditions, with one necessarily following from the other. The chief executive officer of a major accounting firm proposed that the federal government adopt a new accrual accounting system so that the public and Congress could monitor the federal budget. He argued that "if citizens were to demand the financial information to which they are clearly entitled, incentives would be created for sound fiscal management—and, perhaps, for more enlightened political leadership. We could then expect to see better-informed decision making—less fiscal recklessness—and a reduction in the risks caused by the misallocation of capital."[12]

Persuasive Evidence   The persuasive speaker in Western cultures not only must structure the persuasive argument but also must support these contentions. What is perceived to be the most persuasive form of supporting material—**evidence**—includes testimony from experts, statistics, and specific instances. Solid data to support your contentions will lend substance to your argument. For example, a speaker who attempts to persuade listeners that the U.S. Food and Drug Administration (FDA) needs more funds to hire inspectors can cite specific instances from the agency's files. Actual cases are on record of potatoes contaminated with insecticide and ginger ale containing mold that were sold to consumers. The speaker also can cite statistics indicating that only five hundred FDA inspectors are available to monitor sixty thousand food-processing plants in the United States.

Two Words That Persuade

Two key words will make you more persuasive. The words: *if* and *then.*

Whether you're trying to sell a car or an idea, the message that works is "If you will take this action, then you'll get this reward."

The next time you're planning to try to persuade someone, think about using these two words to get what you want.

Source: Adapted from *Overcoming Resistance,* by Jerald M. Jellison, Simon & Schuster, 1230 Avenue of the Americas, New York, NY 10020.

Reasoning Fallacies   Speakers sometimes, intentionally or not, present material that contains flaws in reasoning. As a speaker, you should be aware that you might fall prey to using these fallacies. Wise listeners are aware that they must protect themselves from accepting fallacious reasoning. Types of reasoning fallacies include hasty generalizations, faulty analogical reasoning, faulty causal reasoning, ignoring the issue, ad hominem argument, ad populum argument, and ad ignorantium argument.

A speaker who makes a **hasty generalization** reaches an unwarranted general conclusion from an insufficient number of instances. For example, a speaker may argue that gun control legislation is necessary and demonstrate this argument with some instances of freeway shootings in Los Angeles, thus limiting the scope and numbers of possible cases in support of the need for gun control.

Another reasoning fallacy is **faulty analogical reasoning.** No analogy is ever totally "pure" because no two cases are ever identical. Speakers use faulty analogies when they assume that the shared elements will continue indefinitely or that all the aspects relevant to the case under consideration are similar. The speaker who, for example, argues that the AIDS crisis is analogous to the bubonic plague that ravaged medieval Europe overlooks the medical advances that make the AIDS crisis very different (although no less serious).

Faulty causal reasoning occurs when a speaker claims, without qualification, that something caused something else. If the claim overstates the case, faulty reasoning has been used. Rather than saying "a common cause" or "a probable cause," the speaker would argue, for example, that the increase in the number of illegal immigrants into the United States is the direct result of liberal welfare laws.

An entire set of reasoning fallacies can result from **ignoring the issue.** In ignoring the issue, the speaker uses irrelevant arguments to obscure the real issue. The **ad hominem argument**—attacks on the personal character of a source—is one example. For instance, some attacks on the proposal for health system reform in the mid-1990s centered on the fact that Hillary Rodham Clinton was one of its codevelopers. Since she wasn't elected by the people, it was argued, she shouldn't have been on the proposal commission, and therefore the bill should not be passed.

The **ad populum argument**—an appeal to people's prejudices and passions rather than a focus on the issue at hand—is another characteristic of ignoring the issue. For example, in 1994, when O. J. Simpson was initially arrested in connection with his ex-wife's murder, many sports fans insisted he was innocent. Their devotion to him as a football hero overshadowed any implicating evidence.

Yet another example of the fallacy of ignoring the issue is the **ad ignorantium argument**—an attempt to prove that a statement is true because it cannot be disproved. For example, supporters of pit bull terriers argue that they are not dangerous pets because dog bite statistics show pit bulls to rank ninth in number of bites, after poodles and cocker spaniels. Of course, the number of pit bulls in this country is minuscule in comparison with the number of more popular breeds such as poodles and cocker spaniels.

[handwritten margin note: — mistakes lack of evidence for evidence to contrary]

Organizing the Persuasive Speech

In Chapter 13 the concepts of organizing a speech were presented. Communication theorists have developed specific organizational techniques that they feel work best with persuasive speaking. Those formats deal with specific types of persuasive speeches.[13]

Power Speaking

People are persuaded by more than facts and statistics. They are also moved by stories.

Source: Frederick Gilbert, *Power Speaking: How Ordinary People Can Make Extraordinary Presentations* (Redwood City, CA: Frederick Gilbert Associates, 1994), p. 20.

Proposition of Fact   A **proposition of fact** states the existence of something in the past, present, or future by giving the reasons that the proposition should be believed.

Here is the format for a proposition of fact (e.g., the Cleveland Browns will win the Super Bowl this year):

I.   Introduction

II. Statement of Central Idea

III. Body
   A. Reason 1
   B. Reason 2

IV. Conclusion
   Speech outline for proposition of fact:

I.   Quotation by Cleveland Browns' head coach regarding winning

II. The Cleveland Browns will win the Super Bowl this year.

III. There are three reasons for my prediction:
   A. The coach
      1. Proven record
      2. The team's improvement since he became head coach
   B. The offense
      1. Quarterback
      2. Receivers
      3. Running game
   C. The defense
      1. Record last year
      2. Additional players

IV. Quotation from *Sporting News* predicting a Browns victory

This method also can be used by applying the cause-effect, problem-solution organizational scheme. In addition, the pro-con and elimination methods may be used. In the **pro-con method of organization,** the speaker not only tells why he or she believes in the proposition but also shares his or her reasons for opposing other proposals. This method is valuable when the speaker knows that the audience is opposed to the proposal.

The **elimination method of organization** centers on the speaker's listing all of the possible solutions and then going through each one and eliminating each by telling the reasons that it won't work. This method is used when "the audience is hostile to the speaker."[14] At best, the speaker can eliminate a solution that is the best of the worst. Sometimes the speaker can do no more than to find agreement on what is *not* the case. An example would be a proposal for how to eliminate impurities from the Cuyahoga River in Ohio. It is agreed that there is no way to eliminate all the impurities because of the boat traffic and industrial sites along the bank; however, there are ways to eliminate many of the impurities. All of the proposals will cause financial problems and inconveniences. With the elimination method, the speaker would attempt to show which would cause the least disturbance at the lowest cost.

Proposition of Value   "A **proposition of value** offers an evaluation of a person, place, or thing."[15] In the proposition of value, there is always a value term (e.g., *good, bad, beneficial, harmful, right, wrong*).[16] There are two methods that can be used for proving a proposition of value: survey of reasons and criteria-satisfaction.

The **survey of reasons method** is a form of the topical arrangement. In this method the speaker lists all of the reasons for the belief. Here is an outline for this method:

I.   Introduction

II. Statement of Central Idea

III. Body
    A. Reason 1
    B. Reason 2
    C. Reason 3
    (additional reasons)

IV. Conclusion

The **criteria-satisfaction method** follows the deductive reasoning pattern in which the speaker identifies the value term. Then the speaker establishes a general definition or set of criteria for that term. Finally, the speaker shows how the subject under discussion fits the definition (or criteria).[17] For example, assume the topic of the speech is "Washington, D.C., is a wonderful place to live." The value term is *wonderful*. The term *wonderful* means invigorating, stimulating, educational, and remarkable. The statement, the speaker contends, is true because of the educational, cultural, employment, and recreational opportunities available.

This would be the outline for the first section of the speech:

I.   Where are the Kennedy Center, George Washington University, the Congress of the United States, and Falls Creek located?

II. Washington, D.C., our nation's capital, is a wonderful place to live.

III. There are four reasons that this is true: the educational, cultural, employment, and recreational opportunities available in Washington, D.C.
    A. Educational opportunities
        1. Fine private and suburban schools
        2. Several of the top fifty colleges and universities
        3. More four-year colleges and universities than in any other equivalent-sized city
    B. Cultural opportunities
        1. National galleries and museums
        2. Close proximity to other cities with cultural venues
        3. The Kennedy Center/Eisenhower Theatre/college and university offerings
    C. Employment opportunities
        1. U.S. government agencies
        2. Nonprofit agencies
        3. Legal and lobbying firms
        4. Internship opportunities
    D. Recreational opportunities
        1. Professional athletic teams in area
        2. Collegiate athletic teams in area
        3. Park services

Proposition of Policy The **proposition of policy** is the most commonly used persuasive method and the easiest to prove. It centers on stating that something should or should not be done. It is most commonly developed by the **motivated sequence,** which is a psychological approach that asks what motivates audiences to change their minds. This sequence illustrates not only that arguments and evidence can be persuasive but that speech structure can also be.[18]

The motivated sequence consists of five steps: attention, need, satisfaction, visualization, and action.[19] The *attention* step, which parallels the introduction of any speech, is intended to arouse the audience's attention. The *need* step establishes that a need for a change or a problem exists by presenting a problem in detail. The *satisfaction* step centers on satisfying the need by presenting a solution to the problem by using examples, statistics, or the testimony of authorities. The *visualization* step creates a picture in the minds of audience members of what life would be like with this solution in place and enhances the appeal of the solution by showing its workability by painting a picture of how balance can be restored through the solution. The *action* step appeals to the audience to do something to help bring about a solution to the problem by indicating how the solution can be put into effect.

As in other organizational methods, each of the steps is organized by one of the internal methods of organization (see Chapter 13).

Here is an outline for a speech developed by the motivated sequence:

◆ Have you ever wondered why you voted for a particular candidate for office? The reason may well be that she used a process called the motivated sequence to convince you. *(attention step)*

◆ It is of great value for you, as a student of persuasive speech, to know how to persuade others, especially members of your class and your instructor, who will be grading your persuasive speeches. *(need step)*

◆ Your grades on speeches will go up, and your classmates will be impressed. *(satisfaction step)*

◆ See yourself coming up to the front of your communication class, feeling comfortable because you are prepared to give an effective speech, getting a good grade on the presentation. Feels good, doesn't it? *(visualization step)*

◆ You now know what to do the next time you prepare a persuasive speech. It's up to you to follow this format to be a successful speaker. *(action step)*

This format can be organized into the four-step process that has been discussed and modeled throughout this book. For example, the *attention step* is parallel to the *introduction*. The *need step* is the *statement of central idea*. The *satisfaction* and *visualization steps* are the *body* of the speech, and the *action step* is the *conclusion*.

Psychological Appeals

The third component of the persuasive message, **psychological appeals,** enlists listeners' emotions as motivation for accepting your arguments. Just as you must select your arguments and enhance your credibility on the basis of what you know about your listeners, so must you select psychological appeals on the basis of what you think will stir their emotions. The purpose of incorporating some emotional appeals in your speech is to keep your listeners involved as you spell out your persuasive plan, even though they may not distinguish the emotional from the rational in your presentation.

People tend to react according to whether their needs are being met. Several theories attempt to illustrate what needs people have, and persuasive speakers can use these as a guide to organizing emotional appeals to trigger need satisfaction.

One approach to understanding need satisfaction is the **Hierarchy of Human Needs** (Figure 15.1) devised by psychologist Abraham Maslow. Based on this view, a speaker must determine the level of need of a particular group of listeners and then select appeals aimed at that level.[20] Although Maslow's theory is hierarchical, these

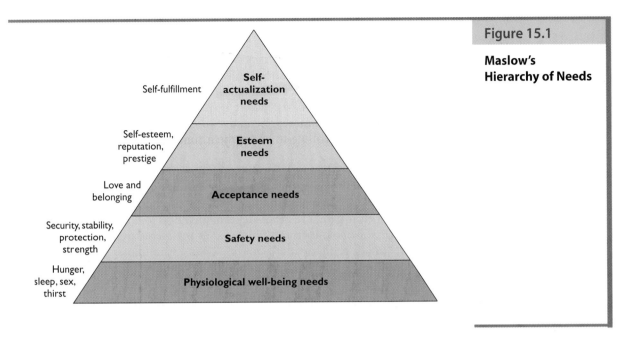

Figure 15.1

Maslow's Hierarchy of Needs

need levels can all function at the same time. Therefore, a speaker need not deal with only one level at a time.

Maslow suggested that all human beings have five levels of needs. The first, most basic level is *physiological needs:* hunger, sleep, sex, and thirst. Normally all of these needs must be satisfied before a person can be motivated by appeals to higher levels of need. For example, the U.S. Agency for International Development offers aid to developing nations in order to persuade them, through appeals to physiological needs, that the democratic form of government offers housing and food and medical care.

Persuasive speakers who use the survival-of-the-species aspect of this theory are appealing to such factors as the physical and psychological safety of an audience member and his or her family.

The second level of human need, *safety needs,* encompasses security, stability, protection, and strength. Organizations that have had to reduce their workforces and lay off employees have found it persuasive to offer seminars on job searches, résumé preparation, and other career skills. Employees concerned about the security of their positions are quick to sign up for such offerings.

The third level consists of *acceptance needs:* the needs for love and belonging. College and university alumni representatives use this need in speeches intended to motivate alumni to contribute to endowment funds for the sake of being part of their alma mater.

Esteem needs form the fourth level that Maslow identified. Human needs at this level involve both self-esteem (desire for achievement and mastery) and esteem by others (desire for reputation and prestige). Athletic coaches use appeals to esteem in their pep talks before games to persuade team members to do their best.

Finally, Maslow identified the fifth level in the hierarchy as *self-actualization needs:* desire for self-fulfillment or achieving one's greatest potential as the ultimate level for which people reach. Recruiters attempt to influence potential military personnel with slogans such as "Be the best that you can be."

The **Ethnographic Theory of Human Drives,** another attempt to explain human needs, indicates that survival of the species, pleasure seeking, security, and territoriality must be satisfied. (See Figure 15.2.)

Persuasive speakers using the *survival-of-the-species* aspect of this theory try to appeal to such factors as the physical and psychological safety of the person and his or her family. Speakers talking to teens, for example, regarding the need for safe sex, use AIDS and sexually transmitted diseases as life-threatening illustrations.

Pleasure seeking centers on the idea that people spend a great deal of their lives seeking happiness. For example, in discussing why a city income tax is needed, a municipal spokesperson might indicate that the funds would be going toward refurbishing the city's recreation facilities.

Security here means keeping things on an even keel, in balance, under control. In analyzing an audience, look for instances of fears about change, insecurity, and uncertainty. For example, during the sniper attacks in Washington, D.C., in 2002, area police, when speaking to the television audience, gave information on how to feel more secure by avoiding open spaces and keeping alert to one's surroundings while also ensuring the listeners that a full-scale investigation was under way.

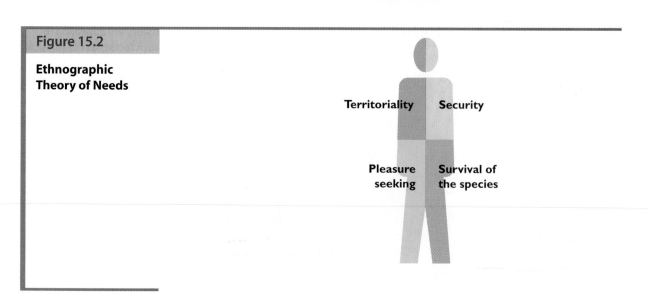

Figure 15.2

Ethnographic Theory of Needs

Territoriality   Security

Pleasure seeking   Survival of the species

We all mark off and defend territory. This is *territoriality*. To activate this appeal, you must ascertain that audience members are concerned about what is already theirs, or you can instill the belief that something will belong to listeners.

Human needs connect with human values and principles that are held in esteem. European American values shape the way persuaders appeal to listeners and establish themes. These values include improvement, practicality, freedom, responsibility, equality, and individuality.[21]

Appeals to Motivate Listeners

Besides using your listeners' need level(s), you can also build into your speech a variety of motivational appeals. Being aware of the most typical appeals can assist you in determining which ones will be appropriate for your listeners:[22]

◆ *Adventure.* The speaker stresses listeners' desire to explore new worlds, see exciting places, take part in unusual experiences, or participate in different events. A speaker in the travel industry might motivate potential travelers by describing a tour to an unusual place.

◆ *Companionship.* This taps our desire to be with other people. A speaker might make this appeal in an attempt to recruit membership for a senior citizens' group.

◆ *Deference.* Showing respect for the wiser, more experienced, higher authority can be a successful strategy. Political candidates who are running for office often emphasize their record of civil service to remind voters that they are the most experienced candidate. Local candidates may also try to get respected community leaders and national office holders to endorse their candidacy and appear with them at rallies and in television commercials.

◆ *Fear.* This appeal is used to raise apprehension in a listener. A representative of the food industry speaking to individuals who have had heart attacks or bypass surgery could use this approach to discuss no-salt and low-cholesterol products. Although the fear appeal can be powerful, there can be a danger in its use. Listeners can become frightened if they perceive the situation as hopeless.[23] Long-time smokers, for example, may assume that because of their long history of smoking, there is no sense in quitting because the damage has already been done.

◆ *Gender.* Appealing to women's rights, stressing the need for understanding the male point of view, or criticizing sexual harassment can all be useful in persuasion.

◆ *Guilt.* People may feel guilty for both doing and not doing something. Clergy turn to this appeal in some sermons.

◆ *Health.* A strong appeal is the need for good health. The complexity and the increasing cost of the health care system serve as strong reminders that individuals need to do all they can to preserve their good health. We're persuaded to slim down and stay fit. A healthy you is the bottom line for motivational appeals in advertising, public service messages, and speeches stressing the need to change the nation's physical and psychological health care system.

◆ *Hero worship.* Audiences are often motivated by hero worship. Referring to a famous person who feels as you do about a subject may be the motivating factor to convince an audience to take a desired action. AIDS fundraisers often refer to the work of Elizabeth Taylor and Magic Johnson on behalf of their cause. Following the September 11, 2001, terrorist activities, speakers who needed a hero image referred to the firefighters and police who lost their lives while trying to save others.

Psychological appeals enlist listeners' emotions as motivation for accepting arguments.

♦ *Humor.* People enjoy laughing and are often taken off guard when they are enjoying themselves. "Humor can engage, entice, coax and persuade."[24] Humor has also been credited with relieving pain, helping aid in the cure of illnesses, and helping in the development of positive mental health.

♦ *Independence.* The appeal to independence ("do your own thing"; "be your own person") is strongly entrenched in European American values. Since the United States was built on a spirit of independence, European Americans like to be able to express their individuality and have a sense of control over their own decisions.

♦ *Loyalty.* Appeals to commitment—to respect the nation, friends and family, or organizations—motivate. The "Buy American" campaign is an example of an appeal to national pride.

♦ *Revulsion.* An appeal to disgust can be effective. A speaker, for instance, can illustrate the effects of water pollution on Chesapeake Bay by showing listeners some water samples in an attempt to motivate them to support legislation to clean up the bay. As with fear, revulsion can arouse such strong feelings that listeners may tune out the message. For example, antivivisectionists risk overwhelming their listeners with photographs of maimed laboratory animals.

♦ *Safety.* Concern for safety ranks high in human needs, as the Maslow hierarchy indicates. Safety—airline safety, school safety, vehicle safety, home safety—is a major issue. Advocates for gun control appeal to parents to ensure the safety of their children by disallowing the sale of firearms. Those desiring controls over the sale of natural herbs as medicine stress the issue of safety because there is no national testing of the ingredients in the products.

♦ *Savings.* Fluctuations of the world economy continue to convince people that they need to save money—both in terms of bargain purchasing power and for retirement. Speakers representing financial institutions appeal to individuals to invest their money. Retail institutions convince us that the "price is right."

♦ *Sex.* Sex sells. Sex is a major motivational appeal in the global marketplace and almost inescapable in advertising messages. A controversial but effective advertising campaign for Candies, a new perfume product, showed a woman in front of an open medicine cabinet filled with condoms. The attention drawn to the explicit sexual nature of the advertisement caused sales to skyrocket.

♦ *Shame.* Related to guilt is the response of shame. "Properly calibrated, shame falls somewhere between mild embarrassment and cruel humiliation."[25] A teen-developed advertising campaign centered on a series of nationally placed billboards showing a smoking teenager with the message "Loserville. Population—YOU." A speaking series in which teens went to schools and spoke on how it was "out" rather than "in" to smoke was also developed based on the theme.

♦ *Sympathy.* By showing photographs or films of starving children or impoverished elderly people, a speaker can compel listeners to give time, money, or other resources. A sympathetic bond, often coupled with guilt, is created with those less fortunate.

Structure of the Persuasive Message

The structure of a persuasive speech should allow the listener to reach the behavioral or mental change the speaker desires. The most common method of developing a persuasive message is to use the problem-solution arrangement. The speaker identifies what is wrong and then presents the cure or recommendation for its cure.

A structure of the body of a speech that develops inductively would be

III. Body
   A. Identify the situation (what is wrong).
   B. Identify the problem (what has to be changed).
   C. List the possible solutions to the problem.
   D. Evaluate the solutions for workability, desirability, practicality.
      1. Workability—Can the proposed solutions solve the problem?
      2. Desirability—Will the proposed solutions cause bigger problems?
      3. Practicality—Can the proposed solutions be put into effect?
   E. Recommendation of the solution that is most workable, desirable, and practical.

When you are listing the possible solutions (section C), two strategies are available: placing the strongest argument first so that it will have the greatest impact on listeners at the outset or placing the strongest argument last to ensure that listeners retain it.

Another consideration is whether to develop section D by simply listing the reasons that the solution to be proposed is workable, desirable, and practical or to investigate both sides of each solution, including the one to be recommended. One potential problem in developing both sides of an argument is that you may raise issues and ideas that your listeners have not previously considered.

An alternative to the illustrated pattern would be to place what is section E at the start of the body, thus beginning by revealing the solution and then explaining why this solution was selected. In general, if you feel that the audience is or may be

Achieve Change with 2-6-2

To persuade a group to accept change, consider the "2-6-2" principle: Two out of ten will oppose it, six out of ten will wait and see, and two out of ten will embrace it. Strategy:
♦ Don't try to sway the opposing 20 percent.
♦ Give the pro 20 percent all they need to make the change work. *Reason:* They'll quickly produce results. And when the fence-sitting 60 percent see that, they'll join the pro team.

Source: Go-Go Tools: Five Essential Activities for Leading Small Groups, by Shigehiro Nakamura, Productivity Press, P.O. Box 13390, Portland, OR 97213. © Communication Briefings, www.briefings.com, 1101 King St., Suite 110, Alexandria, VA 22314. Used with permission.

on your side, state your arguments first and allow your listeners to believe along with you for the rest of your presentation (a deductive mode of reasoning). But if you perceive your audience to be hostile to your position, build the background and then present the arguments when you think that your listeners are ready for them (a more inductive line of reasoning).

Persuasive Process in Action

Psychological appeals, coupled with a speaker's credibility and well-reasoned and well-supported arguments, provide a sound, honest approach to influencing others to change their beliefs or actions. The sample speech outlined in Table 15.1 illustrates the interaction of these persuasive elements.

Table 15.1	The Persuasive Process in Action
Statement of Central Idea: To persuade the audience that the United States should be prepared for biological terrorism by explaining that the United States is not adequately prepared for a biological attack on the American public, why the country must strengthen national preparedness, and what can be done to solve the problem.	

Attention material to involve listeners	I. Introduction
	    A. Attention Material:
	        According to Stephen Schwartz, publisher of the *Bulletin of the Atomic Scientists,* since September 11, the hands of the Doomsday Clock have moved closer to midnight. These hands have not moved in three years, and they symbolize an immense threat to the human population. If bioterrorism is unleashed on our nation, the Doomsday Clock surely will strike midnight.

Orienting material to relate topic to listeners and to establish speaker credibility Topic of speech	B. Orienting Material: Approximately thirty years ago, 143 countries signed the Biological and Toxic Weapons Convention (BTWC), certifying that they would not produce or store agents of bioterrorism. Yet none of these countries were held accountable to this agreement, and numerous countries continue to develop biological weapons.
Central point of speech	II. Central Idea: In the wake of the terrorist events of September 11, we must acknowledge the gravity of the threat of biological terrorism in the United States and prepare ourselves.

Statement of the first issue: the problem
 	
Ways in which the problem is defined
	III. Body
	    A. The United States is not adequately prepared for a biological attack on the American public.
	        1. Doctors and hospitals are not prepared to deal with bioterrorist attacks on civilians.
	            a. The limited resources and supplies currently available are not sufficient to treat thousands of infected people.
	            b. Public health agencies would not be able to devote the necessary time or labor resources to investigate an actual or suspected outbreak.

　　　c. Medical personnel lack the training or experience to treat diseases like anthrax or smallpox. Therefore, it is nearly impossible to predict how an outbreak would be handled.

　2. There is not enough communication among federal, state, and local health agencies and the public.

　　　a. Currently, it is not possible for large numbers of medical professionals to communicate vital information among themselves in a manner similar to that of members of law enforcement agencies.

　　　b. There is currently no clear and efficient plan of action to alert and instruct the public in the event of an attack, leaving people vulnerable to such an attack.

　　　c. There is not enough communication between the physicians who would see the first signs of such an attack and the biomedical researchers developing treatments, a situation that could potentially make the number of casualties higher.

Definition of biological warfare

　3. Definition of biological warfare

　　　a. Biological weapons are any infectious agent, such as a virus or bacterium, that is used to intentionally cause bodily harm to others.

　　　b. Biological weapons are immensely destructive.

　　　c. In a conducive environment, they can multiply and self-perpetuate.

　　　d. Thus, weapons of bioterrorism naturally mutate, making even the smallest amount of an agent deadly.

Elaboration demonstrating inconsistency between government preparedness and the problem

　4. Does the American government realize the gravity of the threat of bioterrorism?

　　　a. If so, why hasn't it allotted more money for increasing American preparedness?

　　　b. If so, why haven't hospital and medical personnel been better equipped to handle a biological terrorist attack?

Transition

　　(As it is becoming apparent, the American public must become better organized and more aware of the risk and reality of bioterrorism.)

Statement of second issue: why it's a problem
Refutation of justifications

B. Why we must strengthen national preparedness and response to bioterrorism in order to preserve our future safety

　1. The Appropriations Bill of 2002 gave the Department of Health and Human Services ten times the previous funding to combat bioterrorism, but this is hardly enough.

　　　a. We must understand that public health agencies are taking on great responsibilities without the necessary resources.

　　　b. In the past, public health agencies have been among the first to lose funding in state budgets.

　　　c. Current funding is only a "down payment" on the true cost needed to confront biological weaponry.

　2. The Commission on National Security determined that bioweapons pose one of the most severe threats to national security in the United States.

　　　a. In the future, biotechnological advancements will only increase.

　　　b. Bioweapons will surely become more powerful, less expensive, and more accessible.

　　　c. Engineering, computing, and capital markets will further biological capability immensely.

| Transition | (As it is clear that we need to be more aware of the potential for biological terrorism to endanger the livelihood of the American public, we must increase our attentiveness to national security against bioterrorism.) |

Statement of third issue: What should be done? Elaboration on solutions to the problem

C. What can be done to solve the problem?
1. Categories of biological defense
   a. Prevention measures, such as disarmament and inspection regimes and vaccinations
   b. Protection, such as protective suits, clothing, and filters
   c. Detection, such as SMART (Sensitive Membrane Antigen Rapid Test) or BIDS (Biological Integrated Point Detection System)
   d. Treatment—only treatable if infection is identifiable; then it may be treated with medication.
2. Defensive and offensive biological warfare programs must keep up with fast-moving technology of the future.
   a. Defensive and offensive programs are no different.
   b. Both require the production, testing, and weaponization of agents of bioterrorism.
   c. Genetic alterations of agents could be beneficial in attaining knowledge or developing antibodies.
3. The Centers for Disease Control and Prevention is and should continue to be in control of providing technical expertise and resources to public health agencies for biological preparedness.
   a. We must support the efforts of the medical professionals and scientists.
   b. We also must demand the development of new systems and strategies.
   c. We also must demand that the federal government monitor the Centers for Disease Control and Prevention to ensure considerable and continued improvement in biopreparedness.

IV. Conclusion

Reiteration of main issues

A. Restate the issues.
1. Currently, the United States is not prepared to handle a biological attack of magnitude.
2. There is a lack of communication between public health facilities and the public, which has the potential to be harmful.
3. Biological weapons are any infectious agents used to cause death or bodily harm and thus can be immensely destructive.

Final appeal

B. Clincher: Since September 11, we have witnessed the terrifying effects of biological weaponry on the United States Postal Service. This was only a taste of what could be in store for the nation if we do not strengthen public awareness and reaction.

In Conclusion

Persuasion is the process by which one party purposefully secures a change of behavior on the part of another party. The basic process of persuasion centers on a speaker's making a claim and backing it up in such a way that listeners accept the claim. Successful persuasive strategies center on the use of speaker credibility, logical arguments, and psychological appeals.

Learn by Doing

1. Prepare a speech on a topic about which you have strong feelings. Propose a change in a current procedure, take a stand on a view concerning the subject, or propose a plan of action. The topic should be one to which your listeners can relate and react so that you can persuade them. An example of a topic for this speech might be "This school should not raise tuition."

2. Select a controversial topic and prepare a speech in which you advocate a particular solution to the problem. Your task is to persuade your listeners to accept your solution. A topic for this speech might be "Euthanasia should be a legal option for terminally ill patients."

3. Prepare a speech analyzing the persuasive strategies used by some group in advocating a particular cause (e.g., gay rights or Native American rights). Select a number of persuasive messages by spokespersons for the group you choose, and use examples from these messages to illustrate your analysis of the persuasive strategies.

4. Find a speech or letter to the editor that illustrates one or more of the psychological appeals described in this chapter.

5. Make a list of what you perceive to be the differences in preparing persuasive speeches and informative speeches.

6. Attend a persuasive speech by someone in a public forum, or analyze a persuasive manuscript in *Vital Speeches of the Day*. Prepare a descriptive analysis of the use of persuasive strategies by this speaker similar to that demonstrated in Table 15.1.

Key Terms

persuasion
persuasive speech
speech of conviction
speech of actuation
theory of field-related standards
group norm standards
individual norm standards
critical thinking
comparative-advantage reasoning
motivated sequence
Elaboration Likelihood Model
ethos
logos
pathos
speaker credibility
charisma
inductive argument
generalization conclusion
hypothesis conclusion
deductive argument
categorical syllogism

enthymeme
disjunctive argument
conditional argument
evidence
hasty generalization
faulty analogical reasoning
faulty causal reasoning
ignoring the issue
ad hominem argument
ad populum argument
ad ignorantium argument
psychological appeals
Hierarchy of Human Needs
proposition of fact
pro-con method of organization
elimination method of organization
proposition of value
survey of reasons method
criteria-satisfaction method
proposition of policy
Ethnographic Theory of Human Drives

APPENDIX 1

The Résumé[1]

20 Seconds Is All You Get!

This is the average time a manager takes to scan a résumé and determine if the applicant should be granted an interview. It's true: you may have spent thousands of dollars on education and training, and all you now have is just 20 seconds to sell yourself to a prospective employer.

For this reason, the materials you use to market yourself *must* project a professional image. Your résumé should present your abilities and what you have accomplished in your jobs. It must make the reader want to meet you by asking, "How did she (or he) accomplish that?"

The Importance of Premium Paper

Because your résumé serves as one of your first introductions to a prospective employer, it needs to present a quality, professional image. This is why the color and quality of the résumé paper you choose are so important:

- High-quality, acid-free, 100-percent cotton, 24-pound paper
- Sophisticated color selections
- Watermark placed one inch above center
- Matching envelopes

Accomplishment Statements: Selling the Sizzle!

When preparing a résumé, most people make the critical mistake of detailing their duties and responsibilities instead of highlighting accomplishments. In advertising jargon, this would be selling the steak instead of the sizzle—a marketing error that could cost you an important interview.

A potential employer has only a secondary interest in the duties and responsibilities you performed in a previous job. So what if you sold widgets to the aerospace industry or were the senior accountant in a candy factory or even vice president of marketing for a furniture company? Titles and duties say nothing about performance (the sizzle)—or what you can bring to this new employer that is unique and worthy of consideration. On the other hand, if your résumé indicates that you increased widget sales by 20 percent, receiving Salesperson of the Year honors, or discovered accounting errors that saved $50,000, or designed a new production system that reduced material costs, saving $200,000 annually, you can bet an interview will follow.

Your accomplishment statements need not be dramatic, but they should always enlarge on your basic duties and responsibilities. The best way to do that is to quantify, by adding numbers or percentages, when possible. Here are some examples of the type of questions you must ask yourself:

- How many payroll checks, involving how much money, did you issue each week?
- How much time and/or money did your new procedure save the company?
- How large a budget did you manage?
- By what percentage and/or number of dollars did you increase sales?

It is this kind of self-questioning that will help you develop accomplishment statements that will generate employer interest. Remember that you're the product: your accomplishments are the sizzle.

Consider This
Résumé Tip

When applying for a new position in the company or somewhere else, be sure your cover letter emphasizes how you can either save or make money for the employer.

Employers usually have three concerns:

◆ Can you make or save money for the company?
◆ Can you fit into the organization?
◆ Can the organization afford you?

How well you address these concerns can determine whether you're made an offer.

Source: Communication Briefings, as adapted from Lawrence B. Fuller, 2904 West 132nd Place, Gardena, CA 90247.

The Do's and Don'ts of Résumé Preparation

Do's

- Make sure your résumé is easy to read. Use concise, unambiguous sentences, and avoid overwriting or flowery prose.
- Know your audience: use the vocabulary and speak the language of your targeted field.
- Keep the overall length of your résumé short. Depending on your experience, one or two pages is ideal.
- Stress your past accomplishments and the skills you used to get the desired results.
- Focus on information that's relevant to your own career goals. If you're making a career change, stress what skills are transferable to support your new career objectives.
- Begin accomplishment statements with action verbs (see the following) instead of pronouns like *I* or *we* or even *the company*.
- Neatness counts. A poorly structured, badly keyboarded résumé is a reflection of the applicant.

Don'ts

- Your salary history or reasons for leaving a previous job should never be included on a résumé.

- If you're considering enclosing a photograph of yourself, don't! You may bear a striking resemblance to someone the reader doesn't like.
- Don't include personal references on your résumé. Potential employers are interested in references only after they are seriously considering hiring you. At that time, you may be asked to provide reference information.
- Don't stretch the truth! Misinformation or untruthful statements will inevitably come back to haunt you.
- Avoid references to hobbies, activities, and memberships that are not business related or haven't any application to your current career goals or job objectives.
- Last, but certainly not least, don't have any unreasonable expectations of what a résumé can do. Employers do not hire résumés; they hire people.

Action Verbs Make a Difference

When describing your accomplishments, using action verbs can make the difference between a statement that attracts attention and one that seems commonplace and uninteresting.

achieved	*designed*	*increased*	*performed*	*strengthened*
added	*eliminated*	*initiated*	*planned*	*supervised*
broadened	*established*	*invented*	*purchased*	*trained*
consolidated	*evaluated*	*maintained*	*reduced*	*transformed*
coordinated	*expanded*	*managed*	*saved*	*utilized*
created	*generated*	*negotiated*	*simplified*	*verified*
developed	*identified*	*organized*	*streamlined*	*worked*

Electronic Screening of Résumés

Be aware that some companies use a technique that electronically screens résumés. The résumés are scanned into computers and sorted by key words to identify candidates with specific abilities and talents.[2] When companies employ this technique, résumés, even when no job openings exist, are being filed in a computer for future reference.[3]

To ensure consideration of your application, it is wise to follow an electronic-sensitive format that includes white-paper-only documents typed with highly readable spacing, nonserif fonts, and no underlining, bolding, italics, or reverse blocking. (Some scanners can't deal with these variations.)[4] Make sure in your cover letter and résumé you use words identical (not similar, *identical*) to the words in advertisements and want ads. This ensures that the electronic processor will react positively to your materials.

Skills-Based Functional Résumé Format

This format is best suited for multi-industry or function careers (different industries and function/skills) and/or when there are gaps in employment history.

ALAN WINTER
2432 Bayard Drive
Edgeware, NJ 10216
(515) 221-6453

An experienced sales executive in the electronic, scientific, and real estate fields. A well-organized individual who utilizes excellent communication and leadership skills to gain the respect and confidence of clients and coworkers.

SIGNIFICANT ACCOMPLISHMENTS

Sales
- Named "Salesperson of the Year" for a real estate firm with 70 full-time associates.
- Developed a new sales territory, achieving a 10% market share among six established electronics competitors in a one-year period.
- Maintained 22 major existing accounts and added seven new customers, exceeding annual sales budget by 72%.

Marketing
- Restructured ten sales territories, resulting in a 40% increase in cost effectiveness.
- Initiated new, more competitive pricing policies, incorporating term and volume discounts, increasing sales by 20% annually.

Training
- Demonstrated technical products at 15 trade shows, resulting in 23% sales increase.
- Trained seven-member technical service staff in effective customer communications, receiving "Staff of the Year" award from CEO.

EXPERIENCE

HALL-MARK ELECTRONICS   1995–Present
Fairfield, New Jersey
- Sales Engineer

HAMILTON INSTRUMENTATION   1983–1995
Newark, New Jersey
- Sales Representative

MAX E. WYNN, INC.   1981–1983
Chester, Pennsylvania
- Director of Development and Finance
- Real Estate Sales Associate

EDUCATION

B.S. in Chemistry, Park College, Kansas City, Missouri
Graduate Coursework, Northwestern University, Evanston, Illinois

Chronological Résumé:
Action Verbs Make a Difference

This format is best suited for single-industry or single-function careers and when there are no gaps in employment history.

SHARON SUMMER
23 Old Colony Road
Los Angeles, CA 90031
(216) 556-7878

A payroll professional with increasingly responsible positions, including five years with a multi-million-dollar cosmetics company.

PROFESSIONAL EXPERIENCE

RICHARDSON-BARRON, INC.   1996–Present
Los Angeles, California

Payroll Administrator
- Resolved several hundred discrepancies in employee pay and benefits, maintaining excellent employer/employee relationships and morale.
- Developed and formatted a new PC compensation tracking system which contained a breakout of salaries and benefits for employees, consultants, and temporary personnel, reducing processing time by 70%.
- Assisted corporate accountants in filing federal and multi-state tax returns, with no requests for government audit.
- Administered the 2,000-employee corporate payroll function during a conversion from an outside supplier to an in-house fully automated system, maintaining full continuity.
- Analyzed corporate financial reports, successfully balancing inter-related accounts for the closing of office.

BARCLAY ELECTRIC   1990–1996
Milwaukee, Wisconsin

Senior Payroll Clerk
- Managed payroll for 250 union employees, including posting hours and auditing payroll with no discrepancies or requests for audit.

EDUCATION

Milwaukee Area Technical College: Major, Data Processing
West Los Angeles College: Major, Travel and Transportation

APPENDIX 2

Basic Rules for APA Style

There are many formats available for footnoting, endnoting, and writing bibliographies. This format, developed by the American Psychological Association, is presented as it lends itself to easy transition into speech oral footnotes and does not require insetting the sources into the body of the material, which would be distracting to speakers.

Sample of APA Entries

Overall Rules:

- Authors' names are inverted (last name first); give the last name and initials for all authors of a particular work.
- Capitalize only the first letter of the first word of a title and subtitle of a work unless the word is a proper name (e.g., *England*).
- Italicize titles of books and journals.

Samples of Specific Entries:

An article in a periodical (e.g., a journal, newspaper, or magazine)

Author, A. A., Author, B. B., & Author, C. C. (Year, add month and day of publication for daily, weekly, or monthly publications). Title of article. *Title of periodical, volume number,* pages.

A nonperiodical (e.g., book, report, brochure, or audiovisual media)

Author, A. A. (Year of publication). *Title of work: Capital letter, also for subtitle.* Location: Publisher.

Part of a nonperiodical (e.g., a book chapter or an article in a collection)

Author, A. A., & Author, B. B. (Year of publication). Title of chapter. In A. Editor & B. Editor (Eds.), *Title of book* (Pages of chapter). Location: Publisher.

Article in an Internet-only periodical

Author, A. A., & Author, B. B. (Date of publication). Title of article. *Title of journal, volume number* (Issue number if available), Article number. Retrieved month, day, year, from http://web address

Nonperiodical Internet document (e.g., a web page or report)

Author, A. A., & Author, B. B. (Date of publication). *Title of article.* Retrieved month, day, year, from http://web address

Part of nonperiodical Internet document

Author, A. A., & Author, B. B. (Date of publication). Title of article. In *Title of book or larger document* (chapter or section number). Retrieved from http://web address

A motion picture or videotape

Producer, P. P. (Producer), & Director, D. D. (Director). (Date of release). *Title of motion picture* [Motion picture]. Country of origin: Studio or distributor.

A television broadcast or television series

Producer, P. P. (Producer). (Date of broadcast or copyright). *Title of broadcast* [Television broadcast or Television series]. City of origin: Studio or distributor.

A single episode of a television series

Writer, W. W. (Writer), & Director, D. D. (Director). (Date of publication). Title of episode [Television series episode]. In P. Producer (Producer), *Series title.* City of origin: Studio or distributor.

A music recording

Songwriter, W. W. (Date of copyright). Title of song [Recorded by artist if different from songwriter]. On *Title of album* [Medium of recording: compact disc, record, cassette, etc.]. Location: Label. (Recording date if different from copyright date).

Journal article, one author

Harlow, H. F. (1983). Fundamentals for preparing psychology journal articles. *Journal of Comparative and Physiological Psychology, 55,* 893–896.

Journal article, three to six authors

Kernis, M. H., Cornell, D. P., Sun, C. R., Berry, A., & Harlow, T. (1993). There's more to self-esteem than whether it is high or low: The importance of stability of self-esteem. *Journal of Personality and Social Psychology, 65,* 1190–1204.

Work discussed in a secondary source

Coltheart, M., Curtis, B., Atkins, P., & Haller, M. (1993). Models of reading aloud: Dual-route and parallel-distributed-processing approaches. *Psychological Review, 100,* 589–608.

Magazine article, one author

Henry, W. A., III. (1990, April 9). Making the grade in today's schools. *Time, 135,* 28–31.

Book

Calfee, R. C., & Valencia, R. R. (1991). *APA guide to preparing manuscripts for journal publication.* Washington, DC: American Psychological Association.

An article or chapter of a book

O'Neil, J. M., & Egan, J. (1992). Men's and women's gender role journeys: Metaphor for healing, transition, and transformation. In B. R. Wainrib (Ed.), *Gender issues across the life cycle* (pp. 107–123). New York: Springer.

A government publication

National Institute of Mental Health. (1990). *Clinical training in serious mental illness* (DHHS Publication No. ADM 90-1679). Washington, DC: U.S. Government Printing Office.

A book or article with no author or editor named

Merriam-Webster's collegiate dictionary (10th ed.). (1993). Springfield, MA: Merriam-Webster.

Daily newspaper article, no author

New drug appears to sharply cut risk of death from heart failure. (1993, July 15). *The Washington Post,* p. A12.

A translated work and/or a republished work

Laplace, P.-S. (1951). *A philosophical essay on probabilities* (F. W. Truscott & F. L. Emory, Trans.). New York: Dover. (Original work published 1814)

A review of a book, film, television program, etc.

Baumeister, R. F. (1993). Exposing the self-knowledge myth [Review of the book *The self-knower: A hero under control*]. *Contemporary Psychology, 38,* 466–467.

An entry in an encyclopedia

Bergmann, P. G. (1993). Relativity. In *The new encyclopedia Britannica* (Vol. 26, pp. 501–508). Chicago: Encyclopedia Britannica.

An online journal article

Kenneth, I. A. (2000). A Buddhist response to the nature of human rights. *Journal of Buddhist Ethics, 8*(4). Retrieved February 20, 2001, from http://www.cac.psu.edu/jbe/twocont.html

Chapter or section of an online document

The Foundation for a Better World. (2000). Pollution and banana cream pie. In *Great chefs cook with chlorofluorocarbons and carbon monoxide* (Chap. 3). Retrieved July 13, 2001, from http://www.bamm.com/cream/pollution/bananas.htm

Message posted to an online newsgroup, forum, or discussion group

Frook, B. D. (1999, July 23). New inventions in the cyberworld of toylandia [Msg 25]. Message posted to http://www.groups.earthlink.com/forum/messages/00025.html

For any format not listed here, refer to *Publication Manual of the American Psychological Association,* Fifth Edition (ISBN: 1557987912) or go online to

http://www.apastyle.org/aboutstyle.html or
http://www.apastyle.org/elecref.html

NOTES

Preface

1. Marilyn Hanf Buckley, "Focus on Research: We Listen a Book a Day; We Speak a Book a Week—Learning from Walter Loban," *Language Arts* 69 (December 1992): 623.
2. John A. Nidds and James McGerald, "Corporations View Public Education," *Artbeat, the Newspaper of the Minnesota Alliance for Arts in Education* 18(4) (December 1995).
3. The Secretary's Commission on Achieving Necessary Skills, U.S. Department of Labor, "What Work Requires of Schools: A SCANS Report on America 2000" (Washington, D.C.: U.S. Government Printing Office, June 1991), p. vii; and Leila Hawken, Robert L. Duran, and Lynne Kelly, "The Relationship of Interpersonal Communication Variables to Academic Success and Persistence in College," *Communication Quarterly* 39 (Fall 1991): 297–308. See also Sherwyn P. Morreale, Michael M. Osborn, and Judy C. Pearson, "Why Communication Is Important: A Rationale for the Centrality of the Study of Communication," *JACA* 1 (January 2000): 1–25.
4. Anita Vangelisti and John Daly, "Correlates of Speaking Skills in the United States: A National Assessment," *Communication Education* 38 (April 1989): 132–143.
5. Ibid.
6. James McCroskey and Virginia Richmond, *Quiet Children and the Classroom Teacher* (Bloomington, IN: ERIC Clearinghouse on Reading and Communication Skills in cooperation with the Speech Communication Association, Annandale, VA, 1991), p. 20.
7. For an extended discussion on public speaking and communication apprehension, see Virginia R. Richmond and James C. McCroskey, *Communication: Apprehension, Avoidance and Effectiveness*, 4th ed. (Scottsdale, AZ: Gorsuch Scarisbrick, 1995).
8. Roy Berko and Carolyn Perry, ed., *Speaking, Listening, and Media Literacy Standards for K Through 12 Education* (Annandale, VA: Speech Communication Association, 1996), p. 2.
9. Ibid.
10. Ibid.
11. Michael Cronin, ed., "The Need for Required Oral Communication Education in the Undergraduate General Education Curriculum," unpublished paper, 1993, available from the Speech Communication Association, Annandale, VA.
12. Wendy S. Zabava Ford and Andrew D. Wolvin, "The Differential Impact of a Basic Communication Course on Perceived Communi-

cation Competencies in Class, Work, and Social Contexts," *Communication Education* 42 (July 1993): 215–223. Also see David R. Seibold, Sami Kudsi, and Michael Rude, "Does Communication Training Make a Difference? Evidence for the Effectiveness of a Presentation Skills Program," *Journal of Applied Communication Research* (May 1993): 111–131.

Chapter 1

1. Rebecca B. Rubin and Elizabeth E. Graham, "Communication Correlates of College Success: An Exploratory Investigation," *Communication Education* 37 (January 1988): 14.
2. Ibid.
3. Jennifer Grubb, "Get That Job," *Young Money* (Fall 2002), p. 11.
4. Jerry L. Winsor, Dan B. Curtis, and Ronald D. Stephens, "National Preferences in Business and Communication Education: A Survey Update," *JACA* 3 (September 1997): 170–179.
5. Valerie Marchant, "Listen Up!" *Time* (June 28, 1999), p. 72.
6. Ibid.
7. Anita Vangelisti and John Daly, "Correlates of Speaking Skills in the United States: A National Assessment," *Communication Education* 38 (April 1989): 132–143.
8. Ibid.
9. James C. McCroskey and Virginia P. Richmond, *Quiet Children and the Classroom Teacher* (Bloomington, IN: ERIC Clearinghouse on Reading and Communication Skills; and Annandale, VA: Speech Communication Association, 1991), p. 20.
10. For an extended discussion of public speaking apprehension, see Virginia P. Richmond and James C. McCroskey, *Communication: Apprehension, Avoidance, and Effectiveness*, 4th ed. (Scottsdale, AZ: Gorsuch Scarisbrick, 1985), Chapter 3.
11. Unisys Corporation, "How Can We Expect Him [Her] to Learn When We Haven't Taught Him [Her] How to Listen?" advertisement reproduced in Roy Berko, Andrew Wolvin, and Darlyn Wolvin, *Communicating: A Social and Career Focus*, 6th ed. (Boston: Houghton Mifflin, 1995), p. 81.
12. "Don't Copy It, Mopy It!" *Hindu* (October 9, 1997), p. 27.
13. Michael Cronin, ed., "The Need for Required Oral Communication Education in the Undergraduate General Education Curriculum,"

unpublished paper, 1993, available from the National Communication Association, Annandale, VA.

14. Based on David K. Berlo, *The Process of Communication* (New York: Holt, Rinehart and Winston, 1960).

15. Advertisement, "WordPerfect–Macintosh," WordPerfect Corporation, Ogden, UT.

16. Factors that cause communication difficulties are sometimes called *interference.* In this text, these factors are referred to as *noise.*

17. "Media Usage and Consumer Spending: 1990–2001," in *Statistical Abstract of the United States, 1998* (Washington, D.C.: U.S. Government Printing Office, 1998).

18. Dita Smith, "How Wide a Web?" *Washington Post,* July 28, 2001, p. A13.

19. See Vinton Certf, "How the Internet Got Started," *Online Success* at <http://www.webmastercourse.com/articles/Internet/history>.

20. Neil Postman, "The Antidote to Trivialization," *NPQ* (Fall 1990): 55.

21. Milt Thomas, "Cultural Self-Identification in the Basic Course," unpublished paper presented at the annual meeting of the Central States Speech Association, Oklahoma City, OK, April 1994, p. 9.

22. Judith Seid, *God-Optional Judaism: Alternatives for Cultural Jews Who Love Their History, Heritage, and Community* (New York: Citadel Press, 2001), p. 46.

23. Guo-Ming Chen and William J. Starosta, *Foundations of Intercultural Communication* (Needham Heights, MA: Allyn & Bacon, 1998), p. 27.

24. Ibid., p. 23.

25. Milt Thomas, p. 8.

26. Ibid.

27. Kim Walters, "Coalescence in the Basic Course," unpublished paper presented at the Western Speech Association Convention, Albuquerque, NM, February 15, 1993.

28. *Oxford English Dictionary,* 2nd ed. (Oxford, UK: Clarendon Press, 1989).

29. William A. Henry III, "The Politics of Separation," *Time* (Fall 1993, special edition), p. 75.

30. Deborah Atwater, "Issues Facing Minorities in Speech Communication Education: Moving from the Melting Pot to a Tossed Salad," *Proceedings of the 1988 Speech Communication Association Flagstaff Conference Report* (Annandale, VA: Speech Communication Association, 1989), p. 40.

31. *Report on the Population* (Washington, D.C.: Reference Bureau, n.d.), and William A. Henry III, "Beyond the Melting Pot," *Time* (April 9, 1990), pp. 28–31.

32. Atwater, p. 41.

33. Larry A. Samovar, Richard E. Porter, and Lisa A. Stefani, *Communication Between Cultures* (Belmont, CA: Wadsworth, 1998), p. 250.

34. Ibid., p. 46.

35. Everett M. Rogers and Thomas M. Steinfatt, *Intercultural Communication* (Prospect Heights, IL: Waveland Press, 1999), p. 76.

36. Samovar et al., p. 200.

37. Thomas, p. 8.

38. Samovar et al., p. 200.

39. Ibid., p. 46.

40. Ibid.

41. Rogers, p. 12.

42. Henry, pp. 28–31.

43. Samovar et al., p. 47.

44. Ibid., p. 46.

45. Ibid., p. 250.

46. Ibid., p. 251.

47. Chen, p. 192.

48. Rogers, p. 226.

49. Ibid., 76.

50. Helen Dewar, "Free Speech Free-for-All," *Washington Post,* October 21, 1993, p. A1.

51. Franklyn S. Haiman, *Speech Arts and the First Amendment* (Carbondale, IL: Southern Illinois University Press, 1993), p. 1.

52. "Sex Policy Raises Questions of Academic Freedom," *Cleveland Plain Dealer,* November 27, 1993, p. A16.

53. Matt Helms, "License to Hate," *National College Magazine* (September 22, 1992), p. 14.

54. Haiman, p. 3.

55. Rich Hodges, "Speech Codes on Campus!" *Washington Post,* November 27, 1993, p. A25.

56. Ibid.

57. Alan Dershowitz, "Imprisonment of Ideas: What Is the First Amendment?" speech presented at the Eisenhower Symposium, Johns Hopkins University, Baltimore, MD, October 20, 1991.

58. Scott Jaschite, "Nominee Reflects on 'Hate Speech,' Sees Supreme Court Taking Up the Issue," *Chronicle of Higher Education* (August 4, 1993), p. A23.

59. "Island Trees School Board *v.* Pico," as reported in Maureen Harrison and Steve Gilbert, *Freedom of Speech Decisions of the United States Supreme Court* (San Diego: Excellent Books, 1996), p. 65.

60. Ibid., p. 79.

61. "Tinker *v.* Des Moines Independent Community School District," as reported in Margaret C. Jasper, *The Law of Speech and the First Amendment* (Dobbs Ferry, NY: Oceana Publications, 1999), p. 62.

62. Scott Barbour, *Free Speech* (San Diego: Greenhaven Press, 2000), p. 27.

63. Ibid., p. 27.

64. Ibid.

65. Ibid.

66. Ibid.

67. Gina Holland, "Free Speech Cases Pile Up on Docket at Supreme Court," *Cleveland Plain Dealer,* August 20, 2002, p. A7.

68. Richard L. Johannesen, *Ethics in Human Communication,* 4th ed. (Prospect Heights, IL: Waveland Press), p. 2.

69. "A Code of Professional Ethics for the Communication Scholar/Teacher," National Communication Association, 1999.

70. Johannesen.

71. Thomas Nilsen, *Ethics in Speech Communication* (Indianapolis: Bobbs-Merrill, 1966), p. 139. This book contains an extensive discussion about being an ethical speaker.

72. Ibid., p. 14.

73. Michael Purdy, "Listening Ethics: Little Things Mean a Lot," unpublished paper presented at the International Listening Association Convention, Boston, March 1994.

Chapter 2

1. Diane Catellano Mader, "The Politically Correct Textbook: Trends in Publishers' Guidelines for the Representation of Marginalized Groups," paper presented at the Eastern Communication Association Convention, Portland, ME, May 3, 1992, p. 4.

2. Ibid., p. 3.

3. B. L. Pearson, *Introduction to Linguistic Concepts* (New York: Knopf, 1977), p. 4.

4. Ibid.

5. Emily Eakin, "Before the Word, Perhaps the Wink? Some Language Experts Think Humans Spoke First With Gestures," *New York Times,* May 18, 2002, p. B7, col. 5, based on Michael C. Corballis, *From Hand to Mouth: The Origins of Language* (Princeton, NJ: Princeton University Press, 2002).

6. Ibid.

7. Ibid.

8. Michael C. Corballis, *From Hand to Mouth: The Origins of Language* (Princeton, NJ: Princeton University Press, 2002). Also see Justin Gillis, "Gene Mutations Linked to Language Development," *Washington Post,* August 15, 2002, p. A13.

9. See Stephen W. Littlejohn, *Theories of Human Communication* (Belmont, CA: Wadsworth, 1999), Chapter 9, "Theories of Social and Cultural Reality." The social construction of reality concept has its roots in Peter L. Berger and Thomas Luckmann, *The Social Construction of Reality: A Treatise in the Sociology of Knowledge* (New York: Doubleday, 1966).

10. Eakin.

11. Ibid.

12. Ibid.

13. Ibid.

14. Jim Wise, "Word Game," *Durham Herald-Sun,* September 6, 1992, pp. 71–E9.

15. Norman Geschwind, "Language and the Brain," *Scientific American* 226 (April 1972): 76–83.

16. Norbert Wiener, *The Human Use of Human Beings* (New York: Anchor Books, 1950).

17. T. R. Tortioriello, *Communication in the Organization* (New York: McGraw-Hill, 1978), p. 13.

18. George Herbert Mead, *Mind, Self, and Society* (Chicago: University of Chicago Press, 1934).

19. Steven Pinker, *The Language Instinct* (New York: William Morrow, 1994).

20. Paul Madaule, *When Listening Comes Alive* (Norval, Ontario: Moulin, 1994).

21. Littlejohn.

22. Wise, pp. 71–E9.

23. Barbara Warnick and Edward S. Inch, *Critical Thinking and Communication* (New York: Macmillan, 1989), pp. 257–259.

24. Mader, pp. 112–113.

25. Ibid.

26. Ibid.

27. Blaine Goss and Dan O'Hair, *Communication in Interpersonal Relationships* (New York: Macmillan, 1988), pp. 67–69.

28. For a complete discussion of doublespeak, see William Lutz, *Doublespeak* (New York: Harper & Row, 1990).

29. National Council of Teachers of English Committee on Public Doublespeak, Urbana, IL, as reported in Lutz (1990), p. 14.

30. Lutz (1990), pp. xii, xiii.

31. Roger Brown, *Words and Things* (New York: Free Press, 1959), p. 22.

32. Howard A. Mims, "On Black English: A Language with Rules," *Cleveland Plain Dealer,* August 31, 1979, p. A21.

33. Ibid.

34. Jospeh A. DeVito, *The Communication Handbook: A Dictionary* (New York: Harper & Row, 1986), p. 94.

35. Richard Stapleton, "You Say Grinder, I Say Hoagie," *USAir Magazine* (November 1993), p. 95.

36. Mims.

37. Randall L. Alford and Judith Strother, "A Southern Opinion of Regional Accents," *Florida Communication Journal* 21 (1992): 51.

38. Material in this section is based on the work of W. Zelinsky, as discussed in Peter A. Andersen, Myron W. Lustig, and Janis F. Andersen, "Regional Patterns of Communication in the United States: A Theoretical Perspective," *Communication Monographs* 54 (June 1987): 128–144.

39. Phil Kloer, "Dictionary Adjusts to Language That Changes 24/7," *Cleveland Plain Dealer,* October 15, 2002, p. E3.

40. Ibid.

41. "People, Etc.," *Elyria (Ohio) Chronicle-Telegram Scene,* April 10, 1977, p. 2.

42. Deborah Work, "Who Call Like?" *Washington Post,* October 14, 1993, p. C5.

43. Amy Reynolds, "Dudespeak: 'Too cool'?" *The Towerlight* (Towson State University, Towson, MD), September 5, 1991, p. 29.

44. Work, p. C5.

45. Work, p. C5.

46. Ibid.

47. "What's in a Word? A Job, Hood Senior's Study Says," *Washington Post,* June 6, 1991, p. Md8.

48. Sandy Banks, "Ebonics Is a Language with Its Own Set of Rules: An Interview with Orlando Taylor, Howard University," *Cleveland Plain Dealer,* January 14, 1986, p. B2.

49. Robin Henry, " 'Black English' Causes Confusion in the Classroom: An Interview with Dr. Howard Mims, Associate Professor of Speech and Hearing, Cleveland State University," *Elyria (Ohio) Chronicle-Telegram,* July 26, 1987, p. G2.

50. Anita Manning, "Schools to Recognize Black 'Ebonics,' " *USA Today* (December 20, 1996), p. 3A; Michelle Locke, "School Board OKs Black English as Second Language," Associated Press, as reproduced in *Cleveland Plain Dealer,* December 20, 1996, pp. 1A, 19A; Jesse McKinley, "Critics Accuse Board of Double Talk," *New York Times,* as reprinted in *Cleveland Plain Dealer,* December 21, 1996, p. 15A.

51. Michael Hecht, Mary Jane Collier, and Sidney Ribeau, *African American Communication* (Newbury Park, CA: Sage, 1993), p. 85.

52. Rene Sanchez, "After Ebonics Controversy, Oakland Seeks Viable Lesson Plan," *Washington Post,* April 19, 1998, p. A10.

53. Ibid.

54. "Teaching Standard English: A Sociological Approach," unpublished handout based on the syllabus for the Basic Communication Strategies course at LaGuardia Community College, New York, Speech Communication Association Convention, Chicago, November 1987.

55. "Teaching Standard English," with reference to Clarence Major, *Dictionary of Afro-American Slang* (New York: International Publishers, 1971).

56. Rachel L. Jones quoting black writer James Baldwin, "What's Wrong with Black English?" *Newsweek,* December 27, 1982, p. 7.

57. William Labov, "Allow Black English in Schools? Yes: The Most Important Thing Is to Encourage Children to Talk Freely," *U.S. News & World Report,* March 31, 1980, pp. 63–64.

58. Hecht et al., p. 84.

59. Ibid.

60. For an in-depth discussion of the syntactic and phonological features of Black English, see Robert Hopper and Rita J. Naremore, *Children's Speech: A Practical Introduction to Communication Development,* 2nd ed. (New York: Harper & Row, 1978), pp. 161–164, 168–171.

61. Hecht et al., p. 87.

62. Ibid., p. 88.

63. I. Sachdev and R. Y. Bourhis, *Language and Social Identification* (New York: Harvester Wheatsheaf, 1990).

64. Janice Castro, "Spanglish Spoken Here," *Time* (July 11, 1988), p. 53.

65. Ibid., as stated by Carmen Silva-Corvalan, University of Southern California.

66. Ibid.

67. Gary Althen, "The Americans Have to Say Everything," *Communication Quarterly* 40 (Fall 1992): 414.

68. Ibid.

69. Steven B. Pratt, "Razzing: Ritualized Uses of Humor as a Form of Identification among American Indians," paper presented at Central States Speech Association, Oklahoma City, April 1994; also in *Interaction and Identity: Information and Behavior,* vol. 5, ed. H. B. Mokros (New Brunswick, NJ: Transactions, 1994), p. 4.

70. Ibid.

71. Gerry Philipsen, "Navaho World View and Culture Patterns of Speech: A Case Study in Ethnorhetoric," *Speech Monographs* 39 (June 1972): 134.

72. Ibid., p. 135.

73. Pratt, p. 2.

74. Ibid.

75. Sanchez, p. A10.

76. Hopper and Naremore, pp. 159–174; Naremore and Hopper, pp. 156–158; Labov, pp. 63–64; and the work of Howard A. Mims, Cleveland State University.

77. Based on research by Sandra Terrell and Francis Terrell.
78. Julie L. Nicklin, " 'Switching' Between Black and Standard English," *Chroncle of Higher Education* (April 20, 1994), p. A6. For further information on this topic and an approach to altering pronunciation and language usage, see Julie L. Nicklin, *Speak Standard, Too: Add Mainstream English to Your Talking Style* (Chicago: Orchard Books and Columbia College, n.d.).
79. Michael Agar, *Language Shock* (New York: William Morrow, 1994), p. 106.
80. Thomas R. Nilsen, *Ethics of Speech Communication* (Indianapolis: Bobbs-Merrill, 1974), p. 105.
81. Sarah Smith, "Words That Sting," *Psychology Today* (September–October 2000), p. 24.
82. Ibid.
83. Ibid.
84. Name of student withheld to protect his identity.

Chapter 3

1. Janet Beavin Bavelas, "Redefining Language: Nonverbal Linguistic Acts in Face-to-Face Dialogue, a B. Aubrey Fisher Lecture," October 1992, Department of Psychology, University of Victoria, Victoria,B. C., Canada, p. 2. Also, an excellent learning aid for gaining awareness of intercultural characteristics is *Intercultural Communicating* (Provo, UT: Language Research Center, Brigham Young University); another is the Language Research Center's "Culturegram" series, which is intended to offer briefings to aid understanding of, feeling for, and communication with people around the world.
2. Judee K. Burgoon, David B. Buller, and W. Gill Woodall, *Nonverbal Communication: The Unspoken Dialogue,* 2nd ed. (New York: McGraw-Hill, 1996), p. 1.
3. Ibid.
4. Ibid.
5. Bavelas, pp. 2–3.
6. Burgoon et al., p. 136.
7. Ibid., p. 1
8. Ibid., p. 136.
9. Ibid.
10. Norbert Freedman, "You Have to Move to Think," report to the Clinical Behavioral Research Unit, Downstate Medical Center, Brooklyn, NY, n.d.
11. "The Pegasus Mind-Body Newsletter", Issue 9, January 4, 2002. For more information on NLP Eye-Accessing Cues, search Pegasus NLP Trainings at <http://www.nlp-now.co.uk/>.
12. Clifford Wright, *NLP Workbook, Introductory Level,* Books 1 and 2 (Portland, OR: Metamorphous Press, 1989).
13. Ibid., p. 4.
14. Ibid.
15. Ibid.
16. For a further discussion of thinking and eye movement, see Eric Adler, "Speak to Me with Thine Eyes (and Head and Arms)," *Washington Post,* November 26, 1998, p. C5.
17. Edward Hall and Mildred Hall, "The Sounds of Silence," *Playboy* 18 (June 1971): 148.
18. Edward Hall, as interviewed by Kenneth Freedman, "Learning the Arabs' Silent Language," *Psychology Today* 13 (August 1979): 53.
19. Discussion based on research reported by Paul Ekman, Wallace Friesen, and John Bear, "The International Language of Gestures," *Psychology Today* 18 (May 1984): 64–69.
20. Mark Knapp and Judith A. Hall, *Nonverbal Communication in Human Interaction,* 4th ed. (Forth Worth: Harcourt Brace, 1997), pp. 13–20.
21. The statement is credited to Sigmund Freud, though no footnote source is available.
22. Scott Sleek, "Psychologists Debate Merits of the Polygraph," the American Psychological Association's *Monitor* (June 1998), p. 30.
23. Ibid.
24. Randolph Schmid, "Lie Detectors Called Too Inaccurate for National Security," *Cleveland Plain Dealer,* October 9, 2002, p. A10.
25. Ibid.
26. Kaja Perina, "Truth Serum, Brain Scans May be Foolproof Lie Detectors," *Psychology Today* (January–February 2002), p. 15.
27. Ibid.
28. No specific identifying channels of nonverbal communication have been universally defined. The names used here are a compilation of those that have appeared in various textbooks on communication.
29. Nick Jordan, "The Face of Feeling," *Psychology Today* (January 1986), p. 8.
30. Knapp, pp. 43–45.
31. The universal theory is proposed by Daniel Goleman, "The Seven Thousand Faces of Dr. Ekman," *Psychology Today* (February 1981), pp. 45–49; the contrary opinion is presented by J. A. Russell, "Is There Universal Recognition of Emotion from Facial Expressions? A Review of the Cross-Cultural Studies," *Psychological Bulletin* 115(1) (January 1994): 102–141.
32. Ibid.
33. Edward Hall and Mildred Hall, "The Sounds of Silence," *Playboy* 18 (June 1971): 148.
34. A research study conducted by Joe Teece, Boston College neuropsychologist.
35. Knapp, pp. 386–390.
36. Hall, pp. 47–48.
37. Based on the theories of Milton Erickson presented by Ron Klein as part of the training units of the American Hypnosis Training Academy, Inc., June 1991; also see Knapp, pp. 375–376.
38. Adler, p. C5
39. Ibid.
40. Knapp, p. 9.
41. Ibid.
42. Ibid.
43. James T. Yenckel, "Fearless Traveler: Sorting Through the Chaos of Culture," *Washington Post,* October 20, 1991, p. E10.
44. Burgoon, p. 41.
45. For an extended discussion of emotions and nonverbal communication, see Burgoon, Chapter 10.
46. Diane Ackerman, "The Power of Touch," *Parade Magazine* (March 25, 1990), p. 3.
47. Roy Berko, Lawrence Rosenfeld, and Larry Samovar, *Connecting: A Culture-Sensitive Approach to Interpersonal Communication Competency* (Ft. Worth: Harcourt Brace, 1997), p. 157.
48. Ibid., pp. 157–160.
49. Yenckel, p. E10.
50. Neal Roese, James Olson, Marianne Borenstein, Angela Martin, and Allison Shores, "Same-Sex Touching Behavior: The Moderating Role of Homophobic Attitudes," *Journal of Nonverbal Behavior* (Winter 1992): 250.
51. Ibid., p. 251.
52. Peter Andersen, *Nonverbal Communication: Forms and Functions* (Mountain View, CA: Mayfield, 1999), p. 47.
53. Ibid., p. 48.
54. Ibid.
55. Stanley Jones, *The Right Touch* (Cresskill, NJ: Hampton Press, 1994), p. 26.
56. Knapp, pp. 273–284.
57. Jennifer Steinhauer, It's 'The Gap' Once You're Hired, But Job Hunters Must Spiff It Up," *New York Times,* April 2, 1995, p. F13.

58. Ibid.

59. Ibid.

60. Ellen Neuborne, "Causal-Clothing Makers Make Pitch to Offices," *USA Today,* February 7, 1995, p. B1.

61. Elizabeth Snead, "Casual Look Suits Today's Businessmen," *USA Today,* August 13, 1993, p. 1D.

62. Mark Albright, "Menswear Sales on Upswing," *Elyria (Ohio) Chronicle-Telegram,* November 25, 1994, p. D8, as reprinted from the *St. Petersburg Times.*

63. Neuborne.

64. Pam Belluck, "Uniform Appeal," *Baltimore Sun,* March 2, 1992, p. 5.

65. Roxanne Washington, "Culture Weighs Body Image," *Cleveland Plain Dealer,* June 18, 1996, pp. 1E, 4E. Also reported in "Black Bodies," *20/20,* ABC-TV, April 19, 1999, available from ABC News Home Videos, #T990419.

66. "The Eyes Have It," *Newsweek* (December 3, 1973), p. 85.

67. Ibid.

68. "Attractive Male Attorneys Earn More, Faster," *GW Hatchet* [George Washington University], January 18, 1996, p. 9.

69. Lynn Sherr, "Short Men," *20/20,* ABC-TV, December 27, 1996.

70. Ibid.

71. Ibid.

72. Mark Knapp, *Nonverbal Communication in Human Interaction,* 2nd ed. (Forth Worth: Harcourt Brace, 1978), pp. 166–167.

73. Jay Mathews, "The Height Report: Short Is Beautiful," *Washington Post.*

74. Some research classifies touch separately as *tactile-cutaneous* rather than as part of proxemics. This discussion, although recognizing this distinction, includes touch within proxemics.

75. Burgoon, p. 224, referring to research by Edward Hall.

76. Ibid.

77. Burgoon, p. 224, based on the work of S. M. Jourjrard and N. M. Genley.

78. Hall and Hall, p. 148.

79. Mark L. Hickson III and Don W. Stacks, *Nonverbal Communication: Studies and Applications,* 3rd ed. (Madison, WI: Brown and Benchmark, 1993), p. 13.

80. Knapp, pp. 204–205.

81. For an extensive discussion of paravocalics, see Knapp, Chapter 11.

82. Stephan Rechtschaffen, "Time-Shifting," *Psychology Today* (November–December 1993), p. 35.

83. Ibid.

84. Burgoon, p. 226.

85. Michael Argyle, "Inter-Cultural Communication," *Cultures in Contact: Studies in Cross-Cultural Interaction,* ed. Stephen Bochner (New York: Pergamon Press, 1982), p. 35.

86. Edward T. Hall and Mildred Reed Hall, *Understanding Cultural Differences: Germans, French, and Americans* (Yarmouth, ME: Intercultural Press, 1990), p. 38.

87. R. Levine, with E. Woolf, "Social Time: The Heartbeat of Culture," *The Nonverbal Communication Reader,* ed. J. A. DeVito and M. L. Hecht (Prospect Heights, IL: Waveland Press, 1990), pp. 332–338.

88. For an extensive discussion on procrastination, see Albert Ellis and William Knaus, *Overcoming Procrastination* (New York: AEI Publications, 1979).

89. Diane Ackerman, "Our Most Mysterious Sense," *Parade Magazine* (June 10, 1990), p. 8.

90. Section based on Joseph DeVito, *Nonverbal Communication Workbook* (Prospect Heights, IL: Waveland Press, 1989), pp. 187–189.

91. Ackerman, p. 8.

92. "The Business of Business Music," "Environmental Music," Muzak Limited Partnership, 1989; Alice Reid, "Unoriginal Sound Tracks," *Washington Post,* January 9, 1998, p. B 1; Ronald Milliman, "The Effects of Slow Tempo Background Music on the Behavior of Supermarket Shoppers," *Journal of Marketing* 46, as reported by Muzak.

93. Carol Austin Bridgewater, "Slow Music Sells," *Psychology Today* 17 (January 1983): 56.

94. Patricia McCormick, "Rock Music Can Weaken Muscles," *Elyria (Ohio) Chronicle-Telegram,* January 12, 1979, "Encore," p. 15.

95. Muzak Limited Partnership, and Reid and Milliman.

96. Loretta Malandro and Larry Barker, *Nonverbal Communication* (New York: Newberry Award Records, 1983), p. 325.

97. Malandro and Barker, p. 329.

Chapter 4

1. Pamela Butler, as noted in Robert McGarvey, "Talk Yourself Up," *USAir Magazine* (March 1990), p. 90.

2. Ibid.

3. Gall Dusa, as noted in McGarvey, p. 90.

4. Dave Grant, as noted in McGarvey, p. 93.

5. Bernie Zilbergeld, as noted in McGarvey, p. 94.

6. Donna R. Vocate, *Interpersonal Communication: Different Voices, Different Minds* (Hillsdale, NJ: Lawrence Erlbaum Associates, 1994), p. 176. For a discussion of the work of L. S. Vygotsky, see Vocate.

7. Ibid.

8. Ibid.

9. Ronald B. Adler, Lawrence B. Rosenfeld, and Russell F. Proctor II, *Interplay: The Process of Interpersonal Communication,* 8th ed. (Orlando, FL: Harcourt, 2001), p. 237.

10. For an in-depth discussion of language development, see Rita C. Naremore and Robert Hopper, *Children Learning Language: A Practical Introduction to Communication Development* (Clifton Park, NY: Thomson/Delmar Learning, 1997).

11. Norman Geschwind, "Language and the Brain," *Scientific American* 226 (April 1972): 76–83; also see Naremore.

12. Mary Duenwald, "Baby Talk Linked to Origin of Language," *Cleveland Plain Dealer,* October 15, 2002, p. E3.

13. Ibid.

14. Mark McKinley, *Crybaby: Analysis of the Cry Language of Babies* (New York: Folkways Records, 1973); also see Marjory Roberts, "No Language But a Cry," *Psychology Today* (June 1987), p. 57.

15. Leon Festinger, *A Theory of Cognitive Dissonance* (Evanston, IL: Row, Peterson, 1957).

16. Sveri Wahlross, *Family Communication* (New York: Macmillan, 1974), p. xi.

17. Long Beach City College of Theatre Arts and Speech, *Communicate,* 3rd ed. (Dubuque, IA: Kendall/Hunt, 1976).

18. William James, *The Principles of Psychology* (New York: Holt, Rinehart and Winston, 1990).

19. Ruth C. Wyle, *The Self-Concept* (Lincoln: University of Nebraska Press, 1979), p. 9.

20. The verb *to be* provides us with our basic label of our self. Native Americans and those from some other cultures, such as West Africans, may have difficulty understanding and applying this concept because of linguistic and cultural differences. Most U.S. Americans, however, should find it an understandable concept.

21. Joseph A. Luft, *Group Process: An Introduction to Group Dynamics* (Palo Alto, CA: National Press, 1963), Chapter 3.

22. Based on Lawrence Rosenfeld, "Relational Disclosure and Feedback," unpublished paper developed by Lawrence Rosenfeld, Department of Communication, University of North Carolina, Chapel Hill.

23. For a discussion of communication and ethnography, see Stuart Sigman, "A Matter of Time: The Case for Ethnographics of Communication," unpublished paper presented at the Speech Communication Association Convention, November 23, 1996, and H. L. Goodall, "Transforming Communication Studies Through Ethnographic

Practices," unpublished paper presented at the Speech Communication Association Convention, November 23, 1996.

24. The description presented is based on a synthesis of theories about ethnography.

25. See, for example, Joe Ayres, A. Kathleen Wilcox, and Debbie M. Ayres, "Receiver Apprehension: An Explanatory Model and Accompanying Research," *Communication Education* 44 (July 1995): 223–235; and Joan E. Aitken and Michael R. Neer, "College Student Question Asking: The Relationship of Classroom Communication Apprehension and Motivation," *Southern Communication Journal* 59 (Fall 1993): 73–81.

26. Joannie M. Schrof and Stacey Schultz, "Social Anxiety," *U.S. News and World Report* (July 21, 1999), p. 50.

27. Beth Azar, "Shy People Have Inaccurate Self-Concepts," *American Psychological Association Monitor* (November 1995): 24.

28. Ibid.

29. Joe Ayres and Tim Hopf, *Coping with Speech Anxiety* (Norwood, NJ: Ablex Publishing, 1993), p. 4.

30. James McCroskey and Virginia Richmond, *The Quiet Ones: Communication Apprehension and Shyness* (Dubuque, IA: CommComp, Gorsuch Scarisbrick, 1980), p. 21.

31. Schrof and Schultz, p. 50.

32. Ibid.

33. Ibid., p. 53.

34. "America's #1 Fear: Public Speaking," *Bruskin/Goldin Research Report* (February 1993), p. 4.

35. "Is Shyness Inherited?" *Healthy Decisions* (Georgetown University Medical Center) (Winter 1997), p. 2.

36. Azar, "Shy People."

37. For an extended discussion of the causes of communication apprehension, see Virginia Richmond and James McCroskey, *Communication: Apprehension, Avoidance, and Effectiveness,* 4th ed. (Scottsdale, AZ: Gorsuch Scarisbrick, 1995).

38. Lawrence R. Wheeless, "An Investigation of Receiver Apprehension and Social Context Dimensions of Communication Apprehension," *Speech Teacher* 24 (September 1975): 261–268.

39. Azur, "Shy People."

40. Ibid.

41. Richmond and McCroskey, pp. 97–101.

42. Ibid., p. 36.

43. Ibid., p. 49.

44. Virginia P. Richmond and K. David Roach, "Willingness to Communicate and Employee Success in U.S. Organizations," *Journal of Applied Communication Research* 20 (February 1992): 104.

45. Schrof and Schultz, p. 54.

46. Ibid.; Anduradha Raghunathan, "Drug Firms Work on Treatment for Extreme Forms of Shyness," *Cleveland Plain Dealer,* May 18, 1999, p. 8A. (Paxil was the first selective serotonin reuptake inhibitor to win approval by the Food and Drug Administration for treatment of debilitating shyness. In addition, the drugs Zoloft and Prozac may be of some value.)

47. Printed by permission of James C. McCroskey. For an in-depth discussion of this and other communication apprehension evaluation tools, see Richmond and McCroskey.

Chapter 5

1. Based on materials developed by Robert Montgomery as they appear in Roy Berko, Lawrence Rosenfeld, and Larry Samovar, *Connecting: A Culture-Sensitive Approach to Interpersonal Communication Competency,* 2nd ed. (Fort Worth: Harcourt Brace, 1997), p. 100.

2. Ibid.

3. Marilyn F. Buckley, "Focus on Research: We Listen a Book a Day; We Speak a Book a Week—Learning from Walter Loban," *Language Arts* 69 (1992): 622–626.

4. For a comprehensive review of information on listening, see the 1990 issue of the *Journal of the International Listening Association;* and Andrew D. Wolvin and Carolyn Gwynn Coakley, eds., *Perspectives on Listening* (Norwood, NJ: Ablex, 1993).

5. Harry C. Payne, "Listening: The Neglected Liberal Art," *Administrator* (May 1998), p. 6.

6. See Larry Barker and Kittie Watson, *Listen Up* (New York: St. Martin's Press, 2001), Chapter 4.

7. *National Strategic Research Plan: Hearing and Hearing Impairment* (Bethesda, MD: National Institute on Deafness and Other Communication Disorders, 1996), 24 March 2002 <http://www.hospital-management.net/informer/breakthroughs/break12/>.

8. Ibid.

9. Interview with Marcia Warren, CCC-A, licensed audiologist, July 10, 2002.

10. "Why Use Active Learning?" Active Learning Online (The Abilene Christian University Adams Center for Teaching Excellence), e-mail: activelearning@acu.edu.

11. James Hill, quoted in Karla Cook, "Want to Remember? Pay Attention!" *Washington Post,* June 19, 1998, p. B5.

12. Berko, Rosenfeld, and Samovar, p. 100.

13. Dorothy Singer and Jerome Singer, "Is Human Imagination Going Down the Tube?" *Chronicle of Higher Education* (April 29, 1979), p. 56. The impact of television on attention is assumed, but it has not been thoroughly researched. See Daniel R. Anderson and John Burns, "Pay Attention to Television," in *Responding to the Screen Reception and Reaction Processes,* ed. Jennings Byant and Dolf Zilman (Hillsdale, NJ: Erlbaum, 1991), pp. 3–25.

14. A. M. Liberman, "The Grammars of Speech and Language," *Cognitive Psychology* 1 (1970): 301–323.

15. Norbert Wiener, *Cybernetics* (Cambridge, MA: MIT Press, 1961); and Norbert Wiener, *The Human Use of Human Beings* (Garden City, NY: Doubleday, 1964).

16. See Andrew Wolvin and Carolyn G. Coakley, *Listening* (New York: McGraw-Hill, 1996), pp. 233–235.

17. Thomas Cahill, *The Gifts of the Jews* (New York: Doubleday, 1998), p. 3.

18. Jack C. Richard, "Listening Comprehension: Approach, Design, Procedure," *TESOL Quarterly* 17 (June 1983): 219–240.

19. For a discussion of left/right brain the theory, see Betty Edwards, *Drawing on the Right Side of the Brain* (Los Angeles: Jeremy Tracher, 1989); Constance Pechura and Joseph Martin, eds., *Mapping the Brain and Its Function* (Washington, D.C.: Institute of Medicine National Academy Press, 1991); and Rebecca Cutter, *When Opposites Attract: Right Brain/Left Brain Relationships and How to Make Them Work* (New York: Dutton, 1994).

20. Satoshi Ishii and Tom Bruneau, "Silence and Silences in Cross-Cultural Perspective: Japan and the United States," *Intercultural Communication: A Reader,* ed. Larry A. Samovar and Richard E. Porter, 7th ed. (Belmont, CA: Wadsworth, 1991), p. 125.

21. Ibid.

22. Edward T. Hall and Mildred R. Hall, *Understanding Cultural Differences* (Yarmouth, ME: Intercultural Press, 1989).

23. Rebecca Reisner, "How Different Cultures Learn," *Meeting News* 17 (June 1993): 30–33.

24. Deborah Atwater, "Issues Facing Minorities in Speech Communication Education: Moving from the Melting Pot to a Tossed Salad," *Proceedings from the Future of Speech Communication Education: Speech Communication Association Flagstaff Conference Report* (Annandale, VA: Speech Communication Association, 1989), p. 41.

25. Ibid.

26. Ibid.

27. Carl R. Rogers and F. J. Roethlisberger, "Barriers and Gateways to Communication," *Harvard Business Review* 30 (July–August 1952): 46–52.

28. Wolvin, pp. 233–235.

29. Harvey Mackay, "Listen Up!" *Successful Meetings* (July 1993).

30. Andrew D. Wolvin and Carolyn Gwynn Coakley, *Listening,* 5th ed. (Dubuque, IA: William C. Brown, 1996). Chapter 3 includes an analysis of the major variables affecting the listening process.

31. Ibid. See also Andrew D. Wolvin, Carolyn G. Coakley, and Kelby K. Halone, "A Preliminary Look At Listening Development Across the Life-Span," *International Journal of Listening* 9 (1995): 62–83.

32. The taxonomy is developed and detailed in Wolvin and Coakley, Part II.

33. Roy Berko and Carolyn Perry, ed., *Speaking, Listening, and Media Literacy Standards for K through 12 Education* (Annandale, VA: Speech Communication Association, 1996), p. 3.

34. Lawrence R. Wheeless, "An Investigation of Receiver Apprehension and Social Context Dimensions of Communication Apprehension," *Speech Teacher* 24 (September 1975): 263.

35. Joe Ayres, "Measuring Patients' Communication Apprehension about Interacting with Physicians: Instrument Development," *Communication Research Reports* 13(1) (Spring 1996): 86–93.

36. Anthony J. Clark, "Communication Confidence and Listening Competence: An Investigation of the Relationships of Willingness to Communicate, Communication Apprehension, and Receiver Apprehension to Comprehension of Content and Emotional Meaning in Spoken Messages," *Communication Education* 38(3) (July 1989): 237–248.

37. Charles J. Wigley, "Student Receiver Apprehension as a Correlate of Trait Argumentativeness," *Communication Research Reports* 4(2) (December 1987): 51–53.

38. Joe Ayres, Tanichya Keereetaweep, Pao-En Chen, and Patricia A. Edwards, "Communication Apprehension and Employment Interviews," *Communication Education* 47(1) (January 1998): 1–17.

39. Edward Addeo and Robert Burger, *Egospeak* (New York: Bantam Books, 1974), p. xiv.

40. *Competent Communication: K–12 Speaking, Listening and Media Literacy Standards and Competency Statements* (Annandale, VA: National Communication Association, 1998).

41. Based on W. James Potter, *Media Literacy* (Thousand Oaks, CA: Sage, 1990), Chapter 18.

42. Based on instruments developed by Paul Torrance, Bernice McCarthy, and Rebecca Cutter.

Chapter 6

1. Rebecca Cline, "Seminar in Interpersonal Communication," unpublished syllabus, Temple University, Philadelphia, n.d.

2. Roy Berko, Lawrence Rosenfeld, and Larry Samovor, *Connecting: A Culture-Sensitive Approach to Interpersonal Communication Competency,* 2nd ed. (Ft. Worth: Harcourt Brace, 1997), p. 16. For additional information on interpersonal communication, see Ronald B. Adler, Lawrence B. Rosenfeld, and Russell F. Proctor II, *Interplay: The Process of Interpersonal Communication,* 8th ed. (Orlando, FL: Harcourt, 2001).

3. Valerie Marchant, "What Bosses Really Want," *Time* (June 28, 1999).

4. Leila Hawken, Robert L. Duran, and Lynne Kelly, "The Relationship of Interpersonal Communication Variables to Academic Success and Persistence in College," *Communication Quarterly* 39 (Fall 1991): 297–308.

5. Ibid., p. 303.

6. For further discussion of the "I," see Calvin S. Hall and Gardner Lindzey, *Theories of Personality* (New York: Wiley, 1957), p. 483.

7. Gerald Marwell and David R. Schmitt, "An Introduction," *Seeking Compliance: The Production of Interpersonal Influence Messages,* ed. James Price Dillard (Scottsdale, AZ: Gorsuch Scarisbrick, 1990), pp. 3–5.

8. For a discussion of the left/right brain theory, see Betty Edwards, *Drawing on the Right Side of the Brain* (Los Angeles: Jeremy Tracher, 1989); Constance Pechura and Joseph Martin, eds., *Mapping the Brain and Its Function* (Washington, D.C.: Institute of Medicine National Academy Press, 1991); and Rebecca Cutter, *When Opposites Attract: Right Brain/Left Brain Relationships and How to Make Them Work* (New York: Dutton, 1994).

9. A theory of Murray Banks, a professional speaker who speaks extensively on leadership, change, performance, and lifestyle.

10. For an extensive investigation of emotional expression, see Berko, pp. 84–95.

11. Berko, p. 428. Also see Robert A. Barraclough and Robert A. Steward, "Power and Control: Social Science Perspectives," *Power in the Classroom,* ed. Virginia P. Richmond and James C. McCroskey (Hillsdale, NJ: Lawrence Erlbaum, 1992), pp. 1–4.

12. George A. Bordon, *Cultural Orientation: An Approach to Understanding Intercultural Communication* (Englewood Cliffs, NJ: Prentice-Hall, 1991), p. 116.

13. Jan Servaes, "Cultural Identity in East and West," *Howard Journal of Communication* 1 (Summer 1998): 64.

14. Deborah Tannen, *You Just Don't Understand* (New York: Morrow, 1990), p. 14.

15. Anne Moir and David Jessell, "Sex and Cerebellum: Thinking About the Real Differences Between Men and Women," *Washington Post,* May 5, 1991, p. K3.

16. Daena J. Goldsmith and Patricia A. Fulfs, as quoted in "Hot Type," *Chronicle of Higher Education* (June 18, 1999), p. A22, from their article in the *1999 Communications Yearbook.*

17. Ibid.

18. For a discussion on the differences between male and female communication, see Lauri P. Arliss and Deborah J. Borisoff, *Women and Men Communicating: Challenge and Changes* (Ft. Worth: Harcourt Brace, 1993); Deborah Tannen, *You Just Don't Understand* (New York: Morrow, 1990); John Gray, *Men Are from Mars, Women Are from Venus: A Practical Guide for Improving Communication and Getting What You Want in Your Relationships* (New York: HarperCollins, 1992); Julia T. Wood, *Gendered Lives: Communication, Gender, and Culture* (Belmont, CA: Wadsworth), 1994; and Lea Stewart, Pamela Cooper, Alan Stewart, and Sheryl Friedley, *Communication and Gender,* 3rd ed. (Scottsdale, AZ: Gorsuch Scarisbrick, 1996). For the American Communication Association's online resource regarding male-female communication, go to <http://www.uark.edu/depts/comminfo/www/gender.html>.

19. Lauri P. Arliss and Deborah J. Borisoff, *Women and Men Communicating: Challenge and Changes* (Ft. Worth: Harcourt Brace, 1993), p. 3.

20. Moir and Jessel, p. K3.

21. Ibid.

22. Arliss and Borisoff, p. 9.

23. Barbara Mathias, "Male Identity Crisis," *Washington Post,* May 3, 1993, p. C5.

24. Gray, p. 16.

25. Mathias, p. C5.

26. Brent Burleson, Kathryn Dindia, and Celeste Conduit, "Gender Communication: Different Cultural Perspectives," panel discussion at the National Communication Association Conference, Chicago, 1997.

27. "What's in a Word? A Job, Hood Senior's Study Says," *Washington Post,* June 6, 1991, p. MD8.

28. Tannen, pp. 43–44.

29. Based on research by H. G. Whittington, James P. Smith, Leonard Kriegel, Lillian Glass, and Hilary Lips.

30. For a discussion on interruptions, see Stewart, Cooper, Stewart, and Friedley, p. 54; and Wood, pp. 31, 144.

31. Based on the research of H. G. Whittington, James P. Smith, Leonard Kriegel, Lillian Glass, and Hilary Lips.

32. Ibid.

33. Ibid.
34. Gray, p. 26.
35. Ibid., p. 25.
36. Ibid., p. 15.
37. Patrick Fanning and Mathew McKay, *Being a Man: A Guide to the New Masculinity* (Oakland, CA: New Harbinger, 1993), p. 13.
38. Gray, pp. 11–13.
39. Gary Kreps, *Sexual Harassment: Communication Implications* (Cresskill, NJ: Hampton Press, 1993), p. 11. For more information, see Mark Walsh, "Court Asked to Define Sex Harassment in the Workplace," *Education Week,* October 20, 1993, p. 37.
40. Kreps, p. 186.
41. Ibid., p. 107.
42. Toni Morrison, Nobel Prize for Literature acceptance speech, December 1993, as reported on National Public Radio.
43. Kreps, p. 1.
44. Ibid., p. 107.
45. Ibid., p. 133.
46. Ibid., p. 13.
47. Ibid., p. 134.
48. Richard Morin, "Harassment Consensus Grows," *Washington Post,* 1992, p. A22.
49. Based on the writings of Rebecca Ray, senior vice president, director of training, American Skandia Corporation.
50. Based on a theory of Jon Nussbaum.
51. Ibid.
52. For a discussion of the economic model of relationships, see Berko, p. 289.
53. Based on the research of Anthony Brandt.
54. The section "The Internet as a Means of Interpersonal Communication" was written with the advice and editorial assistance of Joan Aitken, University of Missouri–Kansas City.
55. John Diekman, "How to Develop Intimate Conversations," *New Woman* 12 (November 1982): 70.
56. "Wiredville, U.S.A.," *Newsweek* (September 20, 1999), p. 62.
57. Sara Sklaroff, "E-mail," *U.S. News & World Report* (March 22, 1999), p. 54.
58. J. B. Walther, "Computer-Mediated Communication: Impersonal, Interpersonal, and Hyperpersonal Interaction," *Communication Research* 23(1) (February 1996): 3–43.
59. Brian Spitzberg, "CMC Competence," Unpublished manuscript draft submitted for the San Diego State University School of Communication Convergence Project, March 23, 1997, p. 1.
60. Lisa Flaherty, Kevin Pearce, and Rebecca Rubin, "Internet and Face-to-Face Communication: Not Functional Alternatives," *Communication Quarterly* 3(46): 250–276.
61. Connie Schultz, "Internet Addiction," *Cleveland Plain Dealer,* based on psychiatrist Nathan Andrew Shapira's study on obsessive Internet use.
62. Martin Corbett and Mike Thatcher, "People Management," *Personal Publications* (June 26, 1997), p. 26.
63. Flaherty, Pearce, and Rubin, pp. 250–276.
64. Corbett Thatcher, p. 26.
65. L. Tao, *What Do We Know About E-mail? An Existing and Emerging Literacy Vehicle* (ERIC Document ED399530), 1995.
66. GeekGirls at <http://www.geekgirls.com/onmail_relationships.htm>.
67. S. Turkle, *The Second Self: Computers and the Human Spirit* (New York: Simon & Schuster, 1984).
68. Based on the theories of Joseph Walther, Northwestern University.
69. Jay Tolson, "The Life of the Mind Goes Digital," *U.S. News & World Report* (March 22, 1999), pp. 58–59.
70. Connie Schultz, based on psychiatrist Nathan Andrew Shapira's study on obsessive Internet use.
71. T. J. Belsare, G. R. Gaffney, and D. W. Black, "Compulsive Computer Use," *American Journal of Psychiatry* 154(2) (February 1997): 289–290.
72. K. Sherer, "College Life On-Line: Healthy and Unhealthy Internet Use," *Journal of College Student Development* 38(6) (November–December 1997): 655–665.
73. Schultz.
74. Ibid.
75. Ibid.
76. Ibid.
77. Ibid.
78. Amy Harmon, "Sad, Lonely World Discovered," *New York Times,* reporting about *Homenet,* a $1.5 million project sponsored by Intel Corporation, Hewlett-Packard, AT&T Research, Apple Computer, and the National Science Foundation.
79. Ibid.
80. The concepts of sociologist Sherry Trukle, author of *Life on the Screen,* and psychiatrist Esther Gwinnell, author of *Online Seductions,* as referred to in Wray Herbert, "Getting Close, But Not Too Close," *U.S. News & World Report* (March 22, 1999), pp. 56–57.
81. Malcolm Parks and Floyd Kory, "Making Friends in Cyberspace," *Journal of Communication* 46(1) (Winter 1996).
82. Corbett and Thatcher, p. 26.
83. Harmon.
84. Marc Silver, "Hooked on Instant Messages," *U.S. News & World Report* (March 22, 1999), p. 57.
85. *1999 Report on Cyberstalking*<http://www.usdoj.gov/criminal/cyber crime/cyberstalking.htm>.
86. <http://www.mgrossmanlaw.com/articles/1997/cyberstalking.htm>.
87. Parks and Kory.
88. Flaherty, Pearce, and Rubin.
89. Herbert, p. 56.
90. Corbett and Thatcher.
91. Sklaroff, p. 55.
92. Adapted from Pamela Cumming, "Empowerment Profile," *The Power Handbook* (Boston: CBI, 1981), pp. 2–5.
93. As conceived by Peggy Post. <http://www.emilypost.com>.

Chapter 7

1. Pam Kruger, "How to Talk to Anyone About Anything," *Redbook* (April 1994), p. 132.
2. Gary Althen, "The Americans Have to Say Everything," *Communication Quarterly* 40 (Fall 1992): 415.
3. Ibid., p. 414.
4. LaVerne L. Ludden and Tom Capozzoli, *Supervisor Savvy: How to Retain and Develop Entry-Level Workers* (Indianapolis, IN: JIST Publishing, 2000).
5. Roy Berko, Lawrence Rosenfeld, and Larry Samovar, *Connecting: A Culture-Sensitive Approach to Interpersonal Communication Competency,* 2nd ed. (Fort Worth: Harcourt Brace, 1997), p. 372.
6. Ibid.
7. William A. Donohue, with Robert Kolt, *Managing Interpersonal Conflict* (Newbury Park, CA: Sage, 1992), p. 2.
8. Ibid., p. 3.
9. Ibid.
10. Diana Rowland, *Japanese Business Etiquette* (New York: Warner Books, 1985), p. 5.
11. Lennie Copeland and Lewis Griggs, *Going International* (New York: Random House, 1985), p. 109.
12. Berko, Rosenfeld, and Samovar, p. 374.
13. For a further discussion, see Joseph A. DeVoit, *The Interpersonal Communication Book* (New York: Longman, 1998), p. 372.
14. Donohue and Holt, pp. 12–17.
15. Harriet Goldhor Lerner, *The Dance of Anger* (New York: Perennial Library, 1985), p. 1.

16. Based on the concepts of Marlene Arthur Penkstaff.
17. A theory of Dr. Susan Forward, media psychologist and author.
18. Ibid.
19. The principles are based on the theories of Sonya Friedman.
20. Roy Berko, "Dealing With Stress," unpublished paper presented in a workshop to the counseling staff at the Alexandria (VA) Social Service Agency, December 1993.
21. This is a principle of Gestalt therapy, as explained by Les Wyman, Gestalt Institute, Cleveland, OH.
22. "Activity 1," handout developed by Mary Adams Trujillo and Laurie Miller and distributed at the workshop "Responding to Conflict Around Issues of Difference," National Conference for Community and Justice, Northern Ohio Region, February 19, 1999, Cleveland, OH.
23. Ibid.
24. Ibid.
25. Ibid.
26. "When and How to Apologize," pamphlet produced by the University of Nebraska Cooperative Extension and the Nebraska Health and Human Services System, n.d.
27. Dennis R. Tesdell, "The Top 10 ways to Apologize to Someone You Have Hurt or Offended," February 2, 1997, lifecoach@coachdt.com.
28. Ibid.
29. Rosamund Stone Zander, "The Power of An Apology," *Parade* (July 29, 2001), p. 8.
30. Discussion based on shyness-workshop materials prepared by Phyllis DeMark, Lorain County Community College, Elyria, OH, n.d.
31. Sharon Bower and Gordon Bower, *Asserting Yourself* (Reading, MA: Addison-Wesley, 1976), p. 87.
32. For a discussion on business negotiation, see Deborah A. Cai and Laura E. Drake, "The Business of Business Negotiation: Intercultural Perspectives," *Communication Yearbook* 21 (1998): 153–189.
33. Code of Virginia, Chapter 20.2, Section 8:01–576.4 (July 1993).
34. For information on mediation, see Jonathan G. Shailor, *Empowerment in Dispute Mediation: A Critical Analysis of Communication* (Westport, CT: London, 1994); and Dorothy J. Della Noce, *Mediation Fundamentals: A Training Manual* (Richmond, VA: Better Business Bureau Foundation of Virginia, 1993).
35. Matthew McKay, "How to Handle Criticism," *Bottom Line Personal* (August 1, 1994), p. 11.
36. Based on theories of Deborah Weider-Hatfield.

Chapter 8

1. Alan Gratch, "The Interview: Who Should Be Talking to Whom?" *Wall Street Journal,* February 29, 1988, p. A8.
2. Ibid.
3. Steve D. Ugbah and Randall E. Majors, "Influential Communication Factors in Employment Interviews," *Journal of Business Communication* 29 (Spring 1992): 145–159.
4. Laura M. Graves and Ronald J. Karren, "The Employee Selection Interview: A Fresh Look at an Old Problem," *Human Resource Management* (Summer 1996), pp. 163–180.
5. Concept and questions are based on Pierre Mornell, "Zero Defect Hiring," *Inc.* (March 1998), p. 78.
6. For an extensive review of employment interviews, see Jeanne Tessier Barone and Jo Young Switzer, *Interviewing Art and Skills* (Boston: Allyn & Bacon, 1995), Chapter 8.
7. Frank S. Endicott, *Making the Most of Your Job Interview* (New York: New York Life Insurance Company, n.d.).
8. "Executive Grooming 101," *Washington Post Magazine,* November 15, 1992, p. 16.
9. Robert McGarvey, "Tailoring an Image," *USAir Magazine* (May 1990), p. 76.
10. Ellen James Martin, "Making a Good First Impression," *Baltimore Sun,* May 27, 1991, p. 3.
11. McGarvey, p. 78.
12. Ibid., p. 80.
13. "Executive Grooming 101," p. 30.
14. McGarvey, p. 80.
15. Charles J. Stewart and William B. Cash Jr., *Interviewing Principles and Practices* (Dubuque, IA: William C. Brown, 1997), p. 248.
16. U.S. Department of Labor, Employment and Training Administration, *Merchandising Your Job Talents* (Washington, D.C.: U.S. Government Printing Office, n.d.), pp. 7–8.
17. Anthony Medley, *Sweaty Palms: The Neglected Art of Being Interviewed* (Belmont, CA: Lifetime Learning Publications, 1978), excerpted in "Spring Job Market '81," *Washington Post,* May 3, 1981, pp. 11, 16.
18. Charles J. Stewart, *Teaching Interviewing for Career Preparation* (Urbana, IL: ERIC Clearinghouse on Reading and Communication Skills, 1976), p. 8.
19. Vernon D. Miller and Patrice M. Buzzanell, "Toward a Research Agenda for the Second Employment Interview," *Journal of Applied Communication Research* 24 (August 1996): 165.
20. Amy Joyce, "How to Keep Cool on the Interview Hot Seat," *Washington Post Business* (June 21, 1999), p. 8.
21. Ron Grant, president, Meridian Resources, Greenville, SC.
22. Ronald P. Lovell, *The Newspaper* (Belmont, CA: Wadsworth, 1980), p. 229.
23. Sandra O'Connell, *The Manager as Communicator* (New York: Harper & Row, 1979), p. 21.
24. Norman C. Hill, *Counseling at the Workplace* (New York: McGraw-Hill, 1981), p. 10.
25. A psychological theory expressed on several broadcasts by Susan Forward, media psychologist.
26. Michael E. Stano and N. L. Reinsch Jr., *Communication in Interviews* (Englewood Cliffs, NJ: Prentice-Hall, 1982), pp. 262–267.
27. For a review of this research, see Lawrence R. Wheeless, Robert Barraclough, and Robert Stewart, "Compliance-Gaining and Power in Persuasion," *Communication Yearbook* 7, ed. R. N. Bostrom (Beverly Hills, CA: Sage, 1983), pp. 105–145.
28. These strategies are spelled out in detail in V. R. Buzzotta, R. E. Lefton, and Manuel Sherberg, *Effective Selling Through Psychology* (Cambridge, MA: Ballinger, 1982), Chapter 5.
29. "Cold Feet," *Entrepreneur* (August 1996), p. 108.
30. Stano and Reinsch, p. 99.
31. Judi Brownell, "The Performance Appraisal Interview: A Multi-Purpose Communication Assignment," *Bulletin of the Association for Business Communication* 57 (June 1994): 11–21.
32. Kate Moore, "Love Those Evaluations," *Washington Post,* January 4, 1998, p. H4.
33. Paul Preston, *Communication for Managers* (Englewood Cliffs, NJ: Prentice-Hall, 1979), p. 254.
34. List based in part on Joan Linder, "Accepting Criticism Gracefully," *Secretary* (May 1990), p. 29.
35. Walter R. Mahler, *How Effective Executives Interview* (Homewood, IL: Dow Jones-Irwin, 1976), p. 118.
36. "Delivering Bad News with the Good in Performance Reviews," *Washington Post,* May 26, 1996, p. H4.
37. Joseph P. Zima, *Effective Interviewing* (Palo Alto, CA: SRA, 1983), p. 281.
38. Ibid., p. 284.
39. Stewart and Cash, p. 286.
40. T. Richard Cheatham and Keith V. Erickson, *The Police Officer's Guide to Better Communication* (Glenview, IL: Scott, Foresman, 1984), p. 37.
41. Richard N. Bolles, *What Color Is Your Parachute?* (Berkeley, CA: Ten Speed Press, 2003).

Chapter 9

1. *Group Problem-Solving and Meeting Dynamics,* blind review manuscript (Cincinnati, OH: Southwestern, 1993), p. 2.
2. J. Dan Rothwell, *In Mixed Company* (Ft. Worth: Harcourt Brace, 1992), p. 6.
3. *Group Problem-Solving and Meeting Dynamics,* p. 3.
4. Ernest Bormann, *Discussion and Group Methods* (New York: Harper & Row, 1969), p. 304.
5. Rothwell, p. 40.
6. Charles H. Kepner and Benjamin B. Tregoe, *The Rational Manager: A Systematic Approach to Problem Solving and Decision Making* (New York: McGraw-Hill, 1965).
7. Irving Janis, *Victims of Groupthink* (Boston: Houghton Mifflin, 1972).
8. For an extended discussion of groupthink, see Irving Janis, *Groupthink: Psychological Studies of Policy Decisions and Fiascoes* (Boston: Houghton Mifflin, 1983).
9. Gregory Moorhead, Richard Ference, and Chris P. Neck, "Group Decision Fiascoes Continue: Space Shuttle *Challenger* and a Revised Groupthink Framework," *Social Psychology 2001–2002,* ed. Mark H. Davis (Guilford, CT: McGraw-Hill/Dushkin, 2001), p. 201.
10. *Group Problem-Solving and Meeting Dynamics,* p. 7.
11. The theory of Bibb Latane, Kipling Williams, and Stephen Harkins.
12. Charles C. Manz and Henry P. Sims Jr., *Business Without Bosses* (New York: Wiley, 1993), p. 211.
13. Ibid., p. 2.
14. William Higgins, "Group Study: Strength in Numbers," *Computer Connection* 4 (October 1990): 1.
15. Marianne Schneider Corey and Harald Corey, *Groups: Process and Practice,* 3rd ed. (Monterey, CA: Brooks/Cole, 1987), p. 9.
16. Marilyn Elias, "Self-Help Groups," *Denver Post,* July 13, 1980, p. 38.
17. A theory of Susan Forward, media psychologist, Talknet Radio Network.
18. "How Cancer Patients Are Talking Their Way to a Longer Life," *Good Housekeeping* (June 1990), p. 251.
19. "Ann Landers," *Washington Post,* March 15, 1990, p. B12.
20. For a discussion on the various definitions of a *family,* see Laurie Arliss, *Contemporary Family Communication: Meaning and Messages* (New York: St. Martin's Press, 1993); Judy Pearson, *Communicating in the Family: Seeking Satisfaction in Changing Times,* 2nd ed. (New York: HarperCollins, 1993); Janet Yerby, Nancy Buerkel-Rothfuss, and Arthur Bochner, *Understanding Family Communication,* 2nd ed. (Scottsdale, AZ: Gorsuch Scarisbrick, 1995); and Kathleen Galvin and Bernard Brommel, *Family Communication: Cohesion and Change,* 4th ed. (New York: HarperCollins, 1996).
21. Rothwell, pp. 55–80.
22. Ibid., pp. 65–66.
23. Matt Helms, "License to Hate," *National College Magazine* (September 1992), p. 61.
24. Ibid., p. 64.
25. Henry M. Robert III and William J. Evans, *Robert's Rules of Order, Newly Revised,* 9th ed. (Glenview, IL: Scott, Foresman, 1990), pp. 52–55.
26. In parliamentary procedure, the term *consensus* means "unanimous." In nonparliamentary use, the term is often assumed to mean "generally." For voting purposes, it is synonymous with *all.* See Robert and Evans, pp. 52–55.
27. Robert and Evans, pp. 399–400.
28. *Part-of-the-whole voting* is sometimes referred to as *2/3 voting.* For a discussion, see Robert and Evans, pp. 396–397.
29. Rothwell, p. 195.
30. Ibid.
31. Janis, p. 197.
32. The classic Dewey inductive process was first discussed in John Dewey, *How to Think* (Boston: D. C. Heath, 1910), pp. 68–78.
33. Janis, p. 219.
34. Ibid., p. 203.
35. A process refined by Roy Berko from a concept of Eileen Breckenridge.
36. Rothwell, p. 221.
37. Michael Mayer, "Behaviors Leading to More Effective Decisions in Small Groups Embedded in Organizations," *Communication Reports* 11 (Summer 1998): 123–132.
38. For a discussion on group meeting spaces, see Dale Leathers, *Successful Nonverbal Communication,* 2nd ed. (New York: Macmillan, 1997), pp. 407–411.
39. Ibid.
40. Mark Knapp and Judith Hall, *Nonverbal Communication in Human Interaction,* 4th ed. (Ft. Worth: Harcourt Brace, 1997), p. 175.
41. Leathers, pp. 407–411.
42. Ibid.
43. Mark Knapp and Judith Hall, *Nonverbal Communication in Human Interaction,* 3rd ed. (Ft. Worth: Harcourt Brace, 1992), p. 168.
44. For a discussion of round and rectangular tables, see Knapp and Hall, 4th ed., pp. 177–179.
45. Leathers, pp. 407–411.
46. Knapp and Hall, 3rd ed., p. 168.
47. Ibid.
48. From the research of R. Sommer, as found in Knapp and Hall, 4th ed., pp. 116–118.
49. Research reported by Janet Fulk, University of Southern California, Annenberg School for Communication, in Barbara Langham, "Mediated Meetings," *Successful Meetings,* January 1995, p. 75.
50. Ron Zemke, "The Rediscovery of Videotape Teleconferencing," *Training* (September 1986), p. 46.
51. Isa Engleberg and Dianna Wynn, *Working in Groups* (Boston: Houghton Mifflin, 1997), p. 345.
52. Fulk, p. 75.
53. Ibid., pp. 75–76.
54. Ibid., p. 76.
55. The 3M Meeting Management Team with Jeannine Drew, *Mastering Meetings: Discovering the Hidden Potential of Effective Business Meetings* (New York: McGraw-Hill, 1994), pp. 114–115.
56. Engleberg and Wynn, p. 345.
57. Lee Fehl, "The World at Your Fingertips," *Successful Meetings* (March 1999), p. 91.
58. Ibid.
59. Ibid.
60. Engleberg and Wynn, p. 345.
61. 3M, p. 115.
62. Ibid.
63. Engleberg and Wynn, p. 345.
64. Fulk, p. 75.
65. 3M, p. 116.
66. Ibid., p. 123.
67. Ibid., pp. 116–118.
68. Ibid., pp. 121–122.
69. *Group Problem-Solving and Meeting Dynamics,* pp. 30–31; and Fulk, p. 76.

Chapter 10

1. George A. Borden, *Cultural Orientation: An Approach to Understanding Intercultural Communication* (Englewood Cliffs, NJ: Prentice-Hall, 1991), p. 133.

2. Larry Samovar and Richard Porter, *Intercultural Communication: A Reader* (Belmont, CA: Wadsworth, 1994), p. 79.

3. Gerry Philipsen, "Navaho World View and Culture Patterns of Speech: A Case Study in Ethnorhetoric," *Speech Monographs* (June 1972): 138.

4. Ibid.

5. Ibid.

6. Borden, p. 105.

7. Ibid.

8. Samovar and Porter, p. 79.

9. Ibid., p. 298.

10. Ibid., p. 291.

11. Ibid.

12. Ibid.

13. Ibid.

14. Ibid.

15. Ibid.

16. Ibid.

17. Janet Fox, "Changing Leadership Styles," *Amtrak Express* (May–June 1993).

18. Pearson, p. 338.

19. Laurie Arliss and Deborah Borisoff, *Women and Men Communicating* (Fort Worth: Harcourt Brace, 1993), p. 168.

20. Lea Stewart, Alan Stewart, Sheryl Friedley, and Pam Cooper, *Communication Between the Sexes* (Scottsdale, AZ: Gorsuch Scarisbrick, 1990), p. 162.

21. Ibid., p. 163.

22. Barbara Bates, *Communication and the Sexes* (New York: Harper & Row, 1988), p. 155.

23. Arliss and Borisoff, p. 168.

24. Ibid.

25. Stewart et al., p. 159.

26. Julie Ann Wambach, *Group Problem Solving Through Communication Styles* (Dubuque, IA: Kendall/Hunt, 1992), p. 150.

27. Based on the work of James E. Sikell, Florida Maxima Corporation.

28. Dorrine Turecamo, "Perfect Timing," *Successful Meetings* (October 1992), p. 119.

29. Kenneth D. Benne and Paul Sheets, "Functional Roles of Group Members," *Journal of Social Issues* 4 (Spring 1948): 41–49.

30. Dale Leathers, *Successful Nonverbal Communication* (New York: Macmillan, 1992), p. 376.

31. J. Dan Rothwell, *In Mixed Company* (Ft. Worth: Harcourt Brace, 1992), pp. 116–119.

32. James MacGregor Burns, *Leadership* (New York: Harper & Row, 1978). For an analysis of leadership by noted social critics and leadership experts, see the March–April 1987 issue of *Liberal Education*. Also see Judy B. Rosener, "Ways Women Lead," *Harvard Business Review* (November–December 1990): 119–125.

33. Burns, p. 4.

34. Charles C. Manz and Henry P. Sims Jr., *Superleadership* (Englewood Cliffs, NJ: Prentice-Hall, 1989).

35. Ralph White and Ronald Lippitt, "Leader Behavior and Member Reactions in Three Social Climates," *Group Dynamics,* ed. D. Cartwright and A. Zander (New York: Harper & Row, 1968), pp. 318–335.

36. Rothwell, p. 147.

37. For a discussion of leadership style, see Fred Fielder, *A Theory of Leadership Effectiveness* (New York: McGraw-Hill, 1967).

38. Arlene Schubert and George Schubert, "Leadership Emergence via Nonverbal Communication," paper presented at the Central States Speech Association Convention, Chicago, April 13, 1978, p. 1.

39. Michael Hackman and Craig Johnson, "Teaching Leadership from a Communication Perspective," unpublished paper, Department of Communication, University of Colorado, Colorado Springs, n.d., p. 6.

40. Hackman and Johnson, p. 2.

41. Schubert and Schubert, p. 3.

42. Based on a concept developed by Patricia Hayes, Indiana University–Bradley.

43. Wambach, pp. 168–169.

44. Contributed by Isa Engleberg, Prince George's Community College, Largo, MD. Used with permission.

Chapter 11

1. Kathleen Kendall, "Do Real People Ever Give Speeches?" *Central States Speech Journal* 25 (Fall 1974): 235. Other follow-up studies have affirmed the conclusion.

2. Kent Menzel and Lori Carrell, "The Relationship Between Preparation and Performance in Public Speaking," *Communication Education* 43 (January 1994): 17.

3. Brigid Schulte, "Web of Cheating," *Cleveland Plain Dealer*, October 8, 2002, p. E1.

4. Ibid.

5. For an extended discussion of demographics, see Andrew Wolvin, Roy Berko, and Darlyn Wolvin, *The Public Speaker/ The Public Listener*, 2nd ed.(Los Angeles: Roxbury, 1999), pp. 85–88.

6. For an extended discussion of speech outlining, see Wolvin, Berko, and Wolvin, pp. 198–202.

7. Based on content of <http://www.owl.english.purdue.edu/handouts/general/gl_outline.html>.

8. Ibid.

9. For an extended discussion of preparing the manuscript speech, see Wolvin, Berko, and Wolvin, pp. 204–209.

10. Based on the teachings and theory of speech coach Dorothy Sarnoff.

11. Stuart W. Hyde, *Television and Radio Announcing,* 4th ed. (Boston: Houghton Mifflin, 1995), p. 81.

12. For an extended discussion of pronunciation and articulation, see Jon Eisenson, *Voice and Diction: A Program for Improvement,* 6th ed. (Needham, MA: Allyn & Bacon, 1992).

13. Hyde, pp. 83–85.

14. For a discussion on using gestures in a speech, see Wolvin, Berko, and Wolvin, pp. 220–222.

15. Joe Ayres and Tim Hopf, *Coping with Speech Anxiety* (Norwood, NJ: Ablex, 1993), p. xi.

16. Debbye Turner, *The Early Show,* CBS-TV, July 31, 2002.

17. Psychologist Shirley Impelizari, appearing on *The Early Show*, CBS-TV, July 31, 2002.

18. Ayres and Hopf, p. 1.

19. Ibid., p. 5.

20. These principles are based on concepts of Morton C. Orman, M.D., as presented in "How To Conquer Public Speaking Fear," <http://www.stresscure.com/jobstress/speak.html>. For additional information on Dr. Orman's theories, see M. C. Orman, *The 14-Day Stress Cure* (Sparks, MD: TRO Productions, n.d.).

21. Ibid., p. 1.

22. Ibid. p. 2.

23. Ibid.

24. Ibid.

25. Ibid., p. 6.

26. Ibid.

27. Ibid., p. 7.

28. Ibid.

29. "America's #1 Fear: Public Speaking," *Bruskin/Goldin Research Report* (February 1993), p. 4.

30. Only anecdotal evidence is available to demonstrate that these activities are effective.

31. Discussion based on information given by Les Wyman, Gestalt Institute, Cleveland, OH.

32. John A. Daly, Anita L. Vangelist, and David Weber, "Speech Anxiety Affects How People Prepare Speeches: A Protocol Analysis of the Preparation Processes of Speakers," *Communication Monographs* 62: 383–397.

33. Kent E. Menzel and Lori J. Carrell, "The Relationship Between Preparation and Performance in Public Speaking," *Communication Education* 43: 17–26.

34. There are mental health centers such as the Public Speaking–Social Anxiety Center of New York (http://www.speakeeezi.com) that specifically deal with public performance apprehension.

35. Menzel and Carrell, pp. 17–26.

36. This is a section of the "Personal Report on Communication Apprehension" (PRCA-24) from Virginia P. Richmond and James C. McCroskey, *Communication: Apprehension, Avoidance and Effectiveness,* 4th ed. (Scottsdale, AZ: Gorsuch Scarisbrick, 1995), pp. 129–130. For a more comprehensive public speaking apprehension test, students should take the PRPSA (Personal Report on Public Speaking Anxiety), which is reprinted in the Instructor's Resource Manual accompanying this text.

Chapter 12

1. *Research on Digital Libraries* (Arlington, VA: National Science Foundation, 1993), p. 1.

2. In *Evidence* (Boston: Houghton Mifflin, 1969), Robert Newman and Dale Newman provide insight into the types of bias present in many sources of information.

3. Pat Guy, "U.S. News to Be on Computer," *USA Today,* November 26, 1993, p. 5B.

4. The catalog can be obtained from ABC News by calling 1-800-505-6139.

5. For a discussion of computer searches, see Carolyn Wolfe and Richard Wolfe, *Basic Library Skills,* 2nd ed. (Jefferson, NC: McFarland, 1986), pp. 113–118.

6. Steven R. Knowlton, "How Students Get Lost in Cyberspace," *Washington Post,* November 2, 1997, p. 18.

7. Ibid.

8. Ibid.

9. Ibid.

10. Ibid.

11. Ibid., p. 21.

12. Christina Pino-Marina, "Online Resources for Legitimate Research," *Cleveland Plain Dealer,* October 8, 2002, p. E3.

13. Ibid.

14. Newman and Newman.

15. Jim Cope, "Data Overload: Separating Gold from Garbage," *Hemisphere* (April 1998), p. 33.

16. Deborah Tannen, *I Only Say This Because I Love You: How the Way We Talk Can Make or Break Family Relationships Throughout Our Lives* (New York: Random House, 2001), p. 98.

17. For an in-depth discussion of styles, see John Bourhis, Carey Adams, Scott Titsworth, and Lynn Harter, *Style Manual for Communication Studies* (New York: McGraw-Hill, 2002).

18. Joanna Slan, *Using Stories and Humor* (Needham, MA: Allyn & Bacon, 1998), p. 26.

19. Norris McWhirter, *1984 Guinness Book of World Records* (New York: Sterling, 1984), p. 28.

20. Rob Rachowiecki, *Ecuador* (Berkeley, CA: Lonely Planet Publications, 1986), p. 13.

21. Darrell Huff, *How to Lie with Statistics* (New York: Norton, 1954), pp. 123–142.

22. For extended discussions of communication research, see Rebecca Rubin, Alan Rubin, and Linda Piele, *Communication Research: Strategies and Sources,* 3rd ed. (Belmont, CA: Wadsworth, 1993); and James Watt and Sjef van den Berg, *Research Methods for Communication Science* (Needham, MA: Allyn & Bacon, 1995).

23. The 3M Management Team with Jeannine Drew, *Mastering Meetings* (New York: McGraw-Hill, 1994), pp. 141–143. For additional material about visual thinking, the design and aesthetics of displaying information, how to present information visually, and the credibility of visual evidence, see Edward Tufte, *The Visual Display of Quantitative Information* (Cheshire, CT: Graphics Press).

24. Russell Shaw, "When the Presentation Went Up in Smoke," *Sky* (November 1996), p. 39.

25. Bill Eadies, "PowerPoint in the Basic Course," *SPECTRA,* National Communication Association (July 2001), p. 7.

26. Ibid.

Chapter 13

1. Charles Petrie, "Informative Speaking: A Summary and Bibliography of Related Research," *Speech Monographs* 30 (June 1963): 79–91.

2. Jack E. Hulbert, "Planning and Delivering Effective Oral Presentations," *Business Education Forum* 50 (April 1996): 43.

3. Richard A. Lindeborg, "A Quick and Easy Strategy for Organizing a Speech," *IEEE Transactions on Professional Communication* 33 (September 1990): 133–134.

4. Morris Mandel, *Stories for Speakers* (New York: Jonathan David, 1964).

5. Senko K. Maynard, "Contrastive Rhetoric: A Case of Nominalization in Japanese and English Discourse," *Language Sciences* 18 (1996): 944.

6. Ulla Connor, *Contrastive Rhetoric: Cross-Cultural Aspects of Second Language Writing* (New York: Cambridge University Press, 1996), p. 45.

7. Melbourne S. Cummings, "Teaching the Black Rhetoric Course," unpublished paper, Educational Resources Information Center, 1983, p. 5.

8. Connor, p. 52.

9. Gerry Philipsen, "Navajo World View and Cultural Patterns of Speech: A Case Study in Ethnorhetoric," *Speech Monographs* 39(2) (1972): 133.

10. Richard Morris and Philip Wander, "Native American Rhetoric: Dancing in the Shadows of the Ghost Dance," *Quarterly Journal of Speech* 76 (1990): 170.

11. Gerald J. Alred, "Teaching in Germany and the Rhetoric of Culture," *Journal of Business and Technical Communication* 11 (1997): 363.

12. Connor, p. 41.

13. Ibid., p. 37.

14. Ibid., p. 36.

15. Annie Lang, "Effects of Chronological Presentation of Information on Processing and Memory for Broadcast News," *Journal of Broadcasting and Electronic Media* 33 (Fall 1989): 441–452.

Chapter 14

1. Connie Koenenn, "The Future Is Now," *Washington Post,* February 3, 1989, p. B5.

2. Richard Wurman, *Information Anxiety,* 2nd ed. (Garden City, NY: Que, 2000).

3. Michael F. Warlum, "Improving Oral Marketing Presentations in the Technology-Based Company," *IEEE Transactions on Professional Communication* 31 (June 1988): 84.

4. Richard Hoehn, *The Art and Practice of Public Speaking* (New York: McGraw-Hill, 1988).

5. Categories are based on those reported in James H. Byrns, *Speak for Yourself: An Introduction to Public Speaking* (New York: Random House, 1981), Chapters 14–17.

6. H. Lloyd Goodall and Christopher L. Waagen, *The Persuasive Presentation* (New York: Harper & Row, 1986), p. 105.

7. Suggestions for structuring a technical report are based on Richard Weigand, *Business Horizons,* School of Business, Indiana University, Bloomington, as reported in *Communicating Briefings* (January 1986).

8. Hoehn.

9. G. H. Jamieson, *Communication and Persuasion* (London: Croom Helm, 1985), pp. 5–16.

10. Hoehn.

11. Ibid.

Chapter 15

1. Bruce E. Gronbeck, Raymie E. McKerow, Douglas Ehninger, and Alan H. Monroe, *Principles and Types of Speech Communication,* 12th ed. (New York: HarperCollins, 1997), Chapter 8.

2. For a review of this research, see Sarah Trenholm, *Persuasion and Social Influence* (Englewood Cliffs, NJ: Prentice-Hall, 1989), Chapters 3 and 10.

3. Richard E. Petty and John T. Cacioppo, "The Elaboration Likelihood Model of Persuasion," *Advances in Experimental Social Psychology,* ed. Leonard Berkowitz (New York: Academic Press, 1986), pp. 123–181.

4. "*New York Times* News Survey," as reported in Andrew J. Cherlin, "I'm O.K., You're Selfish," *New York Times,* October 17, 1999, pp. 44, 46, and 48.

5. Robert B. Cialdini, "Harnessing the Science of Persuasion," *Harvard Business Review* 79 (October 2001): 72–79.

6. Aristotle, *The Rhetoric of Aristotle,* trans. Lane Cooper (New York: Appleton-Century-Crofts, 1932).

7. Based on a speech given by an inmate of the Grafton Prison Farm, Grafton, OH. Name and setting withheld by request.

8. Robert B. Maxwell, "The 'Graying' of America," *Vital Speeches of the Day* (September 15, 1987), p. 710.

9. Jim Courter, "Step by Step," *Vital Speeches of the Day* (July 15, 1987), p. 581.

10. Donald M. Stewart, "Good Writing," *Vital Speeches of the Day* (August 1, 1987), p. 633.

11. James A. Baker III, "America and the Collapse of the Soviet Empire," in a speech presented at Princeton University, December 12, 1991, published in *Vital Speeches of the Day* (January 1, 1992), p. 167.

12. Duane A. Kullberg, "Accounting and Accountability," *Vital Speeches of the Day* (July 15, 1987), p. 608.

13. Barbara Breadon, *Speaking to Persuade* (Ft. Worth: Harcourt Brace, 1996), p. 237.

14. Ibid.

15. Ibid., p. 109.

16. Ibid.

17. Ibid., p. 110.

18. Monroe's Motivated Sequence, as explained in Breadon, p. 112.

19. The discussion that follows is based on Breadon, pp. 112–113.

20. Abraham Maslow, *Motivation and Personality* (New York: Harper & Row, 1970), pp. 35–58. How Maslow's hierarchy is reflected in societal needs is demonstrated in M. Joseph Sirgy, "A Quality-of-Life Theory Derived from Maslow's Developmental Perspective," *American Journal of Economics and Sociology* 45 (July 1986): 329–342.

21. John Harmon McElroy, *American Beliefs* (Chicago: Ivan R. Dee, 1999), p. 220.

22. Discussion adapted from the theories of Gronbeck, McKerrow, Ehninger, and Monroe as described in all editions of *Principles and Types of Speech Communication* (Glenview, IL: Scott, Foresman/Boston: Little, Brown).

23. A comprehensive summary of research on fear appeals is provided in James P. Dillard, "Rethinking the Study of Fear Appeals: An Emotional Perspective," *Communication Theory* 4 (November 1994): 295–323.

24. Eugene Finerman, "Humor and Speeches," *Vital Speeches of the Day* 62 (March 1, 1996): 313.

25. Jonathan Alter and Pat Wingert, "The Return of SHAME," *Newsweek* (February 6, 1995), p. 22.

Appendix 1

1. This material is a reprint of materials available from Kinko's, a registered trademark of Kinko's Graphics Corporation. Permission granted by David Bowman, President of TTG Consultants, Los Angeles, CA, a career management and human resources consulting firm. Dates on the résumés have been updated.

2. Robert E. Steinman, "The Latest Wrinkle in Job Search," *Cincinnati Enquirer,* October 8, 1995, p. G1.

3. Ibid.

4. Ibid.

Appendix 2

1. *Using American Psychological Association (APA) Format* (updated to the 5th edition of the *Publication Manual of the American Psychological Association,* 2001), Purdue University Online Writing Lab.

GLOSSARY

1-3-6 Decision-Making Technique   A format for decision making in which each participant works alone (1), then in a group of 3 and then in a group of 6.

Accent   The pronunciation and intonation used by a person that may cause some difficulty in understanding; sound is clearly identifiable yet often is not always understood by those outside a geographic area, such as what happens with a "Southern accent."

Accenting relationship   The relationship of verbal and nonverbal communication in which the nonverbal message stresses the verbal one, such as turning the person to look at you while commanding, "When I speak to you, look at me!"

Action chain   A behavioral sequence with two or more participating organisms, in which there are standard steps for reaching a goal, such as the sequence of two businessmen meeting and greeting each other.

Action questions   Devices used in the presentation section of a speech that are intended to get the audience involved in the presentation by making the listeners think and respond.

Action-reaction principle   A theory that indicates that if someone acts in a particular way toward another person, the other person will react in a parallel manner. For example, when we smile, others are likely to smile back.

Ad hominem argument   Developing an argument by attacking the personal character of a source.

Ad ignorantium argument   An attempt to prove that a statement is true because it cannot be disproved.

Ad lib speaking   A speech given in which a speaker has no time to organize ideas and responds immediately when answering a question, volunteering an opinion, or interacting during an interpersonal experience.

Ad populum argument   An appeal to people's prejudices and passions rather than an effort to focus on the issue at hand.

Adaptors   Movements that accompany boredom, show internal feelings, or regulate a situation. For example, those who are bored often tap their fingers on a table or bounce a crossed leg.

Adjourning   A group's temporarily or permanently going out of existence.

Aesthetics   The communication of a message or mood through color or music.

Affect displays   Facial gestures that show emotions and feelings such as sadness or happiness; pouting, winking, and raising or lowering the eyelids and eyebrows are examples of affect displays.

Agenda   The list of the topics to be discussed in a meeting or the problems that must be dealt with in the order in which they will be acted upon.

Aggressive behavior   Acting in a way to dominate, to get your own way at any cost.

Alphabetical language   A language system in which letters are combined to represent a single word; languages that are alphabetically based recognize the differences between vowels (e.g., in English, *a, e, i, o,* and *u*) and consonants (e.g., in English, *r, b,* and *m*); English, Greek, and Hebrew are examples of alphabetical languages.

Ambiguity   Vagueness caused by use of a word that has more than one interpretation.

Analogy   Information used to clarify a concept for listeners in which the speaker compares an unfamiliar concept to a familiar one.

Analytical thinking   Thought patterns emphasizing analysis, which dissects events and concepts into pieces that can be linked into chains and categorized; typical of Euro-American cultures and people descendent from those cultures.

Androgyny   The internalization of both masculine and feminine language and characteristics so that both men's and women's speech falls further from sex-type extremes and closer to some ground in between.

Anger   The feeling of being mad at yourself and/or others.

Anxiety   Excessive worry or concern; an important variable that may affect a person's perceptions and performance since negative anxiety causes stress.

APA footnote, endnote, bibliographical method   A format for inscribing research notations that was developed by the American Psychological Association.

Apologizing   One person expressing that he or she is sorry to another person.

Appraisal interview   An interview format that helps the interviewee to realize the strengths and weaknesses of his or her performance.

Appreciative listening   The attempt of a person to engage in enjoyment or sensory stimulation of a message, such as listening to humorous speakers, comedians, or music.

Arbitration   An attempt to solve a conflict by involving a third party to settle a dispute by hearing the evidence and making a decision on how the conflict will be resolved.

Artifacts   A person's clothing, makeup, eyeglasses, and jewelry, each of which carries distinct messages.

Asian American dialect   English as spoken by immigrants who speak one of the Asian languages.

Asking   Seeking out information by inquiring in order to eliminate misunderstandings, aid in receipt of an intended message, and gain the proper information.

Assertive communication   Communication in which a person stands up for and tries to gain personal rights without damaging others; centers on a person's realizing that an individual has the right to choose and control his or her own life.

Assertiveness   When a person stands up for and tries to achieve personal rights without damaging others; centers on a person's realizing that an individual has the right to choose and control his or her own life.

Assignment of meaning   The process of putting the stimulus received during listening into some predetermined category.

Asynchronous conference   Meeting participants contribute to an online conference or to database-centered meetings at different times.

Attention (listening)   The focus on a specific stimulus selected from all the stimuli received at any given moment; a listening phase in which the other stimuli recede so that the listener can concentrate on a specific heard word or visual image.

Attention span   The capacity of the short-term memory; rarely lasts more than forty-five seconds at any one time.

Attitudes   A person's perspective and viewpoints.

Audience analysis   Assessing the demographic, psychographic, and rhetorographic characteristics of your prospective listeners.

Audio aids   A representation or the real duplication of a sound, such as a voice or music, which appeals to the listener's sense of hearing.

Audiovisual aids   A film, videotape, and/or tape-slide presentation that combines the dimensions of sight and sound.

Authoritarian leader   A leader who dominates and directs a group according to personal goals and objectives, regardless of how consistent these goals are with group members' goals.

Behavioral interview   An interview to allow employers to know what specific skills the potential employee has and how these skills would translate into performance on the job.

Behavioral kinesiology   A theory that holds that particular kinds of food, clothes, thoughts, and music strengthen or weaken the muscles of the body.

Beliefs   A person's convictions.

Bipolar question   A closed question that requires a yes or no response, such as "Would you like to work for this company?"

Black English   An alternative name for Ebonics; the primary language used by many African Americans.

Body of a speech   The section of a speech that develops the major points as well as any subpoints pertaining to a speaker's central idea.

Body synchrony   The study of posture, walk, and stance.

Boolean search   A computer-based search that combines multiple words connected by *and* or *or*.

Brain dominance   The brain has two hemispheres by which a person processes information, the left (linear) and right (global) sides; brain dominance accounts for learning and listening in patterned ways based on which side of the brain is being used.

Brainstorming   The generating of possible solutions without evaluation of them at the time of their proposal.

Case interview   A potential employee is asked to work through a particular case study or set of case studies; often used by investment and consulting companies.

Case method of organizational speech structure   A method for organizing a speech in which the speaker discusses the central idea without breaking it into subpoints.

Categorical syllogism   A type of deductive argument in which an argument is presented that contains premises and a conclusion.

Causal method of issue arrangement   A way of organizing the body of a speech that shows how two or more events are connected in such a way that if one occurs, the other will necessarily follow.

Centralized decision-making process   A decision-making process that views authority as being inherent within the individual, not his position; a technique used by many Mexicans.

Centralized group communication networks   A group communication pattern in which all information flows toward and through the leader of the group.

Channel/channels   The five senses by which messages are carried from and to the sender and receiver.

Charisma   The quality held by people who are compelling and have the ability to entice others.

Chart   A visual representation of statistical data that gives information in tabular or diagrammatic form.

Chatrooms   Group interactions that allow simultaneous communicating among people on the Internet.

Chronemics   The study of the way people handle and structure their use of time.

Circular time   A societal use of time in which there is no pressing need to achieve or create newness or to insatiably produce more than is needed to survive; such societies have successfully integrated the past and future into a peaceful sense of the present, such as is the case with many Native Americans.

Clincher to a speech   The final statement made during a public speech; it gives the speaker one more chance to reinforce the major ideas she or he has presented and to wrap up the presentation with a final message to clinch the selling of the central idea.

Closed question   A question that provides alternatives, narrows the possibilities for a response, and probes for opinions on opposite ends of a continuum, such as "Do you think that knowledge of a product or possession of communication skills is the most important asset of a salesperson?"

Cluster   The grouping together of nonverbal signals such as gestures, posture, eye contact, and movement in order to interpret a nonverbal message.

Code switchers   Individuals who can change the language or accent they use as is appropriate for a situation; for example, selectively using Black English or mainstream American English, depending on the situation.

Coercion   A leadership power method in which a number of choices, all of which are undesirable, are offered to solve a problem.

Coercive power   Power based on negative outcomes that are used as weapons; such outcomes could include knowing what weapons the other person fears most, acquiring them, communicating that the weapons have been obtained, and persuading the other person that they will be used against him or her.

Cognitive dissonance   The imbalance among a person's values, attitudes, beliefs, and actions.

Cognitive language   Language used to convey information; tends to be denotative.

Cognitive modification   A method that teaches people who have learned to think negatively to think positively; a useful tool to aid in overcoming communication anxiety.

Cognitive processing   The comprehending, organizing, and storing of ideas.

Committee   A small group that has been selected from a large group to be responsible for study, research, and recommendations about an issue.

Communication   Conscious or unconscious, intentional or unintentional process in which feelings and ideas are expressed as verbal and/or nonverbal messages, sent, received, and comprehended. This process can be accidental (having no intent), expressive (resulting from the emotional state of the person), or rhetorical (resulting from specific goals of the communicator).

Communication apprehension   Speech anxiety that may be situation specific, as when a person is anxious about communicating in a specific setting (e.g., giving speeches), or general, as when a person is anxious about communicating in all situations.

Communication stoppers   Statements that put down the ideas of others in a way so that they stop participating; may cut off valuable input. "That will never work," "We've tried that before," or "That's ridiculous" are communication stoppers.

Communication system   A pattern of rules and methods that is set up in communicative relationships and that describes how the relationship is functioning; a pattern of communication determined by who is participating, the setting, the purpose, and how these elements interact.

Comparative-advantage reasoning   A method of persuasion in which the speaker states possible solutions, then demonstrates how the proposal is the most workable, desirable, and practical solution.

Comparison-contrast method of issue arrangement   A method of organizing the main points of the body of a public speech by telling about both similarities and differences of two or more items.

Comparison method of issue organization   A way of organizing the body of a speech in which the speaker tells how two or more examples are alike.

Competitive turn-taking   Interrupting another speaker.

Complementing relationship   The relationship of verbal and nonverbal communication in which a nonverbal message accompanies a verbal message and adds further dimension to communication, such as the nodding of the head vertically as a person says the word *yes*.

Compliance gaining   Getting others to do something for us, agree with us, or otherwise engage with us.

Comprehension listening   The attempt to recognize and retain the information in a message; to comprehend a message, the listener must first discriminate the message to recognize its auditory and visual components.

Computer-based retrieval system   An electronic information search system that allows the researcher to compile a bibliography or a set of facts relevant to a specific topic.

Computer conferencing   Meetings in which participants log on to a central conference database through their personal computers and send or receive electronic mail.

Computer-mediated communication (CMC)   Electronic mail, instant messages, and computer conferencing.

Computerized graphic programs   Programs such as PowerPoint that provide speakers with the opportunity to outline a speech, create slides with animated bullets that follow that outline, and import visual graphics, photos, video or audio clips, and Internet connections.

Conclusion of a speech   The section of the speech that summarizes, pulls thoughts together, or motivates listeners to take a prescribed action.

Conditional argument   A form of deductive argument that sets up an if/then proposition; the establishment of two conditions, one of which necessarily follows from the other.

Conflict   Any situation in which a person perceives that another person, with whom they are interdependent, is frustrating or might frustrate the satisfaction of some concern, need, want, or desire.

Conflict accommodation   A conflict-resolution style in which an individual puts the other person's needs ahead of his or her own, thereby giving in.

Conflict-active societies   Societies in which conflict is accepted as an important part of life; common in most of the Middle Eastern, Mediterranean, Central and South American, and Arabic countries.

Conflict avoidance   Dealing with conflict by not confronting the conflict; putting up with the status quo, no matter how unpleasant, in order to avoid conflict.

Conflict-avoidance societies   Societies that believe that face-to-face confrontations are to be avoided, a belief common in many Asian societies.

Conflict competition   An attempt to resolve conflict by exerting power.

Conflict compromise   An attempt to resolve conflict by bringing concerns out into the open in an attempt to satisfy the needs of both parties.

Conflict integration   An attempt to resolve conflict by being concerned about the needs of all the participants; an attempt to resolve a conflict through a win-win solution.

Conflict smoothing over   An attempt to resolve conflict by preserving the image that everything is okay above all else.

Conflicting relationship   The relationship of verbal and nonverbal communication in which the verbal message and nonverbal message are in contrast, such as when a child says, "I didn't steal the cookies" while he is looking at the floor and squirming.

Confucian principle of i   A principle that requires that a person be affiliated and identify over long periods of time with a small and tightly knit group of people who aid and assist each other when there is a need. This aid leads to a mutually implied assistance pact among group members.

Congruency   The relationship between present and past patterns of behavior, examined in order to ascertain whether a person's present verbal and nonverbal patterns are parallel to his or her past patterns.

Connotative meanings   Understandings that are associated with certain words or to which an individual attaches particular implications (e.g., the word *cat* as referring to your love for your own cat rather than referring to cats in general).

Connotative words   Words that have an implied or suggested meaning (e.g., *love, hate, beautiful*).

Consensus   A voting procedure in which every member of a group agrees on a proposal.

Contact culture   Those cultures characterized by tactile modes of communication that sanction touching, hugging, and close space proximity (e.g., Latin American, Mediterranean, French, Arab).

Context   Who is present, where the communication is taking place, and the general attitude of those assembled.

Contrast method of issue arrangement   A method of organizing the main points of the body of a public speech by giving specific examples of differences between two or more items.

Conversation   A communication interaction with at least one other person.

Counseling interview   An interview designed to provide guidance and support to the interviewee. It is used by mental health professionals, friends, and family members, among others.

Criteria-satisfaction method   A technique used in a proposition of value persuasive presentation. It follows the deductive reasoning pattern in which the speaker identifies the value term by establishing a general definition or set of criteria for that term and then shows how the subject under discussion fits the definition or criteria.

Critical listening   A listener's attempt to comprehend and evaluate the message that has been received; a critical listener assesses the arguments and the appeals in a message and then decides whether to accept or reject them.

Critical thinking   A process of reaching conclusions in which criteria are established and then solutions are matched with the criteria.

Criticism   The act of judging another person, decision, or process.

Cultural noise   Communication difficulty caused by preconceived, unyielding attitudes derived from a group or society on how members of that culture should act or in what they should or shouldn't believe.

Cultural relativism A view that professes that individuals should judge another culture by its context and not by comparing one culture with another; this view holds that neither culture is right or wrong.

Culture All those individuals who have a shared system of customs and communication.

Cutaway A visual aid that allows the listener of a speech to see what he or she would normally have to imagine.

Cyberaddiction Compulsive preoccupied usage of the Internet, chatrooms, and the World Wide Web. Also referred to as *Computer Addiction, Impulse Control Disorder,* or *Internet Addictive Disorder.*

Cybernetic process The theory indicating that the process of acquiring and using language functions much like a computer in that the cortex stores, computes, and eventually processes incoming signals and puts forth the necessary information; starts to develop in humans at about the third month after birth.

Cyberstalking Following and harassing individuals by use of the Internet.

Dale's Cone of Learning A graphic illustrating the principle that the most effective method of learning involves direct, purposeful learning experiences, such as hands-on or field experiences.

Decentralized group communication networks A group communication pattern in which ideas flow freely among all members of a group.

Decode Translating of a received message.

Deductive argument A system of reasoning that is based on logical necessity; a conclusion is stated in the form of a premise, and proof is given to prove that the premise is correct.

Democratic leader A leader who directs a group according to the goals of its members and allows them to form their own conclusions.

Demographics Factors that make the listeners of a speech unique based on their descriptions and backgrounds; includes such factors as their ages, genders, religions, ethnicity, educations, occupations, and race.

Denotative meanings The interpretation of words that have direct, explicit meanings (e.g., *dog* carries the denotative meaning of a "four-legged, furry animal, canine").

Denotative words Words that have direct, explicit meanings (e.g., *book, dog*).

DESC scripting A way of dealing with interpersonal conflicts that centers on the process of Describing, Expressing, Specifying, and stating Consequences.

Dialect A social or regional variation of a language; each language is a collection of similar dialects; like languages, dialects differ from each other in terms of pronunciation, vocabulary, grammar, and accents or tones.

Direct aggression The outward expression of dominating or humiliating communication.

Direct intervention A method used by mental health professionals in which the counselor takes the stand that there should be active probing, that specific activities should be carried on outside the counseling session, that there should be role-playing and activities during counseling, and/or that therapeutic hypnosis should be used in some cases to deal with certain types of problems.

Direct question A question that requires explicit and specific replies; for example, "Where did you last work?"

Directions Instructions for accomplishing a task, achieving an effect, or getting somewhere.

Discriminative listening The listeners attempt to distinguish among auditory and visual stimuli.

Discussion question The issue or problem that a group is to deal with at a meeting.

Disjunctive argument A type of deductive argument that is based on establishing an either/or argument in which true alternatives must be established.

Doublespeak A special form of language vagueness that is deceptive, evasive, and/or confusing; a conscious use of language as a weapon or tool by those in power to achieve their ends at the expense of others.

Dyad A pair of people, such as two persons engaged in a conversation.

Dysfunctional system A relational system that is not functioning because of the structure or roles being played by the participants.

E-commerce Conducting business online.

E-lingo Use of keyboard letters or symbols to send abbreviated or symbolic messages in e-mail correspondence. Sometimes called *e-bbreviation,* it includes letters or symbols such as *brb* ("be right back"), *jk* ("just kidding"), :(("surprise"), and :) ("happiness").

E-mail An Internet messaging system that allows people to speak to each other in letter like form via computer connections.

E-mail ignoring Takes place when someone does not write back after receiving an e-mail. It is particularly identified with discussion lists.

Ebonics Ebony phonics; the primary language used by many African Americans; sometimes referred to as Black English.

Economic model of relationships A theory that contends that people make judgments about interpersonal contacts by comparing relational rewards and costs. As long as rewards are equal to or exceed costs, the relationship becomes more intimate; however, once costs exceed rewards, the relationship begins to stagnate and eventually dissolves.

Egospeak The art of boosting our own ego by speaking only about what we want to talk about.

Eight-legged essay A Chinese mode of presenting ideas through a variety of indirectly related views; often takes the form of an opening-up, amplification, preliminary exposition, first argument, second argument, third argument, final argument, and conclusion.

Elaboration Likelihood Model Model that explains how listeners process persuasive messages depending on their motivation.

Elimination method of organization Method used in persuasive speaking. The speaker lists all of the possible solutions and then goes through and eliminates each by telling why it won't work.

Emblems Nonverbal acts that have a direct verbal translation or dictionary definition (e.g., making a circle with your thumb and pointing finger while extending the other three fingers upward, signifying "okay"); an emblem's meaning in one culture may not be the same as that same emblem's meaning in another.

Emotive language Language used to express the feelings, attitudes, and emotions of a speaker; employs emotional connotative words.

Empathic assertion A statement that may follow a simple assertion or be the first step in the assertive process that recognizes the other person's problems or rights.

Employment interview An interview that is used as a way of entering the job market or changing positions, getting promotions, or achieving salary increases as well as for gaining admission to colleges and universities, internships or assistantships, or graduate or professional programs.

Encode To put ideas into message form.

Enthymeme A form of syllogism in which a premise is not directly stated since it is already shared by the communicators and therefore does not need to be verbalized.

Entry relational development phase The phase of a relationship in which biographical information and general attitudes are exchanged.

Environmental noise Outside interference that prevents the receiver from gaining the message.

Ethical communicators Those who conform to the moral standards that a society establishes for its communicators.

Ethical value system The basis for a person's decision making and understanding of why she or he will or will not take a particular stand or action; the basis for one's communication ethics.

Ethics The systematic study of what should be the grounds and principles for right and wrong human behavior.

Ethnocentrism   The belief that one's culture is primary to all explanations of reality.

Ethnographers   Researchers who study cultures.

Ethnographic Theory of Human Drives   A theory that attempts to explain human needs, which indicates that survival of the species, pleasure seeking, security, and territoriality must be satisfied.

Ethos   Credibility; one of the three speaker components in Western culture's system of persuasion.

Evidence   Proof that includes testimony from experts, statistics, and specific instances.

Exit relational stage   The phase of a relationship in which questions concerning the future of the relationship are raised and resolved.

Expert   A person who, through knowledge or skill in a specific field, gains respect for his or her opinions or expertise because his or her knowledge has been acquired through personal experience, education, training, research, and observation.

Expert power   The capacity to influence another person because of the knowledge and skills that a person is presumed to possess.

Exposition   Information presented in a speech to give the necessary background to listeners so that they can understand the material being presented.

Extemporaneous mode of speaking   The preparation method and reference aids in which a speaker develops a set of "talking points," such as notes or an outline to assist in presenting ideas.

Eye-accessing cues   Cues based on Neurolinguistic Psychological (NLP) research that indicates whether a person is thinking in images, sounds, via self-talk, or through his or her feelings as the eyes move in patterns. Most people will look up for visual accessing, down for linguistic accessing, to the left for past experiences, to the right for future perceptions, and straight ahead for present-tense thinking.

Eye contact   A speaker's looking into the eyes of the audience as he or she speaks.

Fabrication   The making up information or guessing at information and presenting it as being true.

Facial Action Coding System (FACS)   A process used to analyze facial expressions that has been responsible for establishing information about facial expression.

Facsics   The study of how the face communicates.

Fair fighting   Conflict in which the participants are concerned about working toward an amicable solution to the problem.

Family   An assemblage of people who have legally been declared a group or who have defined themselves as such; typical kinds of families include natural families, blended families, single-parent families, extended families, and self-declared families.

Faulty analogical reasoning   Reasoning that establishes that no analogy is ever totally "pure" because no two cases are ever identical.

Faulty causal reasoning   Occurs when a speaker claims, without qualification, that something caused something else.

Feedback   Response to a message.

Feminine traits   Those identifiable verbal and nonverbal tendencies that are identified as being "female," versus those that are "male."

Fight-or-flight mechanism   A neurological reaction to fear or endangerment that causes an individual to stay and battle it out or run away.

Flaming   When individuals exchange hostile or insulting remarks via the Internet.

fMRI   Functional magnetic resonance imaging is a medical process that scans the brain. Forensic experts predict that because fMRIs measure complex mental processes rather than just skin and blood pressure changes, fMRI will develop into an accurate predictor of lie detection.

Focus groups   A group designed to test reactions to a particular product, process, or service offered by an organization.

Follow-up assertion   A restatement of the simple or empathic assertion followed by a statement of your own position, which may include a direct statement of the action you need or want.

Forecast   A statement that alerts the listeners of a speech to ideas that are coming.

Formal time   The way in which a culture divides its time, such as by centuries, years, months, weeks, days, hours, and minutes.

Forum   An interaction during which participants field questions from each other as well as from any audience members present.

Frame of reference   A combination of factors that act as a perceptual screen; allows each communicator to understand another's message from her or his unique perspective; the basis on which persons assign meaning to words, phrases, and sentences; contingent on a person's background, experiences, and perceptions.

Freedom of speech   The protected right to speak without restrictions; to be free to say what we want.

Functional system   A relational system that is operating to the general satisfaction of the participants.

Funnel schedule   The interview outline that formats questions beginning with the more general and moving (funneling) to the more specific.

Gender   One's psychological, social, and interactive characteristics; not the same as *sex,* which is one's biological or physical self.

Genderflex   The temporary use of communication behaviors typical of the other gender.

Generalization conclusion   A conclusion that is derived from predicting some future occurrence or that explains a whole category of instances; the assumption that what holds true for specific instances will hold true for all instances in a given category.

Gestics   The study of the movements of the body that includes such factors as posture, walk, and stance, which can provide clues about a person's status, mood, ethnic and cultural affiliation, and self-perception.

Gestural Theory   A theory suggesting that long before early humans spoke, they jabbered away with their hands. The theory also contends that speech was an ingenious innovation but not quite the freakish marvel that linguists have often made it out to be.

Gestures   The use of hands, body movements, and facial expressions while one is speaking.

Global listeners/learners   The right hemisphere of the brain is responsible for intuitive, spatial, visual, and concrete matters; those with this listening/learning dominance prefer examples rather than technical explanations, prefer knowing whether information can be useful and applied, are creative, rely on intuitive thinking, can follow visual or pictographic rather than written instructions, like to explore information without necessarily coming to a conclusion, and enjoy interaction rather than lecturing.

Goal of the speech   Terms that express the expected outcome of a speech, which usually is to inform or to persuade.

Group   An assemblage of people who communicate face to face in order to fulfill a common purpose and achieve a goal.

Group cohesion   The interconnectedness of the members of a group.

Group communication networks   The patterns that are developed by members of groups to pass information among members.

Group conforming   The stage in group operation during which the group settles such issues as norms, the group's purpose, and how to handle the role of power.

Group norming   The stage in group operation in which the group members come together and start a group or welcome new people into an existing group.

Group norms   The rules by which the group will operate; the norms will state the obligations of the members, what they can and can't do, and the mode of operation normally decided upon; norms can be explicit or implicit.

Group norm standards   The habits of the thinking of a particular group that a persuasive speaker may use as a guide when developing arguments.

Group performing   The action stage of group process during which the group is working toward its goals with clearly established rules of operation.

Group storming   The stage in group operations during which conflicts erupt; it most commonly takes place during the process of setting rules or working toward the group's goal.

Groupthink   The mode of thinking by members of a group engaged in the process of decision making in which concurrence seeking becomes so dominant that it tends to override realistic appraisal of alternative courses of action.

Groupware   Specially designed software that meeting participants use to perform tasks such as brainstorming and decision making.

Guilty conscience   A person's real or perceived fear that she or he is going to get caught, be punished, or be "found out."

Gustorics   The study of how taste communicates. It includes the communication aspects of such factors as the classifications of taste, the role of culture in taste, and the roles of food deprivation, food preferences, taste expectations, color, and textures as encouragers or discouragers of eating and drinking.

Haptics   The study of the use of touch as communication.

Hasty generalization   An unwarranted general conclusion drawn from an insufficient number of instances.

Hearing   A biological activity that involves reception of a message through sensory channels; the first action in the listening process.

Hidden agenda   An objective or purpose that goes beyond the constructive interests of the group as a whole.

Hierarchy of Human Needs   Abraham Maslow's theory of needs satisfaction; based on this view, a speaker must determine the level of need of a particular group of listeners and then select appeals aimed at that level.

High-context cultures   In countries such as Japan and Saudi Arabia, it is the responsibility of the listener to understand information as it is assumed that meaning is situated in the communicators themselves and in the communication setting, so fewer words are necessary.

High-prestige dialects   Language and accents used by the mainstream members of a society.

Holistic thinking   Thought patterns that do not dissect events or concepts but that regard information in totality; a thought process typical in South American and Asian cultures and people descendent from those cultures.

Hypothesis conclusion   A conclusion that is reached by taking into consideration all available evidence.

Ideal self   The person an individual would like to be or thinks he or she should be; the "perfect self."

Identifying language   Language that names things, thus providing the sender with the ability to clarify exactly what is being spoken about.

Ignoring the issue   Reasoning fallacies that can result from using irrelevant arguments to obscure the real issue.

Illustrations   Detailed stories used in a speech to clarify a point, not to offer proof.

Illustrators   Kinesic acts accompanying speech that are used to aid in the description of what is being said or to trace the direction of speech.

Impromptu speaking   A speech given with little or no preparation.

Inarticulates   Sounds, words, or phrases that have no meaning or that do not help the listener gain a clear understanding of the message; fillers that cover up the speaker's inability to think of what to say or fill in thinking time or that are bad vocal habits—for example, "you know" and "stuff like that."

Individual norm standards   The concept indicating that certain people within any group influence the thinking of a group.

Inductive argument   A reasoning system based on probability; a conclusion that is reached by deriving the expected or believed from the available evidence.

Inferences   Results derived when we interpret beyond available information or jump to conclusions without using all of the information available.

Informal time   Flexible expressions of time such as "soon," or "right away," which can cause communicative difficulty because such terms are arbitrary and mean different things to different people.

Information-gathering interview   An interview that sets out to obtain information from a respondent; an interview format that is important to journalists, law enforcement authorities, health care workers, students, businesspeople, and mental health professionals.

Information highway   An assemblage of networks linking primary and secondary schools, public and private institutions, commercial enterprises, individuals in their homes, and foreign institutions together for collaboration.

Informative briefing   An information public speech that presents information to a specialized audience, which is followed by the exchange of data, ideas, and questions among participants.

Informative speaking   A public speech that imparts new information, secures understanding, or reinforces accumulated information.

Ingroup   The collectivity with which an individual identifies. The ingroup's beliefs are perceived to be right.

Innate neurological programs   Those automatic nonverbal reactions to stimuli with which individuals are born.

Inner speech   The acts of mumbling, daydreaming, dreaming, fantasizing, and feeling tension by which, awake or asleep, a person is constantly in touch with himself or herself; sometimes referred to as *self-talk*.

Instant messaging   Simultaneous computer messaging of information sent to and from individuals in a chatroom or on special e-mail systems.

Interactional model of communication   A drawing indicating the process in which a source encodes and sends a message to a receiver (through one or more of the sensory channels); the receiver receives and decodes the message, encodes feedback, and sends it back to the source, thus making the process two-directional; the source then decodes the feedback message. Based on the original message sent and the feedback received, the source then encodes a new message that adapts to the feedback (adaptation).

Intercultural communication   When a person speaks to those with whom he or she has little or no cultural bond.

Internal summary   A short restatement of what has just been said in the section of a speech before proceeding to the next segment.

Interpersonal communication   Communication that takes place between two persons who establish a communicative relationship that includes conversations, interviews, and small-group discussions.

Interrogation   An interviewing technique that uses leading questions in an attempt to discredit or incriminate an interviewee by asking questions that elicit information outside his or her factual knowledge; a technique used by law enforcement officers and trial attorneys.

Interrogation interview   An interview format designed to secure information from an interviewee through extensive use of probing techniques; used by lawyers, credit officers, tax specialists, and law enforcement officers.

Interview   A purposeful conversation between two or more persons that follows a basic question-and-answer format; interviewing is more formal than most conversations because the participants usually share a preset purpose and use a focused structure.

Interview format   An outline of the procedures that will be used to achieve the interaction's purpose.

Interviewee   The person who is being interviewed; she or he should prepare for the session by knowing the purpose of the meeting and what her or his role and responsibilities are.

Interviewer   The person responsible for an interview's arrangements; person who takes the lead in conducting the activity; usually establishes the time, location, and purpose of the meeting.

Interview's conclusion   A summary of what has been accomplished during an interview, which may also indicate the next step to be taken after the interview has ended.

Intimate distance   The space varying from direct physical contact with another person to a distance of six to eighteen inches that is used for our most private activities—caressing, making love, and sharing intimate ideas and emotions.

Intracultural communication   Communication in which a person interacts with those with whom she or he has a cultural bond.

Intrapersonal communication   Communication with yourself that includes thought processing, personal decision making, listening, and determination of self-concept.

Introduction to a speech   The beginning section of a speech that attempts to gain the listeners' attention and orient them to the material that will be presented.

Intuitive-affective decision-making approach   An approach to decision making that attempts to develop a solution by using broad issues that do not appear to be directly related to the issue; these issues are linked together on the basis of whether or not the speaker likes the issues; a technique used in many Arabic cultures.

Inverted funnel schedule   A technique used in reprimanding that starts out with a clear, specific statement of the performance problem so that there is no question as to what the problem is and then works toward a solution.

Johari window   A method of illustrating that allows a person to ascertain his or her willingness to disclose who he or she is and whether the person is interested in allowing someone else to disclose to her or him.

Kinesics   The study of communication through body movement.

Laissez-faire leader   A leader who uses a nondirective style and lets group members "do their own thing."

Language   A system of human communication based on speech sounds used as arbitrary symbols; does not remain static; it is constantly changing.

Language distortion   Confusion caused by language ambiguity, vagueness, or unclear inferences.

Language-Explosion Theory   Proposes that humans build communication skills from the core of language developed early in life.

Language Instinct Theory   A theory that argues that language is a human instinct wired into human brains by evolution. Thus, language is a biological adaptation to communicate information.

Large groups   An assemblage of more than a dozen people who form to achieve a common purpose or goal.

Leaders   Those who guide a group.

Leadership   Those who influence a group to accomplish its goal.

Leadership power   An enforcing of obedience by the group leader through the ability to withhold benefits or to inflict punishment.

Leading question   A question that encourages a specific answer because it implies the way in which the interviewee should answer the question—such as "You wouldn't say you favor gun-control legislation, would you?"

Lecture   An informative public speech that facilitates learning.

Legitimate power   Stems from one person's perception that another person has the right to make requests because of the position that the other person occupies or because of the nature of the relationship.

Lie detection/Lie detector   The attempt to read the body's nonverbal reactions by measuring changes in blood pressure, respiration, and skin response; attempting to detect a conflicting relationship between the verbal and the nonverbal.

Linear learners/listeners   The left hemisphere of the brain is most responsible for rational, logical, sequential, linear, and abstract thinking; people who tend to be left-brain dominant listen and learn best when materials are presented in structured ways and tend to like specifics and logic-based arguments.

Linear model of communication   A drawing representing the process in which a speaker encodes a message and sends it to a listener through one or more of the sensory channels.

Linear time   A societal use of time that is concerned primarily with the future; societies utilizing it focus on the factual and technical information needed to fulfill impending demands; used in most of Western Europe, North America, and Japan.

Linguist   A social scientist who studies the structures of various languages in order to provide concepts that describe languages.

Linguistics   The study of the structure of human language.

Listener apprehension   The fear of misinterpreting, inadequately processing, and/or not being able to adjust psychologically to messages sent by others.

Listening   A process that involves reception, perception, attention, the assignment of meaning, and response by the listener to the message presented.

Litigation   Adversary communication in which a dispute is settled by presenting evidence to a judge or a jury, who are given the responsibility of deciding who is right.

Loaded question   A type of leading question that is designed to elicit an emotional response, such as asking a job applicant who was president of the union at a previous job to defend this company's policy of nonunion affiliation.

Logos   Logical arguments; one of the three speaker components in Western culture's system of persuasion.

Lose-lose negotiation   A way of attempting to deal with problems that centers on one person's getting what he or she wants while the other comes up short; neither person is satisfied with the outcome.

Low-context cultures   In countries such as the United States and Canada, it is the speaker who is responsible for making sure that the listener comprehends since these cultures perceive that most message information is contained in words.

Low-prestige dialects   Language and accents used by people who do not employ mainstream language patterns; individuals who use nonstandard dialects.

Maintenance dimension of groups   The social responsibilities of a group that center on meeting the interpersonal needs of the members.

Majority vote   A voting procedure in which the winner receives more than half of the possible votes, excluding the votes of those who abstain (i.e., do not want to vote).

Manuscript speech mode   The preparation method and reference aids in which the material for a speech is written out and delivered word for word.

Masculine traits   Those identifiable verbal and nonverbal tendencies that are identified as being "male," versus those that are "female."

Media   The various means of mass communication, including radio, television, the Internet, magazines, newspapers, and film.

Media conference   A technique that allows a group to conduct meetings via telephones, computers, or television.

Media interview   An interview that is broadcast on radio or television in which the interviewer asks questions of a guest.

Mediated meetings   Audioconferences, videoconferences, or computer conferences that allow for meetings to be conducted through electronic channels.

Mediation A process in which a neutral person who has no vested interest in the outcome facilitates communication between parties and, without imposing a solution on the parties, enables them to understand and resolve their dispute.

Meet-while-standing A method of decision making in which participants are forced to stand while making decisions so that they will work more rapidly because they will get tired and want to finish their business and find someplace to sit.

Memorized speech mode The preparation method and reference aids in which a speech is written out word for word and is then committed to memory.

Messages The material or information that is communicated.

Method of issue arrangement for the body of a speech A way of organizing the body of a speech, which usually takes one of six forms: spatial arrangement, chronological/time arrangement, topical arrangement, causal arrangement, comparison-contrast arrangement, or problem-solution arrangement; the sequencing of the body of a speech for listener clarity.

Method of speech development The structure of a speech, which can be chronological, spatial, cause-effect, problem-solution, or topical.

Mind mapping A method of arranging materials visually rather than in list form either for developing a speech or for use during the presentation stage of speaking.

Mirror question A form of question that is intended to get a person to reflect on what he or she has said and expand on it. For example, the interviewee may say, "I've worked for this corporation for years, and I'm getting nowhere." The mirror question might be "Do you feel you're not moving ahead in the corporation?"

Mockup A visual aid that shows the building up or tearing down of a real object or model.

Modes of speech presentation The preparation method and reference aids used during the speech; impromptu or ad lib, extemporaneous, manuscript, and memorized modes.

Monotone A flat, boring oral sound resulting from constant pitch, volume, and rate.

Motivated sequence A psychological approach to speech organization that proposes not only that arguments and evidence can be persuasive but that speech structure can be as well.

Multiculturalism A political and attitudinal movement to assure cultural freedom so as to eliminate the feeling of disfranchisement of people of color, gays and lesbians, and people from cultures other than the mainstream culture.

Multiculture A society consisting of varied cultural groups.

Nationality The nation in which one was born, now resides, or has lived or studied for enough time to become familiar with the customs of the area.

Native American/American Indian languages Languages used by Native Americans/American Indians; there is no one language since Indian identity is not the same as tribal identity, and all tribes have differing languages and customs.

Negotiation The act of bargaining to reach an agreement in which at least two people work on a mutual problem.

Neurolinguistic programming The theory that indicates that many nonverbal actions are inborn; part of the neurological system.

Noise Any internal or external interference in the communication process, including environmental obstacles, physiological impairment, semantic problems, syntactic problems, organizational confusion, cultural influences, or psychological problems.

Nominal Group Technique of Decision Making A group decision-making procedure that encourages generation of ideas from all individuals but avoids criticism, destructive conflict, and long-winded speeches.

Nonassertive behavior Attempting to resolve conflict by avoiding conflict.

Noncontact cultures Those cultures characterized by nontactile modes of communication, thus stressing little touching, hugging, or close space proximity (German, English, North American).

Nondirective technique A counseling technique in which the interviewer does not take an active role in a solution; can work only if the troubled person accepts that a problem exists, has the skills to identify what is wrong, and deals with it.

Nonstandard dialects Pronunciation and intonation used by individuals who are not part of the mainstream society.

Nonverbal communication All messages that people exchange besides the words themselves.

Ocalics The study of how the eyes communicate.

Olfactics The study of smell.

One-on-one briefing A speech given to a person or a small group of individuals on findings or recommendations.

Open question A question that specifies only the topic and invites the answerer to respond as he or she desires—for example, "What is your educational background?"

Oral footnote A statement that identifies the source of the material being presented in a speech.

Oral history interview A procedure of audio, video, or in-person interviewing of an individual in order to preserve family or historical information.

Organizational noise The result when the receiver fails to understand the message because the source failed to realize that certain ideas are best grasped when presented in a structured order.

Orienting material The section of the introduction that gives the audience the background necessary to understand the basic material of the speech; often provides a historical background, defines terms that will be used in the presentation, ties the speaker's personal history to the subject, and illuminates the importance of the ideas to the listener.

Other-perceived Me The person whom others perceive you to be; he or she may be the same as or different from your self-perceived I.

Outgroup A collectivity with which an individual does not identify. The outgroup's beliefs are perceived to be wrong by the ingroup.

Paraphrases Someone else's ideas expressed in a speaker's own words.

Paraphrasing The listener's summary of the ideas she or he has just received.

Paravocalics All the vocal effects made to accompany words—such as tone of voice, rate (speed), volume (power), pitch (such as soprano or bass), pause (stopping), and stress (intensity)—but not the words themselves.

Part-of-the-whole voting A voting procedure in which a specific number or percentage of those who are eligible to vote agree on an action to be taken.

Participants Those members of a group who interact to bring about the actions of the group.

Partitioning organizational speech structure A method for organizing a speech in which the speaker starts with the introduction, leads into the central idea, then states the central idea, restates it, and divides it by listing the main issues to be covered in the order in which they will be covered, which divides a speech into topical sections.

Partitioning step The restatement of the central idea of a speech and listing of the main points to be covered in the presentation.

Passive aggression Pretending that nothing is wrong but derailing any attempt to solve a problem that isn't to your liking in a way that doesn't appear to be aggressive—including using sarcasm, withholding, or being sweet and polite—but that, in fact, controls what is being done.

Pathos Psychological appeals; one of the three speaker components in Western culture's system of persuasion.

Paxil   The first selective serotonin reuptake inhibitor to win approval by the Food and Drug Administration for treatment of debilitating shyness.

Perceptions   The factors that combine to allow each individual to view the world that are determined by a person's culture, communication skills, physical and emotional states, experiences, attitudes, memory, and expectations.

Perceptual filter   The device in the brain that strains the stimuli received and separates what makes sense from what doesn't based on a person's background, culture, experiences, roles, mental and physical state, beliefs, attitudes, and values.

Personal distance   A zone of eighteen inches to four feet between people in which most North Americans feel most comfortable when talking with others.

Personal relational phase   The phase of a relationship in which information about central attitudes and values is exchanged.

Persuasion   The process of influencing attitudes and behaviors.

Persuasive interview   An interview format that attempts to change a person's beliefs or behavior.

Persuasive speech   A speech intended to influence the opinion or behavior of an audience.

Phatic language   Language used to reinforce the relationship between the participants in a communicative exchange; greetings, farewells, and small-talk exchanges such as "Hello, how are you?" and "Have a nice day."

Physical characteristics   A person's height, weight, and skin color, which communicate information about that person to others.

Physiological-impairment noise   A physical problem that blocks the effective sending or receiving of a message.

Pictographical language   A language system, such as Chinese, in which symbols represent a single word; in contrast to alphabetical languages, in which letters are combined into units called *words*.

Plagiarism   Takes place when a speaker uses the ideas and words of someone else while offering them as her or his own without giving credit to the originator of the material.

Plurality   A voting procedure in which the winner is the person who receives the most votes.

Pollyanna-Nietzsche effect   A group phenomenon in which there is excessive optimism *(Pollyannaism)* and an idealized belief *(Nietzschism)* that the group is superhuman and can do no wrong.

Poster session   A session in which a speaker prepares a poster that visually highlights some research or idea at a school or professional conference. The poster is set up in a room with other posters. Speakers each give a short presentation, and listeners ask questions.

Postspeech analysis   Information following a speech that enables a speaker to determine how a speech affected the audience.

Power   The ability to control what happens—to cause things you want to happen and to block things that you do not want to happen.

Power role   The ability to influence another's attainment of goal, which normally centers on controlling another person or persons, influencing the efforts of others, and accomplishing a goal.

Presentation graphics   A series of visuals that are projected via an overhead projector while the speaker is discussing each point; may be computer generated through a program such as Microsoft's PowerPoint.

Primary group tension   The normal jitters and feelings of uneasiness experienced by members when groups first congregate.

Primary signal system   The tools used to send and receive messages; the senses: seeing, hearing, tasting, smelling, and touching.

Primary sources of information   Sources of information that represent the original reports of the observations or research.

Prior to the speech analysis   The process of finding out the demographic, psychographic, and rhetorographic characteristics of the prospective listeners before the speech is given.

Probe   A question used in interviews to elicit a more detailed response, such as "Why do you feel that way?"

Problem-solution method of issue arrangement   A way of organizing the body of a speech in which a speaker attempts to identify what is wrong and to determine how to cure it or make a recommendation for its cure.

Problem-solving interview   An interview in which the interviewer and interviewee meet to solve a problem.

Process of the speech analysis   Observing the audience for feedback during a speech.

Pro-con method of organization   Used in persuasive speaking. The speaker not only tells why he or she believes in the proposition but also explains why he is opposed to other proposals.

Professional papers   A speech, usually given at a conference, in which the presenter briefs his or her audience on some findings that relate to the listeners' area of interest.

Proposal-counterproposal negotiating   Negotiation in which a plan or solution is presented and then a counteroffer is made.

Proposition of fact   A statement declaring the existence of something in the past, present, or future by giving the reasons why the proposition should be believed.

Proposition of policy   A persuasive technique that centers on stating that something should or should not be done.

Proposition of value   A persuasive technique that offers an evaluation of a person, place, or thing.

Proxemics   The study of how people use and perceive their social and personal space.

Psychographics   Attitudes and beliefs of the audience members. This profile can be determined by analyzing the listeners.

Psychological appeals   Appeals that enlist listeners' emotions as motivation for accepting of persuasive arguments.

Psychological noise   Stress, frustration, or irritation that causes us to send or receive messages ineffectively.

Public communication   Characterized by a speaker's sending a message to an audience; it may be direct, such as a face-to-face message delivered by a speaker to an audience, or indirect, such as a message relayed by radio or television.

Public distance   A spatial separation between individuals of that may be as little as twelve feet but usually is more than twenty-five.

Public meetings   Assemblages of interested individuals attending a meeting in which there is no restricted membership.

Public self   The image a person lets others know; based on the concept that "if others believe the right things about me, I can get them to like me; I can persuade them and generally get my way."

Public speaking anxiety   A phobia, known as *speechophobia,* that is characterized by (1) persistent fear of a specific situation out of proportion to the reality of the danger, (2) a compelling desire to avoid and escape the situation, (3) a fear that is recognized as being unreasonable and excessive, and (4) a fear that is not due to any other disorder. As with most phobias, it is curable.

Pupilometrics   A theory that indicates that pupils dilate when the eyes are focused on a pleasurable object and contract when focused on an unpleasurable one.

Purpose of the speech   The speaker's expected outcomes for the presentation.

Question-and-answer session   An on-the-spot set of unrehearsed questions and answers that measure a speaker's knowledge, alert a speaker to areas in a speech that were unclear or needed more development, and give listeners a chance to probe for ideas.

Question of fact   A proposal for action by a group in which something is established as true and to what extent.

Question of policy   A question for action by a group of whether a specific course of action should be undertaken in order to solve a problem.

Question of value   A question for action by a group of whether something is good or bad, right or wrong, and to what extent.

Quotations   Material written or spoken by a person in the exact words in which it was originally presented.

Razzing   A communication technique used by some members of the African American culture in which humorous stories are told. The razz may be from a present or past experience, but it must relate to someone in attendance.

Real self   What a person thinks of herself or himself when being most honest about her or his interests, thoughts, emotions, and needs.

Real-time conference   Participants are all at their computers at the same time to participate in a mediated meeting.

Recalibrated system   A relational system that has been restructured.

Recalibration   The process of restructuring a communicative system by altering the rules and methods by which the system is operating.

Receiver   The recipient of a message.

Reception   The initial step in the listening process; includes the receiving of both the auditory message and the visual message.

Red flag words   Words or phrases that evoke emotional biases in a person based on her or his culture, religion, ethnic beliefs, or biases.

Referent power   Power based on personal loyalty, friendship, affection, and admiration.

Reflective actions   Nonverbals that mirror the society from which they were learned.

Reflexive actions   Automatic nonverbal reactions caused by neurological drives, such as a person's blinking her eyes when a pebble hits the windshield while she is driving.

Regulators   Nonverbal acts that maintain and control the back-and-forth nature of speaking and listening between two or more people; nods of the head, eye movements, and body shifts are all regulators used to encourage or discourage conversation.

Relational costs   An individual's investment of money, time, and emotion in a relationship; the investment as a part of the economic model of relationships.

Relational fusion   When one partner defines, or attempts to define, reality for the other partner in a relationship.

Relational rewards   An individual's profits from being involved in a relationship; the positive gains received as a part of the economic model of relationships.

Reprimanding interview   An interview format that helps the interviewee to analyze his or her problems and develop techniques to correct them.

Requesting   The process of expressing a desire for something.

Reward power   Requires that a person be perceived as the best or only source of desired rewards.

Rhetorical language   The use of appropriate language based on the participants, setting, and purpose to accomplish the desired goal.

Rhetorical question   A device used to gain the listener's attention at the start of a speech in which a question is asked for which there is no expectation of an outward response.

Rhetorographics   The place, time limit, time of day, and emotional climate for a speech.

Risky shift phenomenon   A theory that decisions reached after discussion by a group display more experimentation, are less conservative, and contain more risk than decisions reached by people working alone.

Robert's Rules of Order   The most commonly used set of parliamentary guidelines for handling procedural agreements and disagreements.

Sales interview   An interview format that attempts to link the customer's needs and interests with a product or service.

Scale model   A representation of a real object that is in exact proportion to the dimensions of the original object.

Schema   Mental scripts a listener uses for processing information.

Schemata   Information that is shaped by the language categories and by the way our brains process information.

Second employment interview   An interview designed to further determine the candidate's fit to the organization and provide more detailed information about the position.

Secondary group tension   The stress and strain that occurs within a group later in its development.

Secondary sources of information   Sources of information that report, but did not generate, the original observations or research.

Selective communication   Choosing the symbol that best represents the idea or concept to be expressed; combining sounds into complicated structures so as to describe events and objects.

Selective perception   The process of the listener's narrowing his or her attention on specific bits or pieces of information.

Self-concept   The view one has of oneself.

Self-confidence   A personal sense of competence and effectiveness.

Self-disclosure   Intentionally letting another person know who you are by communicating self-revealing information, which can be done through verbal or nonverbal messages.

Self-fulfilled person   The person who confidently chooses what to reveal and to whom; a self-fulfilled person is not intimidated into a negative self-concept and realizes that there will always be problems, frustrations, and failures in life.

Self-love   The acceptance of oneself as a worthy person.

Self-perceived I   The image a person projects; the way a person perceives herself or himself.

Self-talk   A nearly constant subconscious monologue or inner speech with oneself; sometimes referred to as *inner speech.*

Semantic noise   Problems in coding or decoding a message caused by either source's understanding of the meaning of words.

Semantics   The study of the relationship of language and meaning.

Sensorium   An approach to perceptual screening, akin to Eastern philosophies, that encourages a person to listen emotionally, with all of the senses, including intuition, as well as logically.

Sentence outline   An outline format that uses complete sentences for all entries and usually uses correct punctuation.

Sex   One's biological or physical self; the sexes (male and female) are different because the brain is constructed differently in men and in women, which allows for the processing of information in different ways; not the same as *gender,* which is one's psychological, social, and interactive self.

Sexual harassment   Generalized sexist remarks or behavior; inappropriate and offensive, but essentially sanction-free, sexual advances; solicitation of sexual activity or other sex-linked behavior by promise of rewards; coercion to obtain sexual activity by threat of punishment; assaults.

Significant-Other Theory   Centers on the principle that our understanding of self is built by those who react to and comment on our language, actions, ideas, beliefs, and mannerisms.

Signposting   A transition device used by a speaker to alert the listeners as to where they have been, where they are presently, and where they are going.

Silent majority   Those members of a group who say nothing during the decision-making process.

Simple assertion   A statement in which a person states the facts relating to the existence of a problem.

Six-Step Standard Agenda for Decision Making   A decision-making procedure that requires a reflective-thinking process, which stresses that a problem be identified and analyzed, solutions sought, and a solution selected and implemented.

Slang   Words that are related to a specific activity or incident and are immediately understood by members of a particular group.

Small-group ecology   The placement of chairs, the placement of the person conducting a meeting, and the setting for a small-group encounter.

Small groups An assemblage of three to twelve persons who form to achieve a common purpose or goal.

Small talk An exchange of information with someone at a surface level that centers on biographics (name, occupation or college major, hometown, college attended or attending) or slightly more personal information (hobbies, interests, future plans, acquaintances).

Smell adaptation When a person gradually loses the ability to detect distinctiveness of a particular smell through repeated contact with it.

Smell blindness When a person is unable to detect smells.

Smell discrimination The ability to identify people, places, and things on the basis of their smell.

Smell memory The ability to recall a previous situation when encountering a particular smell previously associated with that situation.

Smell overload Takes place when an exceptionally large number of odors or one extremely strong odor overpowers a person.

Social Anxiety Disorder Sometimes referred to as *Communication Apprehension* or *shyness*, it is the third most common mental disorder in the United States, behind depression and alcoholism.

Social Construct of Reality Theory Theory that suggests that our world and how we deal with it are shaped by how we talk about its various components. Our meanings and our understandings result from our communication with ourselves and with others.

Social distance A four- to twelve-foot zone that is used during business transactions and casual social exchanges.

Social loafing Occurs when group membership leads some people to work less than they would work individually.

Social phobia A term sometimes used to describe Social Anxiety Disorder, it is the third most common mental disorder in the United States, behind depression and alcoholism.

Source The originator of a message.

Spanglish A common linguistic currency used by Spanish Americans.

Spatial arrangement A method of organizing the body of a speech in which the presenter sets a point of reference at a specific location and then follows a geographic pattern in developing the material.

Speaker credibility The reputation, prestige, and authority of a speaker as perceived by the listeners.

Speaking setting The place where the speech is given, the time limit, when the presentation is made, and the emotional attitude of the audience.

Specific instances Condensed examples that are used to clarify or prove a point.

Speech-independent gestures Those gestures not tied to speech but that carry their own meaning, such as holding up one finger when asked how many scoops of ice cream you want; emblems.

Speech of actuation A persuasive speech whose objective is to move the members of the audience to take the desired action that the speaker has proposed.

Speech of conviction A persuasive speech whose objective is to convince the listener to believe as the speaker does.

Speech of introduction An informative public speech that identifies the person who will be speaking to the audience and gives information that may spark listeners' interest in the speaker and/or the topic.

Speech participants The speaker and the members of the audience.

Speech planning outline A brief framework used to think through the process of the speech.

Speech presentation outline A framework in which the speaker fleshes out the speech planning outline details through examples, illustrations, internal summaries, and forecasts.

Speech-related gestures Those gestures directly tied to or accompanying speech, including illustrators, affect displays, regulators, and adaptors.

Speeches about concepts An informative public speech that examines theories, beliefs, ideas, philosophies, or schools of thought.

Speeches about events An informative public speech that informs about something that has already happened, is happening, or is expected to happen.

Speeches about objects An informative public speech that describes a particular thing in detail, such as a person, place, animal, structure, machine—anything that can be touched or seen.

Speeches about processes An informative public speech that instructs about how something works, is made, or is done.

Speechophobia The term used to define public speaking anxiety.

Spiral form of explanation A mode of organizing a speech in which a statement is made, then a story or analogy that deals with that statement is presented, and then it is often left up to the listener to apply the parallels and draw outcomes related to the original statement.

Spiral structure of argument A narrative communication pattern commonly used by Hispanics and Arabs in which stories are used to explain ideas; strikes many Standard American English speakers as abstract and imprecise since it does not set up a clear purpose and use evidence to clarify and prove.

Standard American English The language generally recognized by linguists as representative of the general population of the United States.

Standard dialects Pronunciation and intonation representative of the mainstream/high-prestige members of a society.

Standing-seated interaction A communicative transaction in which the person in control stands and the other person sits, such as in teacher-pupil and police officer–arrestee transactions.

Statement of central idea Defines the subject and develops the criteria by which to evaluate the material included in a speech; a statement that centers on what a speaker wants the audience to know, to be able to do, or to believe.

Statement of the speech's central idea The section of the speech that is intended to keep the speaker on course for developing a purposeful and well-organized speech; indicates the response the speaker wants from listeners.

Statistics Any collection of numerical information arranged to indicate representations, trends, or theories.

Stress interview An employment interview format designed to determine how the interviewee functions under pressure.

Study groups Small groups established to enable individuals to work together to study and learn with the assistance of others.

Study of language The study of meaning based on words.

Substituting relationship The relationship of verbal and nonverbal communication in which the nonverbal replaces the verbal, such as performing the action meaning "yes" (nodding of the head vertically) for the spoken word *yes.*

Summary of a speech The final segment of a speech in which the major points of the speech are restated.

Superleadership A leadership style in which people are led to lead themselves and thereby release the self-leadership energy within each person.

Supplementary speech aids Visual, audio, audiovisual, and computer-aided graphics that are intended to facilitate listener understanding.

Support group A system that allows people to interact with others in order to increase their knowledge of themselves and others, assists them in clarifying the changes they most want to make in their lives, and gives them some of the tools necessary to make those changes.

Supporting speech material Ideas whose purpose is to clarify a point being made in a speech.

Survey of reasons method A technique used in proposition of value presentations in which the speaker lists all of the reasons for a belief.

Symposium A group discussion format in which participants give prepared speeches with no interaction among themselves or with the audience.

Syntactical noise Inappropriate grammatical usage that can interfere with clear communication.

Synthetic model A representation of a real object that is not in proportion to but nevertheless is representative of the original object.

Systematic desensitization A method used to aid people in overcoming or controlling their communication apprehension in which they are taught how to first recognize tension in their bodies and then relax.

Tag question   Question added onto the end of a statement—such as "That movie was terrific, don't you think?"—with the intent of getting the partner to enter the conversation.

Task dimension of groups   The action responsibilities of a group, which include decision making, informing, appraising/examining, problem solving, and creating interest in staying on track.

Taste adaptation   Takes place when a person becomes used to a taste to the degree that he or she can eat a substance and not taste it.

Taste blindness   The inability to taste.

Team briefings   Speeches presenting findings or recommendations given by a group of speakers to school, corporate, or organizational teams.

Technical report   An informative public speech that is a concise, clear statement explaining a process, explaining a technique, or discussing new elements, either to people within a business or industry or to people outside it.

Technical time   Precise time, as in the way some scientists look at how things happen in milliseconds.

Technobabble   Computer language used for other meanings.

Teleconferencing   A media conference conducted on television.

Telephone job interview   An option to the face-to-face job interview in which the interviewee is contacted by telephone.

Testimony   A direct quotation or a paraphrase from an authority.

Theme statements   A device used to gain the listener's attention at the start of a speech that indicates exactly what the speaker is going to talk about.

Theory of field-related standards   A concept that proposes that not all people reach conclusions in the same way and thus may react differently to the same evidence or psychological material.

Therapeutic listening   The attempt to be an empathic listener by putting oneself in the emotional and intellectual place of the sender; requires a listener to learn when to ask questions, when to stimulate further discussion, and when, if ever, to give advice.

Time method of issue arrangement   A way of organizing the body of a speech that orders information from a beginning point to an ending one, with all the steps developed in numerical or time sequence.

Topic of a speech   The subject to be covered in a speech.

Topic outline   An outline format that uses words or phrases for all entries and usually uses little or no punctuation after entries.

Topical method of issue arrangement   A way of organizing the body of a speech in which a speaker explains an idea in terms of its component parts.

Touch   The placing of a hand or another body part on another's body.

Touch avoidance   The degree to which an individual refrains from touching or being touched.

Town meeting   A public meeting in which a presenter opens with some short prepared statement that establishes the framework for the meeting. Following this, individuals in the audience engage in a forum with the speaker.

Transactional model of communication   A drawing representing the process in which messages are processed simultaneously by the communicators. Communicator A encodes a message and sends it. Communicator B then encodes feedback and sends it to A, who decodes it. These steps are not mutually exclusive; encoding and decoding may occur simultaneously.

Transformational leadership   A leader who serves as a transforming agent because he or she can change both the behavior and the outlook of his or her followers.

Transitions   Statements made during a speech that provide a connection between the points being made.

Two-valued orientation   The understanding that life is multidimensional and that meanings vary as the backgrounds and experiences of the communicators differ; the ability to classify ideas and contentions in an either/or orientation rather than to assume everything is right or wrong.

Unfolding organizational speech structure   A method for organizing a speech in which the ideas bridge from one to another.

Vagueness   Ambiguity that results when words or sentences lack clarity.

Values   What a person perceives to be of positive or negative worth.

Videoconferencing   Meetings conducted with one-way video and two-way audio as well as those conducted with fully interactive two-way video and two-way audio.

Visual aids   Aids used in a speech that appeal to the listener's sense of sight.

Voting   A procedure that takes place when members are given an opportunity to indicate agreement, disagreement, or no opinion on an idea or candidate.

Win-lose negotiation   A way of attempting to deal with problems that centers on one person's getting what he or she wants while the other comes up short.

Win-win negotiation   A way of attempting to deal with problems that centers on all participants' satisfying their wants.

Work teams   Small groups of workers who function as teams to make and implement decisions about the work to be done.

Yes-response question   A form of leading question that is stated in such a way that the respondent is encouraged to agree with the interviewer—such as "You would agree with me, wouldn't you, that this company's policies are fair?"

INDEX

Note: Definitions of all key terms used in the text, as well as other important terms, may be found in the Glossary of this book.

Aesthetics, 78–79
Aggressive communication, 194
    defined, 193
    direct aggression, 193
    figure of, 194
    passive arguments, 193
Anger
    dealing with another's, 186
    figure of, 185
Apologizing, 190–193
    defined, 190
Appraisal interview, 227–229
Approval seeking, 141–142
Arbitration, 198
Aristotle, 393
Artifacts, 71–72
Asian-American Dialect, 49
Assertive Communication, 193–198
    defined, 193
    DESC scripting, 196
    figure of, 194
    principles of, 193–197
    types of responses for, 196

Berko-Wolvin-Wolvin Leader/Leadership
    Relationship Model, 279
Bibliographies, 332
Black English, 48–49
Body synchrony, 69, 71
Brainstorming, 253

Chronemics, 76–77
Communication
    components of, 6–13

components of, model, 8
context of, 13
decoding in, 6
defined, 5
encoding in, 6
ethics, role of, in, 29–30
figure of, 7, 16
interactional model of, 17–18
intercultural, 22–23
intracultural, 22–23
linear model of, 15–16, 17
male/masculine-female/feminine, 146–151
models of, 15–20
noise in, 10–13
power, role of, in, 144–146
relational, 157–158
system of, in 14–15
transactional model of, 18–19
Communication anxiety, 97–101
Communication apprehension, 97–101
    causes of, 98–99
    defined, 97
    help for, 99–100
    spectrums of shyness, figure of, 98
Compliance gaining, 142–143
Computer conferencing, 259–261
Computer-based retrieval systems, 326–329
Computer-mediated communication (CMC),
    159–167
    cyberaddiction, 162–163
    cyberstalking, 164
    defined, 162
    effective strategies in using, 165–167
    e-mail ignoring, 163
    flaming, 163
    internet use, in, 159–160

negative aspects of, 161–164
positive aspects of, 160–161
relationship development, using,
    164–165
Confucian principle of I, 265
Conflict, 179–190
    accommodation style in, 188
    approaches to resolving, 187–190
    arbitration, rule of, in, 198
    avoidance style in, 188
    causes of, 181–182
    competition/aggression style in, 190
    compromise style in, 188–189
    dealing with others in, 186
    defined, 179
    fair fighting, 186–187
    integration style in, 190
    levels of, 182–184, figure of, 183
    litigation, role of, in, 198
    managing of, 192–201
    mediation, role of, in, 198–200
    negotiation, role of, in, 197–198
    personal anger in, 184–186
    personal styles, figure of, 189
    styles of, 201–203
Connotative word, 40–42
Conversations, 172–177
    listening skills needed in, 174–175
    nonverbal skills needed in, 175
    small talk, as used in, 172–174
Counseling interview, 225
Criticism, 200–201
Culture, 22–27
    conflict styles in, 180–181
    groups, as affected by, 265–269
    nonverbal as affected by, 73–74

role of in listening, 113
    role of in speech structure, 352–354
Cultural relativism, 26–27
Cyberaddiction, 162–163
    symptoms of, 163
Cybernetic process, 36
    model of, 36
Cyberstalking, 164

Dale's Cone of Learning, 107
    figure of, 107
Denotative meaning, 40
DESC scripting, 196
Dialects, 44–51,
    Asian American dialect, 49
    Ebonics/Black English, 48–49
    effects of speaking, 50–51
    inarticulates, role of, in, 47–48
    Native American languages, 49–50
    nonstandard, 45, 48
    regional pronunciation, 46
    slang, 46–48
    Spanglish, 49
    standard, 45
    Standard American English, 45–46
Direction giving, 175–177
Doublespeak, 43–44

Ebonics, 48–49
E-commerce, 160
Egospeak, 124–125
Emotions, 143–144
Employment Interviewing
    answering questions during, 217
    behavioral interview, 218–219
    case interview, 219
    defined, 212
    dressing for, 215–216
    legal restrictions concerning, 217–218
    preparing for, 213–215
    stress interview, 219
    telephone interview, 219–220
Ethnocentrism, 24–27
Ethnographic Theory of Needs, 95–97,
        404–405
    figure of, 404
Ethical communicators, 29–30
Ethics, 29–30
    defined, 29
    ethical value system, 29
    public speaking, 292–294
Ethnocentrism
    cultural relativism, role of, in, 26–27
    defined, 24
Ethos, 393
Eye-accessing cues, 58

Fabrication, 293–294
Facsics, 64–66
Fair fighting, 186–187
Feedback, 9–10

First amendment speech, 27–29
Flaming, 163
Freedom of speech, 27–29

Gestics, 67–68
    defined, 67
    touch avoidance, 69
    touch avoidance scale, 70
Global/linear thinking/listening, 111–112,
        128–129
    testing of, 128–129
Group communication, 237–263, 265–285
    adjourning, 248
    agenda setting in, 249
    brainstorming, 253
    committees, 242–243
    communication networks, 275–276, figure
        of, 275
    Confucian principle of I, 265
    culture, role of, in, 265–269
    decision-making techniques, 251–255
    defined, 237
    difficult members in, 276–279
    family as a, 243–244
    focus, 243
    hidden agenda, 273
    individual communication versus,
        237–240
    leader, 279–285
    leaders, responsibility of, 283–285
    leaders, role of, in, 265
    leaders, types of, 280–281
    leadership, 279–285
    leadership, role of, in, 265
    maintenance tasks, 271–272
    making decisions in, 248–255
    male and female roles in, 268–269
    norming, 245
    1-3-6 decision-making technique, 253–255
    participants, role, of in, 165, 269–279
    participating in, 265–285
    performing, 248
    performing tasks, 272–274
    proposal/counterproposal negotiating, in,
        267–268
    public meetings, 244
    risky-shift phenomenon, 238
    setting in, 255–257
    silent majority, 269–270
    Six-step standard agenda, 252–253
    storming, 245–248
    study groups, 241
    superleadership, 280
    support, 241–242
    town meetings, 244
    transformational leadership, 280
    types of groups, 240–245
    voting in, 250–251
    work teams, 240
Groupthink 238–240
    framework for, figure of, 239
Gustorics, 79–80

Haptics, 68–69
Hearing, 106
    defined, 106
Hidden agenda, 273

I-Me Theory, 139–141
    figure of, 140
    options in, 140–141
    other-perceived me, 139
    self-perceived I, 139
Interrogation interview, 230–233
    legal interrogation, 231
    media, 231–233
Information-gathering interview, 220–222
Informative speaking, 370–386
    characteristics of, 372
    classification of, 372–382
    concept of, 371–372
    developing, 382–383
    informative briefings, 375–376
    lecture, 378–379
    one-on-one briefings, 376
    professional papers, 377–378
    question-and-answer session, 379–381
    sample speech, 384–385
    speeches about concepts, 375
    speeches about events, 375
    speeches about objects, 373–374
    speeches about processes, 374
    speeches of introduction, 381–382
    team briefings, 376
    technical reports, 377
Interactional model of communication, 17–18
Intercultural/Intracultural communication,
        22–23
Internet, see computer-mediated communica-
        tion (CMC)
Interpersonal Communication, 135–167,
        172–201
    apologizing, 190–192
    approval seeking, 141–143
    basic concepts of, 135–137
    computer-mediated communication
        (CMC), 159–167
    conflict, dealing with, 179–190
    conflict management, 192–201
    conversations, 172–177
    criticism, role of, in, 200–201
    defined, 5, 135
    direction giving, 175–177
    emotions, role of, in, 143–144
    gaining compliance, 142–143
    power, role of, in, 144–146
    self and others, 139–141
    self-disclosure, 137–139
    sexual harassment, 151–154
    uses of CMC in, 159–160
Interviewing, 207–233
    appraisal interview, 227–229
    counseling interview, 225
    defined, 207
    employment, 212–220

format for, 208–211
information-gathering interview, 220–222
interrogation, 230–231
interviewee, role of, 207
interviewer, role of, 207
persuasive, 225–226
problem-solving interview, 222–223
reprimanding, 229–230
sales interview, 226–227
types of, 211–233
Intrapersonal communication, 83–101
cognitive processing, 86–88
communication apprehension, 97–101
defined, 5
need drives affecting, 95–97
self-concept, 88–90
self talk, 83–88
understanding the self, 90–95
willingness to communicate, 100

Janusik/Wolvin Student Listening Inventory,
129–131
Johari Window, 90–95
defined, 90
figure of, 92
Language, 34–53
accents, used in, 45
concepts of meaning, 39–42
connotative words, 40–42
defined, 34
denotative meanings, 40
dialects of, 44–45
distortion of, 43–44
emotive, 42
functions of, 42–43
identifying, 42–43
origins of, 34–35
phatic, 42
rhetorical, 42
symbols, learning of, 37–42
symbols, processing of, in, 35–36
symbols, role of, in, 35–37
symbols, selection of, in, 35
using verbal, 51–53
Language-explosion theory, 37–38
Language instinct theory, 38
Linear model of communication,
15–16, 17
Linguistics, 44–45
Listening, 105–127
appreciative, 122
apprehension, role of, in, 122–123
comprehensive, 119–120
critical, 120–122
defined, 106
discriminative, 118–119
hearing versus, 106
importance of, 105–106
improving, 123–127
influences on, 116–118
memory techniques, used in, 114–116
paraphrasing, role of, in, 109, 126
process of, 106–118
purpose of, 118–122

test of your, 129–131
therapeutic, 120
Litigation, 198
Logical arguments, 395–399
Logos, 393

Male/masculine-female/feminine communication, 146–151
differences between, 148–151
influence of in groups, 268–269
perceptual differences between, 149
sex and gender as related to, 147
Maslow's Hierarchy of Needs, 403–404
figure of, 403
Media, 20–22
Media Interview, 231–233
Mediated meetings, 258–262
computer conference, 259–260
defined, 258
teleconference, 258–259
types of, 258–262
videoconference, 259
Mediation, 198–200
Mind mapping, 306, 308–309
figures of, 308, 309
Multiculturalism, 23–24

Native American languages, 49–50
Negotiation, 197–198
lose-lose style of, 197
resolutions, figure of ,197
win-lose style of, 197
win-win style of, 197
Neurolinguistic programming, 56, 59
eye-accessing cues, 59
Noise, 10–13
cultural, 12
dealing with, 12–13
defined, 10
environmental, 10
factors of, figure of, 13
organizational, 11
physiological-impairment, 10
psychological, 12
semantic, 10–11
syntactic, 11
Nonassertive communication, 193–194
defined, 193
figure of, 194
Nonverbal communication, 56–80
actions chains, in, 59
aesthetics, as factor in, 78–79
artifacts, as factor in, 71–72
attractiveness, as factor in, 72
body synchrony, as factor in, 69, 70
categories of, 63–80
categories of, figure of, 64
chronemics, as factor in, 76–77
congruency, as factor in, 57
culture, role of, in, 58–60
defined, 56
emotional influences on, 60–61
facsics, as factor in, 64–66

gestics, as factor in, 67–68, 68–69
gustorics, as factor in, 79–80
height, as factor in, 73
kinesics, as factor in, 64–72
neurolinguistic program, role of, in, 56, 57
ocalics, as factor in, 66–67
olfactics, as factor in, 77–78
paravocalics, as factor in, 75–76
physical characteristics, as factor in, 72
proxemics, as factor in, 73–75
pupilometrics, as factor in, 66–67
small-group ecology, as factor in, 75
sources of, 57–60
touch avoidance, as factor in, 69
using, 80
verbal/nonverbal relationships, 61–63
Note-taking, 119–121
format for, 121

Ocalics, 66–67
Olfactics, 77–78
Oral history interview, 223–224
Outlining, 303–306
sentence outline, 305–306
topic outline, 305

Paraphrasing, 109, 126
Paravocalics, 75–75
Pathos, 393
Perceptions, 8–9, 110
defined, 8
male/female similarities and differences of,
149
Persuasive interview, 225–226
Persuasive speaking
comparative-advantage reasoning, use in,
390
components of, 393–407
example of, 408–410
group norm standards, use in, 390
individual norm standards, used in, 390
influence, role of, in, 392–393
logical arguments, used in, 395–399
motivated sequence, used in, 390–391
process of, 389–391
proposition of fact, used in, 400
proposition of policy, used in, 401–402
proposition of value, used in, 400–401
psychological appeals, used in, 402–407
strategies for, 391–392
structure of, 407–408
theory of field-related standards,
389–390
Plagiarism, 293
Pollyanna-Neitzche effect, 239
Power
coercive power, 146
defined, 144
expert power, 145
legitimate power, 146
referent power, 145
reward power, 145–146
testing your power, 168–169

PowerPoint, 312–314, 339–343
  designing, figure of, 342
  developing, 341, 343
Problem-solving cycle, figure of, 223
Problem-solving interview, 222–223
Pronunciation, 311
Proposal/counterproposal negotiating, 267–268
Proxemics, 73–75
  culture, role of, in, 73–74
  group setting, factor of, in, 255–257
  meeting setting, factor of, in, 155–256. 257
  space distances, 74–75
  space distances, figure of, 74
Public communication, see public speaking, 291–411
Public speaking, 291–411
  ad lib mode of, 302–303
  anxiety concerning, 315–317
  anxiety scale, 320
  bibliographies for, 332
  body of, 347, 352–359
  case method for organizing a, 365–366
  computerized graphics, 339–343
  conclusions for, 347–359–360
  defined, 5
  demographics, 294–295
  difficulties, confronting of, during, 318–319
  ethics of, 292–294
  extemporaneous mode of, 303–306
  eye contact in, 312
  fabrication in, 293–294
  forecasting, 337
  formatting methods, used in, 360–366
  gestures, as used in, 311–312
  impromptu mode, used in, 302–303
  informative speaking, 370–386
  interval summaries, 337
  introduction of, 347, 347–351
  issue arrangement, method of, used in, 354–359
  language selection in, 298–299
  magic V eye contact technique, 313
  manuscript mode of, 307–310
  memorized mode of, 310
  modes of presentation for, 301–310
  oral and physical presentation, 310–314
  oral footnotes, 331
  paraphrasing in, 331–332

parameters of, 292
partitioning method for organizing a, 360–363
persuasive speaking, 389–410
physical elements used in, 311
plagiarism in, 293
postspeech analysis, as a factor in, 301
PowerPoint use in, 312–314, 339–343
preparing a, 291–292
prior analysis, as a factor in, 294–300
process analysis, as a factor in, 300–301
pscyhographics, 295–296
recording research for a, 330
rehearsing a, 317–318
researching for a, 323–326
rhetorographics, as used in preparing a, 296–297
signposting, 337
speaking inventory, preparing a, for use in, 319–320
speech planning outline, 303
speech presentation outline, 303–305
statement of central idea, 299–300, 347, 351–352
statistics, use of, in, 334–336
structuring, 347–367
supplementary aids, use of, in, 337–342
supporting materials for, 333–337
topic selection for, 297–298
unfolding method for organizing a, 363–365
visual aids, use of, in, 338–339
Public speaking anxiety (stage fright), 315–317
Public speaking inventory, 319–320
Pupilometrics, 66–67

Question-and-answer session, 379–381
Question asking, 177–178

Relationships, 154–158
  communication in, 157–158
  continuing of a, 155–156
  developing an online, 164–165
  developing of a, 154–155
  ending of a, 158
  positive, 156–157
Reprimanding interview, 229–230

Requesting, 177–179
  asking questions, 177–178
  asking for clarification, 179
  asking for definitions, 178–179
  asking for information, 177
  asking for restatement, 178
Rhetorographics, 296–297
Risky shift phenomenon, 238

Sales interview, 226–227
Self-concept, 88–90
  defined, 88
  ideal self, 88
  Johari window, 90–95
  public self, 88
  real self, 88
  selves, figure of, 88
Self-confidence, 88
Self-disclosure, 137–139
  defined, 138
  self-love, 138
Self-talk, 83–88
Semantics, 41
Sexual harassment, 151–154
  defined, 151
  responding to, 152–153
Shyness, 97–101
Significant-other theory of language learning, 38
Silent majority, 269–270
Small-group ecology, 75
Small talk, 172–174
Social construction of reality language theory, 38–38
Spanglish, 49
Speech of Introduction, 381–382
Stage fright, see Public Speaker Anxiety, 315–317
Standard American English, 45–46

Teleconferencing, 258–259
Transactional model of communication, 18–19

Videoconferencing, 259
Voting, 250–251

ACKNOWLEDGMENTS

Photo Credits

Chapter 1: page 2, James Marshall/The Image Works; page 3, Walter Hodges/Tony Stone Images; page 6, Louise Gubb/The Image Works; page 10, Getty Images; page 14, Mary Kate Denny/Tony Stone Images; page 23, Bob Daemmrich/The Image Works; page 28, Dick Blume/The Image Works; *Chapter 2:* page 33, Will Hart/PhotoEdit; page 37, Lawrence Migdale/Stock Boston; page 40, Steve Allen/Liaison/Getty Images; page 43, Bob Daemmrich Photography; page 51, Eric Neurath/Stock Boston; page 52, AP/Wide World Photos; *Chapter 3:* page 55, Jeff Greenberg/PhotoEdit; page 56, Spencer Grant/PhotoEdit; page 62, Bob Daemmrich/Stock Boston; page 66, David Young-Wolff/Tony Stone Images; page 72, Gerard Pile/Tony Stone Images; page 76, Dion Ogust/The Image Works; *Chapter 4:* page 82, Jeff Greenberg/PhotoEdit; page 84, Tony Freeman/PhotoEdit; page 89, John Boykin/PhotoEdit; page 90, David Young-Wolff/Tony Stone Images; page 96, Miro Vintoniv/Stock Boston; page 97, Penny Tweedie/Tony Stone Images; page 101, SmithKline Beecham; *Chapter 5:* page 104, Getty Hulton Images; page 109, Bob Daemmrich Photography; page 110, Jeff Greenberg/PhotoEdit; page 114, Paula Bronstein/Tony Stone Images; page 116, Jeff Greenberg/PhotoEdit; page 122, Zigy Kaluzny/Tony Stone Images; page 124, Bob Daemmrich/Stock Boston; *Chapter 6:* page 134, Charles E. Pefley/Stock Boston; page 136, David Young-Wolff/PhotoEdit; page 139, Fabian Falcon/Stock Boston; page 144, David Young-Wolff/PhotoEdit; page 154, Esbin/Anderson/The Image Works; page 154, Bob Daemmrich Photography; page 159, David Young-Wolff/PhotoEdit; *Chapter 7:* page 171, Bonnie Kamin/PhotoEdit; page 172, David Young-Wolff/PhotoEdit; page 176, Richard Lord/The Image Works; page 178, Jose L. Pelaez/The Stock Market; page 181, Esbin/Anderson/The Image Works; page 188, Jeff Greenberg/The Image Works; page 198, Bob Daemmrich/The Image Works; *Chapter 8:* page 206, Bob Daemmrich Photography; page 208, Chuck Savage/The Stock Market; page 212, Bob Daemmrich/The Image Works; page 222, Kevin Horan/Tony Stone Images; page 227, Don Smetzer/PhotoEdit; page 230, Spencer Grant/PhotoEdit; page 232, Getty Hulton Images; *Chapter 9:* page 236, Najlah Feanny/Stock Boston; page 240, A. Ramey/Stock Boston; page 241, Walter Hodges/Tony Stone Images; page 243, David Young-Wolff/PhotoEdit; page 251, David Young-Wolff/Tony Stone Images; page 252, Michael Newman/PhotoEdit; page 256, Bill Aron/PhotoEdit; page 261, ©Syracuse Newspapers/Gloria Wright/The Image Works; *Chapter 10:* page 264, Kevin Horan/Tony Stone Images; page 266, Bob Mahoney/The Image Works; page 269, ©Fujifotos/The Image Works; page 271, Michael Newman/PhotoEdit; page 273, Bob Daemmrich Photography; page 281, Derke/O'Hara/Tony Stone Images; page 284, Jim Smalley/Index Stock Imagery; *Chapter 11:* page 290, John Madere/The Stock Market; page 291, Jeff Greenberg/PhotoEdit; page 296, Paul Conklin/PhotoEdit; page 297, A. Ramey/Stock Boston; page 304, Najlah Feanny/Stock Boston; page 312, Jose Louis Pelaez/Stock Market; *Chapter 12:* page 322, Roger Ball/The Stock Market; page 330, Stewart Cohen/Tony Stone Images; page 335, Spencer Grant/PhotoEdit; page 338, Charles Gupton/The Stock Market; page 340, Cleve Bryant/PhotoEdit; *Chapter 13:* page 346, Larry Kolvoord/The Image Works; page 349, Bob Daemmrich/The Image Works; page 350, David J. Sams/Tony Stone Images; page 353, E.A.Kennedy III/The Image Works; page 358, David Young-Wolff/PhotoEdit; page 363, Bob Daemmrich Photography; *Chapter 14:* page 369, Nancy Sheehan/PhotoEdit; page 371, Amy Etra/PhotoEdit; page 373, David Young-Wolff/PhotoEdit; page 375, Jeff Greenberg/PhotoEdit; page 379, Zimbel/Monkmeyer Press Photos; page 381, Bruce Ayers/Tony Stone Images; *Chapter 15:* page 388, Steve Skjold/PhotoEdit; page 390, Bob Deammrich/Stock Boston; page 394, Marilyn Humphries/The Image Works; page 395, Ed Bock/The Stock Market; page 396, Don Bosler/Tony Stone Images; page 403, Cleve Bryant/PhotoEdit; page 406, Jonathan Nourok/PhotoEdit.

Art credits

Art on pages 7, 13, 16, 20, 24, 39, 58, 61, 65, 74, 85, 88, 106, 140, 155, 183, 197, 216, 239, 245, 257, 342, and 404 created by Uli Gersiek.

Illustrations on pages 7, 13, 16, 65, 85, and 140 created by Sonja Gjokaj-Taormina.

All cartoons created by Bob Vojtko.